DR. J. E. HODGES, *President*
Catawba County Historical Association, Inc.

A History
of
Catawba County

Compiled and Published

by

CATAWBA COUNTY HISTORICAL

ASSOCIATION, INC.

Edited by

CHARLES J. PRESLAR, JR.

Southern Historical Press, Inc.
Greenville, South Carolina

This volume was reproduced from
An 1954 edition located in the
Publisher's private Library

All rights reserved. No part of this publication may be reproduced,
stored in a retrieval system, transmitted in any form, posted
on to the web in any form or by any means without
the prior written permission of the publisher.

Please direct all correspondence and orders to:

www.southernhistoricalpress.com
or
SOUTHERN HISTORICAL PRESS, Inc.
PO Box 1267
375 West Broad Street
Greenville, SC   29601
southernhistoricalpress@gmail.com

Originally published: Salisbury, NC, 1954
Copyright 1954 by Salisbury County Historical Association
ISBN #0-89308-282-1
All rights Reserved.
Printed in the United States of America

In Memoriam

J. YATES KILLIAN
First President
Catawba County Historical Association, Inc.
Elected President 1936. Died September 24, 1953.

Dedication

To that hardy band of pioneers, who braved the dangers and inconveniences of the wilderness to develop a country where posterity might live in peace and comfort and security, this book is reverently dedicated.

In Memoriam

RAYMOND L. HEFNER
Second President
Catawba County Historical Association, Inc.
Elected 1948. Died December 1, 1953.

PUBLICATION COMMITTEE
CATAWBA COUNTY HISTORICAL ASSOCIATION, INC.

Mrs. J. C. Plonk

Mrs. Pearl M. Tomlinson

Jesse W. Warlick

G. Sam Rowe

Judge Wilson Warlick

Dr. J. E. Hodges

1954 OFFICERS

OF THE

CATAWBA COUNTY HISTORICAL ASSOCIATION, INC.

President..Dr. J. E. Hodges
    Maiden, North Carolina

Vice-President..Mrs. J. C. Plonk
    Hickory, North Carolina

Secretary..Mrs. Pearl M. Tomlinson
    Hickory, North Carolina

Treasurer..Mrs. J. M. Ballard
    Claremont, North Carolina

Custodian..G. Sam Rowe
    Newton, North Carolina

Treasurer Publication Funds..Jesse W. Warlick
    Hickory, North Carolina

J. McDowell Ballard
Dean of Catawba Historians . . . has been collecting local history for more than fifty years, and at age 92 is still active.

Charles J. Preslar, Jr., M.A.
Editor

Philip Moose
Pulitzer Prize Art Winner
Illustrator

Contents

Chapter One..............................Natural Characteristics.
Chapter Two..............................National Stocks and Early Families.
Chapter Three..........................Pattern of Settlement and Basic Economy: Agriculture.
Chapter Four.............................Contribution to the American Revolution.
Chapter Five..............................Early Religious Life.
Chapter Six................................Early Education Methods.
Chapter Seven..........................Early Transportation Facilities
Chapter Eight............................Early Trades and Industries.
Chapter Nine............................Early Professions.
Chapter Ten...............................Contribution to the War of 1812.
Chapter Eleven.........................Formation.
Chapter Twelve........................Government, Judicial and Political Development.
Chapter Thirteen.....................Contribution to the Confederate Cause.
Chapter Fourteen....................Municipalities, Villages and Crossroads, Then and Now.
Chapter Fifteen........................History of Post Offices
Chapter Sixteen.......................Contribution to the Spanish-American Conflict.
Chapter Seventeen.................Contributions to Twentieth Century World Conflicts.
Chapter Eighteen....................Morals and Manners.
Chapter Nineteen....................Notable Community Institutions.
Chapter Twenty.......................New Era: The Twentieth Century

Foreword

For many years there has been a general realization throughout Catawba county, that one of the great needs of our several communities was a recorded history of the area, tracing local development from the first known settlers to the present time.

The only published account of this kind was "The Catawba Soldier," a book compiled and published by the late Professor George W. Hahn, in 1911. Invaluable as the work of Professor Hahn has been during the past four decades, it was never meant to be a comprehensive history of Catawba county—the contents being largely limited to information concerning the Catawbans who saw service in the War Between the States.

This new volume, for which I have been invited to write a brief preface, is as comprehensive a history of Catawba County as available records make possible at this time, edited by Charles J. Preslar, Jr.

In producing "A History of Catawba County," a really vast and foreboding array of manuscripts, and materials of all kinds and description had to be sifted meticulously and studied to determine their significance from the standpoint of inclusion in a running account of important happenings in what is now Catawba county, over the years.

Philip Moose, art editor, is likewise entitled to high praise for the painstaking manner in which he has given the reader visual concepts of various phases of pioneer life concerning which most persons are totally ignorant today.

The Catawba County Historical Association spearheaded the movement that has resulted after many years of effort, in bringing to fruition the long-time dream of a comprehensive county history such as this. Raymond L. Hefner, late president of the Association and one of its organizers, is along with Dr. J. E. Hodges, and others entitled to special mention. It is not our purpose in this foreword to assume any responsibility of giving credit where credit is due, but we could not resist the temptation to mention the names of these two "brave souls" who have for more than two decades carried the torch in drumming up interest in getting a county history published.

It represents an enormous amount of work, and even though there may be oversights and other causes for justifiable criticism we certainly have no disposition to look for them. We are much too happy in having a valuable volume we can hold in our hands and refer to on occasion for many years to come.

It is my great pleasure, therefore, to salute the two gifted young men who have collaborated in producing "A History of Catawba County" and say to them with confidence that they have made a contribution which will grow in the appreciation of the people of Catawba County.

L. C. GIFFORD

CHAPTER I

NATURAL CHARACTERISTICS

Needles of sunlight were streaking the morose September morning when Adam Sherrill shouted the order which halted his wagon team.

The robust man, whose face was furrowed by many physical endurances, looked west upon an expanse of gray-blue water, and lush-green vegetative growth which met its farther shore.

His son, Adam Sherrill, Jr., slid from off the wagon and joined him in apparent, but subdued, excitement. He unconsciously slid his hand into his father's brawny hand, and stood alongside in quiet respect for a development he could not understand.

No sound was audible in the strange land but the slush of water against the river bank. Not even a bird screamed a greeting to the people who would lay the first permanent hearth west of the Catawba river in what now is Catawba county.

The mind of the elder Sherrill seethed with conflicting thoughts—anticipative, yet apprehensive for judgment.

Having led his family from Virginia in this year of 1747, he now had them facing a land which in essence was a wilderness. Ten days ago he had set forth from Augusta county, Virginia, intent upon the plan of establishing himself and his family in a new, productive home. This, however, he could have done throughout a vast portion of North Carolina, into which he lashed his horses. But somehow he was driven—through unexplainable motive—farther west.

Perhaps the suggestion of William, Sr., the Sherrill father, and William, Jr., the son, made time and time again the night before, was advisable. These men already were talking of clearing for a home site at the immediate point—after admitting, quite frankly, that to cross the stretch of water would cut off intercourse with civilization as surely as would living a 100 miles west in the foreign land. The Indian's arrow can pierce in a second, and the fording of a stream is a matter of minutes or hours, they reasoned. The women and children were to be considered, they contended. Surely sufficient land was available here on the east side for all members of the Sherrill family.

Yet, Adam Sherrill could not feel prone to alter what maybe were predestined plans.

The sturdy frontiersman had no visions, or even the remotest dreams, of communities with thousands of souls, and the development of mineral and other natural resources of the opposite shore, to be sure. But he did, no doubt, see the fording of the river as the conquering of another barrier, and the opening of the way for a neighbor whose children might someday marry his children. Who knew, anyway, the number of fur animals that were at home in the adjoining forests, and what new trade routes might be opened with the exploration of the river?

From the first minute of the difference of opinion concerning the site of settlement, Adam had conceded that he would go little farther than across the river. He would then be situated on one bank, and William would be located, along with the eldest Sherrill, on the other. The arrangement doubtless would be advantageous.

The father and brother now stood at hand to help with what they considered both a useless and rather mad scheme. Adam loosened his hand from his son's, and gently pushed the boy into the direction of the wagon. The sudden action gave evidence of the father's decision.

With a look of confidence in his eyes, Adam Sherrill turned to William, Sr., and announced: "It will take us less than a day to cross, if we test and find that we can ford it."

Thus, 206 years ago the first permanent settler west of the Catawba river entrusted his rickety wagon to the hazards of an unknown body of water.

The picture was one of adventure and romance.

The entourage no doubt prayed as it set forth upon mild-appearing yet risky waves, petitioning aid beyond that which lay in the sunburned muscles of the men who directed an unsteady path.

Saul, the senior Adam Sherrill's able and trustworthy Negro man, was coaxing two heifers and a bull to venture the slight current. A calf of one of the heifers had been hoisted onto the wagon and was getting a free ride, although the mother kept an attentive eye on it and bawled out her concern. The team of horses blundered and neighed disapproval as they struggled for the distant shore—one being ridden by William, Jr. Screams from Saul, the shouts of instructions from the Sherrill men, plus the audible happiness of Adam, Jr., lent a dramatic effect to the introduction to the history of Catawba county.

Although based on historical data, the account of the advent of the Sherrill family is fictionized. Some persons doubt the use of the covered wagon, expressing the belief that the area of Catawba afforded too rough terrain to be traversed by these vehicles without trails or roads. They forward the opinion that the Sherrill family moved by way of pack horse train. One tradition, moreover, is that Adam Sherrill found an accessible fording point by watching buffaloes cross the river.

It generally is conceded that Henry Weidner, father of one of Catawba county's most distinguished families, came into the Catawba territory about the same time as the Sherrills. Some believe, in fact, that Weidner came as a member of the Sherrill entourage.

Of course the territory into which the pioneers entered was not known in the 1740s as Catawba county. It was then a part of Bladen county, and was just in the midst of an evolution of name changes.

The area's position in the picture of the American development is as follows:

It is believed that there was no civilized man in America prior to its discovery in 1492. For almost 100 years after this date, the country remained unexplored.

England's Queen Elizabeth was instrumental in its exploration. She gave a countryman, Walter Raleigh, privilege to make an expedition to the "New World."

In 1548, Raleigh claimed for the crown of England the territory now comprising the states of North Carolina and South Carolina. Raleigh was knighted at this time and the region was named Virginia in honor of Queen Elizabeth. In 1629. King Charles of England granted Carolina (Latin for "land of Charles") to Robert Heath.

When Charles II came to the throne, he gave Carolina to eight "Lords Proprietors" in two separate charters — dated March 20, 1663, and June 30, 1665.

King Charles allowed in the charters that the western boundary "was to the South seas" (the Pacific ocean). Thereafter, when a county was formed to the westward, its western boundary was the "South seas."

During the last of the 1700s, a western county extended to "the Blue Ridge" or Tennessee.

A subdivision of the colony was called "a precinct." The first political subdivision in what is now North Carolina (or in "Carolina") was called "The County of Albemarle" (consisting of Chowan, Pasquotank, Perquimans, and Currituck precincts), and extended from the Virginia line southward to the dividing line of North Carolina and South Carolina (the points of which were agreed upon by the two colonies (or "provinces") in 1689—consisting of the mouth of Little river on the seashore, 30 miles south below the mouth of the Cape Fear river). That part of "The County of Albemarle" north was called North Carolina, and all below was called South Carolina.

The eastern part of the boundary line between North and South Carolina was run in 1735. The line began at the point agreed upon previously and extended northwest 64½ miles to a branch of the Little Peedee. In 1737, the line was extended in the same direction 22 miles, erroneously supposed to be at the point of intersection with the 35th degree parallel of north latitude.

The line was run due west to the Peedee river afterward by colonial authorities representing the two colonies, and, thence westward to the Catawba river. It has been asserted that the zig-zagging line was due to private plot, but the real explanation is to be found in an agreement that the Catawba Indians must be placed in South Carolina.

In 1738, the "Precincts" were called "Counties," and the chief executive officer—the provost marshal—became the sheriff. It is significant that the first county of North Carolina, Albemarle, the mother of all the other counties, no longer exists.

Six counties absorbed "Albemarle": Chowan, Currituck, Perquimans, and Pasquotank, formed in 1670; Bath (which no longer exists), formed in 1696; and Tyrrell, formed in 1729.

Bath soon was subdivided into a number of counties, one of which was New Hanover. In 1735, Bladen county was formed of New Hanover. Bladen county was to become the mother of 55 counties in the state.

Until the time of the coming of Adam Sherrill to the area which is now Catawba, the colonial legislature had taken little interest in the western portions of North Carolina. However, in 1749, the situation changed.

In this year, Bladen was divided by a line equidistant from Saxapahaw (also called Haw) and Peedee rivers—the western part to be the new county of Anson. Anson then included the whole of the western part of North Carolina from the Virginia line to the South Carolina line and evidently west to the Pacific. But in 1753, Rowan county was cut off from Anson, taking with it all the territory north of Earl Granville's line, which had been fixed at latitude 35°34'.

In 1762, Mecklenburg was cut off from Anson, its eastern boundary being "a line beginning at Lord Carteret's (Earl Granville's line) six miles Northeast from Capt. Charles Hart's plantation on Buffalo Creek, and to run from thence to the mouth of Clear Creek which empties itself into Rocky River, below Capt. Adam Alexander's, and from thence due South, to the bounds of the province of South Carolina." Mecklenburg's northern boundary was evidently Earl Granville's lines; its southern boundary, the South Carolina line; and its western boundary, the Pacific ocean.

In 1768, effective April 10, 1769, Tryon county was cut off from Mecklenburg. Tryon's eastern boundary was a line "beginning at Earl Granville's line where it crosses the Catawba River, and the said river to be the line to the South Carolina line." The northern boundary was Earl Granville's line. The southern boundary was the South Carolina line. The western boundary was indefinitely westward. In 1777, this western boundary was, however, fixed by the formation of Washington county, comprising all the territory west of the mountains, and the western boundary of Tryon became approximately what is now the boundary line between North Carolina and Tennessee.

Named for General Benjamin Lincoln, a hero of the American Revolution, Lincoln county was formed in 1779. Tryon county was abolished and Lincoln and Rutherford counties were organized out of its territories. The object of eliminating the name of "Tryon," obviously, was to put into disuse a name which was most unfavorable to the patriots of the Revolution. William Tryon was a royal governor.

The county of Tryon was cut by a line "beginning at the South line near Broad River on the dividing ridge between Buffaloe Creek and Little Broad River, thence along the said ridge to the line of Burke county." All of Tryon to the west of this line became Rutherford county; all to the east became Lincoln.

The western boundary of Lincoln then ran through the middle of what is now Cleveland county. The northern boundary was Earl Granville's line. The southern boundary was the South Carolina line. The eastern boundary was the Catawba river.

In 1782, the size of Lincoln county was increased by addition of a part of Burke county. The northern line of Lincoln was to run as follows: "Beginning at Sharrol's Ford, running with the road leading towards Henry Whitner's as far as Mathew Wilson's; thence a direct course to Simon Horse's on the waters of Clark's creek, thence a direct course to the fish-dam ford of the south fork of the Catawba river, between James Wilson, and David Robinson, and from thence a Southwest course to Earl Granville's old line." This line was amended in 1784 so that "the boundary line between the counties of Burke and Lincoln shall hereafter be as follows, to wit, beginning at the Horse-Ford on Catawba river, running thence to John Hawn's on Henry river, thence to William Orr's on Jacob's river, and thence to the intersection of the counties of Burke, Lincoln, and Rutherford." These two enactments were somehow interpreted as extending the county northward to the Catawba river, and the county is so shown on maps dated about 1820. Thus from 1784 until the formation of Cleveland in 1841, the county included all of what is now Lincoln, Catawba, and

CATAWBA COUNTY 23

Gaston, and a large part of what is now Cleveland. This is an area about 56 miles long and about 33 miles wide.

In 1841, Cleveland county was cut off from Lincoln and Rutherford. The part of the line that affected Lincoln was to run with the dividing line of Burke and Rutherford to the Lincoln line, thence to the 13 mile post on the Lucas Ford road, thence to the 12 mile post on the New Post road from Rutherfordton to Lincolnton, thence to the 12 mile post on the road from Lincolnton to Quinn's Ferry, thence to the 12 mile post on the road from Morganton to Yorkville, S. C., thence with the road passing Abernathy's store by the Gold Mine at King's Mountain to the South Carolina line.

Catawba county was cut from Lincoln in 1842. All that portion of Lincoln north of an east and west line running one and one-half miles north of Lincolnton was taken away. A part of this territory was returned to Lincoln when Gaston was formed four years later.

The history of the establishment of Catawba is dealt with in chapter eleven of this volume.

In 1846, Gaston county was cut off. All that portion of Lincoln which lay south of an east and west line running six miles south of the dividing line between Lincoln and Catawba (that is, four and one-half miles south of Lincolnton), was taken away. At the same time, the dividing line between Lincoln and Catawba was moved four miles north, to a line five and one-half miles north of Lincolnton. The consequences were a Lincoln county only ten miles wide.

Easily the most impressive geographic feature of the area into which Adam Sherrill pioneered was the river which he crossed to complete his journey.

This winding body of water—which rises in the mountains to the west and flows into the neighboring state of South Carolina—was to influence much the lives of early settlers.

The earliest known reference to the Catawba river is on a French map bearing the date of 1712. Held by the Map Division of the Congressional Library, this map shows the Santee, Wateree, "Catamba" and the Congree. The second known mention of the famous Catawba in historical documents is 1749, the date of issuance of the first land grants.

The county, without doubt, takes its name from the Catawba river.

The river, in turn, is said by many to be named for the Indians who once inhabited the section. The Catawbans, an offshoot of the Sioux Indians, constituted a powerful tribe when the white men first invaded their territory. Their relations with the whites were consistently friendly and their aid against unfriendly Indians and in the war against the French and British was invaluable to the pioneers.

There is some conjecture concerning the meaning of the word "Catawba." Some historians say it is a Choctaw word meaning divided, set apart, or separated. Others say it means "river of grapes." Those of the latter conviction say the Indians so named the river because of the profusion of grapes which grew wild along its banks.

The United States Department of the Interior, Geological Survey, Washington, D. C., replies thus to inquiry about the Catawba river:

"... The Survey is unable to give any definite answer (about the earliest time the name is mentioned) for it has neither conducted research into such historical matters nor compiled records thereon. As a matter of map information, however, it is known that among the earliest maps of Carolina, now on file in the Library of Congress, one by John Thornton, Robert Morden, and Philip Lea of 1685 and another by S. Siena of 1690-1799 show the name the Watere (Wateree) from the Atlantic coast as far North as Indian town called at that time Esaw, about where Catawba, South Carolina, is now located. Neither map, however, either shows or names the Catawba river. The map of North America of 1755 by Dr. John Mitchell is the first of record here that both shows and names this river, and this map also changes the Indian town of Esaw to Watere Town.

"From the earliest period the Catawba Indian tribe was known as the Esaw or Issa (Catawba, Iswa - 'River') from its residence in the locality known as the Catawba region, divided by the river of that name. The name given by this tribe to both the Catawba and the Wateree rivers was Iswa. The name Catawba probably is from the Choctaw 'Katapa' meaning divided, separated, or division. Lynche Creek, between the

Catawba and the Peedee rivers, was anciently known as Kadapau and it is possible that the name Catawba was originally given to the Indians of that region by some tribe living in Eastern South Carolina from whom the colonists first obtained it . . ."

The tribal name "Catawba" has been variously spelled—Catamba, Cadapouce, Calabaw, Cataba, Cataapaw, Cataube, Cattaba, Cautawba, and Cuttawa.

Lawson's "History of North Carolina" refers to the Catawba Indians as the "Kadapau."

Perhaps nowhere in the history of North America does an area owe more to a particular tribe of Indians than do Catawbans to the Catawba Indians.

In addition to the giving of their name to the river which skirts Catawba county, for which the county ultimately was named, the tribe of Indians befriended the people's forefathers, and with few exceptions, proved their unequaled friends.

The same does not hold true for the Cherokee Indians of sections farther west in the state. Their plunderings of what now is Catawba county prior to the Revolutionary war, during the Revolutionary war, and following the Revolutionary war are cited in other portions of the history, namely the attack on one of Catawba's earliest settlers, Henry Weidner, and the killing of several early and brave pioneers, including Matthias Barringer.

The Catawbans were the largest and most important tribe of Siouan stock in Piedmont North Carolina.

According to a tradition of the tribe, as recorded by Douglas L. Rights, author of "The American Indian in North Carolina," they migrated from the North, and as the Siouan tribes were noted as buffalo hunters, it is thought that the southern branch of this stock came from the Midwest on their hunting expeditions and settled in the piedmont country. They were first mentioned in the account of the expedition of Juan Pardo.

It is generally agreed that about 1,000 members constituted the Catawba tribe at the time Adam Sherrill crossed the Catawba river.

Primarily an agricultural people, the Catawba Indians are described as being trustworthy, courageous, and friendly, though regarded by some as being more easy-going and lacking in energy than many Indians. Lawson records that the women were "reasonably handsome," taking great delight in feather ornaments and industrious in domestic pursuits. Among the skills of the Catawba women were pottery-making and basket-weaving.

Fortunately for the early white settlers, the Catawbas were traditional enemies of the Cherokees. The Cherokees had claimed that they held the country about the headwaters of the Catawba river to below the present city of Morganton until game became scarce; then they retired farther into the mountains and afterward "loaned" the eastern territory to the Catawba.

Evidences of Catawba-Cherokee battles remain still in what has become Catawba county, notably in the river sections of the area.

Rights points to the history of the Catawbas, thus: "Relations with the colonists, except during the Yamassee War of 1715, were uniformly friendly. With the exception of this one brief outbreak of hostility they have maintained a meritorious record for friendliness toward their white neighbors. They aided in the campaign against the Tuscarora in the East and served as a barrier against tribes of the West. The flood of immigration that poured into the Piedmont area about 1700 was little opposed by the friendly Catawba. Although constant encroachment on their hunting territory called forth repeated protests, there was no serious outbreak except the minor defection already noted.

"They aided in expeditions against the French and their Indian allies at Fort Duquesne and elsewhere during the French and Indian War, and in the same struggle they helped to protect the Piedmont Carolina settlers from invasions by the Cherokee. In 1756, Governor Dobbs stated that no attacks had been made on the frontier, owing principally to the frontier guardsmen and 'the Neighbourhood of the Catawba Indians, our friends.' A single mention from the colonial records of the same year, which tells of their aid in pursuit of a roving band of Cherokee marauders, of the recovery of goods stolen from settlers, and of the return of the goods to Salisbury for distribution to rightful owners, indicates the Catawba good will and protection which have made the people of the Carolinas ever indebted to them. If in this time of danger the Catawba nation had made alliance with enemy Indians and had taken up arms against the settlers instead of fighting valiantly for them, there is no doubt that many a family of the Piedmont, whose descendants dwell happily in the region today, would have been massacred.

"In 1763, it was proposed to use them and the Cherokee against the lake tribes under Pontiac. During the Revolution they assisted the colonists against the British, and were forced to leave their homes, with their families, and to seek refuge in Virginia until peace was restored. Catawba scouts led the way for General Greene to the battle of Guilford Court House. Their warriors were prominent in Williamson's expedition against the Cherokee. Catawbans served with valor in the Confederate Army. In the First World War, several of their young men were enlisted out of a total surviving population of less than two hundred, and made an honorable record in the United States Army. In the Second World War, their response was no less praiseworthy. This is a notable record, hardly surpassed by any other tribe of the American continent."

For their kindnesses, the Catawbas were repaid with greediness on the part of frontiersmen, in most instances. Moreover, the white man introduced diseases, especially smallpox; and liquor. The once populous tribe suffered a rapid decline.

The remaining tribesmen saw their holdings—which once included the territory between the Broad and Yadkin rivers, from the headwaters of the Catawba, far into South Carolina—reduced to one square mile. In 1943, however, under protection of the Federal government, their reservation in South Carolina was increased to two thousand acres.

Perhaps the most famous Catawba Indian was Chief Haiglar, who became leader of his tribe a year following Adam Sherrill's entry into the area of the current study.

His friendly and helpful attitude toward the governments of North and South Carolina and his honorable conduct made him respected and trusted throughout the territory. He is described as a "man of sterling character, just in his dealings, and true to his word, acting the part of a father to his people, by whom he was greatly beloved."

Evidence is to the effect that the roving, plundering Cherokee nation never was interested in the area now comprising Catawba county except in terms of a game source. These Indians truly were a mountain fold, and in fact called themselves "Tsalagi," or "Tsaragi," denoting "Cave people." For a long time they possessed or controlled all the region of the Alleghenies in Southwest Virginia, Western North Carolina, Northwestern South Carolina, Eastern Tennessee, and Northern Georgia and Alabama. Their settlements overflowed into the game-abundant valleys of the foothills—and it was thus that they encountered the Catawba. An estimate of their population in the seventeenth century is given as 22,000. They controlled 40,000 miles of territory and claimed much more.

An apt description of the present Catawba county area in 1752, five years following Adam Sherrill's advent, and in the interim, others, is provided in the notes of Bishop A. G. Spangenberg, who made a survey of the western piedmont region seeking a location for a Moravian settlement.

Bishop Spangenberg and several companions wrote when they reached the Catawba river west of the present Statesville: "Hitherto we have been on the Trading Path, where we could find at least one house a day where food could be bought, but from here we were to turn into the pathless forest."

The area which is now Catawba county is 17 miles in breadth, north and south, and 27 miles in length, east and west. In addition to its boundary formed by the fast-flowing Catawba river, it is bordered, on the south, by Lincoln county, and, on the west, by Burke county. The county contains an area of 435 square miles.

Catawba is in the western-most piedmont belt of North Carolina and is in latitude 80° 15' 00", and longitude 35° 38' 00".

The highest elevations of the county are Bakers mountain (formerly McNary mountain), 1,812 feet; Anderson, or Little mountain, 1,567 feet; Linn mountain (in Bandys township), approximately 1,060 feet; and Plateau, 1,010 feet.

The terrain of the section is high and rolling, with an elevation averaging around 1,000 feet.

Authenticity is lent to the claim that the Catawba area once was the home of the buffalo herd by *The Colonial Records of*

North Carolina. Bishop Spangenberg, who is referred to previously, is recorded in Volume Five as writing: (Speaking of the Little River section in what now is Alexander County) ". . . Upon the whole the bottom has an abundance of water courses, not only from the creek which has such steep banks as to render it too steep for fording—(except where buffaloes have made a ford) but it abounds in springs also . . ."

(Speaking of portions slightly west of Catawba county) ". . . Our survey begins 7 or 8 miles from the mouth of the River where it flows into the Catawba. What lies farther down the river has already been taken up. The other line of the survey runs close to the Blue Ridge. I must add that we were compelled to take in a number of high hills which are bare of trees and useless for cultivation. But this is not to be avoided. This piece thus consists of about 6,000 acres. We can have at least 8 settlements in this tract and each will have water enough, wood enough and land enough;—very good land and meadow land in abundance; and I calculate to every settlement 8 couples of brethren and sisters. How the roads are to be laid out I know not. We crossed high and steep hills in coming here, and calculate the distance from the Catawba land to be about 18 miles; the road lies in a N. W. direction (but why do I speak of road, when there is none but what buffaloes have made) . . ."

The geography of the area of Catawba directly affected its development.

The land's fertile soil was responsible for the primary business of farming. The western and northwestern portions of the county have cecile sandy loam soil, the central portion, cecile clay, and the eastern and southeastern portions (with the exception of a small area north of Anderson mountain which has cecile clay), also cecile sandy loam. Along all rivers and major streams is meadow loam soil.

The valleys naturally follow the area's water courses. None is especially significant geographically.

Beneath Catawba soil was to be found, during the course of history, gold, iron, mica, kaolin and lime, among other mineral deposits.

A matter of conjecture is Catawba's virgin forests. A theory is advanced that the area literally was covered with valuable timber in the year 1747, and another is advanced that worthwhile trees were found principally along the water courses.

Those who hold the first opinion point out that records of early settlers emphasize the difficulty of travel due to "thickets and forest parts." It will be recalled that Bishop Spangenberg referred to the Catawba area as a "pathless forest."

Those who hold the second opinion believe that the Indians burned vast areas of woodland in order to drive out game. They say the biggest trees were along the water sources, where the effects of fire were least apt to be suffered. Also, the suggestion is forwarded that herds of buffalo, traveling east in winter and west in summer, grazed on and trampled down forest growth.

The story is told that, in 1804, John Wilfong, of Catawba county Revolutionary war fame, was interested in purchasing a large tract of land along the banks of the South Fork river. He is said to have taken his son, John Jr., 15, along as he inspected the property.

Riding horseback with his son behind him, John Sr., said: "Boy, do you reckon these saplings will ever make timber."

The younger Wilfong is supposed to have replied, "Yes, papa, if you give them time."

The two were referring to small oaks and hickorys, which, it is related, later made some of the most valuable timber to have been produced in Catawba county.

This story is told in connection with the theory that Catawba's great forest lands were to come during the nineteenth century, generally following the era of the Indians and the buffaloes.

No one denies, however, that tremendous poplars long have grown along the banks of area streams.

When the white man came to the Catawba section, the oak, hickory, poplar, chestnut, walnut, dogwood, persimmon, cedar, holly, ash, willow, elm, beech, gum, locust, sour-wood, maple, birch, pine and sycamore were found. It is a discredited theory that the pine was to be found more in abundance in 1747 than in 1953. This species of tree was the product of over-used and unproductive land.

The early settler chose a home site most often near a body of water for several reasons. One was the necessity of water for human consumption and home use. Another was protection against fire, often caused by the Indians. Another was the watering of crops. Still another was a source of food.

Early fish of the Catawba area included catfish; sucker, or red horse; horney-head; sun perch; bass; and carp. The eel was found also. Concerning the last, it is said that those who sought the eel greeted the fish with sand in their hands. This was done to hold the slimy, wiggling creature.

The Catawba county area always has ranked among the first of the catfish counties in North Carolina. There is, in fact, a portion of the county known as the Catfish section.

Most pioneers who settled along water courses took advantage of bottom land for meadows. Native grasses were utilized for hay.

The land animals of the Catawba area about the middle of the eighteenth century included deer, rabbit, squirrel, raccoon, buffalo, o'possum, mole, rat, mouse, weasel, bear mouse, otter, musk rat, and water rat. There were a limited number of beaver, fox, wildcat, bear, panther, wolf, and polecat. The deer was as plentiful in Catawba forests in the middle eighteenth century as rabbit is today. It generally is believed that there were fewer foxes in the days of the pioneers than now, due to a popular custom of today of importing the animal for hunting purposes. The bears which were here, as well as panthers, wolves, wildcats and polecats, are said to have been strays from the western mountains.

A joke among the citizens of the late eighteenth and early nineteenth centuries, according to oldtimers, was the "blind tiger." This so-called animal was, in reality, the farmer's still house.

Edible fowl of the Catawba area included turkeys, geese, ducks, pheasants, partridges, and mallards.

Birds included the hawk, sparrow, blue-jay, turtle dove, thrush, woodpecker, mocking bird, catbird, blue bird, wren, crow, blackbird, redbird, bat, humming bird, owl, and whippoorwill.

Fruits included wild apples, pears, cherries, grapes, strawberries, blackberries, mulberries, dew berries, raspberries, goose berries, figs and plums.

Nuts included hickory, walnut, chinquapin, chestnut and hazel nut.

Reptiles included the rattle snake, the water moccasin, the black snake, the green snake, the copperhead, species of scorpions, species of frogs, and species of turtles.

Flora of the Catawba area included some mountain laurel and rhododendron, particularly on the north sides of hills of the western areas; maple bloom; ivey bloom; dogwood bloom; honeysuckle; violets; wild species of roses; and jessamine.

Principal streams within or on the boundaries of Catawba county, listed alphabetically, are as follows: (Name, tributary of, head and general direction)

Allen creek (north and south forks)—Maiden creek; about four miles east of Maiden; west.

Anthony creek—Later Hildebran creek.

Bakers creek—Lyles creek; five miles northeast of Conover; southeast.

Balls creek—Catawba river; two and one-half miles east of Carsons crossroads, which is located about five miles east of Newton; easterly.

Battle Run brook—North fork of Mountain creek; near old lime kiln; south.

Beaver Dam brook—South fork of the Catawba river; one and one-half miles west of Maiden; west.

Betts branch—Clarks creek; near Startown; southeast.

Bills branch—Clarks creek; midway between Newton and Maiden; southwest.

Bradys branch—Lyles creek; northeast of Conover; northeast.

Browns creek—Lyles creek; north of Claremont; east.

Butts Shoal creek—Henry river; Longview; south.

CATAWBA COUNTY 33

Camp creek—Jacob Fork river; South mountains of Burke county; southeast.

Catawba river—Wateree river, S. C.; Blue Ridge mountains; southerly.

Clarks creek—South fork of Catawba river; southeast of Hickory; south.

Clines creek—Clarks creek; one mile west of Conover; south.

Elk Shoal creek—Catawba river; northeast part of county; east.

Falling creek—Catawba river; northeast part of Hickory; northeast.

Frys creek—Horseford creek; Arneys springs; northeast.

Grassy creek—Snow creek; six miles northeast of Hickory; northwest.

Haas creek—Potts creek, northwest Blackburn; southeast.

Hagan Fork—McLin creek; three miles east of Newton; northeast.

Henry Fork river—South fork of Catawba river; South mountains of Burke county; southeast.

Herman branch—Clarks creek; three miles east of Hickory; southerly.

Hildebran creek—Clarks creek; southwest of Conover; south.

Hop creek—Jacob fork of Catawba river; five miles southwest of Hickory; southeast.

Horseford creek—Catawba river; north Hickory; north.

Howards creek—South Fork river; southwest Catawba county; southeast.

Jacobs Fork river—South fork of Catawba river; southwest part of Catawba county; easterly.

Jonas' Little creek—Lyles creek; four miles north of Conover; southeast.

Lippard creek—South Fork river; south of Highway 16 and west of Anderson mountain; southwest.

Little Potts creek—Potts creek; ten miles southwest of Newton; southeast.

Long Shoal creek—Catawba river; seven miles northeast of Hickory; northeast.

Lyles creek—Catawba river; one and one-half miles east of Hickory; east.

Maiden creek—South Fork river; seven miles east of Maiden; southwest.

McLin creek—Lyles creek; southeast Conover; northeast.

Mountain creeek—Catawba river; nine miles east of Newton; southeast.

Mulls creek or fork—Lyles creek; one mile east of Conover; northeast.

Naked creek—Catawba river; seven miles north of Conover; north.

Pinch Gut creek—Maiden creek; five miles east of Newton; southwest.

Potts creek—South fork of Catawba river; ten miles southwest of Newton; southeast.

Reed creek—Mountain creek; east side of Anderson mountain; southeast.

Rhodes Mill creek—Potts creek; two miles south of Plateau; east.

Rocky (Stony) creek—Henry Fork river; southeast part of Hickory; southerly.

Sampson creek—Potts creek; one mile south of Plateau; northeast.

Shoal creek—Catawba river; seven miles northeast of Hickory; northeast.

Shook branch—Rhodes Mill creek; one and one-half miles south of Plateau; southeast.

Smyre creek—Town creek; two miles southeast of Newton; west.

Snow creek—Catawba river; near junction of Springs and Sandy Ridge roads; northeast.

South Fork river—Catawba river; junction of Henry Fork and Jacobs Fork rivers; south.

Terrapin creek—Catawba river; two miles northwest of Sherrills Ford; east.

Three Forked branch—Lyles creek (frequent reference made to "The Three Forks of Lyles Creek"); four miles north of Conover; easterly.

Town creek—Clarks creek; north part of Newton; south.

Whiteners creek—Henry Fork river; four miles southeast of Hickory; southerly.

CHAPTER II

CATAWBA'S NATIONAL STOCKS AND EARLY FAMILIES

The dotting of Catawba county's hills and rolling valleys has been due principally to immigration of "Dutchmen" who in reality are Germans and "Irishmen" who in reality are Scots.

Strangely enough, the Pennsylvania Dutch lines of family lineage stem directly from German stock, and the Scotch-Irish strains in the population come directly from the British plantation of Ulster in North Ireland.

The "Pennsylvania Dutch" are so called because they were "Deutsch" (the German word for "German") who settled in the colony of Pennsylvania.

First German immigrants to the United States settled around ports of debarkation. One of these was Philadelphia, an area which knew quick settlement about the beginning of the eighteenth century, and an area which, several years later, was due to spill over its migratory masses into the Southland.

Germans sought refuge in America due to almost as many causes as there were individuals who braved the Atlantic to enter the new land. It is a false assumption to declare that the peoples were motivated to leave their loved ones and their customs and traditions solely because of religious persecution, the desire for liberty, or the lust for adventure. To be sure, these factors played a part. But it is equally sure that there were many and varied private reasons for the decisions on the part of individuals to seek a totally new existence.

It may be said that many Germans came to enjoy the liberty of a land which was not torn by political wars and controlled by arrogant land and government overlords. A distinct characteristic of the German is that he is a retiring and peaceful citizen, opposed to bickering and strife. He will patiently suffer wrong for a time, but he will not always be imposed upon.

Some Germans came to seek new homes, as an outlet for the crowded population of their homeland. The German is noted for his devotion to personal freedoms which are associated with ownership. He is industrious, economical and thrifty, and works continuously with the aim in mind of promoting his, his family's, and his community's interests. He is not afraid or ashamed of hard work, but wishes for it to show dividends. Particularly he is a home-lover, and is slow in making changes. The first German settler, it will be noted, held tenaciously to the practices and habits and modes of thought practiced by his ancestors, when often more modern ways were better.

Along this line, the German was slow to yield his native language, especially where he lived in settlements of other Germans. For this reason, he retained for a long time his peculiar traits of character, his religious codes, his social convictions and his moral attitudes. Also for this reason, he was to lose prestige and standing in the professions and official life. Early county office holders were those persons who had a knowledge of the English language.

Nathaniel Wilson Talking at Muster Ground

Some Germans came to escape religious restrictions. The German especially is a devout worshipper of God. His honest background, bequeathed by heredity, and upright manner of dealing with his fellowman, likewise bequeathed by heredity, determined that one of his first considerations in the new world was spiritual sustenance. By nature a pious man, the German was constitutionally endowed with love of freedom of conscience. Hostilities between the home government and outside countries, and the political impositions incident to warfare, had unbearably restricted liberty of conscience. Thus cruelly imposed on at home, the German was ready to brave hardships to secure his coveted ideals.

Likely few Germans came to satisfy longings for adventure. Because of his stable and persevering characteristics, the German was not apt to break family ties simply because of the desire to learn more of the distinctions and delights of the world. There are few records of German hunters and trappers.

It is feasible that some Germans came to escape their just recompense in the courts of justice; leaving, it might be said, "for the good of the homeland." Others came to escape the military services demanded of all young men in Germany.

Underlying all causes of immigration, actually, was a desire on the part of the individual German to acquire a free start. Perhaps, in final analysis, he was searching for liberty of conscience, enjoyment of civic rights, and better welfare.

Concerning the German nationality, Rev. R. A. Yoder, writing an essay on the German element in Catawba county's population in Professor George W. Hahn's "The Catawba Soldier in the Civil War," points out: "The . . . immigration fortunately brought here that German stock which for morality, perseverance, simplicity and contentment is easily first among the nations."

The current of German immigration from Pennsylvania into the piedmont section of North Carolina was a full tide about the middle of the eighteenth century.

Germans who came into what now is Catawba county were of families which sprang primarily from the enterprising Pennsylvania Germans, who had years before settled in Montgomery, Berks, Lancaster, and York counties.

The course of travel Southward pursued by the early Germans is described by Colonel W. L. Saunders in his "Prefatory Notes" to *The Colonial Records of North Carolina*. He writes: "The route these immigrants from Pennsylvania took to reach their future home in North Carolina is plainly laid down on the maps of that day. On Jeffrey's Map, a copy of which is in the Congressional Library at Washington City, there is plainly laid down a road called 'The Great Road from the Yadkin Valley thro' Virginia and Pennsylvania to Philadelphia, distance about 435 miles.' It ran from Philadelphia thro' Lancaster and York to Winchester, thence up the Shenandoah Valley crossing the Fluvanna River at Looney's Ford, thence to Staunton River, and down the river through the Blue Ridge, thence Southward crossing the Dan river below the mouth of Mayo River, thence still Southward near the Moravian settlement to the Yadkin River, just above the mouth of Linville Creek, and about ten miles above the mouth of Reedy Creek."

Those persons who came on to the land which is now Catawba county, of course, crossed the fertile valley of the Yadkin. The sturdy Germans settled chiefly the South Fork valley of Catawba county.

An excellent description of the nationality is provided by Col. George M. Yoder, whose ancestors were among the first of the county:

"John Yoder, one of the original trustees (of Grace Union church), who was a son of Conrad Yoder, who left Switzerland and went to Rotterdam in 1751, and there embarked on a sailing vessel for the American continent, landing at Philadelphia in 1751, came to this section between the years 1755 and 1760. He was a single man, and in 1762 bought the southern portion of the Henry Weidner entry on the waters of Jacob's Fork river. He married a Miss Cline about the year 1762, and settled on the farm.

"I had the privilege and opportunity of examining an emigrant register, containing the emigrant register of 30,000 emigrants, who had left at Rotterdam from various portions of the Old World, and landed at Philadelphia from 1727 to 1777.

"Before any emigrants could leave the ship they had to take the oath of allegiance to the Crown of England, as he became very jealous of so many emigrants flocking into the American continent. They had to subscribe their name thereto, and many of them could scarcely write, and what few could write did it in German, and generally written very badly. Many could not speak the English language, and what little they did speak was so broken that an Englishman could scarcely understand.

"In writing the German language the letter 'Y' often resembles the letter 'Z' or 'K,' so I found in the register that in the translation of these names many of them were spelled wrong, and beginning with another letter than that of the original.

"Now, Conrad Yoder who was the father of John Yoder. This name appears on the register 'Conrad Koder' living in Philadelphia in 1757. Then I found the name spelled Zoder, Soder, Jedor, Jotter, Yoner, Yetter. I remember yet that in my boyhood days they were called 'Yotters' by those German people . . .

"Now again to John Yoder, the original trustee on the Presbyterian or German Reform (of Grace Church), was born in October 1761, and was the first white child born on the Jacob's Fork river. He was a farmer by occupation, and spoke the German language.

"During the Revolutionary War, he volunteered as a soldier at the age of 16, into the American Army. But he never got into an engagement as peace was declared between the two nations. He was married to Mary B. Beib (Reep), who was raised near Lincolnton on the South Fork river. She was a German lady and heard the first gun fire at the battle of Ramsours mill, on the morning of the 20th of June, 1780. . . . (John Yoder was the grandfather of Col. Yoder)

"He (John Yoder) was a surveyor, and of this he did a great deal. He was appointed by the legislature, with Mr. Pearson of Burke county, to establish the present line between this and Burke county. He also was a militia captain for a long time. He never spent his money in Negro property (slaves), but always invested in real estate. At his death he owned nearly 1,300 acres of land.

"He was an elder at Grace church as well as one of the founders and builders of it. During Rev. Loretz' administration for a number of years, and after Loretz' death, when the

German Reformed congregation had no regular minister for some fifteen years, he and his family went to St. Paul's church where Rev. Bogers preached. . . .

"About the year 1825 the German Reformed congregation at Grace church called a meeting to use some effort at getting a regular German Reformed minister. They unanimously elected him (John Yoder) as a committee to write to the Pennsylvania Synod for a minister, which he committed with and they sent them the Rev. John Fritchey. About the year 1830 or '32, Rev. Fritchey wanted to take the negro into the church, which he (Yoder) strenuously opposed. At last the church altar called an election to vote upon the question. . . .

"He (Yoder) was one of all those determined men, as he had passed through an American struggle for liberty and was not afraid to express his opinion on any subject. So after the ballot was announced, and he (Yoder) was defeated, he made the following declaration in the German language:

"'Ian h auben de kerchem helfen bauchem, an d ich stageninde theren cin staungel briggel und slaug dare ars en Nager um das do ui gaen wall.'

"Translated: 'Helped to build this church and will take my stand in the door and the first Negro that attempts to go in I will knock him over with a snake pole.'

"Then at this juncture many of the Yoders withdrew from the congregation because they did not like Fitchey's negro proclivity, and went to the Lutheran church. Fritchey and his friends acquitted to his declaration and did not attempt to force the negro question any further, and he did not attempt to come into the church building until after his death which occurred on the 31st day of December, 1835. He was buried at Grace church on the first day of January, 1836, in his 72nd year, and Rev. Fritchey preached his funeral. The text was from John's Gospel, 10th chapter and 1-2-3 verses. He was a faithful Christian passed away. His wife survived him about six years and was buried at Grace church, and John Crawford preached her funeral."

In his "The German Settlers in Lincoln County and Western North Carolina," Joseph R. Nixon points out that the Germans encountered many perplexing obstacles that they had to overcome as a result of settling among people new to them.

One of these difficulties was to learn the most extensively used language. Since the predominant race in the colony of North Carolina was English, a knowledge of the English language was necessary. The Germans experienced a great disadvantage and much embarrassment in such important matters as society, commerce, customs and politics until they acquired a practical knowledge of the chief language.

It generally is conceded that the area of Catawba contained the most predominantly Pennsylvania Dutch population in the colony. Historians have noted that a dividing line of the German and Scot populations in the piedmont section of the colony was the Catawba river. The Germans crossed the river, and the Scots, for the most part, remained on the eastern side.

Equally necessary for the Germans was the Anglicizing of their own names and many of the words and idioms they knew best. As the Germans were ignorant of the English language, so likewise the English were unlearned in the German speech, and there was no mutual arbitrator or conventional device to serve as a medium for Anglicizing German names and idioms.

According to Nixon, the Germans generally followed the sound of words in learning the English language and in transforming the names and idioms into English. So then, whether translating German words into English or acquiring the new English term, the Germans usually spelled and pronounced the new word according to its articulate elements.

"To obtain recognition in society and politics, the task of Anglicizing the names was first necessary," Mr. Nixon explains. "Retention of the original German appellation was considered too unprogressive. The rendition of the names into English was effected by different methods. In many cases, the English sound of the German word became the permanent name. For instance, the name Cantzler was given the English sound Cansler; in the same way, Pfeiffer became Phifer; Kneip, Canipe; Krauss, Crouse; Huber, Hoover; Roedisill, Rudisill; and Jundt, Yount. In many other cases, a translation of the German name into its English meaning occurred. As an example, Zimmerman was translated into its English equivalent

Carpenter; likewise Kuhn became Coon; Weiss, White; Stein, Stone; Schneider, Taylor; and Freytag, Friday. Different members of the same family sometimes employed both of the above methods, one adapting his name after the English sound and the other choosing the English translation. Later, other changes were made in one or both of these adaptations; so that in the course of time many German names originally the same were, and are today, spelled in a variety of ways. As an example, one name is variously spelled as follows: — Haas, Hass, Hase, Haws, Hoss, Hoes, Hose, House, Hauss and Huss. Along with the thoughts of these changes in names, one must also remember that some Germans held to the original cognomens, as Arndt, Reinhardt, and Hartzoge."

Although the newest generation of Germans do not employ them, they remember that their grandparents, and, in some cases, their parents, customarily interchanged v's for w's, d's for t's, and b's for p's. These letters have given the Germans considerable difficulty.

Among examples are winegar for vinegar, wery for very, vin for win, Waldese for Valdese, de for the, dat for that, robe for rope, peer for beer, paddle for battle, and papy for baby.

The German is devoted to his church. This is evidenced by the fact that among his first concerns in his adopted country was the establishment of houses of worship. The pioneer German was Lutheran or Reformed. These denominations often used the same houses of worship, with one congregation having charge one Sunday and the other having charge the alternate Sunday.

A mistaken belief is that the German places little value on education. The idea is dispersed when one uncovers records of schools being held in conjunction with the church activities. Often a church served both as a place of worship and as a school building.

Still another unjust appraisal of the German is that he is adverse to mutual cooperation in advancement of public benefits. This erroneous belief likely arose to his slowness in accepting the English language and his natural constitutional reserve.

The first Germans to settle the area which now is Catawba county were farmers by occupation. As the country developed and people became more numerous, the Germans turned to other livelihoods. They were the familiar occupations of the day: Operation of grist mills, conducting of tan yards, operation of saw mills, conducting of blacksmith shops, manufacture of furniture, manufacture of shoes, etc.

As eagerly as he labored, the German sought sport and amusement. His social entertainments possessed little if none of the caste system. Every one was treated equally in a community. Special occasions that brought the Germans together included quilting parties, spinning matches, corn shuckings, log rollings and house raisings.

It is to be noted that, often, the German profited materially as he amused himself. As an example, his social gatherings entailed projects of making a livelihood—such as corn shuckings. The sport was added by his test of skill in completing his particular work at hand first. Of course such events also afforded opportunity for free interchange of social discourse.

Sports favored by the German were horse-racing, foot races and hunting, wrestling, and square dancing.

The distillery was an important adjunct of the German farm. Liquor was plentiful. The "corn liquor" the German drank was in most cases for health and happiness. It was virtually a requisite of the domestic board; a "tram" was a symbol of hospitality.

The sometimes unusual characteristics of the German marked him in a community. A familiar phrase that is today remembered by grandparents is: "Well, that's to be expected; they're 'Dutchie' folks."

The fear of James VI of Scotland and James I of England, one and the same, directly is to be credited for Catawba county's Scot-Irish (Scot) ancestry.

James, the only son of Mary, Queen of Scots, sat upon a throne more or less insecure by reason of the fact that the Roman Catholics of the realm were disloyal subjects who always were planning to take the throne from Protestant hands and turn it over to a Catholic king. Ireland, which was part of James' realm, almost solidly was of the Roman Catholic faith, and, so, persistently was a threat to his authority.

Consequently, James looked about in his kingdom for some group of people whom he might settle in Ireland, and who would be a shield against this annoying threat to his royal power. In Scotland he found the answer. The Scots were Presbyterians who were as uncompromisingly attached to their faith as the Roman Catholics were to theirs, and as loyal to a Protestant king as the Roman Catholics were disloyal. Then, too, there was no danger that they would every intermarry with the Irish, for the Scots looked down upon the Irish with that disdain with which the conqueror generally looks down upon the conquered.

Accordingly, James drove the Irish from that part of Ireland known as Ulster. During the decade from 1610 to 1620, he brought 40,000 Scot Presbyterians into that seized Irish territory, and settled them there. These people later became known in America as "Scot-Irish," although they actually were pure Scot and Irish only in the sense that their ancestry once lived in Ireland.

The plantation of Ulster was a brilliant success. The skill and thrift of the Scot raised it high above the rest of Ireland in wealth. As a result, its industry became a threat to England.

By the beginning of 1700, the Scot industrial enterprises had become competitors of the similar enterprises of England. Moreover, the tenacious, uncompromising stand for the Presbyterian faith by the Scots brought them into sharp conflict with the authorities of the Episcopal church, which was then the established church of England.

Consequently, the British Parliament passed a series of acts which limited greatly the output of the Scottish factories and put the people at the mercy of their rivals. The English made laws which made it impossible for the Presbyterians in Ireland to hold office, practice law, teach school, or exercise many other civil and religious rights.

The impositions caused the "Scot-Irish" to leave Ireland by the droves. Many came to America, to North Carolina, and to the Catawba territory.

Hundreds of Scot-Irish peoples were caught in the stream of emigration which flowed from the European world to the province of Pennsylvania. A good number of these came to North Carolina by the same route followed by the "Pennsylvania Dutch."

A part of these finally found their way into the Catawba area by way of Sherrills Ford and other points on the Catawba river. The settlers established homes, for the most part, in the southeast portion of the county. Thus it happens that in the town of Catawba such family names as Bandy, Love, McNeil, Keener, Ervin, Boggs, Ballard, Rabb, Drum, Sherrill, Eads, Wilson, McGinnis, Beard, Bradshaw, Bridges, Carson, Hamilton, and Harbinson are found.

Among the strongest characteristics of the Scottish people is their unerring desire for freedom. A strong, brave, honest and loyal people, the center of their interest is religion.

Like other nationalities of Europe, they had been Catholic until the sixteenth century. Then, through the preaching of one of their countrymen, John Knox, they turned to the Presbyterian faith. This became the established religion of Scotland.

The Presbyterians, upon their advent to the new country, based their faith on the Bible as they understood it. Plain and practical in their everyday lives, the Scot did not care for elaborate church services like those of the Roman Catholics or the English Episcopalians. They were too calm, thoughtful and slow moving to get highly excited or emotional in their religion. But once they had built up a system of beliefs, they could defend it with never-ending arguments, and cling to it with the earnestness and loyalty for which they were noted.

This kind of religion demanded education. The Presbyterians, therefore, were among the most earnest of all churches in their support of schools and colleges. "Let the people be taught!" said John Knox; and his followers ever since have repeated his plea.

Doubtless, the religion of the Scots strengthened their interest in democracy. As they had to work hard for a living in the old country, the people had learned to place a high value upon the rights and interests of every individual.

Along with their sincerity in religion, their belief in education, and their democracy, the Scots were noted for their industry and thrift. They were familiar with work. They not only worked in the fields, but were among the first in the new country to establish the industries of the day. Due to their connections in the old country, they often entered fields allied to the manufacture of clothing.

The pattern of settlement of the Scots in the area now comprising Catawba county generally took the same form as the Germans. Although there is no accurate method of measuring, it is believed that, by 1842, the date of the formation of the county, about one-third as many Scots were in Catawba as Germans.

Settling in the forests as the Scots did, far away from the trade routes of the coast, and with only rough trails for roads, they could not have sold large harvests if they had produced them. So they had to be content, for a while at least, with small farms cultivated by their own families; and with relatively simple living.

The Scot homes were small, built mostly of logs and rough-hewn lumber. Their furniture, too, was simple, and so were the utensils and implements of home and farm. But they soon had workshops of various kinds, where they made the cloth for which they were famous and the household furnishings to supply their needs.

Such people were not long without community enterprises. In each area of settlement a school house and church—usually the same building—went up along with the dwellings and workshops. The minister and teacher—often the same person—generally supplied several communities, traveling at intervals from one to the other.

Admirers of the Scot-Irish have attributed to them many of the virtues which have appeared in Catawba county, and for that matter, North Carolina, society.

"They were the most efficient supporters of the American cause during the struggle for independence," wrote Rev. Eli W. Caruthers in 1842, "and they have done more for the support of learning, morality and religion than any other class of people."

It should be pointed out that the Catawba county stock of the Scot was of the Lowlands in the old country. Also settling in other sections of North Carolina, particularly in the Eastern part, were the Scottish Highlanders. Due to closer ties with the British—including an economic one—the Highlanders generally were Tories, or loyalists, during the Revolution.

Different from other sections of the colony, again the Eastern part, the English settlement in the area which is now Catawba was relatively small. Nevertheless, because the English made the first settlements in North Carolina and occupied the territory for almost a century without interruption, their political and social institutions were fastened to an extent throughout the entirety of the colony. English customs molded the form of local government, the system of courts, and the colony's legislation.

The Catawba county area had few if any Dutch (Hollanders), Irish and French settlers.

Pioneer families of the county, which are listed from the first United States Census of 1790 and other sources, are as follows:

A—Abernathy, Adams, Alexander, Allen, Anthony (Antony), Arndt, (Arnt), Armstrong and Ashbranner.

B—Baker, Ballard, Barnes (Barns), Barrier (Berrier), Barringer, Bendy, Bates, Baxter, Beard (Baird), Beaty (Beatty), Beckman (Beekman), Beck, Belcher, Benfield, Best, Bisanar (Bysinger), Blackburn, Blanton, Boggs, Bolch (Bolick), Bolinger (Bullinger), Borland, Bost (Bast), Bowman (Baumann), Buttz (Bott, Butt), Boyd, Bradburn, Bradley, Bradshaw (Bradsha), Brilhart, Bridges, Brown, Buff, Bumgardner, Burns and Byers.

C—Cagle, Caldwell, Call, Campbell, Carson, Cathey, Cellars, Chapman, Chester, Clark, Clay, Cline (Klein), Coburn, Cobb, Cogdahl, Cole, Collins, Cloninger, Clubb, Conrad, Cook, Coons, Coulter, Corpening, Cowan, Creseman, Cressman, Crunkleton, Cumins (Cummings), Crouse and Cumberland.

D—Davis, Dawfey, Deitz (Deets), Deal (Diehl), Dellinger, Dillinger, Dorsey, Douglass, Doty, Drum and Duncan.

E—Eslinger, Earnest, Earwood (Erwood), Echard (Eckerd), Edwards and Ervin.

F—Falls, Farley, Feigley, Finger, Fish, Fisher, Fitspatrick, Fleming, Freeman, Fry (Frey, Frei) and Fulbright.

G—Gabriel, Gant, Garner, Gilbert, Goforth, Goodwin, Gordon, Gorman, Gortner, Graff, Graves, Grider, Gross, Grount (Grundt, Grunts), Gyger.

H—Hafer, Hafner (Heavner, Hefner), Hamilton, Hampton, Harris, Hart, Harbison, Harman (Herman), Harwell, Haun (Hahn, Hawn), Hagar (Heager), Hedrick, Hedick, Henson, Hessian, Hill, Hiltebrand, Hogshed, Holler, Holman, Holsclaw, Hopp, Hoover, Horse (Haas, Hass),

Indians and Weidner Oak

Eli S. Coulter's Mill, purchased December 8, 1856, from Lawson Hollar who in turn had purchased it in 1853 from John Wilfong. It was equipped with French buhrstones for both wheat and corn. A mill was erected on this spot before the Revolution.

CATAWBA COUNTY

Horton, Hoselberger, Houk (Houck), Hubbard, Hunsucker, Hutson (Hudson), Huyet (Hewitt), Hyde and Huffman (Hoffman).

I—Icard (Ikert) and Isenhour (Eisenhower).

J—Janet, Jarrett, Johnson, Johnston, Jonas and Jones.

K—Kasler, Kaylor (Caler), Keiner (Keener), Keller, Kennedy, Killian, Kirkendahl (Kuykendal) and King.

L.—Lagle (Lael, Lail), Lang, Launce, Laurence, Levaun, Lineberger, Link, Litten, Lockhart, Loller, Long, Longcrier, Low (Lowe), Lowrance, Lauchanore, Lutes (Lutz), Lyons, Lynn and Lyle (Lyall).

M—McCasland, McCorkle, McCormic, McDonald, McGee, McGahey, McKissick, McMullin, Martin, Mass (Moss), Matthes, Mehaffy, Miller, Milroy, Minges, Moore, Moses, Mouser, Moyer, Mull (Moll), and Murphy.

N—Neall (Neill), Ney (Neigh), Null (Noll).

O—Olliver, Orr, Osborn, Owin (Owen), Overwinter and Oxford.

P—Padget, Pain (Payner), Pattern (Patton), Pierce, Perkins, Peterson, Pfifer (Phifer), Phillips, Pilgram, Pope (Bope), Poovey (Bovey, Boovey), Potts, Plunk, Propst (Bropst) and Punch (Puntch).

Q—Queen and Quinn.

R—Ramsour, Rankin, Ramsey, Reid (Reed), Renabaugh, Rennick, Rauch (Rowe), Rider, Rinehart (Reinhardt), Ring (Rink), Robinson (Roberson), Rose, Rosemond (Roseman), Rudessil (Rudisill) and Rutledge.

S—Sander, Seagle (Sigel), Seitz (Sides), Setzer, Sharp, Shell, Sherrill, Shull, Shuke (Shook), Shoup, Shuford, Shuffler (Sifala, Shifala), Sigmon, Sloan, Smyre (Smyer), Smith, Snider, Speigle (Speagle), Spencer, Spilman (Spellman), Stafford, Star, Starnes, Stamy (Steamy, Staway), Steel, Stricker, Stocking, Stroup (Stroap), Summy (Summey), Summers, Sumerow (Summerrow), Stoner, and Syps (Sipe).

T—Taylor, Tepong, Tomlinson, Trefflestaat (Travis), Turbyfield (Turbyfill), and Turr (Derr, Durr).

V—Vanhorn.

W—Wagner (Wagone), Wason, Warlick (Warleigh), Weaver (Webber), West, White, Whitener, Whitley, Whitworth, Wilcocks (Wilcox), Wilbrooks, Wilfong, Williams, Wilson, Winkler, Winebarger, Wise, Wittenburg (Whittenburg), Witheron, Withers, Witherspoon and Woodring.

Y—Yoder (Goder), Young and Yount (probably same as Grundt, Grunts).

Z—Zimmerman (Carpenter).

CHAPTER III

PATTERN OF SETTLEMENT AND BASIC ECONOMY: AGRICULTURE

Although the latter-day Catawban generally is compelled by the whir of industry, he has not, and likely never will, forget his hereditary love of the soil. His ancestors were men and women who took proud cognizance of their familiarity with the earth. As they commanded the land, they realized its worth as the supreme tangible wealth.

Agriculture was the prevailing industry in Catawba county as late as 1900. Even today, its importance as an economic factor determines that the area ranks among the first in North Carolina in farm production.

The county's agriculture is prompted, of course, by its physical characteristics. The gently rolling hillsides, fertile and watered valleys, and plateaus are suitable for the growth of many crops. Agriculture also is prompted primarily by the mental nature of the early settlers: German and Scot pioneers were accustomed to farm life and were attracted locally due to the desire to pursue the tilling of the soil in productive and peaceful surroundings.

It is indeed fortunate that Catawba has such a stable basic economic element. History has proved, particularly in the instances of the reconstruction period following the War Between the States and the great depression of the 1930s, that reliance on the soil as a means of livelihood has just reward. The county's people never have suffered at length due to adverse national and international economic conditions.

Although lately the economies of machine industries have taken hold firmly here, Catawbans have not neglected even temporarily their farming interests. The machine age has actually enhanced the attractiveness of agriculture by introducing power-driven equipment and scientific methods which alleviate much of the drudgery of farm endeavor.

Rather than be hindered by machine industries, which now occupy much of the citizens' time, the improvements introduced to agriculture by this machine age have sparked the tempo of the industry. New techniques, learning and machinery have determined that farm production is up an estimated 200-300 per cent over production at the time of the formation of the county in 1842.

But the evolution of the agriculture industry was a slow procedure. Its process affords an interesting study.

The tools with which the pioneers began the subjugation of the forests and swamplands were hand-made. Metal tools were made from iron which had been smelted and hand-forged. This type included a cross-cut saw, a mattock, the common axe, a rather crude brier and brush hoe, a scythe and a single-footed plow with wooden beam using slender bull-tongue and shovel plow attachments.

Tools needed for house and house-furniture construction included the hand saw, trysquare, auger, broad axe and hammer.

The method of land-clearing incorporated by Catawbans to almost the twentieth century was the "burning-off." Indians bruised the bark on trees and caused their deaths, prior to the coming of the settlers. The bark and limbs of trees fell, as a result. The settlers, then, set fire to effect a clearing.

The axe, however, was used to fell some forests, to cut the trees into firewood and log length. The "new-ground burning-off" again followed in this instance, often affording occasion for neighbors to get together and combine work with a social frolic.

In building the house for the family, logs were cut and notched and pulled into place on poles with rope. The cracks were daubed with clay. For windows only rough shutters were obtainable. Contrary to common belief, cabin-type structures were unknown to, or certainly unused by, New England colonialists. Carolina and Catawba settlers adopted this type of house building, generally credited as being introduced from the Swedish forests, because of its relatively easy construction process. With the aid of a "house-raising" party, a family might easily find itself in a new home in the brief span of a single day.

The earliest attempts at cultivation of the soil were by the mattock, the hoe and the plow. The idea prevailed that "new ground" contained all that was needed by crops to be planted and cultivated successfully. When, after a few years of use, a field became eroded and worn out, it was abandoned back to nature and more new ground was sought. The waste of land hardly concerned pioneers when it was so much in abundance.

Corn first was planted with a hoe. Later, rows were run off with a ripper or bull-tongue plow. Corn was dropped by hand and covered with the same type plow. The plow ran about five times between rows. General rules of agriculture were that corn be plowed three times during a season.

Wheat sheaves were dried like hay and hauled to a building with a tight floor. The crop was spread out on the floor and horses were employed to tramp it until the grain fell out. Usually, a colored boy watched the horses to ascertain that manure fell into a basket and not upon the wheat. The straw then was raked away from the wheat with forks. Threshers came later with a homemade wind blower that blew the chaff and dust from the grain. The wheat then was ready for the mill.

Thriftiness of the frontiersmen prompted them to make use of every natural substance which promised usefulness, even grass. Grass was cut by hand with scythes which were broad and of iron, hammered out and ground to a sharp edge. When the grass dried, it was raked with home-made, wooden, long-toothed rakes. The weeds were forked onto two poles which served as stretchers and carried to the stack pole to be saved for future use.

Frontiersmen raised cotton and flax and wool for clothing. It was necessary to pick seeds from the cotton by hand, card the cotton, and then spin it.

Numerous types of herbs were planted for medicinal use. These plants, as foodstuffs, were planted close together so that only the width of the hoe was allowed between them. The Germans brought with them virtually every known type of seed.

Gardens were small spaded with spade forks, four prongs of about one inch wide and 12 inches long. No horse, dog, chicken or person other than the gardener was allowed in the garden. Gardens and fields had to be fenced because of the absence of stock laws until the 1870-80s. Fences sometimes were live hedges. Others were formed of plaited, split staves placed together and bent around three rails. Bored holes in the posts were used for rails, as nails had to be made by hand were extremely scarce.

After gardens were planted, the pioneers had squashes, pumpkins, potatoes, and cabbage. These were cooked in the big iron pots, with pork, venison, bear meat, and wild geese or turkeys, and made a tasty dish. When dumplings were added, this was called "potpie," the standard dish at all logrollings, house-raisings and corn-huskings. Venison was "jerked" or cured Indian fashion by cutting it into thin strips and placing it on a framework of sticks over a bed of live coals.

In the fall, cabbage, potatoes, turnips, and like foods, were stacked and covered with straw and dirt to keep them from freezing for winter use. Fruit, pumpkins, small baking sweet potatoes, snap beans, corn and strings of beef were dried and hung in bags about the cabin walls. Hutzels were dried whole peaches; snits were dried apples. Kraut, pickles, vinegar, and molasses were stored in large earthen jars or barrels in smoke houses. The smoke house also was used for the keeping of salted and smoke cured meat. Hickory chips were used for smoking the meat.

Teas were made from spicewood, sassafras, and other herbs, but were used principally for the sick. If milk was scarce, a gravy of meat juices or a little wild honey was served with the mush or hominy which was the usual supper dish. Cabbage was made into sauerkraut, apples were made into apple butter, and quinces and apples were preserved. Sorghum and maple sugar were made at home.

Pioneers of Catawba county were proud of their lush meadows. Horses, cattle and hogs grew fat without extra feed. Even in the winter, wild peas were in abundance, as was cane grass. Nevertheless, livestock noticeably became leaner in the winter months.

Lucky pioneers owned flint lock guns. Many, however, were reduced to bow and arrow for shooting game. Traps and snares aided in the obtaining of meat. Fish were brought to the shore either in baskets or on gig poles.

Farmers made a practice of hauling their corn, rye and apples to the "still house," having them distilled, and selling the product—liquor—to whomsoever they pleased. About 1850, whiskey sold for 25c a gallon, and brandy for about 50c.

Brandy was made of apples and peaches and wine from grapes and berries. It was believed that every product of the earth should be used to some advantage and nothing wasted. Brandied peaches were made. Peach leather was made by crushing ripe peaches on a board and mashing them out flat. Strips were cut and dried.

The Catawba area was, and remains, rich in natural foods and timber. Its staple fruit crops have been from the beginning peaches, apples, pears, grapes, plums and berries. Its best timbers were, and some still remain, blackwalnut, poplar, ash, gum, hickory, chestnut, elm, wild cherry, oak, and pine.

When fall came, pioneer families busied themselves gathering corn, bringing in the vegetables, butchering the hogs, piling wood, and repairing cabins. These were joyful preparations, for the gloomy months of winter meant safety from Indian attacks and generally respite from work. It did happen, however, that sometimes after the cool weather had set in, there was a period of warm weather, called the "smoky time," or "Indian Summer." It was given the second name because it gave the Indians another opportunity to attack. The warm weather, or thawing days at the end of February, the pioneers likewise called "powwowing days," because they supposed the Indians were then holding their war councils, getting ready for spring fighting.

It was the custom to give lodging and a hearty welcome to strangers who came along. They were offered the best food in the house and made as comfortable as possible. After a pleasant evening by the fireside, the best sleeping accommodations in the house were made ready for the visitors and this was theirs as long as they desired to stay. It was considered an insult to offer to pay at the end of a visit for hospitality. Even little children were taught to refuse money.

Mills were constructed on streams for the purpose of getting water power. Overshot water wheels came into common use. The saw mill usually was operated by means of water wheels.

The saws were up-and-down pitman saws, not the circular saws used today. About 30 minutes were required to saw one plank. The log was set and needed no watching, as a bell rang when the plank was sawed. There were no planes. The smoothing of the surfaces had to be done by hand.

Two large round rocks were employed for grinding the grain, the bottom one being stationary and the top one moveable by means of a wooden screw that could be raised or lowered. Stones were grooved and needed sharpening or their grooves made deeper occasionally. Corn was ground with the stones some distance apart. Ground grain fell down into the center of the stones and was thrown onto a seive or bolting cloth where it was sifted.

A settler with a small water power on his land often would make a water wheel and connect with a small wood lathe. Thus, the making of furniture was easier. Many four-poster beds, tables with turned legs, chair rounds and legs, cradles and other items of small furniture were made by smart and thrifty men.

For tanning hides of animals, small neighborhood tanneries were built. These later became private enterprise. Leather for harness and for shoe uppers and shoe soles would be tanned by extracting the acid from oak bark after it was dried, pounded and soaked in water.

Every member of the family, old and young, had work assigned. After providing shelter for his family, the pioneer had to clear the land, plow, and plant. The mother not only had the work of the house to do, but she helped to care for the sheep, chickens, and other animals. She had to do the washing, carding, spinning, winding, knitting, and weaving of the wool. She made coverlets and blankets. Sugar making, candle-dipping, soapmaking, cooking, preserving, and caring for the sick were some of her other duties. She was used to the heaviest labor, helping with the planting and harvesting when she was needed. Marriage came early, and very often the women, who worked so hard, died young. All pioneer boys and girls learned to do their share of work as a matter of course. The girls shared the household work with the mother, and the boys learned to use the axe and rifle at an early age. They knew how to hunt and trap, prepare the skins and furs of animals for use, and preserve the meat for food. They helped with the plowing and planting and cared for the domestic animals. A pleasant task for the children was to gather plants and herbs for drying. There was little time for idleness.

Necessities for the home included a bedstead, a few chairs or benches, and a few cooking utensils. A chest of drawers sometimes was included because of the desire to lodge safely the few luxuries, such as an extra dress or articles of bed furnishings, settlers owned.

Occasionally, a journeying tinsmith might stop and visit and in barter leave behind a set of candle moulds, a candle snuffer and possibly a few cups. He also might have for trade a few pewter spoons and mugs and plates. Provided with moulds, the matter of getting animal fat for moulding candles was no problem. Wicking for candles could be made from soft inner bark of trees or home-grown flax.

Cooking was done in pots by an open fire. Baking was done in skillets with coals below and on top. Hot ashes were also used for baking. Potatoes especially were cooked in this manner. Corn or wheat dough often was wrapped in corn shucks and baked in ashes. Later, dutch ovens were built outside homes. Bread and pies were prepared with these. The dutch ovens were built of rock. When the fire built within them became extremely hot, bread and pies were placed for cooking. Bread sometimes was baked on cabbage leaves or corn shucks. Pottery dishes were used. Tuesday and Friday usually were "baking days."

The spider was the handiest and most commonly used of all pioneer cooking utensils. It was made just like a skillet, except that it had a very long handle. It also had legs on it and could be set right over the open fire. There was an iron rim on the cover, so that hot coals could be piled under the spider and on top of the lid. No flame was allowed to blaze around it. The griddle was much like the spider, but had no legs or cover.

An iron crane on the side of the fireplace extended out over the logs, with hooks of various lengths hanging from it. Thus the kettles could be hung in the best position with regard to the fire. The crane could also be drawn out over the hearth away from the fire so that the kettles could be tended.

Iron cast pots, kettles, skillets, pans, spiders and other kitchen utensils were the work, generally, of foundrymen and iron workers.

Spoons were made of cow horns, and usually were just a long scoop. Some were made of wood, iron, brass and silver. Knives and forks were carved from iron. Originally the forks had only two straight prongs. Later the prongs were curved. Some forks actually were only forked branches of the dogwood tree peeled and dried to harden.

Gourds served the purposes of cups, dippers, salt boxes, egg boxes and many other things. Some people grew gourds as a crop.

Tables and benches generally were only split logs. Legs were placed in bored holes. The product was dressed smooth by hand.

Spool furniture was used extensively.

Wooden barrels of course were made with wooden hoops. Some also were made by weaving white oak splits.

The women endeavored to make an entire outfit for each member of the family each year. Wool jeans suits and lindsey dresses stood many years' wear. Stockings were knit by hand of cotton and wool. Coon skin caps set off the men's outfits often. Buttons were moulded of lead like bullets. Women made hats of shucks and bullrushes. Many had only bonnets quilted or with wooded splits to hold them straight. The men wore long drawers of cotton or wool in the winter, wool or cotton shirts, and pants. A knitted jacket or coat tightly fitted completed the outfit. The women wore a chemise, a combination underwaist and skirt, and long drawers made from cotton cloth. They wore an extra woolen petticoat in the winter. With the changing fashions, bramble briars were used for hoops in women's skirts. Some wooden hoops and wire hoops also were used. Imported shawls were worn for wraps by women, when they were obtainable. Cloth was dyed several colors. Walnut hulls effected brown coloring, cedar effected gray coloring, and indigo effected blue coloring.

The pioneer woman's task of providing clothing kept her busy. In the summer she and the children went barefoot, and in the winter they wore moccasins or shoepacks similar to those of the men. Before flax could be raised and wool grown, hair from cattle, and even lint from the wild nettle, were spun and woven into cloth. In taking these unusual materials which grew at hand, and making use of them for clothing, the pioneer woman displayed the imagination and independence which were among her strongest assets.

The spinning, weaving and dyeing of woolen cloth was a long process from the time the wool was clipped or sheared, washed, picked, combed, and carded, until it was sent through the spinning wheel to make fleecy wool yarn. Weaving was hard work too. If there were enough clothes to go around there were always blankets and coverlets to be made. The preparation of flax required a special set of tools. By drawing the flax fibers through the hatchel, a sort of comb with six-inch teeth, the woody parts of the stalk were removed and the long threads remained in smooth piles. The spinning wheel used for this linen tow thread was called the "little wheel." On it, too, was spun linsey-woolsey.

Every spring, enough soap was made to last a year. Wood ashes saved during the winter were put into an ash-hopper. Water was poured through the ashes and allowed to trickle out through a hole near the bottom. This brown liquid, or "lye," was then boiled in a large kettle with fats and grease saved from the year's cooking and butchering. The mixture was cooked until it thickened slowly to form a soft, jellylike soap.

The occasional traveling artisans lent their talents in barter for provisions for food and what small amount of cash that had gotten in circulation. Journeying shoe makers, or cobblers, would visit at the homes in fall and make the winter's supply of shoes for the family. There were no left and right shoes; all were made straight. Each morning it was necessary to change shoes in order to keep them straight. Brass tips were put on the outside of shoe toe tops for children to protect the leather. Wooden pegs held the soles on. Shoes were sewed with waxed thread. Leather strings were used.

With the passage of time, a few musical instruments and books were brought in by these traveling "salesmen," and gradually the arts added to the comforts and pleasures of the people.

Although the early settlers were busy, they found time for play—oftentimes by combining work and frolic.

Among the social events were husking bees (corn shuckings), taffy pulls, quilting parties, log-rollings, house-raisings and barn-raisings, community dances, cotton pickings, horse racing, contests of strength, etc. Church also was made into a social affair, since preaching was irregular. Virtually every season with its different tasks brought opportunities for get-togethers.

Pioneers developed great skill in the manipulation of Indian war gear, such as tomahawk throwing and in using the bow and arrow. Feats of strength were ever popular. Even after a hard day's work, men and boys ran races, wrestled and enjoyed weight-lifting contests.

When a fiddler was present, a dance often ended the day's work and play. Community gatherings were always popular.

One of the most popular sports was shooting matches. When a farmer had a beef to sell, he put out the word. Immediately this meant a "make up" of chances, and a "shoot." Shooting usually was done at a 100 yards distance. The man who "drove" the center of a marked paper was entitled to the choice of the beef's hind quarters. The second best shot got the other hind quarter, the third, a choice of the fore quarters, the fourth, the other fore quarter, the fifth, the hide and tallow, and the sixth, the lead of the shooting if he cared to chop it out of the tree.

Hunting, which served primarily as a means of procuring fresh meat, also was considered a sport. Wild game was abundant in the Catawba area, especially deer, squirrel and rabbit. Fowl and fish also were sought.

Neighbors were always ready to help newcomers and newly married couples build their homes and barns. When a new home or barn was to be built, men, women and children from miles around gathered together. Usually the house was finished between sunup and sundown. At noon, and at evening, a feast was spread, and everyone sat about, eating, telling stories, and playing jokes on one another. At the housewarming parties, they would often dance until late in the night, with a fiddler calling the dances.

The husking bees are said to have been a favorite pastime of Catawbans, serving the utilitarian purpose of preparing food for the long winter months and, at the same time, affording one of the most pleasant socials of the season. Neighbors gathered at a farm house soon after dinner, set to work at shucking, and were usually through the task by nightfall. The evening meal was served—"piping hot"—by the host. Following supper, men would entertain themselves by foot racing, wrestling, jumping and playing horseshoes. Women bided their time by conducting quiltings, cardings and sewing—supplemented, of course, by exchanging community gossip. Young people "carried on" by dancing, giving plays, and attending to matters of the heart.

Weddings gave an opportunity for fun and hilarity. On these occasions, the pioneers attended in their best clothes, the men in coarse shoes, leather breeches, leggings and hunting shirts. The women came in linen dresses (if fortunate enough to have them), coarse shoes, stockings, and sometimes buckskin gloves. Frequently there was a march in double file to the cabin of the bride. In some instances, the neighbors thought it was fun to delay the ceremony by placing trees or grapevines across the path over which the wedding party must travel. After the ceremony, a feast was held, at which beef, pork, fowl, roasted and boiled with potatoes, cabbage, and other vegetables, was served. Occasionally, neighbors not asked to the wedding cut off the manes and tails of the horses belonging to the guests.

The early settlers were particularly observing of "signs." An old rheumatic pain was their most reliable weather forecaster. They believed a pale red setting sun foretold a plague, and the crackling of the burning backlog meant a coming storm. Thick corn-husks, low-hanging hornet's nests, and busy woodpeckers were taken as signs of a severe winter. Fruits and vegetables were gathered in the dark of the moon so they would not spoil. Journeys were not started on Friday, neither was sewing done; and debts were not paid on Monday. Many people carried charms.

Due to the fact that certain articles could not be produced in the home or community, and because no railroads existed in the early nineteenth century, trips had to be made to distant markets such as Charleston and Camden, S. C., and Fayetteville.

CATAWBA COUNTY

There were those who made two trips to these markets each year—one in the spring and one in the fall. Often, virtually the entire community was served by one or two such trips, because the residents cooperated in the matter of hauling to and from markets.

W. A. Day, an Iredell county native who later moved to Catawba county, and an accurate historian, affords an interesting description of the market journeys:

"They usually drove six horses to their heavy wagons, and had a load to haul to market and a load for the merchants to haul back. They had a certain meeting place where they all met and camped the first night. Next morning they all started off together, with food enough packed on top of the load to last the round trip. They had regular camping places where they camped every night, both going and coming.

"On leaving their first camp, they would leave enough food in the care of some man living near, to feed on their return, and so on at every camp they would leave feed until at the end of the trip they had just enough left for one feed. Their last camp was generally close to the city, where they could easily get back to it on their return. Their back loads, as they called them, consisted of almost everything sold in a store, besides salt and leather for their neighbors.

"The rules of the road were for the front wagon today, to travel in the rear tomorrow, and so on through the whole train, an empty wagon to give the road to a loaded one; two loaded wagons meeting, each gave half the road turning to the right, a loaded wagon going down hill gave the road to a loaded one going up hill. When they came to a long steep hill they doubled as they called it, they would take the two lead horses from the second wagon and hitch them in the lead of the first wagon, thus having some times eight horses to one wagon, after pulling the first wagon up, the third would help put the second one up, and so on till all the wagons were all up but the last one, then the first man would take his horses back and help pull the last one up. Then all started off together.

"It generally took them about three weeks to make the trip to Charleston."

That weather was severe occasionally is attested by Day. He gives the following illustration:

"It was about the first of January, 1856; it began to snow on Friday evening, and snowed all night and next day till late in the evening when it stopped; the snow was then about 16 inches deep on the level, but in places it drifted up high as the fences; it had begun to settle down some when on the next Friday evening, another just like it fell on top of it, and kept on until it snowed four successive Friday nights and Saturdays. And when it finally ceased, it was nearly three feet deep. It settled till it became so firm that a wagon scarcely made a track on top of it. Everybody got out of wood and had to go to the woods, and for years afterwards until the stumps rotted away you could tell every tree that had been cut in the deep snow: The stumps were four feet high."

Catawba county was never owned principally by a few people. Only seven persons are believed to have had possession of more than 1,000 acres of land.

Immediately following the War Between the States, principal land-holders were: W. M. Huitt, 1,042 acres; Joseph Bost, 1,831 acres; David Wike, 1,722 acres; H. W. Robinson, 2,475 acres; Jacob Setzer, 1,319 acres; F. D. Reinhardt, 537 acres; M. W. Wilson, 552 acres; Frederick Smith, 572 acres; E. E. Deal, 529 acres; W. P. Reinhardt, 779 acres; John Stine, 462 acres; Samuel Blackburn, 471 acres; R. P. Reinhardt, 335 acres; Pinckney Wilfong, 200 acres; J. J. Sigmon, 189 acres; Andrew Fry, 227 acres; Elias Longcryer, 620 acres; John J. Shuford, 1,075 acres; Elisha Sherrill, 955 acres; J. E. Paine, 1,109 acres; J. S. Bridges, 771 acres; B. A. Abernethy, 771 acres; Joseph H. Moore, 460 acres; John Ward, 590 acres; and Jacob Mull (the exact amount is unknown).

Most land tracts had been sliced by the middle of the 1870s. According to Branson's North Carolina Business Directory, the principal farmers than and the valuation of their properties were:

Catawba Station—F. A. Yount, 632 acres, $4,300; D. Roseman, 820 acres, $4,700; Jesse Bost, 255 acres, $2,000; D. C. Cochran, 263 acres, $3,150; William Long, 553 acres, $3,000; W. E. Lawrence, 194 acres, $1,500; Powell and Sandford, 273 acres, $1,600; Jacob Setzer, 1,136 acres, $3,728; and Andrew Yount, 405 acres, $1,900.

CATAWBA COUNTY 63

Hickory Tavern—Joel Miller, 637 acres, $1,900; W. A. Reinhardt, 388 acres, $5,500; H. W. Robinson, 1,257 acres, $8,600; John Ward, 590 acres, $3,300; and Jacob Sandford, 412 acres, $3,200.

Jacob's Fork—L. R. Whitner, 196 acres, $1,800; Henry Cansler, ——, ——; Jacob Mull, 1,500 acres, $4,170; Jacob Mosteller, ——, $2,400; Jacob Anthony, 763 acres, $5,800; and Samuel Blackman, 571 acres, $4,500.

Newton—M. M. Hunt, 1,270 acres, $8,900; F. D. Reinhardt, 493 acres, $5,700; M. E. McCorcle, 450 acres, $3,500; F. Smith, 400 acres, $4,000; H. F. Carpenter, 894 acres, $5,000; F. D. Reinhardt, 537 acres, $6,000; Logan Smyre, 491 acres, $3,500; F. Smith, 406 acres, $3,250; F. L. Hennon, 203 acres, $1,200; M. L. McCorkle, 740 acres, $9,000; R. A. Bost, ——, ——; Joseph Bost, 744 acres, $5,500; Frank Carpenter, 977 acres, $6,000; P. W. Whiten, 175 acres, $2,000; Caleb Rhodes, 510 acres, $5,000; E. P. Coulter, 280 acres, $2,500; John Smyre, 375 acres, $6,000; J. J. Sigmon, 189 acres, $2,500; John Wilfong, 389 acres, $5,000; V. P. Wilfong, 200 acres, $3,000; S. T. Wilfong, 284 acres, $2,500; L. R. Whitner, 175 acres, $2,000; D. B. Gaither, 506 acres, $3,140; George Hennon, 385 acres, $2,500; M. M. Hunt, 975 acres, $7,525; and G. A. Ikerd, 420 acres, $3,400.

Sherrills Ford—D. W. Shelton, 257 acres, $1,200; Lewis Holdsclaw, 534 acres, $2,500; Thomas Beaty, 475 acres, $1,900; S. J. Caldwell, 443 acres, $3,600; E. F. Sherrill, 210 acres, $2,000; L. A. Lockman, 500 acres, $5,000; and J. M. Gabriel, 310 acres, $2,000.

The first assistance from the state in regard to agricultural matters was afforded in the 1870s. Catawba county's "Correspondent for the Agriculture Department," the forerunner of the agencies for farm, home demonstration and related aid, was W. P. Reinhardt of Hickory. He was holding office as early as 1877.

Reinhardt's report to Raleigh at approximately this time put Catawba land acreage at 247,415 with a value of $1,044,388, and town property at $94,655.

He listed 1,851 horses, worth $103,439; 1,160 mules, worth $75,509; 16 jacks, worth $1,475; 18 jennetts, worth $387;

48 goats, worth $48,; 7,042 total cattle, worth $47,305; 13,075 hogs, worth $17,493; and 8,301 sheep, worth $8,167.

A North Carolina state department of agriculture report during the 1870s placed the county's farm acreage and its production as: 5,175 acres of cotton, producing 2,012 bales; 21,248 acres of corn, producing 358,210 bushels; 7,566 acres of oats, producing 64,236 bushels; 181 acres of rye, producing 783 bushels; 15,154 acres of wheat, producing 101,770 bushels; and 49 acres of tobacco, producing 26,388 pounds.

The county contained 78,080 acres of improved land and 141,593 acres of unimproved land at this time.

During the 1880s and 90s, Catawba county began to obtain state agricultural honors and "first" records. By 1884, the area was considered to be one of North Carolina's top wheat growing counties. Catawba was the pioneer Jersey cattle center of the state, and for more than 70 years the area's herds of this animal have been nationally known. Equitable climate made the well-watered section in which Catawba county is located the natural home of livestock. The Holstein and Hereford breeds of cow also have earned great boosters here.

Although it is known that the list is incomplete (omissions especially notable in Hickory and Cline townships), an indication of the distribution of farms is obtainable from a compilation by Branson for his Directory. The report purports to provide the names (many of which are obviously mispelled) of the county's farmers, according to their post office addresses, in 1885. The writing is as follows:

Catawba—F. A. Yount, D. Roseman, Jesse Bost, D. C. Cochran, William Long, W. E. Lawrence, ——— Powell, Jacob Setzer, Andrew Yount, Barbara Abernethy, Pharr Abernethy, A. J. K. Thomas, S. N. Thomas, Franklin Yount, Henry Baker, Jones Cochran, Pink Milagan, John Sherrill, W. G. James, Uriah Long, Sidney Bridges, James Moore, Lewis Lollar, A. M. Powell, A. M. Lewis, E. F. Sherrill, E. Sherrill, M. Martin, A. House, H. Setzer, D. Little, Thomas Long, B. Turner, I. H. Sherrill, J. S. Bridges, C. M. Lawrence, Henry Pitts, M. B. Trollinger, F. M. Alley, W. H. Aderholdt, J. H. Aderholdt, Jno. Blackwelder and L. A. Shuford.

Clinesville—H. W. Caldwell, J. Howard and John Dambwood.

Conover—C. Hinkle, ——— Hill, Daniel Hoover, D. Harman, P. Little, David Drumm, John Smithdel, Dr. ——— Ellurte, J. Isenhour, M. A. Abernethy and company, L. Hunsucker, N. Hunsucker, David Hunsucker, Daniel Deal, Sylvanus Deal, N. Sigmon, E. Sigmon, L. Sigman, E. Smith,

Old Mathias Barringer Home, erected in the 1760's. Catawba County was organized here March 13, 1843.

Newton Court House with Whipping Post

CATAWBA COUNTY 65

Mark Smith, John Stine, Logan Dellinger, George Moser, Moses Herman, Elijah Herman, Elijah Cline, Daniel Cline, Lafayette Yount, Joshue Little, Peter Drum, Jacob Little, Cicero Simmons, John Simmons, Noah Rowe, Henry Isenhour, Jacob Isenhour, G. M. Welfong, J. Cline, E. Gant, W. H. Morrow, J. W. Blackwelder, Jesse Bost, Alfred Bridgers, W. G. Jarus, Phillip Pitts, M. Rufty, David Smith, Jacob Setzer, John S. Sherrill, J. H. Sherrill, Eliott Sherrill, S. S. Yount, Andrew Yount, F. A. Yount, J. G. Bynum, A. D. Shuford, M. B. Trollinger, J. H. Pitts, J. H. Aderholt, Robert Cook, Alexander Blackley, S. C. Brown, Jacob Brown, Logan Kale, T. S. Long and John Null.

Farm—C. J. Frazier, N. Huffman, John Killian, V. M. McBee, H. P. Rudisill, O. P. Bost, Max Huffman, Abel Fry, W. Lawers, Philip Gilbert, Philip Burns, George Whitner, Logan Whitner, Caleb Rhodes, John Whitener, Joe Whitener, H. Whitner, Jonas Harrison, Samuel Lutz, Ben Whitner, P. C. Rudisill, Lansen Yount, P. Setzer, John Sims and William Blackburn.

Flemmings—O. W. Asbury, John T. Cochran, B. F. Cornelius, J. H. Cornelius, H. F. Cornelius, M. M. Gabriel, John Gabriel, Spencer Munday, Thomas Beattie, Franklin Beattie, John Little, F. G. McCaul and W. Mundy.

Hickory—R. W. Johnson, R. B. Davis, Daniel Hawn, Joe Moore, Jackson Huffman, R. W. McCombs, E. Rhine, Laban Holman, R. Holman, Thomas Alexander, A. Flowers, E. Towman, C. Hawn, W. W. Ellis, S. Fry, A. W. Marshall, H. Welfong, S. P. Welfong, Mick Bullinger, F. Harmon, R. J. Wilton, R. Yoder, M. Yoder, A. Yoder, F. Burns, John Sapock, M. L. Been, Daniel Morgan, A. Morgan, N. M. Seagle, W. P. Rheinhardt, William Whitener, L. Whitner, R. P. Hunter, A. C. Link, Andy Cleverd, G. W. Sapock, John Lingle, John Lyerly, M. L. Cline, A. G. Shuford, John Bohannon, Noah Halmand, S. A. Suttlemyer, A. Sigmon, A. Y. Sigmon, Moses Abernethy, John Corpening, J. W. Mouser, Joel Miller, R. B. Davis, H. S. Suttlemyer, W. A. Reinhardt, H. W. Robinson, J. Ward, Jacob Sandford, and A. A. Shuford.

Jacob's Fork—L. R. Whitner, Henry Cansler, Jacob Mull, Jacob Masteller, Jacob Anthony, Samuel Blackman, T. Anthony, Abram Anthony, F. K. Beck, A. G. Corpening, John Canseller, P. W. Delinger, Peter Finger, A. K. Finger, John Fulbright, John Kistler, A. Love, V. Love, J. M. Leonard, A. Smiller, J. W. Propst, J. J. Reinhardt, A. L. Ramsour, D. W. Ramsour, J. S. Shuford, M. Shuford, D. C. Shuford, D. H. Shuford, P. M. Sharpe, Jacob Silfong, R. M. Whitner, D. E. Warlick, Q. A. Wilfong, S. T. Wilfong, L. R. Whitner, M. Yoder, G. M. Yoder, P. M. Yoder, L. Masteller, Jacob Masteller, R. J. Helton, C. E. Hunsucker, R. Yoder, and G. L. Shuford.

Jug Town—J. F. Hudson, Dr. F. Foard, Miles Huffman, D. M. Wyant, J. C. Hoyle, E. F. Ramsour, John Mosteller, J. F. Hedson, W. A. Wray, Jacob Masteller, Lawson Mosteller, P. Baker, Barton Baker, Eli Burnes, Jonas Brittan, and John Rocket.

Keeversville—James Keever, D. E. Warlick, Daniel Keever, and Jacob Masteller.

Monbo—A. E. Sherrill, S. C. Brown, L. H. Shuford, Joel Fisher, Miles A. Abernethy, and J. Stiles.

Mountain Creek—Dr. J. A. Sherrill, Powell Sherrill, D. W. Shelton, John Gabriel, Hosea Lineberger, Rev. John Crawford, M. A. Sigmon, Tyler Beath, James Crouhleton, J. E. Paine, D. W. Shelton, and J. A. Sherrill.

Mull Grove—B. Baker, P. Baker, D. M. Brittan, E. Burns, Jonas Brittan, W. L. Chapman, N. Hildebrand, M. F. Mull, A. B. Mull, P. M. Mull, and B. Baker.

Maiden—Jacob Rudisill, R. W. Boyd, Marcus Boyd, M. V. Ramsour, Ambrose Bolick, J. D. Caldwell, Rufus England, and John W. William.

Newton—F. D. Reinhardt, M. E. McCorkle, F. Smith, H. F. Carpenter, Logan Smyre, F. L. Hennon, M. L. McCorkle, R. A. Bost, Frank Carpenter, P. W. Whiten, Caleb Rhodes, S. T. Welfong, L. R. Whitener, D. B. Gaither, George Hennon, F. C. Icard, Adam Hagan, Jacob Setzer, Reuben Setzer, M. Witherspoon, Jacob Clapp, Daniel Little, Jno. Carpenter, B. Whitner, Frank Carpenter, John Hoss, S. Wilfong, Daniel Hoss, G. Yoder, Mary Sigmon, Robert Reinhardt, Frank Reinhardt, F. Herman, M. Wilfong, Philip Burns, Noah Huffman, John Thomison, Eli Coulter, M. M. Wilson, Logan Wilson, William Self, Joseph Bost, R. P. Reinhardt, Noah Barringer, Moses Huitt, Lewis Huit, W. Whitener, Franklin Setzer, Daniel Setzer, John Aurnt, Caleb Rhodes, Silas Smyer, Abel Icard, Cyrus Fraizer, Franklin Icard, Rufus England, Winfield Boyd, William Boyd, E. Cline, Mark Wike, Robert Cline, Jonas Cline, Andy Bolch, Jonas Deal, Lewis Sigmon, Abel Huit, Noah Huit, and Sidney Yount.

Oxford's Ford—John Stine, C. Sigmon, A. A. Reitzel, J. R. Hermon, J. Little, J. Coons, David Fox, D. Hedrick, and P. Little.

Sherrill's Ford—E. L. Sherrill, John N. Sherrill, G. M. Beatty, L. A. Lockman, W. J. Holdsclaw, J. N. Sherrill, A. J. Caldwell, Henderson Cornelius, Alex Clark, Jason Sherrill, Thomas Beatty, G. M. Beatty, Tyler Beatty, Frank Beatty, Osborn Flemming, Archibald Flemming, James Harwell, H. F. Cornelius, B. F. Cornelius, J. H. Cornelius, Thomas Kozzle, Newton Sherrill, Whit Sherrill, M. W. Sherrill, Elisha Sherrill, Thomas Sherrill, Mrs. ——— Sherrill, A. E. Sherrill, Mrs. Sallie Sherrill, Jacob Sherrill, Wesley Sherrill, Claud Sherrill, J. H. Sherrill, J. Setzer, P. C. Shuford, L. Shuford, A. D. Shuford, Thomas Shelton, John Allen, Lee Allisn, Alexander Bradburn, H. Brotherton, Alexander Litten, John Bymen, Francis Brown, J. Turner Byman, Alex Clark, John Crawford, A. J. Caldwell, Frank Caldwell, Edmond Caldwell, W. P. Caldwell, Lewis Holdsclaw, W. J. Holdsclaw, Robert Holdsclaw, Alexander Holdsclaw, Osborne Day, W. A. Day, Dallas Day, Hanan Day, Joseph Edwards, John Edwards, Miles Edwards, Jacob Edwards, Herbert Edwards, B. P. Edwards, David Fisher, Tom S. Fisher, William A. Fisher, Thomas

CATAWBA COUNTY 67

Gilleland, Thomas Gilleland, Jr., Joseph Gabriel, J. W. Gabriel, M. M. Gabriel, Mrs. Francis Gamble, Julius Hildebrand, W. P. Gabriel, C. C. Farwell, Joseph Johnson, George W. Jones, Eveline Jones, Allen Jones, Abel Jones, Sigmon Gabriel, L. A. Lockman, W. M. Robinson, Newton Robinson, James Robinson, John Robinson, George Robinson, George Moss, Julius Moss, Freeman Brown, J. W. Long, Joseph Little, Pinkney Robinson, Osborne Gilleland, Sidney Whitner, E. L. Sherrill, Alexander Clarke, James Crunkleton, F. Howard, Robinson Sherrill, and J. N. Sherrill.

Sparkling Catawba Springs—E. O. Elliott.

Yount's Mill—W. H. Rockett, N. E. Sigmon, G. D. L. Yount, Dr. M. Yount, G. H. Moser, D. Roseman, J. M. Ornt, W. J. Carpenter, L. Dellinger, A. Deal, P. G. Herman, B. Huffman, and P. M. Hoke.

An appraisal of Catawba's agricultural scene is afforded by an article in an 1890 Press and Carolinian newspaper: "With upland and bottom very fertile and varied in composition, agricultural pursuits have been followed with much success, notable among the products being wheat, oats, cotton, corn, tobacco and the grasses. Fruits of all kinds grow in rich profusion, and there in 1801 was discovered the famous grape and its natural consequent which Longfellow so elegantly praises in the lines—

" 'Pure as a spring, Is the wine I sing, and to praise it,
" 'One needs but to name it. For Catawba wine, has
" 'need of no sign, no tavern-bush to proclaim it.'

"The mineral deposits of bountiful mother nature have also challenged the attention of our thrifty people; several gold mines have been worked with profit, the iron furnaces have turned out large quantities of this valuable ore, while kaolin, lime, and graphite are among the discoveries. The amethyst, too, sparkles on almost every hillside. The noble forest trees, including almost every kind of wood which stood so long in silent dignity, stretching out their vast arms to greet each other and shelter the beasts and birds, are now being fashioned under the mechanic's hand into dressed woods of all designs and greatest beauty. Furthermore we have by no means fallen behind our sister counties in the erection of large factories for the consumption of our own material products, thus carrying out the policy so nicely pursued by all the South for her resurrection from the effects of what we look back upon as a thing long past and calmly call 'the late civil struggle'."

New machinery and improved methods were to expedite farming beginning about the middle of the nineteenth century. One of the first changes was the making of a "turn-plow." Such an instrument was hand-forged and was called a "twister." The new plow turned the soil over, whereas its predecessor only had "ripped" open the soil. The next development of the plow was the cast chilled mould-board plow, that required two horses or mules to draw it. Agriculture scientists look upon this improvement as one of their greatest advances.

Another farming improvement was the power grain binders, which required three or four horses to pull, and which antiquated the old manner of hand cradling wheat and oats. Following in this line was the threshing machine, that was first powered by horses. About 1890, the thresher powered by steam engines was introduced in the county. One such machine was capable of cleaning 1,000 bushels of wheat in a day. Usually the owner of the machine contracted with farmers to do their threshing.

Cotton has been Catawba county's leading money crop for many years. Tobacco growing became profitable during and after the War Between the States. Large areas of the sandy soil were cultivated in the latter crop. Hickory was at one time a good leaf tobacco market. But, upon the organization of the American Tobacco company, the tobacco factories began to wither and finally completely disappeared from the scene. When the factories began to disappear, the farmers discontinued the cultivation of tobacco on a large scale. Among the trade names of tobacco products manufactured in Catawba county in the long past were "Carolina Special," "Cinderella," "Marshall's Favorite," and "Carolina Indian Chief."

As encouragement for Catawba farmers to produce quality farm products, agriculture fairs were sponsored as early as 1871 or 1872. For a number of years, both a Hickory and a Newton fair were held.

A Press and Carolinian newspaper article of 1890 points out: "The Hickory Catawba Industrial Association has decided to hold the seventh annual fair. The following officers were elected: L. R. Whitener, president; J. F. Moore and J. F. Click, vice-presidents; S. E. Killian, secretary; J. W. Mouser, assistant secretary; C. C. Bost, treasurer; James Wilfong, H. C. Killian,

D. W. Shuler, J. G. Hall, L. P. Seitz, executive committee; Mrs. William H. Ellis, Mrs. J. F. Murrill, D. W. Shuler, S. E. Killian, J. F. Click, H. C. Killian, and J. W. Mouser, committee to prepare the premium list."

A Press and Carolinian report of October 9, 1890, explained:

"The Hickory Fair is now in full swing.

"Despite rainy weather, the third annual fair of the Catawba Agriculture and Industrial Association at Newton was a success. A. B. Saunders had thirty-five varieties of chickens on display, while M. M. Cline, Reinhardt & Son and Holt and Homeward led among the exhibitors of porkers. The bovines were worth seeing even in rain and mud.

"M. M. Cline, V. P. Bost, J. C. Wilbury, R. L. Shuford, R. P. Reinhardt and S. L. Yount are among those who had fine horses. The Floral Hall was a centre of attraction. It is impossible even for a married man to describe accurately the wonderful and sometimes mysterious things made by women. In the manufacturers hall the basket made by John Warlick was indeed a wonder, and the sheep skins belonging to Jacob Cooks were things of remarkable beauty. Side Draught beat Jack High in one horse race, while Jay Bird beat Coral in the best two out of three.

"In the way of speeches, the people had a feast. The idol of North Carolina, Senator Zeb Vance, explained his position on the sub-treasury bill, proving that he is the best friend the farmer has in North Carolina. Hon. A. Leaser of Mooresville showed that the contraction of money is the cause of hard times. The Republicans demonetized silver in 1873, and so that party must be blamed, he said, for the now demoralized condition of the country."

The 1891 Newton fair also pleased a writer of The Press and Carolinian. The October 1, 1891, issue of the newspaper announced: "The fair opened Tuesday morning in Newton under very favorable auspices. The array of fine stock, cattle, horses, hogs, and poultry is simply grand. Our agricultural interests are represented and illustrated by samples liberal, excellent and curious, embracing every product of the soil in this portion of the state. The Association certainly bid fair to do their work effectually, successfully and acceptably."

Since the beginning of the twentieth century, agriculture in Catawba county has been revolutionized. Among the improvements have been knowledge of soil and water conservation by land terracing; the introduction of heretofore unknown grasses and legumes to start upward the restoration of the fertility of the soil; the assistance of national, state and county agricultural schools and experimental stations, plus the employment of persons especially trained to assist farming by giving personal supervision; the use of chemistry in soil preservation by fertilizers; and the introduction of many and varied pieces of farm machinery.

CHAPTER IV

CONTRIBUTION TO THE AMERICAN REVOLUTION

The first sacrifice in Western North Carolina to America's altar of freedom was made in the area which was to become Catawba county.

Isaac Wise, at the age of seventeen, was hanged in 1776 when he refused to align himself with the Tory cause, of which his own father was a staunch supporter.

Although living in a neighborhood of Tories, Isaac, according to substantiated history, declared his purpose of aiding the patriots. He was captured by a band of Tories near the home of Pioneer Simon Haas and hanged on a tree near the old Haas homestead, located about two miles southeast of Newton.

Pioneer Haas, according to tradition, took the body down, conveyed it to his home, and prepared it for burial. His wife supposedly furnished her best linen sheet for a shroud. The young patriot was buried in a plot of land which 60 years later was deeded by George Haas, Pioneer Haas' grandson, for burying ground purposes.

Three years following young Wise's death, the pioneer died, and his body was interred by the side of the young martyr. Descendants of the old pioneer say that he met his death when he stopped at a small branch to drink while enroute to a fulling mill located on Smyre creek, formerly Sigman creek, Bullinger Mill creek, and Smyre Mill creek (near Newton). He was thought to have lain down to drink and was stricken, probably by a heart attack. When found dead, his face was in the water. It was never known whether he died as a result of a heart attack or other sickness, or whether he was rendered helpless physically and drowned in the water.

Scant facts are available concerning the short but significant life of Isaac Wise. Only through diligent research by members of the Catawba County Historical Association was his name learned. In 1951, the Association marked with an impressive stone the site of the hero's grave.

Apparently, the people of the area of Catawba, following the Revolutionary war, were intent upon forgetting its misery. The section almost was equally divided as to Whig and Tory elements, and bitterness was easily stirred. This likely is responsible for the silence concerning the Wise death. The horror episode probably was never recorded in writing in contemporary times, and was remembered only because it was passed by word of mouth from fathers to sons and became a community legend.

Some historians express the belief that young Wise was fleeing from the South Fork section to the region around Salisbury. It is known that he and his family were not natives of the area which now comprises Catawba county. The opinion is expressed that they had fled earlier from Bertie county.

Tradition is that when Wise was captured, there was no rope available for hanging. Tradition also records that another young man broke his nose in an attempt to secure this needed facility.

A leader of Tories of the South Fork region ran his horse so fast over a bridle path in search of a rope that this mount stumbled, and threw its rider. The rider fell on a tree root face down and broke his nose.

The incident, although it did not stop the hanging, had its consequences. The Tory, whose nose was to lay to one side, acquired the name of "Crooked Nose." He later was mortally wounded at Ramsour's Mill fighting "for the King." He died the second day after the battle.

Because of the unfortunate circumstances surrounding Wise's death, such as his age, historians of future generations likely will give the account deserved glorified treatment. Nevertheless, in its connection, it should be emphasized that the Tories who hanged the innocent lad likely were subjects of mob frenzy.

Actually, some of the best and most useful citizens of Catawba county are descendants of Tory forebears. Their fathers were as thoroughly convinced of the worthiness of the King's cause as the patriots were compelled by conscience to sanction the movement for independence.

CATAWBA COUNTY 73

In the Shuford family, as an example, the youngest of the sons, David, was a brave Whig. Meanwhile, all of the other sons were staunch Tories. David, who, like Isaac, refused to take the oath of allegiance, was to become a very popular man after the peace. He represented Lincoln county in the House of Commons, and received other honors through serving his fellowmen in public office.

The Whigs of North Carolina were not to be slackers when a showdown was forced in the matter of the desire for freedom. When war clouds loomed on the horizon, after the port of Boston had been closed and the charter of Massachusetts abrogated, bold John Harvey of Perquimans county called a meeting of the representatives of the people to meet in New Bern in August, 1774.

The meeting was held in defiance of the royal governor. It was the first such meeting to be held in North Carolina and one of the first in America. Its result was the advice that counties elect or appoint committees of safety to take charge of public affairs. Such was done, and, until the adoption of a constitution, all governmental, legislative, executive, judicial and military power was to be vested in these organizations. The committees were charged with the responsibilities of making all the rules and regulations for the government of the people and enforcing them.

Drum and Rifle

Rowan county, of which the Catawba territory was then a part, was the first county in the province to appoint a committee, composed of the best and most trustworthy men of the region. Men of the Catawba area who are known to have served are Francis McCorkle; Christopher Beekman; Matthias Barringer, until he was killed by the Indians; Peter Mull; Robert Blackburn; Josias Black; and Peter Ikerd.

The first citizens of present-day Catawba to be killed in battle were Captain Matthias Barringer, a man named Lipiscom, a man named Adam, a man named Grunt, a man named Haas, a man named Wilson, and another man whose name is not known. These men were massacred at John's River, in the Quaker Meadows area near Morganton in Burke county. They were participants of General Rutherford's forced march against the Cherokee Indians. The date of the massacre was July, 1776.

One of the contingent of Commanding Officer Barringer's party, Philip Fry, escaped by the grace of God and a blessing of fate.

It was during this period that the Cherokees were crossing the Blue Ridge into the upper Catawba Valley area, where they carried on a reign of terror among the white settlers. The red men were allowed provisions by the King's army, and were encouraged to fight the Whig sympathizers.

General Rutherford's march was aimed specifically at freeing Colonel Charles McDowell and nine other men, plus about 125 women and children, who were withstanding an onslaught in Cathey's Fort in Turkey Cove of what now is McDowell county.

Prior to the Rutherford arrival, Captain Barringer and his group of soldiers encountered the Indians on a scouting mission. The Indians, who now had rifles and ammunition, were as well armed as the Whig soldiers. As the advance guard was marching through the woods, the savages, from their hiding places behind trees, suddenly fired upon them. Captain Barringer, being in front, was the first killed. The others of the party returned the fire, and a fierce battle ensued.

When the Indians saw that all the white men were dead but one, they left their shelter behind the trees and came yelling toward him. He happened to be near a large chestnut tree that had blown down. On the back side of this the leaves had drifted until they were more than two feet deep. When he saw the Indians coming, Fry, according to legend, ran to the big log and rolled over on his back, keeping perfectly still, hardly daring to breathe.

According to folklore, he could see out a little through the leaves, and while the Indians were scalping the dead men, one of them came and stood on the chestnut log. Fry was supposed to have said afterwards that he looked square into the Indian's eyes, but the savage did not see him.

In a short time the main army came up, and the Indians fled. General Rutherford ordered some of his men to remain behind and bury the bodies of the dead captain and his comrades. This they did, scraping out the soft earth with their frying pans. They covered the shallow graves with stones to mark the place, but to this day no one knows the last resting place of Captain Barringer and his men.

General Rutherford was successful in his march against Cathey's Fort. The Indians took to their heels when they learned that the army was approaching. Whereupon, General Rutherford followed the Indians and drove them across the mountains into Tennessee.

Tradition relates that Captain Barringer's wife, who was at home with her children, Matthias and Catherine, told her friends on the day of the battle that she knew her husband was either dead or badly wounded, because she had heard him groan.

The people of Catawba county, on July 2, 1897, erected, in the courthouse square in Newton, a monument of granite to the massacre victims.

The territory which now is Catawba was part of three different counties—Rowan, Burke, and Lincoln—during the Revolution. As a result of zig-zagging of county lines, historians virtually find it impossible to record the actions of persons who lived within the borders of present-day Catawba during this important period of history. Both Burke and Lincoln counties were formed during the seven-year span of the war. No military engagements occurred within Catawba's present borders. This fact has operated to produce a lack of records to give light on the activities of the times.

In 1776, Catawba county was frontier country. Only 29 years had lapsed, in fact, since the first smoke from a white man's chimney west of the Catawba ascended to the sky.

Shortly prior to the difficulty of the American colonies with England, about 1771, settlers living west of the Catawba had presented a petition to the Colonial Assembly requesting that a new county be set up composed of territory covering the present counties of Catawba, Burke, McDowell, Caldwell, the greater portion of Alexander, and half of Wilkes.

Western North Carolinians set forth the argument that the county, if authorized, would be 100 miles in length and 60 miles in width and would contain approximately 2,000 taxables (males) between the ages of 16 and 60 years, white and colored.

Contrary to common belief, Caldwell and Burke county territory was as thickly settled in 1770 as the Catawba county area. It is estimated that present-day Catawba county comprised slightly more than 200 families. Due to the fact that the population was almost equally divided politically (Whigs and Tories), it is understandable why so few Catawbans served in the Continental army. They were needed to protect their homes from the depredations of Tory neighbors. Likewise, they were deemed necessary in their homestead land to handle Indian outbreaks which were encouraged by British agents.

Although general Revolutionary history is somewhat silent on Catawbans' efforts during the seven years of the heartbreaking struggle, it must not be supposed that Catawba patriots were idle. Colonial records substantiate that militia troops of Catawba, Burke and Lincoln were not surpassed in enthusiasm, bravery and availability.

The matter of the absence of records concerning local patriots likely needs explanation. Virtually all Whigs of the area were members of the militia, and subject to call at any time. Each militia company was divided into four classes—One, Two, Three and Four. When a need for men arose, a class would be summoned. When the need for the particular class was terminated, the men were "mustered out" until called again. Men

CATAWBA COUNTY   77

lately "mustered out" were exempt from another call until all the other classes served. When the situation was sufficiently urgent, two or three classes or all the clasess were called at one time. Such a case, however, arose seldom. As the "tours" of the classes most often were short, and for a definite purpose, there are few existing records of them. Because the area was pestered constantly by Indian and British threats, no calls for extended operations of the local militia were made.

However, the King's Mountain battleground drew rather heavily on the section. Among those serving in the engagement which soundly discouraged the Britishers were Major George Wilfong, Captain John Sigmon, Captain Peter Mull, Captain William Sherrill, Lieutenant Isaac Van Horn, Palsor Sigmon, Daniel Whitener, Abram Whitener, John Dellinger, Michael Cline, Benedict Hahn, Michael Shell, Joshua Hahn, John Setzer, Francis McCorkle, John Wilfong, John Wilson, Andrew Wilson, Christian Arney, Samuel Caldwell, Caspar Bolick, Martin Coulter, Benjamin Bowles, Conrad Tippong, John Turbyfill, Conrad Yoder, John Dobson, Jacob Lutz, Simon Haas, Uriah Sherrill, Philip Fry, John Haas, and William Simpson.

Captain Daniel McKessick, who lived between the sites of Maiden and Providence Mill, was seriously wounded at Ramsour's Mill battle and was not sufficiently recovered to be at King's Mountain. Captain McKessick is said to have been an active patriot.

Francis McCorkle was active in both the battles of King's Mountain and Ramsour's Mill. Following the War, he continued his leadership in the militia, and attained the rank of major.

A tradition has come down to the effect that soldiers of the Catawba area collected at the South Fork region home of Henry Weidner, among the most illustrious of pioneers, to march from there to the Battle of King's Mountain.

At the same time, history records that Colonel Charles McDowell's force of 160 militiamen were refugees in the Watauga Settlement, in what is now Tennessee, and were marched from there with the "Mountain Men" (among whom was the principal body of men of Catawba) to the battle.

The tradition is partially true and partially false. An explanation is necessary.

When the men under Campbell, Shelby and Sevier began to gather at Sycamore Shoals, near the present town of Elizabethton, Tenn., for the march to find Ferguson, Colonel McDowell left his men to come on with the other forces. He crossed the mountains to his home at Quaker Meadows and there tried to collect any additional men he could by the time the "Backwater Men" (western Carolina patriots) arrived.

As soon as he was at home on the Catawba river, he started a messenger to find Colonel Cleveland and hurry him on to the rendezvous at Quaker Meadows. He also sent other messengers to rouse the country.

There were, perhaps, a few scattered militiamen in Catawba, who were not with Colonel McDowell when he went from Cane Creek over the mountains to escape Ferguson. (Although the entire militia force of the region had been called for the September 11 rendezvous).

These few militiamen doubtless received Colonel McDowell's Quaker Meadows message, and it is logical to suppose that they collected at the home of the old South Fork Whig to start on their march to join their comrades at Quaker Meadows.

This explains how it was possible for some men to congregate there, even though the principal body of the militia was already in the field.

Only a single resident of the area which was to become Catawba county served as a Continental soldier. He was John Wilfong, who was born April 8, 1762, and died June 8, 1838.

Military records of Wilfong, given by his application for pension, afford information concerning Revolutionary war activities in western North Carolina and elsewhere. Wilfong's data include the following:

1780—Enlisted September 1, under Colonel Charles McDowell, Captain John Sigman and Lieutenant Van Horn. The military detachment went to Cane Creek, Burke county, where it was in a skirmish; moved on to Watauga Settlement; returned by the same route to join Colonels Sevier, Shelby and Campbell; came again to Cane Creek; went to Gilbert Town,

Rutherford county; continued on to Cowpens where it joined Colonels Cleveland and Williams and Lincoln county troops; crossed the Broad river; and finally fought the Battle of King's Mountain. Wilfong was wounded in the left arm and went home October 8.

1781—He enlisted on July 15, under Colonel Hammond and Captain Cowan. From Lincoln county, he was ordered to Augusta, Ga., and then into South Carolina where he joined General Greene at Eutaw Springs. He was in battle there on September 8, 1781. He also went to White Hall in South Carolina the same year.

1782—He went to the Cherokee nation under Captain Jesse Johnson in March. He returned to General Pickens in South Carolina.

Wilfong was only 18 when he fought at King's Mountain, and only 19 when he enlisted in the Continental line of 1781. The Continental, or regular, soldiers enlisted for three years, or the duration of the war.

Following the Battle of Cowpens, it is substantiated that Continental forces of General Daniel Morgan and Colonel William Washington crossed the Catawba territory.

The route of General Morgan is described in the "Revolutionary Papers of General Joseph Graham," edited by his grandson, Major W. A. Graham, as follows:

"Cornwallis delayed several days—from the 10th to the 23rd of January—in the country between Gilbertstown and Tryon Court House. He probably expected Morgan to retreat on the south side of South Mountains as the nearest route to reinforcements. Gen. Greene's main body of troops had been held at Cheraw. Morgan, however, went around the South Mountains, came to where Morganton is now located, then along the 'State Road' by the site of Maiden, to Mrs. Bolick's. Here he sent the prisoners on to Island Ford, where they crossed on the 29th of January, he with a portion of his troops took the Sherrills Ford road, placing himself between Cornwallis and the prisoners, and crossed the Catawba on the 30th while Cornwallis was at Forney's."

General Graham was at Sherrills Ford when Morgan crossed and when General Greene arrived.

General Graham is corroborated in his description of Morgan's route by Major Joseph McDowell, who was with Morgan, in command of a body of militia.

While Morgan was at Sherrills Ford, and before he crossed, two of the Maryland Continentals died and were buried on the Adam Sherrill farm near the ford.

If Catawba county was able to furnish only one Continental soldier, the area did furnish a final resting place for two of the finest soldiers who followed Washington and Greene, for the Continentals of Delaware and Maryland were the most daring and hardest fighting troops in the American army.

Contrary to the opinion of some, it was no small cavalcade that streamed down the new State Road from Quaker Meadows. General Morgan's little army contained approximately 850 men, and approximately 500 British prisoners these soldiers had captured.

It is estimated that the entourage, in addition, was composed of from 700 to 800 horses. General Morgan had his own cavalry, the horses of many of the militia men who were mounted, the teams of his own baggage wagons, 100 captured dragoon horses, four-horse teams of 30 captured baggage wagons, and captured artillery horses. Moreover, the small army had 12 baggage wagons of its own, and, while the men burned a few of the captured wagons, they retained enough to carry the most valuable part of the booty captured, and the arms and ammunition which the patriot forces so badly needed.

Likely it is no exaggeration to say that the 40 wagons, two captured cannon and caissons, 800 horses and 1,400 men presented the most imposing military line the area of Catawba county had or has witnessed. It probably would have stretched two miles or more along the road.

A tradition has come down from the old people who lived in the vicinity of Island Ford that Continental soldiers gave the area the name of "Catfish." A story goes that there had been a recent freshet, and there were a number of shallow pools, left when the high water had receded. These pools contained catfish. The soldiers caught the fish with their hands and by using their blankets as nets. Hence, the place was labeled "Catfish."

CATAWBA COUNTY 81

Wonder often has been expressed as to the reason so few Catawbans were fighters in the Ramsour's Mill engagement, the place where actual combat came nearest the area.

The matter has been explained thus: General Rutherford had ordered Colonel Locke and other officers of Rowan and Mecklenburg to embody a force of militia from local counties to attack the Tories assembled at Ramsour's. Therefore, the Whigs who fought there chiefly were from the eastern side of the Catawba.

No effort was made to embody troops in Catawba territory. A few men of Burke and Lincoln, possibly 15 or 20 (exclusive of McDowell's 20 men), probably were engaged.

Captain McKissick is known to have been there as a private. He received a severe shoulder wound.

Any estimate as to the total number of men who served as soldiers at any time during the seven years of the war would be a guess. But, of the nine companies of militia in Rowan county in 1775, two may reasonably be assumed to have been composed of Catawba men. Captain McCorkle's outfit is believed to have contained about 64 men, and Captain Matthias Barringer's, approximately 88 men.

Catawba county men who are known to have borne arms in the name of freedom are:

Adams, Conrad; Adams, Philip; Allen, Vincent; Arney, Christian.

Barringer, Matthias, Capt.; Beekman, Christopher, Col.; Bolick, Caspar; Bowles, Benjamin; Black, Josias; Blackburn, Robert; Bradshaw, Jonas.

Caldwell, Samuel; Cline, Boston (Sebastian); Cline, Michael; Corral, William; Coulter, Martin.

Dellinger, Henry; Dellinger, John, Capt.; Dobson, Elias; Dobson, John; Drum, Philip.

Edwards, Nathaniel; Ekard, Martin.

Fye (Fey, Fie), Jacob; Flemming, Mitchell; Fry, Philip; Fry, Nicholas.

Gabriel, James; Grunt, Adam; Haas, John; Haas, Simon; Harmon, John; Helton, Abraham; Herman, George; Hoppes, Adam; Houk, Michael; Houk, Nicholas.

Ikerd, Henry.

Killian, Leonard; Killian, Samuel; Krunkelton, James.

Lipscomb, ———; Little, Peter; Lutz, Jacob; Lytton, J. L.

McCorkle, Francis, Major; McKissick, Daniel, Capt.

Maiden, Lawrence; Maples, Marmaduke; Mason, Thomas; Mays, William; Moore, Alexander; Moore, James; Moore, John; Moore, William; Mull, Peter, Capt.

Pope, George.

Reip, Audolph, Commissary; Robinson, David; Robinson, James; Robinson, John.

Setzer, John; Sides, Adam; Sigmon, George; Sigmon, John, Capt.; Sigmon, Paulsor; Simpson, William; Shell, Michael; Sherrill, Adam; Sherrill, William, Capt.; Sherrill, Uriah.

Tippong, Conrad; Turbyfill, John.

Van Horn, Isaac, Lt.

Wasson, Joseph; Whitener, Abram; Whitener, Benjamin; Whitener, Daniel; Whitener, Henry, Capt.; Whitener, Michael; Wilfong, George, Major; Wilfong, John; Wilkinson, James; Wilson, Andrew; Wilson, Matthew; Wilson, John.

Yoder, John.

Yunt, Russell.

Perhaps most favorable folklore has been built around Frances McCorkle than any other person of the Catawba territory of the Revolution period.

It is told that a group of men rode up to the McCorkle home, located on Mountain creek, immediately following the Battle of Ramsour's Mill, and called the militia man out. The group pretended to be a band of Tories, and told McCorkle he had been "sent for." In turn, the captain was asked his sentiments. McCorkle is said to have answered them curtly: "I will not die with a lie in my mouth—I'm for liberty."

Someone of the group reputedly laughed, and gave away the hoax of neighbors who had come to celebrate and rejoice with the captain of his brilliant military victory. The incident is pointed to by historians as indicating the real worth of McCorkle's patriotism.

True stories and other traditions and folklore have come from Revolutionary days.

During the early days of the war, Lemuel Jones and William Coyle, two of the Catawba area's most notorious Tories, found Major George Wilfong away on a military expedition when they travelled by his home in the South Fork region.

Deciding to take advantage of what appeared to be an advantageous situation, the pair stole two of the major's horses and all they could carry in household articles.

The major had so carefully concealed his bridles that the thieves failed to locate them. As a substitute, Jones and Coyle took the major's clothes line as halters for the stolen mounts.

But the major returned home a bit too soon. When he discovered what was done, he collected a few of his neighbors and set out in hot pursuit. The avengers narrowly missed their subjects at the home of James Harwell, a Tory living near Wilkesboro. Harwell had been harboring them, and assisted them in escaping.

Major Wilfong, nevertheless, recovered his horses and all other property, including the clothes line. As a token of his desire, he left the two pieces of rope with the directions that they be used in hanging the Tories.

Sometime later, Colonel Benjamin Cleveland's scouts captured Jones and Coyle. The colonel promptly followed the major's request. The Tories were hanged—by clothes line—at the "Tory Oak" near the courthouse in Wilkesboro.

The action on the part of Colonel Cleveland, history records, almost caused a murder charge to be lodged against him. It appears that he hanged the marauders, and also gave Harwell a lashing, without a court martial, or trial of any sort. Major Wilfong's word apparently satisfied the patriot colonel.

Friends of Coyle and Jones set about immediately to obtain retribution and prepared to have the enthusiastic, hard-boiled Cleveland arrested.

The General Assembly, however, was sitting at the time at Halifax, and came promptly to the rescue. In the records of the Assembly of October, 1779, is an act directing Governor Caswell to pardon Colonel Cleveland, Colonel Herndon, and others, for killing and whipping the Tories. As originally drawn, it is interesting to note, the act provided for paying the Whigs for executing the Tories. But it failed to pass in that form. Apparently, the Assembly meant to protect the colonel from any inconveniences about the matter, but did not intend paying the young state's scant money for something it indicated was justifiably done.

Another story concerns William and Reuben Simpson, brothers who married daughters of Captain William Sherrill, a renowned Whig. Reuben was a Tory, and William subscribed to the Whig conviction. As a result, a deep hatred arose between the men. It is told that William was on a scouting party when he learned that his brother was engaged in the Battle of Ramsour's Mill. William made straightway for the battlefield, according to tradition, almost running his horse to exhaustion. The horse finally fell, and William jumped off and continued on foot in a run. He reportedly was attempting to get a chance to shoot his brother. Nevertheless, the battle ended before the Whig supporter could carry through his wishes.

Still another story concerns romance. John Wilfong, son of Major George Wilfong, was wounded in the arm at the Battle of King's Mountain. In coming home, he stopped at the home of Captain John Sigmon, in the South Fork region, and called for a drink of water. Hannah, the pretty 16-year-old daughter of the captain, ran to the spring and brought the young soldier his desired refreshment. John was impressed with the young lady, and started to inquire concerning her interests. Eventually, he was to lead Hannah to the altar. Prior to the marriage, John joined the Continental Army.

That Catawba Tories early were embroiled in the courts is proved by North Carolina state records.

Volume Twenty-two of the records reveal that at the March, 1777, term of Rowan county court:

"Melchoir Tarr (Derr), John Rose, John Shuford, Sr., Martin Shuford and Daniel Wise, appeared before the court charged with signing a petition to Governor Josiah Martin, injurious to the independence of this State, and other misdemeanors against this State, said misdemeanors being confessed by the accused, they prayed the application of the pardon offered by the Governor's proclamation, it was adjudged by the court that they were within the proclamation, whereupon they were discharged, having given security for their good behavior, and the preservation of the peace."

Of the men, Derr, Rose and Wise are said to have lived near the South Mountains, near the head of Jacobs Fork river, probably in the edge of Catawba county or immediately across the present county line of Burke. Derr is supposed to have moved into Rowan county after the war ended. Wise came to the region about the beginning of the war, from the eastern part of the province, after having been entangled with the Committee of Safety at his former home. Tradition fixes that he was shot by either John or Andrew Wilson who captured him in the South Fork community where he probably had been spying on Whig houses. He was the reputed father of the young patriot Isaac Wise. Following the peace, Rose moved into the foothills of the Blue Ridge in the upper part of Burke county. Martin Shuford, who apparently later switched sides again, was killed at Ramsour's Mill. John Shuford, Sr., father of Martin, was "cleared" and continued to reside in the Catawba county area.

The Tryon, Lincoln and Burke areas (of which Catawba was a part) generally are conceded to have been "hot-beds" of Toryism. A study of pension applications reveals that each year from 1776 to 1782, there were "tours" of from a few days to three weeks into these counties to put down uprisings and to disperse Tory groups. During the years 1779 to 1781, inclusive, there were expeditions every two or three months for this purpose.

An idea of the importance of local militia in this section may be gained from the fact that, in 1790, Burke county had 13 militia companies, Lincoln, 12, Rutherford, 14, and Wilkes, 16.

During the early 1780s, the Catawba county area became a station of the sinister and despicable Sam Brown, plunderer of war. Actually, the infamous Brown, who was aided in his waste exploits by his sister, Charity, and other culprits, operated for some time from a cave at the Lookout Shoals on the Catawba river.

Natives of old Tryon county and members of a Tory family, the Browns carried on the business of stealing before the days of the Revolution, according to some. Their efforts only were intensified under the cloak of war. Prizes of the pair and their helpers most often were horses, bed clothes, wearing apparel, pewter-ware, money and other valuable articles.

The spoils from the pillaging forays in this section were hidden about three miles about the Island Ford at the Lookout Shoals, where a bluff on the western side of the Catawba river rose—at that time—more than 300 feet. About 60 feet from the base of this bluff under an overhanging cliff was a cave of considerable dimensions, large enough to hold several persons. Later, it is said, the opening of the cave was partially closed by a large mass of rock sliding down from above. Now, the river closes the entire cave.

The depredations of the Browns extended from the shallow ford of the Yadkin to the region embracing the several counties of the northwestern portion of South Carolina.

Tradition has it that Sam Brown was married to the daughter of a pioneer who lived near Island Ford. Unable to accept the life Brown led, she fled and returned home to her father. Brown swore that he would have revenge. He went one night and killed all the stock belonging to his father-in-law, whose name is not known.

Brown's achievements became so notorious that he was known throughout the region as Plundering Sam Brown. But among the Tories, he was known as Captain Sam Brown.

Persistent efforts of Whigs of this general section determined that Brown was to be banished to Green river, in what is now Polk county in the southwestern part of North Carolina. With the coming of Colonel Ferguson to the up-country of South Carolina, Brown was given certain protection to carry on his terrifying work in his new section. The hardened wretch now could dignify his plundering with the sanction of his Majesty's faithful servants—Colonels Ferguson and Innes and Major Dunlap.

Brown ultimately came to his end in the region of Tyger river in South Carolina. He was shot by Josiah Culbertson, brave Revolution Whig whose wife had been threatened by the robber. Brown also had apprehended Mrs. Culbertson's father, Colonel Thomas, soon after the fall of Charleston, and carried him, two of his sons, their Negroes and horses to the British at Ninety-Six.

Money and other loot hidden by the Browns at Lookout Shoals were supposed to be precious. Many searching parties were made to seek the treasure, but it was never found.

Tradition has it that Brown kept a mistress in his secluded cave. It is reported that she was questioned and that she professed ignorance of his robber activities.

After the death of her brother, Charity Brown fled westward to the mountain region of what is now Haywood and Buncombe counties.

The superstitious of the Lookout Shoals section once told that weird noises came from the general location of the cave when one attempted to near it. Folklore also says that the wind once blew down a large tree at the cave premises and 12 sets of pewterware fell from its hollow body.

CHAPTER V

EARLY RELIGIOUS LIFE

An unfaltering faith in God and certainty as to its beneficial manifestations are perhaps the most basic characteristics of Catawbans.

Original settlers concerned themselves immediately in the new land with a worship program for themselves and their children. Until facilities could be provided, they used private homes or open groves or barns as places of worship. Anxiously they waited for the passing of a traveling minister who would baptize their children and hold memorial services for loved ones who had died and been buried in the absence of a preacher.

History bears out the fact that the building of a church almost invariably preceded the construction of other institutions in a community. The church edifice, in fact, served in the earliest days as a general center. Schools were conducted in church buildings.

Catawba's religious life closely is related to the story of its early settlers, most of whom were Germans, of the Reformed and Lutheran faiths, who migrated to this section from Pennsylvania. Three of the first four pioneer churches were built by members of these faiths.

A rather baffling aspect of the religious scene is that the spread of Presbyterianism has not been as pronounced as some other Protestant denominations, in spite of the fact that a strong "Scot-Irish" population was present almost from the founding of the county.

Particularly due to the fact that early Presbyterians were uncompromising in their beliefs, it is thought strange by some that the southeastern portion of Catawba county—where the "Scot-Irish" settled thickly—contains only one Presbyterian church. This church, in fact, has been built in comparatively recent years.

The answer appears to lie in the fact that Presbyterian ministers for America were difficult to obtain in colonial days, and the ministers of that sect who did come to the new land felt obligated to preach to the larger groups of their people in

Iredell, Rowan, Forsyth and other counties. Consequently, Catawba Presbyterians generally were without a minister of their faith. Many drifted into the memberships of other denominations.

Another answer doubtless is the fact that Presbyterians required that their pastors have a complete theological education, whereas, in some other denominations, laymen were allowed to hold services and do the work of a minister.

Education and religion were closely allied in the beginning of the county's history. Men of education often performed the dual functions of teaching and preaching. Sometimes they were ordained ministers who later entered also the teaching professions. Sometimes they were teachers who, because of the esteem bestowed upon them by their neighbors, felt the desire to enlarge their services by ministering to the spiritual needs of their friends.

But, then, some earliest communities had neither preachers nor teachers.

In this case, laymen assumed the duties, as pointed out before. In the instance of church, persons who in essence preached, yet were unlicensed, were termed "class leaders."

Services usually were opened by the singing of a hymn, the speaking of a prayer, and a session of "exhortation." Church then was adjourned for lunch on the grounds. Following the meal, the class meetings were held. All who were not members of the church retired during the class session. The church doors were closed.

Class leaders enthusiastically set about their duties. They went through their congregations inquiring into spiritual conditions, and transacting any business in regard to the church which was person-wise or community-wise.

Early records reveal that persons remaining away from class meetings without adequate excuse were expelled from the church.

Most often, Catawba churches were built by more use of the congregation's brawn than its cash. Such luxuries as ceilings and uniform seats were purchased years after churches had been in use.

Some of the area's first churches were "union churches," where congregations of usually two faiths shared the use of the same edifice, generally on alternate Sundays. There have been instances in which the congregation of one church has "loaned" the use of its church structure to an infant congregation which was in the process of building its own meeting house.

The religious forces of the county have always been Protestant, primarily. Among the faiths are found the Lutheran, Evangelical and Reformed and Methodist, Baptist, Presbyterian, and Episcopalian, with a few lesser sects. A negligible amount of the population has been Catholic and Hebrew.

The first church west of the Catawba river was built in what now is Catawba county. This church was St. Paul's church near Newton, a union Lutheran and Reformed church.

It is not know when the first church building was erected. It has been ascertained that a Swiss minister named Martin, a member of the German Reformed church, preached there in 1759. Also, in 1764, Rev. Richard DuPert held services in the same locality, probably in the same place where the Rev. Mr. Martin preached.

The next pioneer church was Zion Lutheran church, the first exclusively Lutheran church west of the Catawba river. The church's deed is dated October 12, 1790.

In connection with the founding dates of early churches, it is to be remembered that, in many cases, congregations were formed prior to the obtaining of places of worship.

Methodism became evident in the Catawba section with the founding of Rehobeth church. The deed for the church is dated August 26, 1791. Some doubt is raised concerning Rehobeth's claim of being the first Methodist church west of the Catawba river, however. There are historians who believe that Moore's Methodist church, which no longer exists, rightfully claims the distinction. It is known that a church by this name once was located near the Catawba river approximately four miles north of Hickory, near the present "steel bridge" on Highway 127. The Moore graveyard affords evidence of this fact. However, no documented records exist concerning the founding of Moore's church, and it generally is conceded that Rehobeth's claim is warranted.

Among the other churches organized by the date of the formation of Catawba county, 1842, and which are the subjects of the present chapter, are Grace Lutheran church (1796), St. John's Lutheran church (1798), Hopewell Methodist church (1811), Union Baptist church (1815), Mt. Ruhama Baptist church (1816), St. Peter's Lutheran church (1816), Wesley's Chapel Methodist arbor and campground (1824), Thessalonica Baptist church (1827), Bethlehem Methodist church (1831), Smyrna Evangelical and Reformed church (1832), Concord Methodist church (1832), Olivet Baptist church (1833), St. James Lutheran church (1834), St. Stephen's Lutheran church (1840), Corinth Baptist church (1840), and Ebenezer Methodist church (1841).

In addition, official records of Lincoln county show that J. M. Smith gave "to Trustees for German Lutheran and Reformed Churches" one acre and 66 poles for the purpose of "a Church School House and burying place" in 1803 "near Smith's flat place on the south side of the South Fork of the Catawba river." Nothing more is known of the church, or, if it was built.

An important aspect of the religious history of this section is campgrounds, which are believed to have originated locally for the Southern part of the United States.

Interest on the part of white people in the religious welfare of the Negro race is not new, and the many well-built, attractive colored churches maintained today throughout Catawba county are but the outgrowth of the encouragement the masters gave to their slaves to attend worship in the days prior to the War Between the States.

Masters were required to have their slave children baptized and to look after their religious training. They took their slaves to church and in many of the houses of worship, both Lutheran and Reformed, the leading denominations of the county at that period of history, special seats were reserved for the colored persons either in the gallery or at the back of the church.

The slaves always took communion, but after their white folks had finished. True to the spirit of Christianity, the congregations believed in saving souls—but frowned on anything that smacked of social equality between races, even in the matter of religion.

In 1838, the North Carolina Classis of the Reformed church adopted the following action concerning the slaves:

"Whereas, there are some churches in our bounds without room for the colored people in the sanctuary, and without provision for their reception into the church, therefore, Resolved that all such churches be recommended to follow the example of their sister Reformed churches and the churches of other denominations generally in the South, in providing room and pews for the colored people in the House of God and in opening the doors for their reception into the communion of the church whenever their knowledge of the truth and personal piety shall render them fit subjects for Christian communion; and if slaves, by and with consent of their masters."

However, the question of admitting colored people into the church during services caused a severe disagreement in one Catawba county congregation. The cause of the division is shown in the minutes of Grace church.

The minutes recorded on February 10, 1838, read as follows:

"After prayer by Rev. J. G. Fritchie the object of the meeting was made known by the chairman. A communication from John Coulter (one of the elders of the congregation) was received and read. After which the discipline of the German Reformed church was read in the audience of the meeting. A communication from Elias Jarrett (Lutheran), one of the trustees of the church was received and read.

"Resolved, that the vote of the meeting be taken upon the question, whether people of color should be admitted into the church at times of public worship, when the German Reformed congregation meets for the purpose, or not. The vote was taken as follows: Those voting in favor of admitting were: Barbara Coulter, Ann Shuford, Sarah E. Shuford, Harriet Ramseur, Philip Shuford, Jesse Whitener, Henry F. Ramseur, Daniel Conrad and David Ramseur. Those opposing were: Solomon Shuford, Lavinia Yoder, John A. Yoder, John Yoder, and David Yoder, Sr. After the vote was taken the following resolution

CATAWBA COUNTY 93

was adopted, viz:—That the blacks be allowed to occupy the two back seats on the gallery fronting the pulpit, whenever they are admitted, and that they shall not be allowed to go in until whites are all seated, and then, if there is sufficient room, they are to be invited in by one of the officers, and to remain in their places until all the whites have gone out of the church."

ST. PAUL'S LUTHERAN AND REFORMED CHURCH (Located one and one-half miles northwest of Newton.)

"The Dutch Meeting House" was the first name given to the Lutheran and Reformed Union church for which a deed was made May 20, 1771. The property was deeded by Paul Anthony and wife, Frony, of the county of Rowan, to be used for school and church purposes. It is in part as follows:

"This indenture made the 20th day of May in the year of our Lord one thousand seven hundred and seventy-one and in the eleventh year of our reigning; Between Paul Anthony and Frony his wife of the county of Rowan in the province of N. C. of the one part and christian churches Lutarin and Presbetaren of the state named commonly called the South Fork in the province aforesaid of the other part; Witnesseth that for and in consideration of the sum of two pounds current & lawful money of N. C. to said Paul Anthony and Frony in hand paid by said two churches at and before the sealing and delivery of these presents the receipt whereof the said Paul Anthony & Frony doth hereby acknowledge and thereby doth exonerate, acquit and forever discharge the said two churches, his heirs, Exe., & admin by these presents that the said Paul Anthony & Frony his wife have given, granted, bargained, sold, aliened released and confirmed & by these presents doth give, grant, bargain, sell, alien, release and absolutely confirm unto said two churches for a meeting house place now being by virtue of bargain & sale to them hereof made by the said Paul Anthony and Frony his wife for one whole year by indenture bearing date the day before the date of these presents and force of the statutes for transferring uses into possession & to their heirs and assigns forever all that tract, piece or parcel of land containing ten acres, situate, lying and being in the county of Tryon in said Province, Beginning at a White Oak in Paul Anthony's line & running W. 60 poles to a stake, thence N. 32 poles to a stake, thence E. 60 poles to a stake, thence S. 32 poles to the Beginning it being a part of a tract of land was granted unto the said Paul Anthony by patent bearing date 25th day of April in the year of our Lord Christ 1767 and all buildings, houses, etc. . . . to the only proper use & behoof of them the said two churches & their heirs and assigns forever and for no other use, intent, or purpose whatsoever.

"Signed by Paul Anthony in German

"Frony makes her mark:"

After the turn of the nineteenth century, "The Dutch Meeting House" was to become known as "South Fork church."

The original meeting house was nothing more than a log cabin. The building as it now stands was remodeled from the old house of worship which became dilapidated about 1818 and was torn away. The sound logs were utilized in the new church, which was constructed a short distance from the original. The remodeled structure was made of huge logs but they were weatherboarded and ceiled. The nails used in the work were home-made. The church was built high to accommodate a gallery above the first floor. The seats throughout the church are crude, straight-backed benches, arranged on three sides of the building. There are five tiers on the first floor and three tiers in the gallery. The building is rectangular in shape, with a door at each end and in the center of the long side. Just inside the end doors are the steep narrow winding stairs to the gallery.

Windows in the gallery are very small square openings. There are three on each side and two on each end. Windows downstairs are longer but no wider than those above. There is only one on each side of the front door and only one at each end, as the steps to the gallery are on one side of the doors. Three windows are on the back side.

There was formerly a goblet pulpit, located very high, which enabled the preacher to be as near the gallery as to the first floor. It has been replaced by a roomier, rectangular pulpit built against the back wall. It is also very high and has to be entered by a flight of steps.

Directly above the place where the goblet pulpit stood is a device made of wood and suspended from the ceiling. It is in the shape of a wine glass inverted, and resembles a chandelier.

CATAWBA COUNTY

It was made for a sounding board to enhance the volume of the exhorter's voice.

No belfry with its significant spire pointing upward adorns the building. Neither does it have a bell to call the worshippers in.

To appreciate the quaintness of the church, now called "Old St. Paul's," one must necessarily see it. It stands tall and white with its ancient "God's Acre" hard by. Many of the tombstones are inscribed in German and the names on the markers are the same as those familiar in the county today.

The graveyard has reached large proportions. The older part of it is shaded by old and beautiful cedar trees. Some markers are home-made from soap-stone and date to the 1700s. Many inscriptions are in German and remain legible.

For many years, St. Paul's had no resident minister. Baptisms, eucharistic and confirmation services, and burial services had to wait upon the arrival of a visiting ordained minister.

A second deed covering the land upon which stands the historic church was made in 1818. It is signed by John Smyre, and made to John Wilfong and John Propst (one a Lutheran and the other a German Reformed) as commissioners. These men were charged with the duty of caring for the church property. The deed, written in a splendid hand, is in legible English.

Just why St. Paul's site was chosen is not recorded. As one views the property today, he thinks it might well have been for its accessibility.

The first resident pastor of St. Paul's, and the first resident minister west of the Catawba river was Rev. John Godfrey Arndt—Johann Gottfried Arends.

A legacy in the form of an old journal, written by the Rev. Mr. Arndt, gives insight into the advent here of the first preacher. The journal was presented Lenoir Rhyne college by Mrs. Jane Erson of Lincoln county, granddaughter of the pioneer educator and minister, who was to be the first Lutheran minister ordained in the state, and the first president of the North Carolina Lutheran Synod.

The book dates before the Revolutionary war and is written in old script, much of the history being in German.

The Rev. Mr. Arndt originally came to America from Germany as a school teacher, but, after two years' work with the children, he was ordained a minister and labored in the religious field until his death, in 1807, in Lincoln county.

The minister's journal corresponds with the "History of the Evangelical Lutheran Synod and Ministerium of North Carolina" in the instance of telling of the visit to Germany of Christopher Rintleman (Randleman) of Organ church, Rowan county, and Christopher Layerly (Lyerly) of St. John's church, of Mecklenburg, now Rowan county. In North Carolina for more than a quarter of a century the German settlers had been without any regular pastors, and were dependent for the occasional administration of the Word and Sacraments upon any preacher who might happen to pass through the country.

Thus, it must have been a season of great rejoicing when Randleman and Lyerly, representing 60 families, undertook the long, hazardous journey, at their own expense, back to the Fatherland to appeal for a pastor, a school teacher, and such pecuniary assistance as they needed to sustain them in order that "they might have the Bread of Life broken to them in their own language."

Leaving their homes in 1772, carrying with them credentials and a letter of recommendation from Governor Tryon of the then Province of North Carolina, they made the journey.

The story of their visit is that they successfully persuaded Rev. Adulphus Nussman, minister, and Johann Gottfried Arends, school teacher, to return with them in 1773.

The Rev. Mr. Arndt was a graduate of the Teacher's Seminary in Hanover, Germany, and a native of Goettingen, where he was born December 11, 1740.

For two years, the Rev. Mr. Arndt taught the children of the congregation of Organ church, and then upon request of the congregation and of Pastor Nussman, he was ordained to the gospel ministry on the eleventh Sunday after Trinity, 1775, by Joachim Beulow, Missionary and Inspector over North and South Carolina.

The Rev. Mr. Arndt served the Organ congregation and others for 11 years and then moved to Lincoln county, then called Tryon, and became the acknowledged founder of the Lutheran church west of the Catawba river.

After coming to the local area, the Rev. Mr. Arndt became the close friend of Rev. Andrew Loretz, Reformed minister, neighbor and associate in the ministry of Daniel's church in Lincoln county.

The earliest record of the appearance in the local area of the Rev. Mr. Arndt is his administration of the Holy Communion to children at South Fork church in August, 1776. In his journal, the Rev. Mr. Arndt lists the partakers as:

"Boys, Jacob Kransster, Johannes Vollbrecht, Johannes Antoni, Michael Hauk, Wilhelm Seigmann, Jacob Killian, Peter Hauck, Michael Klein, Johannes Haas, Conrad Winkler, Johannes Seigmann, Samuel Tritt, Johann Georg Siegmann, Henrich Wittenburg, Johann Miller. Girls, Sibilla Schuken, Anna Margaretha Bolicken, Maria Barbara Wittenberger, Rosina Tiehlen, Katharine Beringern, Anna Maria Siegmann, Eva Mahnen, Anna Millern, Dorothea Vollbrechten, Elizabeth Hahnen, Susanna Neuen, Elizabeth Hahnen, Susanna Neuen, Elizabeth Luxen, Anna Katharina Luxen, Maria Dorothea Scheuflern, Katharina Dormeyern, Maria Marlena Dormeyern, Maria Margaretha Schmidten, Philipa Adams, Anna Katharina Tritten, Elizabeth Bolichen, Christina Bolichen, Anna Katharina Weinbergen."

Among the pioneer ministers of other denominations were the Rev. Mr. Loretz; and Rev. Daniel Asbury, Methodist.

In 1901, the Reformed congregation moved from the historic Old St. Paul's church to the Startown community and built a handsome house of worship where the present St. Paul's Reformed church stands. In about the year 1905, the Lutheran congregation also moved from the original spot to the Startown community and erected a substantial house of worship. The Ohio Synod Lutheran church worshipped in the original St. Paul's church until it recently occupied a handsome brick structure almost adjoining the old church's land.

Virtually all the Reformed and Lutheran congregations in Western North Carolina are grandchildren or great-grandchildren of the historic St. Paul's church.

ZION LUTHERAN CHURCH (Located five miles south of Hickory.)

The deed for the church grounds of Catawba county's oldest strictly Lutheran church was made by Christian Neigh (Ney), to Johannes Hahn and Martin Speagle, as trustees for "The Deutsch Lutheran Congregation," and specified ten acres of land. The "consideration" was five pounds.

The edifice was completed during the latter part of 1791. A granddaughter of Trustee Hahn, Saloma Weaver, daughter of Conrad Weaver, was born March 18, 1791, and the grandfather was especially anxious that the child be baptized in the new church. The father, however, not being pleased with the idea of deferring the baptismal, had the child baptized at St. Paul's church.

The first church structure was a two-story log affair, about 30 by 36 feet, finished with neatness and considerable ornament for that period of time. There was a balcony across the south end, but only those who sat on the front row of the balcony could see the pastor, the beauty of the pulpit, and the chancel. A sounding board was placed over the pulpit.

Organization of the church is credited to Rev. John Godfrey Arndt. A historic document dated January 1 and July, 1800, written in German script, lists those who were contributing to the support of the Rev. Mr. Arndt as follows: Jacob Miller, Jacob Yoder, Jacob Gortner, George Whisnant, Daniel Gross, Nicholas Frey, Conrad Weaver, Jacob Weaver, Daniel Ashabranner, Adam Hartzoge, Benjamin Whitener, Casper Schell, Henry Whitener, Philip Speagle, Christian Hahn, Joshua Hahn, Johan Barger, Johan Dellinger, Jacob Hahn, Johannes Dintz, Henry Miller, David Hahn, Jacob Miller, Peter J. Hahn, Peter Fry, Johannes D. Hahn, Martha Yoder, Peter D. Hahn, Johannes J. Hahn, Johannes Ashabranner, Johan Yoder and ———— Hofman.

In the spring of 1807, it is known that 26 members partook of Holy Communion.

Trustee Hahn was one of the first to be buried in the church cemetery. Among other trustees who served early in the history of the church were Conrad Weaver, Benjamin Whitener, Jacob Hahn, Abram Cook, David Hahn and Michael Link.

Construction of the second church was begun in early summer, 1883. The cornerstone was laid on April 30, 1884. The dedicatory service was held March 29, 1885, with Rev. J. M. Smith presiding.

It has been established that brick for the new structure was made by Reuben Yoder, Noah Hahn, Abel P. Seitz, S. Augustus Hahn and James Jarrett. It was carried by Lawrence Jarrett and Charley Yoder, young sons of Reuben Yoder and James Jarrett. Lank Rowe, a Negro, moulded the brick.

Noah Hahn was in charge of carpentry, assisted by Pink Deitz and others. Brick work was in charge of Campbell Brothers of Hickory. Boniwell and Company also of Hickory furnished seats for the church.

The first communion service held in the new church was on November 8, 1884.

Zion church in its long history has never been a large congregation. But many other congregations have grown from it.

REHOBETH METHODIST CHURCH (Located two and three-fourths miles northwest of the mouth of Mountain Creek.)

Rehobeth church, the first Methodist church west of the Catawba river, is situated in the center of a fine farming section settled by industrious and intelligent pioneers whose descendants possess fine traits of character.

What St. Paul's church is to the Lutheran and Reformed denominations and the central part of the county, Rehobeth is to the Methodist denomination and the Sherrills Ford and Terrell sections.

Little is known about the religious activities of the Rehobeth community for the first few decades after the first land grant was received by William Sherrill in 1749. This does not say, however, that the residents neglected religious worship for awhile until homesteads were established. In 1780, a traveling minister held religious services near Terrell, using as his pulpit the top of a large boulder that projected a few feet above the surface of the ground.

In 1789, Rev. Daniel Asbury, a pioneer Methodist minister of the Old Brunswick, Va., area, organized Rehobeth congregation where he found a number of Methodist families which also were of Virginia. The Rev. Mr. Asbury married a daughter of one of these families, a Miss Morris.

The Rev. Mr. Asbury started the campmeeting movement at Rehobeth in 1794, when was held the first campmeeting of which record is known in the section. Campmeetings were continued at Rehobeth for four years, then moved to a new location in Lincoln county. The frontier campmeeting survives in Rock Springs campground at Denver.

The Rev. Mr. Asbury, born in Fairfax county, Va., in 1762, had some harrowing experiences during his youth.

When only 16, he went to Kentucky where he was captured by Shawnee Indians and held captive for several years. He was carried to Canada where he was captured by the British and confined in irons and brutally treated.

Escaping, he made his way back to Virginia. He came in contact with pioneer preachers, joined the Methodist church, and, in 1784, became a minister himself. He preached over a large territory from Virginia to Georgia.

He was moving spirit in the great "spiritual awakening" of 1802, at which time, historians point out, "the Methodists and Presbyterians combined to overcome the wave of iniquity and skepticism that followed the Revolutionary War."

During this period the campgrounds movement mushroomed, and a great revival swept over much of North Carolina, Tennessee, Kentucky, Southern Virginia and other locations.

The new church in the Terrell community was called Grassy Branch, the name being taken from the name of a small stream just east of the church so-called for the unusual fine grass growing along its course. No information is available as to when the church name was changed from Grassy Branch to Rehobeth.

The first church building at Rehobeth was erected in the year 1790. The structure was of hewed logs cut on the grounds. The building stood 100 yards back of the present building—at the south side of the cemetery. It appears to have been the custom with the early settlers to lay out the cemetery rather in front of the church building. This is evidenced at both St. Paul's and Rehobeth.

The first church house was built by members of the congregation and their neighbors—a free work system common in early days. At a meeting to decide how to build the new house of worship and when to begin the work, the slogan for the occasion was "Who will cut down the first tree?" It was a challenge given to all who would help. In the instance of Rehobeth, on the day appointed, a Mr. Howard arose "when the morning star got up," went to the church grounds, and cut down his tree before daylight. When the other workers came, he had his tree ready for hewing.

As time passed, the log church was replaced by a new building. The second building gave way to a third, and the present, structure in 1889.

The Rev. Mr. Asbury died April 15, 1825, and is buried in the churchyard of old Rehobeth, where he served his people more than a third of a century.

He was described by a biographer as ". . . an eloquent speaker . . . (whose) . . . fervent appeals to the wicked almost were irresistible."

An interesting feature of the deed of Rehobeth church, made by John Pinner, and Winnie, his wife, is one of its conditions. The deed places "the lately erected church, with yard, grave yard, walks and ways, under the special trust . . ." and stipulates "that they permit the preachers known by the name of Methodists, appointed and approved by the yearly conference of the Methodist Episcopal church, and *no other person* . . ." to use the church.

GRACE LUTHERAN AND REFORMED CHURCH (Located eight miles southwest of Newton.)

The third monument to the memory of Rev. John Godfrey Arndt is exemplified in the history of Grace Lutheran church. The earliest resident minister west of the Catawba river was instrumental in the establishment of Catawba county's third Lutheran church body, believed to have been organized in 1796.

The deed to the first Grace church lot is dated January 14, 1797, and it is assumed that there was an organization prior to that time.

The congregation owned its property jointly with the Evangelical and Reformed church, and the respective bodies worshipped on alternate Sundays. This arrangement continued until about 1941-42, when a mutual division of property was agreed upon.

The old Log Church House was constructed about 1797. An interesting description of its dedication service is provided by Rev. Paul Henkel in his Journal. The Rev. Mr. Henkel and several of his descendants were to follow in the ministry of Grace church and were to assume a significant role in its development.

The description is as follows: "Thursday, September 10, 1807. Today I went with Philip (his son) to a newly built church erected jointly by the German and English people. Today is the day appointed for its dedication. An English Presbyterian minister came to represent the English part of the community. Philip and I had difficulty in making him understand how we conduct a service of the kind. They do not have exercises of this kind and therefore they have no idea of how to go ahead. We informed him that he was to deliver the first sermon. His two long prayers that he spoke before the sermon were applicable enough, but his sermon was not at all appropriate. His text was 'Rejoice that your names are written in heaven!' It was unusually long. The English people in the audience were few in number, and still fewer on the part of the Germans. It was nearly sunset when the services concluded; I gave but a brief exhortation in German. I returned to the city with my son but it was late when we arrived as the distance was twelve miles." The Rev. Mr. Henkel was then pastor of Abbotts Creek church in Rowan, now Davidson, county.

Carrying out a Synodical resolution passed May 2, 1803, the Rev. Mr. Henkel came to Lincoln county to assist the Rev. Mr. Arndt. He succeeded the pioneer minister as pastor at Grace church.

In speaking of the Rev. Mr. Henkel, one writer says: "He was, in early life and for many years, a laborious missionary among the scattered Anglo-German population of the South. He may indeed be considered as one of the pioneers of the church in that region, which was in those days truly desolate."

The earliest Reformed minister is recorded as Andrew H. Loretz. Scant information is available concerning this pioneer, whose work in the ministry in Catawba county inspired a progressive denomination. A small pamphlet entitled "History of Daniel's Evangelical Lutheran and Reformed Churches, Lincoln County, N. C.," prepared by A. Nixon, includes the following general information about the minister:

"So far as I can learn the first Reformed pastor was Rev. Andrew Loretz, a native of Switzerland. (The Rev. Mr. Loretz was pastor of Daniel's church and was, at the same time, pastor of the Reformed congregation at Old St. Paul's church. He was to become pastor of the Reformed congregation at St. John's later.) He came about the same time of Mr. Arndt and discharged the duties of his sacred office until death. He built the Fox residence a few hundred yards to the south on the plantation adjoining the (Daniel's) church land. On this building today are the initials of his name and the date of its erection, ('A. L. 1793'). Only the German was used during their (the Rev. Mr. Arndt and the Rev. Mr. Loretz) pastorates. Rev. Loretz died March 31, 1812, aged fifty years and is buried in the church-yard here. He was a man of remarkable energy, great endurance, and zealous in the performance of duty; a preacher whose sermons were strong in thought, chaste and learning...." It is also known that the Rev. Mr. Loretz entered somewhat into the political life of his day. Records reveal that he was three times a member of the state House.

The first Grace church was a log house, about 25 by 30 feet, with two stories. It was said to have been inconveniently arranged. Traditional history relates that members of the congregation were instructed to procure the number of logs and deliver them to the church site. Others were engaged in making and delivering shingles.

The second Grace edifice was constructed in 1857-58, and is now used by the Evangelical and Reformed congregation. Following periods of both slack and growth, the new building was deemed necessary when Dr. A. J. Fox stimulated intense religious interest in the community. The congregation decided that a brick house of worship would be begun when $200 was raised collectively. When the church was completed, it cost $1,400 all told.

Following the division of property by the Lutherans and Reformed members, the Lutherans erected on land on the east side of the highway just opposite the Brick Union church the New Brick Lutheran church. It was opened for service on Easter Day, April 5, 1942. The building was dedicated on June 6, 1943.

The Lutheran church was destroyed by fire on March 7, 1948. Rebuilding was begun immediately, and, on September 16, 1951, the beautiful and utilitarian new Grace Evangelical Lutheran church was dedicated.

ST. JOHN'S LUTHERAN CHURCH (Located three miles northeast of Conover.)

Because of the absence of records, St. John's Lutheran church may be deprived forever of its rightful position among early churches. It generally is accepted that this church was the fifth established in the area which was to become Catawba county, although lately certain evidence has become uncovered which tends to indicate that the church is entitled to recognition for earlier birth, possibly due the distinction of being the second congregation created in the county.

Records of the establishment of the congregation and of the building of the first church, if any were kept, have been lost. The only record that has escaped the ravages of time is the deed to the land, about six acres, upon which the church stands. This deed was executed in 1798 by Henry Bobe (Pope), who had obtained the land by king's patent from Governor Tryon.

The deed points out: "This indenture made this 25th day of November in the year of our Lord 1798 between Henry Bobe of the County of Lincoln and State of North Carolina of the one part, to the elders of the United Congregation of St. John's and their successors in office forever in trust for the said congregation consisting of Episcopalians, Lutherans and Presbyterians . . ." The words of the deed plainly indicate the organization of a congregation prior to its writing, even to the selection of trustees. Further suppositions that make the formation of St. John's likely before 1798 include the facts that the members of the church's congregation, "Pennsylvania Dutch," made their entrance into this section as early as 1760; and the church cemetery contains the remains of persons born as early as 1741.

Recently discovered by members of the Catawba County Historical Association is a reference to St. John's made in the diary of Rev. Paul Henkel, which gives rise to speculation that possibly some sort of edifice bore the name of St. John's as early as 1789. Writing of his travels in this section during 1805, the Rev. Mr. Henkel points out: ". . . The next morning I drove through the hills for several miles to my old friend Peter Mack on the Great Catawba, and spent the day there. I was visited here by his son-in-law and his wife. The son-in-law had been instructed with others and confirmed in St. John's Church last August (which would have been August, 1804); the wife in the year 1789, as she was still at home with her parents. . . ." The Rev. Mr. Henkel, a "missionary" in the South, preached at St. John's, and was to be followed by kinsmen who held regular pastorates—Rev. David Henkel, Rev. Phillip Henkel and Rev. Polycarp C. Henkel.

The church was a union church when it was begun, with the property being owned by Lutherans and German Reformed members, and possibly by others. The greater portion of the members who began this congregation originally belonged to St. Paul's church. "The History of the Reformed Church in North Carolina" points out: "About 1812 when the first house of worship at St. Paul's (west of Newton) gave place to the one still standing, that part of the Reformed and Lutheran congregations which lived in the bend of Catawba River, erected for themselves a commodious log building six miles northeast of the mother church." The "commodious log church" was St. John's.

Concerning the building of the church, Rev. C. O. Smith, a recent minister of St. John's and a native of its area, has written: "Here it is said that the first church was erected 'about 1812.' Whether that is correct I do not know, but I do know that this first church was built of logs. I was baptized in it, and confirmed in the brick church which was erected when the first church was torn down. This log church was weatherboarded and ceiled: Was two-stories high; had a gallery with a floor space more than half the size of the first floor; had a 'goblet' pulpit, entered by a little stairway from the rear, and in it the minister was in position to address the audience on both floors. The slaves sat in the gallery. This pulpit was a real work of art in workmanship. Every plank and every nail used in the church and in the pulpit was made by hand. A certain Mr. Sigman made the nails in his blacksmith shop."

In 1883, the log church was replaced by a commodious brick church which seated approximately 600 persons. In 1949, the old brick church was remodeled and enlarged, but soon after it was completed, it was destroyed by fire. Without delay, however, the congregation erected a new and better church.

Due to a charge of immorality against a minister, Rev. Adam Miller, in the mid-1800s, a split occurred in the St. John's congregation. Concerning this difficulty, the Rev. Mr. Smith writes: "... This (the charge) he (the Rev. Mr. Miller) denied. The majority of the congregation thought he was guilty as charged, and refused to have him as their pastor. He and his followers got one Sunday in the month. So, the services at St. John's ran thus: The Lutheran majority two Sundays; the Lutheran minority one Sunday and the Reformeds one Sunday...."

HOPEWELL METHODIST CHURCH (Located two miles north of Sherrills Ford.)

Established 1811.

UNION BAPTIST CHURCH (Located one mile north of Bakers Mountain.)

The fourth major religious sect to appear on the Catawba county scene was the Baptist denomination. The first records of the activities of this denomination date to 1815. It is believed, however, that "preaching stations" (usually at members' homes) were conducted prior to that time.

Union or "Mountain Meeting House" was organized principally under the leadership of Rev. Hosea Holcombe, who came from Virginia. The Rev. Mr. Holcombe is said by the writers of Baptist history to have been the most influential and best educated minister of the denomination of his time.

Because of its location, the church was usually called the "Mountain Meeting House." The name "Union" is said to have been given in order to unite the Baptists in and around the mountain.

The Rev. Mr. Holcombe baptized Alexander Abernethy in 1817. Abernethy soon became pastor of Union church and served it for 50 years.

In 1881, the congregation reorganized under the name of Mountain Grove church.

MT. RUHAMA BAPTIST CHURCH (Located one mile west of Olivers Crossroads.)

Organized in 1816, Mt. Ruhama is the second oldest Baptist congregation in Catawba county.

Two traveling Baptist ministers, Drury Dobbins and Berryman Hicks, followed the practice of spending the night in the community where Mt. Ruhama is located as they ministered to the newly formed Union church and a church located near River Bend. While riding their circuit, the ministers visited a Killian family in the Mt. Ruhama section.

They began to hold services in the Killian home, and in the homes of others whom they visited.

The Killians gave the lot on which the first log church was erected, and for many years it was known as Killians Meeting House.

Mt. Ruhama church is said to have sent into the field more ministers from its membership than any other church in the county.

ST. PETER'S LUTHERAN CHURCH (Located eight miles north of Conover, near Oxford Ford.)

Although St. Peter's church was not deeded until 1827, and, the deed, in fact, was not recorded until 1857, it has been established that some sort of religious edifice existed in the locale of St. Peter's as early as July, 1816.

The following road order is entered on county records in Lincolnton: "July Session 1816—Ordered by Court that Peter Harmon be Overseer of the Road leading from Oxford Ford past the Old Meeting House to Lincolnton from Sandy Ford to Isahours Old Saw Mill, and that Joseph Isahour be Overseer from the Old Saw Mill to the Burke Road to the Old Mailing House—and that they call on all hands, within three miles of said Road. . . ."

Moreover, the oldest marked grave in the graveyard is that of Leban Wineberger, a one-year-old child, buried in 1816.

It generally is conceded that the original St. Peter's church was built about 1825. This was a log structure.

Records reveal that the first child baptized was Elizabeth Heffner, daughter of Elias and Sarah Heffner, born August 18, and baptized August 28, 1825.

It generally is conceded that the church was established by Rev. R. J. Miller, one of the four pastors who organized the North Carolina Synod in 1803.

The second church was erected in 1873. The present large brick building was dedicated in 1940.

Church records reveal that during the War Between the States the congregation was greatly disturbed and almost went to pieces. In 1865, a meeting was held under the direction of Rev. J. M. Smith, and the following resolution was adopted:

"Whereas we have just passed through a most cruel and bloody war, by which the church has been torn and scattered, leaving us almost without knowledge who are and who are not members of this congregation, St. Peter's; therefore, we the members of St. Peter's, Cat. Co., N. C., do RESOLVE that we form a new list of all the members of this congregation, making it the duty of each member to come forward and re-enroll his or her name; any one neglecting or refusing to do so, after suitable opportunity, shall not be allowed church privileges as members of this congregation."

WESLEY CHAPEL METHODIST ARBOR AND CAMPGROUND (Located seven and one-half miles southwest of Newton and seven and one-half miles south of Hickory.)

Established 1824. Name later changed to Wesley Chapel Methodist church.

THESSALONICA BAPTIST CHURCH (Located four miles southwest of Newton.)

Thessalonica Baptist church was organized as an "arm" of Mt. Ruhama Baptist church. Andrew Yoder is credited as giving the congregation a lot of three acres of land for the church, which was erected in 1827.

The church no longer exists, but a burying ground remains.

BETHLEHEM METHODIST CHURCH (Originally located two

miles east of Claremont, later moved into the incorporate limits of the town of Claremont.)

Established 1831.

SMYRNA EVANGELICAL AND REFORMED CHURCH

An offshoot of Old St. Paul's church, Smyrna Evangelical and Reformed church was organized in 1832 by Rev. John G. Fritchey.

The first elders were John G. Shuford and William Edwards.

A large church building of logs was erected. It was weatherboarded, but never ceiled. This old building still stands.

The church was the county's first exclusively Evangelical and Reformed church.

A second of three churches was erected during the pastorate of Dr. J. C. Clapp. The congregation, according to records, was "moved" to undertake the work when Mrs. Catharine Hartman, a daughter of Jacob Lentz, after a Sunday morning service came forward and laid $50 upon the altar, saying, "This is for a new church." The present church was dedicated in 1953.

CONCORD METHODIST CHURCH (Located 2 miles west of Long Island.)

The first traceable history of Concord church goes to 1832, when services were being held in a log building. A minister by the name of Parker was pastor of the church at the time.

Cyrus Pede was superintendent of the Sunday school at the same period. Described as extremely strict, Pede was of the opinion that Sunday school should be kept as strictly as day school.

In 1856-58, a frame church was built just back of the present building. It was constructed by Henry Kale, assisted by local carpenters. A small structure, it was partitioned off back of the pulpit for colored people. It was in use a number of years before it was ceiled. The church was divided by a railing resting on the back of the seats and running lengthways through the building. The men came in through the right door facing the pulpit and sat on the right side, and the women came in through the left door and sat on the left side, a common custom at the time. The land on which the church was built was owned by Dr. A. M. Powell, one of the owners of Long Island Mill.

OLIVET BAPTIST CHURCH (Located three and one-half miles northwest of Sherrills Ford.)

Olivet Baptist church was organized near Sherrills Ford on August 17, 1833. The first deacons of the church have been ascertained as William Lytton, Miles Jones, Jacob Brown, Jephthae Clark and David Wilkerson. The first pastor was Rev. Edward Hugh Quinn.

The first church building was a log house. About the year 1883 a new house of worship was built, and, in 1950, the third church—a modern, brick building—was constructed.

During the construction of the second Olivet church, the congregation worshipped in the Concord Methodist church. In appreciation of the use of the neighbor church, the congregation adopted the following resolution:

"Resolved: That we extend our thanks to Concord Methodist church for the use of their house in which to hold our meetings, and for their efficient aid in conducting the same;

"That a copy of these resolutions be spread on our church book and one presented to the Clerk of Concord church."

The seriousness with which the early families regarded their church life is evidenced by additional excerpts from the minutes of Olivet church. It appears that one had to walk the "straight and narrow," or be "dealt with." It was not unusual for Olivet and other early churches to expel their members for such offenses as drinking and dancing, or even for failure to attend church regularly.

Three articles from the Olivet constitution are:

"Article 3. Any brother failing to attend church meetings twice in succession will consider himself liable to be dealt with, except in sickness.

"Article 4. And if three times shall give satisfaction for his absence.

"Article 6. Any member who shall be guilty of the practice of drinking at public gatherings, or found about wagons, shall be dealt with by the church."

The following excerpts from the church minutes give an idea of how the constitution was carried out to the letter:

"October 4th, Saturday, 1856. The church met according to appointment and had preaching by Bro. Logan. The church called to order, and fellowship asked for. A report says Bro. Wm. Kile is guilty of drinking too much and dancing, for which the church thought it expedient for some of the brethren to see him and know the certainty of the matter. Whereas, Brethren Jos. T. Sanders and Jacob Brown were appointed to see him and report at the December meeting."

"Saturday, April 25th, 1863. Church had preaching, then sat in conference. Brother Little stated to the church that it had been reported to him that Brother John Ervin had been hauling fruit juice to the still and had been selling some of the spirits, which we consider contrary to our rule and usage. It was moved and seconded that he be expelled, which move was sustained by an unanimous vote of the church."

"Saturday, September 24th, 1881. The hand of fellowship withdrawn from Dr. Tate Powell for getting drunk."

ST. JAMES LUTHERAN CHURCH (Located one and one-half miles southeast of Newton.)

Originally known as the Old Haas church, a log building, St. James Lutheran church history dates from 1834. The deed, executed in Lincoln county in the name of David Haas and George A. Ikard, also in 1834, verifies the ownership of land about one mile south of the present St. James church.

The church was to be used by both Lutheran and Reformed members until 1845, when the Reformed members withdrew and built a church of their own in Newton.

The change from the old location to the present one came in about 1867. Records reveal that a communion service was held in the Haas church September 23, 1866, and that another such service was held May 23, 1867, at St. James church. The land on which the new church was built was deeded to the church by M. M. Hewitt.

The present concrete block building was constructed soon after the turn of the twentieth century and was dedicated on May 8, 1910.

St. Stephens Lutheran Church

The establishment of St. Stephens church and its ultimate development is responsible for Catawba county's unusual circumstance of having three Lutheran churches virtually adjoining each other.

The congregation of the first Lutheran church in the present-day St. Stephens section near Hickory was organized in 1840. Its first building, a log structure, contained a gallery floored with loose boards. It stood a short distance to the east of the present St. Stephens church of the North Carolina Synod.

The first church was especially crude, having seats made of slabs, with legs for support but no backs. No provision was made to heat the building.

The land for the church building was given by Frederick Miller, who requested that it be called "Miller's church."

A disturbance arose in 1845 over the conduct of one of the ministers of the Tennessee Synod, causing a number of members of the first congregation to form a new congregation, which later united with the Ohio Synod.

Following the War Between the States, the two congregations cooperated in the building of a new church, which was to be octagon shaped and was to be located almost opposite from the present Miller's church. When the groups prepared to dedicate the new edifice, however, they could not agree on a name. Those who had left the Synod wished to retain the name Miller's, but those who remained loyal to the Tennessee Synod wished to change the name to St. Stephens. As a result, the church was dedicated one day in 1868 as St. Stephens, and, a few days later, as Miller's.

Another disturbance arose in 1890-1903, and again the church split, resulting in a third Lutheran congregation in the same community. This change brought upon the scene the Missouri Synod.

Corinth Baptist church (Located 12 miles southwest of Hickory.)

Established 1840. The congregation recently erected a new rock structure.

EBENEZER METHODIST CHURCH (Located 13 miles southwest of Hickory, one mile east of Burke county line.)

Established 1841 as Mt. Pisgah Methodist church.

Although the date is not known, it is believed that a church, known as Providence Methodist church, existed one and one-half miles southwest of the town of Catawba, on present Highway 10, prior to the formation of the county. A graveyard remains. The Catawba Methodist church and Shiloh Methodist church grew out of this pioneer church.

It is believed that Lebanon Lutheran church, located a mile south of Anderson mountain, also existed prior to the formation of the county. About 1866, the Baptist denomination took over the church. Its present name is Mountain View Baptist church.

CAMPGROUNDS

Any attempt at church history of this section would be incomplete without some reference to the famous campgrounds, especially those of Rock Springs (of Lincoln county, but begun in Catawba county) and Balls Creek. Perhaps the most famous of county campgrounds is Balls Creek, where thousands trek each year to participate in a custom almost as old as the county itself.

A "campmeeting in the forest, for a number of days and nights," was held in 1794 at the site of Rehobeth Methodist church in the Terrell section. The meeting was held four years in succession at this place. Rev. Daniel Asbury, traveling Methodist minister, who founded Rehobeth, conducted the first meeting.

Site of the camp was moved, in 1827, some ten miles west, where it was known as Robey's campground. It continued there until Rock Springs campground was equipped in Lincoln county. Historians generally agree that the establishment of Rock Springs came as direct result of the Rev. Mr. Asbury's campmeeting held at Rehobeth in the pioneer days of Catawba county.

It appears that the campmeeting was begun at Rehobeth as a make-shift measure until a church could be built. The Methodists worshipped in the grove, and "these meetings resulted in great good and were often continued throughout the day and night." Perhaps the recollections of meetings in the grove, the inadequacy of the little church, and inconvenience of walking or riding back and forth many miles to the services and the desire to devote all their time for a while to religion, were factors in the decision to hold the first regular campmeeting.

Since the inauguration of the Rock Springs campmeeting, every year, without a break, the annual meeting has been held, even during the war periods.

In August, 1853, the campground at Balls Creek was established by the Methodists of the community and the first campmeeting was held there under a brush arbor.

Very few permanent tents had been built at that time and the people camped mostly in canvas tents and in covered wagons.

Preaching at the first campmeeting was done by Rev. H. H. Durant, and Rev. Lewis Scarborough. Enthusiasm was so great that before another year rolled around a group of men consisting of F. M. Abernethy, David L. Edwards, Willis Gantt and G. P. Routh deeded to a committee of men consisting of B. B. Smith, John Marshall and James Keever a tract of land consisting of about 40 acres to be used for a campground for the Methodist Episcopal church. Signatures were witnessed by Henry Keever, A. L. Lackey and Drury Hamilton.

Alexander Lineberger and Lawson Lowrance were employed by the trustees to build an arbor in the center of the tract for the purpose of a public place of worship. This arbor was 60 by 80 feet, and all the frame work was made from logs that had been cut and hewn. These were mortised and pinned together. There was also a section in the arbor that was used for the Negro slaves who came with their masters to worship.

Lighting for the new arbor was made by burning pine knots together with tallow candles that were brought in by those who attended the services.

Since its beginning, only two years have passed in which campmeeting has not been held, the first of these was during the early part of the War Between the States, the other when one of the ministers opposed it, and succeeded in having it suspended for a year.

As time went by some of the most interested attendants conceived the idea of building "cook sheds," the first of these being erected by J. T. Hewitt of Maiden. These "cook sheds" were maintained for some time but were ordered discontinued several years ago by the trustees. In later years wood and oil stoves replaced the old method of cooking on an open fire.

Before the days of prohibition, rowdyism was part of the campground scene. Not a few individuals settled their difficulties by the fist and skull method. During the history of the camp, one man lost his life as a result of homicide.

Records show that three people have died at the campground during campmeeting. It is also said that one child was born at the campmeeting during the late 1860s.

Aside from religious festivities the campground stands out in two particulars: It has plenty of fresh water from the big spring near the campground and from which the name originated, and, second, the good eats that are carried to the campground by those who camp there during the week.

Another fact of no less importance is the excellent conduct of the people who attend these meetings in later years. Although a regular police force is maintained during the series of meetings, it is very rare whenever an arrest is made.

Other campgrounds which have operated at some time during the history of the county include a German Reformed campground on the east side of Clines creek, about three miles west of Newton; Wesley's Chapel Methodist campground; Dry Pond campground, two miles west of Hickory; Motts Grove campground (Negro), between Terrell and Sherrills Ford; and McKenzies campground (Negro), four miles southeast of Catawba.

Among the ministers who are believed to have served Catawba area churches prior to the section's designation as a county are the following, listed alphabetically:

Rev. Alexander Abernethy, Rev. John Godfrey Arndt, Rev. Daniel Asbury, Bishop Francis Asbury, Rev. C. E. Bernhardt, the Rev. Mr. Beuthahn, Rev. Joachim Beulow, the Rev. Mr. Bogers, Rev. Drury Dobbins, Rev. Jacob Christian, Rev. Richard Dupert, the Rev. Mr. Easterly, the Rev. Mr. Frohock, Rev. Henry Goodman, Rev. David Henkel, Rev. Paul Henkel, Rev. Philip Henkel, Rev. Berryman Hicks, Rev. Hosea Holcombe, Rev. John Lantz, Rev. Andrew Loretz, Rev. Isaac Lowe, a Swiss minister named the Rev. Mr. Martin, Rev. Adam Miller, Jr., Rev. Robert Johnstone Miller, Rev. Daniel Moser, Rev. Adolph Nussman, Rev. Jacob Sneider, the Rev. Mr. Suther, and Rev. Christian Theus.

Many churches were established in the county from the date of its formation until 1900. Among these, including those now extinct, are:

Baptist—

- 1869 Upper Smyrna, Newton area.
- 1870 First, Hickory.
- 1872 Providence, about two miles southwest of the town of Catawba.
- 1873 First, town of Catawba.
- 1874 First, Newton.
- 1874 Mull's Chapel, in Bandys township.
- About 1869 Mountain Grove, probably earlier known as Bakers Mountain, located one mile north of mountain.
- 1882 Startown.
- 1887 East Hickory.
- 1888 Penelope, in Longview.
- 1891 First, Maiden.

Date Unknown   Morning Star, in Hickory.

Catholic—

- 1880 St. Joseph's college and church, in Hickory.

Episcopal—

- 1872 Church of the Ascension, in Hickory.

Evangelical and Reformed—

1845	Grace, in Newton.
1848	Bethel, five miles south of Hickory.
1869	Corinth, in Hickory.
1886	Memorial, in Maiden.
1892	Trinity, in Conover.

Lutheran—

Date Unknown Lebanon, acquired by Baptists in 1872, near Anderson mountain.
1850 Beth-Eden, in Newton.
1863 St. Mark's, in Claremont.
1867 Sardis, about 11 miles southwest of Hickory. (First Tennessee Synod, now North Carolina Synod.)
1868 St. Stephen's, about three miles northeast of Hickory.
About 1868 Thyatira, about one and three-fourth miles west of Island Ford, probably also known as the White church.
About 1872 Hope's, probably in Newton area.
1874 Bethel (first known as Piney Grove), about one and one-half miles southwest of Lookout dam.
1876 Holy Trinity, in Hickory.
1878 Concordia, in Conover.
1880 New Jerusalem, four miles southeast of Hickory.
1885 Mt. Olive, four miles north of Hickory.
1887 St. Timothy, about two miles west of Conover.
1889 Ebenezer, near Bandys crossroads.
1893 St. Andrew's, in Hickory.
1893 St. Martin's, in Maiden.
1898 St. Stephen's (Missouri Synod) about three miles northeast of Hickory.

Methodist—

1853 Mt. Pleasant, in Mountain Creek township.
1853 Balls Creek campground.
1854 Bethel (formerly Providence, Dry Pond campground, Arneys Chapel), in Longview.

1854 First, Newton.

1856 Fairgrove, midway between Hickory and Newton.

About 1869 Pisgah, near Balls Creek campground.

About 1869 Smyrna, probably in Newton area.

About 1870 Brown's Chapel A.M.E., two miles north of Terrell.

1870 Mays Chapel, two miles northeast of Maiden.

1872 St. Paul's A.M.E. Zion, in Hickory.

1872 Lanier's Chapel, five miles northeast of Hickory, near Catawba river.

1872 Oak Grove, probably in Newton area.

1873 Mt. Nebo, southwest of Newton in Rocky Ford area.

1874 First, Catawba.

1875 Mt. Zion A.M.E. (McKenzies) campground and church, four miles southeast of Catawba.

1879 Marvin, four miles northwest of Conover.

1879 Mt. Pisgah A.M.E., in Hickory.

1881 Friendship, five miles east of Newton.

1883 Prospect, in Startown community.

1883 Mt. Zion A.M.E., in Maiden.

Prior to 1886 Coulter's Grove A.M.E., about one and one-half miles south of Startown.

Prior to 1886 Mott's Grove A.M.E. campground, about one and one-half miles north of Terrell.

Prior to 1886 Shiloh, four miles southwest of Catawba.

Prior to 1886 Mt. Olin A.M.E., four miles east-southeast of Newton.

1887 St. Paul's A.M.E., in Newton.

1888 Center, three miles southwest of Catawba.

1889 Zion A.M.E., in Newton.

1892 Houck's Chapel, two miles northwest of Hickory.

1893 Lanier's Chapel, in Jacobs Fork township on waters of Potts creek.

1895 Zion A.M.E., in Catawba.

CATAWBA COUNTY

Presbyterian—

1858   First, Newton.
1873   First, Hickory.
1890   First Sherrills Ford.

Protestant non-denominational—

1884   Union, Sparkling Catawba Springs, eight miles northeast of Hickory.

Among the ministers who have served Catawba county since its formation until 1900 are the following:

Baptist—Abernathy, William; Allison, Elijah; Berry, L. M.; Cashwell, C. S.; Cobb, W. B.; Faulkner, J. K.; Gardner, C. S.; Green, G. W.; Gwaltney, W. R.; Hawks, R.; Howell, J. K.; Jones, J. R.; Jones, R. B.; Jordan, Rev.; Lequeauz, H. D.; Marsh, J. B.; Richardson, J. B.; Rector, J. A.; Shell, Rev.; Wilkie, G. I.; and Woodruff, C. E.

Catholic—Mother Augstine.

Episcopal—Bland, Rev.; Drake, Rev.; Falls, Neilson; Griffin, Rev.; Huske, John; Joyner, Edmund N.; Lyman, Theo B. (Bishop); McBee, Vardry; and Weston, James A.

Evangelical and Reformed—Clapp, J. C.; Crawford, J. H.; Crooks, David; Bennet, William C.; Butler, T.; Foil, J. A.; Fox, J. C.; Fritchey, John G.; Gurley, G. D.; Hedrick, Michael; Heller, C. E.; Horn, A. P.; Ingold, H.; Ingold, Jeremiah; Leonard, J. C.; Murphy, J. L.; Rankin, William C.; Reitin, Lewis; Romoser, G. A.; Rowe, W. W.; Shuford, Julius H.; Shuford, Q. A.; Trexler, P. M.; Welker, George William; Wolfinger, A. D.; and Vaughn, A. S.

Lutheran—Arney, Benjamin; Barb, J. E.; Beck, A. R.; Bernheim, C. H.; Bolick, A. L.; Brown, B. S.; Cline, W. P.; Cromer, T. L.; Crouse, A. L.; Coyner, E. T.; Darr, Rev.; Dau, W. H. D.; Deaton, J. L.; Deaton, W.; Deitz, John C.; Fespermann, J. H.; Fox, A. J.; Fritz, R. L., Sr.; Goodman, John; Groseclose, L. C.; Hall, John; Hease, S. L.; Henkel, D. F.; Henkel, Polycarp; Hopkins, B. N.; Huffman, D. C.; Hunt, G. L.; Kistler, Paul; Keissler, S. S.; Koiner, J. S.; Lentz, Rev.; Linn, J. A.; Little, Marcus L.; Long, George; Lutz, W. A.; Miller, J. P.; Moretz, Christian G.; Moser, J. C.; Moser, J. R.; Moser,

Timothy; Price, J. P.; Reitzel, C. G.; Roof, F. K.; Rudisell, J. A.; Settlemyer, D. T.; Scherer, Simon; Smith, J. M.; Smithdeal, T. L.; Sox, E. J., Sr.; Stirewalt, M. J.; Swicegood, John; Wannamacher, J. H.; Wessinger, J. C.; Wike, Jacob; Wike, P. C.; Yoder, Robert A.; and Yount, Adolphus.

Methodist—Abernathy, Alexander; Abernathy, J. W.; Abernathy, R. L.; Asbury, H.; Barnette, R. G.; Boone, F. A.; Bonner, T. P.; Bristoe, J. E.; Carpenter, J. D.; Dagnall, Richard R.; Davis, F. M.; Doggett, R. R.; Durant, H. H.; Ervin, J. S.; Hartsell, J. C.; Helton, Robert; Herman, P. L.; Hughes, J. P.; Ivey, G. W.; Jones, B. G.; Little, C. G.; McClellion, W. T.; McKenney, J. H. C.; Nelson, J. S.; Page, Jesse; Paynes, John E.; Payne, Jordan N.; Ricaud, T. P.; Scarborough, Lewis; Shell, Lemon; Sherrill, J. A.; Sherrill, J. S.; Sherrill, W. L.; Stamey, E. L.; Terrell, Rev.; Townsend, F. L.; Warlick, David E.; and Watts, John.

Presbyterian—Anderson, R. B.; Gibbs, G. M.; Matthews, W. T.; Munroe, C. A.; Ramsay, T. Alston; and Thurston, T. G.

Denominations unknown—Anderson, Charles M.; Bennick, Augustus R.; Brindle, J. H.; Callihan, G. W.; Cline, James M.; Clark, Jephthue; Davis, R. N.; Finger, J.; Hildebrand, Amos; Hill, Jacob; Killian, W. L. C.; Mason, J.; Patterson, W. C.; Parker, Joseph; Robinson, J. H.; Stemey, Alexander; Stinson, D. C.; Terrell, Rev.; and Triplet, T. L.

CHAPTER VI

EARLY EDUCATION METHODS

The dramatic and challenging history of education in Catawba county is backgrounded by a struggle of the common man against the difficult circumstances of inherited aristocracy and tradition, a language barrier, and an undependable economy.

The pioneer population came into the Catawba territory as blazers of a new empire. Their educational wants, if not their needs, were small. The desire to expand their mental capacities not seldom was subjugated to the desire to expand their financial resources. The population, of course, contained a limited number of men of letters, and it is known that a few settlers actually held college degrees. But these persons were vastly in the minority and their contribution to the whole of the population was likely only a convincing argument, which ultimately was to pay dividends, that the education processes are rewarding. It is assumed by many historians that pioneers who signed the ships' registers with "X's" upon their voyage to the new world, and subsequently used the same method of identifying themselves for legal purposes, were illiterate. This is not necessarily true. In the instance of the Germans, the language barrier prevented the new citizen from understanding directions. So, when no interpreter was immediately available, an English receptionist usually wrote the German's names himself (often, incidentally, incorrectly).

The settler of the Catawba region had the unfortunate experience of being part of a greater region of which the people knew a certain culture that was hindered in its expansion by both economic and geographic forces. Located on the northern end of the county of Lincoln, the Catawba territory was settled chiefly by Germans who were extremely clannish and who were devoted to rural living. The distance from the Catawba area to Lincolnton, the seat of justice, was foreboding. Mental makeup of the average Catawba frontiersman made him ill at ease among luxuries. He had little time to consider the void created by a lack of educational advantages since his mere existence depended upon the strength in his arms and his success with the soil. He was to attain his wealth and position in society in his new locale; he did not bring it with him.

The German language slowed the creation of a school system, although it did not hinder the establishment of individual schools. This does not indicate that the German people generally did not basically appreciate the advantages offered by schools. But, the Catawba area Germans found it difficult to accustom themselves to a predominantly English-speaking society, and actually, the fact that the English language should become the accepted tongue in the new world. It required considerable time for them to realize that their children were to be considered "different" due to language. Also, they likely resented the fact that their children and themselves were to live in a country in which all social, commercial and legal transactions were carried on in the English tongue.

Until the 1800s, the German language held an edge over the English language, particularly in Pennsylvania, from which the Catawba county Germans migrated. It was not, in fact, until 1798 that the first English school was opened in North Carolina—in Cabarrus county. Ultimately English was to "win the day" completely, however, and, in time, not only ousted the German from schools, but took its place in the daily affairs of the Germans themselves until their very surnames became Anglicized.

That persons of the German nationality were interested in education is attested by numerous records proclaiming the anxiousness with which they went about establishing individual schools. Their teachers were described as men of ability and profound scholarship. Usually, the teachers were also ministers.

The Germans came in congregations and settled as communities. This fact enabled them to organize churches and schools much more readily than those who settled on widely scattered plantations. It is said that one of the first concerns of one of these colonies was to establish a "community house" for the purposes of both church and school.

The Germans, in final analysis, brought a highly developed, very native, culture with them to their new home, and they guarded it tenaciously.

Economic factors discouraged the development of education perhaps as much as did either Lincoln's aristocratic influence, or language. Primarily a rural area, the Catawba section was settled chiefly by persons who were absolutely without financial means.

With the passage of time, a feeling grew rapidly in Catawba county in support of the free, or "common," school. The general population did not sanction the "private tutor" system of the "plantationers," who employed private teachers, established academies of quality early, and sent their sons to Northern institutions and their daughters to the Moravian school at Salem.

The sympathy in behalf of the free schools stemmed from a proud independence of the Catawban and was not apologized for as advocating "charity." The German reasoned that he fought to make America free, even in the instance of education.

To acquire a correct prospective of the evolution of local schools, one must periodically consider the same subject on the scene of the larger governing body of which the Catawba territory and Lincoln county were a part—the state.

North Carolina was settled chiefly by the English who had brought with them to the new country deep-seated class distinctions, a repugnance to public taxation, and the firm belief that education was a private and not a public matter. The elements of the population which were not English, the Moravians in Forsyth, the Swiss in Craven, the Scotch-Irish in the southern and western sections, and the Germans in the south-central and piedmont sections, likewise, did not see education as a responsibility of the government. These persons believed that education was a family and church affair.

Utter indifference to education prevailed among the people of North Carolina from 1790 to the establishment of the ante-bellum common school system of 1840. R. D. W. Connor, in his *Ante-Bellum Builders of North Carolina*, points out that in 1786 "a traveler of uncommon intelligence, after making a tour from Edenton to Charlotte, entered in his journal the assertion that no state in the Union at that period had done so little to promote the cause of education, science and the arts as North Carolina, and he observed that the great mass of the people were in a state of great mental degradation." It is recorded, also by Connor, that a governor of the state in 1826, the semi-centennial year of independence, told the legislature that it was more difficult to obtain a primary education in North Carolina at that time than it was in 1776. It was estimated, moreover, that as late as 1835 one-third of the adult population of the state could neither read nor write.

The deplorable conditions of the state's educational scene was to arouse public indignation finally and call to the state's helm men of exceedingly excellent ability. The noble efforts of Vance, Jarvis, Aycock, Mebane, Caldwell, Murphy, Battle, Wiley, McIver and Graham were to reward North Carolinians' movement of educational uplift to the extent that they created the first complete state public school system in the South. To do this, these men had to overcome two primary obstacles: The low educational standards of the time; and indifferent legislatures.

The first school houses of which record is known in Catawba county are those of Phillipe Henry Greder (or Grider), who is credited as the county's first teacher, located about one and one-half miles southeast of Newton (on land now owned by Emmett Seitz), and one located at St. Paul's Lutheran and Reformed church, situated about a mile and a half west of Newton.

Records in the land grant office in Raleigh reveal that a survey was made by Peter Johnston on July 20, 1767, of 60 acres of land "including the school house" of Grider's. Evidently, Grider had built a house of learning, incorporating the right of the "squatter," sometime earlier. The school master ultimately purchased the property from Matthias Barringer and George Pope, for whom Johnston made the survey. The property then was sold by Grider on May 23, 1773, to Henry Bollinger, Nicholas Frye, Peter Ikerd, John Shuford, John Deal, Frederick Markel, Martin Coulter, Michael Grindstaff, and William Deal, all planters. In his deed to the planters, Grider stipulated that the land was to be forever set aside for school purposes and for the benefit of the public.

Grider's grant begins ". . . On a black oak in Conrad Mingus line, west side of the School House Branch." This proves that a school house had been located on the stream for sufficient time to give to the stream the name of "School House branch." In 1791, John Haas sold to Simon Haas a tract of land on the east side of Clarks creek, both sides of Bullinger's Mill creek, running with Bullinger's line to a white oak near the school house. This assisted in locating the branch and proved that the school house was standing as late as 1791.

It is known that a school was conducted at St. Paul's Lutheran and Reformed church, the first church west of the Catawba river, early in the history of that institution. Land was deeded for the church by Paul and Frony Anthony on May 20, 1771.

Land surveys specify "school land" as early as 1779 within the present corporate limits of the city of Newton. The same surveys refer to a small branch, which runs on the east side of the Carolina and Northwestern railroad tracks.

Zion Lutheran church was built at the site of a school in 1791. The teacher, Jacob Weaver, had constructed a single room at one end of the school for his abode, according to information recorded by Colonel G. M. Yoder.

A land survey made April 28, 1797, for Henry Hallman, makes reference to "an old school house." It is believed that this property is located one-half mile south of the Catawba river, about four miles from Hickory, on the Icard Ferry road.

In 1803, Whitener's school house was located in the forks of Jacob Forks river, in the Zion church area, on land belonging to Daniel Whitener.

J. M. Smith conveyed a tract of land, consisting of one acre and 66 poles, for the purpose of establishing a "Church School House and burying place," located on the south side of the South Fork of the Catawba river, in 1803.

It is known that a Sides school house existed in 1816, for a road order recorded in Lincoln county during this year instructs that "John Slagle be overseer of the Charleston road at the cross roads near Sides school house. . . ." The school was located near Philip Anthony's.

Mention is made in processioner books among Lincoln county records of a "road leading by the school house on waters of Sherrills Ford" in 1818.

In 1822, Daniel Hallman made a deed to his "Good Neighbors" conveying to them a school house. The deed reads, in part: "In consideration of the esteem I have for 'learning' and in order to promote and encourage Education, I have given and granted unto my Good Neighbors the privilege of building a school house on my land which House is now built and nearly finished. . . ." The location of the school is unknown. It is believed to have been in the Catawba territory, inasmuch as some of the witnesses were persons of that area.

The Hop Creek school house was built about 1823.

A school house was constructed in 1823 at Grace Lutheran and Reformed church, located on the south side of Jacobs Fork river about nine miles southwest of Newton.

The Yoder school house was constructed about 1833. The deed for the property from John Yoder, Sr., to John Yoder, Jr., and David B. Whitener, trustees, "in consideration for five cents, on the waters of Jacobs river," points out: "Use of the School House in that neighborhood and inhabitants of that neighborhood. The duty of the trustees to take charge of the School House and if any thing is to be done they shall give notice to the inhabitants of that neighborhood if any one of the trustees should die or remove out of that neighborhood, the inhabitants to hold an election to elect another trustee, the School House to be known as the Union School House to hold forever. . . ." The site of the school is near the present Rhoney Negro School. (The name later was changed to Yoder School house.)

Among the Catawba territory's other earliest teachers were Antoine Has, Frederick Linebaugh, William G. Conley, Samuel Jarrett, Frederick Deitz, and Martin Greder.

The hardships of pioneer life did not permit much time for education. Every pair of hands had to supply the daily needs of the family. Children could not be spared from farm work to attend school at length.

The early school houses were made of logs, with a rough puncheon floor and "cat and clay" chimney. For light, a log was left out of the building, and in severe weather a greased paper was pasted over the opening. The seats were crude benches made of split logs with pegs driven in the corners for legs. For desks, boards were laid on pegs driven between the logs about four feet from the floor. These desks were used by the older "scholars." Younger students sat on blocks or benches made of logs. Fireplaces provided heat. The wood was chopped and carried by the big boys, who also could be persuaded to make the fires "for free."

Children wore garments made of homespun linsey-woolsey and homespun flax. Sometimes the big boys wore leather breeches. Because the material of these breeches, deer skin, was cold, and hard to care for when wet, linsey-woolsey was used as a lining.

Paths were blazed to the school houses by the community's elders. "Blazing" was done by chipping pieces of bark on some of the trees along the way to the school. The blazed trail later became a path and, sometimes, even a cartway.

The one-room school house also was a one-teacher school. The teacher, or "master," sat in the middle of the room, his desk placed on a platform. Students' seats lined the walls. It appears that, during this period, the tutor was held in esteem by some patrons while he was considered a "no-good" by those members of the community who scoffed at the value of education. In the first instance, the master was a law unto himself and a neighborhood oracle. In the second instance, the teacher was considered a person too lazy to seek a livelihood in fields which required strenuous physical labor. Often, teachers were lame, and, even oftener, they were eccentrics.

As salaries were low, the school was "kept" only three or four months, and the early teacher was compelled to travel from one section of the county to the other in order to obtain employment (schools were not held simultaneously, but their most customary time was from November 15 to January or February, or, during the slack period of farming).

As an example of the values placed by the common man on education, historians cite that a teacher was considered desirable if he was simply a good scribe. Thus, many teachers became, to satisfy school committees, masters of the quill. One of the first questions asked by a school committee to a prospective teacher was: "Let us see your hand-writing."

A second, incidentally, was: "Can you whip well?"

There were some excellent "quill-masters" in the Catawba territory, to whom many of the area's earliest successful businessmen owed their ability to write well. Near Hickory lived Professor Stephen Harris, and, in the Vale section lived Isaac Clay. These men were able to execute the most difficult swirls of the day.

The master prided himself upon his knowledge and ability in teaching the three R's—readin', 'ritin', and 'rithmetic (the last commonly referred to as cyphering). In the earliest schools, grammar and geography were unknown. Even as late as 1880, a teacher in a Catawba county school sent a note by a pupil asking that the parents of the pupil buy a geography book, and received this reply: "Hit (the pupil) ain't going ter be no geographer, ner cross the sea, ner be no Philadelphy lawyer."

Older students were given the most attention, with the "juniors" being called upon to recite but seldom. When the master was ready for recitation, he would rap on his desk and shout above the noise of voices, the ages of which ranged from five to 21. It is said that boys and girls during pioneer days spelled and read at the tops of their voices, and that the roar of lessons could be heard half a mile away. Their schools were sometimes referred to as "blab" schools.

Schools contained no maps, pictures or blackboards until about 1820. Among the earliest texts were the Bible (used as a reader), McGuffey's Reader, and the Blue Back Speller.

Prior to 1840, the date of the coming of the common, or free, or district, or state, or public, schools, types of educational institutions were as follows: The field, or blab, or subscription schools; the private or plantation schools; and the academy or classical schools.

The field school was an institution conducted, and crudely, by a single teacher who charged a minimum tuition. The one-room, log structure usually served an entire countryside, with sometimes as many as 100 students being crowded into the small structure. Many parents were financially able to "take" only a single "subscription," yet they divided it among all their children. In this way, as many as six or seven youngsters were permitted several days' school each. The field school is described in the immediately preceding section of the chapter.

The private school was conducted by one or more instructors on the same principle of the field school but on a grander scale.

Bible and Bible Box

Glasses and Glass Case

Writing Case

Cruet Set

Early School Equipment

Highland Academy and Administration Building, Lenoir College

The school was exclusive and conducted among pleasant surroundings. It catered to wealthy persons, and, in fact, often was conducted for the convenience of a single family, almost on the principle of the private tutor basis.

The academy was an instituion conducted on the same principle as the field and private schools but on a sounder financial basis. It most usually was chartered by the legislature and was governed by a board of trustees. The academy sought to give a well-rounded education, and is credited with having served an exceptionally useful purpose in the evolution of today's school system. Sometimes the school was conducted in elaborate, many-room buildings designed especially for teaching purposes. Emphasis was laid in curriculum on a study of the classics. The Greek and Latin languages were held in high esteem by academy instructors. (It is to be noted that some academies served exclusively as high schools or preparatory schools.)

An advertisement published in The Lincolnton Transcript of March 25, 1837, points out what is believed to be the Catawba area's first academy. It is as follows: "Female School—The public are respectfully informed that the subscriber has opened a School near Archibald Ray's in Lincoln County, five miles south of the Island Ford, on the Lincolnton road, where the usual branches of an English education will be taught.

"From having had several years experience in teaching, the subscriber flatters herself that she will be able to give satisfaction to all who may employ her. She can furnish good testimonials as to character and qualifications.

"Terms of Tuition, per Session of Five months, $5.00.

"Board can be had in respectable families convenient to the Academy, at reasonable prices.

"Signed—Nancy Campbell."

This academy is believed to have been located near the present town of Claremont.

Among the academies were the Pleasant Hill academy, believed to have been established before 1840 in the area of the present Oxford Ford at the bend of the Catawba river; a classical school on Mountain creek, taught by Matthew L. McCorkle; an academy at Wilfong's Mill, located one and one-half miles west of Startown, taught by Rev. Jeremiah Ingold; and a classical school in Newton, opened by David Berrier.

As noted previously, the birth of North Carolina's progressive school system of today came in 1840, with the application of the terms of the first school law. For a correct prospective of this legislation, it is necessary that another glance be taken toward education on the state scene.

It will be recalled that the development of the ideal of public education in the state was slow, although it began early. The first significant step in the growth of this ideal was the adoption in 1776 of a constitutional provision for legislative establishment of schools and for a university. This provision of the constitution, which was adopted in December of that year, was "That a school or schools shall be established by the Legislature for the convenient instruction of youth, with such salaries to the masters, paid by the public, as may enable them to instruct at low prices; and all useful learning shall be duly encouraged and promoted in one or more universities." This provision was kept in the revised constitution of 1835. The university was chartered in 1789 and organized six years later. With but a single exception, no additional legislative action was to forward the movement of schools until the passage of the first public school law of the state in January, 1839.

The exception was an act creating the "literary fund." Passed in 1825, this act aimed at establishing a permanent public endowment for educational purposes, deriving its sources thus: "The dividends arising from the stock now held by the State in the banks of Newbern and Cape Fear and which have not heretofore been pledged and set apart for internal improvements; the dividends arising from stock which is owned by the State in the Cape Fear Navigation Company, the Roanoke Navigation Company, and the Clubfoot and Harlow Creek Canal Company; the tax imposed by law on licenses to the retailers of spirituous liquors and auctioneers; the unexpended balance of the Agricultural Fund, which by the act of the Legislature is directed to be paid into the public treasury; all moneys paid to the State for the entries of vacant lands (except the Cherokee Indians); the sum of twenty-one thousand and ninety dollars, which was paid by this State to certain Cherokee Indians, for reservations to lands secured by them by treaty, when the said sums shall be received from the United States by this State; and of all the vacant and unappropriated swamp lands in this State, together with such sums of money as the Legislature may hereafter find it convenient to appropriate from time to time."

The historic school law may be said to have caused two miracles, educationally speaking. It proved the democratic principle that education is the function of the state rather than a family function or a parental obligation; and it proved that the state has the power and the right to raise by taxation on the property of its members sufficient funds for adequate school support.

Principal aspects of the bill were:

That each county of the state was to vote either "for School" or "No School," and ". . . if a majority (of each county) shall be found in favor of Schools, it shall be the duty of the Sheriff to furnish a certificate of the same to the next County court of his County. . . ."

That if the county voted for schools ". . . at the first Court . . . a majority of the justices of such County . . . (shall) proceed to elect not less than five nor more than ten persons, as Superintendents of Common Schools, for such County. . . ."

That if the county voted for schools ". . . said Superintendents or a majority of them, shall meet within a reasonable time . . . and shall have power to choose one of their number as Chairman, and shall proceed to divide their respective Counties into School Districts, for the purpose of establishing Common Schools, containing not more than six miles square. . . ."

That if the county voted for schools, the Board of Superintendents ". . . shall appoint not less than three, nor more than six School Committee Men, in each district. . . ."

The provisions of the law made it possible for a county to receive from the literary fund $40 for each school district, provided the county raised by taxation the sum of $20 for each district.

Unfortunately, Lincoln county, of which Catawba county was a part, was one of the seven counties of the state which failed to adopt the state system. Historians generally cite this factor as a contributing cause to the movement for Catawba "independence."

When division of Lincoln and Catawba came, in 1842, the new county was quick to accept the districting plan as a means of developing free schools. Its first board of Superintendents of Common Schools met in December 1844. The first board was composed of John Coulter, Jonathan R. Moser, William P. Reinhardt, Major Hull and A. H. Shuford. The first chairman of the board (the first superintendent of public schools) was Hull. This is substantiated by a statement given Hull by John Coulter, the second superintendent of public schools, on October 7, 1845, a photostat of which is held by the Historical Association, acknowledging receipt of $300.01 1/2 as "part of the Tax laid for Common Schools for the said county 21st of July 1845." In his receipt, Coulter refers to "M. Hull" as "former ch." In the first book of record of the "Free School of Catawba County, N. C.," the introduction is signed: "By Major Hull Chairman of the Board of Superentendants of Common Schools In the year A. D. 1845."

The first superintendent's report was submitted by Coulter and revealed the status of schools in 1846-47. The report showed there were 38 districts in the county, of which 35 featured sessions of school. Three districts had two-teacher schools, and four other districts had more than one teacher but they taught at different periods during the same year. The average teacher's salary per month was $12.55.

The report of 1851-52, filed by George P. Shuford, who was elected chairman (succeeding Coulter) in 1851, showed that the number of districts had increased from 38 to 44 and that school was taught in 39 of the districts. The report for 1861-62 revealed 47 districts, 43 active schools, and 3.2 months of average yearly term.

In 1847, there were 38 districts in the county and only 37 in 1868. There were 3,772 school children reported in 1847 and 3,621 in 1868. The report for 1868 pointed out that the 37 districts of the county had "tolerably good houses in the districts."

Shuford was to serve as the third superintendent until 1865. He was succeeded by E. P. Coulter.

CATAWBA COUNTY

A history of the formation of the earliest school districts in Catawba county follows:

DISTRICT No. 1—Land was purchased from Daniel Sane for $6; school house was built by Henry Young; earliest payment of cash appropriated was December 10, 1845.

DISTRICT No. 2—Land was purchased (two acres) from Henry Reep for $5; school house was built by Samuel Tucker; earliest payment of cash appropriated was September 5, 1845.

DISTRICT No. 3—Land was purchased from George Lantz for $4; school house was built by Eli Yoder; earliest payment of cash appropriated was June 7, 1845.

DISTRICT No. 4—School house was built by John Lutz, Hosea Hallman and M. Reinhardt; earliest payment of cash appropriated was December 15, 1845.

DISTRICT No. 5—School house was built by Elisha Painter; earliest payment of cash appropriated was December 10, 1845.

DISTRICT No. 6—School house was built by Elijah Kirksey; earliest payment of cash appropriated was April 27, 1845.

DISTRICT No. 7—Land was purchased from Temple Shelton for $55 (evidently a structure stood on the property which was to be converted into a school house); school house was "finished" by Hosea Linebarger and John M. Rankin; earliest payment of cash appropriated was October 21, 1845.

DISTRICT No. 8—School house was built by R. E. Birch; earliest payment of cash appropriated was March 3, 1846.

DISTRICT No. 9—School house was built by Enoch Hudson; earliest payment of cash appropriated was September 29, 1845.

DISTRICT No. 10—Land was purchased from J. Hoyle for $12.50; school house was built by Turner T. Abernathy; earliest payment of cash appropriated was February 3, 1845.

DISTRICT No. 11—School house was built by H. L. Ramsour, Absalom Propst and David Yoder; earliest payment of cash appropriated was November 18, 1845.

DISTRICT No. 12—School house was built by Peter Yount; earliest payment of cash appropriated was December 10, 1845.

DISTRICT No. 13—Land was purchased from Peggy Sulivan for $8.68; school house was built by Joshua Wilson and M. C. Abernathy; earliest payment of cash appropriated was December 10, 1845.

DISTRICT No. 14—School house was built by P. G. Bumgarner; earliest payment of cash appropriated was September 27, 1845.

DISTRICT No. 15—Land was purchased from Gilbert A. Milligan for $22.50; school house was built by Robert Nixon; earliest payment of cash appropriated was November 18, 1845.

DISTRICT No. 16—Land was purchased (five acres) from "the Widow Hudson" for $5; school house was built by Peter Warlick; earliest payment of cash appropriated was December 10, 1845.

DISTRICT No. 17—School house was built by Michael Yoder; earliest payment of cash appropriated was February 28, 1846.

DISTRICT No. 18—School house was built by Daniel Rader, Soloman Shell, Jonas Frye, David Huffman, Jacob Huffman and David Robinson, Jr.; earliest payment of cash appropriated was November 4, 1845.

DISTRICT No. 19—Land was purchased from Elias Smyre for $10; school house was built by Avery Propst, George Setzer and David Hass; earliest payment of cash appropriated was January 24, 1846.

DISTRICT No. 20—Land was purchased from Thomas Ward for $15; school house was built by Jacob Rowe; earliest payment of cash appropriated was November 1, 1845.

DISTRICT No. 21—Land was purchased (three acres) from Nathaniel Edwards for $12; school house was built by Wilson Gabriel; earliest payment of cash appropriated was September 27, 1845.

DISTRICT No. 22—School house was built by Thomas Ward; earliest payment of cash appropriated was March 7, 1846.

DISTRICT No. 23—School house was built by L. A. Sides; earliest payment of cash appropriated was December 10, 1845.

CATAWBA COUNTY 135

DISTRICT No. 24—School house was built by Jacob Huffman and Rufus Hawn; earliest payment of cash appropriated was December 10, 1845.

DISTRICT No. 25—School house was built by David Setzer and John Taylor, earliest payment of cash appropriated was March 7, 1846.

DISTRICT No. 26—School house was built by J. E. Robinson; earliest payment of cash appropriated was December 10, 1845.

DISTRICT No. 27—Land was purchased (two acres) from Miles O. Abernathy for $4.50; school house was built by Abram Wyckoff and William Wyckoff; earliest payment of cash appropriated was October 21, 1845.

DISTRICT No. 28—Land was purchased (four acres) from Cyrus Peed for $20; school house was built by Gabriel Brown, Sr.; earliest payment of cash appropriated was December 27, 1845.

DISTRICT No. 29—School house was built by William Boovey; earliest payment of cash appropriated was November 1, 1845.

DISTRICT No. 30—Land was purchased (two acres) from John Smith for $5; school house was built by Alfred Huffman and Isaac Bolick; earliest payment of cash appropriated was September 3, 1845.

DISTRICT No. 31—School house was built by Frederick Smith; earliest payment of cash appropriated was October 7, 1845.

DISTRICT No. 32—School house was built by Jonas Ramseur; earliest payment of cash appropriated was December 17, 1845.

DISTRICT No. 33—School house was built by Joseph Killian and Elias Hafner; earliest payment of cash appropriated was September 20, 1845.

DISTRICT No. 34—School house was built by Jacob Null, Robert Thompson and Jacob Hetrick; earliest payment of cash appropriated was September 27, 1845.

DISTRICT No. 35—School house was built by Thomas Yarborough, Lawson Reinhardt and Soloman Deal; earliest payment of cash appropriated was January 1, 1846.

DISTRICT No. 36—School house was built by Daniel Sipe and Adam Shook; earliest payment of cash appropriated was August 30, 1845.

DISTRICT No. 37—School house already existed and J. B. Varner was employed to "repair" it; earliest payment of cash appropriated was December 28, 1846.

DISTRICT No. 38—School house already existed and Israel Holler was employed to "repair" it; earliest payment of cash appropriated was April 20, 1847.

What is believed to be a complete list of teachers employed in the county from the formation of the district school system until the close of the War Between the States is as follows:

Benjamin R. Allen, A. F. Abernathy, Logan Abernathy, R. L. Abernathy, Rufus Abernathy, S. T. Abernathy, William Abernathy, William A. Arent, sons of Jacob Arndt (based on entry: "To an order to Jacob Arndt for his sons assisting to teach—$8), and Elijah C. Austin.

Martha A. Ballew, Abel Barger, J. Warren Barger, David Barger, William Barr, Perry R. Baringer, A. B. Benick, David J. Benick, J. S. Benick, Miss Bisinger, George Blackburn, J. R. Blackburn, Robert Blackburn, Isaac Bolick, Legion Bollinger, William F. Boovey, J. H. Bost, Amsia Bost, James Bradshaw, Bettie Bridges, Dr. C. Brinkle, John R. Brinkle, Anderson A. Brown, J. M. Brown, and M. L. Brown.

Franklin Caldwell, Job D. Caldwell, Mary E. Cansler, W. W. Carpenter, Jeptha Clark, Harriet J. Cline, Henry Cline, Miss H. I. Cline, I. R. Cline, Michael L. Cline, L. P. Cloninger, Thomas Cloninger, H. W. Connor, William Correll, Joel Corriher, J. F. Cox, and James F. Crawford.

Edward David, Alonzo Deal, M. S. Deal, William L. Deal, W. S. Deal, Adolphus Douglass, Franklin Douglass, David Downs, James Drum, and John Drum.

George A. Ekard, Henry Ekerd, Simon P. Eckerd, Rufus England, and Wilson England.

CATAWBA COUNTY

Clara T. K. Fry, Emanuel Fry, H. A. Forney, Miss P. E. Forney, and Sarah C. Forney.

Ann V. Gantt, William W. Gilbert, John E. Goodman, James D. Goodson, Johanan Goodson, Matthew Goodson, Malinda A. Gosset, and Isaac H. Grant.

William Hale, H. H. Hallman, H. M. Hallman, Drury Hamilton, T. J. Hamilton, C. W. Harmon, Amzi A. Hawn, George W. Hawn, J. L. Hawn, Noah Hawn, Robinson C. Hawn, George Heedick, John Heedick, Valentine Helderman, P. C. Henkel, Caleb W. Herman, Franklin L. Herman, H. A. Herman, Moses Herman, William P. Herman, Eusebius Hetrick, F. A. H. Hewet, F. A. Hewitt, William D. Hickman, J. J. Hicks, Martha E. Hicks, Noah Hildebrand, Henry Hill, William Hinkle, Daniel L. Hoke, Franklin Holler, Henry E. Holler, Israel Holler, Martin A. Holler, Robinson Howard, F. W. Houston, Eli Hoyle, Jane E. Hoyle, Sarah Ann Hoyle, Rheuben Hoyle, Susan Hoyle, Huldah Hubbard, Enock Hudson, William J. Hudson, A. S. Hufman, John A. Huggins, F. A. Huitt, William F. Hull, and C. A. Hunsucker.

G. A. Ikerd, W. A. Ikerd, and Rev. Jeremiah Ingold.

Elias Jarrett, A. J. Johnson, John D. Johnson, J. Jones, J. F. Jones, M. A. Jones, and F. P. Julian.

Rufus Kids, S. Q. Keever, N. W. Killian, William L. Killian, and B. T. Kirby.

Edmond Lanier, Jacob Lantz, Rev. John Lantz, M. L. Laxton, F. Leeman, J. M. Leonard, M. A. A. Lewis, W. H. Lindsey, T. J. Linebarger, Emma Link, Henry Link, J. E. Link, Sidney A. Link, C. S. Little, Daniel A. Little, George Little, J. B. Little, Lafayette Loftin, David Lore, D. A. Lowe, T. L. Lowe, T. S. Lowe, C. E. Lowrance, Cany M. Lowrance, H. C. Lowrance, J. M. Lowrance, Mark E. Lowrance, William C. Lowrance, Henry F. Lutz, Henry L. Lutz, John B. Lutz, Mary R. H. Lutz, and Martha E. Lutz.

H. McCaul, James H. McCaul, John C. McCaul, Jeptha McClanahan, William Marshall, Berry Medlin, William L. Mehaffy, Adam Miller, Catharine Miller, Frances Miller, Kate F. Miller, Mattie C. Miller, S. G. Miller, Gilbert A. Milligan, G. A. Moser, George H. Moser, J. P. Moser, J. R. Moser, Marcus

M. Moser, Rev. Timothy Moser, D. F. Moose, J. A. Moose, Rev. Christen Moretz, M. L. Morrison, J. W. Mouser, William H. Mouser, Fletcher Munday, and J. E. Murphy.

P. F. Norwood and Williamson Norwood.

Noah Page, Elisha Painter, J. W. Paine, Watesel Palmer, Thomas Parker, Charity Peterson, Daniel Peterson, Jacob Peterson, J. R. Peterson, Rhoda C. Peterson, L. W. Porter, Lewcinda Porter, Eliza Potter, Joseph D. Punch, and I. J. Purcell.

M. S. Ramsour, O. A. Ramsour, Peter S. Ramsour, S. H. Randleman, Henry Reinhardt, Morris Roberts, Ann M. Robinson, Aron Robinson, David Robinson, C. W. Robinson, G. M. Robinson, George W. Robinson, Harvey Robinson, John A. Robinson, John H. Robinson, Kate L. Robinson, Manuel Robinson, Marcus W. Robinson, Miss O. C. Robinson, Miss S. A. Robinson, Sarah C. Robinson, T. A. Robinson, Huldah Rockett, S. A. Roper, D. F. Roseman, Daniel Rouch, J. E. Rouch, J. Dallas Rowe, Lizzie Rowe, T. C. Ruddock, and Marcus Rudisill.

Elisha Saunders, I. C. Scronce, Daniel Seagle, Jacob C. Seitz, A. J. Settlemyre, George Setzer, J. S. Setzer, E. Shell, John T. Shell, Manuel E. Shell, A. R. Sherrill, Elbert L. Sherrill, Elisha Sherrill, H. Sherrill, Jeptha Sherrill, Moses Sherrill, M. C. Sherrill, V. M. Sherrill, W. F. Sherrill, W. W. Sherrill, A. P. Shuford, E. D. Shuford, E. R. Shuford, George P. Shuford, Henry F. Shuford, J. J. Shuford, Marcus C. Shuford, Mary Ann Shuford, P. C. Shuford, William H. Shuford, P. H. Shuford, Quincy A. Shuford, W. P. Shuford, William C. Simmons, D. R. Smith, F. F. Smith, J. A. Smith, John M. Smith, Peter F. Smith, E. E. Smyre, G. S. Smyre, George Smyre, M. W. Smyre, S. L. Smyre, L. L. Steward, Oliver Stacy, E. B. Stiles, M. I. Stirewalt, and James C. Stroup.

A. A. Tallant, M. A. Thornburg, M. C. Tolbert, and G. H. Turner.

Job W. Umphrey.

James E. Veniker.

Benjamin Wagner, Willie J. Walker, David E. Warlick, Elia A. Warlick, Peter Warlick, E. Wells, Harriet E. Wetherspoon, A. P. Whisnant, Alvin Whitener, A. B. Whitener, A. J. Whitener, David R. Whitener, Eli Whitener, Henry Whitener, Jane Whitener, Jesse Whitener, Z. B. Whitener, William Wike, Henry Wilfong, A. W. Wilkey, G. H. Wilkie, George J. Wilkie, S. J. Wilkie, A. Mc. Wilkinson, G. M. Wilkinson, John P. Wilkinson, Thomas Wilkinson, James Williams, James Williams, Elmina Wilson, Jasper Wilson, J. I. Wilson, J. J. Wilson, Noah Winebarger, Abram Wycoff, J. B. Wycoff, and W. J. Wycoff.

Daniel A. Yoder, George M. Yoder, Robert A. Yoder, Rheuben Yoder, Lawson H. Yount, D. McD. Young, E. Yount, J. A. Yount, and Peter L. Yount.

An apt description of the days of the district schools is given in writings of Mrs. Cordelia Clay Miller. She points out:

"I have heard my mother and grandmother speak of people who were too lazy to work and thought that teaching was a soft snap. One man called himself 'squire' and spelled 'school' 'skule' and 'chair' 'cheer,' yet he pretended to be able to teach. After all, there was some money in the job.

"Once the county court appointed a committee to examine teachers. One of the men stood up and addressed the court: 'May it please your worships to examine the teachers further than "baker"?'

"The old schools, even when I first went to school, were very poor. But most of the teachers were of a high order and did unusually well for the chance they had. The schools were the one-room-one-teacher variety and were very meagerly furnished. The outsides were usually made of logs and the insides were just the logs in the rough state. The master's desk was the best piece of furniture in the room, usually placed in the center where he could see all over the room from his platform. Nearby stood the 'dunce stool' which was used to ridicule unruly scholars who could not learn or who misbehaved in school. On a bench near the door stood the wooden water bucket and dipper from which all quenched their thirst, and never thought of germs. To ward off disease, all small girls and many boys wore tied around their necks asafetida tied in a rag. Naturally they did not 'catch' diseases for no one could get near them, so wild were they. The boys would slip and remove theirs, but little girls faithfully wore them until they were black with dirt.

"Near the master's desk stood his supply of red switches which he used liberally. Some of the older boys took turns in coming to school early and sweeping and building the fires. Usually the school house had only one chimney but the larger ones in the more prosperous communities had two. The floor was made of puncheon and the seats for the scholars had no backs. They were made of split logs with small posts driven in each end. Around one side of the room, near the window, was placed a desk known as the writing desk. It had a supply of home-made ink, and the master would cut fresh goosequill pens every day. Much practicing had to be done, before anyone was allowed to really write anything. So at recess all the younger children would play 'school' and write and cypher on a smooth place on the ground. Some of the fathers and older brothers would smooth off a nice white piece of plank, bore a hole in one end and tie a string in it and hang it around the necks of the small ones. . . .

"The school day was very long. Children started to school soon after sun up and got home after dark. School was usually kept in the winter months when the crops were 'laid by' and they could be spared at home. During the war, everyone had to work twice as many hours but schools went on just the same. Many people said that the Yankees said the war had come to the South because the people were ignorant, so they were determined that their children have a better chance at education. As there was no money for private schools, most people were glad to send to 'free schools.' They did not feel that the 'free schools' were beneath them.

"My mother said that once she went to Lincoln county to visit her relatives who lived on a large plantation. The children had so many dolls and fine toys they didn't care for them. When the Lincolnton kin came up to return the visit, naturally the children asked to see mother's dolls. Mother said she told them: 'Surely you don't think we are going to take out our fine dolls just any old time.' That satisfied the guests and they went home never knowing that mother's 'fine dolls' were just made of corn cobs. The people of this section may have been poor, but they were proud; proud of family and country, and true patriots. Many times I have heard grandmother say 'I am poor, but my head will never be bowed.' She said she hated to act like a Pharisee but there were people living in near-by counties who thought the 'hogs ate everybody but them.'

"Since all children had to go so far to school and had to stay so long, they had to take plenty of food that would 'stick to the ribs.' Everyone in those days made large biscuits and it was no uncommon sight to see children tugging along large baskets of these big biscuits with ham, lean-side meat, whole 'punkin' and 'tater' pies as well as baked 'taters' to school. They had nothing to drink except the spring water.

"After they were fed, the big recess was spent in playing games such as 'anty-over,' 'town ball,' marbles, etc.

"Friday afternoon was the day chosen to hold spelling matches, exhibitions, speaking pieces and dialogues. Finally the long-awaited Friday arrived. The room had a festive air. The children and teacher had sand-scrubbed the floor until it was almost clean enough to eat from. The fire place had been filled with pungent pine branches. The morning had been spent in reviewing for the great occasion. The children had eaten their lunches and had put away their lunch buckets and baskets. The wooden water buckets and gourd dippers had been scrubbed and were now filled with fresh cold water from the spring. The boys and girls had washed their faces, hands and feet, and had slicked back their hair. Much doubling up on benches had to be done to make seats for the parents and visitors. Special seats had been provided behind the teacher's tall desk. Parents and relatives were seated. Several of the 'big boys' were sent out to meet the minister and school committeemen, and to be on hand to tie up the horses and to carry in the saddle bags to places of safety.

"The signal was given that 'they had arrived and a stillness suggesting "death" greeted the visitors as they took their appointed places on the platform. The teacher timidly made the 'speech of welcome.' Two of the best scholars were asked to come forward and be the captains who would choose up sides. The best scholars were chosen first, and the others followed.

"The boys and girls, trembling, 'toed the mark'—a large crack in the floor. The old Blue Back was handed to the Chairman of the Committee. Not a sound could be heard except the buzzing of flies and the occasional neigh of the horses outside. All down both sides of the line, the words were given out, and one after another was 'spelled down.' Finally, it was time for the hard words to be given out—like Constantinople, reprehensible, reprehensibility, victual. These words all had to be spelled in syllables.

"The last one up was the winner, and proud were the parents of the child who had won. This was not only a test for the children, but also a test for the teacher, whose aim was to please the committee and teach the required subjects well. The teacher was judged also on how well he used the switch. The motto of the day was 'spare the rod and spoil the child.' Many teachers owed their jobs because they could whip well.

"The dunce cap was not the only means of making an erring scholar an object of ridicule. He was often ordered to 'ride the ass,' or to 'sit on nothing.' 'Riding the ass' was done by straddling an old wooden horse supported by legs. . . ."

During the period 1845 to 1865, Catawba county's first college was established. The people of the Reformed church, early interested in the education of their children, opened the doors of Catawba college in the "old Academy building" in Newton in the fall of 1851. This achievement was the culmination of a movement which began almost 20 years before. As early as 1834, a program was inaugurated to foster education, particularly the education of young men for the ministry. The result was the setting up of an "education society." It is recorded that the first suggestion was made for the founding of the college at St. Matthew's Arbor near the Catawba-Lincoln line in 1849, when M. L. McCorkle, then a recent graduate from Davidson college, suggested: "Why not found a college of our own in our midst." On December 17, 1852, the college was formally chartered by the state legislature. In a few years, buildings were erected and a library and necessary equipment were added. But the scholarship plan on which the school was started failed to furnish sufficient funds, and the curriculum was soon suspended. The school then assumed the status of a high school. Rev. A. S. Vaughan of Pennsylvania raised an endowment of $25,000 and restored the college curriculum in 1859. The War Between the States severely hindered the progress of the school. In 1865, Rev. J. C. Clapp, D.D., reorganized the school, and called it Catawba High school. The name of

Catawba college was restored in 1885. The school operated as a college in Newton until the early 1920s, when it was closed to re-open in Salisbury in 1925.

Presidents of the college were Professor C. H. Albert, 1851-52; Dr. H. H. Smith, 1852-55; C. W. Smith, 1855-59; A. S. Vaughan, 1859-61; J. C. Clapp, 1861-1900; Charles H. Mebane, 1900-04; George A. Snyder, 1904-08; W. R. Weaver, acting president, 1909-10; John Frederick Buchheit, 1910-13; James D. Andrew, 1913-18; A. D. Wolfinger, 1918-23 (moved to Salisbury).

The War Between the States, although it did not stop schools, caused the processes of education to be slowed. Schools still lived, as is evidenced by scattered records, but the attendance on the part of students dropped considerably. The absorbing interest in the war naturally decreased the attention given to school affairs on the community level. Men teachers quickly dropped their academic careers and joined the army. Females were now to come on the education scene in the roles of teachers in increasing numbers. On account of the more reliable citizens being at war, it was most difficult to get school committees to serve. By 1863, the counties had been released from the obligation of laying taxes for schools and the small amounts received from the distribution of the literary fund income were insufficient to maintain schools as long as usual. The state superintendent urged on local authorities that they keep in order the framework and machinery of their county systems; that they supply the places of male teachers called to the war with qualified female teachers and to continue schools wherever female teachers could be found; that they license only competent and loyal teachers; and that they maintain as high a standard of qualifications for teachers as the conditions would allow.

Fortunately, a strong educational sentiment continued during the days of 1861-65.

But, the disaster was to come at the war's close. Although the state literary fund had been guarded jealously by education-minded men in state officialdom, still earmarked specifically for schools, it was to be lost after the war. The principal of the fund was invested in bank and railroad stocks, but the banks had themselves invested heavily in Confederate securities, and, in the wreck of the banking system, the literary fund disappeared. The state throughout 1866-67 made efforts to establish its relations with the Federal government in the instance of education, but other matters absorbed public interest and the means of education received little attention.

The only school legislation of the short session of the state legislature which met on November 27, 1865, and continued until the middle of March, 1866, were orders which abolished the offices of the superintendent of common schools and the treasurer of the Literary Fund; and an act which allowed the justices of the county courts to lay and collect taxes at their discretion for common school support. During the legislature of 1866-67, two acts of educational importance were passed. The first of these was an act authorizing towns and cities to establish school systems to be supported by taxes collected or authorized to be collected for corporation purposes. Provision was made for local trustees, for a local board of education and for other features of a modern school system. In addition to the powers of taxation, authorization was given to levy and collect a poll-tax on every white male over 21 years of age of not more than $2 for the use of the public schools. The second act proposed to "protect certain interests in common schools." Among the features of this law was the stipulation that the county courts appoint a county superintendent, whose services were similar to those of the old chairman of the board of superintendents.

The constitution of 1868 facilitated a complete school law. County commissioners were to order a tax for sites and for building or renting school houses, to be assessed and collected in the same manner as other county taxes. Local township committees were to establish and maintain, for at least four months in every year, a sufficient number of schools at convenient localities "which shall be for the education of all children between the ages of six and twenty-one years." A county examiner was to be appointed by the commissioners, to examine the teachers and to issue certificates, etc.

In conformity with the new law, the Catawba county commissioners levied a public tax of eight and two-thirds cents and a county school tax of one-half cent on the one-hundred dollars property valuation. The provision dealing with the four-month school, unfortunately, conflicted with another clause of the

The Spelling Match

School Master

1865
Typical Costume

Early Log Schoolhouse

CATAWBA COUNTY   145

new constitution, and was usually unheeded, in Catawba as elsewhere.

Generally, schools locally underwent a darker period during the reconstruction period than during the war. The county was without the work of a school leader for two years. Records of the May court of 1869 point out in relation to school matters: "May 26, 1869: The appointed committee met with E. P. Coulter, chairman of the board of superintendents of common schools. We find that E. P. Coulter was appointed chairman of the board of common schools on April 15, 1865, but owing to the state of the country he did not take charge of the office or funds at that time but was re-appointed in 1867 by the County Court and then took charge of the books, papers, funds of the former chairman, George P. Shuford, deceased . . ." Coulter served as superintendent until 1869.

The seriousness of the situation is revealed in the fact that orders from school committees to the county treasurer, filed as late as 1872, called for salaries to be paid for services rendered by teachers during 1865 to 1871. These faithful masters included:

Miles A. Abernathy, H. D. Abernathy, M. A. Abernathy, J. F. Abernathy, E. Baker, Pinkney Baker, T. L. Bandy, Hugh M. Blair, Sarah A. Bridges, H. Brotherton, Sim Browne, David F. Barringer, A. V. Campbell, James Cansler, W. B. Cauble, J. M. Clampitt, W. P. Cline, Mary Clute, Jane O. Cox, B. H. Culbreth, Hosea Deal, Lazabe Deal, Miles Deal, F. J. Dellinger, John A. Edwards, N. B. England, J. A. Epps, William Fite, M. Fulenwider, Pink Fye, J. P. Greene, J. Hallman, James P. Harwell, E. T. Hawn, P. C. Hawn, Irene Herman, J. F. Herman, J. P. Herman, P. S. Herman, Sally Herman, D. Hettrick, John E. Hoke, P. P. Hoke, A. R. Holshower, and H. T. Hoover.

W. N. Houston, Frances M. Hudson, Mrs. E. Huitt, D. C. Huffman, L. C. Huffman, B. F. Ingold, W. P. Ivey, Charles Jarrett, Mattie Jarrett, John Johnson, W. Johnson, L. C. Kale, D. E. Kaylor, A. P. Keever, M. J. Keever, Jasper Killian, James Kistler, C. S. Little, H. Mc D. Little, M. L. Little, S. D. Little, Max H. Lutz, William A. Lutz, George Long, Mollie Long, Elkana McCorkle, M. L. McCorkle, Daniel May, T. E. May, J. L. Miller, M. C. Miller, B. M. Morrow, F. P. Moser, P. W. H. Mouser, I. T. Munday, J. L. Murphy, W. C. Paine, Callie

Powell, J. Y. Propst, W. F. Reep, M. W. Robinson, E. W. Rockett, H. Rockett, M. I. Rowe, and John A. Rudisill.

H. G. Seitz, George W. Setzer, J. M. Setzer, W. J. D. Scherer, J. H. Shuford, L. G. Sigmon, Mary Sigmon, W. H. Sigmon, J. K. Smith, Peter F. Smith, William A. Smith, Julius Smyre, Robert Smyre, Alice Summerow, Alex Summit, M. A. Thornbert, M. Tolbert, W. A. Tweiksbury, H. D. Wagner, James M. Wagner, Josephine Ward, D. L. Warlick, Julius Wike, G. M. Wilkinson, L. M. Williams, Sally Wilson, E. A. Witherspoon, P. T. Witherspoon, Able Whitener, Augustus Whitener, E. L. Whitener, J. A. Whitener, O. W. Whitener, S. Joseph Whitener, Pope Woods, F. A. Yoder, A. L. Yount, Ephraim Yount, and Hattie Yount.

M. E. Lowrance became Catawba county's fifth superintendent of education in 1869. He served until 1880.

School districts were in a state of flux following the war. A report made in 1873 showed six school districts in Hamilton township; eight districts in Clines township; six districts and one private school in Mountain Creek township; eight districts, two academies and one college in Newton township; five districts and one private school in Bandys township; six districts and one private school in Caldwell township; ten districts, one private school and two academies in Hickory Tavern township; and five districts and one private school in Jacobs Fork township. The total number of districts was 54, and only one was without a school. The number of white male students was 1,780 and the number of white female students was 1,819.

The salary of the county superintendent was fixed at $2 per day in 1870 and for the year the superintendent worked a total of ten days in the schools. Thus, his total salary for the year was $20. In 1879-80, he worked only nine days, for $18. After this date, the superintendent began to devote more time to the schools, although as late as July 5, 1897, the pay of the supervisor, as the officer then was called, remained fixed at $2 per day. The county superintendent received $96 in 1884-85; $121.50 in 1889-90; and $174 in 1894-95.

The average length of the school term was 12 weeks in 1880 for both the white and colored schools. Only a few days had been added to the length of the term ten years later. In 1894-

CATAWBA COUNTY 147

95, however, the term of the white schools increased to 15 weeks. But, at the same time, the term of the colored schools decreased to ten weeks.

The average salary paid the teachers in Catawba county during the period of 1870-95 actually decreased. In 1870, teachers holding first grade certificates received an average of $30 per month, and those holding second grade certificates received $22.50. In 1894-95, the white men teachers received an average of $25.80, and the white women, $22.35. The low salary paid during the period determined that more women began to take positions as teachers and men withdrew into more remunerative positions. Twenty-one out of a total of 84 teachers in 1894-95 were women.

That the Negro was given attention in the county's schools is evidenced by the large, and authentic, list of persons who taught in colored institutions beginning about 1870 and ending before the turn of the century.

The teachers were Albert Abernathy, J. H. Abernathy, A. L. Beatty, W. S. M. Blackburn, Frank L. Bost, J. H. Smith, John L. Bost, Joseph Bysander, Hall Chambers, James Cline, John E. Connor, J. H. Cornelius, Meridan Coulter, Jason Cowan, John Derr, Laura Dodge, Elbert Edwards, Elizabeth Forney, J. A. Gabriel, D. J. Graham, T. S. Grier, B. Harren, J. M. Henderson, Lucy Hoke, David Hull, John F. Hull, H. A. Hunsucker, S. A. Hunsucker, S. L. Hyatt, Bob Ikerd, David Johnston, Samuel Kale, W. H. Kennedy, Martha Lintan, Banford McCorkle, R. L. McCorkle, E. P. Mayo, M. C. Munday, A. L. Newby, J. W. Poe, Luther R. Reinhardt, Lewis Robinson, J. W. Rose, W. S. Shuford, Solomon Shrum, Alice Slade, Mayfield Slade, Phebe Smith, Amanda Smyre, R. L. Smyre, Cora M. Steel, Clara Turner, A. A. Vaughn, Adolphus Waugh, J. W. Wells, Andrew Whitener, Frank Wilson, Sallie Willson, Mary Jane Woodford, and Frank Yount.

The period of 1870 to 1900 featured the popularity of the academy, or preparatory, school, and the private school. Prior to this period, in 1863, Dr. Brantley York operated the Log Academy near Catawba. M. A. Robinson taught here for 30 years.

Among the other schools of this type were:

Dr. J. C. Clapp and S. M. Finger operated the Catawba High school in Newton as early as 1865.

The Wesley Chapel Academy, located in the Vale section, and the Kate McCloud school and the Jennir Caldwell school, both located in Newton, were known to be operating in 1870.

The Intermediate Preparatory school, located in Hickory Tavern, was known to be operating in 1871. George W. Hawn and M. L. Little were in charge.

The Terrapin Institute, located on Terrapin creek, was known to be operating in 1872.

The Mary Clute school, located at Hickory Tavern, was opened in 1873.

About 1873, Professor J. W. Mauser started a school in Hickory Tavern.

In 1874, Alice Ingold began a select school for girls, also located in Hickory Tavern.

The Union Academy, located on Lincoln street (now First Avenue, S. E.) in Hickory Tavern, was known to be operating in 1877. Hugh M. Blair and Thomas Lacy were the masters. Lacy withdrew in 1878, and was succeeded by W. P. Ivey.

The Female High school, with a preparatory department for girls and boys, located in Newton, was known to be operating in 1879. J. Dallas Rowe was the master.

The Cochran school, located in Newton, was known to be operating in 1880. This school was sponsored by Mr. and Mrs. G. W. Cochran. Miss Matt Cochran opened a new school here in 1898.

St. Joseph's Academy, a girls' school and convent, located in the southwest part of Hickory (building still stands), was established January 14, 1880, by Dr. B. F. Cobb, and sponsored by the Catholic church. The school was taken over by the Ohio Lutheran Synod January 27, 1888, and renamed St. Paul's Seminary. The new establishment was sponsored by Rev. M. L. Hunt, Professor S. M. Hamrick, Professor H. K. G. Doerman and Rev. J. E. Barb. After this school passed out of existence, its structure was used temporarily as the free Hickory High school.

The cornerstone of Highland Academy, located at the site of the present Lenoir Rhyne college campus in Hickory, was laid March 25, 1882. Major J. G. Hall was the sponsor. Land for the site of the school was given by Capt. Walter W. Lenoir. Col. H. C. Dixon was the first master, opening the school July 24, 1882. Succeeding heads were R. K. Bryan, Richard K. Meade, Jr., and Rev. T. G. Thurston.

A Mr. Shinn opened a school in the Reformed church in Hickory on January 19, 1885.

Keeversville Academy, located at the present Plateau, was known to be operating in 1886. J. M. Clampitt was the principal.

Witherspoon Academy, located in Newton, was known to be operating in 1887. L. L. Witherspoon was the sponsor.

The Beard School for Girls, located at Hickory, was known to be operating in 1892. Lucy Morgan Beard was the organizer.

District schools began to assume community names. Included were Abernathy, Bandys, Bargers, Barringers, Bolicks, Bollingers, Bosts, Bowmans, Clines, Cloningers, Concord, Danners, Ebenezers, Fishs, Freemont, Huffmans, Hopewell, Jacobs Fork, Josh Chapel, Keeversville, Killians, Hickory Tavern, Minerva, Hog Hill, Lead Mine, Links, Littles, Lores, Lutz, Millers, Mountain Creek, Nulls, Piney Grove, Rehobeth, Robinsons, Sherrills, Setzers, Soap Stone, St. James, St. Johns, St. Pauls, Thyatira, Wilkinsons, Townsends, Wilsons, Whiteners, Yoders, and Zions.

Catawba county figured prominently in state education circles during the 1880s and 1890s by virtue of the fact that two of its citizens filled the important post of state superintendent of public schools. Sidney M. Finger, who held the position from 1885 to 1892, was noted for his interest in higher education for women and is given much credit for the advancement of Woman's college of the Greater University of North Carolina at Greensboro. Charles H. Mebane, who held the position from 1896 to 1900, became the first individual to appear before the state legislature in behalf of the state-wide system of public schools, and he set precedent in his biennial reports.

Progress in public education during the eight years of Finger's administration was slow. Superintendent Finger himself was well aware of the lack of educational facilities as well as cognizant of the needs that would have to be met before the school system could be improved. In a preliminary report to Governor Scales immediately after taking office, he said: "Upon the whole, our educational outlook is encouraging in every respect except one. There is not enough money applied to meet the constitutional obligation of four month's schooling."

A revival in education, leading ultimately to the movement which placed North Carolina as the leader of Southern education in the 1900s, is credited to the efforts of Mebane. Going into office under the Fusion ticket of 1896, Superintendent Mebane was determined from the start to devote his full time to education, as completely divorced from politics as possible. His success won the admiration of leaders of the opposing political faith and friends of the public schools everywhere.

"State School Facts," published monthly by the state department of public instruction, points out regarding Mebane's administration "It was during Mebane's administration that the first $100,000 was appropriated for public schools. Mebane prepared the bill to appropriate this money and it was introduced by Senator McIntyre of Robeson County. This is considered by educational historians as the beginning of State aid for public education in North Carolina, even though the public schools had begun in 1839 with aid from the State Literary Fund and a small amount had been used to match local taxes and subscriptions in accordance with the 1897 law, since this was the beginning of appropriations from the general fund which succeeding Legislatures have continued to make, until now such appropriations exceed $50,000,000 annually."

The office of county superintendent of schools was filled by five men from 1880 to 1900. J. C. Clapp, succeeding Lowrance, served from 1880 until 1885; R. A. Yoder served from 1885 until 1894; J. A. Foil served from 1894 until 1895; the schools were under the jurisdiction of the county commissioners from 1895 until 1897; J. D. Rowe served from 1897 until 1899; and A. P. Whisnant served from 1899 until 1903.

During the same period, three colleges were established in Catawba county, one of which continues today.

CATAWBA COUNTY 151

Claremont college, which was suspended May 24, 1915, was chartered as Claremont Female college on August 25, 1880, and formally opened in the fall of that year with classes held in the Corinth Reformed church in Hickory.

Rev. A. S. Vaughan was its first president, and after the brick building was erected in 1883 he resigned. From 1888 until 1892, W. H. Sanborn was president of the institution which was the only school exclusively for girls in Hickory. A complete literary course and a teacher training course were included in the curriculum, together with instruction in the arts. Rules and regulations were rigid, and altogether a high ideal was set for the school.

Florence L. Chase became acting president of the institution in 1883. She was succeeded by Alice Thurston, who served from 1884 until 1885. Katharine Van Rensselaer Bonney served as president from 1885 until 1887. She was followed by W. H. Sanborn, who held the position from 1887 until 1892. Rev. J. L. Murphy became president in 1892, and held the position until 1896. In 1900, the school was leased to S. P. Hatton (president from 1896 to 1900) who, in turn, leased it to M. W. Hatton, president from 1900 to 1902. Again in 1902 the lease changed hands, this time going to A. J. Bolin (president from 1902 to 1905), whose lease expired in 1905 when Professor D. W. Reed became president. Rev. W. B. Duttern and Rev. J. H. Keller jointly controlled Claremont college until 1907, when it was transferred to the Classis of North Carolina, and, in 1909, Dr. Murphy again became the president, until 1915, when Dr. J. M. L. Lyerly became president. In May of that year, the North Carolina Classis meeting at Newton suspended work of the institution.

The present Claremont High school of Hickory is located at the site of Claremont college.

Concordia and Lenoir Rhyne colleges are an outgrowth of the educational awakening that stirred the Lutherans of the Tennessee Synod and resulted in the establishment of Concordia High school at Conover in 1877. Concordia High school was converted into a college and chartered as Concordia college in 1881.

Presidents who served Concordia college were Dr. P. C. Henkel, 1881-85; Rev. J. C. Moser, 1885-88; Dr. R. A. Yoder,

1888-91; no president, 1891-1892; W. H. T. Dau, 1892-99; G. A. Romoser, 1899-1911; C. A. Weis and Ad. Haentzschel, acting presidents, 1911-13; H. B. Hemmeter, 1913-17; O. W. Kreinheder, 1917-28; C. O. Smith, acting president, 1928-30; and H. B. Hemmeter, 1930-35.

In 1935, the school's administration building burned at a time when the Missouri Synod of the Lutheran church was already producing more young men for the ministry than it could use. Consequently, the Synod meeting at Cleveland, Ohio, thought it unwise to rebuild the institution. The school was discontinued the same year.

The school was sponsored by the Tennessee Synod in its early days, but, in 1892, it came into the possession of the Evangelical Lutheran Missouri Synod.

Lenoir Rhyne college was formally opened September 1, 1891, in Hickory (temporarily, the school was known as Highland college). Its beautiful campus was the gift of Captain Walter W. Lenoir, in whose honor the college was originally named Lenoir college. The will of Captain Lenoir stipulated that an initial $10,000 for buildings and equipment be deposited with his executor, Colonel J. G. Hall. This amount was provided by the founders, Drs. R. A. Yoder, J. C. Moser, W. P. Cline, and Rev. A. L. Crouse, by discounting their individual notes, involving as collateral their entire possessions. Laboring along with the founders from the beginning was Professor R. L. Fritz, an alumnus of the school.

The institution was incorporated January 4, 1892. Rev. R. A. Yoder served as president until 1901. Professor Fritz succeeded Dr. Yoder as head of the institution. While the foundations of the institution were laid under Dr. Yoder's administration, the super-structure was erected by Dr. Fritz. Under the administration of Dr. Fritz came a period of building enlargement, reorganization and recognition.

In 1910, Lenoir college graduates were first accepted for post graduate work without examination by the University of North Carolina. In 1915, after government survey and inspection, the college officially was rated one of the ten A-grade colleges of the state along with the state university and other leading educational institutions.

In 1916, a preliminary campaign for endowment resulted in $50,000 and laid the foundation for future endowment work. A forward movement for adequate endowment and a greater Lenoir college was completed in the fall of 1919, when D. E. Rhyne of Lincolnton, a pioneer cotton mill executive of the state, contributed $100,000, and other friends of the institution raised $200,000. In 1923, the name of the institution was changed to Lenoir Rhyne, in honor of Rhyne.

The college became a member of the Southern Association of Colleges and Secondary Schools in 1929. The institution was unconditionally accredited in 1940.

Presidents, following Dr. Fritz, were Dr. J. C. Peery, 1920-25; Dr. P. E. Monroe, acting president, 1925-26; Dr. H. B. Schaeffer, 1926-34; Dr. P. E. Monroe, 1934-49; and Dr. V. R. Cromer, 1949, and still serving.

The school was sponsored by the Tennessee Synod of the Evangelical Lutheran church until 1921, when, through a merger of Lutheran Synods in North Carolina, it became the property of the United Evangelical Lutheran Synod of North Carolina.

The Negro was to become an important political factor in North Carolina in the middle 1890s—and by the same token influence the education scene. The Negro vote of about 120,000 ballots is credited with establishing a General Assembly in 1895 which bore a close resemblance to law making bodies of reconstruction days. The legislature of that year abolished the office of county superintendent and placed the duties of his office in the hands of the clerk of the county board of commissioners.

The same act abolished the county board of education, and placed the duties of that body also in the hands of the commissioners.

But the Negro population in Catawba county was not large enough to change the political affairs of the county, and the area was spared a dangerous reaction which had disastrous results upon the schools in many counties of the state.

The Catawba county commissioners took over the work of education with little interruption to the schools resulting from the change of boards. The first official act of the commission in regard to the schools was that there be ordered ". . . no changes in the districts today. . . ."

Public schools were again turned back to a board of education in 1897. Rowe, who was elected "supervisor" (the new designation for the head of the education board) then received $2 per day—the same rate which had been fixed in 1870, 20 years previous. During his term of office, the board fixed the salary of first-grade certificate teachers at $33 per month.

One of the most important legal controversies in the history of Catawba county education began in January, 1898. The argument arose between the county board of education and the town of Hickory and dealt with the apportionment of school funds. The county board had decided to apportion school funds to Hickory according to the per capita distribution, as to the other districts of the county. Hickory, however, came before the board and pressed its claim for an order from that body for all funds collected by taxation for school purposes within the corporate limits for the benefit of the graded schools of that place. After considerable consultation and discussion, the board held to the original order. Hickory then appealed to the Superior court. The amount in controversy was $722.85. The case was argued at the spring term of court in 1898 and was decided in favor of the board of education. This decision was a signal of victory for the rural schools of the county in that it made the apportionment equal to all school children and allowed the rural child his just benefits of the corporation taxes of the town. This decision also kept the authority of the county board of education from becoming decentralized to the point of weakness and settled once and for all a vexatious problem that has never again risen to injure the county's schools.

Near the close of the nineteenth century, the leading people, not only in Catawba county but throughout the state, began to take an awakened interest in public education. Reconstruction almost had succeeded where war had failed to check the ardor of the masses for public schools.

Consolidation, which now virtually is required by statute in the state, was attempted in the county as early as 1902. In April of that year, records reveal that the board of education spent two entire days measuring a county map for the purpose

CATAWBA COUNTY   155

of consolidating and arranging districts. The plan proposed at that time by Superintendent Whisnant was a great advancement over the prevailing school practice and actually embodied the principles of consolidation recognized by the state legislature in 1923. But the consolidation plan was not accepted by Catawbans so readily. As late as 1920, there were 78 school districts in the county.

The community of Startown led the way in the instance of a special tax for schools. In 1904, the Crab Orchard school and the Wilson school were consolidated, and the district voted a special tax of 30 cents on the $100 property valuation and 90 cents on the poll to maintain a better school. Charles H. Mebane, former state superintendent of public education, was superintendent of the county schools and president of Catawba college at the time. In the consolidation, he was assisted by Governor Aycock, who took a personal interest in the establishment of the district, W. L. Killian and his son, J. Y. Killian, Craig Shuford, Dr. R. A. Yoder, who had also served as county superintendent and president of Lenoir college, and many other interested citizens. The school first was organized as a two-teacher school under the Guilford county act for establishing such schools in 1914, and became a County Farm Life school in 1921.

Hickory became a special charter district in a school election held in 1903. Men who have held the position of superintendent from the date of establishment until the present are D. K. McKrae, Charles M. Staley, C. E. McIntosh, Dr. R. W. Carver, J. Loy Sox, and W. S. Hamilton. Newton became a special charter district in a school election held in 1905. In 1933, the Newton city administrative unit was organized to include Newton and Conover and the rural districts of St. Johns and Charity. Men who have held the position of superintendent from the date of establishment until the present are R. C. Cox, A. S. Ballard, M. S. Beam, L. M. Epps, W. S. Snipes, M. C. Campbell (who later was to serve as superintendent of the county system), and R. N. Gurley.

Additional superintendents of the present Catawba county rural school administrative unit are Mebane, 1903-05; R. R. Williams, 1905-07; George Long, 1907-25; J. A. Capps, 1925-37; Campbell, 1937-52; and H. M. Arndt, 1952.

Today, one of North Carolina's most education-minded counties, which is sponsoring a $5 million consolidation and improvements program, looks back upon a history of sacrificial struggle.

CHAPTER VII

EARLY TRANSPORTATION FACILITIES

The Catawba county wilderness in the mid-seventeen hundreds was punctured only by rivers and waterways, natural vegetative vacancies and Indian trails.

The Indian trails usually were no more than 12 to 18 inches wide. Their locations generally were buffalo paths. It long has been recognized that buffaloes are among the ablest engineers.

In areas where travel was heavy, it is believed that Indian trails sometimes were worn a foot deep! Over such trails Indian runners were able to travel more than the length of the present-day county between a sunrise and sunset. In comparison, the first extensive movements of settlers locally, in parties including women and children, averaged only a mile an hour on foot.

It is doubted that Catawba waterways were ever used to any degree by settlers for purposes of transportation. Few rivers and streams were of sufficient depth for extended distance to enable boat travel, and the principal waterways were clogged at points by jutting land. However, there is evidence that portions of the Catawba, the South Fork, the Jacobs Fork and the Henrys Fork once accommodated the poleboat, or bateau—a transportation facility which was extremely popular elsewhere in early America. The poleboat derived its name from the manner in which it was pushed upstream by means of long poles. These boats seldom ranged in size larger than rafts. Traveling downstream in a poleboat required almost no effort, but upstream against a current was quite another matter.

Of course, settlers used—frequently—the paddle type of boat, from canoe to passenger variety. These facilities were employed principally for local travel. Too, they were employed for fishing and for sport.

Pack horses likely were the first means of transportation in this section—both for humans and for freight. There is some conjecture that Adam Sherrill made his advent into the local area by such a means.

Pack horse trains were not uncommonly seen in mass migration. The first horse in a pack train was ridden by the driver.

Each of the other horses in the procession was led by a rope tied to the one in front. Bars of iron were sometimes lashed to the backs of the horses and then bent around their middles so that barrels, kegs, and creels could be fastened on either side. The routes, variously called tote roads, pack roads, or horseways, in many places were no more than paths several feet wide, winding tortuously over hill and down valley.

Wagons came into use in America soon after 1700, and it is likely that they were used here either at the beginning of local settlement or soon thereafter.

The most famous of these was the Conestoga, which played an important role in the settlement of the new world between 1750 and 1850.

From the standpoint of size alone, the Conestogas with their six-horse bell teams were impressive. Team and wagon together measured 60 feet in length. The top of the front hoop was 11 feet from the ground, and the top ends of the wagon were some 16 feet apart. Rear wheels stood five to six feet high. Colors were almost a trademark: The underbody always a vivid blue, while the upper framework was bright red. It was topped with a dull white cloth cover about 24 feet long.

An apt description of the wagons, which were manufactured in Pennsylvania and doubtless purchased there by numerous pioneer Catawbans prior to their trek South, is provided by John Strohn in The United States Agricultural Report of 1863:

"The capacious wagons which the Conestoga farmers then had in use, were the best means of land transportation which the times and circumstances of the country then afforded. These wagons and teams attracted attention and commanded admiration wherever they appeared; and hence the origin, as I conceive, of the horse and wagon to which the appelation of 'Conestoga' has been attached. The harness was constructed of the best materials, with an eye to show as well as quality. In the harness and trimmings of these teams the owners frequently indulged in expenses that approached to extravagance—It was, indeed, an animating sight to see five or six highly fed horses, half covered with heavy bear skins, or decorated with gaudily fringed housings, surmounted with a set of finely toned bells, their bridles adorned with loops of red trimming—prancing as

CATAWBA COUNTY 159

if half conscious of their superior appearance, and participating in the pride that swelled the bosom of their master."

While it is quite certain that the show aspects of the Conestogas were not the deciding factors in minds of local purchasers, the facts that the wagons were equally practical and durable made their indulgence extremely probable.

It is believed that the earliest road of the Catawba territory was the State road, the Catawba county portion of which was constructed in 1763. The road entered Catawba county in its southwest part, traveled in an easterly direction through Bandys, Jacobs Fork, and Newton townships, to and through the present town of Maiden, and on east to Sherrills Ford.

Other Catawba area roads prior to 1780 included:

The Island Ford road, which intersected the State road east of Maiden, and traveled in a northerly direction to Island Ford on the Catawba river.

A road from a point on the north cove of the Catawba river to Salisbury by Sherrills Ford. The Minute Docket of the Court of Common Pleas and Quarter sessions, Rowan county, for 1768 to 1772, points out: "On petition of Sundry Inhabitants of the upper part of the Catawba River for to view and lay off a Road from a Point called the Cove on the North Fork of the Catawba River the nearest and best way to Salisbury by Sherrills Ford on the Catawba River and that the following Jury be appointed as follows to wit: Capt Adam Sherrill, James McClane, Michael Lithen (or Litten), Jacob Sherrill, John Bridges, Sen, William Simpson, Peter Lorance, Uty Sherrill, Richard Linn, Samuel Brown, Bostain Clyne (Cline), Jr.; and Aquilla Sherrill be a Jury to view and lay off the said Road to as far as the Forks of Silver Creek Road and that John McDowell, John McPearson, George Cathey, Robert Patton, Frances Patton, William Moore, Abram Scott, Andrew Killian, John Pearson, Joseph White, William Ruhey and Robert Branch be and is hereby appointed a Jury to view and lay off the said Road from the Forks of Silver Creek Road to the waters of Balls Creek, and Robert Bingham Perkins from the end of Simon Jonas District to Sherrills Ford. This the 10th day of May (Wednesday), 1769."

A road from the Silver Creek road, at the present site of Hickory, traveling in a northwesterly direction by Horse Ford on the Catawba river to Lenoir. The Minute Docket of the Court of Common Pleas and Quarter sessions, Rowan county, also for 1768 to 1772, points out: "On Petition, Ordered that a Road should be laid off from the Forks of Silver Creek Road, over the Horse Ford and up to the Middle Creek and the Jury is as follows to wit: John Morgan, James Blayor, William Shook, William Baldwin, Moses Perkins, Avington Perkins, Henry Pearson Sen, Vezy Husbands, Thomas Whitson, John Conley, Joseph Wilson and George Reives. Saturday May 13 1769."

A road from the present site of Hickory leading by the Henry Weidner residence to Charleston, S. C. The road, by 1779, had become known as the Ramsour road.

The Crowder road intersected the Ramsour road about two and one-half miles southeast of Hickory on its route from the point of intersection in a southeasterly direction to some destination which is undetermined.

A road from Ramsours mill in Lincoln county to Salisbury, crossing the extreme southeastern portion of the county, about one mile south of Little Mountain by Sherrills Ford.

A road known as Three Creek road which traveled from an undetermined point in a northerly direction through the present city of Newton, intersecting with the Island Ford road near the present site of the town of Conover. This road is shown by land surveys bearing a 1779 date.

With the passage of time, Catawba's Indian paths were widened into the white man's tote path, and later into the wagon road. But they were still made of nothing but natural soil. In an early effort to improve wagon roads, particularly in low places, evidence is found that small logs were placed side by side on the trail and covered with a two- or three-inch layer of dirt. It was then called a corduroy road, but the improvement was not very significant. The labor involved in cutting enough trees to cover a sizeable stretch was staggering. Besides, when the rains came, the dirt washed down between the logs. It was doubtful which was to be preferred, having your wagon stuck in the mud or having it jolted to pieces bumping over the bare logs!

Although stagecoaches were as much a part of the American travel scene as the Conestoga wagon and enjoyed a similar hey-

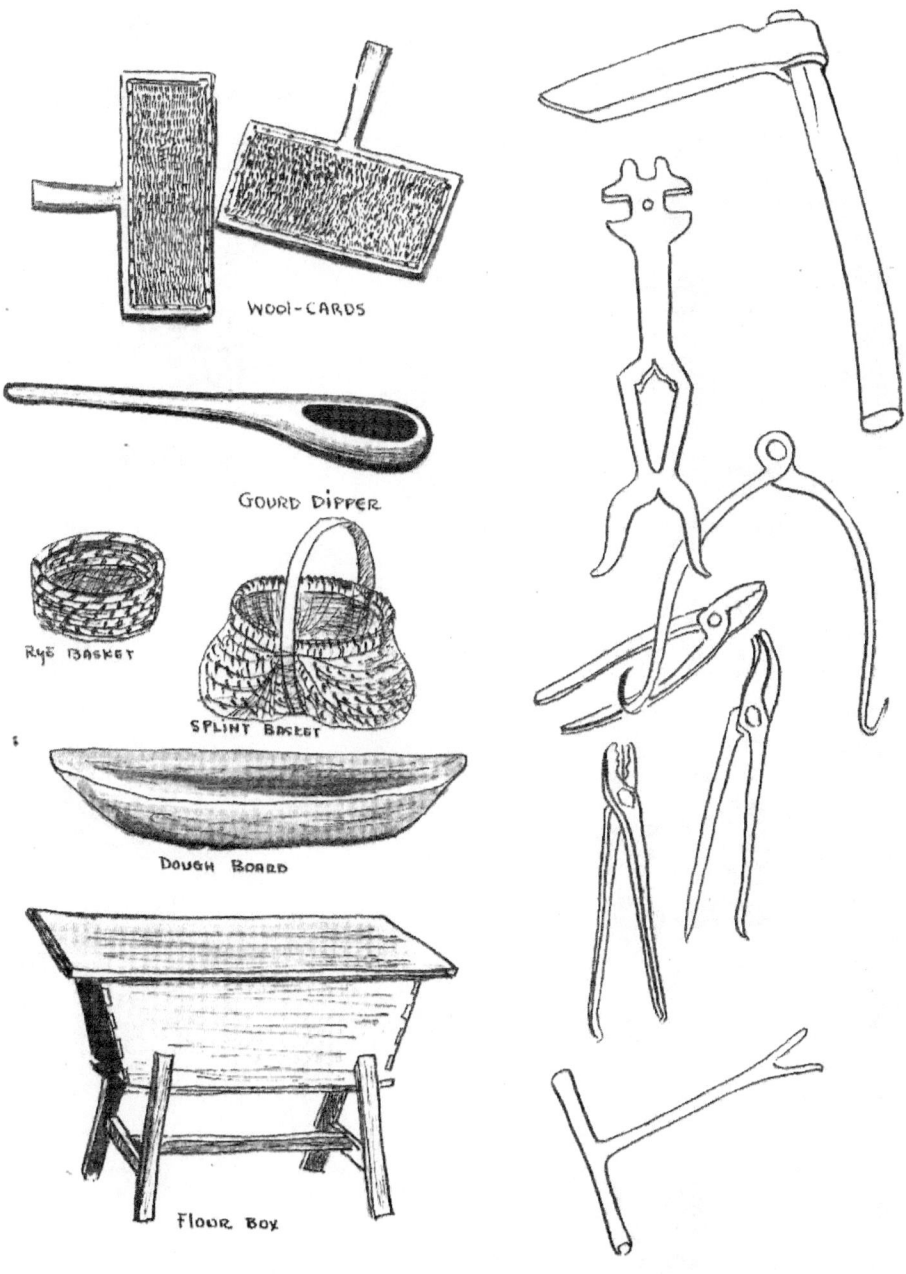

Early Implements

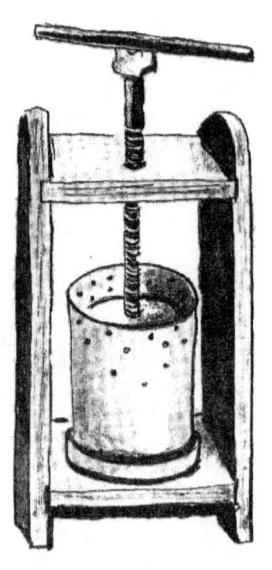

Cheese Press

Old Well

Cheese Box

Cutlery Holder

Salt Gourd

Brass Pot

Pump

CATAWBA COUNTY 161

day, their influence on Catawba county was infinitely less than the family-owned conveyance.

Catawba county never significantly figured as important pivot points for stagecoach companies. However, coaches did traverse certain sections of the county.

Perhaps the most important stage stop in the Catawba territory was at the present site of Hickory. Here was a tavern, operated by John Bradburn (who was licensed as an "ordinary" keeper in 1786). The tavern later became known as the Hickory Tavern.

Coach traffic through the Catawba area principally was from Salisbury, Lincolnton, and Morgantown. Catawba communities served by coach lines or branch lines included the present communities of Hickory, Sherrills Ford, Maiden, Newton, Conover, and Plateau.

It is known that official stage stops were located at two other points in the present county, by virtue of the fact that taverns existed.

The Halfway Tavern was located prior to 1797 about six miles northeast of Maiden, at the head of Maiden creek. The tavern was operated by John Byers.

The Coffee House Tavern was located in the present Plateau area at an early date. This establishment was operated by the Hilton family.

Concerning stage lines in the Catawba territory, Walter A. Hahn has written: "It is not definitely known at what period of time the stage coach lines were established through Catawba county.... When the Western Railroad was finished to Hickory, N. C., Dunn and Company of Abbington, Va., opened a stage coach line from Hickory to Abbington. Their stables were located where the Hickory hotel now stands. This line must have done quite a little business, as the records of the Catawba Toll Bridge Company show that the stage line paid toll to the amount of $100 from January to July in the year 1859. However, it is believed the line was discontinued sometime the next year.

"About the same time another Stage Line was established by C. S. Brown and Company of Salisbury, N. C., this line being known as the Great Western Stage Line. It ran from Hickory to Morristown, Tenn., via Asheville. Local stables were located at the present Harper Motor Company.

Prior to the Revolution, the stagecoach was known as the stage wagon. This vehicle had three or four wooden benches extending from side to side for passengers. There were no backs and no springs. The wagons had straight sides covered with a tunnel-shaped cloth top.

Improvements which transformed the wagon into a coach designed primarily for human transportation were a flat top and side curtains made of leather. Later, seats were made of leather or wool and benches were fitted with back rests of wood or leather. Still later, seats were on wrought-iron springs or held up by pliable leather straps. Coaches were usually drawn by four horses and the teams were changed every few miles.

It is said that Catawba county's coach stops were caused more often from the need for horse-changing than from the pressure of passenger trade.

That persons of the section of Catawba desired to cross streams is evidenced by the astounding number of ferries which operated shortly after the county became a governmental unit, some of them for financial gain. Between 1850 and 1900, it is estimated that 20 ferries and toll bridges were at the disposal of the citizenry. Numerous fords also were used.

The Catawba river claimed by far the greatest number. They included: Cornelius ferry, about one mile north of the county line; Robinson ferry, about three and one-half miles north of the county line; Sherrills Ford, near the present-day village of Sherrills Ford; Sherrills ferry, near the present-day village of Sherrills Ford; Catawba toll bridge, near Monbo; Brown ferry, above Monbo; Lewis ferry, near the town of Catawba; Little ferry, about one and one-half miles below Island Ford; Island Ford; Island Ford ferry, just above Island Ford; Arnt ferry, operated by John Arnt, after a Mr. Houston and a Mr. Cowans; Little ferry (second ferry by this name), below Oxford Ford; Oxford Ford; Oxford ferry, at Oxford Ford site; White's ferry, about a mile above Oxford Ford, operated by Tilford White; Bowman's ferry, about a mile northwest of Catawba Springs, operated by Jacob and Poly Bowman; Baker ferry,

CATAWBA COUNTY 163

near the mouth of Snow creek, operated by Luther Baker; Clark Ford, in Moore ferry area; Moore ferry, bridge site on present-day Highway 127, operated by Joseph Moore; Seitz ferry, about a mile above Moore ferry site, operated by Abel Seitz; Icard ferry, at the Seitz ferry site, operated by Fate Icard; Horse Ford (Haus), near the Catawba-Burke line; Horse Ford toll bridge, at Horse Ford site; and Shuford ferry, at Island Ford.

The South Fork river could be crossed at five points, as follows: Blackburn bridge, about one mile from county line; State Ford, about three miles north of county line; Fish Dam Ford, at the site or near the site of State Ford; Rocky Ford, about one and one-half miles north of State Ford; and Simpson bridge, about two miles above Rocky Ford.

The Jacobs Fork river was crossed at Ramsour's bridge, about one and one-half miles above the junction with Henry's Ford; and Warlick's Ford, just above the mouth of Camp creek.

Among the points of crossing of the Henrys Fork river were the following: Sandy Ford, about four miles below the present site of Brookford; Fisher's Ford, probably about a mile below Brookford; Hanging Rock bridge, the site of Brookford bridge; Rowe's Ford, just above Brookford; Ward's Ford, just above Rowe's Ford; Whitener's Ford, between Ward and Link Fords; Fry Ford, just below the east of Link Ford; and Link Ford, near the Burke county line.

The practice prevailed during the eighteenth and nineteenth centuries of covering bridges with wood canopies. It is supposed that more than ten bridges in the area of Catawba carried this addition during their periods of use. The best known were those of Horse Ford, Sandy Ford and Bunker Hill bridges, the last of which still stands and its preservation is a project of the Catawba County Historical Association. The Bunker Hill bridge is one of four covered bridges which remain in North Carolina.

Several reasons are advanced as to why bridges were covered with wood ceilings.

Some years ago the United States Bureau of Public Roads asserted that timber bridges were constructed with roofs and sides to protect them from the weather. According to that agency, effective housing usually adds many years to the useful life of wooden bridges, which is borne out by the fact that most of the surviving covered bridges are among the oldest bridges in use. Formerly timber was cheap, and it cost very little extra to roof a bridge.

Some suggest that bridges were covered also to provide shade and shelter for man and beast.

A favorite theory among those who like to speculate on the purpose of the roofs on bridges is that they were covered to induce livestock across streams. The roof and barnlike appearance of the bridge, it is said, prevented skittish horses from shying at the sight of water on both sides of them, and it would be easier to drive sheep, hogs and cattle across a covered bridge than across an open one. A difficulty with this theory is that not all the wooden bridges on the way to market were covered, and besides, this purpose would have been served just as well by a sided bridge without a roof.

Some of the early wooden bridges were built without the use of a single nail, the timbers being cut in such a way that wooden pegs were sufficient to hold them in place.

The inimitable "great iron horse," which made its appearance in North Carolina in the early 1840s, did more than scare the real thing. It is credited with developing Catawba county more effectively than any other transportation facility and determining that Hickory is the area's principal city.

At first, the "iron horse" slighted Newton. Due to the county seat city's natural barriers, the railroad lay two miles north of its limits. After crossing the Catawba river, the railroad ran directly west to Hickory, through the places where the present towns of Catawba, Claremont and Conover are located. A spur from the main track was built from Conover to Newton, and the train would "run in" to Newton and "back out" to the main line.

The coming of the railroad may be translated as introducing a new era to Catawba county, in many ways.

In Hickory, for instance, it afforded a trading outlet. The people of the western part of Catawba and the eastern part of Burke counties had no trading point nearer than Newton, except a small store kept by William Hale, near the present intersection of First avenue and Third Street, S. E., and the store of Phillip Warlick five or six miles west of Hickory in Burke county.

In the early 1850s, North Carolina had only a few disconnected railroads—all in the east and none in the west. On this account, the state embarked in railroad building on a liberal scale for that day. The North Carolina railroad was first undertaken—running from Goldsboro to Charlotte via Greensboro. This road still belongs to the state, although leased to the Southern Railway Company. After completion, the Western North Carolina Railroad was undertaken, from Salisbury to Asheville, and ultimately to Knoxville. The charter of the Western North Carolina Railroad Company was granted in February, 1855.

Certain Catawbans figured prominently in the establishment of the Western North Carolina Railroad. These include D. B. Gaither, M. L. McCorkle, Jonas Cline, George Setzer, Dr. Ogburn Campbell, Jonas Bost, George Wilkie, John Wilfong, and Henderson Sherrill. McCorkle and Cline served as early directors.

Audit reports of the railroad show payment for contract work, materials, services, etc., to the following Catawbans:

David Barker, Moses Barger, Sim Barger, N. C. Bollinger, Eli Bost, Jonas Bost, Ab. Cook, E. Connor, Eli Deal, D. B. Gaither, J. L. Gaither, Gaither and Company, William Hale, Moses Harman, John Hewitt, J. P. Hilterbran, P. Huffman, John Hunsucker, Paul Hunsucker, Henry Laigle, J. Longcrier, C. M. Lowrance, G. S. Little, N. C. Lowrance, M. L. McCorkle (he built the Newton depot for $950), J. Miller, William L. Mehaffey, P. Mull, H. L. Robards, Peter Rowe, H. W. Robinson, George Setzer, Joseph Setzer, Levia A. Shufird, M. C. Shuford, J. M. Smith, George Smoyer, Logan Smoyer, William Turner, Daniel Whisnant, David Wike, C. A. Wilfong, and J. Wilfong.

Persons paid for stock killed include Moses Barger, J. V. Barringer, Marcus Bost, Emeline Huffman, G. M. Sherrill, George White, G. J. Wilkey, and F. A. Yount.

The first local agents for the railroad were G. M. Sherrill of Catawba, who was paid $250 for a year; T. A. Bradburn of

Newton, who was paid $450; and A. L. Shuford of Hickory Tavern, who was paid $250.

In determining the path of the railroad through Catawba county, two surveys were made. The surveys were made from a point one and one-half miles east of Hale's store. One was designated the Ridge Line and the other the River Line. The Ridge Line was finally adopted. It is the present bed of the Southern railroad. The River Line suggested a route which would have led to the vicinity of the Horse Ford bridge and up the south side of the Catawba river to Morganton.

Difficulties, primarily engineering, developed many times before the railroad was to wind through Western North Carolina. The question of "bypassing" Newton created quite a furor. The chief engineer of the railroad project suggested in a report to the company board in March, 1856, that a line for the road about three miles from Newton could be located which would cost some $160,000 less than the route then surveyed via the town. It was alleged by the subscribers of Catawba county that there was an understanding between themselves and the other individual stockholders before they subscribed their stock that the road would pass through the county seat city and that the company board was in affirmance of that pledge or understanding.

Concerning the difficulty, a later writer observed: "The Board of Directors appreciating fully the public spirit and patriotic zeal which animated the citizens of . . . Catawba in making their subscriptions, wished to support them in their interest, but higher obligations impressed their consideration upon them."

The matter of the Newton service finally was settled by Legislative enactment.

The engineer's report to the company president and directors on August 27, 1856, included the following:

". . . From this point our next endeavor was to get to Newton by the most direct, practicable and direct line. The Topographical features controlling its direction to the Catawba River, I have stated on a former occasion.

"Suffice it to say, we recross Third Creek by a viaduct 65 feet high; thence over the ridge to Back Creek; passing it 37 feet above its surface, we quickly approach the main water shed, which throws off the waters to the East to the Yadkin, 35 miles distant, and on the West to the Catawba, only five miles distant. Cutting through this ridge, the line descends along Clark's Creek, crossing and recrossing its meanderings to maintain its directness, until it approaches the Catawba, where inclining to the right, it enters the valley of that river—crossing Buffalo Shoal Creek near its confluence with the river, which here runs West to East, and offers great facilities for the economical construction of a Rail Road. Thence up this valley, we cross the Catawba near the mouth of Lyles Creek, 48 feet above the surface of the water by a Bridge 500 feet in length, founded on rock. And although at this point, the valley of Lyles Creek approaches us favorably as to direction, we are prevented from pursuing it on account of high and back water, and must maintain a high elevation along the senuosities of the slopes skirting Lyles' Creek, to a point a short distance above its junction with Mecklin's Creek, which we cross by a viaduct 50 feet above its surface, in order to gain the summit of the ridge between those two creeks. Thence along the ridge to Longerier's; thence in the vicinity of the stage road to Newton.

"A line crossing the River at the Buffalo Shoals was also traced, but it was found to be longer and more expensive. The town of Newton being situated on a spur of the main ridge dividing the great Catawba from the South Fork, its peculiar being about one mile distant from the Beaty's Ford ridge, which is crossed on the East, and 4000 feet distance from Smoyer's mill creek on the West; and the relative elevation of these points being respectively, 1025, 1021, and 886 above tide, the line necessarily must pass Newton on the maximum grade, by cutting 23 feet in the ridge and filling 70 feet at Smyer's mill creek. And thence across the ridge between the last named creek and Clark's creek, it ascends to the Crowder town ridge, another spur of the main which separates the South Fork from its tributary, Clark's creek. And here for about 1800 feet a 5 degree curve is used, the first and only instance on the line where it is necessary. Thence the crest of this ridge is followed to its junction with the main ridge near Hale's, and the same from which the line departed at Longorier's.

"This ridge, though occasionally varying in character, is that of an elevated and narrow ridge, with numerous spurs and indentations on either side, the former projecting out, undulating and irregular between the vallies of the streams which have worn down and flow through the latter.

"Its general course conforms to the direction we desire, and along its crest our line is located, the plains of the road being very nearly coincident with its slope until we reach Hog Hill, the first of a succession of high peaks some of which rise several hundred feet above the general level of the country...."

The company president's report of August 25, 1859, included:

"The grading and Masonry are completed to 'Hale's Store.' The track was laid and the Road put in full and complete operation to Statesville on the first day of October last.... The track-laying is temporarily suspended at the River, awaiting the completion of the Bridge.

"The cross-ties, however, are all laid to Hale's Store, and the laying down of the iron will progress very rapidly, so soon as the Engines can cross the Bridge. Some of the largest of the embankments, West of the River, were not finished by the contractors until about the month of May, and are full green for the reception of the Iron....

"We think we may safely ensure the passage of the Cars across the River in time to complete the track-laying to Newton the 10th November next, and to 'Hale's' during the present year....

"Iron, sufficient to lay the track to Hale's Store, has been purchased on favorable terms, and the greater part of it has arrived at Portsmouth and will be delivered on the road in due time...."

The company president reported on August 30, 1860:

"At the period of your last Annual Meeting, the grading and masonry had been completed to a point near 'Hale's Store,' and the cars were running, and the Road in full operation as far as Catawba River. Shortly thereafter the bridge across the River was completed, and the track-laying was resumed and prosecuted with energy; and on the 22nd day of February, the cars reached the terminus of the first section, one and a half miles East of Hale's Store, as located under the original Charter.

Passengers and Freight were transported, for a while, only as far as Newton.

"The Board of Directors had established a Depot at a station now known as 'Hickory Tavern,' two miles West of said terminus, upon the line of Road contracted to Mr. Fisher; and by an arrangement with him, his part of the line as far as Hickory Tavern station, was in readiness to receive the Iron immediately after the completion East of his contract; and he proceeded at once to lay down the Iron and complete the road to the last named station.

"Since that time Mr. Fisher has prosecuted the work with great dispatch, having constructed the Road and put the same in complete running order from 'Hickory Tavern' to a point within 13 miles of Morganton. . . ."

At the beginning of the War Between the States, the Western North Carolina Railroad was completed 17 miles west of Hickory. During the war, the road was continued to Camp Vance about two miles east of Morganton. Soon after the war, work was resumed on the road, principally with convict labor. The railroad was completed to Old Fort in 1871 or 1872.

Even more serious engineering difficulties confronted the builders from this point westward, where the road, like a thread of steel, winds through a spur of the Blue Ridge till near its summit, when it plunges headlong through roaring gorges and finally pierces the backbone of the Blue Ridge through Swannanoa tunnel.

During the interim while Old Fort was the terminus of the road, there was only one train a day each way through Catawba county. This was a mixed freight-and-passenger train, consisting of five or six freight cars and one dilapidated passenger coach at the rear. This so-called passenger coach had a partition across its center—the front compartment being second class, while the rear end was for first-class passengers. In that day, first-class and second-class tickets were sold, first-class costing one cent per mile more than second-class. There was a "turn-table" at Old Fort and at Salisbury, where the locomotives were reversed or turned around. But the passenger coach was not turned. It therefore followed that the rear-end when going west was first-class, but when going east the same compartment was second-class. As paradoxical as it may seem, some preferred first-class.

The great Z. B. Vance traveled over this road frequently, and always traveled second-class. It is said that a friend had observed this peculiarity of the governor, and on one occasion asked him why he always traveled second-class. The governor, with a twinkle in his eye, quickly replied: "Because there's no third."

At the time when there was only service between Salisbury and Old Fort, the railroad company gave the locomotives names instead of numbers (as now). Seventy-five years ago the road had three engines or locomotives. One was used for a work-train. The other two were for the regular daily East and West runs. The engines bore their names, printed in large gilt letters. One was named "Swannanoa.' The other engine bore the name of "Catawba."

Earliest locomotives were wood-burners. Wood was purchased from farmers along the road and piled at convenient points. When fuel ran low, the train would stop where a supply was available and the train crew would fill the tender. The wood-burners were changed to coal-burners in 1879.

When the Western North Carolina was completed to Asheville, the mixed-train service was discontinued and a regular passenger train was run daily each way; likewise regular freight trains, and a larger complement of engineers and conductors were brought into service.

The old mixed-train service was thoroughly bad. Liquor was sold everywhere at that time and the railroad management put no restrictions on liquor-drinking by any of the employees. It is said that upon one occasion a train from Salisbury arrived in Hickory and it was found that the engineer was too thoroughly "soaked" to continue the trip safely. A work train happened to be on the siding, and its engineer was pressed into service and carried the train through, while the incapacitated engineer crawled into the freight depot and sprawled out on a pile of grain sacks and slept off his drunk.

The first agent of the Western North Carolina Railroad was A. L. Shuford. He was succeeded by John Dickson of Morganton. The next agent was A. A. Yoder, followed by A. W. Muse,

CATAWBA COUNTY 171

who was succeeded by J. S. Tomlinson, who at the same time published The Piedmont Press and also manufactured "Sweet Sixteen" smoking tobacco.

An 1875 "Railroad Schedule—Time Table Western N. C. Railroad" points out the arrival and departure in Catawba county of its two trains.

The Western train, according to the schedule, left Salisbury at 7 a.m.; arrived Third Creek, 7:35 a.m.; left Third Creek, 8:02 a.m.; arrived Statesville 8 a.m. (?); left Statesville, 9 a.m.; arrived Catawba Station, 9:52 a.m.; left Catawba Station, 9:58 a.m.; arrived Newton, 10:48 a.m.; left Newton 10:53 a.m.; arrived Conover, 11:11 a.m.; left Conover, 11:14 a.m.; arrived Hickory, 11:42 a.m.; left Hickory, 11:50 a.m.; arrived Icard, 12:28 p.m.; left Icard, 12:33 p.m.; arrived Morganton, 1:11 p.m.; left Morganton, 1:18 p.m.; arrived Bridgewater, 1:55 p.m.; left Bridgewater, 2 p.m.; arrived Marion, 2:40 p.m.; left Marion 2:45 p.m.; arrived Old Fort, 3:25 p.m.; and thus reached the point of destination.

The Eastern train, according to the schedule, left Old Fort at 4 a.m.; arrived in Marion, 4:41 a.m.; left Marion, 4:46 a.m.; arrived in Bridgewater, 5:27 a.m.; left Bridgewater, 5:32 a.m.; arrived in Morganton, 6:10 a.m.; left Morganton, 6:17 a.m.; arrived in Icard, 6:55 a.m.; left Icard, 7 a.m.; arrived in Hickory, 7:38 a.m.; left Hickory, 10:30 a.m. (?); arrived in Conover, 8:28 a.m.; left Conover, 8:30 a.m.; arrived in Newton, 8:48 a.m.; left Newton, 8:53 a.m.; arrived in Catawba Station, 9:43 a.m.; left Catawba Station, 9:55 a.m.; arrived in Statesville, 10:48 a.m.; left Statesville, 11 a.m.; arrived in Third Creek, 11:50 a.m.; left Third Creek, 11:55 a.m.; arrived in Salisbury, 12:55 p.m.; and thus reached the point of destination.

Directions were afforded for the meeting of the aforementioned trains, as follows:

"Trains pass at Catawba 9:55 a.m. If the up-train is behind time, down-train will wait thirty minutes and proceed, running thirty minutes behind its time, till up-train is met and passed. If both trains are behind its time, the train bound East will have the right to the road indefinitely, as against train bound West; and train bound West will lie off till train bound East passes or is heard from. . . .

"Going West, Breakfast at Salisbury, 6:30 a.m., Dinner at Hickory at 11:50 a.m. Going East, Breakfast at Hickory, 7:30 a.m. . . ."

The theory that the Hickory Western North Carolina Railroad depot initially was planned in the Longview section is proclaimed by a veteran county newspaperman of the early twentieth century, J. F. Click, as

"I see where one says the land on which Hickory is located, was owned by a Mr. Bonniwell. I have always heard and still believe it was owned by a Mr. Robinson.

"When the railroad was built, the company decided to locate the depot at what is known as Longview, fronting where the Hickory-Howard Nursery now is. Old man Miller (I think it was) owned all that land, and refused to give, or to sell them the land to build it on—he didn't want it there.

"Robinson heard of it, and told them if they would build the depot here (Hickory), he would give them the land. The company accepted the proposition and put it there. Hence Miller's mistake was Robinson's good fortune. . . ."

In early railroad history, there was no regulatory agencies for controlling freight and passenger rates, and railroad patrons suffered as the result.

The State of North Carolina through the legislature leased the North Carolina railroad, from Goldsboro to Charlotte, to the old Richmond and Danville railroad, which was controlled by Morgan and Drexel interests—the Morgan member of the firm being the original J. Pierpont Morgan, father of the present financier. Under the Morgan and Drexel control, the Richmond and Danville was so oppressive that the state became hostile toward the road until its very name was anathematized.

At the time, the state was anxious to sell or lease the Western North Carolina from Salisbury to Paint Rock. The R and D railroad was anxious to buy or lease the road, but the state had experienced enough of the R and D, and refused to sell or lease to that road on any terms or conditions.

Whereupon a slick gentleman, John W. Best, came on the scene and made a spot-cash offer for the entire road from Salisbury to Paint Rock. The state legislature promptly accepted Best's offer, and the public complimented itself on escaping the clutches of the despised R and D road.

As soon as the Western North Carolina was transferred to Best, it was found that he was merely a "front" and had bought the road for the Morgan and Drexel company. The Richmond and Danville quickly became owners.

The Catawba county public's first knowledge of the piece of jugglery was when freight and passenger trains passed through the area displaying the signs of "Richmond and Danville Railroad."

At a later date, the R and D went into receivership, and the Morgan interests reorganized the system, consolidating it with several other roads. From this consolidation came the great Southern Railway Company.

The present Carolina and North Western railroad originally was the Chester and Lenoir Narrow-Gauge railroad. It was, as its name implied, a narrow-gauge road. For many years, it ran only from Chester to York, S. C. Later it was completed, little at a time, to Lincolnton, and, after another long stop, was extended to Newton. From Newton to Hickory a third rail was laid on the Southern Railway roadway, completing the narrow-gauge from Chester to Hickory in 1881. In a short time, the road was completed to Lenoir. A few years afterwards, an independent section was built between Newton and Hickory, and the third rail was discontinued.

Not many years later, the company was re-organized, and the firm assumed its present name. At this time, the Southern acquired control of the road, and the independent link between Hickory and Newton was abandoned—all trains passing over the Southern's tracks between these two points.

The usefulness of the railroads locally were supplemented by the telegraph, which is believed to have begun operations in Hickory in 1878.

As an example of the activity about Hickory Station, the following produce was shipped from the train depot during a 12-month period in the early 1870s:

Butter, 18,170 pounds; eggs, 5,140 dozen; beeswax, 4,666 pounds; honey, 1,780 pounds; bacon, 16,898 pounds; apples (green), 253 barrels; oats, 879 bushels; rye, 637 bushels; corn, 6,886 bushels; flour, 198 sacks; dried fruit and berries, 215,430 pounds; roots and herbs, 168,286 pounds; and chestnuts, onions, potatoes, flax seed and other miscellaneous articles, 300,000 pounds. There were 300 sacks of salt sold during the period of time. (This data is obtained from a letter from A. H. Shuford, railroad agent, printed in The Western Democrat of Charlotte on January 18, 1872.)

The importance of the "iron horse" to Catawba county was unsurpassed in history until the automotive age, that may, in turn, yield its throne to an atomic air age.

CHAPTER VIII

EARLY TRADE AND INDUSTRIES

The early tradesmen of the Catawba area, who were few in number, depended more upon skill than equipment for proficiency. Industry in the sense known by the modern Catawban, particularly the aspect of mass production, was unpremeditated.

The manufactured articles which were indispensable, and which the settler could not make for himself, were produced by the few tradesmen who were present. Such tradesmen generally learned their businesses by having served seven years with "master workmen."

As communities formed, tradesmen arrived on the scene. But some, of course, were adventurers themselves and joined pioneers in their treks to new areas of settlement.

The earth and forests of the local area furnished most of the raw materials needed. A notable exception was iron, which was obtained for the Catawba territory prior to 1770 at Cross Creek (Fayetteville). About 1770, a small iron works was established on the Yadkin river, near the present town of Elkin, known as the Allen Iron Works. This enabled the blacksmith to get a supply of iron nearer home. After the Revolution, the great ore-beds of Western North Carolina were discovered.

The Catawba area's early tradesmen included the blacksmith, the miller, the shoemaker, the cooper, the millwright, the tanner, the tailor, the hatter, the wheelwright, the saddler, the gunsmith, the silversmith, the fuller, the weaver, the clock maker, the joiner or cabinet maker, the carpenter, the felt maker, the miller, the mason, the potter, and the merchant. Usually their services and products were those which the unskilled citizen had neither the knowledge nor the facilities to provide and manufacture.

Perhaps the most important industry in a new settlement was a mill to facilitate meal-making. First devised was the hominy beater, which crudely prepared the corn for bread and grits. In the beginning, this process was accomplished by scooping a hole in the top of a stump, into which water-soaked grain was placed and beaten with a pestle of hard wood. Later, the pestle was attached to a long pole, or beam, and made to work up and down by a crude water wheel. The beaten mass was then dried and rubbed through a sieve, made by puncturing with a red hot wire a dressed deer skin stretched over a hoop.

The finer particles that passed through the small holes of the sieve were used as meal to make bread, while the coarser parts were boiled for hominy, similar to the modern grits.

As the settlements were built, and millwrights could be obtained, mill stones were prepared and small tub mills were erected on small streams, where they were operated by crude, overshot water wheels.

At many of these frontier mills sash saw mills were erected, which supplied the settlements with sawed boards.

No records relate when the first grist mill was put into operation in the county, but tradition fixes that an early mill was located on Mountain creek, and, also, Peter Mull is said to have built a small mill on the site of what was later known as Wilfong's Mill, and still later as Coulter's Mill. The latter mill was located a few miles west of Newton. Also, Jacob Shuford is known to have operated a grist mill at this Bunker Hill farm in the 1820s and 1830s.

Among the first millers of the Catawba section, and the year they were known to have been active, are: John Shell, prior to 1780; Jacob and Henry Bullinger, 1798; and Daniel Smyre, 1840. Early millwrights, persons who planned, built and fitted out mills, especially grist mills, include Adam Gross, Lawrence Yount, and David Yoder.

While the settlers evidently came with an adequate supply of clothing, the deerskin being the most practicable and plentiful, no great length of time passed until the weaver was an essential adjunct to the community. So, the weaver set up his loom and subsequently began the manufacture of rough cloth from thread spun of flax and the wool of sheep. This necessitated the fulling mill. All thread for weaving was spun by hand and was seldom uniform in size. Therefore, the cloth was not uniform in thickness. Wool often was greased to cause it to work better in the cards and at the spinning wheel.

Flax

Breaking

Swingling

Hackling

Spinning

Catawba Pottery   Early Iron Utensils

CATAWBA COUNTY   177

The function of the fulling mill was to remove the grease and dirt and to make the cloth of a uniform thickness and give it the effect of a tighter or closer weave. This was done by, first, scouring the cloth with water, soap and fuller's earth and shrinking with hot water; second, by pounding it in a machine with stampers or pestles; and, third, by running it between rollers. Following its trip through the fulling mill, the cloth was clean, shrunk and of an almost perfect uniform thickness.

The single fulling mill of which information is available is Joseph Steele's, located at the George Sigmon homeplace, a short distance from the present Catawba hospital. Steele was serving as a fuller in 1775. Pioneer Peter Ikerd, who came to the Catawba territory with Simon Haas in the 1740s, also was a fuller. The area's first citizen who was a weaver by trade, according to records, is Johannes Hahn, who is known to have served in this capacity in 1765. John Harmon was a weaver in 1774, and Lewis Throneburg in 1818.

The most familiar trade today of the occupations of pioneers doubtless is that of blacksmith, the "calling" which has been immortalized by a legion of writers. The "smiths," who worked in or welded wrought iron for the purpose of making or shaping small utensils, shoeing horses, etc., included John Sigmon, in the year 1775; Jacob Baker, Barnet Sigmon and George Harmon, in the year 1790; George Sigmon, in the year 1795; John Mingus, in the year 1798; John Seitz, in the 1790s; and Philip Baker, John Drum, and Philip Baker, in the year 1800. That hundreds of anvils have sounded throughout Catawba's history is no exaggeration.

Early shoe makers or cobblers, who made or mended the settlers' boots and shoes, included Peter Ikerd, who was active in this capacity in 1760; Adam Bolch, Sr., who followed the trade in 1770; and Reuben Reynolds, who served in this trade in 1820.

Coopers were tradesmen who made or mended vessels of stave sand hoops, such as casks, barrels and tubs. Men who followed this trade, and the dates they were so actively engaged, include John Allen, 1770; John Haas and Jacob Seitz, both in 1790; and George Seitz, 1795.

The art of "tanning" came to the Catawba county area early. It is known that Boston Cline plied the trade in 1753. Among other practitioners were Isaac Lowrance and Peter Little, in the 1790s; David Ramsour, in 1800; Daniel Lutz and Daniel Blackburn, both in 1805; and Isaac Lowrance, in 1816. Indians of the Catawba region made leather from deerskin by a process which some of the early settlers used individually. The Indians piled their skins in packs so that the tissue surrounding the hair rotted off. They scraped the flesh from the inner side of the skin by hand. They tanned this leather by pounding oil and brains of animals (usually deer) into the skin. They completed their deerskin leather by smoking it. The leather, which was called buckskin, was soft and remarkably good. Official tanners generally subscribed to the "bark" tanning process, however. The process is called "bark" because practically all leather for shoe soles, bags, straps, harnesses, etc., was tanned with an extract of some kind of bark. Chiefly used were the leaves, nuts, barks, and woods of hemlock, oak, and chestnut. All vegetation contains a bitter ingredient called tannin. It has the property of combining with proteins to form a compound that will not rot easily. In this instance, the protein is the hide or skin, and the compound is leather. The tannin was extracted from these natural vegetable materials with hot water.

It is believed that tailors were introduced to the Catawba section only after specialization as the result of an enlarging population developed. It is known officially that James Douglas practiced the trade in 1820. Other early tailors included Leon Davidson, William McMullen, John Sigmon and Joseph Hartley, Daniel Seagel, and Isaac Douglas.

Due to the difficult process of hat manufacturing, pioneers could not supply this item as readily as they could other clothing. Hence, hatters are recorded in the territory as early as 1785, when David Carpenter, Jacob Frye, and Adam Bolch were so employed. Later hatters included Robert Wills and John Cunningham, who served the public about 1799. A man by the surname of Moody also was a hatter in the Catawba region prior to 1800. Jacob Hunsucker served in this capacity in 1825.

Diversification of industry was to cause the advent of the wheelwright, a person whose business it is to make or repair

CATAWBA COUNTY 179

wheels and wheeled vehicles, as carriages, carts and wagons. Early wheelwrights included Conrad Wagner, John Gantt, David Bolch, and George P. Clay, Sr. Diversified industry also brought about the trade of saddlery, the business of manufacturing saddles, harnesses, etc. This trade sometimes was practiced in conjunction with others, notably the tanning trade. An early saddler was Jacob Fye, who was also a hatter. Fye was in the area in 1785. Other saddlers were John and Henry Dellinger.

The tradesmen whose work was necessitated by nature's first law, that of self-preservation, were gunsmiths. The "long rifle," designed especially for the woodsman, was most often the product of their remarkable ability in the mid-1700s. The fabrication of a rifle using the crude tools of the century was no easy or unskilled task.

The barrel was forged from iron, by wrapping a red-hot bar of the metal around a mandrel or rod and welding the edges to form a tube. Additional forging gave this rough barrel blank an octagonal cross-section, after which the outside was finished by grinding and filing. The bore was then "sized" with a short, spiral-bladed reamer called a "short bit," followed by a square bodied reamer known as the "long bit," these being rotated by a device resembling a bit-brace.

After straightening, the barrel was clamped on one end of a rifling machine or "banch." An iron rod fitted with a short "rifling saw" on one end was attached to the spiral guide and inserted in the barrel as the guide was moved forward by the operator. The saw was shimmed with thin paper until it pressed firmly against the inside of the barrel, whereupon the guide was withdrawn; the saw making a spiral cut as it was dragged through by the guide. Then the guide was turned by means of the index head into position for the second groove and a cut made by entering the saw and withdrawing it as before. In this manner each groove was begun. To deepen the cuts a slip of paper was inserted under the saw and the entire procedure repeated until the grooves reached the proper depth. The fitting of a breech-plug and sights was the final step in barrel-making.

Constructing the lock was the next undertaking. Every part—lock-plate, cock, frizzen, springs—all but the smallest screws were heated in a charcoal fire and shaped on the anvil by skillful blows of a heavy hammer, then, filed, hardened, tempered, and polished.

Generally the butt-plates, trigger guards, and the bridle plates were cast of brass in sand moulds while the thimbles, patch-boxes, fore-end cap, shin-plate, etc., were formed from sheets of the same metal.

Possibly the most trying operation was the making of the stock, due mainly to the difficulty of working the highly figured maple. First the roughly shaped stock blank was grooved with narrow planes, rasps, and chisels to accommodate the barrel and ramrod, and the lock was carefully fitted. Then with hatchet, drawknife, spokeshave, and rasp the gunmaker shaped the stock to approximately its final dimensions. With the desired shape attained the various pieces of furniture were fitted into place. This installation of patch-boxes, etc., was an extremely painstaking task, yet so flawlessly were they inlaid that even today there are no visible spaces between wood and metal on many ancient flintlocks.

Next the carving was executed and the wood stained with vegetable dyes or acids to enrich the color. A common practice was to scorch the wood lightly to accent the grain. Then came the tedious job of engraving the patch-boxes, inlays, etc., with oil or varnish, the former being most common on early pieces.

The earliest gunsmith of record in the Catawba area was Captain Daniel McKissick, who practiced the trade in 1775. Captain McKissick was followed by Arthur and John Peterson, both in 1780; Matthew Brown, in 1783; and Henry Huffman in 1840. Henry Gross also practiced the trade at an early date which is not known.

The art of the silversmith, who produced silverware and silver ornaments, was not too much in demand by the first residents of the Catawba territory, whose domestic desires were subjugated to the foremost desire of survival. The same is true of the clock maker. But it is known that the area had a silversmith—John Boyd—as early as 1775. The section's first clock maker was Lyman Woodford, who plied his tools in 1800.

Pottery, one of the Catawba area's most famous products, was made by Jacob Weaver, in 1770; John Dietz, in 1790; John Hefner, in 1786; and Jacob Throneburg, in 1800.

The early joiners or cabinet makers, tradesmen who finished the woodwork of houses, etc., included John Paine, Electious Connor and Soloman Yoder. An early felt maker, who produced fabric by interlocking or compacting wool, fur, or hair, by rolling or pressuring, without weaving, was Nathan Armatige, who is known to have been employed in this trade in 1789.

Another early industry prevalent in the Catawba area, though not as extensively as in eastern North Carolina, was the burning of the "rich" pine wood for tar. Having prepared a sufficient quantity of pine trees, an excavation was made in a red clay bank. The bottom of this sloped from each side to the center, as the letter "V," the front being a little lower than the back. The wood was then placed in this hole in the bank, properly crossed and stacked, and fired. The tar which ran from the burning wood escaped from the lower end of the "V" and was caught in a proper receptacle. Tar wood was obtained from dead trees. Its product was manufactured for local use.

Prior to 1790, John Penland was a spinning wheel maker in the Catawba territory.

Few tinsmiths were located in the local area prior to the formation of the county. It is known, however, that L. D. Marlow was engaged in this trade as early as 1840.

Among the earliest stone masons were Conrad Yoder, who is known to have plied his trade prior to the Revolution, and David Yoder and Levi Hoover, who are believed to have served in the trade after 1800.

One of the most colorful tradesmen of the Catawba area was Sally Michaels, who lived for a period in the present Vale section. An Irishwoman, Mrs. Michaels was noted for the manufacture of clay pipes, tavern style.

In connection with trades and industries, it is interesting to note what people of the Catawba territory possessed in 1750 and 1760 that they could sell to obtain money for necessary articles they were unable to produce themselves. When the distance to markets is considered, it is realized that there were only a few commodities the residents could carry to market and exchange for cash or the manufactured articles they needed. These included the various skins of wild animals, cattle hides, tallow, beeswax, butter and feathers. Deer skins, both raw and dressed, were a particularly staple commodity. During this period, a large, well-dressed deer skin sold for 12 to 15 shillings, while the raw skins sold by the pound. However, colonial currency was in use, and this circulated at three-fourths sterling value, making the price of a good dressed buck skin about $2.75 and a good raw skin between $1.25 and $1.50.

The store of the Moravian settlement near the present city of Winston-Salem was one of the local folks' trading points. There is frequent mention in Moravian diaries of wagons from the Catawba arriving at the distant point with commodities. In exchange for their market produce, the traders received manufactured products, such as pottery. One instance is recorded where a wagon from the Catawba river came for a load of pottery and the product of the kiln was sold out before the wagon arrived. Hence, the visitors were forced to return home without crocks, jugs, etc.

Unquestionably Catawba county's most romantic industrial history relates to the mining, manufacturing, and transportation of iron products. To the average resident, perhaps, such terms as ironworks, iron forge, iron mine, or furnace are unfamiliar in relation to his native area. Nevertheless, it is a fact that mining provided an income for many early settlers and was significant factor in the Catawba section's first economy.

Just when the orebeds of this section were first discovered is impossible to determine definitely. But the pioneer locally is said to have been John Fulenwider, a native of Switzerland.

It is recorded that Fulenwider, who was born about 1756, came to Rowan county (of which Catawba then was a part) as a very young man and participated in both the Battles of Ramseur's Mill and King's Mountain. Evidently, he was acquainted with the iron industry from his youth, and was attracted to the local scene by the immense deposits of iron ore. He was to become a large manufacturer of pig iron, and to be one of the first to produce it in this form, using charcoal to reduce the ore.

It is said that Fulenwider also was interested in gold mining, but history relates that he did not experience a like success with gold as iron. One of his primary accomplishments is that his forges in Lincoln and Catawba counties produced cannon for use of the United States government in the War of 1812. At one period of his life, he owned a vast tract of land amounting to more than 20,000 acres. This asset, along with his slaves, forges, and much other personal property, made him one of the most aggressive and wealthy business leaders of his day.

The Swiss established Catawba county's first iron industry in 1804. Known first as the Jenny Lind Forge and later as the Maiden Creek Forge, the concern was located on the site of the present Providence Cotton Mills, about one and one-half miles from the center of Maiden. It was an efficient and prosperous business.

Following Fulenwider's death in 1826, the Jenny Lind Forge passed to his son, William, together with more than 6,000 acres of land in Catawba and Lincoln counties. But William seems not to have carried on the great financial success of his father, and the property was sold to John Hayes. Hayes operated it for years, but whether profitably is not known. In 1850, the heirs of John Hayes sold it to Robert and Ephraim Brevard, who produced all the forms of iron for farm and other uses common to the day.

In 1853, William Williams, a native of New Jersey, came to King's Mountain to take charge of the great iron foundry established by Benjamin Briggs there. He was an experienced iron manufacturer, having come of a long line of men engaged in this business for generations, some of them working in the forges and furnaces in New Jersey and Pennsylvania during and long before the Revolution.

Williams is credited as introducing many new and valuable ideas into iron manufacturing in the South, and about 1857 was persuaded to become the manager of the Jenny Lind Forge. He purchased the plant and a large body of land from the Brevards in 1860, and reorganized the iron industry.

With the help of his son, John Williams, the forge's output was greatly increased, and included practically every type of metal work used in the section. Such articles as "shovel molds," bars, rods, and plates of iron were kept on hand. Account books of the Williams' operations reveal that business was done with farmers and businessmen of many counties and from several adjoining states.

Production was to suffer a sharp revision with the coming of the War Between the States, however. The younger Williams, who was production manager, enlisted and served during the entire four years of the conflict. His father then was left short-handed.

Mrs. Fanny Ransom Williams, writing of Williams and his forge, said: "During the . . . war, his iron works were pressed into the service of the Confederate government, and were required to be run at full capacity in the production of 'blooms' to be used in the construction of gunboats and other implements of war, where a superior quality of iron was required. One of the war histories records the fact that the best iron that could be procured by the Confederacy was made at this forge."

The forges were located near beds of ore. The process of manufacture was laborious. The iron was dug out of the ground, and hauled to the forges in wagons. Limestone was used as the fluxing material in the process of mining. In the beginning, the limestone was hauled from King's Mountain, and although it gave employment to many, its haul was an added cost of production. Limestone later was discovered on the farm of Lawson Keener in Lincoln county, and the product more locally obtained was used.

With the reduction of cost brought by an area supply of limestone, iron began to play an important part in the development of commerce. Farmers, blacksmiths, small manufacturers, merchants and others began to trade with the various forges in Catawba and Lincoln counties. They paid cash for much of the metal, but barter was not neglected. All manner of products were brought in from the counties in every direction, from the mountains to the seashore, to be exchanged for the shovel molds, bars, rods, bolt material, etc. The forges began to be the center of industrial, economic, and even social life. This concentration of trade made the whole community prosperous, just as the big tanyards and mills did in other sections.

Among the other early Catawba county ironmasters was Clisby Cobb.

CATAWBA COUNTY 185

The forges employed many persons in the mining of ore and limestone and the hauling of it to the furnaces. And, there were related or complementary iron businesses.

The metal was melted in the crude crucibles by charcoal, fanned to white heat. The making of the charcoal was an art in itself. In the proper season (and perhaps in the right sign of the moon) the pine trees were cut, later piled high in the shape of "hogans," covered with leaves and dirt, then fired and allowed to char. This manner of burning or charring pine produced a fragrance not known to moderns. But, to their forebears, it was a favorite scent. There are today in the old Piney Woods section of the county evidences of the "coaling grounds" or pits at which thousands of cords of wood were burned for this purpose. The farmers who burned this charcoal were paid, at the beginning, five cents per bushels for the coal delivered at the furnace, and later, when wood became scarce, ten cents.

Heated in the crucibles, the iron was poured out on the sand box in molten state, and as it began to solidify, was picked up with tongs, placed on the anvil, and beat into the desired size and shape by the huge hammers. These were no ordinary hammers, but enormous ones, weighing several hundreds of pounds, with eyes or openings large enough to take as handles logs 30 or 40 feet long.

Above the anvil was a spring made by another log set on an upright post, and extending back the full length of the handle. The power for operating the hammer came from a waterwheel. As the wheel turned, it raised the hammer by pins set in it, and the hammer was given added force by the long spring above, so that the impact on the redhot iron was enormous. It is said that the ringing of the hammers could be heard for miles around.

When the Bessemer process was introduced into Pennsylvania mining industries, and the railroads were extended into the South, the iron manufactured in the North began coming into the country cheaper than it could be produced here, and the open furnace, like all other small manufacturing establishments which had made the South prosperous in the 1800s, was driven out of business. The Jenny Lind Forge held out until about

1880, and is said to have been the last in the state to succumb in the deadly contest with the North.

Among the county's other iron forges were Mount Carmel Forge and Rough and Ready Forge. Soon after the turn of the nineteenth century, Turner Abernathy, a Lincoln county ironmaster, built Mount Carmel on Mountain creek near the east end of Anderson mountain. This was operated by his son, John D. Abernathy, until the latter's death in 1843, when it was sold to Isaac Payne and operated until 1880. Colonel Ephriam Brevard, also of Lincoln county, built Rough and Ready farther down Mountain creek about 1840. After operating it for a period, he sold it to J. Madison Smith.

Principal ore banks of the Catawba section were the Morrison, the Tillman, the Deep Hollow, the Mountain Creek, the Abernathy, the Little John, and the Powell.

The eastern portion of the county early was proclaimed a noted gold bearing area, and this caused Catawba county to become one of North Carolina's most productive (sporadically-speaking) early gold mining centers. Among the most productive of the mines was Shuford's, located four and one-half miles southeast of the town of Catawba. Among the many additional gold mines were the McCorkle mine, the England mine, the Rufty mine and the Abernathy mine. Although mechanical processes involved in gold mining operations were relatively primitive, and few records of them have been kept, some of the mining endeavors were successful. As an example, it is estimated that between $50,000 and $100,000 worth of gold was retrieved from the Catawba country-side in more than 20 mining enterprises.

In the western part of the county were and are occurrences of magnetite ore, usually slightly titaniferous. Such were the Barringer and Forney mines. Brown hemstite ores also occurred and occur in Catawba county in the cyanitic hydro-mica schists of the western part.

Gem stones provided a minimum income for some early Catawbans. Among the stones which were and are to be found in the county are:

The garnet—Desirable shades included.

Quartz—Under the heading of quartz, reference may properly be had to several gems belonging to this classification.

CATAWBA COUNTY

Sagenite, Venus' hair, arrows of love and reutilated quartz are the names usually applied to one of the most striking of the quartz gems. It occurs as a crystal or mass of quartz holding as inclusions scores of acicular crystals of rutile; these are brown, red and yellow in color and are meshed in confusing lines of fiery brightness which are effective in artificial light. Catawba county has supplied many fine specimens.

Citine topaz (known locally as yellow quartz)—Found in small quantities, rarely in deep colors.

Smoky topaz—Occurs in shades of brown from very deep, almost black fading into limpid white.

Amethyst—Known as purple quartz; widely distributed. It has been found in deep and pale shades of purple. Catawba county has produced many handsome clusters.

It is told that somewhere on the lower slopes of Turkey mountain, a spur of Anderson mountain, is a vein of free lead. This was reportedly discovered by a man named Lawson Long in the 1870s. Frank Drum of Maiden, who lived in the Anderson mountain area at the time, says he has seen Long go off with a small basket or bag and a small hatchet to return a few hours later with a load of pure lead in pieces of varying sizes, showing that it had been cut, apparently from a vein between two layers of stone. It is said by Drum that Long would melt the lead and pour it into large cane joints, thus making a rod of lead the length of the cane joint and one-half to one inch in diameter. Long supposedly sold and traded this lead over the country and realized a "neat" sum. Long reportedly never told where his find was located, nor allowed anyone to go with him on his trips. He left the country without divulging his secret.

Among the other deposits of nature from which Catawbans have profited are aluminum, lime, graphite, granite, limestone (little), and mica.

Branson's North Carolina Directory indicates the quantity of mines in Catawba county during 1850 and 1900. The periodical lists the mines, post office addresses and owners, as follows: (The compilation is from several Directories, so managerial changes, and subsequently the renaming of mines, is likely.)

Gold Mine, Catawba Station, A. M. Powell; Gold Mine, Catawba Station, Williams and Tweksbery; Gold Mine, Sherrills Ford, Jno Holdsclaw; Gold Mine, Sherrills Ford, Perkins Robinson; Gold Mine, Newton, D. Barringer; Iron Mine, Newton, William Williams; Gold Mine, Catawba Station, Jacob Fry; Iron Mine, Hickory Tavern, William Hall; Gold Mine, Hickory Tavern, Henry Propst; Aluminum Mine, Hickory Tavern, M. Lowrence; Gold Mine, Mountain Creek, Hoover and Sigmon; Gold Mine, Catawba, W. A. Sweet; Garnet Mine, Hickory, J. A. Martin; Gold Mine, Newton, G. W. Setzer; Gold Mine, Newton, Lanier's estate; Gold Mine, Maiden, D. M. Carpenter; Gold Mine, Hickory, Menzies, Crowel and company; Gold Mine, Mountain Creek, Shuford, McCorkle and Barringer; Gold Mine, Newton, Noah Barringer; Gold Mine, Catawba, M. Rufty; Gold Mine, Mountain Creek, M. A. Sigmon; Iron Mine, Hickory, Shuford Hardware company; Iron Mine, Drumsville, J. W. A. Paine's estate; Lime Mine, Catawba, Mrs. M. B. Trollinger; and Mica Mine, Lincolnton, the Northern company.

The growth of Catawba county manufacturing may be traced during the period 1850-1900 by aid of Branson's Directories.

The source lists only two plants as early as 1867. Two cotton factories, the firms were placed near Catawba Station, "one owned by Powell and Shuford" (the Long Island textile plant, which was established about 1839) "and the other owned by Powell and Tate" (the Granite Shoal textile plant).

Diversification, however, was to come after the War Between the States.

Cotton ginning was done in Newton by H. F. Carpenter; iron works were operated in Newton township by William Williams and in Jacobs Ford township by A. L. Ramsour; lime works were operated at Catawba Station by A. M. Powell (making 100 tons per month); saddle and harness making was done in Newton by Levi Plank and M. M. Rauch; shoe making was done in Newton by ——— Haller and ——— Abernathy, James Murphy and A. J. Helton; tanneries were operated in Newton by ——— Seagle, ——— Clapp and ——— Finger, J. S. Cobb and Sons, David Pitts, H. F. Carpenter and T. D. Marlow, and in Hickory Station by David Link; carriage manufacturing was done in Newton by J. M. Berry and Jones Baker; cabinet making was done in Jacobs Fork township by Henry Reichert; and threshing machines were manufactured in Newton by M. Herman.

Although not recorded in Branson's list, it is known that the Catawba Woolen Mills was organized by Rev. David Warlick and Jacob Mosteller, of near Wesley's Chapel campground, in the year 1872. The mill was a two-story frame building, built on Potts Creek near Plateau. It is interesting to note that the mill also was located near Keeversville, which, in 1886, had a population of 700 and was the third largest community in Catawba county.

New industries introduced in 1875 included tin-ware making, brought to Hickory Tavern by H. (Hiram) Hofner and company; and cigar manufacturing, brought also to Hickory Tavern by J. Flaum.

In 1877-78, Branson lists blacksmithing among the "manufactories." S. M. Abernethy was named as blacksmith in Hickory during those years.

During the ensuing decade, many new industries and trades became established in Catawba county. Among these were plug tobacco making, building and contracting, foundries, shingle making, sash and blind making, whiskey manufacturing, marble yard operations, stoneware production, and "undertaking." Flour and corn mills and saw mills also flourished.

"Manufactories," their post offices and proprietors, in 1884, were:

Cotton (Granite Shoal), Monbo, Turner brothers; cotton (Long Island), Catawba, Powell and Shuford; cotton (Maiden Manufacturing company), Maiden, H. T. Carpenter and Son; cotton (Newton Cotton Mills), Newton, W. H. Williams and S. M. Finger; tobacco, Newton, Michael, Sherrill and company; cigars, Newton, ——— Cretchner; cigars, Hickory, J. Flaum; smoking tobacco, Hickory, J. S. Tomlinson and company; smoking tobacco and cigars, Hickory, Keachy, Davis and company; plug tobacco, Hickory, Hall and Daniel; and plug tobacco, Hickory, A. W. Marshall.

Shoes and harness, Hickory, L. Hawn; shoes and harness, Hickory, Luther Flanagan and Spirs Murphy; wagons, Hickory, Piedmont Wagon company, J. G. Hall and F. B. Alexander; building material, Hickory, Hickory Manufacturing company; sash and blinds, Hickory, Robert Hallman; tannery, Newton, A. J. Seagle and company; tannery, Newton, C. Geitner; tannery, Newton, W. H. Williams and company; tannery, Jug Town, Alexander Hood; tannery, Jug Town, E. F. and R. O. Ramsour; tannery, Sparkling Catawba Springs, Paul Sigmon; and tannery, Catawba, Moore and company.

Shoes, Newton, J. A. Garvin; shoes, Hickory, A. Miller; shoes, Hickory, Seagle brothers; blacksmithing, Hickory, S. M. Abernethy; blacksmithing, Jug Town, John Bullinger; blacksmithing, Jug Town, Jacob Fullbright; blacksmithing, Sparkling Catawba Springs, D. Hynes; blacksmithing, Sparkling Catawba Springs, Jacob Lael; blacksmithing, Jug Town, Emanuel Speagle; blacksmithing, Jug Town, George Wilson; blacksmithing, Catawba, J. H. Utley; foundry, Hickory, Marshall and Lanier; foundry, Newton, W. R. Self; shingles, Hickory, G. M. Whitener; building and contracting, Jug Town, A. Baker; and building and contracting, Sparkling Catawba Springs, Seth Baker.

Building and contracting, Hickory, G. C. Bonniwell; building and contracting, Hickory, A. Y. Sigmon; building and contracting, Sparkling Catawba Springs, A. H. Davis; building and contracting, Sparkling Catawba Springs, Martin Hoke; building and contracting, Newton, Sam Jarrett and Son; building and contracting, Newton, A. H. Sherrill; building and contracting, Jug Town, L. Martin; building and contracting, Catawba, C. H. Shuman; coopering, Sparkling Catawba Springs, John Hynes; coopering, Sparkling Catawba Springs, Adam Hynes; coopering, Sparkling Catawba Springs, Monroe Reinhardt; marble yard, Newton, George E. Coulter; and marble yard, Newton, J. T. Webb and Son.

Whiskey, Newton, M. M. Cline; whiskey, Newton, J. P. Fry; whiskey, Newton, R. C. Setzer; whiskey, Newton, W. A. Huit; whiskey, Hickory, D. W. Rowe; whiskey, Hickory, J. H. Scott; Iron Forge, Newton, William Williams; Iron Forge, Newton, A. L. Ramsour; Lime, Catawba, M. B. Trollinger; millwrighting, Hickory, C. C. Bonniwell; millwrighting, Sparkling Catawba Springs, A. H. Davis; millwrighting, Hickory, J. C. Fry; millwrighting, Catawba, J. H. Irvin; mill-

CATAWBA COUNTY   191

wrighting, Catawba, John Irvin; millwrighting, Catawba, J. W. Irving; millwrighting, Jug Town, Jacob Masteller; millwrighting, Newton, A. W. Wilson; millwrighting, Newton, A. W. Wilson; millwrighting, Newton, Avery Wilson; and millwrighting, Newton, L. N. Wilson.

Saddles and harness, Hickory, M. A. Johnson; saddles and harness, Newton, G. W. Lowe; saddles and harness, Hickory, Seagle brothers; saddles and harness, Newton, L. Plonk; saddles and harness, Sparkling Catawba Springs, N. Sigmon; saddles and harness, Newton, M. M. Rowe; furniture, Hickory, Moore and company; stoneware, Jug Town, Wade Johnson; stoneware, Jug Town, Henry Ritchie; stoneware, Jug Town, Thomas Ritchie; stoneware, Jug Town, Frank Smith; tinware, Hickory, P. L. Hefner and company; undertakers, Hickory, F. D. Ingold; wool-carding, Jug Town, Mosteller and Warlick; carriage and buggy, Newton, W. A. Scronce; carriage and buggy, Newton, J. Bolch; carriage and buggy, Newton, J. Baker; and carriage and buggy, Hickory, A. Abernethy.

Joseph Steel probably operated the first regular store in the area of Catawba county in connection with the operations of his fulling mill. This was prior to the Revolution.

Likely the county's first "traveling salesman" was Joseph Hughes, a one-armed merchant of Salisbury. Hughes opened his Salisbury store about 1760. He peddled goods, tinware and dry goods from a two-horse covered wagon from 1765 to 1790, going wherever he could find roads. It is known that he operated as far west of Salisbury as 60 miles, and that he drove through the country each spring and fall.

Colonel Christopher Beekman operated a "mailing house" (dealing primarily in skins) at the present site of Conover and John Wilfong operated a store, probably in the Zion church area, during the period of the Revolution and after. Jacob Shuford and his son, Elkanah, conducted a store at Bunker Hill as early at 1825. As evidenced by an old bill for goods purchased from Connor and Company, this concern operated a general store in the Rehobeth section likely before 1803 (it is believed that the Connors were merchants from the beginning). David Abernathy operated a store on Mountain creek about 1806. Jacob Shuford operated a store in the Bunker Hill area in the 1820s and 1830s. When Eavesville postoffice near Conover was established in 1832, Lawson Eaves was appointed postmaster and the office was kept in his store, which had been in business for a number of years. George Smyre is known to have operated a general merchandising house at Eavesville prior to the formation of the county. Isaac Hill conducted a general store in the Mt. Pleasant church community on Mountain creek at an early date. Dr. Caleb Fink, a physician, is known to have operated a store in connection with his practice of medicine in the Mountain Creek section also at an early date.

Catawbans who were engaged in the "sale of commodities" in 1885, as listed by Branson's Directories were:

Newton—Abernethy and Williams, drugs; J. Baker, general stock; Ballinger brothers, general stock; Miss Mary Berrier, rock quarry; H. F. Carpenter, leather; Coulter, Lowe and company, lumber; George E. Coulter and company, general stock; C. Detter, general stock; Garvin and Seagle, shoes, books and stationery; J. R. Gaither, general stock; J. M. Hanks, painter; Henkel and Corpening, livery; Adam Hagan, agricultural implements; G. W. Holler, boots and shoes; J. W. Hardister, jewelry; J. H. Hightower, stove and tinware; Jarrett and Selt, general stock; George A. Lowe, drugs; T. B. Marlow, tinware; and Marshall, Lanier and company, tobacco.

Murray brothers, general stock; ——— Marlow, painter; T. D. Marlow and brothers, painters; A. McIntosh, photographer; T. D. Marlow and brothers, stoves, etc.; Dr. G. W. Michael, insurance; Levi Plonk, harness and shoes; L. Plonk, groceries; M. M. Rowe, general stock; W. H. Rockett and company, general stock; G. and J. L. Setzer, millers and general stock; Seagle, Garvin and company, shoes; M. O. Sherrill and company, general stock; Charles Tilman, painter; Mrs. Jane Wright, millinery; R. W. Wilson and company, livery; W. H. Williams, general stock; Williams and Finger, general stock; H. A. Whitener, tailor; W. P. Wilson, general stock; Warlick brothers, general stock; H. A. Whitener, groceries; J. H. A. Yount, general stock; and Yount and Shrum, general stock.

Hickory—A. Abernethy, carriages and buggies; ——— Abernethy, general stock; Abernethy, Rockett and company, general stock; J. F. Abernethy, groceries; Abernethy and Whitener, groceries; Abernethy Brothers, general stock; Aber-

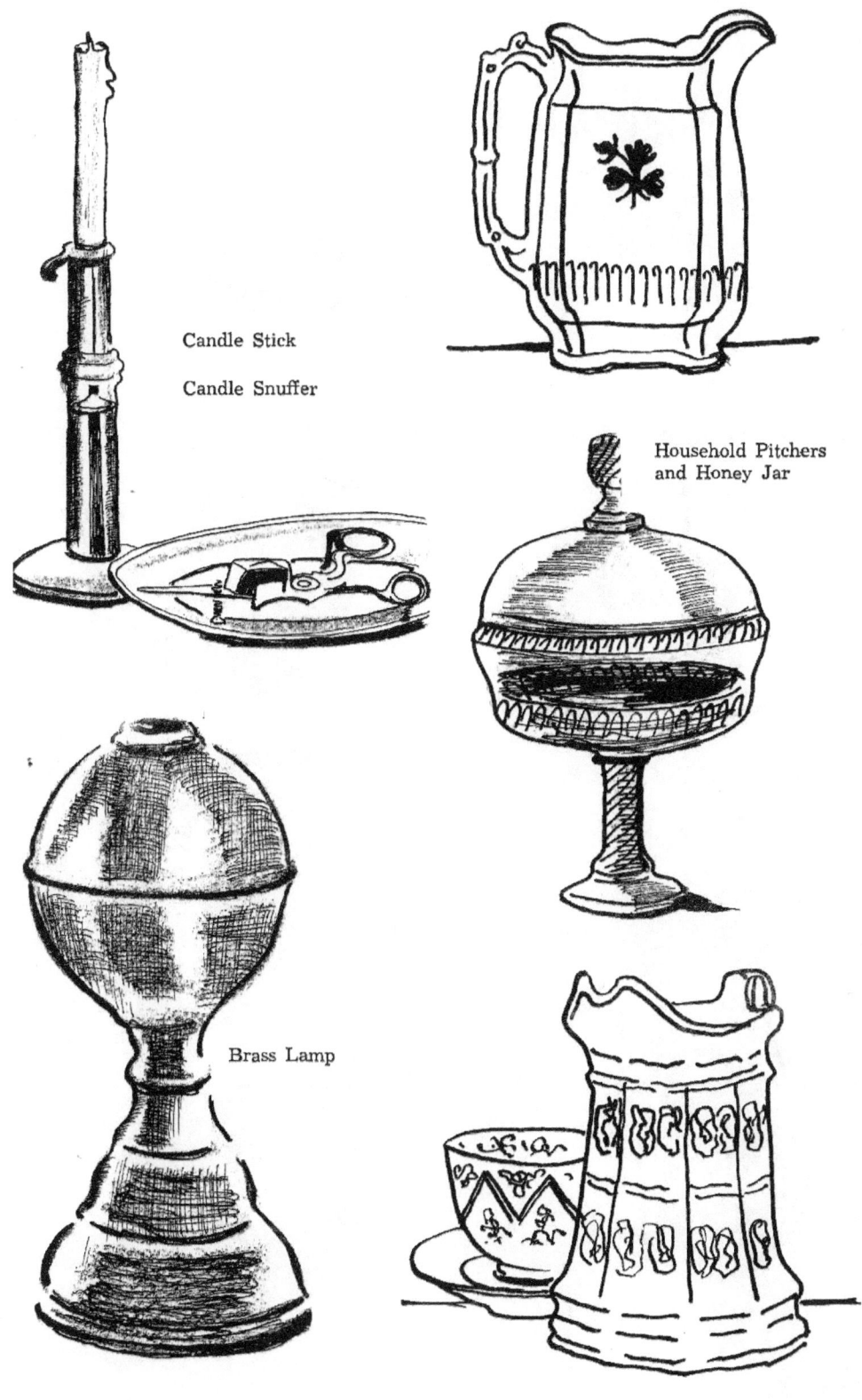

Candle Stick

Candle Snuffer

Household Pitchers and Honey Jar

Brass Lamp

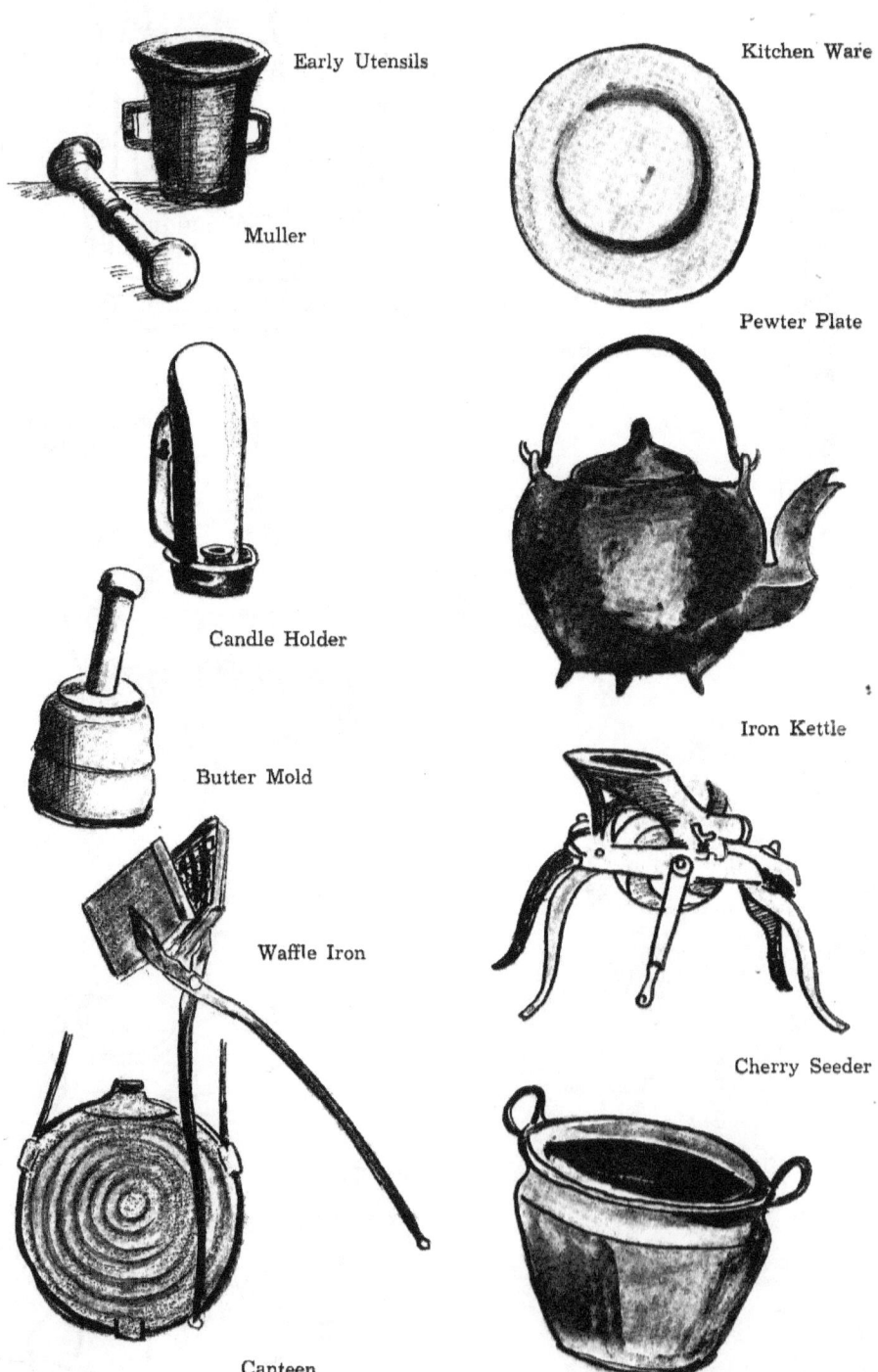

Early Utensils

Muller

Kitchen Ware

Pewter Plate

Candle Holder

Butter Mold

Iron Kettle

Waffle Iron

Cherry Seeder

Canteen

Copper Pot

CATAWBA COUNTY 193

nethy Brothers, livery stables; Blair and Clinard, groceries and confectionaries; J. H. Burns, liquors and general stock; J. B. Baker, drugs; M. L. Bean, lumber; Bobbitt and company, drugs; S. A. Chandler, furniture and general stock; F. A. Clinard, tobacco warehouse; E. O. Elliott, miller and general stock; W. H. Ellis, general stock; Fields Brothers, general stock; J. Flaum, leather and general stock; Fields Brothers and Deal, general stock; M. L. Flaigan, groceries; A. Flaum, general stock; Luther Flanagan, confectionaries; W. W. Goldsmith, jewelry; A. C. Gunter, agent for Signer Manufacturing company; L. Hawn, shoes and harness; and Poly L. Hefner, tinware.

Hall brothers, groceries and Com.; Hayes and Hardy, general stock; Hill and Hill, clothing; R. W. Johnson, agricultural implements; Kerr brothers, livery stables; R. H. Lanier, saloon; Latta and Beard, general stock; Latta and Bean, tobacco warehouse; J. M. Lawrence, jewelry; Moore and company, furniture; O. M. Royster and company, drugs; W. P. Reinhardt, flour; H. W. Robinson, flour; D. W. Rowe, livery stables; H. S. Suttlemyer, confectionaries and general stock; A. Y. Sigmon, general stock; A. A. Shuford and company, general stock; A. A. Shuford, hardware; Seagle brothers, general stock, shoes and harness; ——— Seagle, jewelry; G. S. White, confectionaries and groceries; and George Whitner, livery.

Catawba—Williams Bandy and Son, general stock; Beal brothers, general stock; Cline, Roseman and company, general stock; J. H. Frolinger, general stock; A. H. Houston, general stock; Little brothers, fertilizer agent; Little brothers, agricultural implements; Little and company, general stock; J. H. Long and company, fertilizers and general stock; J. H. Long and company, agricultural implements; Thomas L. Long, livestock; W. L. Moon and company, general stock; Frank Powell, leather; A. M. Powell, lime; H. F. Powell, livestock and leather; Pitts and Irvin, lumber; Sharpe brothers and company, general stock; J. H. Sherrill, livestock; Turner brothers, general stock; and W. H. Williams, fertilizer agent.

Conover—Cline, Roseman and company, general stock; Smith brothers, general stock; C. Simmons, livery stables; and Yount and Hunsucker, general stock.

Chronicle—A. C. Dellinger, general stock.

Jacobs Fork—W. H. Blackburn, general stock; J. and D. Keever, general stock; and B. H. Shuford and company, general stock.

Jug Town—Monroe Britton, general stock; Hudson and Wyant, lumber dealers; and Daniel Lutz, general stock.

Keeversville—W. S. Jarrett, general stock; and A. Propst, general stock.

Maiden—Yount and Shrum, general stock.

Mountain Creek—Franklin Beatty, leather.

Oxford Ford—A. J. Stine, ———.

Sherrills Ford—E. L. Sherrill and son, general stock; and E. L. Sherrill, lumber.

Sparkling Catawba Springs—E. O. Elliott, fertilizer agent; Dr. E. O. Elliott, furniture dealer; and Elliott and McGee, lumber.

Eighty-odd mills, including grist, flour and corn, and saw mills (some with steam), operated during the half-century. Their owners and post office addresses were as follows:

Flour and corn—Noah Rowe, Newton; S. Smyre, Newton; Logan Wilson, Newton; P. M. Hilderbrand, Newton; D. Roseman, Newton; Noah Hawn, Newton; Daniel Rowe, Hickory; R. McKinzie, Catawba; W. G. James, Catawba; ——— Keener, Sherrills Ford; Setzer and Setzer, Newton; George Berrier, Newton; W. Bostian, Newton; Eli S. Coulter, Newton; Boyd and Propst, Maiden; McNeil and Wike, Catawba; Collinger and Suttlemeyer, Hickory; Conner and company, Catawba; J. P. Cline and company, Conover; L. L. James, Catawba; P. L. Jones and company, Catawba; James Keever, Catawba; Powell and Shuford, Catawba; G. C. McNeil, Catawba; P. M. Mull, Mulls Grove, Rhyme and Mchafferty, Newton; Ostwald and Bradburn, Catawba; J. P. Rabb, Maiden; Ramsour and Loie, Jacobs Fork; Daniel Roseman, Younts Mill; Mrs. L. Rowe, Hickory; W. R. Self, Newton; E. L. Sherrill, Sherrills Ford; Silas Smyra, Newton; A. J. Stine, Oxford Ford; Fry and Rowe, Hickory; George Whitner, Hickory; Wagoner and Huffman, Sparkling Catawba Springs; and G. D. L. Yount, Younts Mill.

CATAWBA COUNTY 195

Flour, corn and saw—D. L. Yount, Newton; E. O. Elliott, Newton; D. A. Little, Newton; A. L. Ramsour, Newton; J. J. Mott, Sherrills Ford; D. E. Warlick, Jacobs Fork; and Fry and Rowe, Hickory.

Saw—C. F. Conner, Catawba; Caleb Rhodes, Newton; A. Y. Sigmon, Newton; J. W. Blackwelder, Catawba; Conner and company, Catawba; J. U. Long and company, Catawba; Daniel Roseman, Catawba; McNeill and Wike, Catawba; W. Setzer, Catawba; Herman, Bost and company, Conover; J. P. Cline and company, Conover; Bumgarner and Wagoner, Hickory; Fry and Rowe, Hickory; E. O. Elliott and McGee, Sparkling Catawba Springs; John Gabriel, Sherrills Ford; Hudson and Wyant, Jug Town; M. Huit, Clinesville; Irvin and Coulter, Catawba; P. L. Jones and company, Catawba; Lyerly and Muller, Hickory; Peeler and Lynn, Hickory; A. Y. Sigmon, Hickory; George Whitener, Hickory; E. L. Sherrill, Sherrills Ford; J. P. Rabb, Maiden; A. J. Cline, Oxford Ford; Wilson and Robertson, Newton; and G. D. L. Yount, Younts Mill.

Corn—E. J. Sherrill, Sherrills Ford; D. Christopher, Oxford Ford; E. O. Elliott, Sparkling Catawba Springs; P. Edward, Catawba; W. E. Lawrence, Catawba; Massey and company, Catawba; W. Setzer, Catawba; J. A. Hartsel, Hickory; and M. Huit, Clinesville.

Saw (steam)—W. R. Self, Newton; J. T. Mehaffey, Newton; A. Y. Sigmon, Newton; and one in Hickory, the owner of which is not known.

Corn (steam)—E. L. Sherrill, Sherrills Ford.

CHAPTER IX

EARLY PROFESSIONS

The professions were the weaklings of the Catawba county frontier.

Any professionalist was quite aware that his "calling," although needed, would lead him into bankruptcy or, at best, render him susceptible to extreme deprivation. Until the 1800s, the area's residents—due to necessity—were self-sufficient, self-reliant persons whose mental tempers fostered individualism. The experience of sharing, with its ultimate result of trade specialization, did not produce a spirit of collectivism until the mid-1800s.

Virtually all the early lawyers, doctors, ministers, teachers and newspapermen supplemented their "profession" with another, more remunerative, occupation, usually farming. This, along with the fact that professionalists customarily did not use their titles, such as "doctor" or "attorney," renders the process of determining early skilled technicians difficult.

It is doubted that a lawyer "hung out his shingle" in the Catawba territory prior to its formation as a county. Lawyers rarely located anywhere except in the county towns, and, prior to 1842, there were no county towns in the area now known as Catawba county. The people of the local section first transacted their affairs of the law at Salisbury, in Rowan county; then, with the cutting of new county lines, attended their legal business at Morganton, in Burke county; and, finally, with an additional county division, did court duty and received the benefits of jurisprudence at Lincolnton, in Lincoln county.

Inasmuch as the first United States law school was not formed until 1784 at Litchfield, Conn., following unsuccessful attempts at establishing legal lectures in colleges, the colonial attorney was a product of the European school. European law, about this time, was a combination of Roman and canon law. Medieval law in England was largely of Teutonic, or Germanic, origin. Later English law was also influenced by Roman and canon law. The Code of Napoleon marked a great step forward in the development of law. Napoleon Bonaparte worked out a simple and uniform system of law during his rule of France in the early 1800s. The Napoleonic Code took the place of the complicated and unwieldly legal system that had developed during the Middle Ages and which European governments had not bothered to change.

If the area's initial lawyers did not come directly from Europe, they studied as students of those who did. "Reading" for the bar was done often in the home of the senior attorney, and the junior's field experience was received as an attendant at the senior's court performance.

Of course, the earliest justices of the peace who administered "justice" were not sufficiently schooled for the task. Their positions were obtained more by virtue of community esteem than from legal acumen. During the late 1700s, custom held that a man who had accumulated wealth and prestige was duly called to sit in judgment on his brother. Early lawyers, in fact, found themselves busier drawing up contracts, wills, and other civil legal papers, serving as executors or trustees, and trying to settle civil disputes without a lawsuit, than representing a criminal who might even be maneuvering for his life. The Mosaic law of "an eye for an eye, a tooth for a tooth" was still firmly entrenched in the mores of the people, who often took it upon themselves to handle law offenders of the more vile nature.

The tempo of the times is reflected in the statutes which men make to govern their own actions. The Revised Statutes of the State of North Carolina, passed by the General Assembly at the session of 1836-37, for instance, called for "death without benefit of clergy" for one who stole a slave or one who concealed a slave with intent to remove him out of the state, yet labeled the killing of a slave only homicide.

The law of the time continued to allow the mutilation of human bodies for repayment of crime. Perjury, considered a crime against heaven as well as men, held the following punishment:

"Chapter XXXIV, Sections 50, 51, 52 and 53: "If any person shall wilfully and corruptly commit perjury on his or her oath or affirmation, in any suit, controversy, matter or cause depending in any of the courts of this State, or on any oath or affirmation made or in any deposition or affidavit taken pursuant to the laws of this State, every such person, so offending and being thereof convicted, shall be fined not exceeding the sum of one thousand dollars, and shall stand in the pillory for one hour, at the expiration of which time both ears of the person so offending shall be cut off and severed entirely from the head, and the ears so cut off shall be nailed to the pillory by the officer, and there remain until the setting of the sun; and the person so offending shall be rendered thereafter incapable of giving testimony in any of the courts of this State, or in any case whatsoever, until such time as the judgment so given against the said offender shall be reversed.

"If any person shall, by any means, procure another person to commit corrupt and wilful perjury, on his or her oath or affirmation in any suit, controversy, matter or cause depending in any of the courts of this State, or on any oath or affirmation made or in any affidavit or deposition taken pursuant to the laws of this State, the person, so offending and being thereof convicted, shall stand in the pillory one hour, have his or her right ear cut off, and shall be fined at the discretion of the court, in a sum not exceeding one thousand dollars; and the person so offending shall be thereafter rendered incapable of giving testimony in any of the courts of this State, or in any case whatsoever, until such time as the judgment so given against the said offender shall be reversed.

"Provided, that it shall not be lawful to sentence the offender to have his ears or either of them cut off, unless the perjury or subornation of perjury, of which he is convicted, shall have been committed upon the trial of some capital offense; and when otherwise committed than on the trial of any capital case, the offender, on conviction, in lieu of having his ears cut off, shall be sentenced to receive one or more public whippings, not less than thirtynine lashes on his bare back.

"Whereas principal felons frequently escape and elude the process of law, whereby accessories cannot be prosecuted and punished: for remedy thereof, it shall and may be lawful to prosecute and punish any accessory to felony as for a misdemeanor, to be punished by a fine not exceeding one-hundred dollars, and corporal punishment not exceeding thirtynine lashes, or standing in the pillory not exceeding two hours, although the principal felon be not before convicted of said felony, which shall exempt the offender from being punished as accessory, if the principal be afterwards convicted."

The same Revised Statutes allowed indictment of overseers of roads who shirked their duties; indictment of owners of water mills who did not keep up bridges; the sentence of death ". . . Provided, that he shall be entitled to the benefit of his clergy, in the same manner and to the same extent as in cases of felony at common law" for one who stole ". . . any horse, mare, gelding, jackass, or mule . . ." etc.

Public opinion about what is right changes from generation to generation. Laws must be changed from time to time if they are to keep up with public sentiment. Law is always growing, or evolving, and no law can be said to represent a final truth.

The earliest lawyers who served the persons who were to become Catawbans "rode the circuit" of the courts. Among those who are known to have come into the Catawba territory, prior to the county's formation, were Attorneys Waightstill Avery, who was of Mecklenburg and later of Burke county; John Dunn, who was of Rowan county; Spruce McKay, who was of Rowan county; James Holland, who was of Rutherford county; Alexander Martin, who was of Guilford county; and William Kennon, who was of Rowan county.

As the young attorneys were first admitted to the bar and sworn in at the county courts, preserved court records reveal some of the beginners. It is known that William Alexander, who was of Mecklenburg county; Thomas McGimpsie, who was of Burke county; and Joseph Spencer, who was of Anson county, procured licenses signed by Judges Williams and Haywood and were admitted to the bar in 1795. John Rees, who was of Lincoln county, was admitted to the bar in 1781, after his license was signed by Judges Samuel Ashe and Samuel Spencer.

William P. Bynum and William M. Shipp were prominent Lincoln county lawyers who were intimately associated with the early Catawba county government.

Consensus is that during the first five years after Catawba county was formed, there were only three lawyers serving its population—Burton Craig, Mark E. Lowrance and Matthew Locke McCorkle. The attorneys were located at Newton prior to 1850. In 1869, the membership of the local bar was increased by the acquisition of John F. Murrill, who set up office in Hickory Tavern. The next county attorney was John B. Hussey, who came to Newton in 1872, later moved to Hickory Tavern and then left the county.

Moses N. Amis practiced in the county, probably Hickory, for a brief period between 1875 and 1883. In 1877-78, J. W. Wright established an office in Hickory, and W. H. Reid, in the town of Catawba. R. B. B. Houston was added to the bar ranks in 1877.

Between 1878 and 1885 the membership of the Catawba bar was augmented by the licensing of F. Lee Cline of Hickory, F. M. Williams of Newton, and by the coming of Clinton A. Cilley and D. Herndon Tuttle of Caldwell county, L. L. Witherspoon of Wilkes county, and William G. Burkehead of Wake county.

In the half decade following 1885 there appeared on the scene Samuel H. Jordan, A. P. Lynch, Robert J. Shipp, E. B. Cline and W. A. Self.

Charles W. Rice of Farmville came to Newton in the late 1880s and was licensed in 1889.

Additional attorneys who served Catawbans prior to 1900 included George McCorkle, Charles Milton McCorkle, Henry C. Denny (a mulatto), Thomas M. Hufham, Marcellus Eugene Thornton, W. C. Feimster, Marshall H. Yount, W. B. Gaither, and A. A. Whitener.

The development of the Catawba County Bar, incorporating the intellect, integrity and valor of some of the area's leading citizens, has proved that counties have been subjected to a just application of jurisprudence.

There was little thought of sanitation or hygiene during America's colonization. Women cared for their families without the aid of a doctor, and frequently with only a few homemade remedies. Bacon rind was often used for a sore throat, flaxseed for poulticing, cobwebs to stop the flow of blood, and boneset tea for the ague. The settlers learned to trim and care for a wound.

CATAWBA COUNTY   201

Always, and apparently without serious consequences, superstition was mixed with medical fact.

The contagious, or catching, diseases were not a major problem because the first pioneers led such isolated lives. But from 1800 to 1850, some epidemics occurred in the Catawba section. Among these were dysentery and diphtheria. Because the pioneers knew little about the spread of disease, their attitude was, "every man for himself; the strong will survive, and the weak will perish."

Physicians were slow in coming to the Catawba territory prior to its status as a county. But, when one considers the difficulty with which medical and surgical training was obtained, he is not surprised. There was not a medical college in America until Dr. William Shippen founded the Philadelphia Medical College in 1765. The second such institution also was a great distance from North Carolina, being the New York Medical College, which was founded in 1769.

During the first 100 years of the Catawba settlement, practically all doctors were trained for practice by another physician. The medical student lived with his preceptor and read his books and helped prepare his medicines for one year. For another year he continued his studies and accompanied the doctor on his rounds to his patients, observing firsthand the experienced man's methods. Following the second year of training, the apprentice was considered competent to practice.

The sparsely settled Catawba county did not afford enough practice during its early days to support the doctor and his family, so, if the physician was morally convicted to settle locally, he was almost forced because of financial circumstances to seek a portion of his living by another type of work.

There is no doubt that the first man to come into the Catawba valley to relieve suffering and restore health was Dr. Hans Martin Kalberlahn, a young Moravian doctor from the settlement near Winston-Salem. Dr. Kalberlahn was a native of Norway, from which country he had obtained all the medical education which was available at that time. It is said that the physician was a hundred years ahead of his time in technique.

The diaries kept by the Moravians mention patients brought to Dr. Kalberlahn from the Catawba river, some 60 miles from the Moravian community; and it is known that the doctor rode distances of more than 100 miles, in all directions, to see patients.

The first resident physician of whom there is positive account is Dr. Joseph Lytle, who is described as an old practitioner in 1840. If an old man in 1840, he probably began practice here by 1800 or earlier.

A second pioneer doctor concerning whom authentic records exist is Dr. Ogburn Campbell. Dr. Campbell was born in 1824, therefore could not have been in practice before the late 1840s.

That pioneers were able to manage reasonably well the problems of health while their nearest doctor was miles away affords the modern no little amazement. The truth is that the early settlers practiced medicine themselves.

Every community had one or more mid-wives, some of whom attained a remarkable degree of proficiency. In every settlement was a man who learned to "set" broken bones and replace dislocated joints. Some member of a community owned a pair of tooth forceps, made by a clever blacksmith, and was quick to offer the "pulling" method to facilitate relief. Bleeding was much in vogue. No half-dozen families of a given vicinity were without a lancet or two between them and an equal amount of persons who knew the instruments' operations. Pioneers knew the medicinal value of certain herbs, barks, roots and berries, some of which grew wild in the forests while others were cultivated in home gardens.

A list of physicians who are known to have practiced in Catawba county during the period of the date of its formation to 1900 are the following:

Henry L. Abernathy, W. Lafayette Abernathy, T. M. Abernathy, and Robert E. Adams.

Richard Browning Baker, James Bivings, Kenneth A Black, T. C. Blackburn, E. H. Bobbitt, and C. Brindle.

C. M. Campbell, James R. Campbell, Ogburn Campbell, ———— Churchill, B. F. Cobb, C. W. Connor, A. H. Crowell.

Esley O. Elliott and James R. Ellis.

Caleb Fink, Fred T. Foard, Sr., A. C. Fox, and Alfred J. Fox. ———— Greenwade.

CATAWBA COUNTY

W. C. Haley, Franklin L. Herman, William Herman, J. C. Hinson, O. L. Hollar, J. B. Houston, Charles Hoyle, D. C. Huffman, C. L. Hunter, and George Huffman.
W. P. Ivey.
J. Theodore Johnson.
A. P. Keever, James H. Keever, and Paul J. Klutz.
J. L. Lattimore, James H. Little, Q. M. Little, and Fred Y. Long and Thomas Walter Long.
J. M. McCorkle, Banks McNairy, and George Campbell McNeil.
———— Marshburn, Henry C. Menzies, G. W. Michael, and D. Marion Moser, and James J. Mott.
George Nichols.
T. M. Parks, J. R. Pearson, A. M. Powell, E. Lee Powell, and Tait Powell.
Archibald Ray, Alex Ramsour, Charles Ramsour, George McNeil Robinson, and E. Reid Russell.
A. M. Sherrill, J. A. Sherrill, W. T. Shipp, Q. A. Shuford, William Shuford, and T. Frank Stevenson.
Benjamin F. Terry, Henry E. Thornton, and Josephus Turner.
George Harris West, Benjamin F. Whitesides, J. C. Whitesides, and W. E. Wilson.
Dr. Brantley York, D. McDuffie Yount, and Peter L. Yount.

The dentistry profession followed some years behind the medical profession. Among the area's earliest trained dentists was J. J. Hicks, J. B. Little, J. Lowenstein, W. A. Marler, Charles Ramsay, and W. B. Ramsay.

Among the county's earliest veterinary-surgeons were Dr. Charles Murray and Harry B. Murray.

The teaching and preaching professions, which are closely identified in early American history, are treated separately in the volume's "Early Education Methods" and "Early Religious Life" chapters, respectively. These two professions led all others in the order of appearance in the county.

Teachers listed by Branson's North Carolina Directory in 1885 were: ———— Alexander of Catawba, Annis S. Albright of Newton, Sallie Bradburn of Newton, Miss Laura Bost of Newton, Mother Augustine of Hickory, Professor J. C. Clapp of Newton, C. E. Connor of Sherrills Ford, Rev. H. C. Dickson of Hickory, Miss Fannie O. Eckard of Conover, Professor J. A. Foil of Newton, Sallie E. Herman of Conover, R. E. Hefner of Catawba Springs, W. L. Killian of Catawba, Miss Sallie McDowell of Catawba, A. V. Rockett of Younts Mill, Rev. A. S. Vaughn of Hickory, and R. A. Yoder of Conover.

Branson lists resident ministers of the same year as: G. W. Ivey, Methodist of Newton; P. L. Herman, Methodist of Hickory; E. L. Stamey, Methodist of Catawba; David E. Warlick, Methodist of Jacobs Fork; Robert Helton, Methodist of Jacobs Fork; Dr. J. A. Sherrill, Methodist of Mountain Creek; James A. Weston, Episcopalian of Hickory; R. B. Anderson, Presbyterian of Newton; T. G. Thurston, Presbyterian of Newton; J. R. Jones, Baptist of Hickory; J. K. Faulkner, Baptist of Newton; H. D. Lequeaux, Baptist of Catawba; J. B. Marsh, Baptist of Catawba; J. A. Rector, Baptist of Catawba; G. J. Wilkie, Baptist of Catawba; Col. R. Hawks, Baptist of Catawba; J. C. Clapp, Associated Reformed of Newton; J. A. Foil, Associated Reformed of Newton; J. C. Fox, Associated Reformed of Newton; J. M. Smith, Lutheran of Newton; R. A. Yoder, Lutheran of Newton; P. C. Henkel, Lutheran of Newton; J. H. Fesperman, Lutheran of Newton; G. L. Hunt, Lutheran of Newton; J. A. Linn, Lutheran of Hickory; and A. S. Vaughn, Reformed of Newton.

None of the professions has experienced difficulties as unfortunate as journalism in Catawba county. No fewer than ten periodicals, which blossomed into being for purposes ranging from reform to the literary, but never expressly for monetary gain, have been buried with the passage of time. Due likely to the people's agrarian living and natural tendencies toward individualism, newspapers seemingly found it impossible to take permanent root in the Catawba field.

Some papers failed because the publishers learned a hard lesson along financial lines and simply turned to a surer method of making livings. The late Major J. L. Latta, who served on the staffs of most of Hickory's papers, referred to his city as a "newspaper graveyard." Several of the papers were started to serve a political purpose, and when that purpose had been accomplished, they "folded" and died. Trouble among business heads, although usually concerning minor policy-making, continually cropped up. The newspaper as an advertising medium was not adequately realized. Printing limitations restricted the types of advertising. Subscribers were not convinced that news came earliest by newspapers; in fact, as one writer records, he subscribed to the community paper not to get the news—which he had already learned at the village store—but to find if it had yet reached the editor.

The printing trade was physically strenuous. Early papers were set in hand type and duplicated by hand.

Often the editor served both as chief reporter and shop foreman. During his spare time he solicited advertising and handled business matters, being subjected always to ribald jokes concerning the quality of his product.

Publishing was a risk, due to the heavy overhead expenses. Capital was to be asked of people who had faltering faith in the enterprise which asked it.

As indication of the fact that early publishers earned a major portion of their incomes through occupations coupled with journalism, it is noted that one also engaged in law, another also was in the insurance business, a third also was a physician, and still a fourth ran a tobacco factory. In addition, some of these farmed on the side.

To be worthy of his "salt," the village editor had to have a vocabulary crammed with six-syllable words sprinkled with classical allusions. He was required to entertain any member of his society for seemingly non-ending periods in his office; be an astute politician; be undisputedly a classicist; be an untiring civic booster; etc.

Types of "news" used was anything the editor could put his hands on immediately, from locally-written amateur poetry to clippings from state, and even foreign, papers.

The publisher not seldom was paid in country produce. It is told that one such unlucky fellow took so many cords of wood in payment for his paper that it was by necessity stacked from the sidewalk of his residence on through the front and back yards and continued down the garden fence to the barn, besides that which was left at the printing office to feed the rusty old stove which warmed up the type. Friends observed that the newspaperman had enough wood to last him ten years.

But, regardless of such obstacles, certain papers did exist for considerable periods of time and during their lives served their communities well. Fearlessly they championed the establishment of waterworks, the use of electric lights, the abolition of saloons, free schools, improved roads, etc. Constantly they boosted the growing town and county.

Catawba county's first newspaper was established in Hickory Tavern in 1870 by the village's initial resident physician, Dr. J. R. Ellis. It was The Carolina Eagle.

Dr. Ellis, who was a cultured and scholarly gentleman but untrained in the newspaper profession, sold The Eagle, with its goodwill, emoluments and other appurtenances, to J. B. Hussey, an attorney, after two or three years of almost continuous journalistic calamity.

Hussey ridded himself of the obvious liability shortly thereafter, when J. F. Murrill, another lawyer, moved to Hickory, and J. S. Tomlinson, an itinerant photographer of Iredell county, bought the publication. This pair, which formed the partnership of Murrill and Tomlinson, changed the paper's name to The Press.

The first Newton paper, meanwhile, which is believed to have been titled The Vindicator, saw birth also during the 1870s. Little is known about this periodical, other than its life was shortlived.

Of journalistic significance, however, is the fact that the county's present oldest newspaper from the standpoint of continuous publication (although it had name changes) also was born in Newton during the 1870s. It is today's Daily Catawba News-Enterprise.

The third Catawba county town to have a newspaper prior to 1900 was Catawba, which nurtured a small, shortlived publication, The Mercury, during the 1880s. J. H. Shannon was editor and proprietor.

Rev. A. W. Setzer began a newspaper in Maiden in 1910, The News, but only a single issue was printed.

The journalistic history of the county may now easiest be followed by municipalities, considering the communities of

CATAWBA COUNTY 207

Newton, Hickory, and Maiden, which became headquarters of additional publications.

George Warlick was responsible for the beginning of the present News-Enterprise. It was on February 9, 1879 that the first copy of The Newton Enterprise came from the press. Consisting of four pages, six columns each, it was a neat, well-ordered newspaper, Democratic in policy.

Warlick remained in the newspaper business a little more than two years, when he sold out in order to enter other lines of business. For a time thereafter, Judge W. B. Gaither edited The Enterprise, but before long, F. M. Williams bought the paper and became its editor. Williams erected a building on the north side of courtsquare on the site where the present Eagles company store now stands, and moved the newspaper and printing office there. Here it remained until consolidation with The Catawba County News in 1919.

Williams' editorship was not continuous, however. In 1896, he held public office and during his term B. J. Summerow occupied the editor's chair. As the new editor, Summerow issued the following signed statement: "The paper will remain Democratic and while we expect to speak our sentiments and assert our principles in a bold manner, we concede the right to all men to think and act as they please, yet we reserve the right to point out their advantages and disadvantages as we see them. . . ."

Williams resumed the editorship of the newspaper upon the completion of a term as federal officer and continued in that capacity until The Enterprise and The News were consolidated.

The News appeared in 1903. It, too, was Democratic in policy, and started as a weekly, published every Wednesday. C. M. McCorkle was its first editor, and J. H. Plonk was the business manager. In the initial issue Editor McCorkle had the following comment to make regarding policies: "It is the intention and purpose of the owners to make it so bright, attractive and readable that before many months have passed it will find a welcome in every home in this and adjoining counties. Its policy, politically, will be Democratic. It proposes to print the truth at all times and under all circumstances, give the news and promote the business interests of the county. In so doing, we feel that it cannot but have the good will and hearty approval and cooperation of every reader of its pages. Its columns will be open to all persons upon all subjects, but it reserves the right to reject any communication which in the judgment of its editor would be prejudicial to its own interests or the interests of the people of the county."

The progressiveness of The News from the beginning is indicated by its use of color-printing as far back as 1903—though it was a different style of color-printing from that used today. On the front page of the issue of August 13 of that year, in bold type, an announcement was printed in red ink across the entire front page—over the usual news printed as usual in black ink. The red letters issued this invitation to attend Soldiers Reunion:

"First at Bethel! Last at Appomattox! A welcome to the Veterans. Every soldier of the Civil War who fought for the cause of the South will be given a hearty welcome by the people of Newton on August 15. Speeches will be made by good orators! A monster basket dinner will be given by the ladies of the county. We want every veteran who possibly can to be here on that glorious day! Come one—Come All."

During the year 1904, C. H. Mebane, who then was county superintendent of schools, began to negotiate for the purchase of The News, and the deal was consummated in 1905. The concern was a corporation at the time, with most of the business men in Newton as stockholders. Mebane assumed management and editorship on January 18, 1905. In that issue of the paper, McCorkle announced his connections with the paper had been severed because of other business, and Mebane briefly stated his intention of promoting three movements through his paper: The education of the people, good public highways, and good citizenship.

On October 3, 1905, The News became a semi-weekly, published on Tuesday and Friday.

Shortly after Mebane purchased the paper, he bought the building in which The Daily Catawba News-Enterprise is still published, and in 1912 renovated the structure, building the front as it appears today.

Outdoor Bake Oven

Kraut Making

Early Type Cabin

In 1919, The News and The Enterprise were consolidated under the name The Catawba News-Enterprise. In the interval between his management of The News, and this period, Mebane had become sole owner of the paper. When the consolidation was effected with the purchase of The Enterprise from Williams, a stock company again was formed, with most of the leading business men of the town becoming stockholders. At the time of the consolidation, Mebane was editor and Charles H. Mebane, Jr., was business manager.

During the years that followed, the senior Mebane again became sole owner of the concern and dissolved the corporation. Until his death he edited the paper which gained a wide reputation for its editorial policy that reflected the strong personality and convictions of the editor.

For several months prior to Mebane's death, when he was too ill to continue his work, the management of The News-Enterprise passed to his son, Charles, Jr., who became editor following his father's death in December, 1926. Two years later, the junior Mebane was joined in the management by G. W. Mann, prior to that time of Winston-Salem, who in 1932 became editor and business manager. At that time, Mebane sold his interest in the paper, and, in 1933, he began to publish the Newton Observer, a weekly newspaper.

In 1936, the ownership of The Catawba News-Enterprise changed from the Mebane estate to G. W. Mann and Mrs. Evelyn Odum (then Evelyn Mebane, daughter of the senior Mebane).

The Observer began publication on the northeast corner of the square. It remained a weekly until 1950, when it changed to a semi-weekly, publishing on Monday and Wednesday, and the name became The Newton-Conover Observer.

Following his graduation from the University of North Carolina in 1948, Cyril Long Mebane joined his father as co-publisher of The Observer. In 1953, the strong semi-weekly began tri-weekly publication, adding Friday as a publication date.

After the death of Mann in 1946, his portion of The News-Enterprise reverted to his widow, Mrs. Ione Mebane Mann, another daughter of the senior Mebane. The two women continued to operate the weekly, which had publication dates of Mondays and Thursdays, as co-publishers.

In 1952, Robert H. Morrison of Hickory purchased The News-Enterprise, and, in 1953, began publication five days a week, Mondays through Fridays.

Hickory's second newspaper, The Temperance Echo, was to appear in 1876. The Echo had an interrupted career of five years and finally quit the game. Hugh M. Blair was owner.

Hickory's initial newspaper, The Carolina Eagle, as previously mentioned, was to have its name changed to The Piedmont Press when J. B. Hussey and J. F. Murrill purchased it in 1874.

Murrill was an ardent prohibitionist. Tomlinson was not so ardent. Their editorial policies disagreed at every turn, and a split became necessary. Murrill, for a time at least, withdrew from the field of journalism. Tomlinson associated with him his brother, W. T. Tomlinson, and the two kept the enterprise off the rocks for a number of years.

J. S. Tomlinson, the elder brother, branched out into other fields as well as newspaper publisher and editor. He became agent for the old Richmond and Danville Railroad (now the Southern). He also embarked in the manufacture of "Sweet Sixteen" smoking tobacco, and at one time did a flourishing business in this line. Finding his hands too full, he sold his interest in The Press to D. H. Tuttle, a young lawyer. After a short time, Tuttle withdrew from the business and entered the Methodist ministry in the North Carolina Conference.

In 1885, J. S. Tomlinson secured a position with the Treasury Department at Washington. He held this position for several years, when he resigned and went into the job printing business in that city, which he conducted until the time of his death in the mid-1930s.

W. F. Tomlinson left Hickory during the same year as his brother. He located in Asheville and for a time published a magazine, Our Country Homes. This venture was not a success, and he secured a position in the Department of Agriculture at Washington, which position he held until his death in the mid-1920s.

CATAWBA COUNTY 211

When the Tomlinsons left Hickory, The Press was sold to R. K. Bryan, who conducted the paper until forced to retire on account of approaching blindness.

Hartwell S. Blair at this time was publishing The Western Reporter at Franklin in Macon county. In 1878, he moved his plant to Hickory and changed the name of his paper to The Western Carolinian. In 1880, he sold The Carolinian to J. F. Murrill, who again entered journalism and associated with him his son, Hugh A. Murrill. Murrill, in 1887, again bought The Press and consolidated it with The Carolinian, changing the name to Press and Carolinian. Blair, after selling to Murrill, moved to Lenoir, where he became editor of The Lenoir Topic for a few years, when he sold and moved to Oklahoma. He became a state senator in Oklahoma, but after a few years he returned to North Carolina. He died in Alexander county in 1935. Murrill continued the editorship of The Press and Carolinian until his death, December 6, 1891.

In 1884, meanwhile, J. F. Click moved from Davie county to Burke county near Penelope, a few miles west of Hickory, where he operated a farm. In 1891, he moved to Hickory and established The Hickory Mercury, in association with W. L. Clay and Connelly Payne. Clay and Payne withdrew from the business a few months later, leaving Click sole owner until The Mercury was consolidated with The Times, forming The Times-Mercury.

The Times was established in 1896 by J. R. Whichard. Whichard did not make a pronounced success of his venture, and withdrew after consolidating The Times with The Mercury. Click became editor of The Times-Mercury. Following the turn of the century, Click was to establish a short-lived newspaper, The Nut Shell.

About 1888, H. H. Crowson established Hickory's first daily newspaper, The Cricket. He later also founded The Clipper. But these two infants died soon after birth. One old-time editor lamented their passing thus: "The forewinds chanted the funeral litany of time before the first volume was completed."

In 1893, Hugh A. Murrill sold The Press and Carolinian to Col. M. E. Thornton, who in turn sold it in 1896 to A. Y. Sigmon, who changed the name to The Hickory Press, and converted it into a Republican paper. William Hale, Jr., was employed to edit the paper for a short time. Sigmon later leased the paper to J. F. Miller, who himself served as editor.

Hale was an accomplished French scholar, and was appointed U. S. consul at Lourdes, France, during President McKinley's administration. After about three years, he returned to Hickory and remained about a year, when he left for New Jersey.

In 1903, Sigmon sold The Press to J. O. Foy, when it again went Democratic. Foy, after wrestling with it for two years, gave it up and sold to The Hickory Democrat.

The Democrat was established by W. C. Dowd, owner and editor, at that time, of The Charlotte Evening News. W. E. Holbrook was employed as manager, and in the beginning the paper was printed in Charlotte by The Evening News. After a time, however, a press and other equipment were bought, and the paper was printed in Hickory. The arrangement between Dowd and Holbrook wound up in a lawsuit to determine the owner. Dowd won, and sold The Democrat to Howard A. Banks, who was a genuine newspaperman and a scholarly gentleman, but not a business man. He was for a time associate editor of The Charlotte Observer. He also edited The Sunday School Times of Philadelphia, and did some work on The Philadelphia Record.

At a later date, he had the courage and audacity to undertake the publication of a Democratic weekly in Harrisburg, Pa. He was private secretary to Josephus Daniels when Daniels was Secretary of the Navy in President Wilson's administration.

In 1912, E. V. Morton bought The Democrat and guided its destinies until 1916 when it was bought with its goodwill by the Clay Printing company, and put to sleep. The Clay Printing company at that time owned The Hickory Daily Record. Morton moved to Oklahoma.

J. F. Miller bought The Times-Mercury in 1912 or 1913, and converted it into a Republican paper, running it a year or two, when he sold it to J. O. Berkeley, a Westerner. C. P. Moore became its editor for a short time.

Soon afterwards The Times-Mercury was bought by F. S. Slate, who continued its publication a few years, when it was sold to a certain Mullen of Lincolnton. It was bought next by R. S. Pickens, who after a short time moved it to Statesville, and its publication soon discontinued.

In the fall of 1915, S. H. Farabee came to Hickory, and with a few local business men, bought additional stock in the then-existing Clay Printing company, which was operated by J. Carl Miller. The publication of The Daily Record was then begun, with Farabee as editor. The publication of The Daily Record was continued by the Clay Printing company until the late 1920s, when the paper was divorced from the job printing plant and bought by the present management, headed by L. C. Gifford, with a few other stockholders.

From the first, The Daily Record has been able to speak for itself, and is now one of the leading papers in Western North Carolina.

Maiden's second newspaper was The News (the second by this name), which was begun in 1923 by Dr. J. E. Hodges. It suspended publication in 1938. Still another small newspaper was established in Maiden after this date, but it was shortlived.

CHAPTER X

CONTRIBUTION TO THE WAR OF 1812

Catawban's assistance with the Second War with England was, actually, to renew a dispute with a people who once were a mutual foe of both the Americans and the Britons: The Indians.

Men of the Catawba area, which then was a part of Lincoln county, formed two companies of the North Carolina regiment that helped suppress the Creek Indian nation in Alabama, then part of the Mississippi Territory. The Indians, whose lands were being gobbled in the American continental development, were sympathetic with the British, and were harassing settlers.

Nonetheless, six companies were drawn at the outset of the war in Lincoln county, which also included the present county of Gaston at the time, as a reserve force for the United States in the general war. But these companies were never armed or drilled, and their members saw no military service.

The War of 1812 was promoted, from the American side, by a great surge of nationalism which resulted from the successes of the Revolution.

The struggle between England and France had resumed in 1803 and its repercussions formed countless insults to neutral commerce. The various decrees and orders of the rivals subjected to capture practically all the vessels trading with Europe.

Moreover, England insisted on the impressment of seamen and on the right of search; the Non-Importation act, the Embargo act and the Non-Intercourse act failed of results and negotiations with England were fruitless.

In consequence, a war party sprang up in the United States, and Congress declared war on June 18, 1812. Five days later, the Orders in Council, one of the most objectionable features of the British policy, were withdrawn. Had the Atlantic cable been in existence at the time, there likely would have been no war.

Having contended with France for years, Great Britain was prepared for war. The United States, however, failing to appreciate the dangers attending a new Republic, had exceedingly small military and naval forces. Besides, the country was not united, and the government was weak.

North Carolina's principal part in the conflict was on the water, through the heroic exploits of such men as Johnston, Blakeley and Otway Burns. The United States government, in 1812, called on the state for 7,000 troops, to be detached from the militia.

State authorities promptly detached these troops, organized them, and assigned officers. There were, however, no arms for these soldiers. The United States government had never deposited any of its standard arms in North Carolina.

With the exceptions of a regiment from Eastern North Carolina which was sent to Norfolk, Va., and a regiment from Western North Carolina which was dispatched to battle the Creeks, none of the troops was mustered into service or served a day.

Lincoln county, according to orders, in 1812, selected a number of companies, many of the members of which were of the Catawba territory. But none of the outfits as such were taken into the service of the United States Government.

The companies were numbered and commanded, as follows: Sixth Company detached from the First Lincoln Regiment, Captain Edward Boyd; Seventh Company detached from the First Lincoln Regiment, Captain Henry Rudisill; Eighth Company detached from the Second Lincoln Regiment, Captain George Hoffman; Lincoln county First Regiment, Captain James Finley; Lincoln county Second Regiment, Captain Daniel Hoke; and Seventh Company detached from the Tenth Brigade, Captain Henry Ramsour.

The Creek war was incited by Tecumseh, a Shawnee Indian chief, an ally of Great Britain, to halt encroachment on Creek lands by American settlers. On August 30, 1813, the Creeks broke into the stockade at Fort Mims, and scalped most of the inmates. The governor of Tennessee authorized an emergency force of 25,000 men, led by General Andrew Jackson, to be sent against the Indians.

North Carolina and South Carolina were each called upon by the federal government, then, for a regiment to be made into a brigade to join the Jackson troops. The North Carolina regiment was made up of two companies each from Iredell, Mecklenburg, Lincoln and Rowan counties, and one each from Randolph, Surry and Wilkes counties. This was known as the Seventh Regiment of North Carolina Militia in the Service of the United States. Major Joseph Graham of Lincoln county, Revolution war hero, was commissioned brigadier general to command the outfit.

The War Department lists members of the two Lincoln county companies who fought in the Creek encounter, as the soldiers from Lincoln county who served in the War of 1812. According to the company muster rolls, Captains Lee Edwin Gingles and John McLane were commanders.

The muster rolls follow:

Captain Lee Edwin Gingles, 1st Lt. Robert Torance, 2nd Lt. Robert Oats, 3rd Lt. Robert H. Ramsey, and Ensign John Hill.

Sergeants—Thomas Hannon, Ezekiel Abernethy, Robert Huggins, John Rankin, and John Brom.

Corporals—Robert Simpson, Jacob Conor, Robert McLough, James Martin, John Vicker, and Samuel Gladen.

Musicians—William Low (fifer) and Isaiah Abernethy (drummer).

Privates—John Acer, Matthew Armstrong, Samuel Armstrong, Thomas Bandy, Robert Beel, Joseph Burk, William Brown, Henry Barkley, John Ballard, John Bays, Benjamin Bard, Archibald Cathey, Joseph Center, Robert Crage, Peter Crytes, David Clyne, Henry Clippard, Elisha Cale, Solomon Clyne, John Crage, James Clark, Abner Camp, John Campbell, Samuel Carson, John Clubb, William Carrel, Alexander Ervin, Jacob Eddleman, Henry Eddleman, Peter Evans, Samuel Edging, Benjamin Edward, George Fisher, William Falls, George Ferguson, Benjamin Fisher, William Fullbright, Isaac Fleming, Martin Grisham, Daniel Henderson, William Hawkins, Matthew Holland, Henry Holland, Thomas C. Henry, Michael Hafner, George Hager, John Hager, Lazarus Hinson, William Hull, John Hafner, John Hoyle, William Huatt, Thomas Kenedy, George Little, Thomas Long, John Leek, Nicholas Lowrance, James Lindsey, John Long, Anthony Moose, Daniel

CATAWBA COUNTY 217

Morrison, Alexander Moore, John Masters, James McGinnis, Gordon Mays, William Neel, Alexander Nail, William Oliver, George Oliver, Elias Plott, John Price, John Rudisill, Isaac Robinson, Thomas Robins, Abraham Sides, William Stephenson, Levi Sides, Michael Sides, Freeman Shelton, Meacan Shelton, William Sifford, John Sifford, Caleb Sifford, Frederic Summy, Jacob Setsor, Jacob Thorn, Daniel Tucker, John Tucker, John Thompson, Paten Vaughn, Jonathan Vandike, Jonathan West, Daniel Walls, William Walker, Jr., William Walker, Jr., John Wilson, Robert Wilson, Silas Wilson, Conrad Yoder, and Adolf Yoder.

Captain John McLane, 1st Lt. John Kerr, 2nd Lt. Alexander Robinson, 3rd Lt. Alexander Brown, and Ensign John Fast.

Sergeants—John H. Crow, Cyrus Henderson, John R. Campbell, John Haun, and Zachariah Walker.

Corporals—Edward Buckner, Jacob Freece, George Sifford, David Masters, James Daulton, and Jacob Cruse.

Musicians—Edward Burgis and Francis Newel.

Privates—Benjamin Aguor, Jesse Arwood, Peter Bain, John Beaugas, Simmons Bradley, William Broyhill, Daniel Bool, Charles Campbell, Isaac Cummons, Jacob Casper, Jesse Cheatwood, Layton Carter, Robert Callihan, Jacob Call, Thomas Calton, John Deer, John W. Davis, William Davis, Henry Ellor, Soloman Ellis, John Fast, Edward Farrington, Thomas Francis, James Guffey, William Glascock, Elijah Hampton, Jacob Hoot, James Haywood, John Huit, Joseph Holbert, John Jarret, James Jackson, Solomon Jacobs, Thomas Johnston, Charles Kiker, George Lewis, Henry Landon, John Layton, Jacob Lierley, John Lewis, Lively Lewis, Thomas Land, William McConnald, Charles Main, James McCroskey, James Martin, John McDaniel, James Mathis, Peter Mowny, Samuel McCurday, Eli Newel, John Nixon, Arther Pippin, Ezekiel Peirce, John Poster, James Panacks, Michael Propts, Robert Porter, Henry Phifer, Robert L. Porter, William Robinson, Joseph Sain, David Sutberry, Benjamin Sims, Colby Sutton, Daniel Shufford, Isaac Storier, Solomon Sparks, Jacob Stough, James Thomson, John Twitty, William Twitty, Benjamin Williams, Daniel Whitner, Ezekiel Waldrook, Nicholas Walter, Samuel Williams, and Thomas Williams.

Following a series of forced marches, General Jackson's troops met a large body of Creeks in the battle of Tohopeka, or Horseshoe Bend, on March 27, 1814, and killed more than 2,000 warriors. In the treaty at Fort Jackson, August 8, 1814, Jackson forced the Indians to cede to the United States approximately 20,000,000 acres, something over half of the old Creek country.

General Jackson continued from this skirmish on to the famous battle of New Orleans, the final major encounter of the war. Jackson's striking services as a soldier and military leader were finally to gain for him the honored position of President of the United States.

CHAPTER XI

FORMATION

"We shall split the lightning rods upon the Lincoln county courthouse!"

This proclamation was repeated by Nathaniel Wilson, fiery proponent of the plan to divide Lincoln county, until he was chosen by popular vote to do so.

Wilson was elected to the House of Commons of the state legislature from Lincoln county in 1842. In December of that year, he introduced a bill entitled "An act to lay off and establish a new County, Catawba."

Catawba county was created when the lower house approved the measure by a vote of 64 to 46, and the upper house approved it on December 12, 1842.

A man of natural ability and courage, Wilson believed the size of the Lincoln area worked a hardship on the people who were located along its borders.

His first speech in favor of a division of Lincoln is believed to have been made upon a log at a point near St. Paul's church. He proclaimed to the settlers the hardships of being forced to pay tribute to a local government from which they were too far removed to feel the good effect.

"Why should we find it necessary to make a long and weary journey in order to reach the seat of justice?" he argued with conviction.

The people listened intently, and caught a glimpse of the vision of the man who was making a bid to the state legislature and using the division question as a leading issue.

With his trusted colleague, John Yount, Wilson "stumped" the hills and vales with the proposition of a northern county cut from Lincoln. Long and fiercely the campaign waged between him and his opponents.

A native of the area which now is Maiden, Wilson was a son of Joshua, Sr., and Rebecca Wilson, who came from Ireland. In 1784, Joshua bought land in the forks of Clarks creek, and

Maiden creek, north of the present town of Maiden. Nathaniel was born in 1801.

The most prominent opponent of the "equal division of Lincoln county" was John Killian. Born in 1796, Killian was a son of Jacob and Rebecca Cresamore Killian of the Salem Lutheran and German Reformed church community in Lincoln county. He was a great-grandson of the pioneer Andreas Killian who received his land grant and settled in what is now Lincoln county in 1749. His son, Jesse, was sheriff of Catawba county from 1902 to 1906.

Killian and Wilson, both public spirited citizens, knew a Lincoln county which was one of the wealthiest and most populous of the state. But, the period was one featuring the division of large counties into small ones.

Lincoln county in 1840 embraced what is now Catawba, Cleveland, Gaston and Lincoln counties—being about 40 miles wide and 55 miles long. Cleveland county was formed in 1841, from Lincoln and Rutherford counties. This gave impetus to further division of Lincoln county.

Killian was an experienced politician, had a large family connection, and strong backing against the division of the county. Wilson was a resourceful speaker, possessing plenty of Irish wit, and a political campaigner who had no superior in the county.

Killian had been elected to the General Assembly in 1838. He sought re-election.

Numerous factors, however, favored Wilson in his bid for office. In addition to being a period when division of large counties was popular, the time was one which witnessed an area, county, state and nation flexing their muscles. The matter of freedom—in any degree—was considered serious to the extent that folks resented even the suggestion of encroachment upon private rights. The tax agent actually was suspected.

Areas of interest—religious, social, commercial and governmental—developed in the northern section of the Lincoln area. Community businesses and trades flourished and obtained their outlets within a few miles of their operations. Peace officers in the various settlements considered the distance to Lincolnton courthouse a deterrent to the expediency of justice. They felt that their law offenders were tried too far away from their crimes and by persons often entirely unsympathetic with pertinent circumstances. Neighborhoods met socially and talked of local happenings, thus directing attention to a relatively small area.

In short, the relationship of people of the northern section of Lincoln county with their southern neighbors was based on the occasional trip to the county seat city and the periodic militia musters. Hindered by the difficulty of poor transportation facilities and the infrequency of musters, this relationship was not sufficiently strong to prevent the rising of a movement for county division.

One of the most famous of muster grounds in the area which was to become Catawba county was located on the property of Matthias Barringer, Jr., son of the Indian massacre victim, located about two miles southeast of the present city of Newton. Here was held not only the semi-annual company musters but also the district muster, when all the companies of the county met for a two- or three-day drill, and for entertainment.

(Additional muster grounds of the Catawba area, from the period following the Revolution to the War Between the States, included one at Wilfongs mill near Startown, one near Terrell or Rehobeth church, one near the home of Barnett Sigmon on Clarks creek, one near Wesley Chapel campground or Propst Crossroads, and one near "Gentleman" John Perkins or Lookout Shoals (Island Ford).

In addition to the fact that Barringer's muster grounds was a focal point of much early Catawba county history, it is significant for being the site of the most powerful speech made favoring the establishment of the county. The musters presented opportunity for politicians to contact their constituents. Their speeches made on these occasions were the most important of their campaigns.

A description of the Barringer Muster of 1842 is described by Judge Matthew Locke McCorkle, one of Catawba county's most respected attorneys, in an address he made at the dedication of the monument which stands on the southeast corner of the court square in Newton as a memorial to the senior Barringer and others who were massacred by Cherokee Indians. The address was delivered on July 2, 1897. It preceded the unveiling of the monument by Mrs. E. H. Curtis of Newton and Mrs. Dessie Cline Merritt of Wilmington, great-great-granddaughters of the senior Barringer.

"Had I the ready pen of Shakespeare or Milton or the descriptive powers of Scott, Thompson or Cowper, I could a tale unfold that would harrow up your souls, make your blood curdle in its veins, or run you wild with delight at the courage and heroism of our ancestors, who once defended and won the soil that we now inhabit," Judge McCorkle explained. "There is scarcely an acre of land, in all Catawba, that does not contain incidents worthy to be handed down to the latest times. . . .

"The broken arrow-heads, the deadly tomahawks, everywhere to be found, give evidence that we are continually walking over great battle fields, but of all the places that could be of interest to you, none can be greater than the history of Barringer's muster ground. . . . When Adam Sherrill, the first white man, . . . crossed the great Catawba river at Sherrills Ford, . . . all west of this stream was inhabited by the Catawba Indians. Their territory extended up and down the river to near the top of the Blue Ridge. On the other side was inhabited by the wild and savage Cherokee Indians. They frequently made raids on the Catawbans and whites, even up to the time of the Revolutionary War. This country was settled up very rapidly by immigrants from other countries, mostly from Pennsylvania and Maryland, from 1751 to 1776. The militia muster was handed down to our fathers from England, and was continued up to the late Civil War. It was necessary to have a fighting force, enrolled and drilled in the art of arms. One hundred men from the time of the Romans constituted a company and the commander was called a centurion or captain. Ten companies made a battalion, and this battalion was commanded by a colonel and was sometimes reviewed by a general.

"As far back as the oldest inhabitants can recollect, there was a battalion muster at Matthias Barringer's. He was the son of the patriot Matthias. . . . Matthias, Jr., lived in his father's old homestead, which is now standing, and is now occupied and owned by John Carpenter, Esq.

"After the death of his father, young Matthias inherited a vast area of land from him. He was the oldest son, and entitled, according to English law, to all the landed estate. He was kind enough to sell to his brother-in-law, John Setzer, who married his sister, Catherine, west of his homestead about two hundred acres of land. John Setzer probably is the ancestor of all the Setzers in this country and first settled where Mr. Charles Bolick now lives and there raised a large family of children and died at a ripe old age. . . .

"Matthias Barringer, Jr., married Susanna Haas and they had several children. . . . All these were of strong and vigorous intellects. . . . (They) stood fair wherever known. . . . Matthias Barringer was a well-to-do farmer and a man of strong mind and integrity. . . .

"Barringer's Muster Ground was a place where the people of the territory, now Catawba, and the surrounding country met on the last Thursday, Friday and Saturday of May for Battalion Muster, and for social please and amusement. Saturday was the great day for the battalion drill. It was the great day for the vast multitude of over five thousand people, to assemble and prepare for war, to hear and discuss the topics of the day, and for all kinds of athletic games, wrestling, jumping and leaping, foot racing, horse racing, and music and dancing.

"It was 'On with the Dance! Let joy be unconfined' from early morning until late at night. The dancing was held in the upper story of the Barringer mansion where there was a room of over twenty feet square. It was a great day for the old and young. The Olympian games at Athens or the Isthian games at Corinth which the great Apostle of the Gentiles witnessed, and from which he drew such a beautiful figure of the Christian race, could not have been of more interest to the people of Athens and Corinth than this great social gathering at Barringer's Muster Ground. Every kind of refreshment could be had. Every kind of wine, every kind of beer, choice brandy, apple and peach, and old whiskey that would not kill, but make alive, and yet you would not see an intoxicated man, a young one, no never. All kinds of cakes from the pound to the savory gingerbread, and chicken pies in abundance, could be had.

"Mrs. Barringer had her table set and filled from Friday morning until late Saturday night. . . . It was loaded with every thing that would tempt and satisfy the most fastidious appetites. The choicest young beef, the fattest chickens and turkeys, sometimes fresh venison from the forest with elegant bread and biscuit and choice vegetables with delicious coffee, graced the table. The bake-oven was kept hot and turned out warm ginger cakes, biscuit and pies from early morning till dewey eve. The price of dinner was an old Mexican quarter. Husbands and wives with their children would buy lunch from the wagons and young men would take their sweethearts and surround the festive board or in their carriages, gigs, or wagons, and 'eat drink and be merry' for Barringer's holiday comes but once a year. There were from thirty to forty wagons, all along in a row from which you could buy every refreshment, and everything to please the appetite. The people came there for amusement, and amusement they must have. It is absolutely necessary, for the enjoyment of life, for people to have some kind of amusement.

"This fast crowd was composed of the best men and women in the land. They were dressed in their best attire. They came in their carriages, gigs, wagons, or horseback as best they could. It was no mean, stinted crowd. Many were rich, nearly all well-to-do. You could see more fine looking men, handsome women and lovely girls than in any other crowd of the same size in Catawba county. . . . More fine blooded horses, well-fed wagon or carriage animals could be found there than any where else in the South. . . .

"It was a grand sight to see one thousand men drawn up in line of battle, armed and equipped as the law directs. It was the business of the Adjutant of the Regiment to organize the battalion.

"Each company had about one hundred men. It requires ten companies to form a full battalion. The companies are named after the first ten letters of the alphabet. The whole battalion was subdivided into twos and platoons. The ensign or color bearer, is placed about the middle of the battalion. The music at the head. When the battalion is formed by the adjutant, a courier is dispatched to the General or Colonel and his staff, informing him of the organization of the regiment.

"He and his staff are situated at headquarters, and upon receiving the information, gallop forward towards the regiment

Ink Well

Brass Locked Book

Locked Bible

Daguerrotype

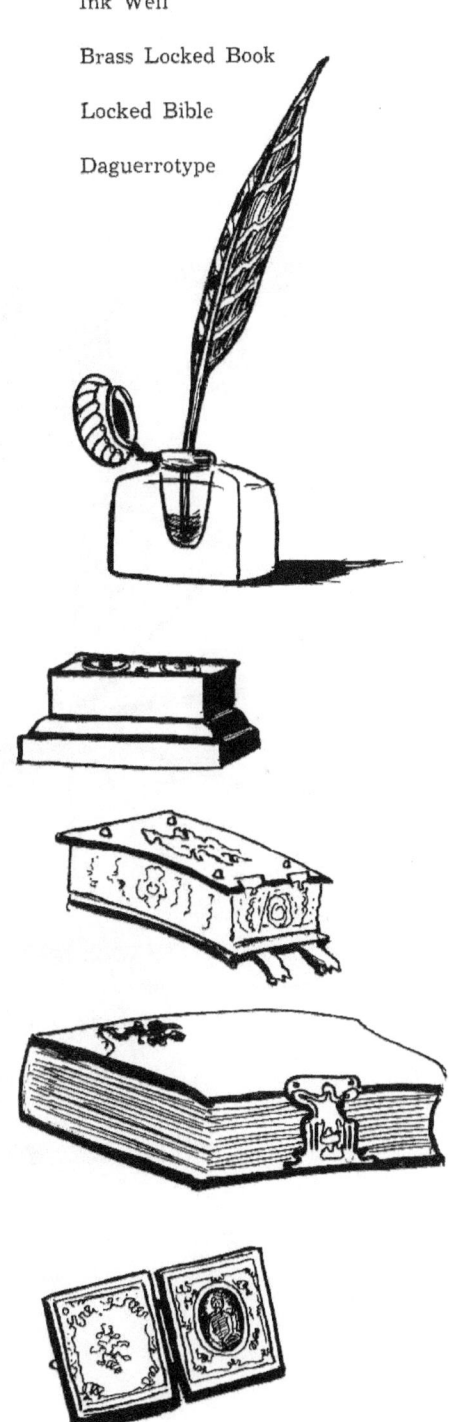

Bettylamps

Tin Lamp

Coffee Grinder

Bed Warmer

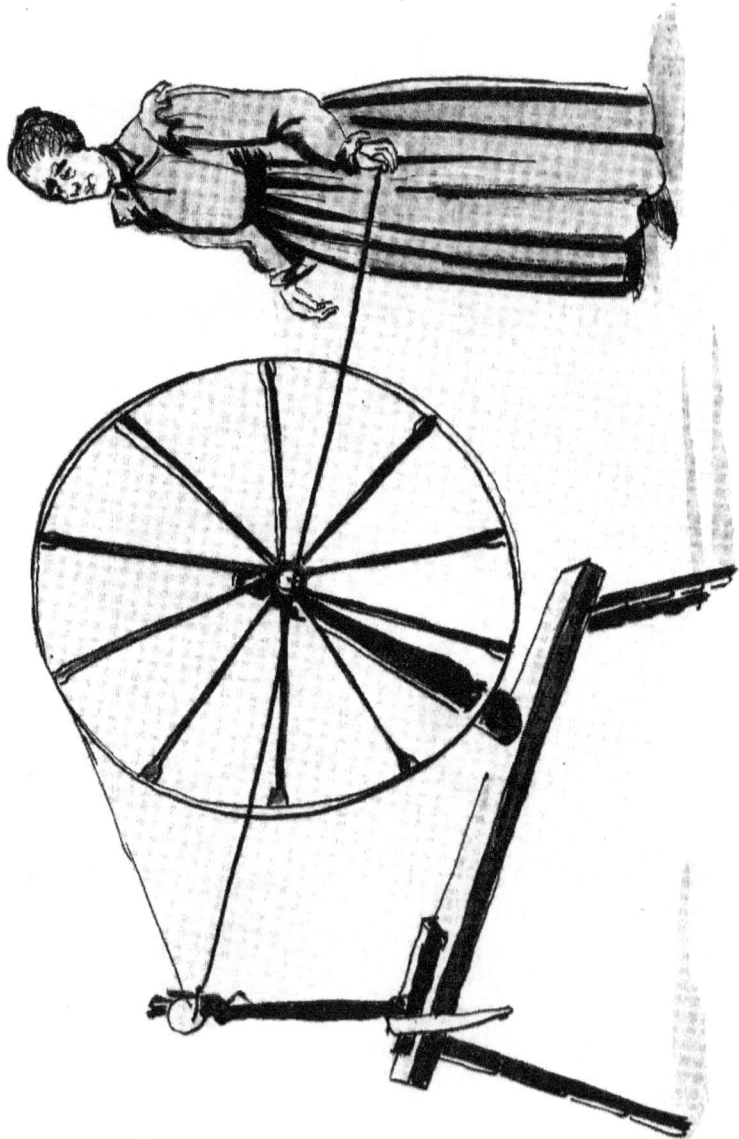

Spinning Cotton Thread

and the Colonel stops about midway of the battalion. As soon as he stops, the whole battalion presents arms. The Colonel then says, 'Attention Battalion! Shoulder Arms! Right Face! Forward March!' Then is heard the ear-piercing fife and heart-stirring drums which arouses every person who hears the sound thereof. Colonel Peter Hoke was the commanding officer of the battalion for many years. He was the son of Squire Frederic Hoke, who built the old rock barn on the Hoke place. Colonel Peter was a gallant, dashing officer. He took great pride in his command. His father was from Pennsylvania, and was Justice of the Peace for a long time. He always tried a case upon its merits. He was the brother of Daniel and John Hoke of Lincolnton and the uncle of Mike Hoke and great-uncle of Hoke Smith, late Secretary of the Interior Department of the U. S.

"After going through a number of evolutions, the battalion drill was ended, and disbanded. After taking refreshments, then all are ready to hear their candidates deliver their addresses under the wide-spreading oaks close by. . . ."

The issue of separation of Lincoln and Catawba counties was of great interest to the assemblage at Barringers. The two candidates for the State Senate were Honorable Thomas Ward and Dr. Archibald Ray. Ward opposed division, and Ray favored it.

Candidates for Commons who favored division were Wilson, Yount, Richard Rankin and James White. Those opposed were Killian, Henry Cansler and two others.

A debate concerning the paramont issue was promoted at the memorable 1842 muster.

History substantiates that Wilson—who was about six feet tall, sharp featured, sandy haired, and spare made—addressed the aggregation with a plea similar to this:

"The county ought to be divided, because it is too large. It is nearly fifty-six miles square and some persons in the extreme part have to go nearly forty miles to get to the courthouse. Many have to go thirty miles. This is too great a tax on people in the extremes to travel so far.

"We hardly ever see a newspaper or hear a judge's charge or lawyer's speech or learn anything about the way that business is done in court. We are literally denied the benefits of the courts of justice. We are compelled to do jury duty and attend as witnesses and take our letters of administration and prove our neighbors' wills.

"We need another county seat. Around this town, made more local, an enlightened and intelligent citizenry will spring up. Witnesses or jurors can go home at night from the courts, and this would be a great saving of expenses to them and a favor to their families.

"Lincolnton has become rich by extortion and high charges. Its people buy property cheap and sell goods dear. If this were all, it would not be so objectionable; but the town is proud, haughty and wicked. The people make sport if you take your eggs and chickens and truck to market. They laugh at your manners, and make fun of your clothing, because you don't dress as fine as they. (Wilson's argument may have been based on a slight personal prejudice, according to writings by Fred A. Olds in the "North Carolina Orphan's Friend," publication of the Masons. In an article "Why Lincolnton Split Wide Open," Olds points out: "To tell the truth Lincolnton and one of its daughters, Catawba, have a very funny history. A man named Nathaniel Wilson, but always called 'Thanny,' lived in what is now Catawba and was a candidate for the legislature from Lincoln. He wore a shirt of home-made linen, with a very large collar, and the Lincolnton boys, some no doubt egged on by their fathers, who were 'agin Thanny,' made a great deal of fun of him when he visited the county-town and shouted that he had on his shirt the wrong way and the collar was really the tail. . . .) They hold caucuses and nominate all candidates for office. They hardly ever nominate a man from our country. They don't give us a fair chance. They make us hewers of wood and drawers of water.

"The town is rotten and corrupt. Its sins are grievous and intolerable, and the town ought to be destroyed.

"I hope to see the day when the grass will grow up in the middle of the street. But if there can be found fifty righteous men in the town, it will not be destroyed, or if forty-five can be found, if forty, or thirty, or if twenty can be found, if ten, it shall not be destroyed. But ten cannot be found!

"It is weighed in the balance and found wanting. The division line must run through the middle of the street. It must be destroyed!"

"Wilson's speech was greeted by wild cheers.

Ward then arose. His address, according to reliable data, was in essence this:

"There are a great many good people in the town of Lincolnton. They are an industrious and plain people. A great many are mechanics and work for a living.

"The town is the greatest manufacturing place in the state. It started the first cotton mill in North Carolina, and its citizens have made their money by economy and industry. We have a large number of prosperous churches in the town, and we have done a great deal for education.

"We have produced some of the greatest men in the State. Daniel Forney got a large part of his education in the Town of Lincolnton. So did Senator William A. Graham. So did that wonderfully bright man Thomas Dews, and also that able man, Pinkney Henderson and that young giant in intellect, Mike Hoke, and that great orator William Lander, and a host of others.

"It would be hard on many people if the town were destroyed. There are women and children that have invested all they have in town property. It is a slander on the people of the town to say they made sport of the country people. If a few bad boys insult some persons, it is wrong to hold the whole town responsible for it.

"Lincolnton people are as friendly, as moral and as religious as any people in the State. We have a large number of churches and church-going people.

"If the people of Mr. Wilson's country do not attend the political meetings, it is their own fault. I have always been treated very kindly by the Lincolnton people and those surrounding the town. I have been elected several times, to the office of sheriff and the legislature. I believe I am going to be elected over my opponent, Dr. Ray, the division candidate.

"No man as bitter and sarcastic and as prejudiced as Mr. Wilson ought to be elected to any office. He has an oily tongue and a wily head and the poison of asps is upon his lips. Don't elect him, for he is a dangerous man. No man can vote for him and his monstrous proposition but the shrubbery and undergrowths."

History records that "Mr. Ward received but few cheers and sat down much discouraged."

The political meeting predicted correctly the fall's elections. Wilson went to Raleigh.

In an exuberant mood, he is supposed to have told his fellow members of the legislature that he had already engaged a famous blacksmith of the day "to split the lightning rods upon the Lincoln county courthouse"—as an effort to keep his pledge of equal division of the county.

The boundaries of the new county were named by statute on December 12, 1842, as follows: " . . . beginning at a point on the Catawba River, and running west, so as to pass within one mile and a half north of Lincolnton, to the Cleaveland County line, and thence with the dividing line between Cleaveland and Lincoln to the Burke line; thence with the line dividing Burke and Lincoln to the Catawba River; and thence with the meanderings of said river to the beginning—be, and the same is hereby erected into a new and separate County by the name of Catawba. . . ."

The first session of the county court was held on March 13, 1843, at the home of Matthias Barringer, Jr. Officers of the county were due to be elected.

Frederick Hoke was appointed chairman of the court and he immediately called upon the magistrates of the new county to produce their commissions from the governor. This they did, and were sworn in as magistrates of the county. Those composing the first circuit of magistrates were Ambrose Lutz, George J. Wilkie, Phillip Burns, Joseph Fisher, Timothy Moser, William Abernethy, Joseph Lorance, Nathaniel Wilson, Thomas I. Hamilton, Eli P. Shuford, Eli Deal, Jackson Whitener, and Franklin Reinhardt.

The election of the officers resulted in the choice of Andrew H. Shuford as sheriff; E. P. Coulter as register of deeds; Joseph A. Reinhardt as clerk; Joseph Wilson as trustee; Joshua Wilson as surveyor; William Shipp as solicitor; Eli E. Shuford as processioner to survey land boundaries; William L. Mehaffey as coroner; Henry Cline as entry taker for lands; Electious Conner as standard keeper; and Jonas Bost, chairman, George P. Shuford, Joshua Wilson, Henry Cline, and John Williams, as members of the select court.

Appointments were as follows: Absalom Warlick, Gilbert P. Rowe, James W. Lowe, and Ephraim Ballard, as constables; Joshua Stamey, John Link, and Isaac Lowe, as deputy sheriffs; and George P. Shuford, John Yount and Jacob Helderman, as rangers to look after strayed stock.

Others generally credited with participation in the county's organization meeting include Fredrick Hoke, Jesse Gaunt, Archibald Ray, Electious Conner, William Harmon, Ephraim Yount, Jonas Bost, John Killian, Absolam Brown, Peter Warlick, Peter Stamey, Henry Cline, John Yount, George P. Shuford, Major Hull, Thomas Ward, Alexander Ward, Nathaniel Edward, John P. Shuford, Joshua Wilson, Jacob Helderman, Wesley Monday, William Long, Lyman Woodford and Thomas Hampton.

On January 14, 1843, a supplemental act to the creation law of Catawba county was ratified by the General Assembly.

It is as follows:

"That the said Commissioners shall have the power to purchase and receive by donation, for the use of the County of Catawba, a tract of land not less than 50 A—upon which a town shall be laid off which shall be called and known by the name of Newton, where the courthouse and jail shall be erected.

"That Joshua Wilson, Isaac Holland, and Eli Shuford be appointed Commissioners to run the lines between Lincoln and Catawba."

The commissioners were authorized to select property within two miles of the county's geographic center. Numerous stories have been handed down to posterity about premeditated discrepancies in calculations. A controversy developed, and the General Assembly ultimately, in 1845, passed an act that approved the site on which Newton was by then developing.

In 1846, Gaston county was formed from the lower part of Lincoln county. The legislative act authorizing division pointed out the new county thus: ". . . Beginning at a point on the Cleveland line, six miles due south of the present dividing line of Lincoln and Catawba; thence running parallel with line to the Catawba river. . . ."

This act would have left Lincoln only six miles wide, but in the same measure the dividing line between Lincoln and Catawba was moved four miles north; that is, five and one-half miles north of Lincolnton. This left Lincoln county about ten miles wide.

John Coulter (an ex-sheriff of Lincoln county, and the second superintendent of public schools of Catawba county), Alexander Lowe of Lincoln county, and Joshua Wilson, Eli Shuford, and George Wilkie, all of Catawba county, were appointed commissioners to survey and mark this last division line between Lincoln and Catawba.

It is interesting to note that the division of Lincoln and Catawba counties was through Killian's farm, but placed his dwelling in the new county. Actually no feeling existed against Killian because of his opposition to forming the county. But he never offered himself again as a candidate for a public office.

Wilson was elected to the General Assembly in 1844 and 1846. In 1852, he again was a candidate for the legislature. But he was killed on July 13 by a son-in-law named Wilson England, who cut him in the bowels. The tragedy resulted from a disagreement concerning family affairs.

After the county division, Lincoln, Cleveland and Catawba counties voted together for legislators until after 1852, as old Lincoln had four representatives in the House of Commons. Wilson's death occurred on the eve of the election. J. A. Caldwell was elected as the fourth representative, along with William Lander, John H. Wheeler and Henderson Sherrill.

John Killian and Nathaniel Wilson were patriotic citizens. Killian, the candidate defeated because he opposed the further division of Lincoln, did not "sulk in his tent," and, Wilson, the victor, did not gloat over his opponent. Both were present at the Barringer house in March, 1843, and both took part in the organization of the new county of Catawba.

Killian and Wilson were members of the same church—Thessalonica Baptist church in Jacobs Fork township.

Killian died in 1884 and was buried at Salem Lutheran and Reformed church. Wilson was buried in Haas' graveyard which was begun by the burial of Patriot Isaac Wise.

After Catawbans had achieved their "independence," they naturally were confronted with the matter of governing themselves.

While the average sturdy, self-reliant citizen plowed his fields and attended to his family duties, there was in evidence a weaker neighbor who crept at night to corncribs of others and committed deeds of dishonesty.

The weak neighbor deserved regulation, and his upright fellow citizens rightfully did administer it.

The first court was composed of magistrates noted more for their honesty and sound common sense then legal acumen. A grand jury was selected to take cognizance of crime. Efficient officers set about their tasks. A courthouse was built.

Interesting early court records include the following:

"March 15, 1843.

"Ordered by the Court, John Yount, Geo. A. Ikerd & John Wilfong, are appointed Commissioners to build a temporary building for holding the Court at the County seat of Catawba by the second Monday in June next 1843.

"Ordered by the Court that Joshua Wilson be allowed $2.00 per day for 12-½ days, and that the chain bearers be allowed $1.00 per day, Matthew McCaslin 3-½ days, John Campbell 3 days and Joshua Wilson $1.00 for expenses and John Campbell 50c for expenses expenses surveying and chain bearing in finding center and that the County Trustee pay the same.

"That E. R. Shuford be allowed $2.00 per day for fifteen days and the chain bearers $1.00 per day, and E. R. Shuford 25c per day for expenses.

"June Session 1843.

"Ordered by the Court that the County Trustee of Catawba County pay the said William R. Hass $133.20 for building the temporary Court House in the town of Newton. It was seconded by the following Commissioners: John Yount, Geo. A. Ikerd and John Wilfong.

"Ordered that Paul Kistler be paid $29.30 for Solomon Hedrick being in jail in Lincolnton.

"On motion Catherine Travenstrett appointed Gdn. for Norah, Joseph, William, and Lida Travenstrett, minor children and orphans of Daniel Travenstrett. Conrad Winebarger and Daniel Travenstrett bondsmen.

"June Session 1844.

"A majority of the Justices of the County being present, ordered by the Court that B. C. Allen, Joseph Wilson, Thomas Cloninger & Lawson Lowrance each be allowed one dollar and fifty cents per day for fourteen days service in locating the Court House for the County of Catawba & that Eli Starr receive one dollar & fifty cents per day for four days service in clerking the sale of the lots for the town of Newton & that Wm. MeHaffy receive one dollar & fifty cents per day for four days service for crying the lots in the town of Newton.

"Superior Court of Law Fall Term 1843. (First in the history of Catawba.)

"Be it remembered that at a Superior Court of Law opened and held for the County of Catawba at the Court House in Newton on the 8th Monday after the 4th Monday in August and the 67th year of the Independence of the U. S. in the year of our Lord, it being the 27th of October A. D. 1843, present and presiding the Hon. Thomas Settle, one of the Judges of the Superior of Law and Equity for said State. The usual proclamation being made, Court was opened and the following Grand Jury drawn, sworn and charged, to wit:

"1. Daniel Coonrod, 2. George Huffman, 3. Henry Moser, 4. George Gilbert, 5. James Wilfong, 6. Henry Bolick, 7. John Mauney, 8. Miles Abernathy, 9. Buckner Brown, 10. Martin Linebarger, 11. Reuben Hoyle, 12. Daniel Rader, 13. Daniel Sumrow, 14. Paul Cline, 15. Joseph Huit, 16. David Hawn, 17. Moses Fry, 18. Conrad Minges.

"Traverse Jury:

"1. Henry Shook, 2. Moses Huit, 3. Philip Whitener, 4. Jonathan Carpenter, 5. David Wike, 6. Andrew Killian, 7.

CATAWBA COUNTY 233

John Boyd, 8. Peter Rouk, 9. George P. Shuford, 10. Aaron Link, 11. William McCaslin, 12. Martin Sigmon, 13. Philip Burns, 14. Alexander McCorkle, 15. John Heffner, 16. Joseph Fisher, 17. Dan'l B. Whitener, 18. Lawson E. Reinhardt, 19. Drury Hamilton, 20. Wesley W. Monday, 21. Thos. E. Mehaffy.

"Isaac B. Wycoff was duly elected Clerk of the Superior Court of Catawba county; came into Court gave his bond and was duly qualified according to law. William A. D. Wycoff was appointed deputy Clerk, and qualified accordingly.

"H. C. Hamilton was appointed Clerk and Master in Equity for the County of Catawba, and the oath of office was duly administered.

"June Session 1844

"The same Court being present proceeded to elect a County Trustee. When the vote was taken it appeared that Joseph Wilson received the largest number of votes and was declared duly elected, who gave bond in the sum of $5,000.00 with Joseph A. Reinhardt & Matthew Wilson as securities and was duly qualified.

"Ordered by the Court that the County Trustee pay to David Setzer the sum of $29.00 for building the jail.

"Jonas Bost was duly elected Treasury of Public Buildings."

Honorable William H. Battle presided at the spring, 1844, court; Honorable Mathias E. Manly presided at the fall, 1844, court, and I. W. Lowe was foreman of the jury; Honorable John L. Baily presided at the spring, 1845, court, and John J. Shuford was foreman of the jury; Honorable Richmond Pearson presided at the fall, 1845, court, and Jonas Bost was foreman of the jury; Honorable David L. Caldwell presided at the spring, 1846, court, and Absolom Brown was foreman of the jury; Honorable Thomas M. Dick presided at the fall, 1846, court; and Judge Settle returned to preside at the spring, 1847, court.

The county's first courthouse, a wood structure, was built in 1843 for $133.20.

It was in 1846 that a second courthouse was built at Newton, which was to remain until 1924. The structure cost $6,000. A writer for The Press and Carolinian in 1890 called the building "substantial." He records:

"We point with pride to our last recent change which gives us the most commodious and handsome edifice of its kind in all this section of the State, containing comfortable apartments for judge, juries and the bar, and ample provision for every suitor and witness whose attendance may be required." (The courthouse was remodeled in 1889. The project cost $3,000.)

New wings were added to the same structure in 1905.

In 1924, the present sandstone, impressively regal courthouse was constructed as a tribute to an industrial and prideful people.

Once moved from the Barringer property, the courthouse was to occupy the same now-famous "courthouse square" in downtown Newton. Its spacious grounds were landscaped ingenuiously.

The population of Catawba county, as shown by the United States Census of 1850, the first after the formation of the county, was 7,293 "Free people," including eight colored males and 13 colored females; and 1,569 slaves. There were 1,257 families and 1,237 dwellings listed.

The population of the county was 10,729 in 1860; 10,984 in 1870 (9,281 white and 1,703 colored) and 14,946 in 1890 (12,472 colored).

Following 1846, no change by state statute altered the course of the Catawba county government until 1865, when the Federal government required a county government reorganization.

CHAPTER XII

GOVERNMENTAL, JUDICIAL AND POLITICAL DEVELOPMENT

The tempo of the evolution of Catawba's governmental, judicial and political systems, insofar as the state and nation did not determine, was in keeping with the conservative German and Scotch natures of the citizenry: Slow and reasoned, but binding in effect.

The Catawban appreciated the American right of allowing those to design a government who would be the governed. Such an attitude determined that the county would have clean and just control.

Prior to the Revolution, the county remained the primary unit of local government. The townships were not yet created. There were military districts, voting precincts and school districts, but none of these had much governmental significance.

The area's civil authority came from the county court, which was composed of justices of the peace. A justice of the peace held a position of influence and dignity. Not only was he important as a local magistrate, but, when acting together with his brother j.p.'s, he constituted the county court.

The county court had both judicial and administrative duties. Its members had the prestige and power of a county commissioner and county judge combined. At least, this could be said of the chairman, who was chosen usually on the basis of seniority.

In his book, *County Government and Administration in North Carolina*, Paul Woodford Wager describes the powers and duties of the county court thus: "When sitting as a county court the justices not only exercised judicial functions, but performed the services now performed by the board of county commissioners, and, in addition, certain duties which grew out of the conditions of the time. . . . (They were) authorized to levy and assess annually between the first of May and the first of November such tax on the taxable persons of the county as should be sufficient to defray the 'contingent charges' of the county. It is to be noted that the tax was assessed on polls and not on property. A law of 1715 defines taxable persons as all males (not slaves) above 16 years of age and all slaves, male and female, above 12 years of age. It is to be noted, too, that there was no limitation on the amount of taxes that might be levied, and no statute which defined the term 'contingent charges.' Of course, as a matter of record, we know that the services of government were very limited and the volume of taxes comparatively small. Other administrative powers included the laying out and construction of roads and bridges, and the operation or control of ferries; the construction of public buildings, mainly jails and courthouses; the licensing of ordinaries (eating houses) and fixing the rates on the foods and beverages to be served; the determining of the location of mills; the regulation of weights and measures; the protection of slaves and indentured servants; the granting of letters of administration; the oversight of orphans and orphans' estates; the proving of headrights; the granting of marriage licenses; the processioning of land (it was the custom to establish the ownership and mark the boundaries of each tract of land every three years); the recording of deeds, mortgages, and other instruments; the establishing and providing for the protection of munition magazines; the determining of the boundaries of governmental areas; the acting as trustee of public endowments; and various other minor powers. The county court also enjoyed large powers of appointment. It appointed the sheriff, the constables, the overseers of the roads, searchers, patrolmen, and inspectors, and sometimes town commissioners. In fact, the court and the register of deeds."

Overseers of roads were charged with the responsibility of "highway" building and sometimes maintenance; searchers were those employed to assist in the finding of strayed animals, and even humans; inspectors generally concerned themselves with matters of community health, particularly as pertained to food in ordinaries and taverns; and the patrolmen were the forerunners of the present-day Highway Patrol, but they laid perhaps more stress on the capture of law-breakers who committed their deeds at places other than public thoroughfares. One of the duties of the patrolmen was to visit the Negro houses in their respective districts, as often as was deemed necessary, and inflict a punishment, not exceeding 15 lashes, on all slaves found off their owner's plantation without a proper permit.

CATAWBA COUNTY

The constable was an important officer, inasmuch as he was the ministerial officer of the justices' court. He often also was the neighborhood police officer.

The j.p.'s generally met at the beginning of the year to design the current Court of Pleas and Quarter Sessions. They appointed a chairman and then designated five members to hold the court for the year. The justices were commissioned by the governor on the recommendation of the General Assembly to hold office during good behavior. Among the criminal jurisdictions of the Court of Pleas and Quarter Sessions were all petit larcenies, assaults and batteries, trespasses and breaches of the peace, and all other crimes and misdemeanors, the punishment of which did not extend to life, limb, or member.

Following the formation of the county in 1842 and up to that period when the War Between the States began, there seems not to have been any particular significant acts done or performed in the county other than those that would commonly follow the development of anything young and just setting out on its course.

Politically, the county was strictly in the Southern Democratic column, having already begun its ascendancy to the position of banner North Carolina Democratic county, which goal it was to attain in the 1880s. Adding popularity to this political philosophy was the rising liberalism that generally manifested itself in northern states and was subscribed to by persons of the Whig Federal and abolitionist creeds. The Republican party, due to its leniency with members who sympathized with the abolition movement, had few followers locally.

Apparently, interest was aroused by national affairs throughout the county in the late 1850s and in 1860, and some persons were predicting war. Secession Democrats, among which Catawbans formed a number, were especially violent.

When counties went to their polling places in the Presidential election of 1860, they had four candidates from which to choose: Whig John Belle of Tennessee, Union Democrat Stephen A. Douglas of Illinois, Secession Democrat John Breckenridge of Kentucky, and Republican Abraham Lincoln of Illinois.

Legend has it that one Catawban exclaimed: "Let war come, we can whip them before breakfast." An editor of a newspaper, later recalling the episode, added: "But the supper bell rang, and they were not whipped yet."

That Catawba county fully was allied to the Confederate cause long before the actual outbreak of hostilities is evidenced by a portion of an address by Honorable Henry W. Connor, who resided for many years in Catawba county and who represented the "old Charlotte District" in Congress for 20 years, from 1821 to 1841. Connor, who had served on the staff of General Joseph Graham in the Creek War of 1812, was an old-time Southern gentleman, possessed of broad culture, pleasing manners and considerable wealth, and was one of the leading citizens of the state.

The slavery question, as seen by a Southern Democrat, clearly is set forth in the following observations of Connor:

"Abolitionism, when I last addressed you (the present address was in the latter 1830s), seemed to be comparatively confined to a few fanatics only, and so absurd seemed to be their views and pretentions, that serious apprehensions could not reasonably have been entertained; but such has been their rapid growth in a short time, that in several of the States they hold the balance of power in politics, and abolitionism has therefore become a political question with the avowed object of striking at the rights and property of the South; and there is reason for believing that they will not be particular as to the mode of getting at their object, whether peacefully or by wading through the blood of man, woman, or child.

"The tables of abolition members, especially Adams', and Slades', are loaded, and thousands and thousands of these petitions, signed by men and women, and children, have been presented within the last two years, asking of Congress to interfere with your rights and your property. This heartless and unjustifiable interference must and will be met at the proper time by the South, by the manly determination to protect and defend at all hazards their rights, that is characteristic of, and known to belong to her.

"In Congress, all that can be done has been done, by the resolutions declaring, 'that every petition, resolution, proposition, or paper, touching or relating in any way, or to any extent whatever, to slavery, as aforesaid, or the abolition thereof, without any other action thereon, be laid upon the table, without being debated, printed or referred.'

"This is strong and decisive of the feelings of a majority in Congress: Though I would myself have preferred that they should not be received at all; but the scruples of many in regard to the right of petition have prevented the passage of such resolutions. The above is the last clause of the last series of resolutions, known as the Atherton resolutions, and the vote on which is considered a test vote; and on this vote the parties of the North exhibit their true colors, the Federalist, and the Abolitionist, side by side, voting against their resolution, and consequently in favor of abolition; while the Democrats of the North, with very few exceptions, are found side by side with us of the South, sustaining us.

"I feel satisfied, if the designs of the abolitionists, equally dangerous to your rights and property, as to the existence of the Government itself, are crushed, we of the South must look to the Republicans of the North to aid and support us in it. The Whig or Federal party there is against us; they are united with the abolitionists, and without them cannot succeed. In the late struggle in Pennsylvania, the abolition candidate was supported by the Whig Federal party and the abolitionist party, as also in the Congressional elections. In Ohio the Legislature before the last had a majority of Whigs and abolitionists. They passed resolutions in favor of abolition. In the last Legislature the scene was changed, a majority of Republicans were returned. They have passed resolutions against abolitionism, and interference with rights guaranteed by the Constitution.

"In the great State of New York, the union of the Whigs and the abolitionists have succeeded in prostrating the Democracy of the State, and obtaining the ascendancy in their House of Assembly; and one of their early acts has been the passage of resolutions condemning the Atherton resolutions in Congress, and therefore, in favor of and sustaining the abolitionists. That union will give in the next Congress an additional number of abolitionists on the floor of Congress with the Lieutenant Governor an avowed abolitionist, and who was within a very few votes, in the convention, of being nominated for the executive chair of the State. And that victory, ominous as it seemed of evil to the South, was hailed with joy and satisfaction by every Whig and Federal newspaper in North Carolina, so far as I had an opportunity of seeing them, and perhaps of that stamp throughout the South.

"But why look and complain in relation to this matter altogether at the North? With pain we have seen a distant and small speck in the horizon, and near home. If the newspapers of the day are to be relied upon, petitions on the subject of abolition, and having for their object interference of your rights and property, were offered in the Senate of your own State, at its last session, by a leading member of the Whig party. Comment is unnecessary. I will pursue this painful subject no further. 'Sufficient for the day is the evil thereof.' " (Paragraphing added.)

But the War Between the States came, and its agonizing course brought defeat to the South.

As a conquered people, Catawbans were due to be subjected to major governmental and judicial, if not political, changes. Less than three months following Lee's surrender, new county officers were named for Catawba, as is evidenced in the following official record:

"State of North Carolina, Catawba county, July 31, A. D., 1865—By authority of his Excellency Governor, W. W. Holden (North Carolina's first reconstruction governor) through the agency of James E. Ellis, Chief Justice in and for the said county of Catawba, the following persons were appointed who met at the courthouse in Newton, and after taking the amnesty oath and oath of office to the United States, to wit—Miles Goodson, V. M. Ramseur, D. F. Moose, Jesse Holdon, David Barringer, Westley Bandy, J. M. Rocket, Daniel Lutz, Samuel Blackburn, Logan Abernathy, Alfred Robinson, Noah Hilterbrand, John Keistler, Eli Coulter, Eli Starr, Daniel Whisnhant, Joel Miller, John Peterson, Thomas Little, J. C. Clapp, D. McD. Yount, P. L. Yount, Noah Hawn, Moses B. Whitener, John Allan, G. J. Wilkie, H. H. Hoyle, G. M. Yoder, Phillip Burns, Moses Abernathy, Jackson Whitener, Nath Hoyle, J. H. Shuford, Alfred Ramsaur, J. D. Caldwell, Phillip Pitts, Logan Wilson, Hiram Hefner, Henry Hallman, E. Yount, James E. Ellis, E. O. Elliot, M. M. Smith, Eusebius Hetrick, W. H. Rocket, F. Smith, E. Conner, James H. Setzer, Alex Frazier, G. D. L. Yount, R. B. Houston, John Hewit, O. Lee, Jonas

Early Fireplace and Utensils

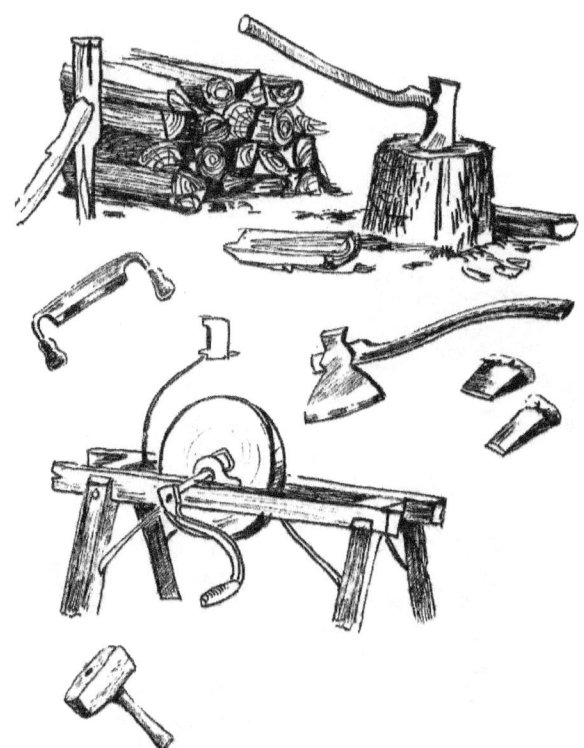

Woodpile and Utensils

Ash Hopper

Moody, A. J. Caldwell, Reubin Setzer, Levi Plonk, Jasper Wilson, Manuel Robinson, J. J. Mott, Franklin Caldwell, and M. C. Abernathy. After being duly organized, proceeded to organize the said county of Catawba by entering the following officers to wit: J. B. Little, sheriff, P. F. Smith, county court clerk, G. A. Ikerd, county trustee, R. Englin, county surveyor, Drury Hamelton, county processioner and M. Robinson, treasurer of public buildings, and John Miller, coroner.

"Special court, G. J. Wilkie, chairman, G. M. Yoder, J. C. Clapp, J. D. Caldwell and E. Connor, whereupon in August, 1865, it being the 7 day and met according to adjournment the court elect specially. Present where upon (record virtually illegible) the officers elected was duly qualified and bonds filed to wit: J. B. Little, sheriff, P. F. Smith, clerk, G. A. Ikerd, trustee, R. Englin, county surveyor, Drury Hamelton, processioner, M. Robinson, treasurer of public buildings.

"Enrolling Board—

"Bandys—V. M. Ramsaur, L. B. Abernathy, A. L. Ramsaur.

"Abernathys and H. Tavern (Hickory Tavern)—A. J. Whitener, J. H. Shuford, E. Yount.

"Springs and Yount—L. N. Wilson, H. Hefner, D. McD. Yount.

Newton and Bridges—M. Robinson, Jasper Wilson and P. I. Pitts.

"Gabriels and Caldwells—J. D. Caldwell, J. J. Mott, Miles Goodson."

The enrolling board members duly qualified citizens as voters.

Members of the local government picked immediately following the war, however, were only to serve until 1868, when a new plan was to be set up by state constitution.

Known as the Township and County Commissioner plan, it provided for a board of five county commissioners to be elected at large by the voters of the county. To this body was delegated all the administrative powers and duties which had belonged to the county court. For instance, the commissioners were given control over the finances of the county, public buildings, roads, schools, bridges and taxes. The voters of the county were authorized to elect the following officers: Treasurer, surveyor, register of deeds, clerk of superior court, sheriff, and coroner.

The new constitution also provided for the creation of townships, which were made bodies corporate for purposes of local government. They were administered by a board of trustees composed of a clerk and two justices of the peace, elected by popular vote in the township. Other township officials included a school committee of three, and a constable. Townships containing cities or towns might elect more than two justices.

The new government setup passed the administration of county affairs from justices of the peace, reducing their positions to those of petty magistrates with only a few administrative duties in connection with the townships, to a board of commissioners; created townships as separate administrative units; made county and township officers elective by popular vote; and transferred the judicial powers of the old county court to the justices of the peace, the superior court and the clerk of the superior court.

There arose at the war's close, and particularly in connection with the new government, due to the people's tendency to suspect its designers, a submerged, semi-political organization known as the Ku Klux Klan. This was an agency prompted by the white Southerner's desire to keep his race supreme in governmental, economic and social leadership; the desire to revenge himself upon his regulators; and the innate desire of one defeated to seek an object to which he may lay blame for his displeasure.

It is known that Catawba county had an active and feared KKK, but little concerning its activities have been handed down to later generations in writing.

Of primary interest and significance is the fact that its membership embodied the county's leading citizenry. The esprit de corps was fostered, it is supposed, by nature's undeniable law of self-preservation.

A feature story in The Hickory Daily Record, published in 1936, gives some insight as to sympathy for the hooded order. It is as follows:

CATAWBA COUNTY 243

"Following the War Between the States, a number of prominent early residents of this section were tried and indicted in United States court at Statesville for being members of the Ku Klux Klan, behooded order charged with attacks on negroes and carpet-baggers during the Reconstruction days.

"Many of the men indicted on these charges received unfair treatment at the hands of federal authorities, however, according to an editorial in The Carolina Eagle of October 31, 1872, which was edited by John B. Hussey. . . .

"The editorial is concerned with the Ku Klux cases on trial that year in federal court at Statesville, with Judge Dick on the bench. Disapproving of the practices of the authorities in regard to the trial of the men charged with participation in Klan activities, the editorial stated that there were 'fifty men within the paper's knowledge indicted who were anxious for a trial and against whom the government had no evidence. Some were dragged from court to court for two years and persistently denied a trial.'

"The early Hickory paper also charged that Judge Dick had adjourned the court to allow Judge Settle, General Barringer and General Bob Douglass an opportunity to intimidate the alleged Klansmen. Pardon and protection by the federal government were promised to the men who would confess and expose their leaders.

"As understood by the men indicted, they were offered the proposition of having the prosecutions pending against them dismissed upon the condition they would vote for Grant. The paper added that speeches of Settle and Barringer simply made more votes for Greeley, that 'several who were doubtful were won over to faithful devotion to Greeley.'

" 'As far as the Catawba men were concerned,' the editorial continued, 'the corrupt propositions were indignantly scorned.'

"A notice in The Eagle was signed by H. C. Cowles, clerk of U. S. court, and was to the effect that $500 bond had to be given for appearance of the indicted at the next term of court, which was to convene on the third Monday in April, 1873."

However evil its effects in principle, the Ku Klux Klan's earliest existence was a saviour to the South. It repaid in part injustices of ill-supervised Northern military administrations. Its underground course oftentimes ferreted to the South's stagnated surface the will to resume purposeful and respectful living.

But as avidly as it was heralded in its inception by Catawbans, its present evil development is detested by the citizenry today.

One may trace the beginnings of Catawba county's government by commissioners, and the development of its township lines, by reading early county records. Among them are the following:

On August 7, 1868: Drury Hamilton was sworn in as chairman of the commission by Anderson Mitchell, judge of Superior court.

On August 10 of the same year: A. G. Copening and M. M. Huit qualified as commissioners and were administered the oath of office by the chairman. At the same time, D. B. Gaither, register of deeds, Miles O. Sherrill, county Superior court clerk, G. A. Ikerd, county treasurer, F. L. Herman, coroner, and Julius F. Cline, county surveyor, also qualified. A. L. Shuford and Joshua Little, commissioners-elect, failed to qualify. They were notified to attend on September 7 "next" and qualify.

August 21 of the same year: "Board of County Commissioners met according to adjournment for the transaction of business. Drury Hamilton, A. G. Copening and M. M. Huit present. . . . Ordered by the Board of County Commissioners that the jurors be drawn to serve at the next Superior court to be held at the Court House in Newton, Catawba county, the first Monday in September next, vis: G. W. Wilkerson, Alsolom Miller, John A. Bumgarner, Milton Jarrett, J. (or I.) M. Drum, Daniel Arnt, G. W. Cansler, Solomon Havner, Marcus M. Rowe, Marion Starr, Sam Blackburn, J. M. (or W.) Bradburn, Sidney Fish, George S. Little, H. S. Settlemire, Fred Smith, J. A. Hamblet, Davidson Cline, Thomas Gilliland, Andrew Yount, L. H. Yount, J. R. Cloninger, C. A. Hunsucker, C. A. Wilfong, Langdon Hoffman, D. F. Moose, Ruben Hoyle, G. W. Jones, Joseph Saunders, E. P. Coulter, D. D. McGee, John H. Powell, R. P. Reinhardt, Noah Yount, Henry Harman, Sr. . . ."

CATAWBA COUNTY 245

September 8 of the same year: ". . . Ordered that the jurors be paid $1.00 per day and five cents per mile for one trip to and from home. Jailor to receive 40c a day for prisoners and 30c key fees. Jonas Cline qualified as Sheriff. . . ."

September 9 of the same year: ". . . Ordered by the Board of County Commissioners office of two County Commissioners be declared vacant, viz: A. L. Shuford and J. B. Little and that the Governor be notified of the vacancy. . . ."

(It is presumed that these two men refused the "reconstruction" offices.)

October 5 of the same year: ". . . The Board of County Commissioners met according to adjournment. Drury Hamilton, M. M. Huit and A. G. Copening present. . . . Ordered by the Board that Registrars and Judges of election be appointed. . . . Newton Precinct—James A. Garvin, Reg., Ruben Setzer, Daniel Rowe, Marcus M. Rowe, William L. Mehaffee, George Setzer and Levi Plunk; Hickory Station—J. J. Sigmon, Reg., G. W. Turner, Peter L. Rowe, John Ward, Henry Link, Daniel Hawn and Moses Barger; Springs Box—Daniel A. Little, Reg., Joseph H. Moore, Elias Hefner, Hiram Hefner, Thomas Cloninger, Joshua B. Little and Jacob Little; Yount's Box—G. McD. Yount, Reg., Daniel Roseman, Frederick Smith, George S. Little, W. G. James, David Hunsucker and Davault Hunsucker; Bridge's Box—Isaac Pearson, Reg., J. S. Bridges, G. W. Caster, Andrew Yount, Alfred Bridges, T. J. Hamilton and Elcana M. Lowrance; Gabriel's Box—Franklin Caldwell, Reg., A. J. Caldwell, Mitchell Wilderson, J. W. Gabriel, Elisha Sherrill, Thomas Beatte and Isaac E. Paine; Caldwell's Box—J. D. Caldwell, Reg., Thomas Wilkerson, Miles Goodson, William Caldwell, Jr., David Drum, Philip Drum and J. Monroe Drum; Loare's (Lore's) Box—V. M. Ramsour, Reg., D. C. Shuford, Daniel Loare, A. L. Yoder, Jacob Jarret, David Loare and G. M. Yoder; Bandy's Box—J. W. Bandy, Reg., Daniel Wyant, F. M. Hull, Franklin Hudson, John Rhoney, William Rhoney and Emanuel Speagle; Abernethy's Box—A. J. Whitener, Reg., Peter Warlick, Jacob Mosteller, Absolom Fratets (?), Miles Abernethy, Jacob H. Shuford and Albert Abernethy. . . ."

October 14 of the same year: ". . . Magistrates appointed and qualified by the County Commissioners: Daniel Whisenhunt, T. J. Pitts, W. H. Lowrance, Manuel Robinson, Drury

Hamilton and Noah Barringer. . . . J. J. (Probably Jacob J.) Sigman appeared, presented his appointment by the Governor as County Commissioner and took the oath prescribed by law. . . . John D. Caldwell appeared, presented his appointment by the Governor as County Commissioner and took the oath prescribed by law. . . ."

November 14 of the same year: ". . . Resolved by the Board of County Commissioners that they commence laying off the county into townships on Monday 22nd November Inst. and that they meet at Auston Corneniu's house on the Catawba River at 12 o'clock M. . . ."

November 30 of the same year: "Ordered by unanimous vote of the Board of County Commissioners that the townships be surveyed whenever necessary and that Drury Hamilton be employed to do the surveying and make the maps, etc. . . ."

December 16 of the same year: ". . . Levi F. Yoder appointed Standard Keeper. . . . The Commissioners having completed laying off the county into townships, eight in number, gave them the following names—Mountain Creek, Caldwells, Hamilton, Jacobs Fork, Clines, Bandy's, Newton and Hickory Tavern. . . . Drury Hamilton, surveyor, made a map of each Township which are filed in this office. The County Commissioners then made their report to the legislature. . . ."

(The townships were named as follows: Mountain Creek, for the stream; Caldwells, for the Caldwell family; Hamilton, for the Hamilton family; Jacobs Fork, for the river; Clines, for the Cline family; Bandys, for the Bandy family; Newton, for the municipality; and Hickory Tavern, for the municipality.)

September 5, 1870: Organization of the second board of county commissioners, for two years' tenure: ". . . Henry Wilfong, Daniel Deal, Andrew Fry, G. M. Wilfong and P. W. Whitener met in the Court House, took the oath of office administered by M. O. Sherrill, Clerk of the Superior Court. . . ." County officials qualifying were J. M. Brown, register of deeds, M. O. Sherrill, clerk of Superior court, J. J. Hicks, county surveyor, Jonas Cline, sheriff, and G. A. Ikerd, county treasurer. ". . . Ordered by the Board of County Commissioners that the line between Hickory Tavern Township and Clines

Township be so changed as to run as follows, viz.: Beginning where the line crosses Snow Creek and run with said creek to Joseph Killian's, thence between Peter Keller's Leah Lanier's to the river according to petition, also to change line between Clines Township and Newton Township to run as follows, viz.: Beginning at a white oak near F. Huffman spring and running with the meanders of Long Branch to the mouth of said branch, thence to the 17 mile post on the Island Ford road, leaving Daniel Little and George Little in Clines Township. . . ."

November 7 of the same year: ". . . F. L. Herman, coroner-elect, refusing to file his bond, the Board proceeded to appoint a coroner, Reuben Yoder being nominated. The vote was taken which resulted unanimously in his favor. . . ."

January 2, 1871: ". . . Two election precincts are ordered in Clines Township—'Springs' at White Sulphur Springs; 'Roseman's' at D. Roseman's. . . ."

February 6 of the same year: ". . . Ordered by the Board that the Sheriff grant J. L. Alexander and Patrick A. Abernethy license to retail spiritious liquors by the small at the Town of Hickory Tavern by paying $25.00 county tax for the year 1871. . . ."

On May 19, 1873, the Commission ordered, on petition, an election for Thursday, September 2, 1873, on the question of county subscription of $100,000 to the Chester and Lenoir Narrow Guage Railroad on condition that the amount be expended within the limits of Catawba county. The sum was to be raised by issuing bonds bearing interest at eight percent for 20 years. However, under date of September 2, 1873, the election was postponed. On October 6, 1873, an election was called for the second Thursday in November, 1873, on the question of a subscription to the same railroad of $50,000. Nothing further is recorded relative to the election.

The Commissioners met at the Granite Shoals Cotton Factory (Claywell, Powell and company) on May 22, 1877, to examine the obstructions or dam in the Catawba river as required by the "Fish Act." The Board ordered a fish-way across the dam.

September 4, 1878: ". . . Jonas Cline Sheriff having failed to settle with the County Treasurer for county taxes for 1877, the Board proceeded to elect a tax collector. . . ." J. S. Bridges was elected.

Hickory Tavern township was changed to Hickory township probably in 1876. Catawba township was first recorded on April 7, 1879. It was recorded as Hamilton township on May 6, 1878, and on March 3, 1879.

(When Hickory Tavern's name was changed to Hickory, the township's name likewise was changed. Catawba township was named for the municipality of Catawba.)

Commission minutes of August 2, 1880, reveal a report on an aspect of welfare work—the caring for the poor. It listed 20 paupers in the "poor house," who each cost the county $3.25 per month; and 40 paupers "outside the poor house," who each cost the county $1.53 per month.

The commissioners granted on June 6, 1881, a change to the Newton-Caldwell township line so as to run with the Island Ford and Lincolnton road from Frank Carpenter's to the Lincoln county line.

On February 9, 1882, a county-wide election was held relative to whether stock laws would be placed in effect. A majority of 229 in the county opposed the action. However, a majority of 109 in Newton and Jacobs Fork townships favored the move. These townships demanded that the law be made effective in their areas. The Commission so ordered, and the expense incurred in fence building was $1,211.39. A 25c tax was put into effect in the two townships. Voters of other townships later adopted stock laws.

On November 6, 1882, the commission ". . . ordered that the passage through the court house be paved with good well broken brick and that George Setzer be requested to procure the brick and superintend the work and report to the Board at next meeting. . . ."

Due more to the fact that Northerners imposed it than because it was inefficient, Catawbans, along with other North Carolinians, were quick to reorganize local government when the so-called "Negro rule of the reconstruction era" was ended in 1875. A state constitution convention was called and, while the delegates did not draft a new constitution, they did add some significant amendments. Principally, they gave the General Assembly "full power by statute to modify, change or abrogate any and all of the provisions" of Article VII, which

CATAWBA COUNTY 249

deals with county and township government, with the exceptions of Sections Seven, Nine, and Thirteen. These sections limit the taxing and debt-making powers of municipal corporations. Actually, the citizens threw almost the entire question of local government into the hands of the General Assembly. Acting on its authority, and beginning in 1876, most important changes were made by the legislature, out of which has finally grown the present county governmental system.

The present plan of local government strips the township of all corporate powers. Elective officers include the sheriff, clerk of Superior court, coroner, register of deeds, surveyor, five commissioners and certain township officers. The county has a board of education with complete administrative control over rural schools. This board, which has five members, elects a county superintendent of schools. (Separate boards administer Newton-Conover and Hickory schools. These units receive their proportionate share of funds provided by the county and their programs are supplemented by local taxes.) Tax assessing is under the administration of a commission. An elections board exists to establish voting precincts, appoint election officers, and receive and canvass returns. A board of health assists in the administering of a cooperative district composed of Catawba, Lincoln and Alexander counties. A superintendent of welfare is provided. The county cooperates with the state in affording agricultural agents, home demonstration agents and a forester. The county also cooperates with the federal government in providing certain other agriculture programs. An attorney is appointed by the commissioners as their legal adviser and he bears the title of "county attorney." Catawba was the second North Carolina county to have a manager, who is elected by the commissioners.

After the adoption of the constitution in 1868 and consolidation of law and equity in the courts, the present-day superior court idea was developed and has continued.

Catawba is one of those counties noted for its judges. Almost continuously the county has had a representative on the superior court bench. Following the War Between the States, Judge C. A. Cilley was a member of the superior court bench. He has been followed by Judge Matthew Locke McCorkle, Judge W. B. Councill, Judge Edward Bost Cline, Judge Wilson Warlick and Judge J. C. Rudisill. Judge Warlick later was named federal judge of the Western North Carolina District.

The Democratic party flourished within the borders of Catawba until the 1890s. In 1892, on the wave of the rise of the Populist strength in North Carolina, many outstanding members of the Democratic party, because of the tragic circumstances of a depression, thought it better for them to become members of a political party which had advanced thoughts. The Populist platform called for rigid economy in government; encouragement of education, agriculture, and manufacturing; a six percent interest law, secret ballot, "purity" of elections, taxation of all railroads, and a ten-hour day in certain industries.

The strength of the Republican party became evident with the decline of the Populist movement locally. Numerous persons who aligned themselves with the Populist cause swung to the Republican ranks after the Populist party began to disintegrate.

In 1894, some offices were filled by the election of the Populist candidates, and in 1894 a combination of the Republicans and Populists was able to bring about the election of an entire county ticket.

In 1898, however, the Democratic party again began to regain its power, and during the next ten years had absolute and positive control of the affairs of the county.

One of the outstanding characteristics of Catawba county is that, without regard to what political party was in office, no scandal has ever attached to any office or any political party. Each member of the administration has undertaken to deal with the affairs of the county in a way that would reflect credit not only on the individual but the institution to which his office was a part.

As Catawba is famed for its judges, it likewise is known for a bar of superb caliber. It has often been said by the various judges who have rotated through Catawba county that the area's lawyers are of keen mind, possess sound legal acumen, and exhibit outstanding courtroom ability.

After the abolition of the "county court" of justices of the peace, Catawba's legal matters—with the exception of minor

CATAWBA COUNTY 251

cases which continued to fall within the jurisdiction of j.p.'s—were handled by the Superior court established by the constitution of 1868. In the beginning, this "high" court convened only once every six months. During the 1870s, however, it became evident that the number of local cases necessitated additional court terms. Whereupon, the sessions were gradually added. Today, the Superior court is in progress almost a third of each year.

The first inferior court of record was established in 1911 when an act permitting such was passed by the General Assembly. This again was the Catawba county court. A Hickory court was established at approximately the same time to have jurisdiction over Hickory township.

The two courts are known today as the Catawba County Recorder's court and the Hickory Municipal court.

Many cases have been tried in Catawba county which were outstanding and which, had the facts been developed in a metropolitan area, would have brought about a great volume of reporting. Included are the cases of State vs. Covington (1895), wherein Covington took the life of James Brown, owner and superintendent of the Long Island Cotton Mill; and State vs. Kale (1898), wherein Kale took the life of George Davis.

Covington was tried before Judge Timberlake at the spring, 1895, session, and was sentenced to death. On the conviction being confirmed, he was hanged in the jail yard in Newton by Sheriff T. L. Bandy.

Kale was tried before Judge Coble at the fall, 1898, term. The defendant escaped and fled to Cuba. His presence was made known to local authorities by a veteran of the Spanish-American war, who mentioned having seen the prisoner in Havana. The convict had, under an assumed name, joined the armed forces and was serving as an enlisted man in the army. On being returned he was tried, convicted, and, on the appeal being sustained, was likewise executed by hanging in the Newton jail yard. The execution was performed by J. W. Blackwelder, jailer.

Possibly the most outstanding political event in Catawba's history was the mammoth rally staged in Newton by five counties on July 4, 1900. Charles B. Aycock, then candidate for governor, was the principal speaker. Numerous persons paraded from the train depot down to the old Academy grounds, where Aycock spoke to an assemblage estimated to have contained thousands. Persons of today's generation remember the sight, and tell of the stupendous preparations made for the favored candidate, such as large banners which necessitated two men to carry. On one such banner, it is related, was painted a huge "A" and, to the right, a large plymouth rock rooster, indicating "A-Cock."

An unusual, or freak, aspect of the county's government in the 1880s was the election of four public officials who each had lost a limb, and a separate one, in the service of the Confederacy. It is said that a picture was made of the quartet—M. O. Sherrill, clerk of court, George W. Cochran, register of deeds, Sidney Yount, sheriff, and Henry Rudisill, treasurer—in such an arrangement as to make two "whole" men.

A list of persons who have held office in the Catawba county government, or have represented Catawbans in other governmental bodies, is as follows:

Processional Officer

Appointed or qualified

March 1843	Eli Shuford
January 1856	Thomas L. Lowe
July 31, 1865	Drury Hamilton, served until the abolition of the office by the 1868 constitution.

Court Clerks (of justices of the peace court)

Appointed or qualified

March 13, 1843	Joseph A. Reinhardt
October 5, 1845	George Setzer
October 1861	M. L. Cline
July 1865	P. F. Smith
February 1866	M. L. Cline (Served until office was abolished under 1868 constitution.)

CATAWBA COUNTY

County Solicitor (of justices of the peace court)

March 1843	William Shipp
January 1851	W. P. Bunum
October 1861	M. E. Lowrance

Standard Keeper

March 13, 1843	Electious Connor
October 1855	Ruffin Brown
January 1859	Logan Pope
February 1866	Alexander Summit
August 1868	Levi F. Yoder

Treasurer of Public Buildings

June 1844	Jonas Bost
January 1865	L. M. Rudisill
July 31, 1865 (Reorganization of county)	M. Robinson
February 1866	E. A. Warlick
January 1867	P. M. Hildebran (Served until organization of the County Board of Commissioners in 1868.)

Sheriff

March 13, 1843	Andrew H. Shuford
December 1843	Lawson Lowrance (Appointed on Tuesday, reported dead on Friday of same week.)
December 1843	Andrew H. Shuford (Resigned June session, 1848.)
June 1848	Jonas Cline
July 1860	J. E. Robinson
July 1863	Jonas Cline
July 31, 1865	J. B. Little (Reorganization of county)
January 1866	Jonas Cline
December 1878	S. L. Yount
December 1888	M. J. Rowe

December 1894	T. L. Bandy
December 1898	John W. Blackwelder
December 1902	Jesse W. Killian
December 1906	Daniel M. Boyd
December 1908	Julius S. Leonard
December 1910	R. Lee Huitt
December 1914	John A. Isenhower
December 1920	John W. Mauser, Jr.
December 1922	George F. Bost
December 1928	L. B. Beal
December 1930	Oscar D. Barrs
December 1938	Ray E. Pitts
December 1950	Austin E. Smith

Clerk of Superior Court

1843	Isaac B. Wyckeff
1847	M. L. McCorkle
1851	Henry Cline
1861	H. A. Forney
1866	David F. Moose
1868	Miles O. Sherrill
1883	P. A. Hoyle
1891	J. F. Herman
1895	John W. Rockett
1899	L. H. Phillips
1907	C. M. McCorkle
1915	J. T. Setzer
1923	J. C. Rudisill
1927	Russell M. Yount (Died while holding office.)

CATAWBA COUNTY 255

1933   Wade H. Lefler (Appointed December 1, 1933, to fill unexpired term of Russell M. Yount.)

Lloyd A. Mullinax, Jr. (Appointed January 3, 1944, upon the resignation of Wade H. Lefler.)

1945   Paul W. Deaton

Register of Deeds

Date	Name
January 13, 1843	E. P. Coulter
January 1851	F. L. Herman
April 1851	David F. Moose
February 1866	D. B. Gaither
November 1868	George W. Cochran
September 1870	J. M. Brown
December 1894	John F. Harwell
December 1896	J. F. Herman
December 1898	P. M. Dellinger
December 1902	J. H. McLelland
December 1906	Jacob E. Setzer
December 1910	E. D. Gamble
December 1914	H. Eugene Sigmon
December 1920	Klutz B. Clippard
December 1922	Mrs. Josephine A. Taylor
December 1924	J. Carroll Abernethy
December 1926	Ralph E. Smyre
December 1928	William S. Robinson (Drowned.)
	Aaron W. Penland (Appointed to fill vacancy created by death of William S. Robinson. Began duties September, 1930.)
December 1930	R. E. Carpenter
December 1934	Carlos W. Murray
December 1936	L. H. Phillips
December 1944	Mrs. Marguerite Trott

County Trustee

March 3, 1843	Joseph Wilson
July 1846	J. F. Ramsour
April 1849	M. M. Wilson
January 1856	George A. Ikerd

County Surveyor

March 13, 1843	Joshua Wilson
April 1846	E. R. Shuford
October 1851	Drury Hamilton
January 1855	Joshua Wilson
January 1859	Rufus England
July 31, 1865	Rufus England (Reorganization of county.)
February 1866	George C. McNeill (Resigned.)
October 8, 1866	Julius F. Cline (Appointed to fill vacancy created by resignation of George C. McNeill.)
September 5, 1870	J. J. Hicks
October 6, 1873	Drury Hamilton
November 18, 1876	T. L. Bandy
December 1884	M. J. Rowe
December 1886	Joseph S. Bandy
December 1888	J. F. Herman
December 1890	G. M. Yoder
December 1892	John Wesley Mauser
December 1896	C. R. Brady
December 1898	A. E. Witherspoon (Resigned)
July 3, 1899	J. F. Herman (Appointed to fill out unexpired term of A. E. Witherspoon.)
December 1900	J. F. Herman (Resigned)
November 6, 1905	Enloe M. Yoder (Appointed to fill out unexpired term of J. F. Herman.)
December 1906	Enloe M. Yoder

Old Mill

Cobbler

Blacksmith at Anvil

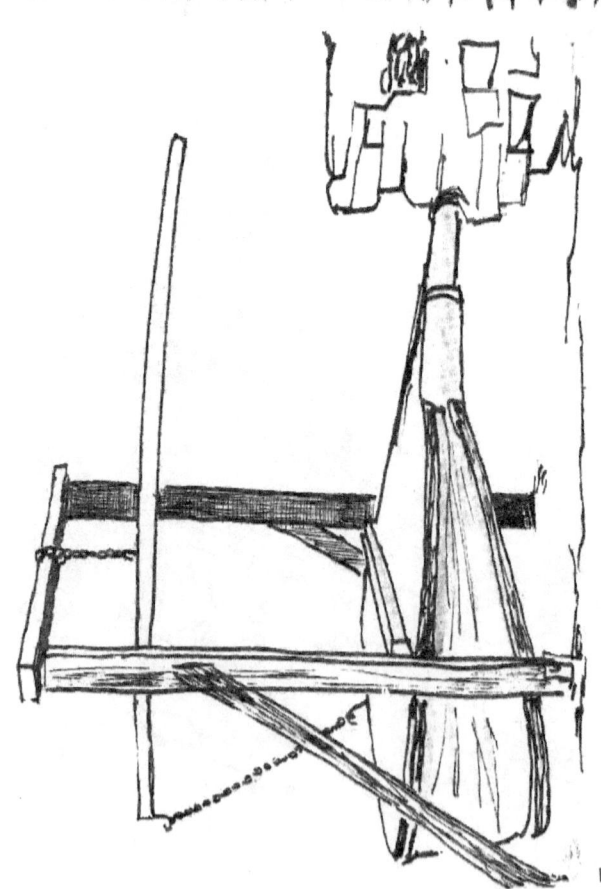

Bellows in Blacksmith Shop

CATAWBA COUNTY

December 1908	J. Alley Gabriel
December 1910	Enloe M. Yoder
December 1914	T. L. Bandy
December 1922	Enloe M. Yoder
December 1928	John F. Carpenter
December 1930	Hubert K. Setzer
December 1932	G. Sam Rowe
December 1938	Hubert K. Setzer
December 1940	G. Sam Rowe

Coroner

March 13, 1843	William L. Mehaffy
June 1845	Daniel Rhyne
April 1846	B. M. Cobb (Resigned)
June 1847	T. W. Bradburn
January 1855	C. M. Rhyne
January 1856	Eli Starr
April 1863	Jonas Cline (Resigned, appointed sheriff.)
July 1863	William Turner
July 31, 1865	John Miller (Reorganization of county.)
February 1866	George M. Yoder
January 1867	F. L. Herman (coroner-elect; refused to serve.)
November 7, 1870	Reuben Yoder
December 1878	John Arnt
December 1880	George W. Lowe
December 1882	D. P. Yount
December 1886	Miles T. Saunders
December 1892	George M. Yoder
December 1894	Q. M. Setzer
December 1898	G. E. Coulter
December 1904	James A. Rice

December 1908	J. S. Campbell
December 1910	Robert Lee Hoke
December 1914	J. Lee Harbinson
December 1916	J. Will Brown
December 1920	Jones W. Shuford
December 1922	S. L. Herman
December 1924	Jones W. Shuford
December 1926	L. S. Sherrill
December 1928	Jones W. Shuford
December 1930	R. L. Washburn
December 1938	B. R. McCreight
December 1942	J. W. Reynolds
December 1950	William E. (Jack) Bass

County Treasurer, and variations

July 31, 1868	George A. Ikerd
September 7, 1874	Henry P. Rudisill
December 1880	George W. Rabb
December 1888	W. L. C. Killian
December 1890	Henry P. Rudisill
December 1892	Q. M. Smith
December 1894	Noah Barringer
December 1896	A. C. Hildebran
December 1898	A. D. Shuford
December 1900	John Sherrill
December 1904	William A. Day
December 1908	J. U. Long
December 1912	W. L. Sherrill
December 1914	W. A. Reinhardt
December 1922	J. Merton Killian
December 1924	D. M. Cloninger (Appointed vice Loy R. Rink who declined to qualify.)

CATAWBA COUNTY 259

December 1926 — D. B. Gaither

April 15, 1929 — Glenn N. Rowe (Appointed county auditor, the position of county treasurer having been abolished.)

December 5, 1932 — Carl H. Cline, auditor.

December 3, 1934 — Joseph Hudson Gilley, auditor.

December 7, 1936 — Nolan Jay Sigmon, county manager, accountant and tax collector.

July 1, 1951 — John F. Carpenter, Sr., county manager, accountant and tax collector.

Board of County Commissioners

August 10, 1868 — Drury Hamilton, chairman, A. G. Corpening, M. M. Huit, A. L. Shuford and Joshua Little named commissioners-elect. They were notified to report September 7 next and qualify.

September 9, 1868 — Ordered by the board that the offices of A. L. Shuford and J. B. Little be declared vacant, and that the governor be notified.

October 14, 1868 — J. J. Sigmon and John D. Caldwell, having been appointed by the governor, were given oaths of office.

September 5, 1870 — Henry Wilfong, Daniel Deal, Andrew Fry, G. M. Wilfong, P. W. Whitener (Chairman not indicated in minutes.)

September 2, 1872 — F. L. Herman, chairman, Daniel Deal, P. W. Whitener, Andrew Fry, G. M. Wilfong.

September 7, 1874 — F. L. Herman, chairman, P. W. Whitener, G. M. Wilfong, W. H. Rockett, Gilbert Beatty.

December 4, 1876 — F. L. Herman, chairman, William H. Rockett, G. M. Wilfong, G. M. Beatty, Daniel M. Wyant.

December 2, 1878 — Levi Plonk, chairman, A. D. Shuford, Moses B. Trollinger, John Lyerly, Alonzo Deal (Plonk resigned. H. R. Forney was elected to fill vacancy on May 3, 1880. John Lyerly was elected chairman. Forney resigned September 6, 1880.)

December 6, 1880	John Lyerly, chairman, C. W. Herman, R. England, John W. Gabriel, G. M. Yoder.
December 4, 1882	George Setzer, chairman, M. L. Cline, M. B. Trollinger, M. F. Hull, C. T. Sigman.

On June 2, 1884, the number of commissioners was reduced from five to three.

December 1, 1884	A. G. Corpening, chairman, A. M. Huit, M. M. Gabriel.
December 6, 1886	A. G. Corpening, chairman, A. N. Huit, M. Abernethy, M. S. Deal.
December 3, 1888	L. R. Whitener, chairman, M. S. Deal, M. A. Abernethy.
December 1, 1890	L. R. Whitener, chairman, S. L. Yount, M. A. Abernethy.
December 5, 1892	L. R. Whitener, chairman, H. S. Gabriel, W. H. Rockett.
December 3, 1894	P. A. Hoyle, chairman, A. A. Shuford, John Sherrill (Shuford declined to serve; person appointed to fill vacancy not noted.)
December 7, 1897	D. E. Sigman, chairman, T. P. Cloninger, A. H. (?) Sigman.
December 5, 1898	John Gabriel, chairman, J. E. Wilfong, D. M. Boyd.
December 3, 1900	D. M. Boyd, chairman, J. D. Elliott, J. H. C. Huitt.
December 1, 1902	J. U. Long, chairman, J. D. Fisher, John A. Cook.

The practice of electing five commissioners was resumed again. Additional members appointed by the governor were A. A. Shuford and Silas Smyre. They qualified March 2, 1903. Shuford resigned soon thereafter and J. D. Elliott was appointed to the vacancy. He qualified April 6, 1903. Elliott later also resigned and J. M. Shuford was appointed to the vacancy. He qualified June 1, 1903.

CATAWBA COUNTY 261

December 3, 1906	I. A. Yount, chairman, J. M. Shuford, Samuel Turner, J. Summy Wilfong, Q. M. Smith.
December 7, 1908	Jones W. Shuford, chairman, D. E. Sigman, J. F. Hudson, John W. Lowrance, P. D. Drum.
December 5, 1910	S. L. Rhyne, chairman, F. A. Yoder, E. S. Little, Julius F. Abernethy, R. E. Gabriel.
December 5, 1912	E. S. Little, chairman, F. A. Yoder, S. L. Whitener, Caleb Setzer, R. E. Gabriel.
December 7, 1914	Osborne Brown, chairman, W. S. Stroup, D. Elias Sigman, Jay Wilfong, John F. Holler.
1916	(Same)
1918	(Same)
December 1948	Carl V. Cline, chairman, G. L. Winters, N. W. Jones, C. E. Rudisill, A. L. Shuford, Jr.
December 1950	L. L. Moss, chairman, Horace J. Isenhower, W. E. Abernethy, A. L. Shuford, Jr., G. L. Winters.
December 1952	L. L. Moss, chairman, Horace J. Isenhower, W. E. Abernethy, A. L. Shuford, Jr., Charles H. Geitner.

Judge of Catawba county Recorder's court (elective office as of 1929)

September 1929	E. M. Bledsoe
December 1930	W. B. Gaither
December 1940	John C. Stroup (Resigned April, 1941)
April 1941	W. C. Feimster (Appointed to fill out vacancy of John C. Stroup.)
June 1942	Eddy S. Merritt
December 1946	Emmett C. Willis
December 1950	Jesse Sigmon, Jr.

Solicitor of Catawba county Recorder's court (elective office as of 1929)

September 1929	Fred Caldwell
November 1930	Wade H. Lefler
December 1934	Russell W. Whitener
December 1944	Joseph L. Murphy
December 1946	W. J. Sherrod
December 1950	Richard A. Williams

Members of the General Assembly

Year	District	Senators	Representatives
1848	46th	Henry W. Connor	
1854	47th		H. Sherrill
1856	47th		Gilbert P. Routh
1858	47th		H. Sherrill
1860	47th		Jonas Cline
1862	47th		George S. Hooper (Resigned.)
			Horace L. Robards (Appointed.)
			W. P. Reinhardt (Took seat in fourth extra session.)
1864	47th	M. L. McCorkle	W. P. Reinhardt
1865	47th		W. P. Reinhardt
1866	47th	M. L. McCorkle	W. P. Reinhardt
1868	37th		James R. Ellis
1870	37th		R. B. B. Houston
1872	37th	James R. Ellis	R. B. B. Houston
1874	37th		Sidney M. Finger
1876	37th	Sidney M. Finger	D. McD. Yount
1879	37th		R. B. Davis
1881	37th	Sidney M. Finger	D. McD. Yount
1883	37th		Miles O. Sherrill

CATAWBA COUNTY

1885	37th	Miles O. Sherrill	A. A. Shuford
1887	37th		M. F. Hull
1889	37th	J. Turner	A. M. Huitt
1891	37th		S. T. Wilfong
1893	29th	Miles O. Sherrill	P. A. Hoyle
1895	29th	A. Y. Sigmon	Lee R. Whitener
1897	29th		Lee R. Whitener
1899	29th		A. C. Boggs
1901	29th		W. B. Gaither
1903	29th		Wm. Augustus Self
1905	31st	C. L. Turner	Walter C. Feimster
1907	31st		Marshall H. Yount
1909	31st	J. D. Elliott	J. Yates Killian
1911	31st		George W. Rabb
1913	30th	W. B. Council	W. B. Gaither
1915	30th		J. Yates Killian
1917	30th		J. Yates Killian
1919	30th	W. A. Reinhardt	J. A. Propst
1921	30th	W. A. Reinhardt	J. A. Propst
1923	25th		W. A. Deaton
1925	25th	A. A. Shuford, Jr.	L. F. Klutz
1927	25th		L. F. Klutz
1929	25th	J. S. Sigmon	L. F. Klutz
1931	25th		Oscar Pitts
1933	25th	John W. Aiken	Herbert L. Arndt
1935	25th		L. F. Klutz
1937	25th	B. B. Blackwelder	Ralph Flowers
1939	25th		Ralph Flowers
1941	25th	J. Henry Hill	Eddy S. Merritt
1943	25th		Harley F. Shuford
1945	25th	John W. Aiken	Harley F. Shuford
1947	25th		Harry Vanderlinden

1949	25th	G. Andrew Warlick	Harry Vanderlinden
1951	25th		Roy E. Leinbach
1953	25th	William B. Shuford	Roy E. Leinbach

Members of Conventions (Constitutions)

1861	P. C. Henkle (resigned, replaced by George Senter)
1865	James R. Ellis
1868	James R. Ellis
1875	M. L. McCorkle

Representatives in Congress

1821	Henry W. Connor
1823	Henry W. Connor
1825	Henry W. Connor
1827	Henry W. Connor
1829	Henry W. Connor
1831	Henry W. Connor
1833	Henry W. Connor
1835	Henry W. Connor
1837	Henry W. Connor
1839	Henry W. Connor
1895	Alonzo C. Shuford

Catawba county is the native land of Hoke Smith, who became governor of Georgia, a senator of the United States, and secretary of the interior in the cabinet of President Cleveland. Dr. Hildreth H. Smith of New Hampshire came to Newton and became dean of Catawba college in 1854. While in Catawba county, he married Miss Mary Brent Hoke of Lincolnton, a sister of General Robert F. Hoke. The couple's first child was Hoke. A state historical marker, located on South College avenue in Newton, indicates the place of birth. Dr. Smith severed his connection with the local institution in 1856 and accepted a teaching position with the University of North Carolina. The Smiths remained in Chapel Hill 12 years. They then moved to Atlanta.

CHAPTER XIII

CONTRIBUTION TO THE CONFEDERATE CAUSE

In the volume treasured by Catawbans as the admirable literary effort of a man who wrote solely to bestow honor upon a country he loved, Professor George W. Hahn, author of *The Catawba Soldier of the Civil War*, relates proudly of the men who are his subjects:

"No flag ever waved over braver boys, and none who wore the grey showed more willingness or promptness than did the heroic sons of Catawba."

Professor Hahn, whose virtually sacrificial efforts resulted in Catawba county's first history text, spoke of some 1,500 men who defended the Southern Confederacy on many of the major battlefields of the Conflict of the Sixties. He recorded the contributions of the Boys Who Wore the Grey, including approximately 300 who gave their lives for a cause that appeared to them righteous and just.

That Catawba Confederate soldiers served gallantly is attested by document. But that they haphazardly and blindly chose this path of action is a misstatement of fact.

Miles O. Sherrill, a Catawba county citizen who served as state librarian, said: "The people of Catawba were conservative, and in 1861 when South Carolina and other states, and even parts of North Carolina, were excited and agitated, our county was calm and cool, but when Mr. Lincoln called on North Carolina for her quota of troops, it was then that the young men of Catawba county were stirred up. When Governor Ellis called for troops it was astonishing how the young men of the county responded. They were encouraged by the patriotic women to do their duty.

"In the soldiers furnished to the cause, those from Catawba county could not be excelled for courage, loyalty and devotion . . ."

The deliberative nature of Catawba's German and Scotch ancestry manifested itself in regards to the most fearful conflict man had yet known in history. The people's reluctance to accept the impulsive decisions of neighbors of certain nearby states, however, generally was shared by the greater governmental unit of which Catawba county is a part — the state.

North Carolina held off from the conflict until war had actually begun and a choice was forced.

It was on December 20, 1860, that the South Carolina Convention, meeting in Charleston, passed its historic ordinance of secession which declared "That the Union heretofore existing between this State and the other States of North America is dissolved." Many other southern states, although reluctant to give up the Union, felt it their duty to stand by the pioneer in the movement against it, and passed ordinances of secession, as follows: Mississippi, January 9, 1861; Florida, January 10; Alabama, January 11; Georgia, January 19; Louisiana, January 26; and Texas, February 23.

In the hope of averting war, numerous peace meetings were held during this period, with Virginia specifically calling a "peace conference" in Washington, D. C., on February 4, 1861. The states represented included most of those in the North, and Delaware, Maryland, Virginia, North Carolina, Tennessee, Kentucky, and Missouri. Ex-President Tyler, of Virginia, was made president of the conference. The proposed terms of settlement were rejected by the North Carolina and Virginia delegates and refused by Congress, which, since the withdrawal of the Southern members, was controlled by the Republicans.

The next step of the Southern conventions was to send delegates to Montgomery, Ala., where they formed "The Confederate States of America," with Jefferson Davis, of Mississippi, president, and Alexander H. Stephens, of Georgia, vice-president. A constitution and flag, both resembling those of the United States, were adopted and all departments of the government organized.

On April 13, 1861, Federally-held Fort Sumter, in South Carolina, was captured by South Carolina Confederates. The day after President Lincoln called on the several states for 75,000 militia for 90 days' service.

The effect in the border states was decisive and immediate. Governors of North Carolina, Maryland, Virginia, Kentucky, Tennessee, Arkansas and Missouri sharply declined to honor the

CATAWBA COUNTY 267

President's requisition for troops to be used against the seven states of the Confederacy. The governor of Delaware reported that he had no lawful authority for calling troops.

North Carolina seceded from the Union on May 20, 1861. The state was received as a member of the Southern Confederacy on May 27, 1862.

Catawbans, by this time, were in accord as to the direction of their loyalty.

The Catawban and his fellow North Carolinians constituted about one-seventh of the soldiers of the entire Confederate forces, even though their state had only approximately one-ninth of the population of the states involved. North Carolina sent into the war about 125,000 men, mostly volunteers, a number larger than its voting population at that time. These troops were in the thick of the fighting and bore themselves bravely on every important battlefield. More than 40,000 North Carolina soldiers lost their lives.

Catawbans and other North Carolinians fought in the state, on the sea, and in the west, but chiefly in Virginia, the most important battleground of the war.

When the conflict began, Catawba county had been established 18 years. Of course changes had taken place since the Revolution and the War of 1812. There were churches, certain public schools, one college, a few cotton gins, a few brick yards, a few blacksmith shops, and a few mills. The railroad had also been built across the county.

Notwithstanding, the county was due few laurels for progressiveness. This situation was created not by the absence of initiative on the part of its people, but, rather, by reason of a tardy economic evolution. The county, whose population of 10,729 in 1860 was almost wholly rural, had known little internal improvement.

There were few large slave owners in Catawba, although major landowning families had sufficient number to tend their big farms and to help about the houses.

Figures show that in 1842, when the county was formed, the slaves numbered 17.7 percent of the population, and from then to 1860 the ratio of slaves to whites actually decreased, numbering only about 15.5 percent when the War Between the States began.

The national crisis virtually halted the county's development. About the only construction done was an iron forge at Maiden to furnish iron for guns, and four commissary buildings at Hickory. Also, a cavalry stock yard was established and a building was designated a commissary in Newton. The commissary buildings were constructed for the express purpose of packing and storing large quantities of meats, grains, and cotton that had been collected as a tithe and which were used for the Confederate army. The commissaries both at Hickory and Newton were later burned.

An article in the August 15, 1909, issue of The Nut Shell, a newspaper published in Hickory, explains the purpose of the Hickory commissary thus: "These buildings were of wood and quite extensive. . . . Very few people in these days realize the hardships suffered by not only the gallant soldiers who were defending their country, but the women and children at home. Think of it! Out of every hundred pounds of meat, you had to give ten pounds, and of every ten stacks of hay, one stack, out of every hundred bushels of corn or wheat, ten bushels, and you had to haul it yourself, to the commissary at Hickory Tavern. Remember that most of this was produced by women and children—working in the fields, supporting themselves and the Confederate army. The commissary buildings referred to were east of the present (train) freight depot on the north side of the railroad, and extended over a thousand feet alongside of the railroad."

Historians express some surprise at the devotion of Catawbans to the Confederate cause in light of circumstances which appear incongruous with such a sentiment. The youthfulness of the county, including the absence of a pronounced esprit de corps, appears a discouraging factor. The people's natural tendency to become angered slowly likewise seems alien. And the county's kinship with mountain areas, which were primarily Union in sentiment because of a feeling of isolation growing out of lack of transportation connections, a lack of influence in the state government, and on the presence of only a small slave population, appears, moreover, unusual. In connection with the mountain people's stand, it should be pointed out that the counties of the extreme western portion of North Carolina and extreme eastern portion of Tennessee were settled by veterans and sons of veterans of the Revolution and they were fiercely patriotic. Fathers taught their children to love their country and its flag, and to give their lives, if necessary, for their defense. They were uncompromisingly opposed to any disruption of the Union and denied the right of secession under any circumstance.

Nevertheless, the war years in Catawba were a time of self-sacrifice and heroism. The people, in fact, were as determined to maintain a civilization against change in 1861-65 as their kinsmen of a later generation were determined to protect Western culture against Asiatic tyrannical regimentation. This sacrificial effort is stimulating and worthy of unending respect and devotion. Yet, it also is deserving of a little sympathy—considering that countians strove to promulgate a system of aristocracy that was utterly foreign to them.

Ante-Bellum social and architectural customs of Catawba county were not as glorious as in other portions of the South, about which legends have been created by ambitious writers. Nevertheless, there was, perhaps, a segment of Catawba population which languished in the comforts of a society composed of gentlemen and workers. Some graceful mansions dotted the countryside, serving as abodes of wealthy landowners. Usually beside these colonial structures, maybe some 75 yards distant from the corner of the garden, stood the carriage house and beyond it lay the barns. On the other side of the mansion, but usually at a farther distance, were six or eight slave cabins, either "hewn and chinked" or constructed of "mud and sticks." The "summer kitchen" also was placed some distance from the house to rid the latter of flies, heat and noise, and necessitated many servants for satisfactory living. The spinning room, lighted by gable windows, was over the summer kitchen, wherein slave women who were not knitting or watching babies carded, spun, beamed, and wove cloth of both cotton and wool. Downstairs, beside the kitchen, there was the loom room. The barns, kept as meticulously clean as the "big house," sheltered the much-prized livestock, with fine horses gaining the most attention.

Catawba county's record as a slave area is unanimously reported by writers as extremely honorable. Slaves were prized property, yet were considered human beings. Their value, supplemented by their masters' affections for them, caused them to be kindly treated. Masters were ever watchful of their slaves' health. Virtually accepted as members of the family, slaves were often included in family gatherings and the older ones were honored with such titles as "aunt" and "uncle." Sometimes the conduct of children was left almost exclusively to trusted slaves' supervision. Never was a slave permitted to suffer after his usefulness was ended. They ordinarily took the names of their masters, and, especially among other slaves, flouted pridefully the accomplishments of such families.

Punishment of slaves was seldom that which would incapacitate them from their plantation duties. In fact, local writers have left no record of actual abuse of the black man under the white master. Usually the deprivation of some privilege constituted the punishment. Whippings of the young, however, are assumed to have occurred.

When slaves were purchased, particularly if they were newly arrived in the country, they were trained with care. They made the "rounds" of household and plantation departments, determining to the master's satisfaction the niche into which they would best fit. Usually they began with household duties, with the kitchen being the first testing area. The especially adept was kept for this service, and such employment was highly prized by the recipient. If his aptitudes were not promising in this area, he was shifted to barn duty or field duty. A pronounced hierarchy is noted among the slaves, the highest position being held by one who was selected to be slave "superintendent" of general plantation chores. Slave marriages were condoned and in reality promoted by masters. Sometimes a slave married another of a surrounding plantation. When such a marriage was approved, a pass was given to the man slave which permitted him to leave his home plantation after dark and return before daylight. The pass held him from suspicion of the "patrollers," persons employed to guard the countryside, being especially instructed to observe the comings and goings of slaves.

The good living of the South resulted directly from its fertile and abundant land. In the Catawba section, the problem of depleted soil was not known, for the area was relatively new in settlement. The practice of the day was to till land for approximately five years, and then discard it for virgin land. Working a new ground was a master craftsman's job. First, the trees were cut almost through with the three-or-four pound axe. Then, they were thrown with ox chains and limbed. The stumps were left, but the top roots were cut away to a depth of some six inches. This was done with a coulter, a cutting instrument attached to the beam of a plow drawn by a steer. Behind came another steer drawing the bull-tongue, a plow. Next came the twister, which was mule-drawn. When the new ground was thus made ready for planting the first crop of corn. Next came oats. The following year, not as a fertilizing agent but as food for the "hands," the field was put in cow peas. Wheat was grown the fourth year, and cotton the next. Then, unless the land was of unusual richness, it was turned out as an "old field."

Industry in Ante-Bellum Catawba county most often was the product of the home, much in the same fashion as during the Revolution period. Few items necessitated "foreign" purchase, particularly in view of the presence of slave labor. Some plantations contained mills for the making of meals, and cotton gins. Most clothes were homemade still, and virtually all foods were homegrown.

Communion among the aristocrats was lavish in some instances. Parties were common, and sometimes lasted an entire week. Schooling was provided children by private tutors. Churches were a center of activity, even recreation.

The restful and graceful pace of living of the Old South was regarded proudly, but not boastfully, by its participants. Generosity was as established among its mores as was chivalry.

Alongside this supple existence, meanwhile, there lived members of a lower social rank. And, if the truth be known, they constituted the majority of the Catawba population. Included were hardy and determined small landowners who did not subscribe to the slave system, being independent of mind and action. They gained a foothold immediately following the war—aided by the cheap sale of plantation lands—and became the nucleus of Catawba's stalwart farming class of later generations.

Whatever Catawbans' social status, it can be said that all alike were unable to realize the impending destructiveness of the war. Few believed that the difficulty could not be settled about conference tables. Fewer believed that actual arms engagements would occur. Still fewer believed that the Northerners would fight.

But, the guesses were miscalculated. American brothers shed each other's blood in history's most pathetic melee.

A sample of the catastrophe is afforded by Catawbans who described it in letters to their loved ones at home, and in diaries, or by reminiscences recorded by them after the war.

A packet of 25 letters written by Sgt. J. Calvin Sides of Company K. 35th North Carolina Regiment, to his wife, Kate Warlick Sides, is preserved by his family. The soldier was killed in battle near Petersburg, Va. His body was never found following the engagement. Sgt. Sides wrote from Kinston on May 11, 1863, an instance of the depredations of the Yankees, as follows: "Down below here a little below where we were on picket the Yankeys made a raid. They run in our pickets. There lived a lady and her daughter, very respectable ladies. Four of the villains went into the house, locked the door and committed deeds that would make the devil shudder, if possible. Who would not fight such scoundrels. If we but had a morsel of bread I could stave a ball or my bayonet through them with good heart. To think they would take their revenge on the innocent women, but the day of vengeance is coming and woe be unto such villains. . . ."

Professor J. Dallas Rowe wrote a paper depicting the battle of the Wilderness through which he and his comrades had fought. Titled "An Evening Scene," the article is as follows:

"Battle of Wilderness, May 5, 1864:

"The sun had set. The first shades of darkness were falling around. Except the firing of a few pickets, the roar of battle on the right had hushed, but on the left, the heavy peals of artillery, the steady roar of musketry, and faintly, the shouts of the assaulting foe, and the cheers of the victorious might still be heard. The ground held by the first line of battle was yielded by the second soon after it relieved the first, that at night left the ground which had been the principal scene of

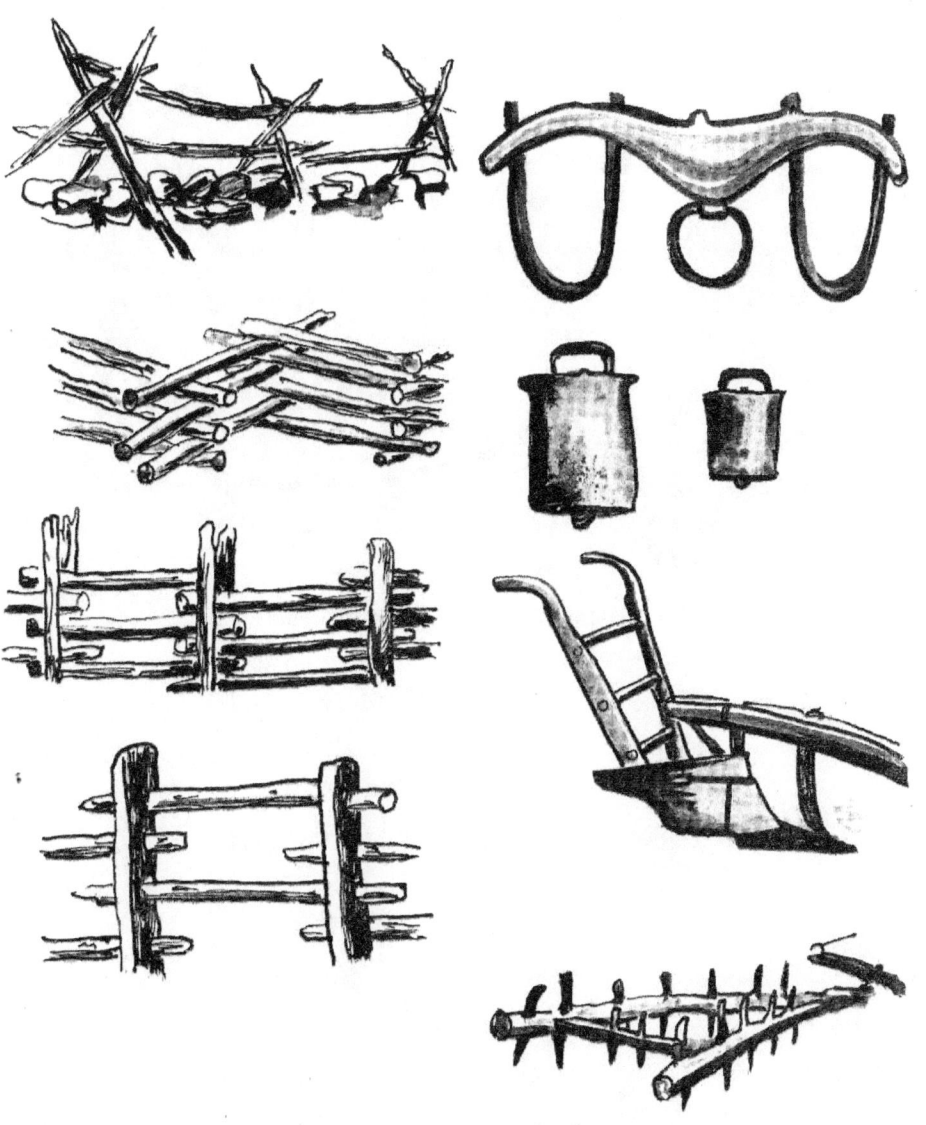

Types of Rail Fences

Ox Yoke

Cow Bells

Plow

Harrow

Home Industries: Basket Making, Churning for Butter, Making Candles

Early Call for the Doctor

conflict during the day between the picket lines of the two armies.

"The killed and wounded of the two armies were not intermingled for the Federals did not advance to the first line held by the Confederates, even after the latter fell back. The dead lay mostly in the line, where they received the fatal shot. Some wounded and returning to the rear, were shot dead a short distance from where their comrades lay. The wounded lay scattered through the wood—some crying piteously for water; others crying vainly for help. Others, in whom the tide of life was fast ebbing, were giving messages to those near them for their friends at home, or sighing for one moment with those who were many miles away. How well that such a scene was unknown to them. What a lively picture of the horrors of war!"

A letter relating the bitterest of war's pathos was written by a Catawba county Confederate soldier immediately before he and his brother were executed. J. E. Lanier, the writer, does not tell the reason for the court-martial, but it is believed he and his brother went just across the line into the enemy territory because they were hungry and hoped to find food.

The letter is as follows:

"My dear friends:—I for your sakes have again determined to write another short Epistol to let you know I am well and my brother is well; however, we expect to leave this sin-stricken world in a very short time. I wrote a letter last Sabbath and started it stating the death notice but it probably did not come to your hand. I therefore must write again.

"You are unaware that we were held in custody and for what crime I am sorrow to informe you the sentence is death to be executed on Saturday, the 26th, but I thank the Lord I have put my trust in Jesus. I hope to meet my friends that has gone before and I hope that you my friends will meet me in Heaven. I would love to see my brothers yet in service and explain the case to them but so it is I can't.

"It goes hard for me to write so solemn a doom but there is not a man in the Regt. that will say we got Justice but the officers have determined to have a better disciplined army than heretofore and so it must needs be that they make example of some to check the remainder and it has fell on our unhappy lot to be an example.

"It is hard but we have to bear it. I know we will get justice in Heaven's judgment. I have spent my time reading the holy bible and in prayer to God. I want you all to pray much and meet me in Heaven. Father, set the example of prayer before your small family. I am exceeding sorrorfull on your account. Read the 88th psalm, the reason plainly to be seen.

"Dear father, dispose of my things that are few and worthless as you see proper to make my debts clear. Now you nor I can do no better than to prepare to meet above. O! then let me exhort you as did Paul in the 12th chapter of Romans. Be yet not conformed to this world but be ye transformed to the renewing of your minds that ye may prove what is that good and acceptable and perfect will of God. Read the chapter throughout."

Next follows a pathetic note to his mother, beseeching her to dry her tears and not to grieve. Expressions of great hope and faith were repeated, as the Confederate soldier wrote bravely that he felt that he was "going home to God."

Praying that blessings might befall them, he wrote messages to his brothers, his sisters and his sister-in-law and ended the letter with the following words: "Farewell, my friends, our parting is at hand. I could write pages to you and then half would not be told; that I would like to have you know but it is hard to write. Don't take it hard. I am willing to go home. I feel bad on your account more than my own. Farewell to friends and world!"

Although their pain was physically greater, Confederate soldiers did not bear all the suffering of the War Between the States. Wives, parents, grandparents and children at home were subjects of austere and even critical economies fashioned with the express purpose of promoting the interests of the Confederate cause. But history has never recorded a more graciously and willingly accepted period of sacrificial living. The home front was convinced that the fighting front was directly dependent on it for superb morale, material and blessing. Young boys gladly assumed men's posts in farming and the day's crude industries; little girls worked tenaciously at producing soldiers' clothing and medical supplies; grandparents and parents persistently watched the soldiers' food supply; and wives and sweethearts continuously wrote letters of encouragement.

Concerning the women, a Southerner wrote in 1861 that never "in any age or country, was there ever witnessed such an intense war spirit as that now prevailing among the women of the Confederate States. . . ." A Federal writer in 1864 noted "that the South stands today quite as much indebted for a successful prolongation of this struggle to her women, as to her generals and soldiers in the field."

Immediately after the war began, women started making flags and presenting them in special ceremonies to military units; they shamed those young men who avoided fighting; they performed men's work to free those fit for uniform; they decorated Confederate graves as early as 1862; they made flags into aprons and wore conspicuous war badges; they entertained soldiers by playing pianos for them, and in captured areas they played "Dixie" when Federal soldiers asked for music; they early organized themselves into clubs and societies, especially to provide soldiers with warm clothing and other home supplies; and they conducted benefits at every turn of the hand. Perhaps their greatest evidence of interest, however, was their joyful giving of prized possessions to be employed in the war effort. In this connection, they gave jewelry, china sets, silverware, watches, vases, and almost anything in the household which could be spared. With many men at the front, the women were left to make a living as well as to take up many occupations primarily to aid the Confederacy. They managed farms and plantations; they made wine, pickles, catsup, and hats of straw, shucks, and various leaves.

An example of the women's determined efforts is afforded in a war edition of The Western Democrat, Hickory newspaper: "Good Idea—We observe the ladies in keeping with the fertility of resources in industry that has immortalized their sex during the war, are making socks from carpet ravellings. They are a little heterogeneous in color, but none the whit less warm for that, and will be acceptable to the soldiers, or those who wear them at home."

Children set about with great fervor to collect wild vegetation to supplement medical supplies at the front and at home.

Medicinal properties of many plants were found to be useful as substitutes for drugs, which become scarce. These included dogwood, boneset, sweet gum, holly (taking the place of quinine), for fevers; sugar from watermelon juice, for colds and diarrhea; etc. Many herbs and barks were collected, such as wild-cherry bark, snakeroot, pokeroots, sassafras, persimmon bark, dandelions, etc. Every neighborhood was expected to garner its valuable materials. Families were encouraged to plant poppies from which to obtain opium.

Blast furnaces and rolling mills are believed to have provided Catawba county's only industrial contributions to the War for Southern Independence.

Upon the outbreak of hostilities, severe limitations were felt in all phases of community life. Schools suffered due both to the scarcity of pupils and teachers and lack of interest. Church services were sometimes held in private homes to conserve lights and fuel. Social events were permitted solely to benefit the war cause.

Yet, with these restrictions, it is said that cheeriness reigned—at least outwardly—among the people. Doubtless due to determination, the Catawba Confederate homefront is recorded as having hidden very well its doubts about the outcome of the war until late in 1864.

But the business of war bore heavily. The mere business of living became enormously difficult. The South was sucked dry by war, strangled by blockade, dismembered by invasion. The breakdown was due to manufactures, transportation, and its medium of exchange.

The "little" things became so aggravating to the general population. White sugar disappeared entirely, sorghum syrup had to be accepted as a substitute. Disease outbreaks, particularly smallpox, were prevalent. Matches disappeared, and flint and steel relics had to be taken from closets and returned to use. Soap was scarce, so the ash hopper was again put to use. As the blockades grew tighter, whale oil became scarce. Beef tallow was saved for greasing cartridges, and fat was needed for soap making, so it was difficult to make good candles.

Toothpowder was substituted by ground sassafras bark and chalk. Shoe polish was made by mixing lamp black with the ripe cortical pulp of chinaberry. Ink was made from oak balls and burnt copperas. For tea, the people used sassafras roots. For coffee, they parched rye and wheat and browned sweet potatoes. Paper became so scarce that wallpaper was removed from homes. Bronze church bells were taken down to be melted and made into howitzers or gun caps. Food portions became small, and clothing became simple. Scraped lint was collected by everybody to be sent to Confederate hospitals for use as absorbent cotton. Communities were urged to collect human urine so that nitre could be procured.

From the beginning of the war, the county government gave certain compensation to soldiers and made provision for their families.

Court records of June 17, 1861, point out that $10,000 was appropriated for the use of the volunteers "who have and may hereafter enter in duty to defend Southern Rites in payment for provisions in pursuance of Act of Assembly ratified, also for aid if necessary . . . of families left behind. . . ." Jonas Bost made the motion, which was approved.

Dr. O. Campbell, John Wilfong, and George Setzer were named a committee to "borrow" the funds.

The school committee was at the same time authorized to "see to the suffering families of any person that has entered on duty as a volunteer, and certify the same to the above named committee. . . ."

M. L. Cline was named agent for the county in 1862 "to secure salt manufactured by the state authorities and to sell same" as he was directed.

Court records of April, 1862, explain: "Ordered by Court that application for 6,000 bushels of salt be made. It will take that amount for citizens of the county of Catawba until Jan. 1st, 1863. Justices appropriated $18,000 to pay for same." Again, Dr. O. Campbell, John Wilfong, and George Setzer were named a committee to arrange for delivery and sale.

In January, 1863, the county court ordered that $500 be paid to D. B. Gaither "to distribute to needy families of soldiers, who are in actual need. . . . The money was to be distributed to "the captain in each District to use as needed."

The court ordered, in January, 1864, that 3,000 bushels of corn be purchased from the Confederate states. The record points out that the grain was to be distributed to wives and children of soldiers in need.

The corn was deposited at Alfred Ramsour's farm and district captains were called upon to distribute it.

Wounded and dying men were continually returned to the county. Their illnesses and deaths were not all attributable to explosives, for disease along the front lines and in prisons was alarming. It is estimated reliably that 20 percent of Catawba's dead were claimed by disease. A record held locally of certain men imprisoned on Johnson's Island points out that the soldiers died of illnesses such as "general disability," fever, consumption, bilious fever, eutietis, dysentery, typhoid fever, chronic diarrhea and phenumonia.

Although its "home guard" was unable to contribute services of magnitude to the Confederate government, Catawba was not without its civilian heroes. Large commissaries at both Newton and Hickory Tavern were stocked with food for the Confederate forces. The Hickory Tavern commissary was a headquarters unit, serving a wide area of Catawba and surrounding counties. Newton also was the site of a Confederate states depository. One of the first letters written by Secretary of the Treasury of the Confederate States George A. Treholm was received by Joseph Bost of Newton in September, 1864. (Treholm succeeded Christopher G. Memminger as Secretary of the Treasury after Memminger was forced to resign because of public clamor about the collapse of the Confederate currency, although he was not wholly to blame.) The letter is as follows:

"Sir: Your letter of the 17th instant, relative to the Old Currency remaining in your hands has been received.

"You will please forward the money immediately by express. . . ."

Catawba Confederates distinguished themselves under fire. Many rose to responsible military positions. The most successful of these was Thomas Lafayette Lowe, who attained the rank of colonel. Serving in a Virginia campaign, Col. Lowe died of pneumonia while sleeping amidst his men in cold and rainy weather. It is told that, although officers were invited into Southern homes, Col. Lowe declined, to remain with his forces.

By the beginning of 1865, there was little room left for belief of any sort in the ultimate success of the Confederacy. The people's deep and tender, almost heart-breaking, solicitude for the noble soldiers seemingly turned to that sentiment which accompanies the realization of an ill-spent illusion. Still, they responded cheerfully again early in January, when an urgent and most pressing appeal was made in behalf of Lee's army. With this supreme effort, every available resource was taxed, every expedient of domestic economy was put in practice.

Following untold suffering for almost four years, the tide of war, at this late date in the conflict, began to roll in upon Catawba. Countians were to learn the rigors of invasion in April, when Stoneman's foragers caused great dismay and widespread terror.

It was at a time that all North Carolina experienced close contact with the war. The fall of Fort Fisher and the occupation of Wilmington, the failure of the peace commission, and the unchecked advance of Sherman's army northward from Savannah, were the alarming features of the time.

In March, 1865, General Stoneman left East Tennessee moving through Taylorsville, Tenn., through Watauga county to Deep Gap in the Blue Ridge. On March 26 he entered Boone and on the day following the column was divided, one division marching toward North Wilkesboro, while the other crossed the Blue Ridge at Blowing Rock and went to Patterson in Caldwell county. Members of this column continued south to harass Catawba countians.

Historians generally agree that the Stoneman Raiders were employed more as a morale-breaking force than as emissaries of conquest. Chiefly, they traveled, apparently without goal, the countryside, pillaging at major points and committing offenses of aggravating, if not serious, nature at other points.

Those members of the Stoneman army who invaded Catawba county are believed to have been stragglers, and likely persons of undesirable character. Stoneman, himself, was not among them.

It is contended by many historians, including Southerners, that Stoneman's personal conduct and his military policies were ethical. Cornelia Phillips Spencer, a North Carolinian, in "The Last Ninety Days of the War in North Carolina," points out: ". . . But General Stoneman's policy toward the inhabitants (of Salisbury) . . . is a very striking illustration of the principles which . . . were the only true and generous and really politic guide for the commanders of an invading army. Private property was protected, guards were stationed, and General Stoneman repeatedly gave strict orders for the enforcement of quiet and protection of the citizens. He himself in person inspected the public stores, which were of course by the laws of war doomed to destruction, and refused to allow the Confederate Quartermaster's depot to be burned lest it should endanger the town. . . . Whatever plundering and insolence the people were subjected to—and there were a number of such cases—was very evidently the work of unauthorized bummers. . . ."

The force which descended upon Catawba did, in fact, deal dastardly with the inhabitants. Newton's encounter with the Federalists is described by George Pope in a newspaper article which appeared in connection with the county's celebration of the 1947 Soldiers Reunion event at the county seat city. It is, in part, as follows:

"On April 5th, 1865, General Stoneman's Cavalry raided Newton. They came up the old Laurel Hill road, which is on the right of the present postoffice, yelling, shooting and swearing. They then began to ransack the town. My mother, who was a very small child at that time, was terrible frightened by the din. The Union soldiers took my Grandfather Beard's cow, hogs and chickens. My grandmother, Nancy Hewitt Beard, went to the commanding officer and tearfully begged for the return of the cow because of her small children. The Yankee officer relented and the cow was returned. Incidentally, Grandmother Beard made costumes for the Ku Klux Klan and which were hidden in the attic of her home when not in use.

"Charley Connor . . . was shot and killed by the Yankee soldiers as he tried to escape on his horse. My mother's aunt, Evie Hilton, was living in the county jail at that time and the Yankee Captain ordered her to move her things out and they burned the jail down and liberated several Union soldiers who were imprisoned there. They also burned down a large Commissary building which was located where the Cilley Hosiery mill now stands. Large supplies of food was stored in the Commissary and hungry children stood by crying as burning mollasses ran down the side of the hill.

"Sherman was right in his version of War—For Such Is War."

Major J. L. Latta affords a graphic description of Hickory's experiences under the heel of the Yankees. It is as follows:

"Just before the close of the Civil War a horde of myrmidons, from God-knows-where, dropped down in the valley above Lenoir, scattering fire and destruction in every direction, and gathering up all the horses, mules and food stuffs that could be found. They burned Patterson factory, and were headed toward Hickory Tavern.

"When the distracted residents learned of their coming this way, they moved everything possible from the Confederate commissary in order to prevent its seizure, but there were many supplies that could not be quickly removed. A great number of heavy sacks of salt were in the commissary and also over one hundred barrels of molasses, vinegar and brandy. The unfriendly visitors arrived on time, April 6, 1865, just three days after Lee's surrender, and Major E. M. Todd, manager, promptly set fire to the commissary building, which was soon reduced to ashes. Before firing the building, axes were used by Major Todd, the commissary keeper, to knock the heads out of all barrels, and the molasses, vinegar and brandy flowed down the railroad track toward the old mineral spring. After the fire, the scorched or roasted salt was gathered up and used by the residents of the village and surrounding community. . . ."

Historians generally agree that Connor was killed following his refusal to halt upon command. Concerning the burning of the Hickory Tavern commissary, E. L. Shuford, in historical writings, said: "This wanton destruction incensed the country around and they appealed to Governor Vance to punish Todd." Todd, however, was not punished.

Numerous tales have been handed down from generation to generation concerning the oppressive heel of the enemy during the April, 1865, "invasion." Generally they tell of the destruction of homes, the stealing of residents' few remaining valuables, and the thefts or killings of livestock. Among such stories is one recorded by Sarah Link in "The Story of My Life During the Confederacy."

"One day as Moll (an old white woman) who lived on her plantation, and I were struggling to get manure out of the stable," the writer begins, "a Yankee officer and two men rode up where we were working and caught us with the horse (they had been after it before but we managed to keep her hidden out in the woods). The officer said, 'So you do have a Cavalry Mare after all, we have come for her.' I said, 'Moll see to the horses,' she picked up a stick and struck at the men as they tried to grab my mare, she hit instead the horses of the Yankees, who became frightened and galloped away. I picked up a pitch fork and started after the Officer, telling him, 'You come one step nearer and I'll run this thing clean thru you. Now Git!' And he 'got.' For some unknown reason they left her and went after their own horses and they did not bother me again about this mare until I went after salt to Hickory Tavern, when they chased me across the Catawba river, shot a hole in my salt bag, and I lost all the salt. . . ."

Even as the Federals still prowled through Catawba county, machinery was put in motion by Union officials to accept the surrender of Confederate armies. The honorable surrender of Robert E. Lee signified to Catawbans finally that their cause was now only a wasted dream.

The same General Lee who admitted the failure of the Southerners had, only several months earlier, paid respectful attention to a Catawba county family. Mrs. Barbara Eva Lavina Wilfong, mother of six Confederate soldiers, received the following letter from General Lee in receipt of a Christmas box of foodstuff:

"Petersburg, 11 Jany. '65.

"My Dear Madame:

"I rec'd. some days since your kind note of the 22 ulte., which has been followed by the box to which it referred. The contents are very acceptable, in excellent condition notwithstanding their long journey, and I am exceedingly obliged to you for them. I am more gratified at your devoting so many sons to the defense of the country. If they are all equal to the one I know, Capt. Wilfong, 12 N. C., you should be truly grateful. I trust a Kind Providence may preserve them all for you and you for them. With grateful thanks for your prayers in my behalf and the success of our cause,

"I remain very respt'
"Your obt. Servt.,
"R. E. LEE."

"Mrs. B. E. L. Wilfong
"Newton, N. C."

The crushing military defeat of the South stunned its people. The wasted energies of four years of strife left them physically and physiologically exhausted. The spirit of a proud people was crushed and stepped upon. Even the bravest tended to view the surrender as the end of all things.

But, naturally, the sun shone on succeeding days, and, as is coexistent with the will to live, the people dragged themselves out of the humiliating circumstances of bondage. The struggle was not easy, for a new pattern of life, complete from economic to social aspects, is not devised immediately upon conviction that it must be attained. The reconstruction years, or the time necessary for the aftermath of war's hatreds to be spent, therefore, were as taxing and as challenging as the miserable tenure of the war.

The War Between the States did more than free the slaves. It also upset a social and an economic order, strengthened the powers of the United States government, and fastened tighter upon the South a colonial status under which it had long suffered.

Unfortunately, the defeated soldier was not allowed to return home after the cessation of hostilities, as he was detained as a prisoner, and the hardest reconstruction tasks fell to women who had suffered equally the deprivations of war. What is more, the women were to be aided no longer by the Negroes, who were now free and from henceforth could go where they willed.

The hardships provided by the scarcities of living's necessities, such as food and clothing, were augmented by sweeping governmental, industrial, political and social changes. An occupation army, quartered for the most part in private homes, neglected or refused to see the ravages of the Northern scum, carpet-baggers and adventurers, who tagged to the tails of the Yankee uniform wherever it went.

Catawba county, because of its scant population and the absence of vital industries, was bothered little by the Union rule in the sense of the presence of soldiers, and it was allowed to attend to its internal affairs generally at its own will.

Change was evident in every aspect of living, from the practices of the family group to the creation of a community-law order. For the purposes of the volume, as an index to the tempo of the times, these two categories are chosen for discussion.

The Ku Klux Klan, which probably originated in Tennessee in 1865, was designed in an effort to combat Northern secret organizations in the South, to "put the Negro in his place," to regain control of government, and to protect Southern womanhood. The order grew rapidly for a period of two years and is known to have had active participants in the Catawba section. Prominent citizens were tried and indicted in United States court at Statesville for allegedly being members of the Klan. Many of these persons received unfair treatment at the hands of Federal authorities. They suffered most from the fact that they were dragged from court to court and persistently denied trial.

A Hickory newspaper listed in 1872 persons indicted under the Ku Klux act and United States witnesses, as follows:

"(1) M. M. Wilson, R. P. Reinhardt, Andrew Yoder, June term, 1871. Bill found.

"(2) Aaron Sigmon, Adolphus Sigmon, Marcus Lynn, June term, 1871.

"(35) Peter Ramsaur, Govan Bost, Albert Smyre, Henry Wilson, John Bumgarner, Benton Clonniger, Keer Setzer, Cain Bost, Franklin Propst, Noah Wise, Bill found. June term, 1871. Act May 30, 1870. Witnesses: Lewis Witherspoon and Julia Ann Perkins.

"(38) Penkney Wilson, Starling Gill, Pinkney Setzer, Edward Bost. Bill found. September session, 1871. Witnesses: George Conley and Abraham Wilson.

CATAWBA COUNTY 285

"(39) Adam Reap, Hosea Whitener, Pinckney Bradburn, Osborn Wilson, Henry Yoder, Sidney Yoder, Joseph Fry, Mat Hoffman, James Wilson and Pinckney Wilson. Bill found. September session, 1871. Act May 30, 1870. U. S. witnesses: James Coulter and Bob Robinson.

"(43) Govan Bost, James Gibson, George Moose, Frank Huffman, Hugh Pence, Caleb Setzer, Cain Moose, Lewis Witherspoon, Thomas Setzer. Bill found. September term, 1871. Witnesses: John Powell, Catherine Powell, Samuel Gibbs.

"(48) Adolphus Abernethy, Lafayfette Abernethy, John Marshall, Marcus Lynn, Noah Hallman, Joseph Childers, Cephas Simmons, James Bowles. Bill found. September term, 1871. Act May 30, 1870. Witnesses: Joseph Abernethy, Jasper Deal.

"(56) Wilborne Boyd and others. Bill found. June term, 1871. Witnesses: Thomas Hope, Lee Clark, Reuben Kirksey, Andrew Davis, B. A. Kirksey.

"(57) O. F. Bost, John Sigman, Adam Reape, Frank Icard, John Propst, David Keistler, John Conrad, P. C. Rudisill, Daniel Shuford, Phillip Hoyle, Henry Yoder, Alfred Jarrett, John Corpening.

"Frank Keistler, Eli Starr, Pinckney Cline, Philip Coulter, Abel Starr, Jacob Huffman, Marcus Huffman, Pinckney Wilson, Max Huffman, Jacob Gilbert, John Hoover, Franklin Smith, S. Bolch, John Bolch, M. M. Wilson, Robert Reinhardt, Julius Helton, John C. Sharpe, J. A. Fry, Abel Fry, John Whitener, Wash Ramsour, Enos Campbell, Jacob Rudisill, Henry Rudisill, Adelphus Rudisill, Phillip Burns, Beorge Fincannon, Noah Huffman, Hosea Whitener, Benjamin Whitener, Philip Gilbert, Franklin Huffman, Adolphus Whitener, Austin Wilson.

"George Rabb, Brock Self, John C. Warlick, David Warlick, Henry Warlick, Loney Carpenter, Thornton Martin, John Rader, John Ramsour, Jefferson Saunders, Daniel Hoover, Pinckney Fry, James Frye, N. D. Lutz, Alonzo Lutz, Benjamin Lutz, Friders Rink, Nelson Keever, Charles Alexander, Wallace Throneburg, G. W. Caldwell, Rufus Self, Monroe Coulter, Daniel Reap, Adolphus Abernethy, Thomas Wilfong. Bill found. November term, 1871. U. S. Witnesses: A. L. Ramsour, John Sims, Albert Angle, R. F. Hamblet, Logan Crouch.

"(59) Adolphus Abernethy, Lawrence Miller, Lafayette Ambernethy, Marcus Whitener, Marcus Lynn, Adolphus Sigmon, Daniel Whitener, Adolphus Propst, Robert Fry, Simon Propst, John Seigler, Sidney Ward, Jasper Deal, John Marshall, Chick Alexander, James Bawles, Cephas Simmons, Poley Hefner, Hiram Miller. Bill found. November term, 1871. Witnesses: Sineon Barger, Joseph Childers, Noah Hallman.

"(63) Cail Setzer, Caleb Setzer, George Fincannon, Charles Setzer, Eli Starr, Pinckney Miller, F. S. Smyre, Henry Wilson, James Gibson, John Conrad, Allen Settlemyre, Pinckney Fry, Peter Ramsour, Thomas Marlow, Sidney Houston, Howell Harris, E. G. Bost, George Throneburg, Richard Wilson, Starr Gill, Abner Smyre. U. S. Witness: Franklin Huffman.

"(64) John Hilton, Daniel Shuford, Henry Yoder, Sidney Yoder, James Wilfong. U. S. witness: Emeline Shuford."

Mrs. Mary Shuford Davis writes interestingly of homes and home life during the reconstruction period, as follows:

"The period after the war was a period characterized by hard poverty in every walk of life, but especially in the home. The Confederate soldier returned to labor and to work. The mothers, wives, and daughters, servantless and poor, took upon their shoulders uncomplainingly the drudgery of the household tasks. Truly it may be said of them that by the 'sweat of the brow did they eat.'

"The daily round of household duties was varied and never-ending, a thousand tasks arose to be completed with every sun. Whatever of clothing, light and food they obtained, whatever of comfort and cheer surrounding them in their homes, was only produced by labor, thrift and saving care.

"Looking back upon this picture of hard toil we see its seting and framework in the typical home of Catawba county as it was then. These houses were small and unpretentious looking, but were made lovely in summer by vines and the beloved old-fashioned flowers that grew in every 'Grandmother's Garden.' The bordered path led up to the door, and here one entered into the general living room, warm, cheery and bright with its glowing open fire in winter and its shadowed cool in summer.

Here the family gathered together when the day was over, about the solitary little candle that so bravely strove to light the depths of gloom. Here the friendly neighbors who came over to spend the day, sat working on half-completed quilts, their knitting or sewing, never idle, but talking of the 'days before the war' or the present news while they worked. Here the social gatherings were held, no fear of boisterous young people doing harm to the rag carpets, the homespun curtains or the split bottom chairs with which the room was furnished. Without doubt these rooms contained many pleasant memories of happy scenes despite 'hard times.'

"Certainly there could be no greater contrast to this cheery room than the gloomy 'best room' or parlor. With its better furnishing of carpet and chairs carefully guarded, its shades drawn down and the few pictures hung precisely on the walls and a few books placed precisely on the table, this sacred precinct was always kept closed and generally locked. Only on such occasions as weddings or funerals was its dark domain invaded and used.

"Passing by the bed rooms with their high, four-poster beds, pretty crazy quilts and old furniture that has been handed down from mother to daughter, we find the old-time kitchen the most important and most interesting place of all. Here was the great open fireplace with its two swinging rods, one on each side, fitted out with hooks on which were hung the many sized pots over the glowing coals. Sometimes there was an old-time stove; but, if so, this was only used for special occasions such as the baking of all the weekly pies and bread on Saturday, or the cake for Christmas season. Generally the daily supply of vegetables and meat was prepared by boiling everything over the open fire.

"Apples, sweet and Irish potatoes were baked in the hot ashes; chestnuts were roasted and popcorn popped over a bed of coals. The Dutch oven, a round covered pan in which biscuits were baked, was often set on these coals with its layer of coals on top. Strings of beef and sausage dipped in brine and hung over the stove or around the room to dry out, were frequent ornaments of the kitchen. Bunches of red pepper also made a cheerful spot. The adjoining pantry was, of course, the realm of delicacies and stacks on stacks of good things to eat.

"Here were sweet pickles and preserves made from every kind of fruit, row on row of dried apples, pears and peaches, fresh tomatoes and fruit saved far into the fall.

"Frequently there was a cellar to the house where winter provisions of potatoes, vegetables and apples were stored. Down in its depths was the place for shelves of peanuts and barrels of sauer kraut, which during the fall was made by filling in alternate layers of cabbage and salt, with the whole pressed down by large rocks. Fruits and melons were often placed in wheat bran in the cellar for preservation and it was a great achievement if some could be saved long enough to grace the Christmas festivities.

"Almost all food was raised on or near the home place. Every household had a garden where the vegetables were raised and fruit trees around the place, if not a regular orchard. As for meat, chickens were an important article and during the winter great supplies lasted over from hog-killing time. Outside the kitchen in the back yard a low, brick oven was generally built, where the baking was done when the kitchen held no stove. Molasses was used a great deal to take the place of the more expensive brown sugar, and once or twice a year a general stock of salt, sugar, coffee and commodities of that sort which could not be 'home-made' or home-grown were laid in. Water in the kitchen or elsewhere was not used so lavishly as at present, because often every bucketful had to be carried from the spring which might be quite a distance from the house.

"If these houses could not boast of beauty, they were nevertheless cheery and home-like. The walls were plastered or ceiled without paper and the few pictures on the walls with occasional portraits of wood, cuts for which the carpenter had sawed out and painted a frame. Books were few outside the family Bible, but those favored persons who had small libraries were usually generous enough to lend reading material around to friends and neighbors. The novel rag carpets were manufactured at home from scraps which had been saved for that purpose. The candles by which light was insured during the long winter evenings were made by dozens and half dozens by pouring the hot tallow into the molds, after the wicks had been fixed in place. Curtains at the windows gave a touch of prettiness and comfort. These, hanging over the figured paper shades, were of certain

Burning of Hickory Commissary, by Confederates

Shown above is the Catawba County Library, completed as a part of the Catawba County War Memorial Center, and formed from the original Barringer home which served as Catawba County's first court house.

material which lasted—as did most things of that day—year in and year out.

"As for clothing in the days following the War, the styles did not change every season as they do now. Clothing which had been one's mother's or grandmother's was handed on down. Woolen dresses when obtained were worn every winter till in rags. Stockings were knitted at home and other clothing when the weaver had finished his job, was put together entirely by hand. Men's suits were usually homespun. Shoes were made by the cobbler of the community and one or two pairs were considered sufficient. Hats were used season after season and every bit of trimming or pretty piece of ribbon was carefully treasured. At social gatherings the young man who wore a 'Northern' or readymade suit was considered a dude and a dandy. Hairdressing in that time was rather severe, the hair being drawn back over the ears in a coil behind. In the case of young girls, curls were preferred, and their few party dresses were made shortwaisted or empire in style.

"The most pleasant side of this picture is the social life of the sixties. Neighbors were friendly—often one good housewife would bring her work and spend the day with another—then a good old country dinner would be prepared; no fancy dishes, but plenty to eat. The young people had social gatherings at each other's homes, quilting and sewing bees and husking parties in the fall. Usually the old people did the work while the young folks played the old fashioned games of 'drop-the-handkerchief' and others. At dances the square dances only were engaged in and the Virginia Reel was the most popular. In the summer, camp meetings were frequently attended and these were a great event in most people's lives, since at these times the country people saw friends and exchanged news and enjoyed social intercourse that was usually denied them. Church during the year was well attended. Whenever an opportunity was afforded as the minister went the rounds of his several charges, the people would drive in for miles around. This was the social side but nowhere could one look at the people gathered together or in their homes but that one saw traces of home labor and toil. From the food they ate to the clothing that kept the body warm one could discern ceasless industry in the thousand lines of household work."

With ingenuity of hands and mind, Catawbans and other Southerners gradually designed a new and satisfying type of living. It was proved that four years of cruel war followed by a decade of humiliation could not blot out the old love of country implanted in South and North alike by the sacrifices of the Revolution and subsequent common problems and experiences.

The Confederacy as a government unit had died completely. Even during the darkest days of reconstruction, Southerners did not harbor the hope of re-establishing a separate country. Although radical leaders of the North hesitated to recognize the fact, the Confederate states had been ready from the day of surrender to resume their positions in the Union.

It can be pridefully said that the New South was devised by the Southerners, and they remain loyal Southerners, though no less Americans.

It is significant that Catawba countians, led by Newtonians, continue to honor the memory of their Confederate heroes through an annual observance—"Reunion" week, staged during August in the county seat city. The event, the chief feature of which is "Reunion Day," Thursday, when friends throughout the county and their friends throughout the nation gather to renew acquaintances, enjoy a parade and other activities, was begun by the Ransom-Sherrill chapter of the United Daughters of the Confederacy.

Concerning the "Reunion," George Pope has written:

". . . They used to set up tables on the old courthouse lawn and gave the old soldiers and their wives dinner on Reunion Day. How well do I remember the old Civil War vet from Taylorsville who used to give the famous old 'Rebel Yell' over at the courthouse. At that time, it was called 'Old Soldiers Reunion.' But now, since all the old Civil War vets are gone, it has been changed to 'Soldiers and Sailors Reunion' in honor of the Spanish American and World War One and Two veterans (now changed to simply Soldiers Reunion). . . ."

Records reveal that the first "regular" reunion was held July 4, 1892, at the county courthouse, when the Confederate veterans organized with J. G. Hall as the first commander and Miles O. Sherrill as first lieutenant. At that time, plans were made for the second reunion to be held a year later in Hickory.

CATAWBA COUNTY

There were 222 veterans at the first Reunion in 1892. Mrs. P. C. Hall, before her death, recalled that as early as 1879 there was a gathering of veterans, but pointed out that the first organized reunion came in 1892.

Another tribute to the patriotism of Confederate soldiers is a beautiful monument on the northeast corner of courtsquare in Newton. This, likewise, was erected by the Ransom-Sherrill Chapter, U. D. C.

Catawba county today claims the distinction of counting among its citizens a past national president general of the U. D. C. This is Mrs. Glenn Long of Newton, whose tireless efforts in the interest of the U. D. C., which organization is dedicated to promulgating the memory of the sacrifices of the Boys Who Wore the Grey, and her worthwhile work in many other realms of civic endeavor, deem her an asset to her county, her state, and her country.

A list of Catawba countians who served in military service during the War Between the States, as complete as possible, is presented. Abbreviations used are:

c ....captured	d ....died	p ....promoted
cm ....commissioned	dg........discharged	pr........prisoner
co ....county	dt ....detailed	r ....resigned
Com........Company	k ....killed	tr ....transferred
e ....enlisted	m ....missing	w ....wounded

Company A, Twelfth Regiment North Carolina Troops—

The first company to be formed in Catawba county to defend Southern Rights was organized in Newton on April 27, 1861. It was called "The Catawba Rifles." The men were sent to Norfolk, Va., where their outfit became designated as Company A, Twelfth Regiment North Carolina Troops.

OFFICERS

Ray, John, Capt, cm April 27, 1861, r August 1861.
Rowe, David Pinkney, Capt, cm Sept 16, 1861, k May 2, 1863, Chancellorsville, Va.
Sherrill, Uriah Franklin, Capt, cm 1861, died Sept 3, 1861, at Norfolk, Va.
Wilfong, Y. Milton, k May 12, 1864, at Spotsylvania Court House, Body brought home.
Bradburn, T. W., p Capt.

Yount, Miles A., 1st Lt, cm Sept, 1861, w at South Mountain, Md., and retired.
Deal, Miles Sylvannus, 1st Lt, cm Sept 16, 1861.
Rudisil, Henry P., 2nd Lt, w at Gettysburg, Pa., lost an arm, and retired.
Brown, James M., 2nd Lt, e April 27, 1861, w at Malvern Hill, retired.

NON-COMMISSIONED OFFICERS

Sherrill, John L., Sgt, e April 27, 1861, w at Hanover Court House.
Wilfong, Sidney Theodore, Sgt, e April 27, 1861, w Cold Harbor, lost an arm.
Bost, Robert A., 1st Cpl, e April 27, 1861.
Lowrance, William E., 2nd Cpl, e April 27, 1861.
Robinson, George W., 3rd Cpl, e April 27, 1861, d Sept 27, 1862.
Smith, Peter F., 4th Cpl, e April 27, 1861.
Abernethy, J. R., 4th Cpl, e April 27, 1861, w at Cold Harbor.

PRIVATES

Abernethy, Patrick E., e April 27, 1861.
Arndt, John M., e April 27, 1861, w at Cold Harbor, lost a leg.
Bailey, John, e April 27, 1861.
Bailey, George, e April 27, 1861.
Barringer, A. M., e April 27, 1861, k July 1, 1862, at Malvern Hill.
Bost, E. Govean, e April 27, 1861.
Bost, Robert A., e April 27, 1861.
Bost, Noah, e April 27, 1861, k July 1, 1862, at Malvern Hill.
Bost, Harvey J., e April 27, 1861, w at Chancellorsville, lost an arm.
Bolick, Salathiel, e April 27, 1861, w at Malvern Hill.
Bowman, Quincey Elcanah, e April 27, 1861, d Sept 22, 1906.
Bowman, Alonza, e April 27, 1861, k at Chancellorsville.
Bowman, Lamden, e April 27, 1861, k July 1, 1863, at Gettysburg.
Bowman, Noah, e April 1, 1862.
Bowman, P. C., e April 1, 1862.
Bowman, William, e April 1, 1862, k May 12, 1864, at Spotsylvania Court House.
Bowman, Wilson, e April 1, 1862, d 1902.
Bowman, E. L., e April 1, 1862.
Bradburn, T. W., e April 27, 1861.
Bradburn, J. M., e April 27, 1861.
Brown, Samuel, e April 27, 1861, transferred to ship Merrimac.
Brown, James, e April 27, 1861, k May 27, 1862, at Hanover Court House.
Brown, C. N., e April 27, 1861.
Bumgarner, Thomas L., e April 1, 1862.
Burch, William, e April 27, 1861.
Burns, William, e Sept 1, 1862, k at Chancellorsville.
Cline, W. H., e April 27, 1861, k Sept 19, 1864, at Winchester.
Cline, Eli Pinkney R., e April 27, 1861.
Cline, Eli (a cousin), e April 27, 1861.
Cline, Perry Robert, e April 27, 1861, w at Malvern Hill, lost an arm.
Cline, Henry, e April 1, 1861, d Sept 1, 1861.

CATAWBA COUNTY 293

Cline, Jonathan, e April 1, 1862, k May 14, 1864, at Spotsylvania Court House.
Cloninger, Elcanah, e April 1, 1862, w at Malvern Hill.
Conrad, Daniel, e April 27, 1861.
Conrad, D. E., e April 27, 1861.
Corpening, Albert G., e March 14, 1863, w at Chancellorsville.
Dailey, Abraham, e April 27, 1861.
Deal, J. Henry, e April 27, 1861, k May 3, 1863, at Chancellorsville.
Deal, Elcannah, e April 27, 1861.
Deal, G., e April 27, 1862, d July 16, 1862, at Richmond.
Deitz, J. B., e April 1, 1862, k in war by his horse.
Dellinger, J. H., e April 27, 1861.
Dixon, Jacob, e April 27, 1861, k May 12, 1864, at Spotsylvania Court House.
Eaton, J. A., April 27, 1861.
Epps, J. A., e April 27, 1861, w at Malvern Hill.
Finger, Daniel, e April 27, 1861, discharged disability.
Fox, George, e April 1, 1862.
Fry, Miles, e April 1, 1862, k at Warrenton, Va.
Fry, Jonas, e April 1, 1862, k at Petersburg, Va.
Gwaltney, G. R., e April 1, 1862.
Hallman, E. D., e Oct 16, 1861, d Dec. 6, 1863.
Harwell, C. C., e April 1, 1862, w at Chancellorsville.
Hawn, E. L., e April 27, 1861.
Hedrick, Sidney, e April 1, 1862.
Hedrick, W. F., e April 27, 1862.
Hefner, W. Sidney, e April 27, 1861.
Herman, Calvin, e April 27, 1861.
Herman, Elcannah, e April 27, 1861.
Hoke, J. D., e April 27, 1861.
Hoke, Julius, e April 27, 1861.
Hoke, B. E., e April 27, 1861.
Hoke, P. C., e April 27, 1861.
Howard, Nelson, e April 27, 1861.
Howard, Levi, e April 27, 1861.
Hoover, Adolphus A., e April 27, 1861, w Spotsylvania, lost an arm, died 1905.
Hoover, D. B., e April 23, 1861, k May 3, 1863, at Chancellorsville.
Hufman, W. F., e Aug 17, 1861.
Hunsucker, W. N., e April 27, 1861.
Hunsucker, Philo, Oct 16, 1861.
Ingold, A. A., e April 27, 1861, d August 1862, at Richmond, Va.
Ingold, W. S., e April 1, 1862.
Ingold, Brite, e April 1, 1862, k at Gettysburg.
Ingold, Luther, e April 1, 1862.
Ingold, Francis, e April 27, 1861, k May 9, 1864.
Isenhower, Hart, e April 27, 1861.
Kale, Pinkney, e April 27, 1861, d 1861.
Kale, John, e April 27, 1861.
Kale, Palser, e April 27, 1861.
Kale, E. P., e April 27, 1861.

Kale, H. L., e April 27, 1861.
Killian, W. S., e April 27, 1861.
Lafon, (or Lefong), T. T., e April 27, 1861.
Lafon, (or Lefong), Timothy, e April 27, 1861.
Lafon, (or Lefong), Noah, e April 1, 1862.
Lafon, (or Lefong), Yoder, e April 1, 1862.
Long, William A., e April 27, 1861.
Loretz, (or Lorentz), D. P., e April 27, 1861.
Lowrance, B. A., e April 27, 1861, w at Gettysburg.
Mathis, Daniel, e April 27, 1861.
Mathis, John, e April 27, 1861.
McGee, Jonas M., e April 27, 1861, w at Malvern Hill and at Gettysburg.
McNeal, T. J., e April 27, 1861.
Michael, Henry, e April 27, 1861, d August 1863.
Michael, Peter, e March 14, 1862.
Michael, L. D., e April 1, 1862.
Miller, J. F., e April 27, 1861, w June 27, 1862, at Cold Harbor.
Miller, Andrew, e April 27, 1861.
Mize, G. W. L., e April 27, 1861.
Moore, D. F., e April 27, 1861.
Moore, W. N., e April 27, 1861.
Moose, Daniel, e April 27, 1861, w slightly several times, surrendered with Lee.
Moose, Elcanah, e April 27, 1861.
Moose, William, e April 27, 1861.
Murphy, William F., e April 27, 1861, w at Gettysburg.
Orant (or Grant), John, e April 27, 1862.
Perry, John, e April 27, 1861, discharged.
Pool, J. H., e April 27, 1861.
Pope, John, e April 27, 1861.
Pope, Elcanah, e April 27, 1861.
Propst, Harvey, e April 27, 1861.
Propst, Noah, e April 27, 1861, surrendered with Lee.
Rabb, George W., e April 27, 1861, w at Chancellorsville, lost a leg.
Reinhardt, Robert Pinkney, e April 27, 1861, d 1902.
Ritzell (Reitzel) Henry, J., e April 27, 1862.
Reitzel, A. A., e April 27, 1861.
Robinson, A., e Oct 16, 1861, d Sept 1862, at Richmond.
Robinson, James Ferdinand, e April 27, 1861, k May 10, 1864, Spotsylvania, Court House.
Rowe, S. H., e June 6, 1861.
Rowe, Daniel LaFayette, e Aug 14, 1861, w at Gettysburg.
Rowe, Noah Isaiah, e Sept 1, 1862, w at Chancellorsville.
Rowe, Sidney Hoke, e June 6, 1861, w at Chancellorsville.
Sapaugh (Seabock), John, e April 27, 1861, w at Malvern Hill, k July 9, 1864.
Settlemyre, D. S., e April 27, 1861.
Settlemyre, Allen, e April 27, 1861.
Settlemyre, J. P., e April 27, 1861.
Setzer, Noah, e April 27, 1861.
Setzer, David, e April 27, 1861.

CATAWBA COUNTY

Setzer, Marcus, e April 27, 1861.
Setzer, Jacob, e April 1, 1862.
Sherrill, Miles O., e April 27, 1861, w May 9, 1864, Spotsylvania, lost a leg.
Sherrill, Thomas, e April 27, 1861.
Sherrill, James Albert, e April 27, 1861, k at South Mountain.
Sherrill, John, e April 27, 1861.
Sherrill, P. R., e April 27, 1861.
Shook, Tobias, e April 27, 1861.
Shook, John, e April 27, 1861.
Shook, Calvin, e April 1, 1862.
Shook, Jacob, e April 27, 1861.
Sigman, Marcus, Sr., e April 27, 1861.
Sigman, Marcus, Jr., e April 27, 1861.
Sigman, Albert, e April 27, 1861.
Sigmon, Wesley, e April 27, 1861.
Sigmon, Calvin, e Oct 16, 1861, w at Chancellorsville.
Sigmon, J. Churchill, e April 27, 1861.
Sigmon, Sylvannus, e April 27, 1861, d Sept, 1862.
Sigmon, J. E., e April 27, 1861.
Sigmon, Newton, e Oct 16, 1861, w at Chancellorsville.
Sigmon, Jethro, e March 19, 1863.
Sigmon, Alfred, e April 1, 1862, w at South Mountain.
Sigmon, W. R., e April 27, 1861.
Sipe, Jacob, e April 1, 1862.
Sipe, Noah, e April 1, 1862.
Smyre, Logan Quincey, e March 4, 1863, k March 25 at Petersburg, Va.
Symre, George S., e April 27, 1861, k at Hagerstown, Md. by Yankee sharpshooter.
Smyre, Silas, e April 27, 1861.
Smith, J. A., e April 27, 1861.
Travis, Nelson, e April 27, 1861, w at Chancellorsville.
Turbyfield, Thomas, e April 27, 1861, k at Chancellorsville.
Turbyfield, W. O., e Oct 14, 1862, d April 1863.
Turner, Joseph, e April 27, 1861.
Turner, John, e April 27, 1861.
Warren, J. Q., e April 27, 1861.
Webb, Curtis, e April 27, 1861, discharged.
White, Wilson, e April 27, 1861.
Whitener, L. R., e April 27, 1861, w at Gettysburg.
Whitener, Peter Wilfong, e April 27, 1861, w at Gettysburg, lost a leg.
Wilkerson, Rufus, e April 1, 1862, w at Malvern Hill.
Wilkerson, J. A., e Aug 14, 1863, w at Malvern Hill.
Wilkinson, John, e Aug 14, 1863.
Wilson, H. J., e April 27, 1861, k at Malvern Hill.
Wilson, D. C., e April 27, 1861.
Wilfong, Maxwell, e April 27, 1861.
Yount, Sidney L., e April 27, 1861, w at Malvern Hill, lost an arm.
Yount, Elcannah, e April 27, 1861, d in 1863 at Charlottesville, Va.
Yount, Hosea, e April 27, 1861.
Yount, Joseph, e April 27, 1861.

Company F Twenty-Third Regiment North Carolina Infantry—

The second company organized in Catawba county was F, Twenty-Third Regiment, under Captain Matthew Locke McCorkle, about June 6, 1861. There were approximately 146 men enrolled, many of whom were killed or died in prison. The most important battles engaged in were Manassas, Williamsburg, Seven Pines, and Seven Days Fight Around Richmond. After the campaigns in Maryland and Pennsylvania, the company returned to Virginia, crippled and reduced in number, but buoyant in spirit. The men were in the battle at Hanover Court House, the Wilderness, and many minor engagements, winding up at the Battle of the Crater, near Petersburg, Va., from which place they marched to Appomattox Court House, and surrendered with General Robert E. Lee, on April 9, 1865.

OFFICERS

McCorkle, M. L., Capt, cm June 6, 1861.
Miller, Jacob H., 1st Lt, cm June 6, 1861.
Wilson, T. W., 1st Lt.
Helton, M. L., 2nd Lt, cm June 6, 1861.
Cobb, R. A., 2nd Lt, cm June 6, 1861.
Clay, G. P., 2nd Lt, cm May 10, 1862.
Wilson, T. W., 2nd Lt, cm May 10, 1862.

NON-COMMISSIONED OFFICERS

Wilkie, L. W., 1st Lt, e June 6, 1861.
Thornton, H. H., 2nd Sgt, e June 6, 1861.
Leonard, J. M., 3rd Sgt, e June 6, 1861, tr. to 57th Regiment.
Pruner, John M., 4th Sgt, e June 6, 1861.
Link, Peter A., 1st Cpl, e June 6, 1861, k in Virginia.
McCorkle, D. N., 2nd Cpl, e June 6, 1861, d July 9, 1862, at Richmond.
Rink, Eli F., 3rd Cpl, e June 6, 1861, w at Seven Pines.
Rowe, Sidney H., e June 6, 1861, tr. to 12th Regiment.

PRIVATES

Abernethy, John F., e June 6, 1861, w at Malvern Hill.
Angel, Marcus L., e March 1, 1862.
Baker, Barton, e June 6, 1861.
Berry, James M., e June 6, 1861, d Dec. 1st of w at Seven Pines.
Benfield, Marcus, e June 6, 1861.
Beatty, Tyler, e June 6, 1861, pr at Gettysburg.
Bolch, William H., e June 6, 1861.
Bost, W. R. D., e June 6, 1861, d July 9, 1862, w at Seven Pines.

CATAWBA COUNTY

Bolch, Israel, e June 6, 1861, d Aug. 1 1862, of disability.
Bolch, Anthony, e June 6, 1861, w at Chancellorsville.
Baker, Alfred, e Sept 1, 1861, d July 4, 1862, for w received at Seven Pines.
Bumgarner, Miles, e June 6, 1861, w at Fredricksburg.
Bumgarner, H. P., e June 6, 1861.
Burnes, Eli, e March 10, 1863, pr at Winchester.
Bruce, F. H., e June 6, 1861, d March 31, 1861, at Orange Court House.
Cobb, Robt. Alexander, 2nd Lt.
Clay, G. P., e Sept 1, 1861, p 2nd Lt, May 10, 1862.
Clay, David E., e March 1, 1862, w and d July 28, 1862, Va.
Cline, Calvin, e June 6, 1861, k July 1863 at Gettysburg.
Cline, Eli, June 6 1861, k May 31, 1862, at Seven Pines.
Cline, William S., e June 6, 1861, w at Chancellorsville.
Crawford, W. J., e June 6, 1861.
Christopher, E. A., e June 6, 1861, w at Seven Pines.
Cummings, G. W., e July 8, 1862.
Deal, J. A., e June 6, 1861.
Dellinger, e June 6, 1861, w at Chancellorsville.
Dagerheart, Pinkney, e Sept. 1, 1861.
Ekard, Wesley D., e June 6, 1861, p Sgt, w at Seven Pines.
Fisher, Jas. C., e June 6, 1861, tr to Com. D.
Fry, John C., e June 6, 1861, w Seven Pines, k May 1863, at Chancellorsville.
Fisher, Joel H., e Sept 1, 1861.
Gibson, Jas. W., e June 6, 1861, dt.
Gross, Daniel, e July 8, 1862, c Gettysburg.
Heffner, Timothy, e June 6, 1861, w Gettysburg.
Helton, A. F., e Feb. 28, 1863.
Hayes, William, e June 6, 1861, d Sept 28, 1861.
Hartsoe, Paul, e June 6, 1861, d Aug 15, 1861 in Va.
Hoyle, Wm. C., e June 6, 1861, d Jan 1, 1862.
Hoyle, Phillip A., e Oct 2, 1863.
Holler, Gilbert, e June 6, 1861.
Holler, M. A., e June 6, 1861, w at Seven Pines.
Hall, John C., e June 6, 1861, dg Sept, 1862, for disability.
Helton, M. A., e March 1, 1862.
Hoover, Jefferson, e June 6, 1861.
Hudson, W. H., e Feb 16, 1864.
Huffman, M. A., e June 6, 1861, w at Chancellorsville, c at Winchester.
Huffman, L. C., e Sept 1, 1861, d July 17, 1863.
Icenhour, M. J., e June 6, 1861, w and d Oct 19, 1864 at Gettysburg.
Jones, Isaac E., e June 6, 1861, c at Winchester.
Johnson, George, e March 1, 1862, w at Gettysburg.
Johnson, Maxwell, e March 10, 1863, d Nov 15, 1864.
Jarrett, George, e March 1, 1862, w Gettysburg, p at Winchester.
Killian, Wm. F., e June 6, 1861, w Seven Pines and Gettysburg.
Killian, Wm. L., e June 6, 1861, p 1st Sgt and C.
Leonard, D. P., e June 6, 1861, d Oct 9, 1862.
Lutz, J. S., e June 6, 1861, w at Seven Pines.
Lofton, Eli, e June 6, 1861, w Gettysburg.

Lofton, Pinkney, e June 6, 1861, d Sept 15, 1861, in Virginia.
Lofton, William, e June 6, 1861, d Oct 20, 1861.
Lael, Alexander, e June 6, 1861, dg.
Lael, Lawson, e Oct 13, 1863.
Moore, George A., e June 6, 1861.
Martin, M. P., e June 6, 1861, k July 1863, at Gettysburg.
Masteller, Lawson, e June 6, 1861.
Mays, William, e June 6, 1861.
Marshall, E. W., e July 8, 1862, d Feb 2, 1863.
Michael, Noah, e June 6, 1861, d July 16, 1862.
Mitchell, Thomas, e June 6, 1861, d Sept 26, 1861 in Virginia.
McGinnis, Albert, e June 6, 1861, d June 1, 1862 at Seven Pines.
McNeill, George C., e June 6, 1861.
Miller, Robert, e June 6, 1861, dg Oct. 18, 1862.
Miller, John R., e June 6, 1861.
Miller, J. M., e April 3, 1864, c May 13, 1864.
Miller, Wesley, e July 4, 1862.
Mosteller, J. B., e March 1, 1861, d May 16, 1862.
McCorkle, F. M., e June 6, 1861, d June 17, 1862, in Va.
Pool, James L., e June 6, 1861.
Pool, John, tr from 12th Reg., d Aug 16, 1862.
Pool, Alexander, e Jan 16, 1863, k May 1863 at Chancellorsville.
Parker, Jacob, e June 6, 1861, m.
Parker, Albert, e March 1, 1862.
Propst, John H., e March 21, 1862, dg Oct 20, 1863, for disability.
Reinhardt, E. F., e June 6, 1861, k July, 1863, at Gettysburg.
Reinhardt, Abraham, e July 8, 1862, k July, 1863, at Gettysburg.
Reinhardt, Elias, e March 10, 1863, d June 2, 1853, w Chancellorsville.
Reinhardt, Levi, e March 19, 1863.
Ramsey, Daniel, e March 1, 1862, w at Gettysburg.
Rink, George F., e June 6, 1861, w at Gettysburg.
Seagle, Adam, e June 6, 1861, w at Gettysburg.
Scronce, Wm. A., e June 6, 1861, w at Seven Pines.
Seitz, Julius, e June 6, 1861.
Seitz, G. L., e March 1, 1862, d Aug 3, 1863.
Seitzer, John F., e June 6, 1861.
Shell, William D., e June 6, 1861, w Chancellorsville & Gettysburg.
Shell, J. H., e June 6, 1861, w at Seven Pines.
Shuford, Philip, e March 1, 1862.
Shuford, Solomon, e March 1, 1862.
Shuford, Able A., e June 6, 1861, p Sgt, w near Richmond.
Sigman, C. C., e June 6, 1861.
Sigman, G. P., e June 6, 1861, d Dec 4, 1861, in Virginia.
Sigman, M. E., e June 6, 1861, d July 1, 1862, in Virginia.
Smith, W. H., e June 6, 1861, d Nov 20, 1861.
Speagle, Philip, e Oct 13, 1863, c Oct 19, 1864.
Towell, W. A., e June 6, 1861, k.
Warlick, G. W., e June 6, 1861, w at Chancellorsville.
Warlick, W. T., e June 6, 1861, p Sgt, w at Gettysburg.
Warlick, M. H., e Feb. 28, 1863, w at Gettysburg.

CATAWBA COUNTY

Walker, James S., e July 8, 1862.
Weaver, John, e March 1, 1862.
Weaver, J. S., e July 8, 1862.
Whitener, D. L., e June 6, 1861, k near Richmond.
Whitener, G. W., e Sept 1, 1861, d Sept 20, 1862, Shepherdstown.
Whitener, Newton, e March 10, 1862, w and pr at Chancellorsville.
Whistenhunt, William, e March 1, 1861, p May 12, 1864.
Wilcoxen, J. B., e July 8, 1862.
Wilson, T. W., e June 6, 1861, p 2nd Lt, May 10, 1862.
Wingate, Albert, e June 6, 1861, d July 13, 1862.
Workman, David, e March 5, 1862, w at Gettysburg.
Yoder, A. M., e Sept 1, 1861, w thrice.
Yoder, Robert, e Sept 16, 1863.

Company E Thirty-second Regiment North Carolina Infantry—

Organized by Mathew Melchisedek Wilson, familiary known as "Chez" about August 1, 1861, this company went first to Norfolk, then returned to North Carolina for some months, before going to Suffolk, Petersburg, Drewry's Bluff, and then to Carlisle, where it had the honor of hoisting the Confederate flag at its fartherest point North. The men did not undergo the hardships of the Maryland campaign, but they did their full share at Gettysburg. After other smaller battles, the company was ordered to Petersburg, and there fought for days, before going to Appomattox for the final roll-call and to surrender with General Robert E. Lee on April 9, 1865.

OFFICERS

Wilson, M. M., Major, cm Aug 14, 1861.
Wilson, Matthew M., Capt, cm Aug 14, 1861.
Shell, Manuel E., Capt, cm May 1, 1862, d July 9, 1862.
Sherrill, Gilbert M., Capt, cm July 9, 1862, d 1864.
Shell, M. E., 1st Lt, cm Aug 14, 1861, p & d.
Sherrill, G. M., 1st Lt, cm May 1, 1862, p.
Little, D. A., 1st Lt, cm July 9, 1862.
Sherrill, G. W., 2nd Lt, cm Aug 14, 1861, p.
Little, D. A., 1st Lt, cm July 9, 1862.
Sherrill, G. W., 2nd Lt, cm Aug 14, 1861, p.
Robinson, John A., 2nd Lt, cm August 14, 1861, p.
Snyder, Joseph E., 2nd Lt, cm May 1, 1862.
Shuford, Pinkney C., 2nd Lt, cm July 13, 1862.
Anthony, Abram, 2nd Lt, cm Dec 15, 1863.

NON-COMMISSIONED OFFICERS

Shuford, Pinkney C., 1st Sgt, e Aug 14, 1861.
Payne, John W. A., 2nd Sgt. e August 14, 1861.

Snyder, Joseph E., 3rd Sgt., e August 14, 1861.
Stiles, Elisha B., 4th Sgt, e August 14, 1861.
Fisher, William G., 5th Sgt, e August 14, 1861.
Gantt, Even, 1st Cpl, e August 14, 1861.
Abernethy, Robert D., 2nd Cpl, e August 14, 1861.
Cansler, Abel J., 3rd Cpl, e August 14, 1861.
Rudisill, Jacob F., 4th Cpl, e August 14, 1861.

PRIVATES

Allen, Frances G., e Dec 14, 1861, dg Aug 17, 1862.
Allen, B. A., e Jan. 2, 1862, d Jan 20, 1863.
Anthony, Abram, e Sept 12, 1861.
Bangle, Henry, e March 13, 1861.
Bolch, Robert, e Oct 18, 1861, d June 4, 1864.
Bridges, H. W., e Aug 14, 1861.
Brown, T. G., e Aug 14, 1861, d in prison in 1864.
Burke, Reeves, e Sept 25, 1862.
Caldwell, J. J., e Sept 25, 1862.
Caldwell, L. J., e Sept 25, 1862.
Caldwell, Gilbert, e Sept 25, 1862.
Caldwell, Henderson, e March 31, 1863.
Canipe, J. A., e Oct 1, 1862.
Carpenter, J. L., e Oct 1, 1862.
Cline, A. K., e Aug 14, 1861.
Cline, W. P., e March 13, 1863, d of w received at Gettysburg.
Clippard, Henry, e March 31, 1863.
Clippard, Marcus, e March 31, 1863, d in prison in 1864.
Clonninger, J. Postel, e May, 1864.
Coonce, Henry, e March 31, 1863.
Cornelius, H. F., e Aug 14, 1861.
Crouse, J. L., e Sept 25, 1862.
Cansler, G. P., e March 22, 1864.
Dixon, William G., e Sept 12, 1861.
Dixon, Samuel, e Aug 14, 1861, d June 13, 1862.
Fink, Caleb, e Oct 18, 1861, d June 13, 1862.
Fry, M. A., e Aug 14, 1861.
Hamilton, M. R., e Aug 14, 1861, d of w at Gettysburg.
Hamilton, Thomas B., e Oct 10, 1861, d of w at Gettysburg.
Hamilton, Leonidas, e March 31, 1863.
Hawn, G. W., e March 31, 1863.
Hendrick, Peter, e March 31, 1863, d Dec 3, 1863.
Hendrick, Levi, e March 3, 1863.
Hewit, Logan, e Aug 14, 1861, d of w in Virginia.
Hewit, A. M., e March 31, 1863.
Hewit, L. L., e March 31, 1861.
Hunt, A. M., e March 31, 1863, w at Gettysburg.
Hunsucker, J. P., e Aug 14, 1861.
Hunsucker, Jonas, e March 31, 1863, d in prison in 1864.
Jarrett, D. P., e Dec 19, 1861.
Jonas, G. W., e Aug 14, 1861, dg Aug 17, 1862.

CATAWBA COUNTY

Little, Albert, e Aug 14, 1861.
Little, William S., e Feb 25, 1863, w at Gettysburg.
Linn, John F., e Sept 12, 1862.
Linn, H. B., e Aug 14, 1862.
Lofton, Edmund, dg Jan, 1862, for disability.
Love, David, e March 31, 1863.
Little, J. A., e Jan 2, 1862.
Little, M. A., e Nov 10, 1863.
McGinnis, G. A., e Sept 5, 1861, w at Gettysburg.
Miller, Rufus, e Oct 6, 1862.
Miller, Absalom, e March 31, 1863.
Miller, Abram, e March 31, 1863.
Mitchel, William J., e Nov 3, 1864.
Moses, M. M., e March 31, 1863.
Mull, Adam, e March 31, 1863.
Propst, John W., e Aug 14, 1863, w Sept 15, 1863, near Winchester.
Reep, Daniel, e Aug 14, 1861.
Reep, Christopher, e Aug 14, 1861.
Reep, Alfred, e March 31, 1863.
Robinson, F. O., e Jan 2, 1863.
Robinson, Jethro, e March 31, 1863.
Robinson, D. S., e March 31, 1863, d at home.
Rudisill, J. F., e Aug 14, 1861.
Setzer, J. S., e Aug 14, 1861.
Sherrill, M. W., e Sept 12, 1861.
Sherrill, E. A., e March 31, 1861.
Sherrill, J. M., e Feb 22, 1864, d at home.
Shuford, David H., e Feb, 1864.
Sigmon, J. Churchill, e 1863 at the age of 18, w March 25, 1864.
Sigmon, J. E., e Aug 14, 1861.
Smyre, Logan, e Oct 26, 1861, dg Aug 17, 1862.
Turner, John, e Aug 14, 1861.
Turner, Josephus, e March 17, 1863, dg Nov 1, 1863, disability.
Wade, W. A., e Aug 14, 1861.
Wade, L. R., e Aug 14, 1861, d July 5, 1863, w at Gettysburg.
Warlick, Lafayette, e Sept 12, 1861.
Workman, S. E., Aug 14, 1861.
Wineburger, N. W., e March 31, 1863.
Wineburger, Silas, e March 5, 1862.
Wilkinson, W. H., e Oct 10, 1862.
Wilkinson, D. D., e March 31, 1863.
Wilson, H. M., e Aug 14, 1861.
Wilson, D. C., e Aug 14, 1861.
Wilson, Newton, e Aug 14, 1861, d of w at Gettysburg.
Wilson, Nathaniel, e Aug 14, 1861, d Aug 16, 1862.
Wilson, A. S., e Aug 14, 1861, dg June, 1862, for disability.
Whitener, D. R., e Oct 25, 1861, d July 24, 1862.
Wyshoff, W. D., e April 1, 1863.
Yoder, Rev. R. A.
Yount, R. L., e Feb 25, 1863, dg Nov 10, 1863, for w.

Yount, A. S., e Aug 14, 1861, dg June, 1863, disability.
Yount, M. P., e Aug 14, 1861, d June 13, 1862.
Yount, J. L., e Aug 14, 1861, d June 25, 1862.

Company F Thirty-second Regiment North Carolina Infantry—

Organized about the same time as Company E Thirty-second Regiment, the history of this company is virtually the same as the former. Its men were in many battles, large and small, before reaching Gettysburg, and, from this time, it engaged in one continuous skirmish and battle. Following the battle at Spotsylvania Court House, Company F had only 52 men, and Company E had only a few more. The companies then were combined, and came together to the surrender ground at Appomattox on April 9, 1865.

OFFICERS

Ray, John, Capt, cm April 27, 1861, r Dec 14, 1861.
Smith, Peter F., Capt, e April, 1861, cm Dec 16, 1861.
Aderhold, John, 1st Lt, cm April 27, 1861.
Lawrence, W. E., 1st Lt, cm May 1, 1862, p from Sgt.
Smith, P. F., 2nd Lt, cm April 27, 1861.
Lortz, Daniel P., 2nd Lt, cm April 27, 1861.
Smith, Julius A., 2nd Lt, cm May 1, 1862, p from 1st Sgt.

NON-COMMISSIONED OFFICERS

Smith, Julius A., 1st Sgt, e April 27, 1861, p 2nd Lt, May 1, 1862.
Lawrence, William E., 2nd Sgt, e April 27, 1861, p 1st Lt, May 1, 1862.
Fish, Henry, 3rd Sgt, e April 27, 1861, d Aug 17, 1862.
Hunsucker, William N., 4th Sgt, e April 27, 1861, pr.
Hall, Palsor, 5th Sgt, e April 27, 1861, dg June 8, 1862.
McNeill, Thomas, 1st Cpl, e April 27, 1861.
Bridges, Alfred T., 2nd Cpl, e April 27, 1861, pr.
Abernethy, Patrick, 3rd Cpl, e April 27, 1861, d April 18, 1862.
Long, J. Uriah, 4th Cpl, e April 27, 1861, w at Gettysburg.
Pitt, Julian V., Drummer, e April 27, 1861.

PRIVATES

Abernethy, Miles A., e Feb 25, 1863.
Aderhold, William H., e Jan 1, 1863.
Aderhold, W. H., e Jan 1, 1864.
Aderhold, F. S., e Jan 1, 1864.
Bynum, John G., e Aug 14, 1861, p Ord Sgt, pr.
Bailey, John, e April 27, 1861.
Bradburn, Jas. M., e April 27, 1861.
Conrad, John, e April 27, 1861.

CATAWBA COUNTY

Conrad, Daniel, e April 27, 1861, d Aug 31, 1862.
Crawford, Jeff, e Aug 14, 1861, dg June 8, 1862, disability.
Dailey, Abraham, e Nov 27, 1861, d July 4, 1862.
Dellinger, John H., e April 27, 1861, pr.
Dellinger, James, e Jan 1, 1863, w at Gettysburg.
Eaton, James, e April 27, 1861.
Edwards, Spencer, e April 20, 1863.
Edwards, Robert, e Dec 1, 1861.
Ennis, J., e April 10, 1864, pr.
Fish, Bryson, e April 13, 1863.
Goodman, Martin, e Aug 14, 1861.
Harwell, Cannon, e Feb 25, 1863, d during the war.
Harwell, Elisha, e Aug 14, 1861, d Oct 4, 1862.
Hefner, Franklin, e Oct 18, 1862, d Oct 4, 1863, w r Gettysburg.
Howard, Levi, e April 27, 1861, pr.
Howard, Nelson, e April 27, 1861, w at Gettysburg.
Hill, Henry D., e Dec 1, 1861.
Hill, Jacob, e Feb 25, 1863, d May 12, 1863.
Hunsucker, James, e Dec 1, 1862.
Irving, John B., e April 27, 1861, p Sgt, dg June 14, 1862.
James, William, e Dec 1, 1861, dg.
Jones, Alfred C., e Sept 20, 1861, w at Gettysburg.
Jones, Burton, e Sept 20, 1861, dg.
Jones, Manuel, e Sept 20, 1861, w at Gettysburg.
Jones, Marcus L., e Sept 10, 1861, p Sgt.
Jones, Levi, A., e Dec 1, 1861.
Kale, Henderson, e April 27, 1861.
Kale, Pinkney, e April 27, 1861, d Oct 3, 1861.
Kale, Noah, e Oct 1, 1862, pr.
Killian, Noah, e Oct 15, 1862, d Dec 14, 1863.
Lael, Calvin, e Dec 1, 1861, dg.
Long, William A., e April 27, 1861, p Sgt.
Lawrence, W. E., pr, 1st Lt, dg.
Moore, William, e April 27, 1861, pr.
Moore, Philo, e Aug 14, 1861, pr.
Mize, Lafayette, e April 27, 1861, p Sgt, pr.
Moss, Julius A., e Aug 14, 1861.
Moss, William, e Aug 14, 1861, k at Spotsylvania.
Miller, Andrew, e April 27, 1861.
Pope, John, e April 27, 1861, pr.
Parker, David, e Oct 15, 1862.
Robinson, Newton, e Feb 26, 1863, pr.
Sherrill, William P., e April 27, 1861, p Sgt, and pr.
Sigmon, John C., e April 27, 1861, p Cpl, and pr.
Sherrill, Thomas, Sr., e April 27, 1861, pr.
Sherrill, Nicholas, e Aug 14, 1861, pr.
Sherrill, Thomas, Jr., e Feb 25, 1863.
Sherrill, Alexander, e Aug 14, 1861, d July 17, 1862.
Sigmon, Daniel, e Aug 14, 1861, dg.
Slewman, Charles, e Aug 14, 1861.
Sherman, Charles, e Aug 14, 1861, p Com Sgt, Aug 1, 1863.

Sutton, Franklin, e Aug 14, 1861, dg.
Wilson, Eli, P., e Dec 1, 1861.
Wilson, Pink, e Dec 14, 1861.
Witherspoon, Henry F., e Aug 14, 1861, p Cpl, d Aug 24, 1863.

Company C, Twenty-eighth Regiment North Carolina Infantry—

Company C, the fifth organized in Catawba county, left Newton on August 13, 1861, for High Point, where it joined the Twenty-eighth Regiment. Thomas L. Lowe was its first captain. The company's strength totaled about 130 men. The company spent the winter about Wilmington, New Bern and Kinston. In the early spring, it went to Richmond. The company was in the thickest of the battles, engaging in conflicts at Mechanicsville, Cold Harbor, Frazier's Farm, Bull Run, Fredericksburg, Chancellorsville, and Gettysburg. The brave men who survived were with General Lee at the surrender ground.

OFFICERS

Lowe, Thomas L., Capt, cm Aug 13, 1861, p Major, Sept 21, 1861.
Linebarger, T. James, Capt, cm May 12, 1862, p from 1st Lt, w at Fredericksburg and Gettysburg.
Linebarger, T. James, 1st Lt, cm Feb 27, 1862, p to 2nd Lt, d of w on July 5, 1863, at Gettysburg.
Kent, John, 1st Lt, cm May 3, 1862, d July 14, 1862.
Gilbert, Jacob H., 2nd Lt, cm May 13, 1861.
Cline, E. Elkanah, 2nd Lt, cm May 13, 1861.
Linebarger, T. J., 2nd Lt, cm Sept 26, 1861, p and k.
Kent, John, 2nd Lt, cm Oct 6, 1861, d July 14, 1862.
Thornburg, M. A., 2nd Lt, cm Aug 4, 1862, p.

NON-COMMISSIONED OFFICERS

Thornburg, M. Augustus, 1st Sgt, e Aug 13, 1861, p 2nd Lt on Aug 4, 1862.
Setzer, Franklin A., 2nd Sgt, e Aug 13, 1861.
Austin, E. Coleman, 4th Sgt, e Aug 13, 1861, p 2nd Lt, k July 3, 1863, at Gettysburg.
Taylor, George E., 1st Cpl, e Aug 13, 1861, d July 19, 1863 at Jordan Springs.
Little, Joshua A., 2nd Cpl, e Aug 13, 1861, p Sgt, w at Ox Hill, d in City Point.
Flowers, Noah F., 3rd Cpl, e Aug 13, 1861, dg July 25, 1862, for disability.
Eckard, Rufus, 4th Cpl, e Aug 13, 1861, p Sgt, k Dec 13, 1862, at Fredericksburg.

PRIVATES

Bolch, Marcus, e Aug 13, 1861, w at 2nd Manassas & Chancellorsville.
Asbury, William
Asbury, Sidney

Sparkling Catawba Springs

CATAWBA COUNTY 305

Bolch, Aaron, e Aug 13, 1861, p Cpl, w at Gettysburg.
Bolch, Abel, e March 15, 1861, w at Cold Harbor.
Bolch, Emmanuel, e March 15, 1861, d Aug 15, 1862, Charlottsville, Va.
Bolch, William, e March 15, 1861, d July 15, 1862.
Bolch, Logan, e March 14, 1863, w and d at Gettysburg.
Bolch, Henkle P., e March 14, 1863, w and d at Gettysburg.
Bolch, N. A., e Dec, 1864.
Bumgarner, Sidney, e Aug 13, 1861, d Aug 1, 1862.
Bumgarner, Allen, e Aug 13, 1861.
Bumgarner, David A., e March 15, 1862, w at Chancellorsville.
Barger, Moses, e Sept 9, 1861, d May 25, 1862 at Charlottsville.
Barger, Josiah W., e March 15, 1862, d May 29, 1863, Guinea Station.
Barger, David.
Barger, Allen, e March 15, 1862.
Barger, Noah, e March 15, 1862.
Barger, Marcus, e March 15, 1862.
Barger, Gilbert.
Bowman, Calvin M., e March 15, 1862.
Bolch, Jordon, e April 4, 1864.
Cline, Sylvanus, e March 2, 1863.
Cline, J. Timothy, e Feb 12, 1864.
Cline, Adolphus, e April 6, 1864.
Childers, Franklin, e Aug 26, 1861, d March 4, 1862 at Wilmington.
Campbell, Adolphus L., e Aug 13, 1861, d July, 1863 of w, r at Gettysburg.
Campbell, Wilburn A., e Aug 13, 1861, dg Dec 20, 1861.
Cook, Abel, e Sept 9, 1862, m May 12, 1864.
Cook, Lawson, e March 15, 1862, w Gettysburg.
Carter, Joshua C., e Aug 13, 1861, w Chancellorsville.
Cline, Monroe J., e Aug 13, 1861, d at Winchester.
Cline, Maxwell A., e Aug 12, 1861.
Cline, John L. H., e Feb 18, 1863, k May 12, 1864.
Cline, Alfred J., e Aug. 13, 1861.
Cline, Ambrose, e March 14, 1863, k near Richmond.
Clippard, John, e March 15, 1862.
Conrad, Henry A., e Aug 13, 1861, k at P. Mills.
Deal, Junius, e Aug 13, 1861, d June 10, 1863.
Deal, Levi, e March 14, 1863, d June 10, 1863.
Drum, David J., e Aug 13, 1861, w 2nd Manassas & Gettysburg.
Drum, Joseph M., e March 15, 1862, w Cold Harbor, k Aug 29, 1862 at 2nd Manassas.
Eckard, Cyrus, e Aug 13, 1861, c and d June 29, 1862 at Governor's Island.
Fry, Jacob A., e Sept 2, 1861, m at Gettysburg.
Fry, Ephraim N., e Aug 13, 1861, w at Gettysburg.
Fry, Andrew J., e Aug 13, 1861.
Fisher, George, e March 15, 1862, d in war.
Fulbright, John, e March 14, 1863.
Goins, Philip P., Aug 13, 1861, w at Chancellorsville.
Goodson, James, e Aug 13, 1861, w at Frazier's Farm.
Grice, James M., e Sept 2, 1861, w Fredericksburg, Chancellorsville and Gettysburg, p Sgt.

Grice, H. Lee, e Aug 12, 1863.
Graburl, A. Alonzo, e March 15, 1862, tr to 23rd Regt, p Sgt.
Hefner, Marcus, e Aug 13, 1861, k May 3, 1863, at Chancellorsville.
Hefner, Serenus, e Aug 13, 1861, w Sept 20, 1864.
Hefner, Levi, e Aug 13, 1861, w at Ox Hill.
Hefner, David, e Aug 13, 1861.
Huffman, Levi L., e Aug 13, 1861.
Huffman, George, w and d at Farmville.
Huffman, John F., e Aug 13, 1861, d of w at Cold Harbor.
Huffman, Jeremiah, e Aug 13, 1861, w at Cold Harbor.
Huffman, Daniel, e Aug 13, 1861, w Manassas.
Huffman, Marcus, e March 15, 1862, d July 2, 1862, pr at Governor's Island.
Huffman, Elijah, e March 15, 1862, d Dec 10, 1862.
Huffman, Elijah J., e March 15, 1862, d June 6, 1863 in Virginia.
Herman, Abel, e Aug 13, 1861, m at Falling Waters.
Harman, D. Monroe, e Aug 13, 1861, w Chancellorsville, p Cpl.
Herman, Rufus E., e Aug 13, 1861, w.
Herman, Phanuel J., e Aug 13, 1861, w Gettysburg, p Sgt.
Herman, George D. E., e Aug 13, 1861, w 2nd Manassas.
Herman, Noah, e 1864.
Herman, D. Alexander, e March 15, 1862, d March 27, 1862.
Herman, W. Henry, e March 15, 1862, d July 8, 1862 at Gordonsville.
Herman, Daniel, e May 6, 1864, d in war.
Hass, John A., e Aug 13, 1861, w Chancellorsville.
Harwell, Watson A., March, 1863, w at Gettysburg.
Hass, Sidney, e Feb 6, 1864.
Hawn, D. Newton, e March 15, 1862, m at Gettysburg.
Hahn, Jesse, volunteered, too old for field service. Exempted. Later guarded prisoners at Salisbury.
Houston, Martin L., e Aug 13, 1861, d July 17, 1862 at Richmond of w, r at Cold Harbor.
Houston, John W., e Aug 13, 1861.
Houston, Jacob F., e March 15, 1862, w at Shepherdstown and Gettysburg, p to Cpl.
Hefner, George, March 15, 1862, m in action May 12, 1864.
Hefner, Wilson, e March 15, 1862, w Chancellorsville, m July 28, 1864.
Holler, Adley D., e April 11, 1862.
Holler, Lemuel, e March 15, 1862, w Gettysburg.
Honeycutt, Solomon, e March 15, 1862, w Chancellorsville.
Kaylor, Alfred, e 1864.
Killian, Elijah, e Aug 13, 1861, dt.
Killian, Calvin M., e Aug 13, 1861, d July 1, 1862 of w, r at Frazier's Farm.
Killian, Joseph, e March 15, 1862.
Killian, Anthony, e Sept 23, 1863, Camp Vance, Burke Co.
Killian, Jasper.
Kent, John, e Sept 9, 1861, p 1st Lt.
Linebarger, Monroe M., e Nov 16, 1863, d in war.
Linebarger, F. Middleton, e Oct 25, 1864.
Linebarger, Levi W., e March 15, 1862, p 1st Sgt, k Farmville.

CATAWBA COUNTY 307

Linebarger, Avery P., e March 15, 1862, w and d Shepherdstown.
Linebarger, Jacob A., e June 22, 1861, tr from 23rd, w at Chancellorsville, d July 5, 1863.
Linebarger, T. James, e Aug 13, 1861, p Capt, w Fredericksburg.
Little, Joshua A., e Aug 13, 1861, d in war.
Little, J. Pinkney, e Aug 12, 1861, w Frazier's Farm and Chancellorsville.
Link, Ephraim M., March 15, 1861, w at Gettysburg.
Lail, Polycarp, e March 14, 1863.
Lail, Abel, e Aug 12, 1863.
Lail, Cicero, e March 15, 1862, w at Ox Hill, m July 28, 1864.
Martin, James W., e Sept 5, 1861, w & d Manassas Sept 22, 1862.
Martin, Robert, e Sept 6, 1861, d July 15, 1862 at G. Island.
Martin, William A., e Aug 13, 1861, w at Gettysburg.
Moose, John B., e Aug 13, 1861, d June 11, 1862 of w at Hanover Court House.
Miller, Marcus, e Aug 13, 1861, d in war.
Miller, William J., e Aug 13, 1861, k July 3, 1863, Gettysburg.
Miller, Samuel E., Sept 9, 1861, d Jan 6, 1863, Lynchburg.
Miller, W., e March 15, 1862, w Frazier's Farm and Gettysburg.
Miller, Caleb, e March 16, 1862, d in war.
Miller, David E., e March 15, 1863, w at Wilderness.
Potts, Conrad, e Aug 13, 1861.
Potts, W. Henry, e Aug 13, 1861, d Aug 31, 1862.
Propst, Alfred, e Aug 13, 1861, d Jan 29, 1863, Lynchburg.
Punch, Robert W., e Sept 9, 1861, d Dec 16, 1862 of w, r at Fredericksburg.
Punch, Joseph L., e Aug 13, 1861, dg June 15, 1862, disability.
Punch, William S., e Sept 9, 1861, d July 15, 1863.
Poovey, Lawson, A.
Poovey, William H., e Aug 13, 1861, w Shepherdstown.
Poovey, Josiah A., March 14, 1862, w Gettysburg.
Poovey, Hiram H., e March 14, 1862, dt.
Poovey, David A., e March 14, 1862, w Chancellorsville.
Poovey, William F., e Sept 1, 1862, d Dec 10, 1862.
Poovey, Julius A., e Jan. 27, 1863, w Chancellorsville.
Poovey, A. Levi, e Jan 27, 1863, w Gettysburg.
Poovey, Henry F., e March 14, 1863, k July 3, 1863, Gettysburg.
Poovey, H. Taylor.
Pollard, Hiram, e Sept 9, 1861, w 2nd Manassas.
Rader, W. Pinkney, e Aug 13, 1861.
Reynolds, James A., e Sept 2, 1861, m at Gettysburg.
Reynolds, F. Harvey, e March 15, 1862, d Nov 19, 1862 in Virginia.
Rinck, Henry, e March 15, 1862, w and pr at Hanover Court House.
Rink, John K., e April 2, 1861.
Seabock, George W., e Sept 9, 1861.
Seabock, J. Pinkney, e Sept 9, 1861, k June 27, 1862.
Seabock, W. H., e March 15, 1862, k.
Seitz, Marcus, e March 15, 1862, d May 3, 1863 of w, r at Chancellorsville.
Seitz, Laban M., e March 15, 1862, dg Jan 26, 1863 for w, r at Sharpsburg.
Short, John, e Sept 2, 1861, pr and d July 30, 1862, at Governor's Island.
Sipe, David, e Aug 13, 1861, k July 3, 1863, Gettysburg.

Sigman, Martin M., e March 15, 1862, w Cedar Run, May 12, 1864.
Sigman, J. Isaiah, e March 15, 1862, d May 29, 1862, Charlottsville.
Sigman, Maxwell H., e Aug 13, 1861, p Cpl, w at Gettysburg.
Sizemore, John E., e Aug 13, 1861, d June 30, 1862.
Summit, Hegler P., e Sept 2, 1861, m May 12, 1864.
Smyer, Jones, e Sept 2, 1861, d May 3, 1863 at Governor's Island.
Spencer, Eli, e Aug 13, 1861, w at Cedar Run.
Spencer, J. Pinkney, e Aug 13, 1861, w Cold Harbor.
Sigmon, Noah, e March 14, 1863, k in war.
Sigmon, Jesse.
Sigmon, Alfred, e April 14, 1864, m in action May 12, 1864.
Simmons, Noah, e March 14, 1863.
Spencer, E. Sidney, e Aug 13, 1861.
Starr, J. Abel, e March 14, 1863.
Starr, Lee, e 1864.
Starr, Elon M., e March 14, 1863.
Starr, Jones.
Thornburg, Augustus M., p to 1st Cpl.
Thornburg, Matthias M., e Aug 13, 1861, p 2nd Cpl, w at Cold Harbor.
Townsend, Solomon, e March 15, 1862.
Townsend, Aaron E., e March 15, 1862.
Turner, George L., e Aug 13, 1861, k in action.
Turner, Laban C., e March 15, 1862.
Turner, David.
Turbyfield, Jones A., e March 15, 1862.
Turbyfield, Elkanak, e March 15, 1862, p Cpl.
Turbyfield, John L., e Sept 10, 1862, w at Mechanicsville.
Turbyfield, Elam A., e March 15, 1862, d June 12, 1862, Richmond.
Wagner, Thomas J., e July 13, 1861, w July 28, 1864.
Wagner, Noah P., e March 15, 1862, d in war.
Wagner, Benjamin, e March 14, 1863, k May 3, 1863, at Chancellorsville.
Watts, Rufus, e Sept 2, 1861, dg March 25, 1862, for disability.
Williams, John W., e Aug 13, 1861, p 2nd Lt, Sept 14, 1863.
Wilson, Benjamin F., e Sept 10, 1861, d May 31, 1862, at Lynchburg.
Wright, Samuel, e March 15, 1863.
Yount, Lawson M., e Aug 13, 1861, w Cold Harbor, dg Dec 5, 1862, for disability.
Yount, Abel E., e Aug 13, 1861.
Yount, Laban A., Sept 9, 1861, k May 3, 1863, at Chancellorsville.
Yount, David, e Aug 15, 1861, dg May 1, 1862, disability.
Yount, Daniel P., e March 15, 1862, dg June 5, 1862, disability.
Yount, Noah, e March 14, 1863, dt.

Company E Fifty-seventh Regiment North Carolina Troops—

Although this company, the sixth, was organized at Salisbury in July, 1862, it contained so many Catawba county men that George W. Hahn in his "The Catawba Soldier of the Civil War" lists it as a Catawba company. On August 13, 1861, the

CATAWBA COUNTY   309

company went to Wilmington, from which point it was dispatched to Richmond and the Valley of Virginia, to Harper's Ferry, into Maryland, and back to Winchester, Richmond, Petersburg, Mine Run, and finally to Appomattox.

OFFICERS

Rhyne, Daniel, Capt, r in 1862.
Yount, Lafayette, 1st Lt.
Cochran, William, 2nd Lt.
Wycoff, William, 3rd Lt.

NON-COMMISSIONED OFFICERS

Huffman, Joel, 1st Sgt.
Cline, Elcanah E., 2nd Sgt, w at Fredericksburg.
Gilbert, Jake, 4th Sgt.

PRIVATES

Anthony, Daniel, e July 4, 1862, d in war.
Anthony, Jacob, e July 3, 1862, p July 20, 1864.
Baker, Henry, e July 4, 1862, p Nov 7, 1863.
Barger, B., e July 4, 1862, d in prison.
Beard, J. W., e July 1, 1862.
Bolick (Bolch), A. E. L., e July 1, 1862.
Bolick, Ephraim, e July 4, 1862, taken pr at battle of Culpepper, paroled March 1865.
Bost, Amzi, e July 4, 1862, d in Camp at Winchester.
Bost, J. C., e July 4, 1862, k at Gettysburg, was color bearer.
Burns, F. A., e July 4, 1862, pr Nov 7, 1863.
Campbell, E., e July 1, 1862 at Fredericksburg.
Cansler, G. W., e July 4, 1862, pr Nov, 1863.
Cline, Cicero, e July 4, 1862, "one of the bravest of his Com."
Cline, Eli, e July 4, 1862, d in Camp.
Conrad, W. J., e July 4, 1862.
Coulter, Philip A., e July 1, 1862, d 1903.
Dietz, Fred, e July 4, 1862, substituted but returned and d in war.
Drum, Joshua, e July 4, 1862.
Drum, Miles, e July 4, 1862, k at Fredericksburg.
Flowers, Henry, e July 4, 1862, taken pr Nov 7, 1863, d in war.
Frazier, C. J., e Nov 1, 1863.
Frazier, H. D., e April 4, 1863, was m at Brandy Station.
Frazier, William, e July 4, 1862, d during war at Petersburg.
Fry, Cain, e July 4, 1862, d in war.
Fry, William, e July 4, 1862, taken pr July 7, 1863, d in camp.
Gantt, J. A., was with Lee at the surrender at Appomattox.
Gilland, H. A., e July 4, 1862, taken pr Nov 7, 1863.
Hallman, E., e July 4, 1862.
Halman, Laban, e July 4, 1863.
Hallman, R. L., e July 4, 1862.
Harbison, Henry, e July 4, 1862.

Hartzoe, Lawson, e July 4, 1862, taken pr Nov, 1863.
Hause (Hass) W. G., e July 4, 1862, d in Savannah, Ga., in 1863.
Hoke, G. A., e July 4, 1862.
Holler, G. W., e July 4, 1863, taken pr Nov 7, 1863, d in 1909.
Huffman, Daniel, e July 4, 1862, taken pr July 20, 1864.
Huffman, Hosea, e July 4, 1862, pr July 9, 1864.
Huffman, Marcus, e July 4, 1862.
Huffman, Max.
Hunsucker, S. A., e July 4, 1862, pr Nov 7, 1863.
Issac, John, e July 4, 1862, d during war.
Issac, Levi, e July 4, 1862, taken pr July 20, 1864.
Killian, L. S., e July 4, 1862, taken pr Nov 7, 1863.
Leatherman, L. M., e March 1, 1864.
Leonard, Daniel, e July 4, 1862, d in prison.
Leonard, Eli, e July 4, 1862.
Leonard, J. M., e June 25, 1862, tr from 23rd Reg to 57th Reg.
Lutz (Luter), M. C., e July 4, 1863, c and d at Fortress Monroe, Nov, 1863.
Mauney, J. S., e July 4, 1862.
McCaslin, A. C., e July 4, 1862, taken pr Nov 7, 1863.
McCaslin, H. F., e July 4, 1862, taken pr Nov 7, 1863.
Michael, Ambrose, e July 4, 1862, d during war.
Michael, Jacob, e July 4, 1862, d in hospital.
Miller, David A., e July 4, 1862, w at Appomattox and at Gettysburg, pr, returned.
Miller, G. W., e July 4, 1862, taken pr Nov 7, 1863, d at home during war.
Miller, J. M., e Aug 1862, taken pr July 8, 1863, d in 1909.
Null, John, e July 4, 1862.
Pitts, David, e July 4, 1862, twice w.
Pope, Daniel, e July 4, 1862, w May 4, 1864, p July 20, 1864.
Pope, Frank, e July 4, 1862, taken pr July 20, 1864, at Fredericksburg.
Propst, Frank, e July 4, 1862, d in Camp.
Propst, F. L., e March 13, 1864.
Propst, Wallace A., e July 4, 1862, taken pr Nov 7, 1864.
Propst, William, e April 1864.
Rabb, Frank, e July 4, 1862, w at Fredericksburg, c a Yankee with an unloaded gun, at Shepherdstown he c four of the enemy, w at Winchester.
Raby, William, e July 4, 1862, taken pr Nov 7, 1863.
Rhinehardt, John J., e July 4, 1862, taken pr Nov 7, 1863.
Robinson, A. J., e July 4, 1862, was a substitute for Conrad, pr Nov 7, 1863.
Roderick, C., e July 4, 1862.
Scronce, Logan, e July 4, 1862.
Self, W. R., e July 4, 1864, w at Gettysburg on first day of battle, at Lynchburg he was w the second day, taken pr at Winchester, for five months was absent from Com with small pox.
Setzer, Harvey, e July 4, 1862, c Nov 7, 1863, d in Hospital while pr.
Setzer, J. C., e July 4, 1862.
Setzer, P. S., e July 4, 1862, taken pr Nov 7, 1863.
Setzer, W. A., e July 4, 1862, p and w.
Shepherd, John, e July 4, 1862, k at Petersburg, was a musician.

CATAWBA COUNTY 311

Sherrill, Wesley, e July 4, 1862.
Shuford, Pinkney, e May 10, 1862, elected 4th Sgt.
Simmons, John, e July 4, 1862.
Sipe, F. C., e July 4, 1862.
Sipe, Sidney, e July 4, 1862, taken pr May 22, 1864, d in prison.
Smyre, Francis Silas, e July 4, 1862, c June 1, 1864, paroled March 4, 1865, just before surrender.
Starr, Marion, e July 4, 1862, pr Nov 7, 1863.
Stowe, W. L., e July 4, 1862, d in war.
Waggoner, William, e July 4, 1862, d in Camp.
Warlick, David Logan, e 1862, w and p.
Weaver, Daniel, e July 4, 1862, taken pr Nov 7, 1863.
Witherspoon, J. H., e July 4, 1862.
Witherspoon, M. C., e Jan 1, 1864.

Company F Thirty-eighth Regiment North Carolina Troops—

This company was organized in September, 1861, under the branches of a large hickory tree in the yard of N. E. Sigmon. It followed General Lee through all the campaigns of 1863 and 1864.

OFFICERS

Little, Joshua Butler, Capt, cm Oct 31, 1861, April 18, 1862, d 1907.
Daniel, McD Yount, Capt, cm April 18, 1862, r Sept 18, 1862.
Bozeman, Daniel F., Capt, cm Sept 18, 1862, p from 1st Lt, w June 26, 1862 at Ellyson's Mill, and July 1, 1863, at Gettysburg.
Deal, Alonzo, Capt, cm March 23, 1863, p from 2nd Lt, and w June 26, 1862, at Ellyson's Mill and July 1, 1863, at Gettysburg.
Yount, McD, 1st Lt, cm Oct 31, 1861, p and r.
Bozeman, D. F., 1st Lt, cm April 18, 1862, p w and r.
Yount, Joshua A., 1st Lt, cm Sept 18, 1862, w June 26, 1862 at Ellyson's Mill, was with Lee when he surrendered at Appomattox.
Bozeman, D. F., 2nd Lt, cm Oct 31, 1861, p w and r.
Yoder, George M., 2nd Lt, cm Feb 8, 1862, p from rank, not re-elected.
Davis, Hiram A., 2nd Lt, cm March 1, 1863, p from Sgt.
Aiken, Joseph, cm Oct, 15, 1861, k at Malvern Hill, July 1, 1862.
Roberts, Harace L., cm Oct 31, 1861, d during the war.
Yount, Daniel F., cm Sept 18, 1862, p from 1st Lt, w June 26, 1862, at Ellyson's Mill, r March 25, 1863.

NON-COMMISSIONED OFFICERS

Bennick, David J., 1st Sgt, e Oct 31, 1861.
Yount, Joshua A., 2nd Sgt, e Oct 31, 1861, p 2nd Lt April 18, 1862, w at Mechanicsville.
Hoke (Hooke), Donald L., 4th Sgt, e Oct 31, 1861, p 2nd Lt.
Smith, Quinton M., 1st Cpl, e Oct 31, 1861, p Sgt and w at Ox Hill and Gettysburg.

Null, Elkanah, 2nd Cpl, e Oct 31, 1861, p Sgt and k June 30, 1862, at Frazier's Farm.
Sigman (Sigmon), Nelson E., 3rd Cpl, e Oct 30, 1861, p and w.

PRIVATES

Airwood (Arrowood) Gilbert, e Oct 31, 1861, w at Chancellorsville and k July 1, 1863, at Gettysburg.
Baker, George H., e Oct 31, 1861, p Cpl and w July 1, 1863, at Gettysburg.
Baker, Jacob M., e Oct 31, 1861, k July 1863 at Gettysburg.
Bost, Miles W. A., e Oct 31, 1861, d after the war.
Clawson, A., e Aug. 19, 1864.
Crawford, Anderson M., e Aug 14, 1863, d at Point Lookout.
Crawford, Sidney H., e March 16, 1863.
Cline, Jefferson, e March 16, 1863.
Cline, J. O., e March 20, 1864, w d in 1899.
Cline, Laban, e Oct 31, 1861, d March, 1862, at Weldon.
Christopher, D., e Oct 11, 1863.
Cloninger, M. H., e Oct 31, 1861.
Dagennart, Noah, e Oct 31, 1861, d March, 1862, at Halifax.
Deal, A. (W), e Oct 31, 1861, d at Point Lookout.
Deal, William, e Oct 11, 1863, d at Point Lookout.
Deates (Deitz) Dan A., e Oct 31, k at Hagerstown.
Drum, Franklin, e Oct 31, 1861, d Jan, 1862 at Raleigh, first death in Com.
Fletcher, P. C., e Aug 19, 1864.
Fox, Adolphus, e Oct 31, 1861, pr.
Fox, Daniel A.
Fox, John, e w 1864.
Fox, Marcus, e Oct 31, 1861, d April 1862 at Petersburg.
George, J. F., e Aug 19, 1864.
Graham, Jacob, e Oct 31, 1861.
Hedrick, Alfred M., e Oct 31, 1861, p Sgt.
Hedrick, Arnderson, e Oct 31, 1861.
Hedrick, Hiram, e Oct 31, 1861, d Aug. 1862, at Richmond.
Hedrick, John C., e Oct 31, 1861, w at Mechanicsville.
Hedrick, Logan, e Oct 31, 1861, d Nov 26, 1862, in N. C.
Heffner, Davanout (Devault), e Oct 31, 1861, dg April, 1862, for disability.
Heffner, Elkanah R., e Oct 31, 1861, p Cpl, d on boat from prison.
Heffner, Herman, e Oct 31, 1861, pr.
Heffner, Peter, e Oct 31, 1861, d Sept, 1862 at Winchester, Va.
Helms, Daniel, e March 6, 1863, k July 1, 1863, at Gettysburg.
Hodge, Charles, e d 1880.
Hoke, George J., e Oct 31, 1861, d Feb 14, 1863 of w received at Harpers Ferry.
Hoke, John A. (D), e March 16, 1863.
Hoke, Martin, L., e Oct 31, 1861, pr d 1908.
Holler, David, e Oct 31, 1861, pr.
Holler, Peter, e Oct 31, 1861, dg April 20, 1863.

CATAWBA COUNTY

Huffman, Alfred, e Oct 31, 1861, w Sept 14, 1862 at Harpers Ferry, dg Jan, 1863.
Huffman, Allen, e Oct 31, 1861.
Huffman, Ambrose, e Oct 31, 1861, d at Richmond.
Huffman, B. L.
Huffman, Burwell, e Oct 31, 1861, k May 3, 1863 at Chancellorsville.
Huffman, David, e Oct 31, 1861, w at Ellyson's Mill or Mechanicsville, d 1905.
Huffman, Jacob, e Oct 31, 1861, k June 26, 1862, at Mechanicsville.
Huffman, M., e Oct 31, 1861, k June 30, 1862, at Frazier's Farm.
Huffman, William S., e Oct 31, 1861, w May 3, 1863 at Chancellorsville, k at Petersburg April, 1865. Last man killed in the Com.
Hunsucker, Carey, e Oct 31, 1861.
Hunsucker, Marcus.
Isenhour, Abel, e March 16, 1863, d June 6, 1863.
Kaniep, Miles, e Oct 31, 1861, k June 13, 1864.
Layel (Lael) Ehas, e Oct 31, 1861, d in Georgia 1863.
Layel (Lael) Jacob, e Oct 31, 1861, k July 1, 1863, at Gettysburg.
Layel (Lael) Lawson, e Oct 31, 1861, w Aug 28, 1862, at Manassas.
Little, Peter, e Oct 11, 1863.
Mozer, Joe.
Moser, Miles, e Oct 31, 1861, w Aug 28, 1862, at Manassas.
Null, Daniel, e Oct 31, 1861, pr d in 1864.
Parker, Augustus, e Oct 31, 1861, d in war.
Phelps, John, e Oct 31, 1861, w at Sharpsburg and d from w.
Pope, David, e Oct 31, 1861, k Sept 17, 1862 at Sharpsburg.
Pope, Elkanah, e March 16, 1863, w July 1, 1863 at Gettysburg, d in 1906.
Pope, George, e March 16, 1863, k at Gettysburg.
Opie, Marcus, e Oct 31, 1861, pr in 1864.
Pope, Miles, e March 16, 1863, w July 1, 1863, at Gettysburg.
Rector, Gilbright, e Oct 31, 1861, d March, 1862, at Goldsboro.
Rector, John E., e Oct 31, 1861, d Feb, 1862, at Raleigh.
Romans, Augustus B., e Oct 31, 1862, (an Italian).
Roseman, Cyrus P., e Oct 31, 1861.
Roseman, Marion J., e Oct 31, 1861, p Sgt, w July 1, 1863, at Gettysburg.
Setser (Setzer), Marcus, e Oct 31, 1861, tr May 1, 1862 to 12th Reg.
Setzer, Alfred, surrendered at Appomattox.
Shook, David, e Oct 31, 1861, dg Nov, 1862, d 1906.
Shook, Franklin, e Oct 31, 1861.
Shook, John, e Oct 31, 1861, d March, 1862, at Weldon.
Shook, Daniel.
Shook, Lawson.
Shook, Philo.
Sigman, Adolphus, e Oct 31, 1861.
Sigman, Alfred L., e April 30, 1861, k May 3, 1863, at Chancellorsville.
Sigman, Anson, e March 16, 1863, d at Richmond in 1864.
Sigman, Devault (Devault) M., e Aug 14, 1862, d at Conover in 1886.
Sigman, Henry L., e Oct 31, 1861, dg Jan, 1862, for disability.
Sigman, Logan H., e Oct 31, 1861.
Sigman, Martin, e Oct 31, 1861, dg April 18, 1862.

Sigman, William, d 1908.
Traffensteat, Peter, e March 16, 1863, w at Chancellorsville.
Traffensteat, William, e Oct 31, 1861, p Cpl and w May 2, 1863, at Chancellorsville, d 1910.
Tulbright, Lenos, e March 16, 1863.
Warren, John Q., e Oct 31, 1861, tr to 12th Reg May 2, 1863, at Chancellorsville.
Winebarger, Daniel, e Oct 31, 1861, pr in 1864.
Winebarger, Noah, e Oct 31, 1861.
Yoder, George M., e Oct 31, 1861, p 2nd Lt Feb 8, 1862.
Yount, George W., e Oct 31, 1861.
Yount, Miles, e Oct 31, 1861, k July 1, 1863, at Gettysburg.

Company K Thirty-fifth Regiment North Carolina Troops—

This company was organized on October 15, 1861, at Hickory Tavern.

OFFICERS

Ellis, James R., Capt, cm Oct 15, 1861, r 1861.
Johnston, James Theodore, Capt, cm Dec 9, 1861, p Major 12, 1862, w at Malvern Hill.
Johnston, Philip J., Capt, cm Oct 15, 1861.
Warlick, Pickney, 1st Lt, cm Oct 15, 1861.
Johnston, P. J., 1st Lt, cm Dec 29, 1862.
Glass, David F., 1st Lt, cm June 30, 1863.
Berry, Pinkney, 2nd Lt, cm Oct 13, 1862.
Glass, D. P., 2nd Lt, cm June 30, 1862.
Hale, William, 2nd Lt, cm Dec, 1861, k March 14, 1862 at New Bern. The first person k from Catawba county.
Johnston, J. T., 2nd Lt, cm Oct 15, 1861.
Link, Julius E., 2nd Lt, cm April, 1862, k July 1, 1863, Malvern Hill.
Rockett, James Monroe, 2nd Lt, cm Dec. 29, 1862.
Stamey, Alexander, 2nd Lt, cm Oct 16, 1861.

NON-COMMISSIONED OFFICERS

Link, Patrick L., 1st Sgt, e Oct 15, 1861, p 2nd Lt, April, 1862.
Bowman, George, 3rd Sgt, e Oct 15, 1861, d Dec 7, 1862 at Charlottesville, Va.
Conley, P. W., 5th Sgt, e Oct 15, 1861, p 1st Sgt Jan 27, 1863.
Bowman, William, 1st Cpl, e Oct 15, 1861.
Franklin, John H., 3rd Cpl, e Oct 15, 1861.
Stuart, William, 4th Cpl, e Oct 15, 1861, pr in 1864.
Seitz, J. C., e July 6, 1862, k July 17, 1864, near Petersburg.

PRIVATES

Abee, Daniel, e Oct 15, 1862.
Abernethy, George J., e May 1, 1861, p Cpl Sept 1, 1863.
Abernethy, John F., e March 1, 1863, d Aug 13, 1863, at Weldon.

CATAWBA COUNTY 315

Abernethy, L. Dow, e May 1, 1861, w July 1, 1862, at Malvern Hill.
Aiken, Joseph, e Oct 15, 1861, k July 1, 1862, Malvern Hill.
Arndt, B. F., e March 1, 1863.
Bailey, R. L., e Oct 15, 1861, k Sept 17, 1862, at Sharpsburg.
Berry, John, e Oct 15, 1861.
Berry, Calvin, e Oct 15, 1861, dg May, 1862.
Berry, Silas, e Oct 15, 1861.
Berry, Waightstill, e May 1, 1862.
Boughman, L., e Oct 15, 1861.
Boughman, T., e Oct 15, 1861.
Brindle, F. L., e May 12, 1862.
Brittain, Jonas, e Oct 15, 1861.
Brittain, Julius, e Oct 15, 1861.
Brittain, Lorenzo, e Oct 15, 1861.
Brookshire, W. A., e Oct 15, 1861.
Burger, R. J., e Oct 15, 1861.
Chester, W. J., e Oct 15, 1861, d Dec, 1861, at Raleigh.
Chester, G. W., e Oct 15, 1861.
Childers, G. F., e Oct 15, 1861.
Childers, Henry H., e Oct 15, 1861.
Choates, N. J., e April 1, 1864.
Clarke, J. C., e Oct 15, 1861.
Cosby, John, e Oct 15, 1861.
Cook, A. E., e Oct 15, 1861.
Cook, Aaron, e Oct 15, 1861.
Cooper, J. H., e Oct 15, 1861.
Deal, Jones, e Oct 15, 1861.
Deal, Sylvanus, e June 1, 1863.
Denton, David, e Oct 18, 1861.
Denton, Jackson, e Oct 18, 1861.
Dietz, C. Frank, e March 1, 1863, dg March 12, 1863.
Dietz, W. Pinkney, e Aug 4, 1862.
Dunn, J. M., e Oct 15, 1861, d Jan 7, 1863, at home.
Erwin, Alexander, e Oct 18, 1861.
Erwin, L. Henderson, e May 1, 1862.
Erwin, Joseph, e Jan 7, 1862.
Fincannon, J. Monroe, e June 1, 1863.
Franklin, A., e Oct 15, 1861, k Sept 17, 1862, Sharpsburg.
Franklin, I., e Oct 15, 1861.
Franklin, L., e Oct 15, 1861.
Franklin, R., e Oct 15, 1861.
Fry, John B., e Oct 15, 1861.
Fry, J. Monroe, e Aug 14, 1862, p Lt June 30, 1863.
Glass, David P., e May 1, 1862, p 2nd Lt, June 30, 1863.
Grady, B., e Oct 15, 1861, dg March, 1863.
Guilford, John G., e Oct 15, 1861.
Hale, John A., e Jan 21, 1864.
Hartzoe, Abel, e Oct 15, 1861, dg June, 1862.
Hawn, Alfred, e April 8, 1862.
Hawn, Amzi, e Aug 14, 1862, k June 17, 1864, at Petersburg.
Hawn, D. Sidney, e April 8, 1862, k at Petersburg in 1864.

Hawn, David J., e March 6, 1862, d during the war.
Hawn, Calvin L., e March 1, 1864.
Hawn, Robinson C., e June 1, 1863, c and d in prison.
Hines, A. R., e Oct 15, 1861, p Cpl Dec, 1862.
Hines, Michael, e Oct 15, 1861.
Hipps, N. M., e May 1, 1862, d June, 1862 at Kinston, N. C.
Holler, Elisha, e Aug 15, 1862.
Holler, Noah, e Oct 15, 1861.
Holler, Paul, e Aug 15, 1862.
Hoyle, John, e Oct 15, 1861.
Hoyle, Nicholas, e March 1, 1862.
Hudson, Pinkney, e Oct 15, 1861.
Huffman, Byrd, e Jan 21, 1864.
Huntley, J. C., e May 1, 1862.
Ikerd, William P., e March 1, 1863.
Ikerd, Sidney J., e Oct 15, 1861.
Johnson, Brycee, D., May 1, 1862.
Johnson, P. J., e Oct 15, 1861, p 2nd Lt Dec 29, 1862.
Lail, Calvin, e Oct 15, 1861.
Link, John C., e Oct 15, 1861.
Laughridge, Larkin, e Oct 15, 1861.
Laughridge, William A., e Oct 15, 1861.
Mace, J. A., e Feb 20, 1861.
Martin, Pinkney, e Feb 20, 1861.
Michael, W. D., e March 6, 1862, w.
Michael, J. H., e March 6, 1862, d.
Miller, Jesse, e March 6, 1862.
Miller, Abram, e May 1, 1861.
Moody, Hiram, e June 5, 1864.
Moody, Harvey, e Oct 16, 1861.
Morris, J. W., e Oct.
Mull, Abram B., e Aug 14, 1862.
Mull, Joseph, Sr., e Oct 15, 1861.
Mull, Joseph, Jr., e Oct 15, 1861, d Dec 4, 1862, Richmond.
Mull, William, e Oct 15, 1861.
Pearson, James A., e Oct 15, 1861.
Pearson, Michael Y., e Oct 15, 1861, d Feb, 1863.
Pitts, Abel, e Jan 7, 1863.
Propst, Riley, e Oct 15, 1861.
Pruitt, A., e March 6, 1861.
Pruitt, D., e March 6, 1861.
Pruitt, S., e March 1, 1861.
Rockett, A. C., e Aug 10, 1862, d July 28, 1863, Petersburg.
Rockett, John A., e Aug 14, 1862.
Rockett, Pinkney R., e Aug 10, 1862.
Seitz, Levi, e March 1, 1863.
Sides, J. Calvin, e July 6, 1863.
Sides, W. Harrison, e, May 3, 1862, d July, 1862.
Sides, George W., e Oct 15, 1861, dg May, 1862.
Sigmon, Esaius, e Jan 7, 1864.
Sigmon, H. Caney, e Oct 15, 1861, p Cpl, 1863.

CATAWBA COUNTY

Smith Samuel, e Oct 15, 1861.
Smith, Robert, e Oct 15, 1861.
Speagle, Osborn, e Oct 15, 1861, d Feb 22, 1863, Wilson.
Suttlemyre, Alexander, e Oct 15, 1861.
Suttlemyre, Harvey S., e Aug 14, 1862.
Suttlemyre, G. Wash., e Oct 15, 1861, d 1862, New Bern.
Suttlemyre, Langdon S., e Oct 15, 1861.
Stafford, George W., e Oct 15, 1861.
Stafford, John, e Oct 15, 1861, w Dec 13, 1862, Fredericksburg.
Stamey, E., e Oct 15, 1861.
Stamey, W. A., March 6, 1862.
Stillwell, H. J., e Sept 1, 1862.
Stillwell, Lucius A., e Oct 15, 1861.
Tolbert, George, e Oct 15, 1861.
Troutman, J. M., e Oct 15, 1861, d Feb, 1862, at Raleigh.
Turney, W. D., e March 6, 1862, d June, 1862, Kinston.
Wagner, Allison, e Oct 15, 1861.
Wallace, Alexander, e Oct 15, 1861, dg May, 1862.
Ward, Anderson, e Oct 15, 1861.
Ward, Anderson, e Oct 15, 1861, k May 4, 1864.
Ward, J. Sidney, e Oct 16, 1861, p 2nd Lt in 1864.
Ward, A. Pinkney, e Oct 15, 1861, p Sgt July, 1863.
Ward, Paul, e Oct 15, 1861.
Watson, James, e Oct 15, 1861, dg May, 1862.
Whitener, Abel, e March 1, 1863.
Whitener, B. F., e Oct 20, 1864.
Whitener, Daniel, e Oct 15, 1861, k at Plymouth.
Whitener, Henry H., e March 1, 1863.
Whitener, J. Laban, e Oct 15, 1861, d Jan, 1863.
Whitener, J. Pinkney, e April 8, 1862.
Whitener, P. Sidney, e Oct 15, 1861, k April 5, 1864, Plymouth.
Wilson, W. Arnold, e Oct 15, 1861, p Cpl Jan, 1863.
Williams, M., e Oct 15, 1861, dg May, 1863.
Whitstine, Marcus L., e Oct 15, 1861.
Whisenhunt, John C., e May 1, 1862, k April 20, 1864, Plymouth.
Yoder, Reuben, e March 1, 1864.
Yoder, Moses, e Oct, 1862.
Yoder, Amzi A., e June, 1863.
Yount, Levi F., e March 1, 1863.
Yount, Walton O., e Dec. 15, 1863.
Zimmerman, David, e May 1, 1862.
Zimmerman, Hartle, e May 1, 1862.

    Surrendered at Appomattox Court House, Va., April 9, 1865.
Arney, B. Franklin.
Arney, J. Franklin.
Abernethy, L. Dow.
Brittain, Jonas.
Childers, Henry H.
Dietz, W. Pinkney.
Deaton, Jackson.
Houck, John A.

Ikerd, William,
Johnson, P. J., Capt.
Laughridge, William A.
Mull, Joseph.
Pearson, James A.
Stafford, John.
Webb, J. R.
Whitener, J. Pinkney.
Yoder, Amzi A.
Yount, Walton C.
Zimmerman, Hartle.

Company K Forty-sixth Regiment North Carolina Troops—

The "Catawba Braves," as this company was called, left Newton on March 13, 1862, for Camp Mangum, near Raleigh, where it became a part of the Forty-sixth Regiment. The "Catawba Braves" first saw action at Reams Station, near Petersburg. Its additional battle areas included Maryland, Fredericksburg, South Carolina (at a point known as Potocaligo), the Wilderness, again at Petersburg, and Appomattox Court House.

OFFICERS

Bost, T. Adolphus, Capt, cm March 15, 1862, w at Wilderness May 5, 1864, k in 1864.
Bost, A. Robert, Capt, cm in 1864, p from Sgt.
Routh, Alexander, 1st Lt, cm March 15, 1862, w at Fredericksburg Dec, 1862, and k in 1864.
Hoover, James M., 2nd Lt, cm March 15, 1862, k in 1864.
Smyre, Marcus M., 2nd Lt, cm March 15, 1862, k in 1864.

NON-COMMISSIONED OFFICERS

Lutz, H. L. (Lentz, Moore sp.), 1st Sgt, e March 15, 1862, d Nov 25, 1862, at Gordonsville.
Wilson, M. M. 2nd Sgt, e March 15, 1862, d Dec 15, 1862, at Richmond.
Shuford, John S., 3rd Sgt, e March 15, 1862.
Routh, Levi W., 4th Sgt, e March 15, 1862.
LeFevers, Isaac, 5th Sgt, e March 15, 1862.
Eckard, Simeon, 1st Cpl, e March 15, 1862.
Bolinger, William P., 2nd Cpl, e March 15, 1863, k 19 Sept, 1862, by accident on the north bank of the Potomac.
Rowe, Dallas, J., 3rd Cpl, e March 15, 1862, p Sgt.
Shuford, William H., 4th Cpl, e March 15, 1862, k on the battle field, 1864.
Hayes, George M. Musician, e March 15, 1862.
Abernathy, John P. Musician, e March 15, 1862.
Yoder, Marcus, e March 1, 1862.

CATAWBA COUNTY 319

PRIVATES

Abernathy, Miles, e March 13, 1862.
Abernathy, Caleb, e March 13, 1862.
Arnts, Jacob, e March 13, 1863, w at Fredericksburg.
Arnts, Henry, e March 13, 1862, dg July 15, 1862, for disability.
Arney, Phillip E. (Averey, Moore sp.), e March 13, 1862.
Armstrong, Turner, e Oct 1, 1862, w at Fredericksburg.
Bost, Robert A., e June 8, 1862, tr from 12th Reg June 8, 1862, p 1st Sgt Nov 21, 1862, p Capt.
Bumgarner, H. L., e March 13, 1862.
Bost, Alfred W., e March 13, 1862.
Barringer, P. R., e March 13, 1862, k Dec 13, 1862, at Fredericksburg.
Banley, Jacob W., e March 13, 1862.
Burch, William R., e March 13, 1862.
Booney, Silas B., e March 13, 1862.
Booney, Miles, M., e March 16, 1863.
Boyd, Marcus, e March 16, 1863.
Booney, Marcus, e Aug 15, 1862.
Boyd, R. Winfield, e March 20, 1862.
Bumgarner, A., e Sept 25, 1862.
Clodfelter, George W., e Sept 25, 1862.
Cobb, Calvin, e March 20, 1862.
Childers, George P., e March 13, 1862.
Cline, Anson, e March 13, 1862, d Sept 25, 1862, at Petersburg.
Cline, W. P., e March 13, 1862.
Caldwell, H. H., e March 1, 1862.
Dagerhardt, Henry, e March 12, 1862.
Deator, William L., e March 3, 1862.
Deal, M. M., e March 16, 1862.
Drummer, George, e March 3, 1862.
Eades, Ransom, e March 12, 1862.
Eckard, Abel S., e Sept 25, 1862.
Finger, D. F., e March 12, 1862, w at Sharpsburg.
Finger, Daniel, e March 13, 1862, d Dec 31, 1862.
Finger, Franklin, e March 13, 1862.
Fry, Calvin G., e March 13, 1862, dg June 23, 1862, for disability.
Fry, Jacob, e March 13, 1862.
Fry, John A. D., e March 13, 1862, d Sept 26, 1862, of w received at Sharpsburg.
Gilbert, P. W., e March 13, 1862.
Gam, Levi, e March 13, 1862.
Gault, J. N., e March 13, 1862, w at Sharpsburg.
Goodman, Columbus, e March 13, 1862.
Garrett, O. M., e March 20, 1862.
Gaither, J. L., e March 16, 1863, d May 30, 1863, at Newton.
Huffman, Noah, e March 13, 1862.
Harrison, Marcus A., e March 13, 1862.
Hall, Humphrey, e March 13, 1862, d June 24, 1862, at Petersburg.
Hass, John M., e March 13, 1862.
Helton, William, e March 13, 1862, dg July 16, 1862.

A HISTORY OF

Helton, Franklin, e March 13, 1862, w at Harrisonburg.
Hewitt, Franklin, e March 20, 1862, d Sept 23, 1862, at Petersburg.
Hewitt, William L., e March 20, 1862.
Hewitt, Anderson, e March 20, 1862, d July 24, 1862.
Hewitt, J. L., e March 20, 1862, w at Sharpsburg.
Hartsoe, Jacob L., e March 13, 1862.
Hobbs, John, e March 13, 1862, d Dec 20, 1862, of w received at Fredericksburg.
Hawn, W. P., e March 20, 1862.
Helton, Hosea, e July 16, 1862.
Hewitt, John S., e Sept 25, 1862.
Isenhour, B. G., e March 13, 1862, d July 24, 1862, at Petersburg.
Jarett, Obida M., e March 20, 1862.
Jones, John A., e March 13, 1862, d Dec 8, 1862, at Richmond.
Killian, Samuel, e March 13, 1862.
Kistler, J. L., e March 20, 1862, w at Sharpsburg.
Keener, Alexander L., e March 20, 1862.
Keener, James M., e March 13, 1862, d Jan 14, 1863, in Catawba county of wounds received at Fredericksburg.
Link, John C., (Lietz, Moore Sp.) e March 13, 1862.
Link, Andrew, e Oct 15, 1862.
Leonard, Robert H., e March 13, 1862, k at Bristow Station.
Miller, John, e March 20, 1862, w at Fredericksburg, d.
Miller, Jesse R., e March 13, 1862, d Nov 10, 1862, at Richmond.
McNeill, James F., e March 13, 1862, k at Fredericksburg Dec 13, 1862.
Martin, Marion, e March 13, 1862, d at Petersburg Aug 10, 1862.
Moore, William, e March 13, 1862, tr June 8, 1862, to 12th Reg at Fredericksburg.
Moore, Martin, e March 13, 1862, k at Fredericksburg, Dec 16, 1862.
Mouser, William H., e March 13, 1862.
Norwood, Robert M., e March 13, 1862, p to Cpl.
Poovey, Silas B., e March 14, 1862.
Parker, Charles, e March 13, 1862.
Parker, John, e March 13, 1862, w at Fredericksburg.
Propst, William, e March 13, 1862.
Parker, Samuel, e March 13, 1862, w Fredericksburg, d Jan 15, 1863.
Propst, John, e March 13, 1862, d April 7, 1863, in Catawba county.
Perkins, Henry, e March 13, 1862, d Dec 14, 1862, at Petersburg.
Rink, C. R., e March 20, 1862, w Sharpsburg, d March 17, 1863.
Robinson, H. H., e March 13, 1862.
Rhinehardt, William A., e March 13, 1862, d Petersburg, Aug 19, 1862.
Reep, Adam, e March 13, 1862, w at Fredericksburg.
Smyre, Cicero M., e March 13, 1862, d Oct 8, 1862, at Winchester, Va.
Smyre, John R., e March 13, 1862, d at Goldsboro, May 28, 1862.
Rowe, A. H., e March 13, 1862.
Seitz, John Q., e March, 1862.
Setzer, R. C., e 1862, c March 25, 1865.
Setzer, Calvin, e March 13, 1862.
Setzer, D. A., e March 13, 1862, k at Fredericksburg, Dec 13, 1862.
Setzer, W. S., e March 13, 1862, w at Sharpsburg.

CATAWBA COUNTY 321

Shuford, M. C., e March 13, 1862, p Cpl, d Sept 8, 1862, at Richmond.
Summit, Pinkey, e March 13, 1862, d at Petersburg, July 4, 1862.
Setzer, Wilburn, e March 27, 1862, w.
Summit, Isaac L., e March 13, 1862, p Cpl.
Sherrill, Robert, e March 13, 1862, d at Winchester, 1863.
Sherrill, Henry, e March 13, 1862, d at Winchester in 1863.
Sherrill, Christopher, e March 13, 1862.
Smith, Isaac, e March 13, 1862, d at Martinsburg in 1863.
Sigmon, Lafayette M., e March 13, 1862, k Wilderness.
Sigmon, Reuben, e March 13, 1862, k Sharpsburg, Sept 17, 1862.
Scronce, Joseph, e March 13, 1862, w Sharpsburg, d at Orange Court House.
Settlemyre, Adolphus, e March 13, 1862, k Wilderness.
Suttleman, John H., e March 13, 1862.
Setzer, Daniel, e March 13, 1862.
Smyre, Walter G., e March 13, 1862.
Sigmon, Louis, e March 13, 1862.
Smyre, Robert A., e March 13, 1862.
Tucker, George, e March 20, 1862, w at Fredericksburg, d at McPherell, S. C., March 25, 1863.
Thornburg, L. L., e March 13, 1862.
Travis, Levi, e March 13, 1862, w at Fredericksburg.
Whitener, Leander, e Sept 25, 1862.
Whitener, Miles M., e March 16, 1863.
Whitener, George L., e March 16, 1863.
Wike, William D., e March 13, 1862.
Whitener, William D., e March 13, 1862.
Wilson, David, e March 20, 1862, k at Bristow.
Wilson, George, e March 20, 1863, w at Fredericksburg.
Wilson, James L., e March 13, 1862, w at Fredericksburg.
Watts, John, e March 13, 1862, d at Jordan's Spring, Va., Oct 2, 1862.
Witherspoon, A. H., e March 13, 1862, d Oct 5, 1862, at Richmond.
Workman, H. J. K., e March 13, 1862, w at Fredericksburg.
Weaver, Henry, e March 13, 1862.
Weaver, Fredrick, e March 13, 1862.
Walker, Elisha, e March 13, 1862, d March 9, 1863, in Catawba county.
Whitener, Logan G., e March 13, 1862.

Company I Forty-ninth Regiment North Carolina Troops—

This company was organized on March 19, 1862, at Catawba, with W. W. Chenault as captain.

OFFICERS

Chenault, W. W., Capt, d Petersburg, Feb, 1863.
Connor, C. F., Capt in Feb, 1863.
Brown, A. E., Lt, cm March 25, 1865.
Connor, Charles F., 2nd Lt.
Connor, C. A., 2nd Lt on March 16, 1863.
Connor, Augustus, Lt.
Sherrill, Jeptha, 1st Lt, d Petersburg, July, 1862.

Sherrill, Jacob, 3rd Lt, w at Sharpsburg, 1862.
Sherrill, James H., 2nd Lt, p to Capt of Co. A.
Sherrill, Jacob, 3rd Lt, r Feb, 1863.
Witherington, Stephen, 3rd Lt, w Fort Steadman.

NON-COMMISSIONED OFFICERS

Caldwell, William J., sgt.
Sigmon, J. W., 3rd sgt, w Petersburg.
Sigmon, J. W., 4th sgt, e March 19, 1862.
Long, W. F., 2nd sgt.
Moody, B. F., 4th sgt, d Richmond Hospital.
Jones, Freeman, 5th sgt.
Lee, J. S., Color Bearer, k Drewery's Bluff, May. 1864.
Brown, Hosea, 1st Cpl, k Petersburg, 1864.
Moss, G. W., 3rd Cpl, w Sharpsburg.
Pool, William, Cpl, p Point Lookout.
Abernethy, Milton, sgt.

PRIVATES

Bandy, Quin.
Benfield, W. P., pr Point Lookout.
Blakely, William L., pr Point Lookout.
Blakely, James M., d Richmond, 1863.
Brady, George, e Fort Steadman.
Brady, John, c Fort Steadman.
Brawley, Peter, tr to 18th N. C. Reg.
Brotherton, Hugh, w Fort Steadman.
Brown, Thompson, k Drewry's Bluff, May 16, 1864.
Brown, Jacob, c Drewry's Bluff, May 16, 1864.
Brown, William, c March 25, 1865, p Point Lookout.
Bumgarner, Monroe, w Malvern Hill.
Caldwell, Abel, w Drewry's Bluff, p Fort Steadman.
Caldwell, James, Sr.
Caldwell, James, Jr.
Caldwell, Lawson, d Brigade Hospital near Drewry's Bluff.
Clark, David.
Collins, Henry, w Petersburg, June 22, 1864.
Collins, James P., w Drewry's Bluff.
Davis, James.
Davis, Andrew, d in service.
Day, William.
Danner, Monroe, k at Petersburg.
Danner, John, w at Yellow House, pr Point Lookout.
Douglas, Elam, tr to 6th N. C. Reg.
Drum, Phillip.
Drum, John, k at Boone's Mill.
Drum, Thomas F., w at Malvern Hill.
Drum, Peter Monroe.
Drum, Rufus.
Edwards, Abel, d in service.

CATAWBA COUNTY

Edwards, Simon, d at Raleigh.
Ellis, W. H., e 1863.
Elliott, John, pr at Point Lookout.
Eller, Alexander, d Brigade Hospital, Drewry's Bluff.
Ellis, W. H.
Fisher, Reuben, k Malvern Hill.
Fisher, Thomas, c Fort Steadman, pr Point Lookout.
Fisher, Joseph, k Petersburg.
Fisher, Elkanah, pr Point Lookout.
Fisher, William, pr Point Lookout.
Fox, Allison, w at Crater at Petersburg.
Freeman, John, dg.
German, John.
Gilliland, Reuben, d Raleigh.
Gilliland, Marcus, k Fort Steadman.
Gilliland, Thomas, pr & d at Point Lookout.
Gilbert, Elbert, pr Point Lookout.
Goble, Lawson, k Petersburg.
Goble, Davidson.
Goodman, Frank, d at Raleigh.
Hagar, John, served in Ambulance Corps, d in 1863.
Hagar, William, k Petersburg, 1864.
Hagar, James, d Goldsboro.
Hagar, Thomas, d from w at Malvern Hill 1862.
Hill, Isaac, c in Stoneman raid.
Hill, John, k at Drewry's Bluff, May, 1864.
Holdsclaw, William J.
Hunsucker, Calvin, pr Point Lookout.
Hull, William, e June 1, 1863.
Jenkins, William, w Malvern Hill.
Jones, William, w Malvern Hill.
Jones, Pinkney L., w Malvern Hill.
Jones, Wilson, d soon after entering service.
Jones, Milton, d in hospital at Petersburg, June 10, 1862.
Jone, Julius, d Goldsboro.
Jones, Bedford, d in hospital at Gordonsville.
Jones, Jeptha.
Jones, Elbert.
Jones, Evelin.
Kale, Ephraim.
Kale, Sydney, c Fort Steadman.
Kale, Jefferson, w Petersburg.
Keever, Andrew, d Petersburg.
Kirksey, William.
Kirksey, Jackson.
Lackey, Theopholis.
Lee, Bird.
Lee, Robert G., member of Ambulance Corps.
Litton, Elijah, d Brigade Hospital, Drewry's Bluff.
Litton, Elkanah, d hospital at Gordonsville.
Litten, Jackson.

Lofton, Franklin, d Drewry's Bluff in 1864.
Marshall, Clark.
McCoy, James.
Null, George, w Malvern Hill, pr Fort Delaware.
Pope, Silas, w Malvern Hill.
Pope, David, d Brigade Hospital, Drewry's Bluff.
Pope, Franklin.
Powell, Tate, w Drewry's Bluff in 1864.
Powell, Andrew, tr to Band.
Powell, A. B., w Battle of Weldon R. R. in 1864.
Reynolds, William, k Petersburg.
Richardson, John.
Robinson, James, dg Raleigh, N. C.
Setzer, Pinkney.
Shelton, Meek, musician.
Sherrill, Wodford, pr Point Lookout.
Sherrill, Elliott, pr Point Lookout.
Sherrill, David J.
Sherrill, Wycliff.
Sherrill, G. P., e Feb 11, 1863, d Sept 7, 1863.
Setzer, Franklin.
Sigmon, Henry, k Malvern Hill.
Sigmon, Julius.
Stewart, Jeptha P., c Five Point.
Stewart, Franklin, w & c Drewry's Bluff.
Stiles, John, w Malvern Hill.
Traffenstat, Noah, d Raleigh.
Traffenstat, Absalum.
Traffenstat, Daniel, d hospital Petersburg.
Turner, James, d Raleigh.
Turbyfield, Jackson, d Brigade Hospital at Drewry's Bluff.
Ward, James, r Petersburg.
Webb, Noah.
Wilfong, John, w Petersburg.
Wilson, Israel.
Wycoff, Andrew, w Bermuda Hundreds.
Wycoff, Wesley.

Company F Fifty-fifth Regiment North Carolina Troops—

Organized April 19, 1862, after the Battle of Bethel, this company was composed of men of Catawba, Lincoln, Cleveland, and Burke counties. The following list includes only Catawba county men.

OFFICERS

Mull, Peter M., Capt, cm April 19, 1862, w in 1864.
Hull, William H., 1st Lt, cm April 22.

CATAWBA COUNTY 325

NON-COMMISSIONED OFFICERS

Mull, Ezra, 4th sgt, e April 24, 1862.
Gross, Ephraim, 5th sgt, e April 22, 1862, d Aug, 1862, Goldsboro.

PRIVATES

Boiles, William M., e April 22, 1862, w Gettysburg, d Sept 4, 1864.
Brinkle, David A., e May 13, 1862.
Bracket, Zach., e Feb 21, 1863, d July 25, 1864.
Goldson, Miles, e April 24, 1862.
Goodson, Calaway, e April 22, 1862.
Hicks, William, e Feb, 1863.
Hicks, R. J., e April 22, 1862.
Hudson, H., e Feb 18, 1864, d Aug 5, 1864.
Johnson, Andrew J., e April 22, 1862, d March 5, 1864.
Johnson Richard, e April 22, 1862.
Keever, James M., e April 24, 1862.
Mull, John M., e May 3, 1862, p Cpl, pr in 1864.
Pope, Lafayette, e April 1862, d Sept, 1862, Goldsboro.
Seagle, William S., e April 22, 1862.
Smith, John, e May 10, 1862, w Gettysburg.
Shuford, Daniel F., e May 13, 1862.
Shuford, Peter, e April 22, 1862.
Shuford, James P., e April 24, 1862.
Swafford, Robert, e April 19, 1862, w at Gettysburg.
Stainny, J. P., e April 22, 1862, pr July 14, 1863.
Williams, A. P., e Jan 10, 1864, d July 4, 1864.
Wise, Levi, e April 24, 1862, k July 14, 1863, at Falling Waters.
Young, Samuel, e April 22, 1862, m at Washington, N. C.

Company E Seventy-second Regiment North Carolina Troops—

Organized on May 21, 1864, at Newton, this company was composed of 17-year-old boys. It was the last of Catawba county's twelve companies.

OFFICERS

Gaither, J. R., Capt, cm May 21, 1864.
Lawrence, J. M., 1st Lt, cm May 21, 1864.
Bandy, J. M., 2nd Lt, cm May 21, 1864.
Wilfong, Charles T., 3rd Lt, cm May 21, 1864, d Camp Chase, Ohio, Prison.

NON-COMMISSIONED OFFICERS

Smyre, J. F., 1st sgt, e May 21, 1864.
Love, G. M., 2nd sgt, e May 21, 1864.
Huitt, N., 3rd sgt, e May 21, 1864.
Horn, J. L., 4th sgt, e May 21, 1864.

Wyant, D. H., 5th sgt, e May 21, 1864.
Moser, R. A., 1st Cpl, e May 21, 1864.
Roney, W. P., 2nd Cpl, e May 21, 1864.
Shuford, J. M., 3rd Cpl, e May 21, 1864.
Helton, J. W., 4th Cpl, e May 21, 1864.

PRIVATES

Abernethy, J., e May 21, 1864.
Angel, A., e May 21, 1864.
Arndt, L. A., e May 21, 1864.
Ballard, J. F., e May 21, 1864.
Berry, M. N., e May 21, 1864.
Bolick, G., e May 21, 1864.
Bolick, G. A. Jr., e Dec 2, 1864.
Bolick, C., e Jan 4, 1864.
Burns, W., e Oct 14, 1864.
Busbee, F. H., e Feb 24, 1864.
Campbell, L. A., e May 21, 1864.
Cantrell, D. C., e Nov 16, 1864.
Carpenter, A. A., e May 24, 1864.
Chapman, G. W., e May 21, 1864.
Chester, C., e Jan 20, 1864.
Childers, M. A., e May 24, 1864.
Christopher, D., e Oct 16, 1864.
Clay, E., e Nov 24, 1864.
Cline, J. Davidson, e Nov 10, 1864, w and dg.
Coulter, J. Summy, e May 24, 1864, c and paroled.
Cranfield, F. G., e Oct 2, 1864.
Crawford, J. E., e Dec 20, 1864.
Deal, J., e May 21, 1864.
Drum, W. C., e May 21, 1864.
Drum, J. M., e May 21, 1864.
Duncan, W., e Oct 16, 1864.
Echard, E., e Jan 4, 1865.
Edwards, G. W., e May 21, 1864.
Erwin, E. L., e May 21, 1864.
Finger, A., e Oct 16, 1864.
Frazier, F. A., e May 21, 1864.
Fry, A., e Oct 30, 1864.
Gabriel, J., e Sept 1, 1864.
Graham, J., e May 21, 1864.
Harbison, H. M., e May 21, 1864.
Harmon, S., e Jan 4, 1864.
Hart, J., e Dec 20, 1864.
Hass, H. M., e May 21, 1864.
Heavner, J., e Oct 14, 1864.
Herman, F. L.
Holler, S. S., e May 21, 1864.
Hoke, Poly, e May 21, 1864.
Huffman, J. M., e May 21, 1864.

CATAWBA COUNTY 327

Huffman, E., e Oct 16, 1864.
Isenhour, D., e May 21, 1864.
Jarrett, J. F., e May 21, 1864.
Jarrett, W. J., e Nov 20, 1864.
Jones, W. E., e Nov 20, 1864.
Keever, C., e May 21, 1864.
Lail, N., e Oct 14, 1864.
Leatherman, S., e Nov 20, 1864.
Leatherman, B., e Nov 20, 1864.
Martin, H. T., e Oct 16, 1864.
Miller, L., e Jan 4, 1865.
Mouser, J. W., e May 21, 1864.
Moore, J., e Oct 19, 1864.
Pope, J. D., e May 21, 1864.
Randall, W., e Oct 14, 1864.
Reep, L. e May 21, 1864.
Rhyne, A. M., e May 21, 1864, k at Fort Fisher.
Richie, J. M., e Oct 14, 1864.
Rockett, C., e Oct 14, 1864.
Rowe, A. E., e May 21, 1864.
Rudisill, C., e May 21, 1864.
Seagle, H., e May 24, 1864.
Seitz, Luther Polycarp, e May 24, 1864, tr to Millers Cavalry.
Settlemyre, N. P., e May 24, 1864.
Sherrill, Adam Tilford, e May 21, 1864.
Shuford, W., e May 21, 1864.
Shook, D., e May 21, 1864.
Shook, W., e May 21, 1864.
Sigmon, J. C., e Oct 14, 1864.
Simmons, C., e May 21, 1864.
Smith, J. F., e May 21, 1864.
Smith, P., e Jan 4, 1865.
Spegle, D., e May 21, 1864.
Weaver, W., e May 21, 1864.
Whitaker, J. W., e Nov 16, 1864.
Whitener, G. M., e May 21, 1864.
Whitener, L. S., e May 21, 1864.
Wilkinson, W. H., e May 21, 1864.
Wilkinson, J., e May 21, 1864.

Many Catawba county men were away from their home county during the war. Hence, they enlisted in other areas. Among these are:

SIXTH REGIMENT

Connor, Rowell P., e April, 1861 in Co D.

SEVENTH REGIMENT

Barger, Joe, e July 7, 1861.
Setzer, Reuben, e June 4, 1861, k March 14, 1862 at New Bern.

EIGHTH REGIMENT

Rogers, Woodson, e March 21, 1862.

ELEVENTH REGIMENT

Avery, Absalom, e May 8, 1862 in Co I.
Ballard, Benjamin Hawkins, e Oct 1, 1864, in Co E (War Dept Record).
Hawn, Christie, e March 13, 1862, in Co I.
Holtzclaw, R., e Aug 14, 1862, in Co E (Moore's Vol. I, p 390).
Mathison, Joseph, e Sept 15, 1864, in Co E (Moore's Vol. I, p 391).
Null, John T., e March 3, 1862, in Co E (Moore's Vol. I, p 391).
Propst, L. H., e Oct 28, 1864, in Co K (Moore's Vol. I, p 391).
Reinhardt, Robert P., e Jan 5, 1863, w July 1, 1863, at Gettysburg (Co I).
Rinck, Noah, e March 21, 1862, in Co I.
Rinck, Daniel, e March 21, 1862, in Co I, pr July 14, 1863, at Falling Waters.
Speagle, Wm. P., e March 15, 1862, in Co I, w July 1, 1863, at Gettysburg, dg.
Speagle, Monroe L., e March 3, 1863, in Co I, k July 1, 1863, at Gettysburg.
Speagle, Aaron, e April 8, 1863, in Co I, w July 1, 1863, at Gettysburg.
Tallant, Aaron A., e April 8, 1863, in Co I, w July 1, 1863, at Gettysburg.

TWELFTH REGIMENT

Brock, H. N., e May 1, 1864, in Co E.
Cline, D. W., e March 10, 1864, in Co E.
Cline, Laban Wilson, in Co E (or Co G).
Horne, W. W., e April 18, 1864, in Co E.
Ingol, F. F., e March 24, 1864, in Co E, w May 9, 1864.
Jarrett, M. W., e Oct 24, 1864, in Co E.
Mann, A. H., e April 12, 1864, in Co E.
Miller, A. P., e March 28, 1864, in Co E.
Miller, Robert, e April 12, 1864, in Co E.
Miller, G. P.
Propst, J. H., e June 17, 1864, in Co C.
Surviance, George, e March 3, 1864, in Co E.
Tonry (or Lowry), J. H., e Oct 25, 1864, in Co E.
Webb, P. B., e April 16, 1864, in Co E.
Wycoff, J. L., e March 12, 1864, in Co E.
Yount, D. P., e Oct 24, 1864, in Co E.

EIGHTEENTH REGIMENT

Beatty, Calvin, e Aug 14, 1862, in Co A, w Sept, 1862 at Sharpsburg.
Beatty, Wilborn, e Aug 14, 1862, in Co A.
Beatty, Cephas, e Aug 14, 1862, pr May 12, 1864 (Co A).
Barkley, John A., e Aug 14, 1862, in Co A.
Bandy, H. Quin, e Aug 14, 1862, in Co A.
Barringer, Hugh Alexander, e Aug 14, 1862, in Co A, d in Nov, 1862.
Cline, Michael L., e Aug 14, 1862, in Co A, d Dec, 1862.
Crawford, R. A., e Aug 14, 1862, m.

CATAWBA COUNTY 329

Deal, Jacob, e Aug 14, 1862, in Co A, m.
Deal, Quinnon, e Aug 14, 1862, in Co A, m.
Deal, William, e Aug 14, 1862, in Co A, m.
Dellinger, J. J., e Aug 14, 1862, in Co A, m.
Fisher, Barnett, e Aug 14, 1862, in Co A, d Nov 18, 1862
Fisher, Noah, e Aug 14, 1862, in Co A, d Nov 11, 1862.
Hawn, Joseph, e Aug 14, 1862, in Co A, m May 6, 1864.
Heffine, John, e Aug 14, 1862.
Hefner, Davault, e Aug 14, 1862.
Huffman, H. N., e Aug 14, 1862, in Co A, m.
Herman, Frederick, e Aug 14, 1862, in Co A, pr May 12, 1864.
Holler, Jacob, e Aug 14, 1862, in Co A.
Huffman, D. J., e Aug 14, 1862, in Co A, d Nov, 1862.
Huntley, J. V., e Aug 14, 1862.
Johnson, John, e Aug 2, 1862.

COMPANY I TWENTIETH REGIMENT

Fry, C. J., e April 3, 1863, w in 1864.
Naugh, W. A., e April 3, 1863, k May 3, 1863, at Chancellorsville.
Sherrill, S. N., e April 3, 1863, dg April 24, 1863.
Thornberg, B. M., e April 3, 1863, d June 17, 1863.
Wood, John, e April 3, 1863, d June 14, 1863, at Richmond.
Young, John, e April 3, 1863, pr July 1, 1863, at Gettysburg.

TWENTY-SECOND REGIMENT

Bruner, James, e March 25, 1863.
Burris, W. P., e April 30, 1861.

TWENTY-THIRD REGIMENT

Barger, Hosea, e Sept 6, 1862, w at Chancellorsville.
Campbell, John, e Sept 6, 1863, m.
Eades, J. N., e Sept 6, 1862, pr at Gettysburg.
Eckard, William, e Sept 6, 1862.
Eddleman, H. M., e Sept 6, 1862, m.
Fisher, James C., e Jan 21, 1861, d April 2, 1863, in Virginia.
Gabriel, Abram, e June 22, 1862.
Gabriel, Alonza, e June 22, 1861, w July 1, 1863.
Gabriel, Munroe, e June 22, 1861, w July, 1863, at Malvern Hill.
Hass, Robert M., e Sept 6, 1862, pr at Gettysburg.
Hayes, Jackson, e Sept 6, 1862.
Herman, Peter, e Sept 6, 1862.
Keever, Milton, e Sept 6, 1862.
Killian, A. L., e Sept 6, 1862 in Co A 23rd, d Feb 14, 1863, at Lynchburg.
Linebarger, Jacob, e June 23, 1861.
Little, James B., e Aug 20, 1862, d in Richmond hospital.
Little, George W., e June 20, 1861, d at Mount Jackson.
Lafawn, Daniel, e Aug 14, 1862, m.
Longcryer, Paul, e Sept 6, 1862, d May 12, 1863, at Lynchburg.

Mathis, James, e Aug 20, 1862, k July 1, 1863, at Gettysburg.
Mathis, Daniel, e Sept 6, 1862.
McCaslin, William, e Aug 14, 1862, d Jan 8, 1863.
McCall, Joseph, e June 22, 1861, d April 10, 1862, at Richmond.
Mundy, Josiah, e June 22, 1861, w and d Dec 21, 1864.
Moore, W. M., e June 6, 1862, d Oct 6, 1862, at Bunkers Hill.
Mull, D. F., e Sept 6, 1862, d Jan 13, 1863, at Fredericksburg.
Mull, Jacob, e Sept 6, 1862, w at Gettysburg.
Parker, J. F., e Sept 6, 1862.
Pollard, Daniel, e Sept 6, 1862.
Pollard, Noah, e Sept 6, 1862, d same year.
Pollard, Samuel, e Sept 6, 1862.
Pope, Frederick, e Aug 14, 1862.
Pope, Franklin, e Aug 14, 1862.
Punch, J. L., e Sept 6, 1862, pr at Gettysburg.
Roney, A. J., e Sept 6, 1862, d in the war.
Scronce, Andrew, e Aug 14, 1862.
Scronce, C. B., e Aug 14, 1862.
Sigmon, W. D., e Aug 14, 1862.
Sigmon, L. K., e Sept 6, 1862, d Nov 1, 1862.
Starnes, David, e Aug 14, 1862, d in prison Sept 15, 1864.
Thornburg, M. A., e July 15, 1863, in Co F, 23rd.
Turner, P. L., e Sept 6, 1862, w.
Turbyfield, Francis, e June 22, 1862, w at Gettysburg.
Weaver, Adam, e Aug 14, 1862, d Dec 11, 1862.
Weaver, David, e Aug 14, 1862, d Dec 25, 1862.
Weaver, S. M., e Aug 14, 1862, d Nov 30, 1862.
Workman, L. H., e Sept 8, 1862, k at Brandy Station.
Young, John, e Sept 6, 1862, pr at Gettysburg and d.
Yoder, Andrew, e 1862.

COMPANY C TWENTY-FIFTH REGIMENT

Fry, Neely Davidson, e March 22, 1862, w at Malvern Hill.
Muse, Dock F., e May 31, 1861.

TWENTY-SIXTH REGIMENT

Burke, James, e Sept 28, 1862, in Co B.
Holler, Max, e in 1862.
Seagle, Noah, e Sept 23, 1862, in Co I, k at Gettysburg (War Dept. Rec).
Sigmon, Jack, e in 1862.
Whisnant, Marcus, e in 1862.
Wyant, S. W., e Sept 28, 1862, d Sept 27, 1864.

TWENTY-NINTH REGIMENT

Mauney, Wallace, e Aug 17, 1862, d Aug 12, 1863.

THIRTY-SECOND REGIMENT

Robinson, John Alfred, e Co E, 32nd Reg.

CATAWBA COUNTY 331

THIRTY-SEVENTH REGIMENT

Cline, Rufus, e July 1861, pr at Gettysburg.
Cochran, George Washington, e Oct 9, 1861, in Co G, 37th, lost a leg.
Cochran, Francis Marion, e Oct 9, 1861, k at Chancellorsville.
Dellinger, Marcus, e 1861.

THIRTY-EIGHTH REGIMENT

Cline, Laban, e March 30, 1861, in Co F, w at Weldon.
Hoke, Daniel Leander, Quartermaster Surgeon, lost an arm.
Rabards (or Roberts), Horace A., e Feb 18, 1862, retired April 21, 1862, Quartermaster.

FORTY-SECOND REGIMENT

Chapman, W. L., e April 22, 1861, w.
Cobb, R. F.
Carpenter, D. E. F., e March 8, 1862.
Finger, J. M., e Feb 27, 1862.
Fry, J. P., e Feb 27, 1862, lost an arm.
Harman, Adolphus.
Huffman, A. F., e April 1, 1864.
Herman, Frederick.
Isenhower, David, e March 8, 1862.
Isenhower, John, e March 8, 1862.
Lowrance, J. M., e March 8, 1862.
McGee, Hosea, March 13, 1862, Brigade Mail-carrier.
McGee, M. M., e March 13, 1862, Courier for Gen. Kirkman.
Miller, John, e March 20, 1862.
Moose, George R., e April 12, 1864.
Propst, J. A., e June 7, 1864.
Reese, George, e Feb 27, 1862.
Reese, Calvin, e Feb 27, 1862
Scronce, Joy, e March 3, 1864.
Shuford, Wallace, e Feb 27, 1862.
Shuford, Avery, e Feb 27, 1862.
Simmons, E., e Feb 27, 1862.
Sipe, Jacob, e Feb 27, 1862.
Sipe, John, e Feb 27, 1862.
Yount, David, e Oct 12, 1864.
Haynes, G. M., e March 13, 1862 in Co C, 46th Reg.

FORTY-EIGHTH REGIMENT

Abernethy, Williford, e Aug 1, 1862, k Sept 17, 1862 (Co C, 48th).

FORTY-NINTH REGIMENT

Ellis, W. H., e 1863.
Hull, William, e June 1, 1863 (Co K, 49th).
Sherrill, G. P., e Feb 11, 1863, in Co G, 52nd.
Connor, John, e May 14, 1861, d May 8, 1862 at Goldsboro, N. C.

FIFTY-SECOND REGIMENT

Higby, George, e March 19, 1862.
Goodson, John W., e 1861 in Co F, 52nd.

FIFTY-SEVENTH REGIMENT

Carpenter, John, e July 4, 1862, in Co B.
Cline, Lawson Henry Graver, e July 4, 1862, d Sept 7, 1863.
Dietz, Christian, e Feb 20, 1864, w Sept 19, 1864.
Hallman, Laban, e Feb 20, 1864.
Setzer, Henry, Co E.
Setzer, William.
Smyre, Francis, e March, 1864.
Warlick, D. L., e July 4, 1862.
Warlick, J. W., e March 4, 1863.
Adderholt, W. M., e July 4, 1862, d Jan 14, 1863, in N. C. (Co G).
Bolch, Joseph, e July 4, 1862, d March 19, 1863 (Co B).
Cline, D., e July 4, 1862, pr July 4, 1864 (Co B).
Hass, H., e July 4, 1862 in Co B, d Jan 10, 1864.
Hinkle (or Henkel), Cicero, e Feb 20, 1864, w Sept 19, 1864.
Leatherman, R. P., e July 4, 1862, in Co B, d Feb 10, 1862, at Richmond.
Reinhardt, John, e July 4, 1862 in Co B.
Setzer, Henry, e 1862 in Co C, 57th N. C. Inf, prison 16 months.
Traffenstadt, Joseph, e July 4, 1862, d Nov 17, 1862, at Culpeper Court House.
Warlick, J. M., e July 4, 1862.
Whisenant, John, e July 4, 1862, d Jan 14, 1863, in N. C.

FIFTY-EIGHTH REGIMENT

Lanier, D. A., e in Co E, 58th.

SIXTY-THIRD REGIMENT

Holsclaw, M. L., e Aug 14, 1862, in Co K.
Hull, J. S., e Aug 25, 1862 in Co K.
Massey, W. F., e Aug 26, 1862 in Co K.
Matheson, J. F., e Aug 12, 1862 in Co K.
Mundy, O. M., e Aug 14, 1862 in Co K.
Nancey, Wiley, e Aug 26, 1862.
Robinson, John, e Aug 18, 1862.
Sherrill, D. H., e Aug 7, 1862.
Sherrill, Moses Whitfield, e Aug 5, 1862.
Sherrill, D. H., Jr., e Aug 5, 1862.
Sherrill, Nelson, Aug 10, 1862.
Traffenstadt, W. A., e Aug 16, 1862.

SEVENTIETH REGIMENT

Burgess, Mathias, e May 25, 1864 in Co B, 70th.
Parlier, J. B., e Co B, 70th in 1864.

CATAWBA COUNTY 333

NORTH CAROLINA CAVALRY

Abernethy, Frank, e March, 1864.
Cline, J. Rome, e Co B, 2nd N. C. Cavalry.
Cochran, William, e in Co D, N. C. Cavalry.
Cochran, John, e in Co D, N. C. Cavalry.
Connor, Charles F., e 1862 in N. C. Cavalry, K in Stoneman's Raid, 1865.
Keever, Daniel, e 1864 in 4th N. C. Cavalry.
Litten, T. B., e in 5th N. C. Cavalry.
Setzer, Franklin, e 1863 in Co D, 49th N. C. Cavalry.
Warlick, Pinkney D., e Oct 16, 1861 in N. C. Cavalry.

CATAWBA MEN ENLISTED IN OTHER STATES

Abernethy, Osborne Franklin, e in Mississippi, Jeff Davis Legion.
Ballard, Robert Seymour, e in Alabama, k by bushwhackers in Tenn.
Bost, Joseph Mehaffey, e in S. C.
Brown, S. C., e in Arkansas from Monbo, N. C.
Bynum, M. P., e in Arkansas from Monbo, N. C.
Holler, Adley, e in S. C.
Hunsucker, Martin, e in S. C.
Killian, Alfred A., e Co A, 5th S. C., April 9, 1861.
Lail, Adolphus D., e in S. C.
McGee, Noah, e June 4, 1861, in 5th S. C. Reg.
Pope, Raneus, e in S. C.
Pope, Mark, e in S. C.
Sherrill, W. B., e in Texas.
Sherrill, William B., e in S. C.
Sherrill, Wm. S., e in Texas.
Smyre, Frank, e in S. C.
Wilfong, V. P., e in Texas.
Wilfong, John Macon, e in Tenn. in Forest's Cavalry.
Wilfong, Henry G., e in Texas Cavalry.
Warlick, Daniel W., e in Alabama, Capt 30th Reg.
Warlick, Monroe P., e 12th Tennessee Inf.

CATAWBA MEN IN UNKNOWN COMPANIES

Canipe, John, d in the war.
Fulbright, Davis, k in war.
Fulbright, Mark, d during the war.
Fulbright, Max, d during the war.
Fulbright, Joseph, d soon after enlistment.
Fry, Abel.
Gantt, Jesse.
Goodson, Daniel Osborn.
Herman, M. M., e Aug 14, 1862, d.
Herman, Benjamin, e Aug 14, 1862, d Nov 2, 1862.
Holler, Lawson, e Oct 5, 1864.
Hudson (or Huffman), Serenius.
Huffman, S. A., e Aug 14, 1862.
Hull, M. F., e Aug 14, 1862, w May 2, 1862.

Ickard, W. A., e Aug 14, 1862, k May 2, 1863, at Chancellorsville.
Johnson, David.
Keener, Ephraim.
Lafon, Daniel, e Sept 8, 1862.
Lanier, Joseph, e Aug 14, 1862.
Lanier, Jacob, e Aug 14, 1862.
Lawrence, Alfred A., e 1861 in Rowan county, k at Seven Pines.
Loftin, Leblume, lost a leg.
Love, James, e in Caswell county, Co D, 13th Reg, N. C. Inf, May 1, 1861.
Lutz, John B., e Oct 5, 1864.
Lutz, Laban, e Oct 8, 1864.
Parker, Lemuel P.
Richie, John, k in war.
Rhyne, Eli S., e Aug 14, 1862, w and pr July, 1863.
Scronce, George, e March 12, 1864.
Seaglr, John.
Sigmon, W. B.
Sherrill, Leander B., e March 15, 1862 in Co B, 23rd N. C. Inf.
Smith, Elisha, died in the war.
Witherspoon, Lawson Alexander, d in Point Lookout prison.
Wilkinson, David Osborn, e March 13, 1863 in Co E, 32nd Reg.
Wilkinson, Wesley, k.
Wilkinson, Sidney, k.
Yoder, Cyrus, e July 14, 1862, d Feb 7, 1865 at Camp Douglas, Ill., buried there.
Bumgarner, Alexander e May 1, 1864 at Alexander, N. C., in Co D, N. C. Jr Res.
Bolch (or Bolick), Abel, e March 15, 1861, in Co C, 28th, w at Cold Harbor.
Bolch (or Bolick), Gerard (not G. A.), e Dec 2, 1864 in Co E, 72nd.
Bolch (or Bolick), Perry.
Bolch (or Bolick), Jeconias.
Bolch (or Bolick), William Pinkney, e March 15, 1861 in Co C, 28th, d July 15, 1862.
Sherrill, Nelson, e March 15, 1862 in Co B, 23rd Reg (Moore's Vol 2, page 259).
Wike, William D., k in war.
Wilke, Miles.
Wike, Silar.
Wike, Marcus.

WAR DEPARTMENT RECORDS

Cline, Calvin, e June 6, 1861, in Co F, 23rd N. C. Inf, born July 15, 1837.
Frazier, Hughey Yerbey, e July 4, 1862, in Co E, 57th N. C. Inf, died in prison Feb 4, 1860.
Fry, Jacob, e March 13, 1862, in Co K, 46th N. C. Inf, w and dg Sept 26, 1864.
Heavner, George Henry, e May 8, 1862, in Co I, 11th Bethel Reg.
Hefner, George, e March 15, 1862, in Co C, 28th Reg N. C. Inf.
Hefner, Franklin, e Oct 18, 1862, in Co F, 32nd N. C. Inf, d Oct 4, 1863.

CATAWBA COUNTY 335

Isenhower, Abel, e March 16, 1863, in Co F, 38th N. C. Inf, d June 6, 1863, Guinea Station.
Killian, Anthony, e Sept 23, 1863, in Co H, 28th N. C. Troops, Camp Vance.
Leonard, Elcanah, e April 5, 1864, in Co B, 6th N. C. Inf at Kinston.
Little, Quintus M., e Nov 10, 1864, in Co F, 3rd Reg, Jr. Reserves.
McGee, Noah Henry, e June 4, 1861, in Co D, 5th S. C. Inf at Orangeburg.
Seagle (Seigel), Noah, e Sept 23, 1862, in Co I, 26th N. C. Inf at Camp Holmes.
Williams, Ransom H., e July 1, 1862, in Co G, 58th N. C. Inf at Burnsville.

Among the members of the Home Guard, some of whom were sent to guard prisoners at Salisbury Prison, are:

HOME GUARD

Bost, William Perry
Cline, Jonas, sent home for sheriff
Cline, Manuel Monroe
Coulter, Eli Summey
Dietz, Mathias
Hahn (or Horn), Jesse
Hollar, Andrew
Hoyle, Humphrey

Kahill (or Cahill) Daniel
Lohr, Ephraim
Propst, Absalom
Propst, Alfred Monroe, blacksmith
Rabb, John
Seitz, Davis
Shuford, Lawson, wheelwright
Smith, Marcus M., **Capt. Sr. Res.**

The roster of soldiers is incomplete and contains errors.

Defeated but Undaunted

CHAPTER XIV

MUNICIPALITIES, VILLAGES, AND CROSSROADS, THEN AND NOW

Chance keynotes the story of the establishment of Catawba county municipalities.

No significant center of population arose without impetus from some outside influence. Hickory, for instance, was the product of the necessity for a trading center between Newton and Morganton and a station of first the stagecoach and later the train. Newton was the product of the need for a center of government. Catawba was caused by the advent of the "iron horse." And Maiden was the result of sound planning by industrious men who saw fit to establish a southern Catawba county trading center.

No one city has held its leadership position always. For instance, Catawba once was the metropolis of the county, due to its focal point on the rail line.

The building of Catawba county municipalities is dramatic. The diligent efforts of persons imbued with civic spirit, their dreams of healthful and pleasant surroundings, and their ultimate successes and failures provide romance.

Of course all has not been happiness in the business of erecting cities and towns. Men's plans sometimes failed. The most notable example, perhaps, is Ulrichsburg, or Crowdertown—which, incidentally, was the county's first "scientifically-planned" town.

The discussion of Catawba's concentrations of population is enabled by a few far-sighted individuals who saw fit to make records for posterity.

Present incorporated cities and towns, listed alphabetically:

TOWN OF BROOKFORD—

A cotton mill may be credited as responsible for the establishment of Brookford, located about two miles south of Hickory. The municipality was incorporated March 1, 1907.

Bunker Hill Covered Bridge, Near Claremont

Old Hickory Tavern

CATAWBA COUNTY 337

The large cotton textile industry was formed as E. L. Shuford and Company in 1898. A short time later it was incorporated as Brookford Mills, Inc., under the same ownership. E. L. Shuford and Henry J. Holbrook were the owners.

The town's name is a portion of each of the owner's names, Hol-BROOK and Shu-FORD.

In 1917, the mill was sold to the A. D. Julliard and Company, Inc., and the name changed to Brookford Mills Company Corporation. In 1953, the mill was purchased by United Merchants and Manufacturers.

During the 1930s, the town sponsored and constructed with Work Projects Administration labor a municipality swimming pool and ball ground. It presently employs a full-time community-worker.

Brookford is the only town within the county which does not make an ad valorem tax levy.

The original officers, as named in the act of incorporation, are Mayor T. J. Leonard; and Commissioners W. H. Shuford, J. W. Ballew, and Charles E. Cole.

Others known to have served the municipality as mayors are Henry J. Holbrook, Wade H. Shuford, John W. Ballew, Yodom Y. Warren, Ed Mitchell (1919-21), David L. Howard (1921-25), A. L. Greene (1925-27), J. Jackson Stepp (1927-31), Mrs. Rena Kendall (1931-35), Marcus A. Bolick (1935-49), J. D. Greene (1949-53) Jr., and Eugene Weaver (1953 and still serving).

The town's population in 1950 was 768.

(For post office information, see succeeding chapter.)

TOWN OF CATAWBA *(first Catawba Station)*—

Catawba, located in the extreme eastern part of the county, is one of the oldest towns between Salisbury and Asheville, having been selected as an early station for the railroads. Trains ran to the town before the War Between the States, beginning probably about 1859.

Branson's North Carolina Business Directory for 1869 lists nine of the county's 15 physicians with Catawba Station addresses.

The town was incorporated as Catawba Station on March 8, 1872. Commissioners named in the act are A. M. Powell, A. D. Shuford, Frank Powell, J. H. Trollinger, William Lowrance, J. K. Howell, and John William Long.

No further record relative to the municipality is found until it is formed as Town of Catawba on February 8, 1893.

Mayors serving since this time are J. L. Pitts (1893), R. H. Trollinger (1894), Trollinger resigned and J. U. Long was appointed to serve, J. U. Long (1894-97), J. H. Pitts (1897), M. J. Cochran (1898-1901), J. H. Pitts (1901), Pitts resigned and Oscar Sherrill was appointed to serve, Oscar Sherrill (1901), Sherrill resigned in 1902 and J. H. Coulter was appointed to serve, J. H. Coulter (1902), Coulter apparently resigned and J. U. Long was appointed to serve, J. U. Long (1902-03), Long resigned and Oscar Sherrill was appointed to serve, Oscar Sherrill (1903-05), A. H. McNeil (1905-07), J. U. Long (1907), James T. Harwell (1908), Harwell resigned and J. H. Pitts was appointed to serve, J. H. Pitts (1908), L. H. Lowrance (1909), C. A. Reid (1910), Reid resigned and A. H. McNeil was appointed to serve, A. H. McNeil (1910), R. R. Boggs (1911), Boggs resigned and J. H. Sherrill was appointed to serve, J. H. Sherrill (1911-12), Sherrill resigned and R. R. Boggs was appointed to serve, R. R. Boggs (1912), Boggs resigned and James T. Harwell was appointed to serve (1912-14), Harwell resigned and Oscar Sherrill was appointed to serve, Oscar Sherrill (1914-1918), W. B. Walker (1919-21), R. E. Carpenter (1922-23), Oscar Sherrill (1924), Sherrill resigned and R. E. Carpenter was appointed to serve, R. E. Carpenter (1924-25), W. L. Sherrill (1926), C. B. Gilbert (1927-30), W. L. Sherrill (1931-32), C. W. Ervin (1933-34), T. E. Harwell (1935-40), E. E. Deal (1941), Deal resigned and R. E. Carpenter was appointed to serve, R. E. Carpenter (1941-44), W. M. Musgrove (1945-47), E. L. Huffman (1948-49), and John S. Danner (1950 and still serving).

The municipality was named for the Catawba river, which flows to its east.

CATAWBA COUNTY 339

The town's population in 1950 was 506.

(For post office information, see succeeding chapter.)

TOWN OF CLAREMONT *(first Charlotte Crossing, second, according to R. A. Yoder's map of 1886, Setzer's Depot)*—

The town of Claremont's first store building was completed the day of the historic cyclone—March 25, 1884. Fortunately, the wind did not destroy it.

The municipality, located in the mid-eastern portion of the county, numbered among its earliest settlers Adolphus and Jonas Sigmon and J. W. Setzer.

Soon after its establishment, the village became known as Charlotte Crossing. The United States Post Office Department would not accept this name due to its similarity with the name of the city of Charlotte. Hence, the post office became known officially as Crossing.

The town of Claremont was chartered in 1893. The act of incorporation names as the first officers J. D. Kelley, mayor, and John W. Setzer, W. A. Hoke, and Jonas T. Sigmon, aldermen.

Succeeding mayors are J. W. Setzer, J. T. Sigmon, W. A. Hoke, W. F. White, J. H. Moser, R. P. Hollar, J. P. Carpenter, W. A. Deal, Sr., J. A. Deal, W. K. Durham, Sam Winters, C. E. Little, John E. Frazier, Lane Moser, Martin Keisler, C. Ray Morrow, T. R. Miller, and C. Ray Morrow (still serving).

The derivation of the town's name is unknown.

The municipality's population in 1950 was 661.

(For post office information, see succeeding chapter.)

TOWN OF CONOVER *(first "Y," then "Canova")*—

The town of Conover is geographically centered in Catawba county.

Concerning its past, Mrs. J. A. Isenhower has written:

"Its history dates to the year 1871 when Frances Smyre purchased of Pink Spencer a lot situated at the "Y," or at the point where the trains of the Southern Railway had a branch line running over to neighboring Newton.

"Clinton Eugene Smyre, son of Mr. and Mrs. Francis Smyre, was the first child born in Conover. As the site chosen by the

Smyres' was situated at a convenient point, in the early years the family operated a boarding house, which won a great deal of popularity.

"Smyre operated a business for making and repairing shoes, and soon other establishments began to grow up. Among the earliest were a general store operated by Townsend, McCreary and Finger; and the following other firms: Henkel, Lippard and Reitzel; Cline Roseman and company; and Smith, Yount and company.

"A first family of Conover was that of Mr. and Mrs. J. Pinkney Spencer. Mrs. Spencer, before her marriage, was Miss Dianah Herman, and, through her father, came into possession of a large tract of land, a portion of which became part of the town of Conover.

"An early resident of the neighborhood was Mose Herman, who owned much of the land between the junction point and the city of Newton along the road leading from Oxford Ford beside which the town of Conover was springing up. The Herman land was sold to John Q. Seitz, a North Carolinian by birth but at that time a resident of Columbia, S. C. . . .

"The Seitz property for many years was the subject of discussion and investigation by local attorneys and citizens as the result of Mr. Seitz' will, the only heir being his son, John Hamilton Seitz. After 1900, Mr. Mueller and Mr. Wagner, of Wisconsin, bought the land. It later was sold to John L. Isenhower, from whom it was obtained for school purposes. . . .

". . . (An early resident) . . . who rendered public service was J. P. Spencer, who served as constable and tax collector for many years.

"A small jail was built near the center of town, but according to stories of the early days, it was seldom used.

"In the year 1883, P. E. Isenhower moved with his family to Conover. For a number of years, he was associated with his brother, J. L. Isenhower and others in the mercantile business. Another of the early merchants was J. A. Yount. His home place on Main Street was among the first handsome residences erected in the town.

CATAWBA COUNTY 341

"M. J. Rowe and S. G. Shell operated the first mill in the community, known as the Burr mill, located near the depot at the "Y."

"Still other establishments of the early days were the blacksmith shop operated by Elkanah Eckard; the Picker Stick and Handle Factory, from which a number of other enterprises have evolved, established by Jonas Hunsucker; and the Jerome Bolick Sons company, the oldest manufacturing concern located in the town.

"During the early years, several physicians located in Conover. Among them were Dr. Alfred Fox, a Dr. Greenwade, and a Dr. Marshburn. In the year 1884, Dr. D. McD. Yount came with his family and remained to practice in the community for 30 years. Dr. Marion Moser was another of the pioneer physicians. He first practiced in Conover, then moved to Claremont. Still another comparatively early practitioner of medicine in the town was Dr. F. L. Herman.

"To enable Newton rail service, the Conover tracks had to be moved from the eastern to the western side of the town in the 1880s. Conover's depot was built in 1889. . . ."

The town of Conover was first known as "The Y," due to the fact that it was the site of a train spur line, which ran to Newton.

It is believed by a majority of historians that the name "Canova" was given the village by Mrs. Mattie Miller Hollar in honor of a famous Italian sculptor.

Those who believe the town was named for the Italian say that the name was corrupted to "Conover" by conductors of the railroad who were careless with their pronunciations.

Others believe, however, including A. L. Barger, who wrote concerning Conover in Hahn's "The Catawba Soldier in the Civil War," that the town was named by a Mrs. Wheisiger of Morganton after the name of a family residing somewhere in the North, probably in Ohio.

The act incorporating the town of Conover was passed January 26, 1877. Persons named as officers are P. F. Smith, mayor, and G. A. Brady, J. P. Cline, J. F. Hunsucker, J. P. Spencer, and Jonas Hunsucker, commissioners.

Succeeding mayors have been J. P. Cline, George A. Brady, Jonas Hunsucker, J. F. Hunsucker, J. W. Rockett, J. S. Coyner, S. H. Jordan, D. M. Moser, Charles L. Coon, Charles E. Sigmon, S. S. Rowe, G. A. Romoser, C. R. Brady, R. M. Hunsucker, John A. Isenhower, R. K. Bolick, P. W. Herman, C. M. Barringer, Glenn N. Rowe, Sr., and John Pharr.

The town's population in 1950 was 1,164.

(For post office information, see succeeding chapter.)

CITY OF HICKORY *(first Hickory Tavern, later Town of Hickory)*—

The present city of Hickory had its genesis in a tavern. Previously, newspaper and other articles have fixed the date of the building of this structure at about 1790.

The Historical Association, however, has located material which may indicate that a tavern, or an "ordinary," existed at the present site of Hickory as early as 1784. In this year, John Bradburn was issued a license to operate an "ordinary" by the county court of Lincoln county. Bradburn purchased the tract of land on which Hickory now is located two years later, in 1786. It is believed, therefore, that he enabled himself to operate the tavern, then probably leased it, and consequently bought it.

The Hickory area land was included in the original tract of 640 acres owned by William McMullin. The grant of land had been issued on October 28, 1782, while the Catawba territory was a part of Burke county. The land was surveyed on June 8, 1779.

It can be said, therefore, that McMullin first owned the property on which Hickory later was to be built.

That a tavern might have been operated even earlier than 1784 is made feasible by the fact that a road first entered the Hickory area in 1769. (See chapter on Transportation.)

The Hickory tavern which remained until about 1875, located at the present 110 and 112 Main Avenue Place, SW, was a rude log, one and one-half story affair.

Major J. L. Latta describes the building further thus:

"In my boyhood days I passed the old Hickory Tavern, which was then standing, twice daily going to school, and at this date the old building with its puncheon floors is distinctly remembered (written in 1932).

". . . The chimney . . . was known as a 'stick chimney'— built of logs and lined with stone for the 'fireplace'—and above daubed or plastered with mud.

"There were no dormer windows on the roof. . . . The porch did not extend the entire length of the building, but a very small one at the door.

"The building was a story and a half high, and a large 'Dutch oven' was in the rear where much of the cooking was done. . . .

"Uncle Joe Miller (an operator of the tavern) did at one time attempt to paint a sign for his hostelry. . . . In crude lettering he painted the words 'Enterdainment for Man and Beast.' It will be noticed that Uncle Joe used a 'd' instead of a 't' in the word 'entertainment! . . ."

Others earlier than Miller who are known to have operated the tavern are John Cline and Simon Haas, a descendant of the pioneer.

Hickory tavern was so named because of a large hickory tree or trees which stood nearby, according to the most generally accepted theory. Major Latta, however, disagrees with this supposition, for he has written: "The spreading hickory tree, so often referred to in legend in connection with the Hickory Tavern, stood at the southeast corner of the building. . . . It so happened, however, that this particular tree was a walnut tree, although it has always been referred to as a hickory tree." In later writing, Major Latta further attests to the fact that Hickory's legendary tree was walnut, not hickory. "The writer is sure of this," he points out. "For he has gathered walnuts from it. The name arose from the hickory forest around the tavern."

Another legend says a large hickory tree stood near the Hickory tavern, and that the tavern keeper occasionally whipped his wife with a hickory switch, thereby leaving the Hickory "impression."

Most historians agree that the village's first name, "Hickory Tavern," came by virtue of the presence of the tavern.

However, there are those who believe that the name of the tavern was in no way associated with a species of tree. They contend that the Germans of Pennsylvania brought the name "Hickory" with them when they trekked south. Where Lancaster, Pa., now stands was once the town of Hickory, due to the presence of Hickory Indians. The town of Lancaster was laid out in 1730.

It is a matter of record that Jesse Robinson bought the land on which Greater Hickory now is situated at a public auction in Lincolnton on May 8, 1798, for approximately 46 pounds in the King's money. The fact is substantiated by an original deed that has been handed down to the present generation of the Robinson family.

An excerpt of the deed reads as follows: "By virtue of an execution issued from the county court of Lincoln county against Joseph Horton for the sum of thirty-nine pounds and ten shillings debt, also the further sum of four pounds and seven pence for coats at the suit of John Moore, assignee, as on record may appear." A description of 360 acres of the tract of land bought by Robinson, the present site of Hickory, is given in the yellowed deed as follows: "A tract of land lying and situated in said county on both sides of the road leading from Lincolnton to Morganton, beginning at a pine and running north 320 poles to the Hickory crossing to the wagon road, then west 120 poles to a stake; then south twenty-eight poles; west 340 poles to a stake; then east to the beginning, containing 360 acres—It being part of a tract of land conveyed to Jo Horton from John Bradburn and sold and conveyed by Lawson Henderson as sheriff to said Jesse Robinson."

The deed states that the transaction was proved in open court by the oath of James Erwin, with Daniel M. Forney, clerk of court, as witness. The names of Martin Huffman and Jesse Robinson likewise appear on the deed. The first sale from the 360 acres after the tract was purchased by Robinson was about 1860, according to the old Robinson plat.

Hickory Tavern existed as a municipality as of the first Monday in January, 1870. However, earlier attempts had been made to incorporate the village. The community's first charter, drawn December 12, 1863, stipulated that the corporate limits of Hickory Tavern should be one mile square, having for its center the depot of the Western North Carolina railroad, and also provided a board of six commissioners invested with all "rights, privileges, powers and immunities" conferred upon commissioners of incorporated towns by their charters. The board of commissioners appointed by the legislature, to serve until their successors were elected, consisted of J. R. Ellis, H. W. Link, A. L. Shuford, A. J. Lindsay, L. Elias, and W. Hall. But, due to the tangling of the state's affairs because of the War Between the States, this charter was never carried into effect.

A second attempt to incorporate the village on July 24, 1868, failed, due to the fact that the governor did not appoint town commissioners. A third attempt on January 3, 1869, likewise was unsuccessful, because the county commissioners failed to appoint judges of election to hold an election on May 4, 1869.

Finally, on December 14, 1869, the original act of incorporation was amended by the state legislature so as to name six commissioners to be in charge of an election on the first Monday in January, 1870. The legislature empowered J. H. Bruns, Abel A. Shuford, Henry Wilfong, W. P. Reinhardt and W. S. Ramseur, or any three of them, to qualify and hold the election. The election was unquestionably held, and it is known that Marcus Yoder was the first mayor and Andrew Shuford was one of the commissioners.

On December 18, 1873, the charter of "Hickory Tavern" was annulled by the enactment of a charter of the "Town of Hickory," prescribing a corporate limit of 1,000 yards in all directions from the "depot warehouse" of the Western North Carolina railroad. This charter also provided that the officers of the town should consist of a mayor and six commissioners, to be elected annually on the first Monday in May.

Hickory became a city by legislative act of March 11, 1889.

Greater Hickory was formed in 1931, when the municipalities of Highland and Brookford were annexed and became a part of the city of Hickory.

Few records document happenings in Hickory prior to the twentieth century. Among the ablest historians who deal with this subject is Major Latta, who was reminisced concerning the founding and development of the city thus:

About the original board of commissioners (named in the act of 1863)—

"The appointed board of commissioners was men of community leadership. Dr. J. R. Ellis was a physician, a soldier and a patriot. In 1861, he organized a company of volunteers and was its captain. He was early discharged, however, in order that he might serve his community as a physician. Although a patriot, he had little confidence in the final success of the Confederacy. While practicing medicine, he also bought all the gold, silver, and 'green backs' he could get in exchange for Confederate money. In the beginning, he would pay $1.50 Confederate for $1 Federal money. As the war wore on, he increased the price. At the close of the war, he was paying ten for one. He became a rich man, but was benevolent and did much for the poor. . . .

"W. Hall moved away from the community soon after its incorporation. He was said to have been a civic-minded individual.

"A. L. (Delph) Shuford was one of the pioneer settlers of the community. He was the first agent of the Western North Carolina railroad, and during the war, was assistant manager of the Confederate commissary. . . . Although called into service in the army, hostilities ceased before Shuford reached the front. This resident was one of the first men of the community to recognize the value and importance of improved cattle, and was the first to import thoroughbred Jersey stock. Nearly all the improved Jersey cattle in the section are descended from his original importations. Shuford built what was known as 'Shuford's Hall,' which was used for shows, general gatherings, etc.

"A. J. Lindsay was a merchant, originally from High Point.

"L. Elias was a Jewish merchant. His store was located west of the present postoffice. His establishment was the largest in the village at that time. Elias was the father of Kope Elias, who was (once) a power in North Carolina politics. . . . In 1893, President Cleveland appointed Kope as collector of internal revenue, but Senator Zeb Vance blocked his confirmation in the United States Senate."

CATAWBA COUNTY 347

Concerning the effects of the War Between the States on Hickory—

"In considering the growth and development of the village of 'Hickory Tavern' and later the town of Hickory, it can be readily seen that little or no progress was possible during the Civil War, but at the close of hostilities conditions were even worse. . . .

"The joyful news of the end of the war spread with the quickness of lightning and prayers of thankfulness, on midnight air, left the lips of myriads of mothers and widows with bleeding hearts. For several years after this event, the history of Hickory is inseparably mixed with the history of the State and county. The war was over, but alas! Nothing remained of the mellow civilization of the ripened South except the fragrance of her memory. The carpet-baggers and adventurers flocked into the state as thick as autumn leaves in a forest wind. They organized the untutored ex-slaves into political groups and with themselves took complete charge of the state government and most municipalities. They elected the memorable W. W. Holden as governor of the state and a legislature that did his bidding, until he was finally impeached. Under his guidance laws were enacted empowering him to declare any county as in a state of insurrection. The first law of nature—self-preservation—forced the best people to band themselves together in an organization known as the Ku Klux, and Governor Holden appealed to the Federal government to furnish troops to subdue an 'insurrection,' whereupon the nefarious Kirk's army was formed in Tennessee, and passed through the State from West to East—like a besom of destruction, arresting and imprisoning multitudes of the most prominent and best people of the State. At this time many of Hickory's very best citizens had to take flight to distant States, and remain away until the storm passed over.

"Under such circumstances . . . no town in the State could be expected to make progress.

"The life and upbuilding of Hickory may be dated from about 1870."

About hotels—

"Hickory's first 'hotel' was erected about 1868. Dr. J. R. Ellis and others erected the Central Hotel on the exact spot where the post office now stands. This was a large, two-story wood structure, and for a few years was operated by a hired manager. Later it was leased to H. C. Elliott. The hotel had a commodious ballroom, and employed a full-time string band.

"At about the same date, the Western Hotel was built by Gabriel Marshall, . . . (diagonally across the street in a northeast direction from the post office). Upon completion of the Western it was operated for a time by A. W. Marshall (son of the owner). After a few years, it was leased to Walker Brothers.

"Both of these hotels for a number of years enjoyed a good patronage and were popular with the traveling public, but after a time their reputations began to decline. . . .

"On November 23, 1887, during a high wind, the Central Hotel caught fire, and in a few minutes time the burning shingles, like lighted torches, were blown across the street and quickly engulfed also the Western in an unquenchable holocaust. This was Hickory's worst fire until this date.

"Immediately after the double conflagration, Field Brothers established the Belmont Hotel. This was a two-story wood structure adjoining the old 'town hall,' where the present municipal building now stands. This was used merely as a temporary hotel. The Hickory Inn was under construction at the time of the fire and was completed a few months later.

(Historians disagree about the building of the Belmont. Some say that it was standing at the time of the big hotel fire, and also was consumed in that blaze. Also, there are some references to a Phoenix Hotel.)

"The Hickory Inn was located west of the postoffice, and was a thoroughly modern hotel for its day. In fact, it was truly an Apollo Belvedere; in interior finish it was unapproached by any hotel in the state. Its office, lobby and dining room were finished in gorgeous fresco, by the eminent painter, F. A. Grace. The dining room walls and ceiling were resplendent in color. The Hickory Inn was built by the merchants of the city, and was opened by McAvoy and company, in January, 1888. It was bought soon thereafter by Frank Loughran of Asheville. After its purchase, Mr. Loughran operated it several years, after which it was leased to different parties. The Inn was destroyed by fire February 25, 1907.

"The New Charter House was opened for business also in 1888. Later known as the Charter House, the hostelry was located directly opposite the original log 'Tavern.' It was owned and conducted by Miss Mollie Evans."

One of the greatest and most far-reaching cooperative achievements in Catawba county was the building of Hotel Hickory by citizens of the city, through community subscriptions and sale of stock, conducted by the local Chamber of Commerce.

The modern, fire-proof, eight-story hostelry, constructed of reinforced concrete and brick, was opened for business on July 15, 1926. Its opening was celebrated by entertaining one of the early conventions of the North Carolina Department of the American Legion, and by inviting the North Carolina Press Association to hold a meeting at the hotel.

Hickory was among the first cities in North Carolina to install electric lights. D. W. Shuler, H. D. Abernethy, J. A. Martin and A. A. Shuford organized the Hickory Electric Company in 1888.

The night of February 4, 1889, was one of achievement. The town's dark streets were electrified for the first time by "bottled" light. An article in the February 7 issue of The Press and Carolinian ably describes the event:

". . . The electric light was turned on for the first time and proved a decided success. The Hickory M. O. Band was out in full uniform, with handsome Charley at the head as drum major, in honor of the occasion which was celebrated in various quarters and in different ways.

"We are proud of our lights. Not so much do we brag on the mere fact of having electric lights for electric lights are common in this progressive age.

"Heaven's artillery has been captured and is being used everywhere and for everything.

"That isn't the point, but this is. There is not another town in the State the size of Hickory that can boast of electric lights. It shows thrift, energy, and prosperity. It shows that the citizens of Hickory are 'right up' and are ready for anything that shows progress. This will do away with 'Old-fogy-ism' and invite people of energy among us. The electric company deserves praise for the thrift they have shown in putting in this plant."

After a number of years, the Hickory Electric company sold out to the late Colonel M. E. Thornton, who operated the business through a stormy period of several years, and finally sold his plant and franchise to the Southern Power company, when the steam plant was discontinued, and the entire lighting and power system was modernized and enlarged.

The city of Hickory installed water works and a complete sewage system in 1904. At that time, water was obtained from the South Fork river, but was changed to the Catawba river about 1927.

The Catawba river, although some distance from the city, has meant much to the municipality. Two of the oldest industries had their birth on the river's murky bands—the Piedmont Wagon company and the Catawba River Lumber company (now Hutton and Bourbonnais company).

Prior to the coming of the railroad, there was almost no industry in the village of Hickory. Practically all of the business was country trade, divided among a considerable number of small stores. The bulk of the business at that date was what was known as "mountain trade." Hickory bought much mountain produce and, at the same time, sold household supplies to many of the mountain counties. It was not unusual to see hundreds of covered wagons, loaded with mountain produce, assembled almost daily on what is now Union Square, and the road from Hickory to the old Horse Ford wooden toll bridge, being thickly lined with more covered wagons—some coming to Hickory, and others returning to the mountains. This was re-enacted almost daily throughout the winter months, and involved a much larger volume of business than would be expected by one unfamiliar with this class of traffic. The mountain produce consisted of apples, cabbage, potatoes, chestnuts, dried fruits, dried beef, feathers, tallow, beeswax, hides, cheese, ginseng, etc. The so-called "mountain trade" came from the counties of Alleghany, Ashe, Mitchell, Watauga, and the upper part of Caldwell. Virtually all of this trade in the early days was handled through Hickory until the completion of the

Chester and Lenoir Narrow-Gauge Railroad to Lenoir, when the mountaineers naturally gravitated to that point.

It was then that Hickory turned its attention to industry. Major Latta writes interestingly concerning industry and people—

"The first laundry in Hickory was operated by Isaac A. Hartsell . . . about the year 1880. Mr. Hartsell didn't find the venture either pleasant or profitable.

"William Hale, Sr., was the first merchant in Hickory. The next general store was opened for business in 1860 by Link, Ellis and company. This firm was composed of W. H. Ellis, Dr. J. H. Ellis and H. W. Link.

"The first dentist in Hickory was Dr. J. Lowenstein, who located in the town in the early seventies.

"If the oldest inventor in Hickory is to be named, the palm must pass to J. F. Abernethy. About 1890, when there was no electric power except from sundown until midnight, Mr. Abernethy devised a method of furnishing a fan to shoo the flies away. He kept a hefty calf in the basement of his store, and constructed some sort of a tread-mill, which with a rope-drive, connected with a homemade ceiling fly fan immediately over his meat counter. At sunrise each morning, the fatted calf was led into the tread-mill, which was so constructed that the calf must keep up a lively trot or be tossed on its head, and as long as the calf kept the lively pace, the ceiling fan revolved and every fly took flight."

The diary kept by C. C. Bost refers to the organization of Hickory's first hook and ladder company—the forerunner of the city's present efficient fire department. Major Latta bases the following story on Bost's material: "The first equipment was a little wagon loaded with yellow home-made ladders which the fire department proudly paraded through the muddy streets upon the slightest provocation. Any housekeeper sufficiently careless as to make a fire in the home that would show ascending smoke above the chimney would be liable to have an immediate visit from the proud volunteer fire department. After the ladders had been tried out a few times without serious casualties, the firemen sent a convoy of their stout-hearted members to appear before the board of commissioners for the purpose of persuading the commissioners to buy a fire pump—something worthy of the town and its volunteer company. After due deliberation something was selected from a catalogue from a mail-order house. It consisted of a small four-wheel wagon, with a rod on each side to be propelled up-and-down by hand power—usually three men on each side. This operated an ordinary suction pump—the water to be discharged through a hose with a beautiful brass nozzle on the end of it. It then occurred to the board that in the event of a fire anywhere in the business section there would be no water available. To avoid a contingency of this kind, the board decided to provide a large underground reservoir for storing a liberal quantity of water. An underground reservoir, 20 feet in diameter and 15 feet deep, was sunk (on Third Street, NW, in the business section). This reservoir was lined with concrete and covered over; water was supplied through gutters from nearby roofs. (Hickory had no water works at this time.) The little hand-operated pump remained in disuse a long time, but finally a fire came. A. Y. Sigmon's dry-kiln was on fire! The little wagon and pump were rushed to the scene and placed over the nearest well. The fire was raging, while six of the volunteers endeavored to operate the hand-pump. Nothing but perspiration came. After the fire died down, examination revealed the fact that dirt-daubers had built a secure nest in the brass nozzle through which the water was supposed to discharge. This was the last trip for the little wagon and hand pump."

Other observations of Major Latta include—

"In the year 1877, R. H. Lanier established himself in business . . . and began the manufacture and sale of 'Old North State Bitters'—doing a very large business as far as volume was concerned. 'Old North State Bitters' was sold as a medicine and shipped virtually everywhere. The concoction was highly recommended for every ailment from in-growing toe-nail to consumption.

"R. H. Lanier's brother, George C., in addition to operating a large tobacco factory, also operated a large corn liquor distillery on Horseford creek, a mile or so from town. A large part of his liquor output was sold to R. H., to be used in the manufacture of the 'Bitters.' In making the medicine, it was only necessary to add to each barrel of liquor a certain amount of wild cherry bark and polygala senega (commonly called

Cable Ferry Across River

Catawba Locomotive

St. Paul's Church, Catawba County, N. C.
Services started here 1759

snake root). Both the bark and the roots were gathered locally from then abounding forests. After standing a few days, a beautiful amber-hued liquid was drawn off and bottled without dilution, the bark and roots imparting a very pleasant bitter taste.

"After bottling, an attractive printed label was attached to each bottle, extolling its virtues—purely vegetable—perfectly harmless—and giving specific directions for using—obstinate cases required larger dosage and treatment should be continued longer. Each bottle, after labeling, was placed in a handsome carton, and included with the bottle was a small pamphlet, describing the symptoms of all ailments peculiar to a sad world. Strange to say, this pamphlet contained scores of bonafied testimonials from grateful users all over the country, testifying to miraculous cures of all sorts of ailments.

"It had no sale locally; the guzzler element knew its contents and preferred to buy the unpolluted article at less cost. While sold strictly as a medicine, it was primarily intended for 'dry' territory. It had an enormous sale and was a money-maker.

"The first watchmaker and jeweler in Hickory was John M. Lawrence. He came to Hickory about 1874. . . . While conducting his jewelry business, he became actively interested and identified with politics, and became a leader of the Republican cause, although at that time Catawba had won the Zeb Vance banner—a beautiful silk affair, presented by the governor to the county having the largest Democratic majority in proportion to population. Catawba county held the Vance banner until 1894, when it was lost, through the fusion of Populists and Republicans. In the early 70's when Lawrence became active in politics, Catawba county had 2,400 voters (600 of them Negroes) and yet the county had a 1,800 Democratic majority.

"Archer McIntosh, who came to Catawba in about 1870 from Lee county, was the first resident photographer in Hickory Tavern.

"The town's first barber was Henry C. Denny, an educated mulatto, from Wilkes county. He located in Hickory in 1876, and while following his trade, he studied law, and was admitted to the bar in the early 90's. Among his race, he was a power in local politics. In 1894, Senator J. C. Pritchard secured him a position in the Postoffice Department at Washington, which position he held until Wilson's administration, when he was eliminated. He then located in Knoxville, Tenn. After receiving his license to practice law, he was employed in only one case while in Catawba county. He was employed by the defense in the famous Cawthon case, the tragedy in which O. M. Cawthon of Selma, Ala., was accused of shooting and killing Sam Tilley, a Negro, near the doorsteps of the Hickory Inn."

The various streets of Hickory were not officially named until about 40 years ago. Prior to that time, they were called by names such as Champion avenue, Church street, College street, Watauga street, Washington street, Jackson street, Atwood street, Peterson street, Ellis street, High street, Railroad street, Martin street, Shuford avenue, Alexander street, Home avenue, Main street, Newton street, Lincoln street, Faith avenue, Hope avenue, Geatle avenue, Charity avenue, and Quiet avenue.

The city manager form of government was adopted by the city in 1913, being the first city in North Carolina to use this system.

Hickory's mayors are as follows: Marcus Yoder, 1870-74; Andrew H. Shuford, 1875; J. G. Hall, 1876; '84, '86, '88, '89; M. L. Cline, 1877, '80; F. A. Wiley, 1880; Isaac A. Hartsell, 1878; John F. Murrill, 1879, '81; J. H. Bruns, 1882; Henry Wilfong, 1883; A. W. Marshall, 1887; Lee R. Whitener, 1890, '91; J. D. Elliott, 1892, '95, 1903, '04, '05, '06, '10, '19, '20, '21, '27; G. H. Geitner, 1893; E. B. Cline 1894-'96; T. M. Huffman, 1897-'98; O. M. Royster, 1899; A. A. Whitener, 1900; M. H. Yount, 1901, '02, '17, '18, '22, '33, '34, '35, '36; J. H. P. Cilley, 1907; J. W. Blackwelder, 1908; J. W. Shuford, 1915; George E. Bisanar, 1909; J. A. Lentz, 1911, '12; C. H. Geitner, 1913, '14; Eubert Lyerly, 1923; S. L. Whitener, 1916, '24, '25, '26; George L. Lyerly, 1928, '29, '30; B. B. Blackwelder, 1931; E. N. Carr, 1932; F. Johnson Suttlemyre, 1937-'38; Walker Lyerly, 1939, '40, '41, '42, '43, '44, '45, '46; R. H. McComb, 1947, '48, '49, '50; and D. S. Menzies, 1951, '52, '53.

The city's population in 1950 was 14,755.

(For post office information, see succeeding chapter.)

TOWN OF LONGVIEW *(officially Long View, but "Longview" commonly used)*—

The municipality of Longview, incorporated March 8, 1907, gains its name by virtue of its geography. It is said that the name was given by Samuel D. Campbell.

Bordered on the east by the city of Hickory and on the west by Burke county, the town is located in the west portion of the county.

The incorporation act names Daniel Morgan as mayor and John Carrier, Frank Lock, and Marvin Morgan as aldermen.

Succeeding mayors are John D. Morgan (1908-10), F. A. Lock (1911), R. M. Barnhill (1912), C. S. Carpenter (1913), Dr. George E. Glowers (1914), J. B. Johnson, Sr. (1915), C. J. Frye (1916), George H. Morgan (1917), John F. Jones (1918-19), H. L. Duncan (1920), Hugh Taylor (1921), S. H. Jones (1922), D. C. Renfro (1923-24), R. B. Gantt (1925), D. C. Renfro (1926), Hershel Fulbright (1927-28), John R. Abee (1929-32), D. E. Brittain (1933-34), Fred J. Dale, mayor pro-tem (1934), John R. Abee (1934-37), W. C. Hollar (1938-46), William A. Lutz (1947), H. J. Frye (1948-51), Dewey A. Houston (1952), and W. A. Lutz (1953 and still serving).

In 1946 and 1950, bonds in the amount of $200,000 facilitated the building of a modern sewage disposal plant. A municipal building was erected in 1953. The municipality has a volunteer fire department.

The town's population in 1950 was 2,291.

(For post office information, see succeeding chapter.)

TOWN OF MAIDEN—

The founding of Maiden was not an accident, but was the result of a definite purpose—the outgrowth of the business experience of several men. It was to be a cotton mill site, and a trading center. The town was incorporated on March 7, 1883.

The area on which Maiden was to be situated occupied chiefly the lands of John Boyd, which were granted in 1782 and 1785, and a small portion of the lands of Daniel McKissick, which were granted in 1781.

Henry Franklin Carpenter, whose large farm lay near St. James Lutheran church, southeast of Newton, had had much experience in manufacturing ventures, and for many years had been a very successful operator of a flour mill and general custom grinding business, a wool carding plant, a cotton gin, and an immense tan-yard. His three sons, D. A., D. M., and Perry A. Carpenter, had been associated with him, working for and with him in these enterprises from early boyhood.

In 1880, D. M. Carpenter, then only 22 years of age, went to South Carolina to work in the Clifton and Converse Mills, the former just having been built. For about six months he was employed at various departments in those cotton mills, performing almost every operation from erecting machinery to running spinning frames. This entirely new field so appealed to him that he decided to make it his life work, and he returned to his home.

With his father and brothers, a partnership was formed, H. F. Carpenter, Sons and company. The concern also consisted of George W. Rabb, well-known Confederate veteran. The purpose of the partnership was the building of a small cotton mill.

There were only two or three families living on land now included in the corporate limits of Maiden—these all being farmers. Among the first families to move in were the Wycoffs, Drums and Keeners, and these became the nucleus of a citizenship which stood faithfully by the management of the mills for more than a generation. With many families moving in to take up employment at the mill, and with business and mercantile establishments springing up to care for the needs of these citizens, it became necessary to name the town. After considerable controversy, involving proponents of Carpenterville, Schrumtown, and several others, the present name was selected.

Some historians believe that the name was taken from Maiden creek. They say the creek took its name from Maiden cane, which grows in profusion (even now) about its banks. The creek flows just north of the town.

Other historians agree that the town took its name from the creek but say that the creek was named for maiden ladies who lived near it.

CATAWBA COUNTY 357

Among the early builders of the town were E. L. Propst, Jim Lohr, Marcus Boyd, Dan Boyd, John Boyd, Frank Rabb, Pinkney Rabb and Logan Rabb.

The first physician to locate was Dr. Alex Ramsaur. Another early physician was Dr. J. L. Lattimore. Dr. Paul J. Klutz began his practice in 1886, and until his death in 1930, was a faithful attendant in every need as well as being identified with business interests.

In 1882, the railroad was finished into Maiden, and for some months was the end of the line. A tragic accident of this period was the explosion of a railway locomotive and the consequent complete dismemberment of the Negro fireman, who negligently fired the empty boiler and filled it with water while it was red hot.

With the coming of the railroad, the volume of town business increased. The original mill also benefitted. After a year of the firm's operation, its plant capacity was more than doubled, bringing the active spindles to 2,200.

Shortly after 1880, the younger member of the firm, Perry A. Carpenter, died. He left a sum of money for the purpose of starting a church in the growing community. The mill provided a lot, and in 1887 the Memorial Reformed church was completed. A new church was built by this congregation in succeeding years. Rev. Joseph L. Murphy, well-known in Catawba county, took over the duties of Memorial church as his first charge. In quick succession, Baptist, Methodist and Lutheran congregations were organized. The mill partnership gave lots for the Baptist and Methodist congregations, and also for the cemetery grounds.

The cotton mill venture was so prosperous that after several years it was decided to build a new mill, and for this purpose they selected the site of the old William Williams or Jenny Lind iron works, on Maiden creek, where for nearly a century iron was manufactured. It was believed that the waterpower which could be developed at this point would overbalance the lack of convenience to the railroad. The new mill was put into production in 1889, with about two thousand spindles. L. A. Carpenter then took charge of the original mill as secretary-treasurer and general manager, a position which he held until

1916. D. M. Carpenter became manager and treasurer of the Providence plant, holding this office until 1917. The owners were the same in each plant, and in 1894, the partnerships gave way to incorporated companies. In this year, the capacity of the Providence plant was trebled, and an auxiliary steam plant added.

Additional cotton mills came on the Maiden scene, most proving successful. Union cotton mills was organized in 1892. Carolina Cotton Mills (now Carolina Mills) was begun in 1916.

From 1892 to 1916, a number of wood-working plants began operations in the town, producing varieties of products from coffins to chairs and millwork. Notable ones were those of the Clay Manufacturing company, the Galls, G. W. Keener, and L. S. Caldwell and son.

Esquire England and associates erected and equipped an up-to-date flour mill in the early 1890s. It had varying managements, including C. F. Williams, W. B. Murray, and Goss Drum.

Maiden's act of incorporation names J. P. Rabb as mayor, and Alexander Keener, Alexander Cline and Amzi Stine as commissioners.

Additional mayors are J. F. Rabb, Dr. P. J. Klutz, D. Martin Carpenter, John W. Williams, William Caldwell, Robert A. Rudisill, James Holshouser, George Drum, Garland E. Mauney (1910), D. Martin Carpenter (1911-12), B. A. Correll (1913), D. Martin Carpenter (1914), Benjamin A. Whitener (1915-19), Dr. J. E. Hodges (1920-21), A. C. Black (1922-23), Wade F. Smith (1924-25), D. H. Thorne (1926-31), Burt M. Ikard (1932), D. H. Thorne (1933), Rufus P. P. Wilkinson (1934), D. H. Thorne (1935), George E. Hunsucker (1936-37), Dr. J. E. Hodges (1939-40), D. Arthur Gilleland (1941-1945), Leonard Jenkins (1946), C. P. Kyles (1947-48), Richard Williams (1949), George E. Hunsucker (1950-51), and Banks Whisenant (1952 and still serving).

The town, located in the south-center portion of the county, had a population of 1,952 in 1950.

(For post office information, see succeeding chapter.)

The City of Newton—

The county seat city of Catawba county, heart of an integral network of governmental agencies, was named Newton, after the son of Representative Nathaniel Wilson.

Newton, according to meager information, was born in 1842, when Wilson was campaigning for the new county, or after his election.

It is claimed by some that the son was named for Sir Isaac Newton. Others believe that the boy was named for the noted minister George Newton, who is known to have been a friend of the Wilsons.

The location of Newton was donated by private property owners and laid off into lots, from the sale of which a fund was realized more than sufficient for the construction of the first courthouse.

On January 14, 1843, certain commissioners were given authority by legislative act to "purchase and receive by donation, for the use of the County of Catawba, a tract of land not less fifty A—upon which a town shall be laid off which shall be called and known by the name of Newton, where the courthouse and jail shall be erected."

On April 18 of the same year, the commissioners met and selected a site for "Newton," including a part of the lands of Mathais Setzer, Jacob Deal and Jacob McGee, "for the consideration of $1.00 in hand to them paid by Jonas Bost, chairman of the county court of Catawba county, . . . wherefore the said town of Newton is to be laid off . . . land lying on the waters of Clarks creek, beginning at a small red-oak on Jacob McGee's line and runs south seventy-six degrees east ninety-one poles to a stake and pointers then north fourteen degrees east eighty-eight poles and five links to a stake in said Jacob Deel's field, thence north seventy-six degrees west sixteen and one-half poles to a stone in old line north thirteen degrees west sixteen and one-half poles to a post-oak thence west forty-eight poles to a stone thence north seventy-six degrees west twenty-seven poles to a stake in the edge of a swamp thence south fourteen degrees west seventy-five poles to the beginning. . . ."

There persists a rumor that when the survey to determine the county seat city was made, the lines were contracted so as to make the center of the county fall at Newton whereas it should have fallen at Conover.

After the selection of the site of the "seat of justice," the court—consisting of George Shuford, chairman, Jonas Bost, John H. Wheeler, Joseph Wilson and Major Hull—appointed, in 1845, a board of commissioners to contract for a house for the purpose of a court. The appointees were Burton Craig, John H. Wheeler, Henry Robinson, Henry Whitener, and A. H. Shuford.

Newton was finally built on land originally granted to William Deal, Conrad Minges, and Joseph Steele. All the tracts were surveyed in 1779.

The town of Newton was incorporated on May 7, 1855. The act named M. L. McCorkle, George Setzer, O. Campbell and S. G. Miller as commissioners. The town was governed by a board of commissioners through 1872 or later, and its chairman is assumed to have been designated mayor.

The first reference in writing to the town of Newton points out that the municipality consisted of 75 inhabitants, 15 dwellings, four tailor shops, a shoe shop, two blacksmith shops, two medical shops, and a law office. Among the 75 inhabitants are the following:

David Dellinger and his wife, Martha, and five children (James Newton Dellinger, the youngest of the five, was the first child born in Newton); Daniel Rhyne, saddler, and his wife, Kathryn, and one child; two apprentices and one boarder; William Lenargin, brick mason (the builder of the county courthouse) his wife and five children; Walter Setzer, his wife and two children; Jacob Scronce, his wife and ten children; Hoyle Witherspoon, tailor, his wife and two children; Anthony Ikard, tavern keeper, his wife, Ann, and one child; Alex Sumit, carpenter, his wife and six children; Jonas Bost, carpenter, his wife, Rosanna, and seven children; Dr. James H. Little, his wife, Jane, and one child; Mrs. Partis and two children; and Philip Hallman and wife. The list of unmarried men included D. B. Gaither, merchant; Dr. C. M. Campbell; L. T. Gaither, merchant; D. W. Rhyne, clerk; John Jones, Clerk; Benjamin

Hallman, tailor; M. M. Wilson, carpenter; Joseph Bost, carpenter; W. Taylor, W. Arwood, shoemaker; M. L. McCorkle, attorney, C. W. Connor, student of medicine; and William Shipp, solicitor of the county court session.

In the instance of railroad service, Newton was to be hindered by natural barriers. The great natural highway lay two miles north of the town, and along this ridge the Western North Carolina railroad was built. Due, however, to the wording of the charter granted to the railroad, the citizens of Newton later forced the trains to run "by Newton." Newton also was to receive service by the Narrow Gauge railroad.

As early as 1860, Newton was site of the Newton hotel, operated by a Captain Bost.

An 1880 copy of The Newton Enterprise sheds certain light on the professions and businesses of Newton. Among the advertisements were:

"A. C. Fox, M.D., Practices Medicine in all of its branches, but special attention will be given to surgery. . . ."

"Dr. George H. West offers his professional services to the citizens of Newton and vicinity. Office at his drug store. . . ."

"Dr. John F. Setzer, dentist, Office south of Bost House."

"M. L. McCorkle, Attorney at Law."

"James R. Campbell, Phyisican and Surgeon."

"High School for Young Ladies, Boys and Girls, J. D. Rowe, Teacher in Charge."

"Bark—Wanted a large quantity of Tan Bark. Will pay Leather or Cash."

"M. E. Lowrance, Attorney at Law, Practices in Catawba and adjoining counties."

"Newton Marble Yard, Produce taken in exchange for work."

Among the businesses listed were Abernethy and Williams; Williams and Finger; D. B. Gaither and Son, general merchandise; Finger's new Boot and Shoe shop; James A. Garvin, boot and shoe store; Tailor shop, owned by L. W. Davidson; and

Yount and Shrum, dry goods, groceries, and general merchandise.

In examining early activities of first citizens of Newton, the following facts have been gleaned:

The first boarding house was owned by Anthony Ikard. He also dug the first well of the town. Called the "Public Well," it was situated on the south side of the courtsquare.

Newton's hotels have been well-known throughout Catawba county history. Among the most famous were the old St. Hubert Inn, built in 1885 and torn away in 1936 to make way for the present postoffice, and the Piedmont hotel, built in 1882. The St. Hubert Inn was a famous hunting lodge at one time and was operated by Joe Stewart and his brother, Herbert Stewart. The Piedmont hotel was one of the most widely known hostelries in piedmont North Carolina about the turn of the twentieth century. The hotel was a popular stopping place for traveling men, better known as "drummers" in early days. Miss Alice Summerrow was proprietor.

The present Newton postoffice building is located on the exact site of its original location, after having completed a "trip around the square." Newton's first office was in the old Bost Hotel building, where the new postoffice now stands, on the corner of South Main avenue and West A street.

Among the mayors who have served Newton are M. L. McCorkle, J. H. Crawford, O. Campbell, Dr. J. C. Clapp, Rev. John Lantz, E. A. Warlick, Levi Plonk, Sidney M. Finger, Osborne Foard, H. A. Forney, W. G. Burkhead, L. L. Witherspoon, George McCorkle, A. D. Shuford, W. B. Gaither, C. M. McCorkle, W. C. Feimster, M. J. Rowe, D. P. Rowe, Clarence Clapp, A. J. Barwick, F. E. Garvin, L. F. Long, S. J. Smyre, L. H. Phillips, W. A. Rhyne, C. M. Rowe, R. J. Shipp, Edward Haupt, George Powell, H. C. Gabriel, John Miles Abernethy, J. R. Gaither, and Ernest B. Clapp (still serving).

The city's population in 1950 was 6,039.

(For post office information, see succeeding chapter.)

Towns which were once incorporated, listed alphabetically:

BERRYVILLE *(later West Hickory, and now Hickory)*—

Berryville was incorporated on March 12, 1895. The act named (Henderson Pinkney) H. Berry as mayor and J. D. Beck, F. S. Miller, and J. M. Maynard as aldermen.

The town was named for its first mayor.

On February 28, 1899, the town's charter was amended by striking out "Berryville" and inserting in lieu thereof "West Hickory." The town then was known as the Town of West Hickory.

Additional mayors who served, listed alphabetically, include Horace H. Abee, William P. Austin, George T. Barger, Charles E. Cole, A. Johnson Drum, Q. A. Hedrick, Forest B. Hicks, F. S. Klutz, John McLemore, Frank S. Miller, Horace Rector, and James M. Walker.

In 1931, the area of West Hickory was annexed and became a part of the city of Hickory.

HIGHLAND—

Highland was incorporated on March 1, 1905. The act named O. T. Rockett as mayor and H. C. Killian, P. C. Coons, Perry L. Hefner, and W. J. Norton as commissioners.

It is probable that the name of the town was taken from Highland Academy, which stood on the campus of the present Lenoir Rhyne college, part of which was embraced within the corporate limits of Highland. Highland Academy, according to tradition, was named by J. G. Hall, trustee of the property on which the institution stood, for the novelist Sir Walter Scott, who wrote of the Scottish Highlands.

John W. Mauser, Sr., drew the charter for the town, and it is said that he suggested using the academy's name.

Additional mayors who are known to have served the municipality, listed alphabetically, are Joseph H. Bolch, Neil W. Clark, Rev ——— Downs, Arthur T. Fox, Charles E. Hefner, Perry L. Hefner, Berry Houston, Junius E. Huffman, Oscar E. Leonard, John W. Mauser, Jr., J. Parks Robinson, William S. Robinson, and William S. Stanley.

Highland lost its identity as a municipality when it was annexed to the city of Hickory in 1931.

KEEVERSVILLE *(now Plateau)*—

The town of Keeversville, which was the third largest town in Catawba county, having a population of 700, in 1886, today is the unincorporated village of Plateau.

Keeversville, named for the Keever family, was incorporated on February 20, 1885. The act named M. A. Poston as mayor, and R. M. Hoyle, James Keever, and Dr. A. P. Keever as commissioners.

The corporate limits of the town were fixed as "one-half mile east, west, north and south from the centre of Keever and Poston's Drug Store."

How long the incorporate status of the town existed is not known.

Plateau, which derived its name from the geography of its locale, is ten miles southwest of Newton and nine and one-half miles south of Hickory.

Present villages and communities, listed alphabetically (additional information on many in succeeding chapter):

BALLS CREEK—Located about eight miles east-southeast of Newton; named for the creek.

BANOAK—Located in Bandys township in the southwest part of the county; named for two school districts, BAN-dys and OAK HILL.

BLACKBURN—Located in Jacobs Fork township about eight miles southwest of Newton; named for Blackburn family. It once was referred to locally as Yodertown, Whitenertown, Hiltontown, and Jarrettown.

COOKSVILLE—Located in Bandys township in the southwest part of the county; named for Cook family.

LONG ISLAND—Located about one and one-half miles southeast of Buffalo Shoals on the Catawba river; name is believed to have come from an island in the river nearby; the area was Catawba county's first industrial section.

OYAMA—Located about five miles east of Hickory; named by the Southern Railway company for a Japanese hero of the Russo-Japanese war; Oyama was the site of a railroad siding and contained a telegraph station for more than 20 years.

MONOGRAM—Located near Sherrills Ford; derivation of name unknown.

MOUNTAIN VIEW—Located about three miles south of Hickory; name caused by geographic location.

PENELOPE—Located about three miles west of Hickory on the Southern railway near the Burke county line; named for Alice Penelope Murchison; although the United States Post Route map shows Penelope post office as being in Burke county, the Historical Association has reason to believe the office was in Catawba county; Penelope was the site of an academy.

SHERRILLS FORD—Located about two and one-half miles west of the Catawba river from the old Sherrills ford site; named for the ford, which was named for the Sherrill family.

STARTOWN *(first Danville)*—Located about three miles southwest of Newton; derivation of name of Danville unknown; why the name was changed also is unknown; name of Startown honors the Starr family.

ST. STEPHENS—Located about three miles northeast of Hickory on the Catawba Springs road; named for area church.

SWEETWATER—Located about two and one-half miles east of Hickory; name derived from unusually good quality of water to be found in the community.

TERRELL—Located about three miles northwest from the extreme southeast corner of the county; named for early minister.

VALE—While the village is located in the extreme northern part of Lincoln county, west of center, portions of the general community reach into Catawba county; derivation of name unknown but it is assumed to have geographic connation.

WINDY CITY *(now Viewmont)*—Located directly north of Hickory; tradition says the community was named for a local braggart; present name taken from area school.

Defunct communities:

JUGTOWN (sometimes spelled Jug Town)—Although there is a "Jugtown" now located in Moore county, there seems to be sufficient evidence to cause residents of Catawba county to believe that their area was the cradle of the original North Carolina "Jugtown" pottery and that the first Jugtown was not in the eastern part of the state but in Catawba county.

M. A. Hilton, owner and operator of the Hilton Pottery at Marion, claimed that the first Jugtown in North Carolina was a section about eight miles square in Catawba and Lincoln counties. In this comparatively small area, which Hilton estimated as lying about 12 miles southwest, about 42 potters have plied their trade, beginning with Jacob Weaver and continuing to the present.

Weaver is credited as being founder of the Jugtown settlement, and also as being instrumental in directing that pottery-making become such an important industry in North Carolina.

Weaver came to this country from Germany. He employed a secret color formula for pottery which was never learned by anyone else.

It is believed that about 115 years ago, there were something like 14 potteries in the southern part of Catawba county.

The Jugtown community was a rich farming center, where much trading was carried on by its people. The Foard-Williams store, later Foard-Whisnant, located a short distance north of the postoffice, did a big business as a general store and is said to have received as much freight as any store in the county.

SPARKLING CATAWBA SPRINGS *(first known as Powder Springs, then Springville, then Elliott Springs, then White Sulphur Springs)*—

The village of Sparkling Catawba Springs, famed resort area of Catawba county, was located eight miles northeast of Hickory.

It is referred to in Jacob Baker's land grant of 1787 as "Powder springs." The next reference to the site is found in land conveyances made immediately prior to the formation of the county. It is then referred to as Springville.

The development of the site came at the hand of Dr. O. E. Elliott, who christened the area Elliott Springs. Dr. Elliott purchased the land in 1853. It was his express purpose to develop a great health resort, employing the use of the available mineral springs.

The name of the resort, which was at its prime from 1870 to 1900, was changed to White Sulphur Springs in 1860. It finally became known as Sparkling Catawba Springs in 1877.

As evidence of the importance of this community, historians point to the facts that documents once located Hickory Tavern as being eight miles southwest of Catawba Springs, and as late as 1905 the state legislature granted the right-of-way for a street railway to be operated by electricity over the public roads from Hickory to the Springs. The latter never materialized.

Frank Vander Linder writing in 1940, records the story of Sparkling Catawba Springs thus:

"Amid a tangle of weeds and underbrush a few miles Northeast of Hickory, is a sulphur springs, and nearby are the remnants of once-handsome buildings, now in a sad state of disrepair.

"Few are the people who ever go there now; but they were many in years gone by, for this is the site of the famous 'Sparkling Catawba Springs'.

"And in a Hickory rooming house, home-sick sometimes for the place she always knew as 'home,' lives Miss Emma Elliott, daughter of the man who made the 'Springs' the favorite rendezvous of hundreds of people half a century ago.

"Miss Elliott's eyes shone through her spectacles and a smile brightened her face the other day as she recalled the happy times when the resort was at the height of its popularity.

"Her father, Dr. E. O. Elliott, came to this section from Charlotte, in the interest of his health, she said. The family first lived near a mill below the springs, and it was there that Miss Emma was born.

" 'But all the home that I remember was at the Springs', she said.

"At the time the Elliotts acquired the property, there was standing near the springs a large house which later was enlarged into the main hotel of the resort.

"Some distance away was another rambling structure known as the 'Castle,' because of its very large rooms.

"Along about 1880, Dr. Elliott began enlarging the facilities to accommodate the many people from miles around who sought rest and recreation at the sulphur springs.

"About a dozen cottages were erected for the guests while onto the main building was added a two-story wing.

"The first floor of this became the dining room, and upstairs was the ball room, which soon became the center of attraction for the fun-loving youth of that era.

"Hear Frank Allen, eighty-three describe the frolics the young folks had in dancing there:

" 'Oh! It was a gay place,' he declared. 'We used to have great times there. All of us boys would go out, and take the girls, and have a fling.

" 'Swing your partner! Cross to the right! All promenade all around!' he laughed. 'By golly, we'd just swing 'em right and left!'

" (Some of the gayest of the gay blades, the retired merchant confided, would take along a little brandy, or rye whiskey, to keep their spirits high. 'It was pure, unadulterated stuff,' he said. 'A swig of that and—oh boy!')

"Square dancing was most popular with the 'jitter-bugs' of the past century, while other steps also were favorites—the waltz, the polka, the schottische, and the Virginia reel.

"To take the visitors to and from the 'springs,' two livery stables regularly ran hacks and other horse-drawn vehicles along the seven-mile route.

"One of these stables was operated by the Abernethy brothers—'Dolph,' 'Jule,' and 'Dr. Hen,' with headquarters on Fourteenth street, near the railroad, in the building now used as a bonded warehouse.

" 'Fate' and 'Tom' Henkel had a livery stable, too.

" 'These hacks would meet all the trains coming in at the station,' said Mr. Allen. 'People would get off the train, into the hacks, and drive to the Springs.'

" 'In that day and time, the place was about the biggest thing around here,' he asserted.

"Visitors from Charleston, Savannah, and places in Eastern Carolina often stayed for several weeks during the season, which lasted throughout the Summer months, according to Miss Elliott.

"The hotel had its own water plant, and its own power system, operated by a dynamo; so it had conveniences not found in many homes of that day.

"Besides the medicinal value of the strong sulphur water, there were the added benefits of bountiful, wholesome food, cheerful companions, and varied entertainment.

"Many people brought their children there, Miss Elliott recalled. 'There were so many, that we had a special dining room for them,' she added. 'And, of course, there were about two hundred other people at the long tables in the main room.'

" 'There was so much space at the Springs, that it was ideal for children.' On the lawn there was a ten-pin alley, as one of the many amusements, 'I used to love that,' said Miss Elliott.

"Croquet was 'all the rage,' then, too, she recalled. Gentlemen in white ducks and sailor hats, and ladies in long, starched gowns both liked to knock the wooden balls through the hoops.

"An octagon-shaped building called the 'music pavilion,' was 'the oddest thing,' according to Miss Elliott.

"Its chief distinction was its unusual stairs, which 'wound 'round and 'round,' she stated. Though called the 'music pavilion,' there was rarely any music played there, for all the dancing was in the ballroom.

" 'Still, everybody had to come and see the pavilion, because of its curious stairs,' Miss Elliott declared. 'People carved their names all over the building.'

"Catawba Springs had its serious aspects, too, for even vacationists in those days went to religious services.

" 'Mother was a great hand at entertaining ministers and missionaries,' Miss Elliott recalled. 'Every Sunday, we would have services in the parlor, and on Sunday nights, we would sing sacred music there.'

" 'I do love a good quartet,' she added, 'and I used to play the piano quite a good deal, also.'

"And so Catawba Springs flourished for several years, as the gathering-place for persons from near and far.

"With the coming of the new century, though, its hey-day began to fade.

"Other resorts farther up in the mountains, such as Asheville and Blowing Rock, began to attract the people who had spent their Summers here.

"Then, too, in 1900, Dr. Elliott himself was stricken suddenly, and passed away.

"The place was never quite the same after that.

"Although it remained a favorite picnic spot, the 'Springs' had declined by the time of the World war. . . .

" 'I declare it makes me blue every time I go back to see the place,' Miss Elliott sighed. 'It's gone to rack and ruin.'

"Still Catawba Springs will always be home to her. 'I'm homesick for it often,' she declared. 'I try to shake it off, but land, it's a job!' "

ULRICHSBURG OR CROWDERTOWN—

One of the most interesting aspects of the county's municipal history is the story of Ulrichsburg, the area "ghost town."

Newton, history bears out, took the place of another municipality. This town was planned as Ulrichsburg, commonly called Crowdertown.

The founder of the town was a German pioneer by the name of Ulrich Crowder of Wilkes county, Ga. Just what year Crowder moved to this state is not known. His first appearance here was in the early 1760s in the Beatties Ford section and in the Henry Weidner neighborhood.

Crowder appears to have been a land speculator rather than a farmer. The Beatties Ford section in the southern part of the territory west of the Catawba river and the Henry Weidner section in the northern part were the most prominent communities in the territory west and south of the Catawba river at this early date. Crowder no doubt intended to lay out a town at each of these places at an opportune time; but, due to various circumstances, other localities suited the conveniences of the settlers more than Crowder's selected places did, and when the opportunity did come for new towns west of the Catawba, other locations were chosen in preference to Crowder's.

New Ulrichsburg was located at the site now owned by the Lutz brothers and used for dairy farms. Its location is a few miles west of Newton.

On December 1, 1764, Ulrich Crowder received a grant for 450 acres of land on the waters of Weidner's Creek. This tract of land lay between Bostian Cline on the east and Henry Weidner on the west. It lay on both sides of the public bridge road running from Lincolnton to a junction with the Salisbury-Morganton road, where the Hickory Tavern later was located.

The first record found as to Crowder's new town is in a deed dated January 3, 1789, given by Crowder to Conrad Heam for 150 acres of land "joining the new town land known as Ulrichsburg." It is supposed that this new town was laid out in lots about the year 1788 as Crowder began to sell lots in the winter of 1789.

Old records point to the fact that the town was laid out in lots twelve poles square according to the four cardinal points of the compass, and each lot containing 144 square poles, the boundaries running due east and west, north and south. The lots were numbered consecutively relative to the place that the lot lay on the east, the west, the north and the south side of the square.

The first lot sold, as recorded, was on March 9, 1789, to Mary Magdalene Stricker, for thirty shillings "in a town newly laid off, lot No. Thirty-four on the northwest square."

Numerous other lots were sold during the following years. From the names of purchasers, Crowder evidently advertised his lots for sale in other sections, as most of the names are not familiar family names at that time in Lincoln county.

Crowder died in the year 1791, and Pioneer John Killian administered his estate. There are no records that he left offspring. His wife's name was Catherine. She died previous to her husband.

Some lots were sold after Crowder's death, but his early demise at the beginning of his enterprise paralyzed the prospects of the new town. By the year 1800, Jacob Fay was about the only one mentioned as running a business in Ulrichsburg, also Crowdertown, although it was referred to as a town as late as 1825.

Why did not Crowdertown survive and become the principal town of what is now Catawba county? It was located on a favorable site—the land lay well for a town, and was in a fine farming section owned by splendid citizens.

Pioneer settlers, it is surmised, immigrated here to make a home and to farm, and were not interested in towns except as places convenient for transacting public matters and to have a "house of justice" reasonably near.

Crowder reasoned well from this desire of the settlers. Charlotte town and Salisbury were too far away, and in the near future the settlers west of the Catawba river would demand a new district or county.

But, Crowder's entry was not located so as to become a proper place for one of the ensuing county seats.

Ulrich Crowder, in essence, was defeated by fate. He had reasoned that soon the citizens of this section would consider Lincolnton and Morganton (following their establishment) too far away for their convenience, and that a new county would be formed between Burke and Lincoln counties. He had laid out the new town of Ulrichsburg on his entry. But he had died before his dream of a new county materialized.

The fact of the matter is, if Crowdertown had survived to a much later date, or to the present time, it would have been isolated by its natural boundaries. With Clarks creek and its tributaries on the east and the South Fork river and its tributaries on the west, it would have been inconvenient, almost inaccessible, to the travel from the eastern and western parts of the state. The watershed between the Catawba River valley and the South Fork valley was a natural highway and lay five miles to the north of Crowdertown. The general public, whether traveling for business or pleasure, follows the ways of least resistance.

Sixty-five years after Crowder laid out lots in his new town, lots similarly named and numbered were being laid out and offered for sale in another new town, "known and named Newton," in Setzer's old field. Thus, Catawba county's present governmental seat took the place that Crowder had planned for Ulrichsburg.

History has borne out that Newton has been handicapped by natural barriers, but to a much lesser degree than Crowdertown.

Other villages have disappeared from area maps. Some scarcely could have been called villages in their "heydays," however. Usually they only were postoffice stations.

Present Crossroads:

The county's present crossroads are Abernethys, Bandys, Canslers, Carsons, Drums, John Browns, Killians, Lippards, Olivers, Propst, Rowes, Rudisills, and Witherspoons.

CHAPTER XV

THE HISTORY OF POST OFFICES

Catawba county's early centers of community activity may be learned by a study of the establishment of post offices, which possessing names that now, in many instances, sound foreign to the population, indicate the pattern of the area's settlement.

The establishment of the first post office in the territory which was to become Catawba county followed within three decades the act of the National Congress setting up a general post office under a postmaster general.

The exact date of the Catawba area's initial office, Mehaffey, is unknown, but reference is made to it in the United States Postal Guides of 1817 and 1819. The last post office to be established in the county, Brookford, was authorized April 27, 1901. During the interim, more than 60 post offices (some of which encountered only name changes) have been set into operation.

History points out that the first step toward setting up a postal system in the American colonies was taken by the General Court of Massachusetts in 1639, when it designated the house of Richard Fairbanks in Boston as the place where letters arriving from across the sea and those to be sent across the sea should be left. Fairbanks was charged with the responsibility of properly disposing of letters left in his care and, for this service, he received one penny per letter.

The first step toward an inter-colonial post was taken in 1692, when Thomas Neale was appointed a sort of postmaster-general by the British sovereigns, William and Mary, and given authority to establish post offices in America.

Benjamin Franklin was instrumental in the organization of the American postal system. In 1737, he was appointed postmaster at Philadelphia, and from that time until the beginning of the Revolutionary War he was closely identified with the postal service. In 1753, he was appointed postmaster-general for the colonies and held the office until 1774, when his sympathy with the American cause led to his dismissal. During his 20 years of service, however, Franklin laid the foundation of the postal system of the United States.

The Constitution gives Congress power to establish post offices and post roads. At the beginning of the Revolution, the colonies took charge of the postal system then in use. By an act passed in 1792, a general post office was established under a postmaster-general. The postmaster-general was not made a member of the President's cabinet until 1829.

The first mail carriers were postmen who traveled either on foot or horseback. These were succeeded by the stagecoach as suitable roads were constructed, and then the stagecoach gave way to the railroad. Locally, sulkies and buggies followed the use of only the horse.

Stores most often served as post offices, but occasionally the mail was deposited in private homes. Politics apparently played a big role in the distribution of postmasterships as it does today, for one may follow the changes of national administrations by the dates of local appointments.

Prior to 1845, rates of postage were extremely high, being six cents a letter for a distance not over three miles, eight cents between 30 and 60 miles, ten cents between 60 and 100 miles, etc. Prepayment of postage was optional with the sender, and the payment had to be made in coin. In 1845, the rates were lowered and based upon weight. The postage rate in effect with this action ranged from six cents an ounce for letters carried 30 miles or less, to 35 cents an ounce for letters carried more than 400 miles.

In 1847, postage stamps were first used in the United States. Since then the rates of postage have been reduced from time to time to meet increasing public demands.

It is interesting to note that the piedmont section of North Carolina was among the first to receive the benefits of rural free delivery. One of the first 15 routes to be established was set up during the first month of operation, October, 1896, at China Grove. At that time Kerr Craige, who was born near Newton and attended school there, was Third Assistant Postmaster General of the United States. It was at his suggestion that Postmaster General Wilson, who served during the last term of President Cleveland, established in North Carolina one of the first rural routes in the United States.

A list of the Catawba area and Catawba county post offices, presented chronologically, follows:

MEHAFFEY: Named for Mehaffey family; located in the area of the present St. Timothy Lutheran church, which is about one and one-half miles west of Conover on Highway 70-A; dates when established and discontinued unknown, although its existence is verified by the United States Postal Guides of 1817 and 1819.

HOKESVILLE: Named for Hoke family; located near the Rock Barn at the Roseman place on Lyles Creek, which is about four miles northeast of Conover; established February 4, 1822; postmasters, Peter Hoke, February 4, 1822, Daniel Hoke, April 19, 1823, Miles W. Abernathy, June 29, 1829, William J. Abernathy, September 28, 1831, and Daniel Roseman, October 23, 1845; discontinued November 11, 1847, and name is later to be changed to Roseman.

ROSEMAN: Named for Roseman family; same location as Hokesville office; established June 23, 1886; postmaster, Daniel F. Roseman; name then changed to Rockett.

ROCKETT: Named for Rockett family; located two miles north of Hokesville; established October 20, 1902; postmaster, Otis M. Rockett; discontinued March 31, 1903, and mail was directed to Claremont office.

MOUNTAIN CREEK: Named for creek; located within the area of the present Mt. Pleasant Methodist church, which is about 11 miles southeast of Newton; established February 7, 1824; postmasters, Lebanon B. Lindsay, February 7, 1824; John McCorkle, December 7, 1826; John B. Abernethy, March 30, 1832; J. F. Gabriel, January 1, 1835; John W. Gabriel, August 5, 1843; John B. Abernethy, September 7, 1848; John W. Gabriel, January 19, 1854; Caleb Fink, December 13, 1855; Robert A. Burton, September 18, 1858; John W. Gabriel, August 10, 1859; Harriet E. Gabriel, January 29, 1866; George M. Wilkinson, May 12, 1870; Mary Wilkinson, July 25, 1870; Any (?) Shuford, November 21, 1873; discontinued May 4, 1874; re-established September 1, 1874; postmasters, John A. Sherrill, September 1, 1874, Jacob Sherrill, October 10, 1883,

John Gabriel, January 2, 1892, Charles M. Beatty, September 12, 1896, Logan P. Eckard, February 18, 1899; discontinued January 31, 1900, and mail was directed to Edith office; reestablished April 27, 1900; postmasters, Woodbury Nance, April 27, 1900, Logan P. Eckard, March 18, 1901; discontinued May 15, 1907, and mail was directed to Sherrills Ford office.

WILFONGS MILL: Named for Wilfong family; located four miles west of Newton; established April 1, 1824; postmaster, John Wilfong, April 1, 1824; discontinued May 15, 1845.

WILLOW GROVE: Derivation of name unknown, but it is assumed that it originated from a grove of willow trees; located three miles southwest of Hokesville, or Roseman's, in the area of Conover; established May 21, 1827; postmaster, Electus Connor, May 21, 1827; discontinued October 16, 1845.

MULL GROVE: Named for Mull family; located one mile north of the present Ebenezer Methodist church, which is about 13 miles southwest of Hickory; established December 12, 1827; postmasters, Jacob Mull, December 12, 1827, John Chapman, June 6, 1866, Margaret Hicks, July 17, 1866, Ruth Jenks, September 25, 1867, Major P. Mull, November 15, 1867, Dolphus M. Brittain, May 9, 1892, Mary A. Mull, June 13, 1893, Amos Sain, September 9, 1897, John C. Wright, September 14, 1903; discontinued August 31, 1905, and mail was directed to Henry office.

WINTERVILLE: Named for Winter or Winters family; located one mile northeast of Claremont, near Lyles Creek; established August 19, 1830; postmaster, Robert Winters, August 19, 1830; discontinued August 10, 1832.

SHERRILLS FORD: Derivation of name, location and other characteristics described in preceding chapter; established May 2, 1831; postmasters, Eldridge Loftin, May 2, 1831, Japtha Sherrill, April 13, 1842, Joel A. Huggins, March 6, 1850, John G. Bynum, December 6, 1857, Elbert L. Sherrill, March 6, 1866, Julia E. Sherrill, November 30, 1874, Mollie E. Johnston, April 3, 1901, Clarence W. Brown, January 18, 1904, Annie L. Saunders, June 2, 1917, Annie L. Gabriel, August 10, 1920, Betty Saunders, acting, July, 1927, Betty Saunders, October 1, 1927, still serving.

FISHERS: Named for Fisher family; located four miles north of Hickory on the Icard Ferry road; established July 17, 1832; postmasters, Henry Fisher, July 17, 1832, Israel Holler, May 9, 1848; discontinued December 6, 1866.

EARLY GROVE: Derivation of name unknown; located three and one-half miles due west of Maiden; established January 15, 1833; postmasters, Maxwell Wilson, January 15, 1833, Adam Miller, September 7, 1839, Joseph Bost, December 6, 1851; discontinued December 6, 1866.

EAVESVILLE: Named for Eaves family; located about 1,000 feet southeast of present Herman-Sipe company on Highway 70-A; established February 10, 1834; postmasters, Lawson Eaves, February 10, 1834, George J. Wilkie, February 17, 1837, George Setzer, December 7, 1841; discontinued April 2, 1844.

BARRINGER: Named for Barringer family; located two miles east of Newton; established July 27, 1834; postmaster, Matthias Barringer, July 27, 1834; discontinued March 31, 1839.

LOWRANCES MILL: Named for Lowrance family; located seven miles west of Sherrills Ford; established January 26, 1837; postmaster, Joseph M. Lowrance, January 26, 1837; discontinued December 11, 1866.

FLINT ROCK: Named for huge flint rock nearby; located one-fourth mile on east side of Oxford Ford road east of the present John Deal's store; established April 13, 1838; postmasters, Daniel Moser, April 13, 1838, Jonathan R. Moser, August 17, 1839, Marcus M. Moser, May 26, 1852; discontinued December 6, 1866.

WARLICKS STORE: Named for Warlick family; located 12 miles south of Hickory; established January 30, 1840; postmaster, Peter Warlick; name changed to Jacobs Fork.

JACOBS FORD: Named for river; located two and one-fourth miles west of Startown; postmasters, Alfred Ramsour, October 4, 1845, Frederick R. Beck, June 6, 1866, George L. Whitener, February 18, 1881; discontinued April 10, 1902, and mail was directed to Newton office.

Three post offices were in Catawba county during 1842-46 by virtue of the fact that Catawba contained a portion of land that reverted in 1846, to Lincoln county. These were CA-

CATAWBA COUNTY 379

TAWBA SPRINGS; named for a spring; located in present Lincoln county; postmaster during the major portion of the four years, Thomas Hampton; BEATTIES FORD; named for the Beatty family; located in present Lincoln county; postmasters during the major portion of the four years, Hugh C. Hamilton, John H. Wheeler; and DRY PONDS; derivation of name unknown; located in Lincoln county at the present site of Denver; postmaster during the major portion of the four years, Hail N. Munday.

SHUFORDS FERRY: Named for Shuford family; located three miles north of the town of Catawba; established September 7, 1847; postmasters, Andrew Shuford, September 7, 1847, Abel H. Shuford, October 27, 1848; name changed to Bunker Hill February 28, 1850.

BUNKER HILL: Opinion as to derivation of name varies; some say it commemorates Revolution battle; located one-fourth mile from the present Bunker Hill bridge; established February 28, 1850; postmasters, Burrell C. Allen, February 28, 1850, James James, August 25, 1885, M. Connor, March 5, 1856; discontinued November 23, 1866.

NEWTON: Derivation of name, location and other characteristics described in preceding chapter; established February 20, 1844; postmasters, George J. Wilkie, February 20, 1844, David B. Gaither, July 16, 1853, Ogburn Campbell, January 31, 1855, Junius L. Gaither, January 15, 1856, David B. Gaither, December 19, 1859, Harriet E. Bost, September 21, 1865, Junius R. Gaither, March 13, 1872, James A. Garvin, August 31, 1877, Rosa Campbell, July 20, 1885, Alphonso C. Hildebrand, June 1, 1889, William B. Gaither, May 17, 1893, J. Edward A. Caldwell, June 1, 1897, Robert P. Caldwell, February 5, 1900, Robert P. Reinhardt, June 4, 1904, Walter H. Everhart, May 10, 1908, Francis M. Williams, May 20, 1913, Wallace A. Reinhardt, February 13, 1922, David M. Cloninger, acting, April 2, 1927, David M. Cloninger, January 4, 1928, Samuel D. Mauney, acting, March 8, 1936, Samuel D. Mauney, April 24, 1936, still serving.

CHESTNUT OAK: Derivation of name unknown, but likely named for species of tree; located at the present site of Hickory, at intersection of First avenue and Third street, SE; established August 15, 1846; postmaster, William Hale, August 15, 1846; discontinued May 31, 1848.

LONG ISLAND: Derivation of name, location and other characteristics described in preceding chapter; established May 3, 1854; postmasters, Abel T. Cansler, May 3, 1854, Avery M. Powell, October 22, 1858; discontinued May 2, 1860; re-established July 25, 1895; postmasters George W. Brown, July 27, 1895, Osborne Brown, March 7, 1898, Thomas N. Horner, August 23, 1929, Filetus B. Tilley, January 20, 1934, James A. Tilley, March 13, 1940, Fred H. Lytton, February 16, 1941, J. Clyde York, November 29, 1942, Mary B. Pope, January 19, 1949, still serving.

MOUNTAIN MILLS: Derivation of name unknown; location unknown; established July 11, 1856; postmaster, George S. Hooper, July 11, 1856; discontinued February 26, 1857.

CHRONICLE: Named for Major William Chronicle, killed at Kings Mountain. Location midway between Maiden and the Catawba river near the Lincoln county line; established August 30, 1857; postmasters, Osborne Munday, August 30, 1857, William A. Warner, February 9, 1869, Archibald L. Dellinger, August 29, 1881, William C. Wentz, March 15, 1892, Jacob F. Killian, November 17, 1894, Richard Frank Beal, December 11, 1894, William C. Wentz, September 14, 1897, David Clark, January 27, 1898, Ernest W. Bost, May 5, 1898, James E. Hicks, April 5, 1899, James S. Abernethy, July 16, 1903; discontinued October 15, 1904, and mail was directed to Maiden office.

ELLIOTT SPRINGS: Named for Elliott family; located eight miles northeast of Hickory; established June 10, 1859; postmasters, Esley O. Elliott, June 10, 1859, Hiram A. Davis, March 13, 1860; name changed to White Sulphur Springs August 1, 1860.

WHITE SULPHUR SPRINGS: Named for springs; same location as Elliott Springs; established August 1, 1860; postmasters, Hiram A. Davis, August 1, 1860, Martha J. Eckard, July 26, 1866; discontinued April 2, 1868.

SPARKLING CATAWBA SPRINGS: Named for springs; located at the site of Elliott Springs and White Sulphur Springs; established December 12, 1877; postmasters, Esley O. Elliott, December 12, 1877, William E. Anderson, September 11, 1900;

discontinued January 31, 1904, and mail was directed to Hickory office.

LONG TOWN: Derivation of name unknown; located approximately a mile north of Conover; established March 7, 1860; postmaster, Cicero Henkel, March 7, 1860; discontinued December 11, 1866.

CLINESVILLE: Named for Cline family; located in the area of the present Drums Crossroads, about five miles southeast of Newton; established April 23, 1860; postmaster, Parson Naylor, April 23, 1860; discontinued January 10, 1861; re-established August 15, 1871; postmasters, W. C. Caldwell, August 15, 1871, Henry H. Caldwell, February 21, 1884; discontinued April 21, 1884, and mail was directed to Drumville office.

DRUMVILLE: Named for Drum family; located in area of present Drums Crossroads; established February 1, 1883; postmasters, Caroline Drum, February 1, 1883, John H. Cline, October 29, 1883; William D. Drum, November 8, 1883, George D. Wilkinson, October 8, 1896, David W. Drum, February 9, 1903; discontinued October 15, 1904, and mail was directed to Catawba office.

YOUNTS TURNOUT: Derivation of name unknown, but likely came from presence of railroad siding about one mile west of Claremont; located in the present St. John's Lutheran church area; established May 11, 1860; postmaster, Emanuel Sigman, May 11, 1860; discontinued February 5, 1861.

HICKORY TAVERN: Derivation of name, location and other characteristics described in preceding chapter; established May 15, 1860; postmasters, Adolphus Shuford, May 15, 1860, Andrew D. Lindsay, June 25, 1860, (Miss) S. V. Tuttle, January 22, 1866, William H. Ellis, January 24, 1867, John M. Lawrence, January 13, 1873; name changed to Hickory.

HICKORY: Derivation of name, location and other characteristics described in preceding chapter; postmasters, John M. Lawrence, May 22, 1876, James B. Beard, September 12, 1877, John M. Lawrence, June 7, 1881, James B. Beard, June 17, 1881, Jacob A. Bowles, January 29, 1887, George D. Smith, May 10, 1890, William P. Huffman, May 16, 1894, Jones W. Shuford, June 22, 1898, Columbus P. Blalock, January 13, 1903, Samuel M. Hamrick, March 14, 1907, Amidas G. Link,

July 25, 1913, Raymond L. Hefner, acting, April 12, 1915, Joseph H. Aiken, April 30, 1915, Raymond L. Hefner, acting, July 1, 1917, William F. Fogle, acting, July 26, 1917, Charles W. Bagby, acting, December 1, 1917, Charles W. Bagby, March 18, 1919, Herbert H. Miller, March 18, 1922, James T. Setzer, December 20, 1930, Willie B. Walker, acting, December 31, 1934, George F. Bost, August 27, 1935, J. Henry Hill, acting, October 1, 1942, J. Henry Hill, October 22, 1943, still serving.

CATAWBA STATION: Derivation of name, location and other characteristics described in preceding chapter; office was first established at Chestnut Grove in Iredell county, May 31, 1856; moved across river and named Catawba Station December 2, 1859; established (in Catawba county) December 2, 1859; postmasters, Gilbert M. Sherrill, December 2, 1859, Elmira A. Lowrance, March 20, 1866, William H. Lowrance, March 23, 1869, Tate Powell, May 10, 1871, William H. Lowrance, August 27, 1872, Jeptha U. Long, July 21, 1873; name changed to Catawba.

CATAWBA: Derivation of name, location and other characteristics described in preceding chapter; postmasters, Jeptha Sherrill, August 6, 1877, Peter A. Little, January 21, 1884, Jeptha U. Long, April 10, 1885, John J. Smith, May 31, 1889, Alexander H. Houston, March 27, 1893, Ceniphar A. Reid, April 23, 1797, Thomas E. Harwell, November 20, 1900, Robert E. Carpenter, April 2, 1914, Thomas E. Harwell, January 5, 1922, Zula S. Glover, acting, February 15, 1934, Zula S. Glover, June 12, 1934, still serving.

CONOVER: Derivation of name, location and other characteristics described in preceding chapter; established May 23, 1873; postmasters, David S. Henkle, May 23, 1873, Noah Townsend, August 17, 1874, John F. Hunsucker, April 29, 1880, Alexander McCrary, December 24, 1883, John F. Hunsucker, December 18, 1884, George A. Brady, May 31, 1889, Peter F. Smith, May 17, 1893, Charles R. Brady, June 30, 1897, John L. Isenhour, March 26, 1904, John F. Hunsucker, April 23, 1914, Preston P. Herman, acting, July 15, 1924, Preston P. Herman, January 26, 1925, Clinton E. Bolick, acting, July 20, 1933, Clinton E. Bolick, February 1, 1934, Claude E. Schell, November 1, 1943, still serving.

OXFORD FORD: Named for Oxford family, located in present Oxford Ford area; established November 5, 1873; postmasters, Marion J. Rowe, November 5, 1873, Allen J. Stine, April 13, 1876, Quintus Hendrick, March 3, 1879, Allen J. Stine, July 8, 1880, Copas S. Little, April 4, 1887, Allen J. Stine, December 24, 1887, Quintus M. Smith, June 30, 1894; discontinued March 31, 1903, and mail was directed to Conover office.

YOUNTS MILL: Named for Yount family; located about one and one-fourth miles northeast of present St. John's Lutheran church, which is about three miles northeast of Conover; postmaster, George D. L. Yount, June 18, 1874; discontinued August 31, 1885.

JUGTOWN (Also referred to as Jug Town): Derivation of name, location and other characteristics described in preceding chapter; established July 19, 1874; postmasters, Alfred A. Havner, July 19, 1874, Amon L. Johnson, August 6, 1875, Wade D. C. Johnson, January 13, 1893, Royal P. Havner, January 11, 1897, Alfred A. Havner, January 19, 1904; discontinued March 31, 1906, and mail was directed to Henry office (in Lincoln county).

FLEMMING: Derivation of name unknown, but likely family name; located about one and one-half miles west of the Catawba river near the Lincoln county line; established August 11, 1875; postmasters, John T. Cochran, August 11, 1875, John F. Harwell, February 28, 1891, John T. Cochran, December 27, 1894, Emma McCaul, January 3, 1899, Dora E. Harwell, April 17, 1900, Alfred R. Thompson, April 17, 1905; discontinued May 15, 1907, and mail was directed to Sherrills Ford office.

MAIDEN: Derivation of name, location and other characteristics described in preceding chapter; established November 12, 1879; postmasters, Frank M. Williams, November 12, 1879, R. A. Bolick, March 30, 1880, Daniel M. Boyd, August 23, 1883, John F. Rabb, January 20, 1886, Christian C. Call, June 1, 1889, Robert A. Rudisill, July 14, 1893, David M. Carpenter, July 20, 1897, James M. Holshouser, June 8, 1905, William L. Bolick, August 23, 1907, John S. Campbell, August 2, 1910, Josephine A. Taylor, April 2, 1914, Grover L. Harbinson, February 3, 1922, George N. Hunsucker, February 16, 1931, Robert A. Rudisill, March 1, 1936, Robert M. McRee, March 1, 1947, still serving.

SHERFORD: Derivation of name unknown, but likely name formed of Sherrill and Shuford; located in the present Long Island section; postmasters, Andrew B. Powell, March 24, 1881, James A. Beal, July 14, 1881, George D. Snuggs, August 1, 1883; discontinued December 13, 1883, and mail was directed to Bandy office.

FARM: Derivation of name unknown; located in area of present Salem Lutheran church, immediately across the Lincoln county line; established April 11, 1881; postmasters, Noah Huffman, April 11, 1881, Hosea Whitener, August 31, 1883, Oliver P. Post, October 6, 1885; discontinued August 13, 1890, and mail was directed to Maiden office.

KEEVERSVILLE: Named for Keever family; located in the present Plateau section; established April 11, 1881; postmaster, William S. Jarrett, April 11, 1881; name changed to Plateau December 7, 1888.

PLATEAU: Derivation of name, location and other characteristics described in preceding chapter; postmasters, John A. Hamblet, December 7, 1888, James S. Goodman, April 10, 1893, Mary Killian, August 2, 1897, James M. Clampitt, May 14, 1903, Charley Scronce, August 24, 1904; discontinued May 31, 1907, and mail was directed to Newton office.

MONBO: Derivation of name unknown; located one-fourth mile southeast of Long Island near the Catawba river; established October 13, 1882; postmasters, Columbus L. Turner, October 13, 1882, Samuel Turner, August 10, 1894; discontinued August 15, 1920, and mail was directed to Long Island office.

BANDY: Named for Bandy family; located in present Piney Grove Baptist church area, which is about four miles southeast of Catawba; established February 1, 1883; postmasters, Perry P. Bandy, February 1, 1883, Maggie Jones, May 26, 1893, William F. Bandy, June 28, 1897, Joseph S. Bandy, November 27, 1897, Burlie M. Cannon, May 12, 1898, Franklin Bandy, January 20, 1899; discontinued August 15, 1905, and mail was directed to Catawba office.

DANVILLE: Derivation of name unknown; located at present site of Startown; established March 5, 1883; postmaster,

Wallace A. Bollinger, March 5, 1883; name changed to Startown October 31, 1884.

STARTOWN: Derivation of name, location and other characteristics described in preceding chapter; postmasters, Wallace A. Bollinger, October 31, 1884, Marcus A. Throneburg, March 6, 1886, John T. Conrad, April 26, 1893, M. A. Throneburg, December 10, 1897, Wallace A. Bollinger, April 27, 1898; discontinued April 10, 1902, and mail was directed to Newton office.

CROSSING: Derivation of name unknown, but likely resulted from fact that it was site of crossing of Oxford Ford-Lincolnton-Charlotte and Island Ford-Morganton roads; name of community was CHARLOTTE CROSSING; location is treated in preceding chapter; established October 1, 1884; postmasters, John W. Setzer, October 1, 1884, William J. Trollinger, September 16, 1885, William A. Hoke, November 5, 1885, Harrison H. Robinson, March 15, 1892; name changed to Claremont August 8, 1892.

CLAREMONT: Derivation of name, location and other characteristics described in preceding chapter; postmasters, Harrison M. Robinson, August 8, 1892, William A. Hoke, April 26, 1893, James H. Rexlode, July 20, 1897, Preston A. Sigman, May 11, 1900, James P. Carpenter, October 28, 1902, Jacob M. Isenhour, May 8, 1906, George E. Setzer, April 28, 1914, Bessie Sigman, acting, December 28, 1925, Bessie Sigman, April 22, 1926, Marion R. Morrow, August 7, 1933, Paul H. Moser, March 17, 1934, still serving.

WHISNANT: Named for Whisnant family; located near Bakers Mountain, about seven miles southwest of Hickory; established March 3, 1885; postmaster, Daniel A. Whisnant, March 3, 1885; discontinued August 20, 1886, and mail was directed to Hickory office.

CATFISH: Legend says Revolutionary soldiers found catfish in mud puddles following freshet and named area Catfish; located about five miles northeast of Claremont; established June 1, 1886; postmaster, James H. C. Huitt, June 1, 1886; discontinued March 31, 1903, and mail was directed to Claremont office.

EDITH: Derivation of name unknown; located one mile west-northwest of Smyrna Evangelical and Reformed church, which is about four miles southwest of Catawba; established June 7, 1886; postmasters, George D. Snuggs, June 7, 1886, Warren M. Gantt, February 15, 1892, Nannie E. Gantt, April 8, 1893, Charlie A. Setzer, September 14, 1897, Jacob Wike, January 2, 1902, Walter L. Alley, January 23, 1904; discontinued May 15, 1907, and mail was directed to Catawba office.

ARNT: Named for Arnt family; located one-half mile northeast of Old Salem Church cemetery, which is about seven miles north of Claremont in the bend of the Catawba river; established August 3, 1886; postmaster, John M. Arnt, August 3, 1886; discontinued March 31, 1903, and mail was directed to Claremont office.

CHESTNUT: Derivation of name unknown, but likely from species of tree; located 11 miles southwest of Hickory near the Burke county line; established August 18, 1887; postmaster, McLelland Hildebrand, August 18, 1887; discontinued August 30, 1904, and mail was directed to Hayseed office.

SHAWNER: Derivation of name unknown; located about three-fourths of a mile northwest of Concord Methodist church, which is about one and three-fourths miles southwest of Long Island; established April 26, 1888; postmasters, Fannie E. Fisher, April 26, 1888, Joel H. Fisher, July 23, 1888, Pinkney C. Kale, February 19, 1892; discontinued May 14, 1904, and mail was directed to Long Island office.

LOUISE: Derivation of name unknown; located in area of present Grace Lutheran and Evangelical Reformed churches, which are about five miles southwest of Newton; established May 10, 1890; postmaster, Louis N. Rudisill, May 10, 1890; name changed to Rudisill October 19, 1893.

RUDISILL: Named for Rudisill family; same location as Louise; postmaster, Louis N. Rudisill, May 1, 1894; discontinued June 30, 1903, and mail was directed to Lincolnton office.

HAYSEED: Derivation of name unknown; located at the present Wade Brittain store in Bandy township; established July 14, 1892; postmasters, James T. Brittain, July 14, 1892, George W. Wilson, April 27, 1894, Daniel W. Brittain, December 10, 1896; discontinued August 31, 1905, and mail was directed to Henry office.

BLACKBURN: Derivation of name, location and other characteristics described in preceding chapters; established June 5, 1888; postmasters, Julius M. Yoder, June 5, 1888, William H. Blackburn, May 10, 1890, Luther S. Ritchey, November 1, 1895, William H. Blackburn, April 17, 1900; discontinued May 31, 1906, and mail was directed to Newton office.

CARSON: Named for Carson family; located at present Carsons Crossroads, about four miles east of Newton; established September 17, 1892; postmasters, John H. Moser, September 17, 1892, Henry J. Sigmon, April 19, 1893, Sarah F. Wilson, October 21, 1893; discontinued April 10, 1902, and mail was directed to Newton office.

LORETTA: Derivation of name unknown; location unknown; established September 25, 1893; postmasters, William E. Jones, September 25, 1893, John F. Hovis, October 21, 1897, Robert B. Jones, June 27, 1898, James C. Tomlinson, August 2, 1900, Wilburn W. Caldwell, September 23, 1901; discontinued October 14, 1904, and mail was directed to Maiden office.

WHITENER: Named for Whitener family; located about four and one-half miles west of Newton; established September 25, 1893; postmaster, David H. Whitener, September 25, 1893; discontinued March 31, 1903, and mail was directed to Hickory office.

TERRELL: Derivation of name, location and other characteristics are described in preceding chapter; established October 16, 1893; postmasters, Thomas F. Connor, October 16, 1893, Thomas C. Sherrill, July 25, 1918, R. Harold Gabriel, acting, December 15, 1933, Robert Harold Gabriel, March 2, 1934, still serving.

MILLSTONE: Derivation of name unknown; located three miles in a southwesterly direction from Wade Brittain's store; established November 11, 1893; postmaster, Sanford Cline, November 11, 1893; discontinued September 9, 1897, and mail was directed to Mull Grove office.

YODER: Named for Yoder family; located eight miles south of Hickory; established April 17, 1894; postmaster, Francis A. Yoder, April 17, 1894; discontinued March 31, 1903, and mail was directed to Hickory office.

COOK: Named for Cook family; located about one mile east of the present Ebenezer Methodist church, in Bandys Township; established February 2, 1895; postmaster, D. Monroe Brittain, February 2, 1895; discontinued August 31, 1905, and mail was directed to Henry office.

PROPST: Named for Propst family; located in area of the present Propst Crossroads, about nine miles south of Hickory; established April 15, 1899; postmasters, Peter M. Sharpe, April 15, 1899, David P. Shuford, September 20, 1900; discontinued January 31, 1905, and mail was directed to Hickory office.

BROOKFORD: Derivation of name, location and other characteristics are described in preceding chapter; established April 27, 1901; postmasters, Henry J. Holbrook, April 27, 1901, Wade H. Shuford, October 18, 1901; discontinued February 14, 1906, and mail was directed to Hickory office.

CHAPTER XVI

CONTRIBUTION TO THE SPANISH AMERICAN CONFLICT

The Spanish-American war differs from any other in history because of at least two aspects: 1. It was begun as a protest of civilization and as a plea for humanity. 2. It ended as an act of unpremeditated national expansion.

Since the close of the War Between the States, Spain's mismanagement of Cuba, which had been in an almost constant state of turmoil or oppression, had so aroused the United States government that it had frequently proposed purchasing the island as a protection to American investments.

Finally in February, 1895, a new rebellion, the sixth in 50 years, broke out in Cuba, and Captain-General Weyler's attempts at suppression were so cruel and ruinous that intervention by the United States was suggested.

But, in his message of December, 1897, President McKinley urged further patience, and the Sagasta ministry, through Captain-General Blanco, proposed home rule for Cuba.

At length, the United States battleship *Maine* was sent to Havana to protect American interests. On the night of February 15, 1898, it was destroyed in Havana Harbor, under mysterious circumstances. An outraged American public believed that Spanish officials were in some way responsible, and it immediately determined to go to war.

President McKinley, then, recommended forcible intervention, Congress declared Cuba independent and sanctioned intervention, and from April 21 war was declared to exist.

By the President's orders, portions of the Cuban coast were speedily blockaded and some 200,000 volunteers were equipped and drilled for service in the camps of instruction which were established near Tampa, Fla., and Chickamauga, Ga.

In Spain it was given out that the South, still mourning the loss of the Southern Confederacy, was ripe for revolt, and that the landing of a Spanish army somewhere on the Gulf coast was only necessary to draw to it a host of rebels waiting for a chance to rise and eager for revenge.

No presumption could have been more wrong. As presented previously, the South, North Carolina, and Catawba county were willing at the failure of their movement for independence to again become a part of the United States. The span of 30 years since the ending of the civil struggle proved Southern patriotism.

Economically, the South had come to be set apart from the rest of the nation by differentials in per capita wealth, income, and living standards that made it unique among the regions. Politically, it had achieved a unity that it had never possessed in ante-bellum times. War and reconstruction, while taking away some of the area's peculiarities, merely aggravated others and gave rise to new ones.

Change was now an accepted part of the Southern scene. The renewal of trade and commerce, the introduction of industries and the revolt against the Eastern manufacturers, etc., produced a profound effect on a once rural economy. To an extent, Catawba county was influenced by this transition in economies, and by at least the last of the nineteenth century, such industries as tobacco and cotton were finding their ways here.

While the South was certainly to be no traitor in the instance of difficulty with Spain, its people were not as incensed with alleged Spanish atrocities as were Northerners. Perhaps this is creditable to the fact that Southerners were so absorbed with their internal affairs.

At any rate, of the seven wars affecting Catawba county, fewest records are kept of the Spanish-American conflict.

Older residents say that they remember only highlights of the short struggle, and seem to regard it as a foreign affair with few local implications. Of course, to those who had loved ones involved, the war was very real and tragic.

A list of Spanish-American war volunteers of Catawba county, with their enlistment dates and the companies to which they were attached, is as follows:

CATAWBA COUNTY

Company A, First N. C. Regiment—Charles T. Bridges (April 21, 1898), James H. Campbell (April 27, 1898), William O. Campbell (April 27, 1898), Gordon H. Cilley (Corporal) (April 27, 1898), Milton E. Deal (April 27, 1898), James M. Edwards (April 27, 1898), John P. Ekard (Unknown), Frederick E. Garvin (April 27, 1898), Avery E. Kale (August 14, 1898), Herbert O. Keever (April 27, 1898), Robert B. Knox (April 27, 1898), Eubert Lyerly (Sergeant) (April 27, 1898), Charles M. McCorkle (Corporal) (April 27, 1898), Coleman O. Moser (April 27, 1898), Charles M. Sherrill (April 27, 1898), Hubert Story (August 14, 1898), John G. Wilfong (Corporal) (April 27, 1898), William H. Williams (April 27, 1898), Henry A. Wise (April 21, 1898), Ainsley T. Yoder (April 27, 1898), Albert O. Yount (April 27, 1898), Lee C. Yount (June 15, 1898), Thomas E. Yount (April 27, 1898), and William H. Yount (April 27, 1898).

Company E, First N. C. Regiment—Robert E. Benfield (Corporal) (April 27, 1898), Esley O. Erwin (April 27, 1898), Fleming W. Gains (April 27, 1898), Frank A. James (April 27, 1898), Lawrence A. Lafon (April 27, 1898), Pinkney E. Lafon (April 27, 1898), Gus W. Payne (Corporal) (April 27, 1898), Robert D. Rufty (Sergeant), (April 27, 1898), Luther E. Seaboch (Corporal) (April 27, 1898), John W. Sigmon (April 27, 1898), and Robert L. Trollinger (Unknown).

Company K, First N. C. Regiment—Hiliary C. Bumgarner (July 23, 1898) (Died September 11, 1898), and Edward T. Pierce (June 15, 1898).

Company M, First N. C. Regiment—J. W. Armfield (April 27, 1898), and Charles W. Hike (April 27, 1898).

Company C, Second N. C. Regiment—Perry W. Hawn (May 15, 1898), John W. Hill (May 15, 1898), David D. Isenhower (May 15, 1898), Joseph O. Jones (May 15, 1898), Daniel H. Lail (July 1, 1898), Thomas G. Miller (May 15, 1898), George P. Mull (June 9, 1898), Horace L. Pendleton (May 15, 1898), Charles E. Talbert (June 2, 1898), Ambrose M. Williams (March 15, 1898), and Rufus I. Williams (June 9, 1898) (Died August 1898).

Company G, Second N. C. Regiment—Hyrle Howell (May 11, 1898), Frank R. Mull (May 24, 1898), Sidney W. Mull (May 24, 1898), and Henry A. Norton (June 29, 1898).

Company M, Second N. C. Regiment—Joseph H. Huffman (Artificer) (May 20, 1898).

Company C, Third N. C. Regiment—James D. Holloway (Colored) (April 27, 1898).

Company F, Third N. C. Regiment—Augustus Bell (Colored) (Musician) (June 23, 1898).

Company G, Third N. C. Regiment—Robert Evans (Colored) (June 23, 1898), Alexander Harshaw (Colored) (June 23, 1898), Robert Lutz (Colored) (June 23, 1898), Thomas Pickenpack (Colored) (June 23, 1898), Clarence Shores (Colored) (June 23, 1898), and James Martin (Colored) (June 23, 1898).

Company B, First Georgia Regiment—Raleigh E. Bollinger (May 6, 1898).

Company D, First S. C. Regiment—Henry R. Triplett (July 20, 1898; re-enlisted Company K, 38th Regiment U. S. Volunteers September 12, 1899).

Second S. C. Infantry—Robert Erwin (Unknown).

Company One, Fourth Virginia U. S. Volunteers—R. Lee Hewitt (Unknown).

Thirty-eighth U. S. Volunteers—Robert Seagle (Unknown).

Company L, 46th U. S. Volunteers—Daniel E. Abernethy (October 4, 1899).

Company M, 46th U. S. Volunteers—Henry Miller (Unknown).

Company and Regiment unknown—Robert Finger (Unknown), Mack Drum (Unknown), and Tull Drum (Unknown).

These men may be said to have assisted America in becoming a self-confident world power, for the Spanish-American war created a position among the great nations for the United States. The country went into the conflict doubtful as to its equipment, resources and capacity. It came out of it assured.

Moreover, the war annihilated sectional lines and solidified the American Union. It dissipated forever the notion that

Americans are a race of mercenary shopkeepers. It announced the arrival upon the scene of the world's action a power which would have to be reckoned with by the older powers in determining the future of civilization. And, it rescued the country from a turbulent discussion of many misleading questions of domestic economy, uplifting and enlarging all its national perspectives.

Catawba county was not exempt from the war's results, particularly the last. The county's industrial development generally dates from the struggle's close.

CHAPTER XVII
CONTRIBUTION TO TWENTIETH CENTURY WORLD CONFLICTS

Wars which were the fartherest in distance from Catawba county have sapped the strength of its manpower more strenuously than any others, and taught belatedly that one man's welfare affects another's a continent away.

Until the Spanish-American war, Catawbans knew war firsthand, having felt its devastating effects in familiar surroundings. But the Spanish-American war was neither exciting nor particularly taxing. Perhaps because of this, Catawbans, and their fellow Americans, began to believe that distance minimizes the cruelties of war, and they generally became disinterested in the world's constant localized conflicts.

The World Wars of the twentieth century brought, therefore, a rude awakening. The First War, which continued from July 28, 1914, until November 11, 1918, was the first great struggle to involve most of the civilized world and it did so in such a way as to have repercussions in virtually all the local communities of the world.

All told, some 65,000,000 men were mobilized for World War One, of whom more than 8,500,000 were killed or died, and more than 21,000,000 were wounded.

Many contemporaries will attest to the fact that Catawbans celebrated the beginning of the First World War almost as much as they did its ending. No one foresaw the horrible slaughter that was to be included in it.

As an example of the enthusiasm with which the local folks sent their sons, husbands, and fathers to war, a June, 1916, article of The Hickory Daily Record is quoted:

"Hickory and Catawba county met on common ground today and gave Company A, First North Carolina Infantry, such a send-off as will be remembered by every man, woman and child for the rest of their lives. The chief event was a picnic dinner in Union Square shortly after one o'clock, arranged by the people of the whole county, and (followed by) short stirring speeches by well known citizens of the section. Temporary tables, placed in the open, literally groaned under their burden of wholesome food and delicacies."

Among those listed as speakers were J. D. Elliott; Dr. J. L. Murphy; W. J. Shuford; Col. Edmund Jones of Lenoir, a veteran of the War Between the States; A. A. Whitener; and Robert Ransom. The speaking was interspersed with music by the Newton band.

"Hickory people woke this morning with the picnic dinner in their bones," the paper's report continued. "Soon they were joined by friends from all parts of the county and other counties, for Company A drew on several counties for its recruits, and by noon the crowd was estimated at several thousand people. If Captain Lyerly and his men ever doubted the interest felt in them, that doubt was removed today. Business was practically suspended. The stores were open, but the proprietors and clerks had as their motto 'Company A First.'"

The scene was repeated many times. The shadows of the cold battlefields of France had not as yet been stretched.

The people, in fact, had not watched too intently the designing of the war. European difficulties seemed remote; their progress was overlooked by a nation of isolationists.

Actually, the underlying causes of the tremendous four-year struggle reach far back into the past and were not to be reduced to any simple formula. Forces which are most generally cited as contributing factors include the economic rivalry among European nations, the maintenance of a system of military alliances, and the clashing of national interests and ideals.

The immediate cause was an assassination. Serbian nationalist propaganda against the Austro-Hungarian monarchy grew more unrestrained after the Balkan Wars. A Serbian group of conspirators determined to assassinate the heir of the Austro-Hungarian throne, Archduke Francis Ferdinand. The opportunity came when Ferdinand and his wife visited Sarajevo, in Bosnia, and on June 28, 1914, the youth Gaurilo Princip assassinated both. The Serbian government, long aware of the plot, had done nothing to suppress it.

The Austrian reaction was immediate, for the imperial government was determined to crush Serbia. Austria first secured the backing of Germany, which believed that the looked-for war could be localized on the assumption that Serbia's ally, Russia, would back down. But, if Russia did go to the aid of Serbia, Germany was prepared to fulfill her treaty obligations by aiding Austria.

This began a chain of events which led all the great powers of Europe to war. With the passage of time, America followed the pattern, declaring war on Germany on April 6, 1917.

Catawba county was hard hit by the result of this decision.

Those men who "fought to make the world safe for democracy," as compiled in the state adjutant general's office in Raleigh, follow: (Although careful screening has been done, omissions are, regrettably, possible. Some men of the county enlisted in other counties, and their names could not be obtained.)

Army:

Officers—

Honor Roll—
  Sigmon, Orin Morrow, 2nd Lt

Wounded in action—
  Reinhardt, John Perkins, Capt
  Warlick, Eli, 2nd Lt
  Williams, Daniel McGregor, 1st Lt.

Additional—
  Abernathy, Claude O., Capt
  Abernethy, Claude S., Lt
  Abernethy, Elon A., Major
  Abernethy, Julius W., 2nd Lt
  Aiken, Hazel R., 1st Lt.
  Aiken, John Will, 1st Lt
  Barringer, Carroll M., 2nd Lt
  Blackwelder, Bascom Barrie, Capt
  Bolick, Clarence P., 1st Lt
  Bowman, Wade V., Capt
  Carr, Earl Nelson, 1st Lt
  Cilley, Joseph E., 1st Lt
  Clarkson, James W., ———
  Cline, Frank L., 1st Lt.
  Cline, Ambrose S., 2nd Lt
  Cole, Grayson Giles, ———
  Coulter, Victor A., Capt
  Councill, Gordon S., 2nd Lt

CATAWBA COUNTY

Councill, William Thomas, 1st Lt
Danner, Clarence E., 2nd Lt
Doll, Jacob Venable, Capt
Elliott, Kerley C., 2nd Lt
Flowe, Bartlette B., 1st Lt
Flowe, Homer P., 1st Lt
Freeman, Charles C., Capt
Geitner, John G. H., 1st Lt
Gwaltney, Philip A., 1st Lt
Hahn, Albert G., Capt
Henderson, Aldis C., 2nd Lt
Hester, Oma H., 1st Lt
Hewitt, Robert L., 1st Lt
Huffman, Arthur M., 1st Lt
Hughey, Clyde O. P., army field clerk
Hunsucker, Charles, contract surgeon
Ingold, Winfred Lee, 1st Lt
Keever, James Woodfin, 2nd Lt
Klutz, Austin Flint, 1st Lt
Long, Glenn, 1st Lt
Lutz, Albert Sherrill, 2nd Lt
Lyerly, George Lafayette, Major
Mauney, Everett George, 1st Lt
Mauney, Samuel Davidson, 2nd Lt
Mauser, Roscoe Frederick, Capt
Menzies, Henry Charles, Capt
Miller, Grover Cleveland, 1st Lt
McCorkle Charles M., Lt Col
McCorkle, Mathew Locke, 1st Lt.
Rowe, Herbert Eugene, 1st Lt
Schell, Frank Royall, 2nd Lt
Shuford, Edward L., ———
Shuford, Jacob Harrison, Major
Shull, Joseph Rush, 1st Lt
Sigmon, Nolan Jay, Capt
Sipe, Harold Gilmore, 2nd Lt
Stearns, Clyde Casey, 2nd Lt
Stevenson, Charles Stuart, 2nd Lt
Taylor, Weston Lenoir, 1st Lt
Turner, Reginald, 2nd Lt
Veach, Milton William, 1st Lt
Warlick, Eli, ———
Warlick, George Andrew, Capt
Warlick, George Clifton, 1st Lt.
Warlick, Wilson, army field clerk
West, G. H., Contract surgeon
Whitener, Joseph Benjamin, 1st Lt
Williams, Macon McCorkle, 2nd Lt
Williams, Robert Ransom, Capt
Wilson, Andrew McCorkle, Jr., 1st Lt.

Winters, Morrison M., 1st Lt
Yoder, Paul Allison

Enlisted Men (white)—

Honor Roll—

Boggs, James Russell, Pvt
Bolick, William A., Pvt
Bonner, Theodore P., Jr., Sgt
Cansler, Adolphus G., Pvt
Carpenter, Thaddius C., Pvt
Cline, Frank E., Pvt
Damerson, Henry P., PFC
Davis, George R., ———
Deitz, Fred J., ———
Ervin, James S., Pvt
Flower, Bergis L., ———
Fry, John V., Pvt
Hass, John A., Pvt
Holbrooks, Jacob W., Pvt
Huffman, John D., Sgt
Hunsucker, Alexander, ———
Jones, Robert, Pvt
Loftin, Bidewell, Pvt
Logan, Hugh Gordon, Pvt
Mace, Joseph, ———
Mann, Ransom L., Pvt
Murphy, Marcus M., Pvt
Null, James Earl, Pvt
Parsons, Marshall C., Wag
Peeler, Lawrence, Cpl
Smith, John I., PFC
Travis, Peter O., Pvt
Whitener, Marion D., PFC
Williams, Chester C., Sgt

Wounded in action—

Buff, Jesse L., PFC
Butler, Charles McDowell, Cpl
Clark, George F., PFC
Cline, Brather E., Pvt
Clippard, Klutz B., Cpl
Denton, Clarence F., Pvt
Edmiston, Raymond E., Pvt
Herman, Oliver C., Sgt
Herman, Preston W., Pvt
Hoyle, Mead S., ———
Huitt, Earl B., Cpl
Jones, Roy Edgar, Pvt
Lael, Lorin T., PFC
Leonard, Alfred B. C., Pvt

CATAWBA COUNTY 399

Lippard, Glenn, Pvt
Mauney, George M., PFC
Reitzel, Perry V., Cpl
Ritchie, John L., Pvt
Sandlin, George Silas, Sgt
Schell, Marshall H., Sgt
Settlemyre, Russell D., PFC
Sigmon, Ralph C., Pvt
Starnes, Russell V., Pvt
Suggs, Carl S., PFC
Tallent, William H., PFC
Turner, Lee E., Pvt
Veach, Robert H., PFC
Wilkinson, Robert George P., ———
Wright, Robert C., PFC
Yount, David L., PFC
Yount, Glenn O., Sgt
Yount, Ross J., Pvt

Additional—

Abee, Hugh Henry
Abee, George H.
Abee, Ephriam Edward
Abee, Julius O.
Abee, Marshal C.
Abee, Mart
Abernethy, Dorse L.
Abernathy, Ernest Henry
Abernethy, Dorton Horace
Abernethy, Jones C.
Abernethy, Robert Glenn
Abernethy, Walter Eugene
Aderholdt, Neil D.
Alexander, Amos H.
Allen, Arnold
Allen, William
Allen, Wilson
Alley, Arthur N.
Alley, Fred L.
Allred, Paul W.
Amos, Frederick W.
Anderson, Thomas
Anthony, Will
Armstrong, John R.
Arndt, Cecil A.
Arndt, Clarence Davis
Arndt, Grover D.
Arndt, Huitt Little
Arney, Edgar C.
Arrowood, George
Ashe, John B.

Asherbranner, Dock
Askew, John R.
Bacon, Edward O.
Bacon, Frank R.
Baker, Clarence V.
Ballard, Charles B.
Banks, John
Barger, Earl C.
Barger, Edgar F.
Barger, Fred S.
Barger, James J.
Barger, Wade
Baumgardner, Campbell E.
Baumgardner, Henry L.
Beard, Allen E.
Beard, Fred E.
Beatty, Cephus
Beatty Custus H.
Bell, John Zebulion
Benfield, Neriah McC.
Benfield, Russell E.
Bentley, Russell E.
Berry, Benjamin Bartlett
Berry, James W.
Berry Ottis W.
Blackwelder, George S.
Blackwelder, William P.
Bolch, Philip M.
Bolich, Marshall Ney
Bolick, Charlie
Bolick Clarence Edgar

Bolick, John W.
Bolick, Rolland K.
Bollinger, George L.
Bonner, Brem
Bost, Cecil T.
Bost, Evans E.
Bost, John V.
Bowles, James H.
Bowles, Otto Lemont
Bowles, Robert H.
Bowman, Arthur L.
Bowman, Floyd A.
Bowman, George William
Bowman, Roby L.
Bowman, Wilkie Grover
Boyd, Arthur N.
Boyd, Claud
Boyd, Richard Crowell
Bradford, Arthur S.
Bradshaw, Jesse Austin
Brady, Frederick E.
Branch, David James
Brittain, Jonas W.
Brittain, Marshall Sylvester
Brittain, Sandford T.
Brooks, Carl L.
Brooks, Thomas M.
Brown, Arthur
Buff, LeRoy
Buff, William F.
Bumgarner, Claude G.
Bumgarner, Elvin L .
Bumgarner, Marvin R.
Bumgarner, Walter E.
Bumgarner, Walter L.
Burch, Samuel H.
Burgess, Samuel L.
Burgin, Robert L.
Burns, Durell E.
Burns, William J.
Burris, Clarence R.
Burris, Clarence F.
Busby, William M.
Butler, Archie A.
Butler, Curthburt E.
Butler, Pink A.
Butler, Joseph D.
Byers, Henry A.
Caldwell, Gaither
Caldwell, James H.
Caldwell, John W.

Campbell, Dick
Campbell, James F.
Campbell, John F.
Campbell, Shelton
Campbell, William C.
Canipe, Avery E.
Canipe, Carl C.
Canipe, Floyd W.
Canipe, Jones A.
Canipe, Omsey W.
Cansler, John Henry
Carpenter, Clyde H.
Carpenter, John F.
Carswell, Frank
Carswell, Walter
Carriker, James F.
Chapman, Ernest E.
Cilley, John H. P.
Cilley, Clinton A.
Clark, Grover Horrell
Click, Francis A.
Cline, Chalmer E.
Cline, Cletus L.
Cline, Curtis F.
Cline, Daras C.
Cline, John M.
Cline, John Merton
Cline, Oscar R.
Cline, Perry E.
Cline, Preston E.
Cline, Raymond R.
Cline, Thomas L.
Cline, Tosso T.
Cline, Vernon O.
Cloninger, Cephas A.
Cloninger, Ralph Adren
Cody, Raymond C.
Cole, Grayson G.
Coley, Charlie G.
Coley, Gabie F.
Coley, James M.
Combs, Robert W.
Combs, Webster
Comer, Joseph William
Conrad, Pierce R.
Cooper, John D.
Cordell, Dewey H.
Cordell, Hardy B.
Corpening, Frank K.
Coulter, Harry B.
Council, Gordon S.

CATAWBA COUNTY 401

Crafton, William D.
Crider, John P.
Crow, Carloss Minifee
Crow, Edison H.
Crow, Ivey O.
Curlee, Claud B.
Curtis, John E.
Dameron, Ellis L.
Danner, Clarence
Davis, Eslie C.
Davis, Forest C.
Davis, Garland Lee
Davis, Jesse
Davis, Ghurman A.
Deal, Charles M.
Deal, Ernest Clark
Deal, Glenn
Deal, Harold G.
Deal, Laurie A.
Deal, Lee A.
Deal, Lester L.
Deal, Ottie C.
Deal, Roscoe
Deal, Russell R.
Deal, Thomas E.
Deal, Vernon E.
Deal, William E.
Deaton, Alfred N.
Deaton, Paul Lewis
Deitz, Claude K.
Deitz, Lester A.
Deitz, Lewis C.
Dellinger, Charles W.
Demeron, Walter
Denton, Lester R.
Denton, Paul
Dietz, Clyde S.
Dietz, John F.
Drum, Dewey L.
Drum, Frank B.
Drum, Houston
Drum, Lee
Drum, Norman E.
Drum, Perry D.
Drum, Ray L.
Drum, Reuben P.
Drum, Roy W.
Drum, Will
Duff, Stephen A.
Duncan, Fife Augustus
Dyson, Adam T.

Eads, James
Eaton, George W.
Eckard, Arthur Cletus
Edwards, Ben
Edwards, Earl T.
Edwards, Ralph L.
Edison, James H.
Ekard, Oliver Columbus
Elders, George C.
Elliott, Robert V.
Ennis, Roby B.
Ervin, Delmar W.
Ervin, John M.
Ervin, Paul P.
Evans, Gordon E.
Finger, Thomas D.
Fisher, Edmond Lloyd
Foard, Frank O.
Fowler, Thomas C.
Fox, Edgar L.
Frazier, Baxter A.
Fritz, Herbert H.
Fry, Perry Oscar
Fry, Pink
Fry, Uris Frank
Fry, William Herbert
Frye, Charles D.
Frye, Leslie J.
Gabriel, Archey Fitzgerald
Gabriel, Heath Cargille
Garbriel, Monroe S.
Gabriel, Thad R.
Gaither, Junius R.
Gaither, William C.
Gamble, Connolly C.
Gamble, Frank
Garis, William M.
Garth, Cornelius V.
Garth, Robert Campbell
Gilbert, Fred Ray
Gilbert, Wade O.
Gilleland, Thomas M.
Glass, Frank B.
Glenn, Robert C.
Goodman, John W.
Goodson, David A.
Goodson, Wade
Griffey, Elmer
Gross, Lowell N.
Hahn, Luke P.
Hamilton, Ellis B.

Hamilton, Thomas T.
Hamrick, William Henry
Harrill, William A.
Harris, Emmett W.
Harris, Truman T.
Hart, Edgar L.
Hart, Jacob A.
Hass, Eugene H.
Hass, Roby J.
Hass, Wilson E.
Hawn, Charles Robert
Hawn, Ernest A.
Hawn, George O.
Hawn, Lester
Hawn, Quincey H.
Hayes, George E.
Heavener, Clarence C.
Hedrick, Carroll W.
Hedrick, Clarence L.
Hedrick, David R.
Hedrick, Lester L.
Hedrick, Roy
Hefner, Arthur F.
Hefner, Edgar L.
Hefner, Henry Jones
Hefner, Herman L.
Heffner, Lonnie
Helms, William H.
Helton, Bartow C.
Helton, James H.
Henderson, William T.
Henkel, Clyde A.
Henkel, Haller J.
Herman, Alvin E.
Herman, Emery C.
Herman, Charles Bernard
Herman, Claude E.
Herman, Harry L.
Herman, Perry E.
Herman, Pinkney M.
Hewitt, Emmitt C.
Hewitt, Carnot Carlton
Hicks, Carlos Alonzo
Hicks, Oscar Reed
Hicks, William A.
Hight, Macy S.
Hilderbrand, Bennie M.
Hilderbrand, Jesse
Hilderbrand, Raymond
Hilton, Robert
Hodgin, Luther E.

Hoffman, Charles L.
Hoke, Harlie J.
Hoke, Harold E.
Hoke, Robert P.
Holden, Brock S.
Holland, Millard F.
Hollar, James J.
Hollar, Homer Frank
Holler, James Clifton
Holler, James J.
Holler, John Alexander
Holdsclaw, Kohler
Holdsclaw, Purtle
Honeycutt, Cleveland
Hoover, Ted P.
Houston, Leslie O.
Houston, Marshall L.
Howard, Carl H.
Howard, James C.
Hudson, Melvin
Huffman, Adrian S.
Huffman, Cecil C.
Huffman, Coy Lester
Huffman, Ewart W.
Huffman, Franklin A. M.
Huffman, Garland L.
Huffman, Glenn R.
Huffman, James H.
Huffman, Noah D.
Huffman, Paul C.
Huffman, Perry Lee
Huffman, Robert L.
Huffman, Roy C.
Huitt, Bura R.
Huitt, John H.
Huitt, Perry D.
Huitt, Ross S.
Huitt, Willie C.
Hunsucker, Clayton O.
Hunsucker, Ezra A.
Hunsucker, Garland H.
Hunsucker, John J.
Hunsucker, Oren O.
Hunsucker, Ray M.
Hunt, Percy Ernest
Ikerd, Franklin R.
Ingraham, Theodore N.
Ingram, Claude H.
Isenhour, Charlie P.
Ivey, Elbert A.
Jones, Avery B.

CATAWBA COUNTY 403

Jones, George G.
Jones, John Lamel
Jones, Offie B.
Jones, Oscar P.
Jones, Tom W.
Kahill, Serly A.
Kale, Charles O.
Kale, Hubbard
Kale, Ralph C.
Kale, Thomas R.
Kaylor, Oren W.
Keller, Marvin G.
Killian, Avery
Killian, Henry R.
Killian, Jesse M.
Killian, Marion Butler
Kirkpatrick, George W.
Kiser, Herman B.
Klutz, Dole Mc
Klutz, Gill W.
Knight, Ernest M.
Kuhn, Harvey A.
Lackey, Guy L.
Lackey, James H.
Lackey, Vernon H.
Lael, Floyd V.
Lael, Otis C.
Lael, Rance M.
Lafevers, John
Laffon, Dexter L.
Lail, Clifford P.
Laney, Noah O.
Laney, William C.
Lawing, Adolphus P.
Leanard, Daniel R.
Leatherman, Fred S.
Leonard, Ernest V.
Leonard, Hyrle S.
Lewis, Brady C.
Lewis, Roby A.
Lewis, Walter T.
Little, Fred O.
Little, Jacob Clifford
Little, Marvin A.
Little, Ross James
Little, Rupert A.
Linebarger, Clyde P.
Lineberger, Avery R.
Link, Oscar
Locke, Beverly C.
Lohr, Arthur C.
Long, David G.
Long, George Everett
Long, Thomas C.
Long, William H.
Longaker, John M.
Lowman, Avery
Lowman, Harley
Lowman, James H.
Lowrance, Carlos U.
Lowrance, Fred
Lutz, Charles F.
Lutz, Claude L.
Lynch, Edward M.
Marlow, William E.
Marshall, John T.
Martin, Posey L.
Martin, Shuford B.
Martin, Stacy D.
Matheson, Willard M.
Mauney, Carl Glenn
Mauney, Robert J.
Mauney, Samuel D.
Mauser, John W.
Melton, Everett L.
Menzies, Henry C., Jr.
Messick, Gordon
Michael, Zeb Vance
Michals, William F.
Miller, Aaron W.
Miller, Carroll O.
Miller, David H.
Miller, Esley L.
Miller, Everett F.
Miller, Hugh M.
Miller, James W.
Miller, Jenks L.
Miller, John C.
Miller, John D.
Miller, John F., Jr.
Miller, Jones W.
Miller, Ralph E.
Miller, Rufus C.
Mingus, Clyde E.
Mitchell, Walter Elwood
Mitchum, Eli P.
Moehlman, Ernest Otto
Moore, Charlie C.
Moore, Grady H.
Moose, Aubery R.
Moose, Everett B.
Moretz, Carl W.

Morrow, Joseph G.
Moser, Frank Bryan
Moser, George A.
Moss, Ira C.
Mowery, Arthur C.
Mundy, James Coleman
Murphy, Joseph L., Jr.
McCall, Glenn M.
McClure, William J.
McComb, Robert E.
McComb, William W.
McCombs, Harvey Ellis
McFall, Uris A.
McFalls, Thomas L.
McRee, Carlos Hobson
Nabors, Earle E.
Nail, George L.
Nantz, John Wesley
Newton, Charles F.
Newton, Ruel David
Parker, Floyd L.
Parker, Robert Lee
Patrick, Bailey
Peeler, John H.
Peeler, Vess
Peeler, Zollie C.
Penland, Herbert E.
Penney, William W.
Peterson, David E.
Pharr, Owen H.
Pierce William Earl
Piercy, Lonnie F.
Poep, Oscar E.
Poovey, Floyd P.
Poovey, Garland O.
Poovey, John F.
Poovey, Marvin T.
Poovey, Charlie A.
Pope, Clyde J.
Pope, Edd C.
Pope, Ernest L.
Pope, Garland H.
Pope, George R.
Pope, George W.
Powell, George R.
Powell, Will C.
Price, Claud W.
Price, Clyde V.
Price, Floyd E.
Price, Gus A.
Price, Henry E.

Price, Joseph L.
Price, Robert L.
Propst, Cletus M.
Propst, Henry L.
Propst, Robert E.
Propst, Walter L.
Propes, Latta L.
Rader, Edgar F.
Ramsaur, Claude B.
Ramseur, David Henry, Jr.
Ramseur, Fred M.
Redmon, Harold V.
Reece, William A.
Reece, William M.
Reinhardt, Clate G.
Reinhardt, James A.
Reinhardt, Joe E.
Reinhardt, John J.
Reinhardt, Lester G.
Reitzel, Charles H.
Reitzel, Earl E.
Reitzel, Guy E.
Reynolds, Charlie K.
Reynolds, Austin M.
Rhinehart, Robert Cecil
Rhodes, Merton P.
Rhodes, Jesse F.
Rhoney, Horace D.
Rhony, George Aden
Rhyne, George W.
Riggs, John
Rinehardt, David L.
Rink, Marvin E.
Rockette, Murphy L.
Rodgers, William
Roper, Amos
Roseman, Tate Lemuel
Rosenbaum, Sidney R.
Rowe, Daniel E.
Rowe, Daniel M.
Rowe, Glenn S.
Rowe, Lloyd O.
Rowe, Mark M.
Rowe, Ray
Rowe, Ray K.
Rowe, Walter E.
Rudisill, Aubrey B.
Rudisill, Glenn Franklin
Rudisill, Joe L.
Rudisill, Justus C.
Schell, Lonnie L.

CATAWBA COUNTY 405

Schell, Richard C.
Schell, Robert G.
Schrum, Forrest F.
Seaback, Ivan R.
Seabock, Alvin V.
Seabock, Earl
Seabock, Hugh
Seagle, Daniel H.
Seagle, Hugh P.
Seitz, Eubert V.
Seitz, George P.
Seitz, John L.
Senter, Earl N.
Settlemyre, Gabriel
Settlemyre, Hubert
Setzer, Claude M.
Setzer, Clyde
Setzer, Edgar
Setzer, Hubert K.
Setzer, James B.
Setzer, Macon L.
Setzer, Roscoe R.
Setzer, Zell T.
Sharpe, Fred
Sharpe, Joe Henry
Shell, Ralph J.
Sherrill, Charlie L.
Sherrill, Don D.
Sherrill, Emory E.
Sherrill, Heubert R.
Sherrill, Hugh C.
Sherrill, Larrie B.
Sherrill, Luther C.
Sherrill, Marion C.
Sherrill, Percy A.
Sherrill, Truman
Shipp, Robert J.
Shook, Loyd William
Shook, Oscar C.
Shuford, Donald E.
Shuford, Harry R.
Shuford, James L.
Shuford, Julius W.
Shull, Beverly
Sides, Charlie B.
Sigman, Walter L.
Sigmon, Adrian Lee
Sigmon, Burley J.
Sigmon, Carlos M.
Sigmon, Caswell F.
Sigmon, Claude W.
Sigmon, Cloyd Richard
Sigmon, Daniel Elias
Sigmon, David S.
Sigmon, Dewey H.
Sigmon, Everett B.
Sigmon, George M.
Sigmon, James R.
Sigmon, James Walter
Sigmon, Marshall Ray
Sigmon, Martin F.
Sigmon, Marvin Festure
Sigmon, Oren Bickle
Sigmon, Oscar Monroe
Sigmon, Quince Edward
Sigmon, Robert V.
Sigmon, Roy E.
Sigmon, Russell E.
Sigmon, Russell G.
Sigmon, William G.
Simmons, David Clyde
Simmons, Ray A.
Simmons, Troy S.
Simpson, Elmer M.
Sipe, David A.
Sipe, Harold G.
Sipe, Vernon Otto
Smith, Ben C.
Smith, Daniel E
Smith, Edgar E.
Smith, Guy F
Smith, James D.
Smith, Loyd J.
Smith, Robert L.
Smith, Ross
Smyre, Earnest D.
Smyre, Leon Everett
Smyre, McKinley
Smyre, Perry L.
Smyre, Robert V.
Smyre, Seth S.
Speagle, Bryson G.
Speagle, James F.
Spencer, Horace M.
Speagle, Joseph L.
Springs, Edwin L.
Springs, John A.
Springs, Miles P.
Staggs, Elmer
Starnes, Floyd G.
Stephens, Patrick C.
Stevenson, Charles L.

Stevenson, Charles S.
Stewart, Jake C.
Stewart, Robert
Stine, Glenn R.
Stine, Perry
Sublett, Roscoe Harvey
Talbert, George E.
Tallent, Bart
Tate, David J.
Taylor, Albert H.
Taylor, George S.
Teague, Alonzo J.
Teague, James B.
Templeton, Roy
Thomasson, Robert Lee
Thornton, Oscar C.
Throneburg, Jacob A.
Tilley, Fred W.
Travis, Frank V.
Travis, Lawson C.
Travis, Macon B.
Travis, Marshall H.
Travis, Robert C.
Travis, Roy E.
Trollinger, Clyde A.
Trott, Wilfong W.
Trott, Willie M.
Turbyfill, Carl M.
Vanhorn, John W.
Wagner, Cletus Edward
Wagner, Theodore B.
Walker, John J.
Walton, Elwood Winfield
Warlick, Frank
Warlick, Simon
Warren, George R.
Warren, Marshall L.
Warren, Paul
Warren, Roy H.
Watson, Kelley
Watson, Nathan L.
Watts, John H.
Weaver, Clayton M.
Weaver, Daniel M.
Weaver, Evans S.
Weaver, Fred L.
Weaver, Russell F.
Webb, Richard C.
Weeks, Paul W.
Wellman, Abram H.
Wells, Daniel L.

Wells, Harry A.
Whisant, Garland
Whisnant, Charlie P.
Whisnant, Richard
White, Woodford
Whitener, Clyde O.
Whitener, Craig S.
Whitener, Daniel J.
Whitener, Fred
Whitener, Henry E.
Whitener, James L.
Whitener, Marion C.
Whitener, Murphy B.
Whitener, Robert E.
Whitener, Roy H.
Whitener, Samuel
Whitener, Zora Babe
Whitener, Henry E.
Whitener, Sidney O.
Whittle, Charles A.
Whitworth, Robert V.
Wilfong, Henry B.
Wilforng, John Edwin
Winkinson, Carl B.
Wilkinson, Jesse G.
Wilkinson, Willie O.
Wilson, Clarence Lee
Wilson, John S.
Wilson, Joseph
Wilson, Mathew M.
Wilson, Robert E.
Wilson, Robert P.
Wilson, Sidney Clyde
Wilson, Thomas R.
Wilson, William L.
Winebarger, Garland
Winkler, Henry
Winters, Morrison M.
Witherspoon, Burgan L.
Witherspoon, Clarence B.
Witherspoon, Edgar H.
Witherspoon, Ivey A.
Woods, Azor C.
Woodward, William R.
Workman, Logan D.
Wright, Samuel E.
Wright, Thomas E.
Yoder, Monroe C.
Yoder, Edwin Moses
Yoder, Eli Charles
Yoder, Grady P.

CATAWBA COUNTY

Yoder, Henry C.
Yoder, Peter L.
Young, Brantley
Young, Theodore
Yount, Clarence E.
Yount, Garland E.
Yount, James G.
Yount, James L.
Yount, Joseph H.
Yount, Raymond E.
Yount, Robert R.
Yount, Vance E.
Yount, William Vance
Yount, Wortha A.

Enlisted Men (colored)—

Honor Roll—
Ader, Anderson L.

Wounded in action—
Hildebrand, Fred M.

Additional—

Abernethy, Blair James
Abernethy, James H.
Angle, Sherilly
Baker, Preston
Bost, Nathaniel
Bowers, Reevese
Brown, Readise
Bullock, Jim
Burton, Henry Casakay
Bryan, Casey
Chambers, Dennis O.
Clark, Albert H.
Clark, Martin L.
Clark, Sylvester
Cloninger, Ezra
Conner, Coot
Cook, Marion B.
Coulter, Alexander
Coulter, Daniel G.
Coulter, David
Coulter, George E.
Covington, Albert
Cowan, Charlie R.
Crider, Frank
Davidson, Ben M.
Davidson, Charlie
Dula, Roosevelt
Fish, Julius William Guy
Foreny, Frank J.
Furgason, Charlie
Gabriel, Erastus
Gabriels, Fred A.
Gaither, James
Goforth, George
Harper, Lewis
Harris, James E.
Hartsoe, James P.
Hill, Berry
Hill, Dock
Holdsclaw, Will
Hooper, Guy R.
Hooper, Tate H.
Hoover, Arater
Hull, Hubert W.
Ikard, Henry Clyde
Ikerd, Less
Johnson, William E.
Jolly, Ike
Lore, Eddie
Lutz, Robert Russel
Mace, Brice
Mahaffey, Furman
McCombs, Clanzelle
McCree, George
Pikcingpack, Thomas J.
Powell, John H.
Propest, Noah
Ramseur, Mart F.
Reel, Harrison
Reinhardt, Robert D.
Rhinehardt, Robert McK.
Roach, Cornelius
Robinson, Jacob
Rowe, Will
Sherrill, John W.
Sherrill, Rome

Shuford, Artis
Shuford, Perry
Shuford, Vance M.
Smith, Arthur
Smith, Ralph
Smyre, Fritz
Smyre, William H.
Thomas, Randolph C.

Transou, John
Turner, Harley C.
Wallace, Fred Henry
Whitener, Dess
Wilson, Ray
Witherspoon, James
Wright, Dixon
Yount, Henry M.

Navy:

Officers—
  Ballew, Ralph Dewey, Ensign
  Councill, Howrad Folk, Lt
  Long, Andrew Theodore, Rear Admiral
  Watts, Steve Lewis

Enlisted Men (white)—
Honor Roll—
  Hunsucker, James Carl, S 1-C
  Lail, George D, ———
  Dellinger, Junius Logan, S 1-C

Additional—
  Abernethy, Craig Lee
  Abernethy, Frank Marion
  Allen, Frank Field
  Attwood, Geter Pritchard
  Barger, Walter Dallas
  Barger, Aaron Seth
  Beck, Daniel Frederick
  Beck, Henry Grady
  Bohannon, John Neil
  Biggerstaff, Joyce Olf
  Bollinger, Grady Earl
  Bolick, Walther Trexel
  Bolch, Charles Carroll
  Bradshaw, Velma Coral
    (Female)
  Bradshaw, James Hugh
  Burns, Noah Claud
  Clark, Nerie David
  Cloninger, Robert Lee
  Crawford, Thomas Jefferson
  Crawford, Claude Ernest
  Dula, George
  Edmisten, Ross Frederick
  Ekard, Walter Burns
  Ervin, John Franklin
  Flowers, Ralph George

  Fritz, Robert Leslie
  Frye, Claude Franklin
  Frye, Thomas Jefferson
  Gregory, James Hade
  Hallman, John Wesley
  Hewitt, Vernon Claude
  Hines, James Burwell
  Hines, Rueal Bunion
  Huffman, Arthur Davis
  James, Robert William
  Johnson, Arabella
  Jones, William Thomas
  Kennedy, Clyde Earnes
  Lowe, Thomas Lee
  McGinnis, Lee F.
  Moehlmann, Gustav W.
  Reinhardt, Frank A.
  Rhinehardt, Laurie
  Rockett, Olin Ray
  Rowe, John Clarence
  Seabock, Hugh
  Sherrill, Joe E.
  Starnes, William E.
  Sox, Jason Loy
  Taylor, Frank Bryan
  Watson, Edgar L.

CATAWBA COUNTY 409

Weatherly, Lyston
West, John Oliver
Whitener, William E.

Wilson, James Robert
Johnson, Joseph H.
Pharr, John Leonard

Marines:

Officers—
Mott, Thomas A., Major

Enlisted Men (white)—
Beatty, Ural Jackson
Deaton, Oscar Claudius
Dellinger, Jacob Cedric
Gabriel, William Gilbert
Long, Edmund Showalter

Menzies, Donald Stuart
Price, James Robert
Seabock, Earle
Shuford, James C.
Shuford, Richard H.

Nurses:

Abernethy, June
Crowell, Lillie H.
Hamrick, Mabel K.
Josey, Ethel M.

Penney, Frances Woodrow
Setzer, Maude B.
Wicker, Ruth

With the ending of the war, Catawbans and their fellow countrymen celebrated as would be expected. Contemporaries remember the eventful September morning when the county's church bells and factory whistles announced at the eleventh hour that the world's bitterest conflict had ended. Many celebrations were staged for returning heroes, an especially memorable one being Hickory's welcome of May 8, 1919. On this day, a miniature Arch of Triumph was built near the railway depot, through which the happy soldiers and sailors marched to meet their loved ones.

Concerning the thrilling occasion, Mrs. C. C. Bost expressed poetically:

"Welcome, our heroes! Welcome home
    "to hearts so true!
"Welcome, thrice welcome! All hearts
    "honor you
"Who in Life's fair morning marched without
    "one backward glance—
"Service flags adorning—to the fields of France.
"Welcome, thrice welcome! Heart and voice in song
    "we raise.
"Lauding our heroes in our songs of praise.

"Your country called you, forth you fared
  "so brave and strong
"Bright, bold and fearless—on your lips
  "a song.
"When we watched you leaving how we fought
  "the gathering tears,
"Fearing War's bereaving or long cruel years.
"No more War's hardships, take the victor's
  "crown you've won!
"Heaven's richest blessings fall on each
  "brave son.
"We will still remember, long as life—and mem'ry last
"How our gallant heroes to the right held fast.
"Yet in our greetings, pause that one
  "fond tear be shed
"For valiant heroes whom we call 'the dead,'—
"Who in far off Flanders, where the bright,
  "red poppies blow,
"They are sleeping under 'crosses row on row.'
"Rest ye, brave heroes! Rest ye, for
  "the victory's won,
"Rest ye, brave heroes! for your work
  "is done."

World-wise, the First War brought the following results: Nationalism was strengthened on the continent. Economic and social reforms were initiated throughout the continent, but not with uniform success in all countries. The United States emerged as the strongest industrial and financial power in the world. And Europe's domination of world affairs lessened.

The events of the next generation showed that Germany was only temporarily weak, for the country renewed the war again in 1939.

The Second World War, which includes American participation after December 8, 1941, was dreaded sincerely by Catawbans, and by Americans generally. It came, nevertheless, and was accepted patriotically.

Those who assisted with its winning have not been listed by official government offices as yet, so the presentation of a roster of the brave men who fought it cannot be presented. But those

CATAWBA COUNTY

who made the supreme sacrifice, recorded sorrowfully by their relatives and friends at home, are these:

Abernethy, Julius F., Sgt
Alley, Sidney Vernon, Lt
Allmon, Herbert, PFC
Anderson, Robert Ervin, RT2
Arndt, Augustus L., Capt
Arndt, Fred H., T-4
Asherbraner, Cecil, Pvt.
Austin, Herman C., Lt
Barb, James E., 1st Lt
Barnette, Howard M., Pvt
Beatty, Willard, T-4
Benfield, James P., Pvt
Black, Robert Bruce, 1st Lt
Bolch, Cyril C., Jr., Pvt
Bolick, Berman W., Pvt
Bolick, Charles M., Pvt
Bolick, Charlie P., PFC
Bost, Joe, Sgt
Bowman, Glenn, S-2C
Bridges, Austin R., Pvt
Brittain, Coone M., Pvt
Brown, Frank, Pvt
Bruner, Warren Dixon, S-1c
Buchanan, William C., Lt
Bumgarner, Fred Lewis, Lt
Burke, John Taylor, PFC
Burney, Duncan L., Jr., Cpl
Burns, Clifton W., PFC
Burris, Cletus L., Sgt
Caldwell, Charles Fay, Pvt
Caldwell, Clinton W., S-Sgt
Campbell, Daniel Marshall, S-Sgt
Canipe, Jolly P., T-5
Carpenter, Bobby James, Pvt
Chronister, Paul J., Pvt
Clarke, A. G., PFC
Cline, Vernon Hugh, PFC
Coffee, Earl C., Pvt
Connor, A. A., Pvt
Connor, James B., Pvt
Cook, Hugh Oliver, SF 2c
Cook, M. B. Jr., Lt
Coulter, Donald Milton, Lt
Cunningham, James T., Jr., Capt
Dagenhardt, Roosevelt, PFC
Davis, James, Pvt
Davis, James Howard, Pvt
Decker, Lester Paul, S-1c
Divenney, Percy E., Ens.
Eades, Ransom Edgar, S 2-c
Eckard, Eugene Ralph, PFC
Eckard, Wilson Clarence, Cpl
Edwards, Clinton Sigmon, T-Sgt
Ervin, Jennings B., PFC
Ervin, Robert M., Sgt
Frye, Clyde H., Lt
Frye, James Wayne PFC
Gantt, Marvin L., PFC
Gilbert, Austin F., PFC
Green, Edgar, S-1c
Gross, Monroe, S-Sgt
Hammond, Frank B., Jr., Sgt
Hart, A. V., Pvt
Hauser, John N., Jr., Capt
Hawn, Iris Leland, Pvt
Hedrick, Paul H., CBM FC
Heffner, Clifford R., Pvt
Hefner, Wade, Pvt
Hendricks, T. C., USCG
Herman, John W., S-Sgt
Hilton, Berlin, S 1-c
Hilton, Wilson W., S 1c
Hoke, Roscoe M., Cpl
Hollar, Thurston, T-5
Hooper, Benjamin, Pvt
Houston, Gus, Pvt
Howell, Marion R., PFC
Huffman, Guy R., PFC
Hudson, Dudley W., S-Sgt
Icard, George Forest, Jr., Pvt
Icard, Frederick M., PFC
Icard, Paul, S-Sgt
Ingle, Jacob Edward, PFC
Isenhour, Bascom M., Sgt
Isbell, William D., Cpl
Isenhour, Charles L., T-Sgt
Isenhour, William W., S-Sgt
Jenkins, James L., Sgt
Jenkins, Leonard, Sgt
Johnson, Clyde Hoey, T-Sgt
Johnson, Floyd C., PFC
Johnson, Julian M., Pvt
Johnson, Orus, Sgt

Kaylor, Vernon Ray, S-Sgt
Kirksey, Charles, PFC
Kistler, Henry Alfred, PFC
Lackey, Vernon H., Jr., Lt
Lail, Charles S., Lt
Lail, Henry A., Pvt
Lawrence, John Dixon, Lt
Lee, Coy C., PFC
Leonhardt, Raymond L., PFC
Lewis, R. P., Sgt
Lindsay, Forest E., PFC
Lineberger, James Arlee, PFC
Little, Felix A., Lt
Little, Peter Philip, Pvt
Loftin, Foy Max, PFC
Lowman, Lloyd J., Sgt
Lowrance, Oswald G., PFC
Lutz, Loy, Cpl
Lynn, Donald J., Pvt
Mayberry, Seth, Sgt
McCaslin, Roy Keith, Pvt
McLeod, James Edwin, Pvt
Menzies, Kenneth Ferguson, Pvt
Middleton, Espey M., Cpl
Miller, William Garland, Pvt
Moose, Ernest Johnson, R 1-c
Morrow, Boyd Deal, PFC
Myers, Reichard Scott, PFC
Nance, Joseph Taylor, A. S.
Newton, Oscar R., Pvt
Norman, Claude, PFC
Overcash, Glenn Long, PFC
Parham, James W., Sgt
Pharr, Lewis H., Sgt
Phillips, Greely C., S. Sgt
Poovey, Marion L., Cpl
Propst, Robert L., S-Sgt
Propst, Thomas H., Pvt
Pruett, Buck H., PFC
Rader, George Andrew, Major
Richard, Howard, Pvt
Richard, Wilburn K., Pvt
Roberts, Walter J., Pvt
Rockett, Marshall Aubrey, F-O

Savoid, Robert, Pvt
Scronce, Ralph, PFC
Scronce, Vernon, Pvt
Self, Olin Franklin, Cpl
Setzer, Harvey Clarence, T-5
Shelton, Jerome Harold, PFC
Sherrill, Boyce, PFC
Shook, Claude Eugene, PFC
Shook, Harold Calvin, PFC
Sides, Wm. Arney, S 1-c
Sigmon, Carl J., PFC
Sigmon, Carter Enloe, Ch. Com. S.
Sigmon, Floyd A., PFC
Sigmon, Jack Pinkney, Pvt
Sigmon, Robert A., Pvt
Sigmon, Robert Stamey, Lt
Simmons, D. E., Jr., AMM 1c
Sloop, Howard Flake, S-Sgt
Smith, Charles Eugene, S 1-c
Smith, Clark Leroy, Cpl
Smith, William H., PFC
Spencer, Odis Odell, PFC
Stewart, Rome W., Pvt.
Taylor, Hugh J., S 2-c
Thompson, Paul W., PFC
Tuttle, Edgar W., Cadet
VanHorne, John P., PFC
Walker, John D., Lt
Walls, William Charlie, Pvt
Ward, Albert Lee, Pvt
Warren, Bryan Little, S 1-c
Whitener, Alfred P., Col
Whitener, Richard M., PFC
Wilfong, Albert Corpening, Sr. PFC
Wilhelm, Early Lewis, PFC
Wilkinson, Clarence A., Jr., C 3-c
Winters, George E., S-Sgt
Wise, Albert Cecil, PFC
Yount, Junius H., Lt
Yount, Zeb Hampton, Jr., Cpl
Zerden, Glenn, Lt

The Korean conflict, so lately experienced, still stuns the citizenry of Catawba county. Although an armistice has been signed, Catawbans are unsure of its meaning, and are solemn in their judgment of the future.

CHAPTER XVIII

MORALS AND MANNERS

Interesting episodes in the lives of Catawbans cannot always be classified categorically for historical purposes.

Yet, it is the habits and customs of people, preferably described by their neighbors, which create the most interesting portions of local histories.

To prepare such a writing, the reminiscences of a few outstanding citizens, who possibly foresaw a need for such material later and diligently recorded the happenings of their day in local periodicals, are the principal source. To such contributors to Catawba county's history text, the appreciative reader owes much gratitude.

Some incidents herewith are factual, and others are legendary. All, however, present a fascinating picture of an area that develops admittedly through trial and error.

A historical pageant, "The Building of Catawba," thrilled countians and their friends in 1925, when it was presented at the fair grounds in Hickory. The pageant was written and produced by Mrs. Pearl Setzer Deal.

(A portion of the pageant's prologue, entitled "In Beautiful Carolina," follows:

"Behold, ye people of Catawba County,
"The building of your present wealth and power.
"A rock foundation did your fathers lay
"That you might e'er the stronger, nobler build.
"O mark you well the struggle, toil, and blood
"That gave to you this land of strength and beauty:
"The land that yields your shelter, clothing, food;
"The streams that turn your wheels and give you light;
" 'Tis Carolina's choicest garden spot
"In the foothills of the Blue Ridge Mountains. . . ."

One of the early defendants of a Catawba county court, one Amos Sweat, is recorded as having felt the lash of the whip due to conviction of crime.

The fall term of the 1850 Catawba county court, according to historical data, included the following case:

"State Vs. Amos Sweat—

"The prisoner Sweat is at the bar and is arrainged and upon his arraingment pleas not guilty. The prosecuting officer enters a nolle Prosequi to the first count in the bill of indictment.

"The following jury sworn and charged, vis: Manuel Robinson, John Killian, Adam Gross, David Warlick, Henry Cansler, Arch Ray, Henry Huffman, George Smyre, David Fisher, George Bowman, John Bibbs and Valentine Lore.

"Who found the defendant guilty in manner and form as charged in the bill of indictment of the felony and grand larceny. The prisoner at the bar being asked why sentence of death should not be pronounced against him—Prays his benefit of clergy; which is extended unto him.

"It is ordered by the Court that the Sheriff of this Court take the prisoner at the bar to the public whipping post between the hours of three and four o'clock and there give him thirty-nine lashes on his bare back and then confine (him) in jail for the space of fifteen days and then take him to the whipping post at the expiration of said time and give him thirty-nine lashes more on his bare back and then he be discharged from custory upon payment of the cost in this (case) and if he be found in this county, at the (next) County Court, that the Sheriff retake him unto his custody and on Tuesday of the County Court that he take him to the public whipping post and there give him thirty-nine lashes more on his bare back."

Catawba county's first and only stocks, pillory and whipping post were constructed by Jonas Bost, who was paid $20 by the county.

R. Vance Whitener, local historian has recorded in his "Tales of Our Ancestry in Catawba County, North Carolina," interesting facts concerning principally his ancestors. Following are some which shed light on the advent here of Heinrich Weidner, one of Catawba county's earliest pioneers.

"Heinrich Weidner Comes to America.

"You will now learn your name. (Whitener's history was written for his kin primarily.)

"The great-great-great-great-grandfather, whose name you bear, arrived in Philadelphia on the ship Molly, October 17, 1741. In the book which Paul and Matthias Barringer afterwards signed, his name appears as Johan Heinrich Weydner. But fifty years later he signed Henrich Weidner at the bottom of his will, and it is so written on his tombstone. In either case he probably pronounced it Hine-rish Wide-ner, while we today call him Henry Whitener.

"It is a tradition of the family that he was a native of that part of Germany known as Saxony. This fact, the account of Colonel Yoder, and the appearance of his grandsons and great-grandsons, whom I knew, leads me to believe that he had blue eyes and yellow hair. The size of his rifle and the life he led in his young days is proof that he was a very large strong man.

"After landing at Philadelphia he lived for several years in Pennsylvania, where he met many old friends and made new ones. No doubt he learned to know John Paul Barringer and often talked with him of the good land and fine climate of Western North Carolina.

"During his sojourn in Pennsylvania he had made for himself a rifle, his signed order for which is still in the hands of the descendants of the gunsmith who made it. This famous firearm has its place in the history of the state and you must know more about it.

"It is more than six feet long and so heavy that only a very strong man can hold it out. It is so constructed that it will shoot either an ounce bullet or buckshot. It is loaded at the nozzle instead of at the breech, like a modern rifle. First, a charge of powder is poured into the barrel. A bit of cloth, greased with tallow, called 'bullet-patch,' is placed over the muzzle. The bullet is placed on the patch and thrust barely inside the barrel. The patch is then cut off even with the end of the gun and the whole is pushed down on the powder with a rod of tough hickory, called a 'ram-rod.' The rod is pulled out and put to its place under the long barrel.

"At the breech is drilled a tiny hole. Just under this is a small spoon-shaped 'pan' which has a hinged cover. On the edge of the cover nearest the hammer a bar of hard steel stands upright.

"When powder is poured into the pan and the cover in place, the gun is said to be 'primed.' When the hammer, which is fitted with a small flint, is pulled back, the gun is 'cocked' and ready to shoot. Hence, the saying that when one is all ready for anything, he is 'cocked and primed.'

"When the trigger is pulled, the flint in the hammer strikes the steel bar, knocking out a shower of sparks. At the same time it lifts the cover of the pan and exposes the powder, which is exploded by the sparks. The powder in the pan sets off the powder inside the rifle and drives out the bullet. If the powder is wet, or the tiny holes are not entirely filled with the grains, the gun does not fire. It may burn in the little pan, but it does no good unless the fire runs through the little holes to the powder inside. Hence the saying about some undertaking that is never finished that it is a 'flash in the pan.'

"You now understand why the pioneers were such good marksmen. It took several minutes to prime and load. Therefore every shot had to count. They often had practice on muster days and at 'shooting matches.' Being often in danger from Indians or wild animals, they were careful of their aim and shot to hit the mark. The powder was carried in a 'powder horn,' a receptacle fashioned from the horn of a cow. The large end was tightly stopped with a block of hard wood, the other end had a small hole stopped with a wooden plug. The bullets or shot were carried in a long slender pouch of leather, called a 'bullet pouch.' The powder and shot were measured for loading in a small wooden vessel about the size of a thimble, called a charger. Powder horn, bullet pouch, and charger were all fastened on a strap which swung from the right shoulder across the body to the left side. On the right side hung a hunter's horn, or a game bag, or sometimes both. A long knife in a leather scabbard was fastened to a belt around the waist. A hunting suit of heavy coarse cloth, or of the skins of animals, completed the outfit of the hunter and explorer of a hundred and seventy years ago (written in 1915 and 1916). It was with such weapons that your ancestors drove the Indians across the mountains into Tennessee, whipped twice their number of Tories at Ramsour's Mill, captured Ferguson's Army at King's Mountain, and made it so hot for them at Guilford Court House that they left North Carolina forever."

"Heinrich Weidner the Explorer.

"The country around Philadelphia was too crowded for the big Saxon who, like Daniel Boone, wanted more 'elbow room.' A few Germans had already settled in the Carolinas, and it is likely that he often heard from travelers of the unexplored lands to the Southward. Whatever the reason, he determined to see for himself what kind of a country it was. . . .

"Imagine him then beginning his journey in the fall of 1745, a big ruddy faced man astride a large long-legged horse. Across the saddle bow was the great rifle; behind him, his blankets and tools. With the eager hounds barking and leaping with joy, and with friends sending messages and letters to far-away kindred, he was a picturesque figure as he made his way through the scattered settlements of Pennsylvania on his five-hundred-mile ride to the South. . . .

"Traveling thus, he finally reached North Carolina. In and around the little village of Salisbury, which was then in Bladen county, lived some German settlers. But here the best land had all been taken up ahead of him. Along the eastern side of the Catawba River the English and Scotch settlers had bought all the best land. These people had come up the river from the older settlements in Lancaster county in South Carolina and Mecklenburg county in North Carolina. . . .

"Weidner crossed the Catawba River into an unknown land. He continued to ride through the dense forest toward the sunset until he reached the South Fork of the Catawba. Following this stream toward its source, he found where it divides. Then for about two miles he followed the east fork which to this day is called Henry river after Henry Whitener, its discoverer. At this point he built his winter camp. . . .

"During this first winter he traveled far and wide, exploring the South Fork valley and gathering a great quantity of furs. He learned to speak the Indian language and to live like them. His hunting suit wore out before the springtime and he had another made of deer skin with the hair turned in. With a coon skin he made himself a warm cap, leaving the striped tail sticking out on top to wave and nod as he walked. His shoes were moccasins made by the Indians of the thickest part of the deer's hide.

"In the spring as soon as the weather turned warm enough to allow him to camp in the open without discomfort, he packed his skins in bundles. Tying them with thongs of deer skin, he strapped them across his horse. With the bridle over his arm, he set out on his northward journey on foot. On the return trip he collected letters from the settlers for their friends in Pennsylvania. When he arrived about a month later, he was a welcome guest with his letters and stories of his life among the savages. And who knows but that one of the most interested listeners was Katrina Mull, a little girl then of only about twelve years old? To her and the other children he was quite a hero in his suit of skins and 'coon skin cap.

"Soon after his arrival, he took his pack to a merchant in Philadelphia and sold it for a handsome sum of money. He remained in Pennsylvania all summer, preparing for another expedition. . . .

"The First Settlement in Catawba County.

"It is a tradition of the family that Heinrich Weidner spent four or five winters in the Indian Country and 'was wont to go back to the civilized world each Spring, carrying his pelts on pack horses.' He lived with the Indians in peace. They seem to have been of a more peaceful disposition than those further west, for during this period he had no trouble with them whatever. They were also Cherokees, and not Catawbas, as one might suppose from the name of the county and river. (Historians are of the opinion that a majority of the Indian population of the Catawba area was in the section likely were stragglers from the Cherokee Nation, which generally occupied the mountainous sections west of the Catawba area.)

"During this time he made some special friends among them who were afterwards of great service to him. He brought them presents of hatchets and tools, always paid them good prices for their furs, dealing as honestly with these simple people as with the wiser white men in Philadelphia. They, in turn, taught him to live in the woods like they did, and to find his way through the dense forests like a red man. He explored the country to the westward as far as the mountains. . . .

"In the year 1749, he bought his first tract of land from the King of England. He brought with him his young wife he had married whose maiden name was Katrina, or Catherine, Mull. She was only sixteen years old while he was thirty-two. This time they came in a big covered wagon, bringing with them tools and everything necessary for a frontier home.

"Having now a pretty young wife, he could not live in a hut. The first task, therefore, was to build a house. This was now possible because he now had tools and help.

"The early settlers always built their houses near a spring to save digging a well. But Weidner did more; he built his directly over one. First he enclosed the spring with a stone wall about six feet high. This wall and the chimney he built is still standing. . . .

"Not long afterward Katrina's brother, Abram Mull, who had married Mary Poffh, came with his bride to settle near them. They built their house on Weidner's land only a short distance away, so they would not be lonesome or afraid. . . .

"The Indian Massacre.

"The little colony were living quietly in their frontier homes when the French and Indian Wars, which spread from Canada to Georgia, broke out. Far away from the other settlements, they heard nothing of the great battles that were being fought. The Indians in Catawba had always been Weidner's friends, and remained so even during this struggle. But back in the mountains lived the greater portion of the Cherokees, a fierce and cruel tribe who had gone on the war path, while our ancestors suspected no danger.

"One afternoon Mary Mull went down to the river, which was about a half a mile from her home, to drive up the cows which generally pastured there. She had started them home and was following at a distance, picking wild flowers by the way and humming a little song. She was very happy in her home in the wilderness, and she had not a care in the world. Suddenly, the cows turned and ran back past her. Thinking some wild animal had scared them, she was herself frightened.

"Slipping cautiously through the woods to where the cows had turned about, she was horrified to see her home in flames, and some Indians in war paint and feathers, dancing around it. Back she raced until she was well out of sight, and taking a round-about way through the forest, made her way to Weidner's house. Slipping through the gate, she called to him.

"When he heard her story, he quickly barred the gate and prepared for a siege. For some reason he never learned, the Indians did not attack him that night. Perhaps they had heard the reputation of the long rifle that never missed, or thought it impossible to climb over the stockade. Or it is possible that they were satisfied with what they had already done.

"Fearing they would make a night attack and find some way in the darkness to set his house on fire also, as soon as it was dark he gathered the women and children together and slipped out the gate to the small stream nearby. They did not yet know the fate of Mary's husband and child.

"They followed the little stream to the river, and then down the river they went through the thick cane brake in the awful darkness, to a cave on the hill side near the bank. Under this shelter the women and children spent the night. Poor Mary Mull slept not at all because she was sure her husband and child had met a horrible fate. Neither did Weidner sleep, but sat out before the cave the live long night, his watch dogs beside him and the rifle cocked and primed. The savages might find him and murder the whole party, but he was determined to sell his life dearly.

"But he had outwitted them. They did not find his hiding place. As soon as the sun arose, he ordered the women to stay in the cave and started back to his home. Slipping through the forest noiselessly as any Indian, he finally reached Mull's ruined home. And what a heart-rending sight! There lay the father dead, and the poor little baby alive but scalped like its father! There was no sign of the savages who appeared to have molested nothing else but some cattle they had either driven off or killed.

"He took the wounded child in his arms and went to his own house. He hitched his horse to the wagon and drove as near the cave as possible and left them. What a horrible story he had to tell the poor widow Mull when he gave her the little mutilated baby! It lived for over a week before death ended its misery.

"As soon as possible, the fugitives entered the big wagon and fled southward. We do not know why they went in this direction, but there could be several reasons. That course took them away from the last sign of the savages. Then Weidner probably dreaded the treacherous ford at Adam Sherrill's where he would also be at a great disadvantage if attacked. Again, it may have been raining and he was afraid the river would be too high to cross. At any rate, he never stopped in his southerly course until he reached the settlement which is now Lancaster, S. C., a hundred miles from his home. Here his family and the widow Mull lived for two years with a Robinson family. Thus was formed the friendship between the Weidner and Robinson families and explains the fact that today the 'home place' of Father Weidner is now owned by a Robinson instead of a Whitener.

"Jesse Robinson married one of the daughters who died without heirs. Father Weidner gave Robinson a deed to the home place."

"The Red Mark of Honor.

"Having found a safe refuge for his women and children, Weidner did not sit idly by, doing nothing. He immediately made preparations to go back and see what harm the savages had done to his home. Taking a few necessities, he started out on horseback once more, following the trail he had made in his flight. He found everything burned to the ground.

"Here he met some of his Indian friends. They told him that it was unsafe for any white man in that part of the country because the Cherokees in large numbers were still on the war path and would kill without mercy any 'pale face' they found.

"The chief of the tribe, who called him brother, assured him protection, but advised him to return to Lancaster and remain until the war was over. Because Weidner had always dealt honorably with him and his tribe, he made a promise that so long as the country was unsafe for 'pale faces,' he would have some of his warriors keep a young white oak tree standing near the ruined fort painted red. By this sign Weidner could at any time learn, by slipping back, whether or not the Cherokees were still angry with the white men. The tree trunk remained red for two years.

"A Hair-Breadth Escape.

"On one of his scouting expeditions from South Carolina, Weidner brought with him a young man by the name of Warlick. This was Warlick's first trip into the wilderness, and he was not provided with as good a horse as he should have been. He thoroughly enjoyed his journey with the experienced frontiersman who was now about forty-four years old. Our ancestor could tell him many stories of both the old world and the new. The time passed rapidly and they reached the forks of the river in a few days.

"As they approached the site of the ruined fort they rode very carefully, watching for the hostile Indians. The war was now over, but there was still danger from roving bands of warriors.

"They were almost in sight of the white oak tree when they were discovered by such a band, who did not for an instant leave them in doubt as to their feelings. All bedecked in war paint and feathers, at sight of the white men they rushed toward them. Weidner, who no doubt was a believer in the adage that 'he who fights and runs away may live to fight another day,' turned his horse about and shouted to Warlick who followed as fast as his horse could carry him. The howling savages followed close behind.

"In that country the upland was firm, affording sure footing for a horse, but along the small streams where low places that at a distance looked solid enough but were really treacherous bogs and swamps. Weidner knew this and led the way on the firmer ground, shouting to Warlick to follow him. He was skirting one of these bogs some distance ahead of the young man who could scarcely keep up. Thinking he could take a short cut and make up the lost ground, Warlick turned his horse straight across the swamp. He had gone but a little way when his horse mired in the soft mud.

"He leaped off and tried to lead the animal out. But it was too late. The Indians, seeing his plight, yelled in triumph and pounced upon him. He leveled his rifle at the howling savages and fired. But he was too excited to take aim and he missed. Weidner, hearing the shot, stopped and turned about just in time to see his young friend go to his death, fighting to the last, using his rifle as a club.

"Not satisfied with killing one white man, the Indians now started after the big Saxon. He waited until they were in range of the great rifle, and taking deliberate aim, fired. A yelling savage fell dead, but the others, having learned in the long war that he would not be able to shoot again before re-loading, now redoubled their efforts to catch him. But Weidner did not propose to be caught. They chased him for miles so closely that he had no chance to re-charge the long rifle. Then it was that he was thankful for the powerful lungs and long legs of his good horse, which carried him to safety.

"To this day the bones of the young Warlick lie in an unknown swamp, though I have heard my grandfather say that he was killed on what is now called the 'Babel Whitener' farm."

"The Return of the Fugitives.

"After about two years, the trunk of the white oak tree was no longer red, and our ancestor knew that he could safely return. With the women and children in the wagon, he made his way through the wilderness back to his home.

"Here he found everything in ashes and all his cattle gone. He had to start again from the beginning. But now he was not alone. To him came Conrad Yoder, who was born in Switzerland but spoke the German language. There also arrived from Pennsylvania George Wilfong, another of your ancestors, who was then about twenty-two years of age. These two young men stayed with Weidner for several years and were a great help to him in re-building his home.

"This was built on the old foundation with the spring under the house like the first. But with such good help, he built larger and better than before. He needed a larger house for his boys and girls were growing up, and now that the country was becoming safe, visitors were becoming frequent. Weidner's house was always open to those who needed shelter. The road he also made from Adam Sherrill's is called in the Colonial Records and in act of the legislature, 'the road to Henry Whitener's'. This was an open road to all who came into the new country and at its end was a cordial welcome.

"These new comers no doubt at one time or another all made their headquarters at the home of the 'King of the Forks,' as they called him, while they looked around for a good place to settle. Of these, several were your ancestors, among whom were

Boston Cline, Matthias Barringer, John Dellinger, and George Wilfong.

"As Colonel Yoder says, everybody came to Henry Whitener's and it was a famous gathering place for the settlers all around. They called him 'Father Weidner' because he was older and more experienced in frontier life. With his princely estate of ten thousand acres, he was by far the wealthiest man among them. He had picked out the best land in the country and the rich soil produced abundant crops with little labor.

"With all his wealth he was simple and unassuming, hospitable to rich and poor alike. Modest and gentle in the true sense of the word, he never made even the humblest of his neighbors feel inferior. In this he showed the spirit of the true gentleman, who, assured of his position and influence, has not the need or desire for vulgar display of wealth or noisy assertion of superiority. As he had dealt fairly with the Indians, he likewise lived honored among his white friends, and to this day, wherever you find his descendants, they proudly claim their kinship with Heinrich Weidner.

The first combat of the mat that white man ever held in Western North Carolina traditionally involved Weidner and a young Scotchman by the name of McDowell. A featured account of the legend was written by Mrs. Mabel Miller Rowe for The Hickory Daily Record, as follows:

"With the increased price of real estate and building costs home seekers are proned to look back upon the good old days in Catawba county when all that was necessary to secure a government grant was to build a rude hut and hang an ordinary tin coffee pot and frying pan on a nail on the wall.

"Henry Blackburn of the Blackburn school community, southwest of Hickory, is author of the 'coffee pot' story. Mr. Blackburn is one of the older residents of his community and before the days of rural free delivery he served as postmaster at Blackburn when it was on star route.

"In the old days, Mr. Blackburn said, a pioneer settler, in order to secure a grant or 'homestead,' had to mark off the land he wanted by chipping the bark off of trees with an axe. Then he had to build a rude hut—possibly six by eight feet—and place therein a frying pan and a coffee pot. These were hung on a nail that had been driven in the wall for that purpose.

"The 'homesteader' then went about his business and lived wherever he pleased until the allotted period had elapsed and the government would issue the land grant to him as the lawful owner.

"According to Mr. Blackburn, Berry Abernethy was the first man to take up a claim in what is now the Blackburn community of Catawba county.

"What is considered one of the most unusual methods of securing a tract took place in what is now Burke county when Henry Weidner, a pioneer settler of Catawba county west of the Catawba river, and a young Scotchman by the name of McDowell wrestled for a piece of land in Pleasant Gardens.

"The story often told around the old firesides and still lingering as a pleasing tradition of early days in this section, says that Weidner lost good naturedly in the bout, and helped the young man survey the coveted tract of land.

"It is told that Weidner met a man by the name of McDowell in Virginia on one of his many trips to Philadelphia from Catawba county, and spent one night at his home. They sat up half the night while Weidner told glowing tales of North Carolina and the South. Young Joseph McDowell listened to the stories with keen interest and on the following morning he informed his father that he was going South with Weidner to see the rich lands himself.

"The two set out and finally came to Weidner's home in Catawba county where they tarried overnight. Next day they left on a trip toward the Blue Mountains as the Blue Ridge was then called.

"Following the Catawba river westward they came to Pleasant Gardens, a beautiful, broad, fertile stretch of land. Weidner immediately craved ownership of the tract but the young Scotchman wanted it too and they fell into an argument about who should enter it.

"McDowell was young and active, fresh from the wrestling bouts of Virginia cornshuckings and the like, so he proposed to Weidner that they wrestle for the land. Weidner, a huge Saxon of great strength, but unused to wrestling, agreed to the Scotchman's challenge to a bout for the title to Pleasant Gardens, rightly named for its fertility. . . .

"In the end, McDowell threw Weidner by using a knee grip and thus won Pleasant Gardens. A gentleman in defeat, Weidner is said to have gladly helped McDowell survey the land which to this day belongs to the descendants of General Joseph McDowell of Revolutionary fame."

Many stories have been written and told about the old Matthias Barringer house, located about two miles east of Newton (later to become the Catawba County Library and Museum which was destroyed by fire in 1952). The house was used as the first courthouse. But none gave a more entertaining account of the pioneer social events that took place there than an anonymous writer of historical events some years back.

Who the writer is remains unsolved. A news dispatch from Newton to The Daily News, believed to be The Greensboro Daily News, was clipped and some years later came into the possession of the family of J. Milt Setzer of Hickory, direct descendants of Matthias Barringer.

The clipping, yellowed with age, bears a February 3 dateline, but there is nothing to identify the year.

The introduction to the news story points out that "a clear interesting view of pioneer days in Catawba county social life is afforded by delightfully written chapters of local history by an anonymous writer. In a recent installment the historian writes of the famous old Barringer muster ground, where the militia of this section gathered after the Revolution for many years to drill and have a good time." A broad, level field on the Barringer place was used as the muster ground.

Everybody attended these annual musters, the writer said. The festivities had a strong hold on the people of the countryside, as social affairs were few and far between in those days. Participants traveled to the grounds in carriages, on horseback, on wagons, and on foot. Thousands swarmed to the place. Those who came from a great distance camped in tents or wagons and stayed several days.

While the young men marched and drilled, said the historian, older men visited each other "discussing crops and politics and swapping horses, while the women had a grand reunion at the big house," which was the Barringer home. After the drills, there would be wrestling matches and not infrequently fights occurred. Around the campfire jokes were bandied about and now and then they doubtless brought on sudden fist-skull performances. There was plenty to eat and a number of things to drink, ranging from cider to applejack and whiskey, abundant and cheap.

After supper the better class of people, old and young, adjourned to the big hall upstairs in the Barringer house and there danced until all hours. Grandparents tripped as gaily as their youngest grandsons and granddaughters, and it is said that a Madame Huitt, who lived to be a hundred, danced as long as she could walk without a stick.

As evidence of the popularity of the Barringer Muster event, it is reported that one young Catawba county matron took her baby in arm and forded a swollen stream to take part in the affair.

The young woman was the wife of Henry Dellinger, a grandson of Pioneer Henry Weidner, she herself being a granddaughter of Captain Barringer.

She had been going to these dances at the Barringer house all her life; and after she married, she still attended the muster balls. On one occasion, Mrs. Dellinger found it necessary to travel from her home across the South Fork river, to the muster place, several miles east, alone. Taking her baby, too young to leave at home, she mounted a horse, and set out.

It had rained heavily and when she reached the South Fork, Mrs. Dellinger found it greatly swollen by flood waters. Instead of turning back, the young matron is said to have doffed her finery and strapped it into a bundle which she placed over her head, and, holding her baby above water, made her horse take the river. The animal swam across all right, and Mrs. Dellinger danced that night.

Tradition does not tell what the young husband had to say about the adventure.

At least two sessions of court were held in the upstairs of the Barringer house. The single room was said to be the largest for miles around. For some reason, Matthias Barringer consistently had refused to divide the spacious hall or room.

The house was constructed of logs and, according to the mode of the day, was mud daubed. No nails were available then and the joints were dovetailed and mortised. There were three rooms downstairs with the large single room covering the second floor. From one end of the house to the other ran a huge beam, of about 20 inches square, while at one end stood a tremendous chimney with a wide fireplace inside.

A smaller building was erected back of the old house which was used as a kitchen and dining room.

Captain Barringer enjoyed his new home only 14 years before he was scalped by the Cherokee Indians.

Rich folklore has developed about the life of "Gentleman" John Perkins, early Catawba territory settler of immense wealth and prestige. Mrs. Pearl Tomlinson describes the pioneer thus:

" 'Gentleman' John Perkins, an early settler who was a large landowner and who owned a race track on an island in the Catawba river, gained his wealth because of kindnesses to and assistance to Bishop August Gottlieb Spangenberg.

"The first record to be found concerning the colorful figure 'Gentleman' Perkins is his meeting with Bishop Spangenberg of the Moravian Brotherhood of Bethlehem, Pa., who had been commissioned to seek land in Carolina. The Brethern had bargained with the Earl of Granville, who owned vast lands in Carolina to sell them 100,000 acres of land in one body. The Bishop journeyed to Carolina where he was joined by a Mr. Churton, the general surveyor, from Edenton. He was advised by Andrew Lambert, 'a well known Scotchman' to employ the young Perkins as hunter and guide. Perkins, although only 19 years of age, was an experienced hunter and guide, having been trained by Pioneer Adam Sherrill in scouting and woods craft. Perkins came to North Carolina with the Sherrill family when he was only 14 years of age. This fact is substantiated by old Sherrill records which bear the date of 1847.

"Spangenberg later said of Perkins: 'I especially recommend John Perkins as a diligent and trustworthy man and friend of the Brethern.'

"Perkins was rewarded for his aid by receiving thousands of acres of land, much of which was in the present county of Catawba.

"W. W. Scott, in his 'Annals of Caldwell County,' states that Perkins was forced to go to South Carolina on account of trouble with the Indians. Some say he lived there for 19 years.

"He returned in 1773 and settled on his vast lands on the western banks of the great Catawba not far from Little's Ferry as Island Ford, rebuilding the home burned by the Indians. This colonial-type home was built of brick imported from England. Perkins believed in blue blood, both in men and animals. At his plantation, he raised his famous race horses, said to have been the finest horses this county has ever produced, for speed, durability, and longevity. His mansion house was so located that he could stand on his piazza and look upon his broad acres of rich bottom land and see his many servants at work and view his race horses make their four miles in the quickest time on the notable race track on the island.

"Perkins' patriotism was doubted at the outbreak of the Revolution. But, on October 17, 1775, the Committee of Safety recorded: 'Pursuant to resolve of last committee, John Perkins appeared and gave account of his political sentiments relative to American Freedom as is satisfactory. . . .'

"It is said that friends of Perkins once prevailed upon him to seek the position of President of the United States.

"Perkins and his wife were buried on the old plantation but their bodies have been removed and re-interred in the Kent plot in the Lenoir city cemetery. This was done in 1941."

That another Catawban promoted the sport of horse racing is attested to in a writing by Mrs. J. A. Isenhower. It is as follows:

"The Look Out section of Catawba County was a gay spot when the debonair sportsman and horse-trainer Jack Wilfong maintained a race-track and game preserve on a 60 acre island in the Catawba river near what was known as Island Ford, according to Perry Deal, aged Catawba county resident, who spent several days with his son, James Deal, here recently. (Written at Conover.)

"Mr. Deal, known to his friends as 'Pel' has spent his entire life within one-half mile of Bethel church in the Catfish section, where he was born the son of Lawson and Susan Deal.... When he was married to Lucy Hewitt the couple acquired 20 acres of land on the original Deal farm and here they resided until the death of his wife, when a daughter Mrs. Marshall Setzer and family came to make their home with him. At that time, Mr. Deal said, everybody selected a home location near a spring, and most homesteads of 100 years ago were located on a branch, as was the Lawson Deal place where the boy grew up.

"It was here that Perry Deal, a lad when the call to arms came in 1861, had his first glimpse of a 'Yankee' when three horsemen drove up and demanded something to eat. The father had warned the family that when the soldiers appeared they were to be treated kindly, and the boy and his mother carried out those instructions to the letter as she baked 'wheatbread' and brought sweet milk from the spring house, 'cutting down' a piece of meat, a shoulder, he said, the hams being safely hidden away. The clank of the swords made a vivid impression as the men rode away, having expressed their thanks for the repast giving the little 'confederate' no cause to be afraid.

"Southern soldiers often stopped at the Deal home in the painful march home after the surrender, Mr. Deal's father being one of the last to go because of his age. He was not called to battle, being stationed at Salisbury as a guard during the last six months of the war.

"Coming to an interesting part of his narrative Mr. Deal related the days of the race track on the Island in the Catawba, telling how Mr. Wilfong's grandmother, Mrs. Barbara Abernethy, lived in a house on a spot now covered by the waters of the Look Out Dam, how the dwelling was burned and later rebuilt by Peter Drum, the widowed daughter, Jack's mother, coming there to live with her handsome young son and several daughters, among them Mattie and Mary, the late Mrs. Shaw Yount and Mrs. John Yount of Newton.

"The old gentleman's eyes twinkled as he related the many happy occasions spent at the home, remembering especially the pies and cakes baked by Sarah, the colored mammy.

"The Wilfong house was moved onto a knoll above the Look Out Dam when waters threatened the place during the 1916 freshet, and is still standing.

"Speaking of Jack Wilfong, Mr. Deal related how the young man grew to be a polite, clever gentleman, always 'mistering old folks' and 'powerful good looking.' 'Everybody liked Jack Wilfong,' the old gentleman repeated, and from his narrative one is led to believe that 'Pel' Deal was a favorite of the young man also, as it seems he was allowed the privilege of hunting the quail and rabbits for which the young sportsman planted grain, and which were zealously protected. On the days of the races great crowds came from surrounding towns to see the blooded horses compete for honors and the countryside turned out en masse.

"While young Wilfong was a man of exceptionally fine manners he 'didn't take no dragging' according to his loyal friends, and the old man showed a genuine sorrow which has lived down through the years as he told how his young friend met a tragic death in an altercation with a group of men while enroute home from Statesville one night.

"'Pel' Deal was spending the night in Conover with his brother, Miles Deal, when word came about daylight one morning, that a man by the name of Church had been slipped out of the Newton jail by a posse of 50 men and hanged to a post-oak tree on the Mehaffey place two miles northeast of Newton. Mr. Deal and his brother visited the spot and found the man still hanging, a red handkerchief tied over his eyes and a folded paper in his pocket. The paper was said to contain a message from the hangmen. Church was said to have killed an old man and his daughter in Alexander county, robbery being the cause of the murders. According to Mr. Deal's recollections, the late Sidney Yount was sheriff of the county at that time.

"Mr. Deal remembers well when there was only one house where Hickory is now a flourishing city, Conover was a 'patch of woods' and the train only came as far as Hosea Yount's store in Claremont. The Deal boys went to this place which was also the postoffice, for war news in the 60s.

"One of a large family who all lived to a ripe age with the exception of a sister, the late Mrs. John Hollar, who it is singulary said was 'born on the 27th of September, married on the 27th of September and died on the 27th of September.' A brother, Reuben Deal, left Catawba county to settle in Mississippi and no message has come from him for more than 50 years, it being the supposition that he, with his family, succumbed to the yellow fever scourge there about that time. One sister died in Oklahoma at the age of 88, and a sister, Mrs. F. P. Moser, is at present one of Hickory's oldest residents.

Afflicted with blindness for the past 25 years, Mr. Deal is otherwise strong and alert, enjoying visits with his three sons here, Messrs. James, Thomas and Charlie Deal at frequent intervals."

Tradition has it that a record auction, or "vendue," was conducted in Catawba county in 1813. The sale of the "goods and effects" of John Mull, who apparently owned a merchandising house, was begun on February 15 and ended on August 9. Lincoln county court records contain 41 pages of lists of articles sold by the administrators of the Mull estate—Peter Mull, Henry Mull and Catharine Mull. It is supposed that Mull resided in what now is Catawba county, but no one has determined the site of his store or home. The sale netted $6,578.50¾.

Among the items sold were "red scarlet cloakes, a side saddle, sewing silk, shawls, muslic cambric, sets of knives and forks, yards of humhumg and durrant, one box window glass, frying panns, one patrol dearskin, curry combs, hatts, coffee potts, many head of livestock, one negro Fillis, one negro man Dick, one negro Bois, one negro girl Sukey, one negro boy Richard, one negro girl Lizzy, one negro woman Mary, one negro boy Dann, one negro boy Allice, one negro girl Peggy, one negro boy Isaac and one negro boy Bobb.

"Fifteen yards of fancy cord, much grain, one parceil shucks, one auger and one chisell, one draw knife, one shovelmoule, hows, sheep shears, soap dishes, pocket flasks, string of beads, one spice box, tobacco boxes, gimlets, wagons, hind geers of wagon and troughts, lead, sheeting, Bibles, spelling books, needles, wagon cloth, parcell straw, a wind mill, cueting boxes, spinning wheels, two setts of horse geers, four raw hides, one fire shovel, a piece of chain, castor oil, two hair combs, hay stacks gunflints, buttons, (much) foodstuffs, snuff boxes, Scotch thread, one-fourth pound of asafascity, hattbands, British oil, dog irons, one house clock, looking glasses, saddle bags, horse trees, bee hives, a flax basket, one rocking cradle, and some old trumpery."

The Burke county area today bears the mark of Catawbans. Ralph T. Shell explains this remark in the following article entitled "Catawbans Founded Communities in Burke County."

"By the time some pioneers were hacking out permanent homesites in Catawba county, there were others staking out claims in the areas to the north and west. For many, the stop after the hop was temporary and but a few years at most, and then another hop. They were especially pushing westward into Burke county and beyond as far and as fast as the Cherokees would permit. The experience of the Moravian Bishop Spangenburg in Quaker Meadows as early as 1752 probably led many adventurers far into Indian country, and McDowell had settled almost at the foothills in 1760. The Indians were sorely feeling the intrusions and the 'crowding' when they staged a terrific fight in 1754, and there were sporadic raids thereafter until 1776. Every boundary treaty made with them was broken by the 'pale faces.'

"When General Griffith Rutherford took an army into the mountains in 1776 to quell the Indians, he subdued their resistance in that area forever after and paved the way for 'land grabbing' in what was still legally Indian territory. Many of the men with him looked upon the new country with eager eyes, and it was not long until they began to stake out large and small entries. Their engagement in the war delayed the new communities by a few years.

"The frontiersmen in upper or northern Burke county were largely from present Catawba county. Mountain tradition has it that these men did not at first come there to make homes, but to hunt for gold, hunt game and to fish. Anyone who has eaten a mountain trout can understand why those pioneers then decided to move there. Some of the oldest stories explain excavations and mounds, some traces of which may still be seen today, as being left by the early golddiggers. Rows of small heaps, some with large trees in them, are 'Indian graves,' etc. It is entirely unsubstantiated that the mountain Cherokees ever buried their dead in such fashion. In fact, contradictory to the grave story, there was another one to the effect that the aged and the sick were thrown over a cliff.

"There was an abundance of wild game in great variety in the mountains in the early days, and immediately after the Revolution, hunting parties made extended trips up there. Such was a favorite sport and they became customary big events, along with 'shootin' matches' until after the turn of the Twentieth century. There existed a few log shacks, called lodges, in which huge logs could be burned. It was no doubt around some of those fires that many large tales were told, some of which could have flavored mountain traditions. One story still prevails of a lode of pure lead, the site of which was marked by a knife in a tree, and many natives have gone looking for the 'lead mine.' Such may be completely true, for one 1783 land grant states that it contains a 'bank of iron ore.'

"There are two communities in upper Burke county which carry names linking them directly to Catawba county pioneers. One lies at the foothills where Steels creek enters Upper creek and is called Steels creek; the other lies around the headwaters of Upper creek and is called Jonas Ridge. A pioneer on Lyle creek, Samuel Steele, had a state's grant surveyed in 1785, which lay on the south fork of Upper creek, later to become known as Steels creek. This grant also referred to a tributary stream as Adams branch, on which Phillip Adams was killed. Now, Phillip Adams had been Steele's neighbor also on Lyle creek. Alexander Harbison and Samuel Alexander were chain bearers. Already, Paul Anthony, formerly of Catawba county, had obtained land there. Whether he was the first Paul Anthony, who gave land for Anthony's church, or the son, is not clear from Col. Yoder's notes on the family. There was a Martin Anthony who got a grant on Clarks creek in 1778, who was not mentioned by Col. Yoder. He did, however, connect the Anthony and Shull families—Anthony Shull, son of Lyle creek Frederick; and, of course, the Thomas Carlton Shull later on Steels creek was of this family.

"Another early Steels creek settler was Benjamin Park, later Parks. He had a grant surveyed in 1779 on the 'south fork of Upper creek,' that is, Steels creek. He got numerous grants, some of which were in the heart of the community previously referred to as Jonas Ridge. Later, there were John Park, Thomas Park, James Park, and William Parks whose heirs had his grants surveyed in 1830. The mountain lying east of Jonas Ridge is today called 'the Park' and said to have been named for John Park who had an early land grant there.

"Jonas Ridge itself, was named after an early Lyle creek pioneer, Simon Jonas, according to the earliest mountain tradition. As an old man he was attempting to go from Steels creek across the mountains to a small settlement near the North Cove, where other early Catawbans had moved. Overcome by the winter's cold, he was assisted to a semi-shelter under the 'Jonas rock,' located near the crest of Jonas Ridge, near a field owned by Julius Barrier. His two companions then went ahead to their destination and sent back help for the 'old man.' Jacob Carpenter was one of them, but by the time they arrived, Simon Jonas was dead. It is said that natives know where he is buried.

"The earliest documentary date of this name for the mountain found so far is 1839, in a survey for George Henry Barrier, the tract lying 'on the west side of Jonases Ridg.' Now, this grantee was but a boy of about 13 at the time, being a son of Henry, who was a son of John Barrier, another early settler on Steels creek. His land was not many miles from the preceding 1839 tract. From the best information available, John was a son of Col. George Henry Barrier, who first got a King's patent in Rowan county in 1761. That location is uncertain, but he later was shown to be near the county line of Burke and Wilkes, some ten miles from Lenoir. There is a Revolutionary War record for him, and a V. A. file, W-3994, shows he was a captain in Col. Francis Locke's regiment on the Cherokee expedition into the mountains. His connection to the Abraham Barrier who with Balser Sigman received a grant on Lyle creek in 1779 has not been learned. However, Sigmans also turned up on Steels creek.

"Other names occurring by 1800 in records for Steels creek and Jonas Ridge were: Jonathan and Benjamin Ross (there may have been a Rose), Jacob Anthony, John and Joseph Dobson, Thomas and Maria Scott, Prichard (father of Buckner Pritchet), James Alexander, Richard Robertson, Henry Inman, Alexander Fox, Richard Waterhouse, and John Graham. It is not known how early George Sigman and John Jonas were there."

Catawba county has experienced two major natural disasters. One was a cyclone which swept through the Newton area on

March 25, 1884, and the other was a disastrous flood in July, 1916.

The cyclone left in its wake one person dead, several severely wounded, and untold property damage. The storm struck about five o'clock in the afternoon. It came from the southwest, a dark cloud appearing to form about three miles from Newton, which approached the town accompanied by a dull roaring sound.

The storm lasted about a minute or two, but the scene it left behind was "fearful to behold." It was estimated that within the town limits, 20 houses were completely demolished, and a large number damaged to some extent.

The first damage reported before the storm hit town on the southwest edge, was the destruction of the barns and stables belonging to W. R. Self. In the outskirts of town, on that side, several Negro homes were also damaged.

The cyclone made a path 200 yards wide through the town, sweeping across the corner of town, unroofing part of the Catawba college buildings, the home of Dr. J. A. Foil and many others. The machine shops of Cline and William were completely leveled, as was the home of a Mr. Jarrett whose wife escaped by leaping through a hole made by a falling chimney. All houses in the path were wrecked, some in peculiar ways, but some were literally splintered.

Reaching the Methodist church and cemetery, the force of the cyclone lifted the church off its foundations and scattered it for miles. The cemetery was described as a complete wreck, and not a tombstone was left standing. It was necessary for the Methodist congregation to completely rebuild and furnish a church, for virtually no furniture was salvaged.

From that point the cyclone swept on across the Snow Hill section of town and over the county toward Buffalo Shoals, gathering force as it traveled. It was said that the path increased to a mile in width, and houses, barns, crops and forests were destroyed.

About seven miles from Newton the center of the storm struck the Hunsucker home, and as it fell in on the family a board struck Miss Lucinda Hunsucker, killing her instantly.

Though the remainder of the town and county were spared the force of the cyclone, the storm caused considerable damage everywhere. Conover residents reported hail on the ground two inches deep, and the rain and hail whipped by the strong winds caused destruction that could not be estimated.

A description of the flood, which made history of dramatic import in Catawba county, as well as throughout the state, is taken from the Tuesday, July 18, 1916, issue of The Newton Enterprise:

"A storm moving northwestward from Charleston, S. C., covering most of South Carolina and cutting across North Carolina with the Charlotte section as a center, caused the greatest rainfall on record Friday night and all day Saturday, putting every stream far far out of bank and causing the most destructive flood in the history of this county. There is no way of accurately measuring the rainfall but vessels in the open measuring from 18 inches up were filled with water.

"The Catawba river rose in wild fury with a giant freshet that swept the river clean of barriers and hurled six great bridges from their high placed beds, cutting its way around the Catawba end of the Look Out dam of the Southern Power Company and liberating a lake of water ten miles long. The Horseford, Moore's ferry, C. and N-W, Southern, Buffalo Shoals and Mooresville bridges are all gone.

"Down the South Fork every bridge went by the board, it was reported yesterday, except Simpson bridge near R. L. Shuford's. Sandy Ford, Fingers and Ramseurs bridges are all gone. The Brookford bridge was cleaned away and $100,000 damage done to the Brookford cotton mill and community. The power house there was washed away.

"At Rhodhiss the dam broke and the cotton warehouse with over 200 bales of cotton went down the river, the house riding as steady as a boat while a string of cotton bales bobbed their way to nobody knows where. Dwellings, some live stock, countless logs and a forest of trees uprooted from the banks all were seen sweeping-down the stream that in its flooded might was a thing of terror to people standing safely on the hills.

"The Southern and Carolina and Northwestern, the Southern Power company, the phone and telegraph companies were all but out of commission. The first break in the Southern occurred near Oyama Saturday when no trains passed after No. 22 going east. . . .

"East of Newton the river bridge of the Southern at Catawba, built in 1901 after the flood of that year had knocked the bridge out, held until after eight o'clock Sunday morning when a part of it collapsed and a little later the rest of it went over. The great steel structure was swept off its immense concrete pillars bedded 30 feet beneath the bed of the river, bobbed up again, sank, and reappeared, the steel 'timbers' were heard snapping and cracking as if in the grip of a giant. These heavy metals can be retrieved, having moved no great distance from the bridge site.

"Below Catawba, where the roads run four miles among the low banks of the river the track is reported as gone, with cuts washed through here and there.

"The Carolina and Northwestern was hit throughout its entire length. There is no communication possible anywhere. The Catawba river bridge above Hickory, a fine steel structure that has stood for many years, was knocked from its piers. Below Newton, the track in low places was submerged, the low bridge at Maiden stripped of its girders but the cross ties held to the rails so that one could walk across. . . . On below Maiden the road was cut to pieces. Trains require an indefinite length of time and it may be several weeks before another train runs.

"No mail reached Newton after No. 11 ran Saturday and the carriers could not make their rounds Saturday, but yesterday while Numbers 2, 3, 4, and 5 attempted to serve as many patrons as possible, none could make their entire routes. No. 1 couldn't operate at all, being unable to cross Clark's creek where Battle bridge used to be.

"This stream carried off that bridge and all others on it except the one at Clarence Ikerd's. It reached from hill to hill and presented a spectacle never seen in its valley before. . . .

"Crop damage throughout the county cannot be estimated. People guess a million, two million, and then do not know whether they are near the loss. Bottom crops are supposed to be absolutely ruined, while uplands were washed very badly.

The corn crop will certainly be vastly reduced when the harvest is counted. . . .

"Hundreds of people motored to the river all day Sunday, watching it with fascination, impressed by the marvelous display of elemental strength, measured its rapid rise. Sunday and Sunday night as reports came in confirming the vast destruction to bridges and telling of the escape of the river at Lookout dam, a feeling of impotence seized on people. Never before had this part of the world experienced such a visitation. In May, 1901, and in August, 1908, there were floods which broke records that had stood for fifty years, but this time the records set by those great floods were smashed, and people wondered. . . .

"Sunday morning at ten o'clock 50 feet of the concrete dam at Look Out broke loose, up-ended and fell into the flood, and the liberated waters roared through, smashing the wing dam on the Catawba side, sending down the stream the immense flood which must have been the waters which overwhelmed the lower cotton mills. Yesterday morning, although the impounded water had rushed all night, there was still an immense pond left. Wes Covington, a colored man living near, said 204 cotton bales were counted, and 45 bales retrieved all of which again got away save six.

"So many stories were afloat yesterday it would be impossible to gather them all and today half that is written may be knocked up by fresh and accurate reports but tales told yesterday of cotton mill damage down the rivers were fierce. . . .

"A farmer named Hedgepeth living on an island at Long Island, with his wife and ten children, were completely cut off Sunday afternoon and his people were seen in their home, with the waters in ten feet of the crest of the hill, his barn and out buildings washed away, but they escaped. There were several houses at Long Island in a flat into which eddy water poured which began floating and men in a canoe went around, fastened ropes to them and anchored them to trees. The fine home of Jason Sherrill at Sherrills Ford with all its contents went down stream."

The next issue of the paper, July 21, had the following story to tell of the damage wrought:

"The Rhodhiss mill and the Brookford mill near Hickory suffered the loss of many thousands; the Long Island mill lost

$50,000 says Osborne Brown, of the company; and the famous old Monbo mill of the Turners was obliterated, with at least $100,000 loss. Henry River mill lost its dam. . . . Along the South Fork every mill was submerged and damaged but none was actually destroyed. . . .

"Out at the great Look Out dam in this county, is a scene beggaring description. Indian Catawba, held captive by Concrete, river guardian of the Paleface, bided his time like a shorn Sampson, until, gathering his strength from ten thousand sources extending to the crest of the Blue Ridge mountains, he hurled himself with titanic energy, but vainly, against the splendid fortifications that held him in bounds; and finding that futile, turned to his kinsman, Earth, in nominal league with Concrete, and Earth gave him passage. The huge dam 86 feet high stands where the engineers place it, only a fraction broken from the Western end, and you might imagine it saying, 'I did all you told me to do—but the Hill was treacherous.' Down through the Catawba hill the ten miles of impounded water four score feet depth, crushed against the Lookout barrier channel that looks to be 600 feet wide and as deep as the dam at the entrance, down to great bed boulders, making an island of the property owned by the company at the end of the dam, where Mr. York lives, leaving about two acres, and turning into the main channel below the dam. The waves swept far beyond the channel cut and in fact almost reached the Gantt dwelling far upon the hill. The water thundered through a tract of timber and what trees were not uprooted as grass, were cut as with a scythe. . . ."

Among the most entertaining writings of Major J. L. Latta in his description of life about Sparkling Catawba Springs, renowned county resort of the 1860s, 70s, and 80s. About operation aspects of the Springs, Major Latta writes:

". . . Dr. (E. O.) Elliott (owner of the development) was a progressive old gentleman, and conceived the idea that if some means of transportation better than the horse and carriage (between Hickory and the Springs) could be provided it would add greatly to the popularity of the resort. With this in view, he ordered the first steam tractor ever shipped to this section—not the caterpillar type that we now frequently see, but the old wood-burning steam tractor such as was formerly used for wheat threshing machines. It was his intention to provide a comfortable coach to be attached to the tractor, and run a regular schedule between the Springs and Hickory—meeting all trains.

"His tractor arrived in due time, and he was enthusiastic over his contemplated method of handling passengers between the two points. In order to try out the feasibility of the proposed plan, he had his 'engineer' fire up the boiler and drive up to the Piedmont Wagon Works, borrow a two-horse wagon, which was coupled to the tractor and the whole affair driven down town to the public square, where the doctor invited the mayor and board of aldermen to take a ride through the town. The town officials accepted the invitation and in a few minutes were all aboard the two-horse wagon, which was used merely as a try-out in lieu of his contemplated coach, which he intended to provide later. True to custom, the 'engineer' blew his deafening whistle, and opened the throttle. The thing started in a jiffy with sparks and fire-brands flying everywhere. In a very few minutes it was found that the clothing of all the city officials was on fire, and all of them jumped off—every man for himself. The same afternoon the doctor instructed his 'engineer' to drive the tractor to the Springs. This was undertaken—sparks flying in every direction. The tractor finally reached a muddy place in the road beyond Highland, where it mired up, 'never to go again.' When dry weather prevailed horses were hitched to the tractor and carried it to a section of timber land, where the doctor used it to run a saw mill—without ever attempting another trip.

"... Sparkling Catawba Springs was strictly a summer resort, although the hotel was kept open throughout the year, and guests were entertained at all seasons, while dances were regular weekly events.

"Fifty years ago, at the Easter season, the young people of Hickory usually held an all-day picnic on the Springs grounds. This was permitted and welcomed by Dr. Elliott, and it was a joyous occasion. Every horse and buggy available at the different livery stables was engaged days ahead by the boys, who would take their best girl out to enjoy the festive occasion from early forenoon till nightfall.

"The grounds were beautiful at this season. The slanting beams of the sun with their rich and resplendent light gave a tinge of beauty even to the repulsive boulders scattered in disorder throughout the lovely forest; the full-blown dogwood emblazoned every hillside with a gorgeous spread of snowy whiteness; a nodding honeysuckle here and there, blushing for the treachery of Judas, shed its fragrance on the quivering air; the multitude of birds splitting their little throats in a joyous song rivalry, while all nature seemed to dance a gay cotillion on the shimmering tide of time.

"The innocent girls knew neither of 'permanent waves,' lipstick or rouge, but they had garlands in their hair and possibly nectar on their lips. The boys and girls spent the day in roller-skating, bowling, tennis, games and in gathering the coveted and elusive trailing-arbutus. 'How dear to our hearts are the scenes of our childhood.'

"Dr. Elliott's son, Frank, who died 15 years ago, was a classical scholar, a princely entertainer and a mechanical genius. He built a small machine shop on his father's estate, and for a quarter of a century worked assiduously in this shop, behind closed doors. He never permitted even his closest friends to know the object of his dreams. It was known for years that he was constructing a machine of some kind for an unknown purpose—but no one knew what it was, or what its creator expected it to do when finished. Finally death intervened and the doors of his shop were opened.

"A massive machine, about 15 feet high, stood in a corner of his shop—a wonder to behold, but as difficult to understand as the pyramids of Egypt. It soon fell into the foul hands of vandals, who stripped it of every removable part, until a mere skeleton of a wonderful machine remains—without a history, explanation or purpose! ... The machine before being stripped of parts must have contained at least 50,000 pieces. It seems a pity and a shame that such a monumental conception of genius should have been destroyed without any serious effort to divine its brilliant builder's idea. Many claim that it was an effort in the direction of 'perpetual motion,' but no one knows. Its purpose, aims and hopes were buried with the genius who conceived it. Again, what a pity!

"Dr. E. O. Elliott was an eminent physician in his day, and he lived and died believing that this particular sulphur water had pronounced therapeutic value in the treatment of many human ailments. Before buying and improving the springs property, he used the water for his own case of stomach trouble, and was completely restored to health.

"Another ardent booster of the springs was Dr. K. A. Black, a physician known by reputation throughout the state. He was a graduate of the University of Edinburgh, Scotland, and lived at Fayetteville. Before the Civil War, he came to Hickory for the purpose of trying-out this water, and became so enthused over the results that he moved his family to Hickory and always used Sparkling Catawba Springs water the remainder of his life. He died about 60 years ago. . . .

"The Indians as far back as 150 years ago, encamped annually near this spring at certain seasons, and their tradition is rich in the account of miraculous cures of the afflicted."

The matter of Hickory law and order, and its deviants, is discussed at length by Major Latta, also. Among his writings are found the following:

". . . Another incident connected with Hickory occurred 45 years ago (written in 1936), and to this day is understood by only a few. In 1892, the 'Hickory Inn' was a beautiful and popular little hotel, operated at that time by Mr. (Frank) Loughran, the owner. Blowing Rock was also a popular summer resort. Many of the present day population will remember the Cowthon killing that took place on the beautiful grounds. There was at the time, and even to the present day, a vast amount of irresponsible and unjust talk.

"A Negro named Sam Tilley was employed by the hotel, doing outside work, and unfortunately this Negro had a very bad reputation for impudence and disrespectful conduct. A young business man from Alabama was on a bridal trip and had spent the day in Hickory and intended to continue his trip next day to Blowing Rock. He had met a number of Hickory people during the day. His bride's mother was with her and Mr. Cowthon. Hickory was a smaller town then than now and it was an easy matter to make a number of acquaintances in a day. It was known that Mr. Cowthon's uncle was governor of Alabama and that he was a prominent gentleman.

"About sunset, Mr. Cowthon and his bride descended the steps leading to the walk. Sam had been mowing the lawn and at the time was raking up the grass. Cowthon, with his bride beside him, addressed Sam as 'Jerry,' saying, 'Jerry, you've done a good job of mowing; now if you will use shears and trim the edges of the walk you will have done a good job.'

"Sam replied, 'Who's doing this job?' Cowthon quickly came back with, 'You black rascal, do you know who you are talking to?' Sam's quick reply was, 'No, and I don't care a d——.' Cowthon's quick rejoinder was a terrific 'bang' from a horrible revolver. Sam dropped his rake and slowly made his way toward the rear of the hotel, but it was apparent to Cowthon that he had missed his mark, and it quickly followed another deafening 'bang,' from his death-dealing revolver. It was evident that Sam was a victim of the cruel bullet. Sam folded his arms across his chest and quickened his steps toward the rear of the hotel, where he faltered and in a minute fell dead.

"In a few minutes' time, fully 500 people had gathered around the hotel. This frightened Cowthon. He thought the vast crowd sought revenge. He quickly made for his room, and refused to surrender unless personally guaranteed protection by the mayor, whom he had met during the day. He further wanted the assurance that a personal guard would be appointed to keep him in custody instead of being locked up during the night.

"The old town hall over the city manager's office was then the mayor's office. The chief of police appointed a large number of guards to provide safe keeping of the prisoner. The chief of police did this in good faith. But even at this late date, let the full, plain truth be told. The mayor knew that a scheme was on foot to allow Cowthon temporarily to escape, with the understanding that he would return to court for trial in Newton when required.

"The chief of police appointed a great number of guards, but as fast as the chief would appoint the mayor would excuse, so that in reality there were no guards at any time except the chief himself. In order to get the chief out of the way at the proper time, a well-known business man went upstairs to the mayor's office, where the prisoner and chief were talking, and the well-known business man told the chief that there was a telegram for him at the old telegraph office. The chief excused himself at once to get the telegram, at the same time leaving the prisoner in charge of the guards who had previously been discharged by the mayor, without the knowledge of the chief.

"This caused much ugly talk about the chief who was altogether innocent of any wrong in the entire matter. Let it be repeated that the chief of police was absolutely innocent of any wrong doing in connection with the Cowthon case. The chief resigned the following day, but there were hundreds that refused to be convinced of his innocence. While the chief was on his way to the telegraph office, another well-known business man whistled a signal to the figurehead guards, who gave the wink to Cowthon, who fled immediately, making his way to Newton in the night, where he hired a team to take him to Gastonia. There he boarded a train and went to his home at Salem, Ala. Our governor endeavored to get the governor of Alabama to grant requisition papers to have Cowthon returned to North Carolina for trial. Governor Jones of Alabama was an uncle of Cowthon. He refused requisition, but assured our governor that Cowthon would be at court in Newton at any designated date—and Cowthon came.

"Thus far the whole story is perfectly true, but when the trial came up, it certainly would take a discriminating judge to ferret out the truth.

"Cowthon sent the finest lawyer in Alabama to this state to find and secure such evidence as seemed desirable. He employed practically every lawyer in this county and they were able to prove that Sam was assaulting Cowthon with a pitchfork amid the screams of his bride, and their lives were endangered. This was a dark shadow that passed over Hickory and stands out in bold blackness. . . .

"In the year 1873 the struggling little village of Hickory Tavern had reached a point in its development where it was felt that some sort of a 'house of detention' was necessary to maintain its 'peace and dignity' and with this in view, the 'board of commissioners' erected its first calaboose or jail.

"It was a small two-room wooden structure, located near the railroad embankment at the entrance of the present downtown underpass. . . . This was long before the underpass was provided. Originally the railroad at this point was a solid embankment without even a culvert of any kind to convey the accumulated waters resulting from heavy rains. As a consequence, a large pond of muddy water formed after continued rains, completely engulfing the little calaboose, which then could be reached in dryness only by means of a wide plank leading from the door to dry ground. The floor of this ancient bastile was about 18 inches above ground, thus safeguarding the luckless prisoners from inundation during the wet season. . . .

"The old wooden calaboose was white-washed inside and out with lime. On each side, near the top, was a small diamond-shaped opening for ventilation and possibly light. Old-timers always asserted that the first occupant of this edifice of sighs was old, lanky 'Bill' Baker—a harmless Negro, but an ardent exponent of inebriety. Whether first or not, every resident of fifty or sixty years ago can safely vouch for the statement that he certainly was among the last, for this was Bill's headquarters. If he was wanted and not found on the streets, it was only necessary to call at the calaboose.

"Around the memory of this sordid structure—Hickory's first effort in self-preservation—cling many dramatic episodes in her early history; for it must be borne in mind that sixty years ago Hickory was a veritable frontier village. The plains of the woolly West did not surpass it in its wild orgies of lawlessness, vandalism and brute display. Dante, when writing the never-dying Divina Comedia, must have visualized youthful Hickory in his matchless vision.

"In the day of the old wooden calaboose, many old-timers will recall a Fourth of July gathering in the old town. It was one of those clear, hot days when the sun in its untempered splendor came down and mingled with the people. There was a saloon on every corner; the sale of liquor was legal and deemed ethical. Jerome Guanziroli was chief of police, and unacquainted with fear. The throng got hot, and most all seemed to believe that temperature could be lowered by the use of liquor.

"In a little while it was evident that trouble was brewing. The leader in the obstreperous activities was a stone-cutter with the muscle of an ox and hard to handle. After much difficulty he was finally subdued and lodged in the little calaboose; whereupon his friends immediately procured axes, and in a few minutes one side of the little jail was cut away, and the stone-cutter emerged to join his friends and continue their hilarity in defiance of the officers. In this instance, at least, the easy accessibility of liquor came perilously near starting a streamline riot.

"Another incident in connection with the old calaboose occurred soon after Howell Harris was appointed chief of police. Two bar rooms were located near where Shuford Hardware company now stands. A very large crowd gathered in one of the saloons, and all 'tarried' long with the wine. After a time they came forth on the street, and two of them were decidedly disorderly in ambulation and loud profanity. The chief took charge of the two most violent, and after much coaxing led them to the prison, and upon unlocking the door the two intended prisoners shoved the chief inside and locked the door. The chief was then inside and the uproarious crowd outside drowned his loud appeals for help.

"Finally the two offenders agreed to unlock the door if the chief would disarm himself by passing his gun out through the ventilation opening. He reluctantly agreed and surrendered his gun through the opening. The two arrested parties removed all cartridges from the gun, unlocked the door and delivered the weapon to the chief, who sullenly walked through the jeering mob and sat down on a nail keg in front of a store, 'disgusted.'

"Finally, the old wooden calaboose was abandoned, and in keeping with the growth and dignity of the municipality a town hall was erected. This was a small two-story soft-brick structure, located on the corner where the present municipal building now stands. The jail was in the east end of the ground floor, while the second floor was used for the mayor's office, also for the meetings of the mayor and commissioners (later called aldermen). It was equipped with a rostrum on which the mayor sat when dispensing justice, before the day of the recorder; also equipped with benches for general gatherings, seating about 450.

"The jail in this building was supposed to be much safer than the old wooden calaboose. However, many will remember a young shoemaker, who had the misfortune of a wooden leg, who also addicted to the use of liquor, and on one occasion was committed to this new jail for safe-keeping. His ingenuity led him to remove his wooden leg and use it for a tool in punching a large hole through the soft brick wall, through which he emerged, replacing the wooden member, walked away.

"On another occasion, about 50 years ago, a near-riot was pulled off around this old town hall. It was a cold afternoon with drizzling rain falling. A circus was in town, and there were four licensed saloons here. The officers arrested drunk after drunk until the jail was completely filled and many stored upstairs under guards.

"Finally home-going time arrived, and about 200 or more gathered in front of the town hall, practically all drunk and demanding the release of their incarcerated friends. Loud threats were uttered, and it was plainly evident that physical force was contemplated.

"Fortunately at this juncture, Sheriff Rowe mounted a two-horse wagon which was driven in midst of the mob, his tall figure standing erect, he urged them to dispense pointing out the serious consequences that would follow their failure to heed. His appeal impressed them, and the howling mob began to slowly melt away. Sheriff Rowe's commanding figure and cool judgment undoubtedly averted a serious affair that would have been attended with bloodshed.

"Another incident of this kind occurred over 55 years ago when the small park on Union Square was about twice its present width. Hall and Daniel, large tobacco manufacturers, employed about 200 Negroes, nearly all of them imported from Danville, and decidedly rough characters. At that time the chief of police was W. S. Ramseur. . . .

"It was a bleak Saturday afternoon—Christmas even; the factory had paid off and closed for the approaching holidays. There were several open saloons in town; nearly all of the Danville contingent filled up with 'Calamity water' and assembled in the little park. One of the myrmidons became very boisterous and threatening; the chief of police attempted to arrest the offender, and immediately his co-workers undertook to rescue him from the police.

"Passing whites saw what was taking place, and rushed to the assistance of the police; the crowd increased in numbers and in two or three minutes there was a free-for-all fight going on all over the park. The late J. G. Hall (probably J. F. Murrill, instead) was mayor and also manager of the tobacco factory. He mounted a goods box and sought to quell the riot by his presence and appeal. Someone jerked the box from under his feet, and the mayor in falling skinned his face badly.

"The prime instigator of the riot was old, long, hammer-heeled Jule Alexander, who also mounted a box and urged the Danville squad to fight-to-kill. At this juncture the late A. S. Abernethy, one of the 'bravest of the brave,' appeared on the scene, and forcing his way through the crowd, leveled a gun at Jule's head, forced him to shut up and leave. The riot subsided at once. The exact date of this tragedy was Saturday, December 24, 1881. Jule Alexander left this locality soon after this episode, and about 50 years ago it was reported that he had been hanged somewhere in Tennessee, although this phase of the matter cannot be verified.

"Sixty years ago, in this locality, there was a 'still-house' on every branch and a bar-room at every cross-roads and one to several in nearly all towns. This was the status until the enactment of the Watts law, which prohibited the sale of liquor within limited proximity to schools and churches outside of the incorporated towns. In effect this confined the sale of liquors to incorporated towns; however, the boot-legger was in evidence the same as now. In that day the stamp tax alone on liquor was $1.10 per gallon, while illicit liquor could be readily bought for $1.00 per gallon.

"Beginning with year 1868 liquor was sold throughout the state with little or no restrictions for several years. Finally serious opposition arose, and in 1880 a state-wide election was held on the question. Prohibition lost. Hickory had been dry several years when the Volstead measure was enacted; but prior to that time it had been wet oftener than dry. After reaching a population of 2,000 it vacillated on the question of wet and dry. . . .

There were two or three years in Hickory's life when boot-legging did not flourish. It was at the time when the late F. B. Ingold was on the board of aldermen. Mr. Ingold was a devout prohibitionist and as unyielding as granite. He had promised that if elected there would be no liquor sold in Hickory. He, with J. S. Propst, was elected, and 'tell it not in Gath, publish it not in the streets of Askelon,' it was dry. No liquor was sold in Hickory except at drug stores, on a reputable physician's prescription. Of course, it was possible to go outside of the city and make purchases clandestinely.

"After Hickory became industrialized Saturday was a great day for business with the saloons. . . ."

Among the intimate sketches concerning the early population of Hickory given by Major Latta are the following:

". . . Back in the days of 'auld lang syne,' hogs, cows, sheep and other stock were permitted to run at large, the cultivated fields alone being enclosed by fences. At that time it was not at all unusual for what is now called Union Square to be thronged with hogs and cows. Hall Brothers operated the largest store in town, and handled considerable country produce. The late F. A. Clinard was bookkeeper for the store. The late Daniel Whisnant lived in a large log house, built on the spot where C. H. Geitner's stone residence now stands. Mr. Whisnant had many hogs that made daily trips to town. On a certain day, Hall Brothers had bought a load of corn, some of which was spilled on the ground and on the store floor. The hogs followed the trail of scattered corn, until possibly a dozen hogs were in the store. The bookkeeper mentioned above had gotten tired of driving the hogs out through the front door, and it occurred to him as being a good time to teach the hogs an object lesson. The back door of the store was ten or 12 feet above the ground. The bookkeeper quickly closed the front door of the store, and at once began pounding the hogs with a large stick, forcing them to make their exit through the back door. Upon striking the ground some of them were killed outright, some escaped with broken legs, others crippled otherwise. About this time Mr. Whisnant was informed as to what happened up to that time and began gathering up the dead and crippled hogs, and immediately a contest in modified profanity ensued, which old timers say reverberated for several hours after the contest, but no further damage was done. . . .

"One incident brings up another. As stated above, 'Uncle Dan' Whisnant's home was a large log house, standing on the spot where Mr. C. H. Geitner's stone residence is located. A short distance from the home on the road toward town, it will be remembered, there is a small branch, where those traveling in wagons would frequently camp for the night.

"Sixty years ago there was an old gentleman named Mullens who did a great deal of trading in mountain produce, buying apples, cabbage, chestnuts, etc., hauling same to Hickory where he disposed of it. There were saloons in those days, and unfortunately the old gentleman was very fond of the stuff sold by these dens, but he would always attend to business first and then steam up. He always drove a little black mule, and on one occasion he came down to Hickory with a load of produce, which he disposed of and made purchases at the saloon. It was a bitter cold day with the pitiless snow falling thick and fast and the howling winds chilling the marrow in the bones. The old gentleman came to the particular branch near 'Uncle Dan's' home, and prepared to camp for the night. He hitched his little black mule behind his covered wagon, crawled in and was soon wrapped in slumber, forgetful of the whistling winds and blinding snow. About two or three in the morning he became aroused by the silence of his little black mule, and looking out toward the rear he was amazed and disturbed to find his mule gone.

"He quickly pulled a blanket around him and began following the mule's tracks in the snow. The howling winds in a short distance had erased every evidence of tracks. He halted in front of 'Uncle Dan's' big log house and yelled loudly 'Hey! Hey! Hey!' Finally 'Uncle Dan' became aroused, opened his door and responded, 'Hey!'

"Through the freezing winds the old gentleman inquired:

" 'Have you seen a little black mule come up this way?'

"Uncle Dan, shivering, yelled, 'No, I ain't seen no little black mule.'

"The old gentleman yelled back, 'No, d———n you, you didn't want to see him!' and he slowly retraced his steps through the whistling winds back to his little covered wagon, looking forward to the coming of the morning when he could have his bottle refilled."

It appears that discovery of a mineral spring near the southwest corner of what is now Carolina Park in Hickory caused the young city to receive certain notoriety.

Major Latta describes the "spring" as follows:

"One small spot, immediately west of Carolina Park, in the long ago, contributed much to the enjoyment and pleasure of the younger people in the summer months. Near the railroad embankment there was a splendid chalybeate spring whose sparkling waters were enjoyed by many. There was a summerhouse near, and its steps led down to the spring. The summerhouse was equipped with comfortable seats, and the surrounding grounds were cleanly kept and provided with benches in abundance in a natural forest of small trees, where squirrels frolicked and birds mingled their joyous notes with the soft south winds.

"It was here that the young people assembled each Sunday afternoon and on moonlight evenings. It was not a clandestine rendezvous, but a gathering place for the best people in the town. There were no picture shows then, no swimming pools, no automobiles, no good roads, but the innocent pastime of the young folks yielded perhaps an equivalent amount of pleasure.

"Their laughter was like rushing waters, their merriment the tincture of summer breezes. In summer evenings, this little spot was particularly enchanting, when the moon held out her silver disc above, casting shadows of the quivering foliage that stenciled weird figures on the trampled ground. This was drowsy, sleepy Hickory in the long ago.

"The spring was a valuable asset to Hickory at one time. Its waters were analyzed by the eminent chemist, Dr. Froehling, and pronounced unmatched as a pure chalybeate water, except by Bola Lake, Scotland. The spring was destroyed about 30 years ago, when the first ice plant in Hickory—just across the railroad—dug a well. The well intercepted the vein leading to the spring, when it stopped, like grandfather's clock, 'never to go again.'"

Hickory drew much of its population from rural sections of Catawba and surrounding counties. Typical of the sojourns into the city was that of Mrs. C. C. Bost. In writing her reminiscences for publication in a newspaper, Mrs. Bost revealed:

"In my long life I have experienced many thrills but none of them surpassed the thrill of moving to Hickory in the March of 1872.

"With my sisters I had spent September, October and November in Hickory attending subscription school taught by my sister, Alice. . . . So I had a taste of town life which made me eager for more.

"The trip from our home six miles north of Lincolnton and 16 miles south of Hickory was made in the family carriage and in the family buggy. Neighbors moved household goods in wagons. The route lay by Grace church crossing Jacobs Fork river at Ramsour's mill; by Zion Lutheran church; by Bethel Reformed church, fording Henry river at Mr. Peter Rowe's and on to Hickory Tavern. When we reached what is now Ninth avenue (now Main Avenue place), the only road to our home, known as 'East Hickory.' . . .

"When walking to and from 'town' every one walked on the railroad tracks. There were two trains daily, so danger from them could easily be avoided.

"But to return to our moving. I have no recollection of the furniture being placed, but I do remember that our beds were of the 'cord' variety and much pulling and tramping was necessary to keep the mattress from swagging. As soon as possible a fire was to be lighted but where had the matches been placed for moving? The sister to whom this had been entrusted was not in reach so a systematic search began. My mother said: 'I will wash and fill the kettle with water to be ready to heat.' Lifting the lid of the kettle she found the matches.

"What trifling things to remember of happenings 60 years ago! . . .

"I have been interested in the whole life of the town—its clubs, its churches, its schools. I have seen Hickory grow from a handful of houses into a busy, bustling little city, and I always have rejoiced that my lot was cast here."

The coming of the Western North Carolina railroad to Hickory in the late 1860s evidently gave the citizens the feeling of becoming "citified." Certain social functions are said to date to about that time.

Perhaps the earliest social life consisted of family entertaining family at dinner or supper, when the menu consisted of such dishes as fried chicken, baked chicken, chicken pie, rice, apple sauce, hot slaw, baked sweet potatoes, Dutch cheese, peach or apple pie, pound cake, sausage, backbones and ribs, and liver mush in season. The art of canning fruits and vegetables still was in a primitive stage. Dried fruits generally were served during the winter. Delicious jellies and preserves were served, and home-made rolls, light bread or biscuits were unsurpassed.

Women guests usually brought along needle or fancy work to "while away" the afternoon. Men folks sat to themselves and talked politics and other topics of general interest.

Young people amused themselves with games, a favorite of which was "Graces," played with sticks, and wooden hoops covered with worsted. Croquet was beginning to be popular.

"Sociables" became the fad a few years after the coming of the railroad. They seem to have been held whenever any occasion offered itself. Often they were formal affairs.

The young lady of the house received by hand of a small boy (white or colored) a beautifully-written note:

"John S. Thompson presents compliments to Miss Mary Montague and requests the pleasure of her company at the sociable at Miss Nancy Booth's home this evening at seven-thirty o'clock."

Miss Montague replied in painstaking hand: "Miss Mary Montague's compliments to Mr. John S. Thompson and she accepts his kind invitation for this evening with pleasure."

The hostess, of course, had an entertaining evening prepared. Among the games she chose were charades, weave the thimble, borrowed furniture, etc.

Among the names familiar to the Hickory "sociable" circle were the Abernethys, Alexanders, Aikens, Blairs, Bells, Butlers, Blacks, Bowles, Beards, Bosts, Baskins, Bakers, Crowells, Dannas, Geitners, Gibbs, Blackwelders, Hales, Ingolds, Hills, Clines, Clays, Ellises, Elliotts, Johnsons, Halls, Links, Robinsons, Wilfongs, Shufords, Ramsours, Roysters, Fields, McCombs, Littles, Reinhardts, Murrills, Wheelers, Seagles, Sherrills, and many others.

The first marriage solemnized in a Hickory church was in the early summer of 1873. The site was the newly-completed

Reformed church on Ninth Avenue. The participants were Miss Gertrude Jones and Frank A. Clinard. The ceremony was performed by Rev. E. N. Joyner. The townspeople were said to have been exceedingly impressed.

Down-to-earth observations characterize the writings of Mrs. Bost. About habits and customs of early Hickory citizens, this historian records:

"Temperance—An organization that did much in molding temperance sentiment was started here in the early 70s, known as the 'Good Templars.' How much of help and safeguard it was to scores of young men in the days when the licensed saloon flourished will not be known till 'the leaves of the Judgment Book unfold.' On election days, especially a Presidential election, ladies did not appear on the principal streets. If they had to go from one part of the town to another, a back street was considered the only proper way to go.

"Union Square—Many interesting memories cling around Union Square. This ground was given to the railroad and to the town for a 'Common' by Mr. Henry Robinson, grandfather of the progressive John W. Robinson of Catawba county. . . .

"A public well was dug about where the drinking fountain is now, and one where the passenger station now stands—these were operated without windlass and bucket. All through the 70s, horses, wagons, buggies, etc., were hitched in the grove in front of the row of stores. In the early 70s it was no uncommon sight to see campfires, and covered mountain wagons camping for the night in the square. Before the stock law was passed, cows and pigs roamed about the town. A favorite sleeping place for the hogs was under the platform of the old passenger depot that is now the freight depot. The enterprising hogs would carry leaves from the square for beds under this covenient shelter.

"Society Life in the 70s—Before taking this topic up, a few recollections about the first Hickory Fair. . . . A good sized area was fenced in with a good display of livestock and farm products on exhibition. 'The Floral Hall,' as the ladies department was called, was very good as well as I remember, and crowds attended. The great feature was the 'Tournament.' I don't remember what they were 'Knights of,' but a number of young men rode. The 'Catawba Station' band furnished music at this fair. Our late townsman, Mr. J. W. Blackwelder, was one of the musicians. At night there was a ball at the Central hotel when the successful knights crowned the 'Queen of Love and Beauty' and her 'maids of honor.'

"It was in the summer of 1873, I think, that the first 'Reading Club' was organized here. Some of the members were Miss Mattie Baskin, Miss Lou Ingold, Miss Ida Ramseur. . . . Mr. Hugh Southerland. There were others, I am sure, but I can not recall them.

"On Hickory generally—Where Bowle's Furniture store now stands, (the present Melville's building on Union Square,) in the early 70s, a general merchandise store was kept by the firm of 'Shuford and Ellis.' In the rear end of this store room, the Hickory Tavern postoffice was kept. In those days, the Western North Carolina Railroad operated two daily trains—one east and one westbound—both of them mixed trains. A little while after the arrival of the train a representative from each family gathered at the postoffice while the postmaster called out the addresses on the letters and afterwards the papers in the same manner. I don't suppose the names were taken alphabetically, but perhaps they were. Just when this method was discarded, I do not know. People were not in such a hurry in those days and the method had one advantage, you could keep tab on your neighbor's correspondence, to a certain extent, if you desired to do so. A very important building was the 'Academy,' built, I think, by the citizens and used for all purposes. Even when Hickory was a very small village, in swaddling clothes, as it were, she 'did things.' This Academy stood at the west side of the old cemetery and was a very primitive structure, being weather boarded but not ceiled for it was only intended for temporary use. Here any and all denominations preached, the Union Sunday school was held, shows were given, etc. A bell was presented to the Methodists before they built a church—before any church was built, in fact. This bell was hung in the wood-shed of the W. N. C. R. R. about where the recently removed passenger depot stood. This was a very convenient arrangement—if there was to be any sort of a service somebody interested stepped over to the shed and rang the bell. It was really hardly necessary to do this, for everybody always knew what was going on—there were no conflicting services."

For a picture of mid-nineteenth century Catawba county life, extremely human because of its straight-spoken facts about prevailing customs, writings of Mrs. A. Y. Sigmon are an aid:

"I was born across the river just below the new bridge, on my father's farm, adjoining that of Mr. Hallman Suttlemyre's. Hallman was the father of Phillip Suttlemyre, and grandfather of Garland and Johnson. My father was the oldest brother of Mr. Bob, Pink, Bill and Bard Winkler, and the son of Abraham Winkler, who lived near the Cliffs. I will be 75 years old the eighth day of April.

"I had two sisters and one brother. My brother, Jeff Winkler, who lives here in town, was born after father went to War. When father heard of the boy baby he wrote mother that she must come with him. He was about three months old and mother had made all plans to leave next morning. That night she was finishing up her split bonnet and accidentally cut a three-cornered hole in it. She began to wring her hands and cry, said that there was no use to go, and laid it away and did not finish it. Next morning early Mr. Suttlemyre came and said word had been received of my father's death. Mother believed in signs and I must admit I do too.

"My first visit to Hickory Tavern was about 1863. I rode behind mother on horseback. There had come a lump, maybe the size of a guinea egg on my throat,—something similar to a goiter, and mother brought me down here where Kenworth is now, to a faith doctor. His name was Dietz. He got a case knife and with the back edge made a cross on my throat,—only pressed lightly. Then we went over by a table and read in the Bible. I remember noticing it for a few days after that, but the next time I thought of it it was gone, and never came back.

"I came a number of times during the war with mother to the cotton gin,—Old Uncle Mose Barger had the only gin for miles and miles around,—none in Caldwell or Burke counties. It was down to the left of Negro-town, going toward Brookford,—some Bargers still live down there. I do not remember the name of the people who ran the Hickory Tavern except

I know mother and I ate dinner there once when we brought cotton and had to wait all day.

"After the war mother married again. I had not been used to work,—we had had slaves to do it, and so I balked and left home and went to grandfather's. There the slaves all gone I learned to spin and weave. I wove jeans, flax, wool blankets and coverlets (colored wool counterpanes) also white cotton counterpanes. All the bed-ticks, sheets, and pillowcases were made of flax homespun, and I still have some things which I spun and wove. I remember the last winter I was at grandmothers I wove 75 yards of jeans from Thanksgiving to Easter, and about six blankets.

"When about the age of 16 . . . I came to Hickory to live with my mother's youngest brother,—Uncle Harvey Suttlemyre. I suppose everybody remembers his milk-shakes. . . .

". . . The train only ran to Old Fort, and only one train each way a day. No train to Lenoir. Dolph Abernethy met the trains and got the mail and took them to Lenoir every day, and a man named Clark in Lenoir got the mail and collected the passengers wanting to come to Hickory to catch the train. . . .

"When I was 19 years old, I met Mr. Sigmon in the fall. He had a store, a sawmill, and was a carpenter, and was then putting up lots of fine houses, besides he dressed quite starchy. Before getting married I went back to grandfather's and was weaving and spinning again. That winter between Thanksgiving and Easter I know I wove 75 yards of jeans and six blankets. It seems they needed me to weave,—anyway even though grandfather thought enough of Mr. Sigmon to loan him all the money he wanted for his business, still they didn't want me to marry him. Grandmother could think of no other way to keep me from marrying him except to hide the homemade soap so I could not wash my clothes. Well, it did cause me much concern until my youngest uncle, Pink Winkler, let me have his fine perfumed face soap. It was clearly understood we would run away and get married at the 'Cross roads' just back of Piedmont Shops, near that church. He would come at two on the dot, the twenty-seventh day of April. . . . Two and three and four o'clock came and he was not there. I decided he had left me asetting for some of the city girls. He was building the Presbyterian church up here in front of the Hotel Huffry (now Hotel Earle).... He was putting on the roof of the steeple and after getting up there found more to do than he thought and didn't realize it was so late until he got down. The steeple was very steep. That completed the church and he got pay for building the church and then came for me. We drove to the Cross Roads and were married. . . ."

Halley's comet, which was seen in 1910, aroused considerable excitement in Catawba county, according to a report of the occurrence in The Times-Mercury of Hickory on June 1, 1910.

Apparently the entire populace was much disappointed at the phenomenon judging from the account, which follows:

"The whole Avenue was out-of-doors to watch for Halley's comet. Some leant on the front gate, some filled up the sidewalks, some occupied a commanding position in the middle of the street. Finally the reporter, true to instinct, yelled 'there it is.' Then the storm broke: 'What? That?' said the seedman. 'If I hadn't had it tagged, I'd never have known it.'

" 'Why, I thought it was as big as the headlight on No. 35,' said the railroad man.

" 'This is perfectly disgusting,' said the lady holding the biggest baby.

" 'I don't think it's right for Mr. Halley to fool people like that,' said the Presbyterian lady.

" 'I believe he fell from grace and saw double when he sized that thing up,' said the Methodist Sunday school superintendent.

" 'Here they've been making a fuss about it a whole year and now expect us to put up with that. Roger Williams wouldn't stand for it,' said the leading Baptist.

" 'Looks like somebody hit it a clip and knocked it into the back of beyond,' said the sporting man.

" 'Just think of the comet of the 80's. Take that thing away,' said two oldest inhabitants.

"But the reporter murmured, "Well, we got through 'syzygy' anyhow!' "

"County Commencement Day" was for many years the big day in the lives of school children of the county, when an enormous parade consisting of children from every school in the county, with their teachers, marched through Newton streets and held exercises at Catawba college.

Following is a description of the 1916 event, as told by a feature writer of The Catawba News-Enterprise:

"In 1916 an unusual feature of the parade was an entry of the Rockett school. On that occasion, Mr. Garland Arndt brought 106 children to commencement on one wagon drawn by four mules. The children were seated on three long benches of a specially constructed float. The entry was awarded a prize for having the largest number of people ever seen in Newton on one vehicle. The girls were all dressed in white, and all of the children carried American flags, and rode through the streets singing patriotic songs.

"As for the rest of the crowd, it was said that 'early on Friday morning the wagons, carriages and automobiles began to roll into Newton. The morning was ideal—the Spring girls were in evidence and never looked better. The young men and boys had on their best Sunday-go-to-meeting fixen's and all made fine appearance.'

"The line of march was formed at the college, and martial music was provided by the Newton Band. And one observer commented in recalling the event 'the courting couples had the times of their lives and made hay while the sun shone and the wind blew on Friday.'

"The line marched around the square and back to the college. It was estimated there were 2,000 children in the parade.

"As the parade reached the college an address of welcome was given by President Andrew of the college. On that particular occasion, Prof. A. O. Reynolds, of Cullowhee State Normal School, was the principal speaker.

"Among the contests staged during the day were a boys declamation contest won by Clayton Helton, of the Yoder school; a girls recitation contest won by Edna Sigmon of the Highland school; singing contest by schools won by the Killian school; baseball game in the afternoon between Catawba and Maryville colleges, happily won by Catawba; high school boys declamation contest won by Keith Hefner of Highland school; and high school girls recitation contest won that year by Katherine Hardin of the Hickory Graded schools.

"Prizes were awarded for the best school exhibits, and they were won by the Highland school, Killian school, and Scronce school. Startown Farm Life school carried off the honors in the high school exhibits, and was rewarded with a good clock,—'A practical thing that the school can use.' . . ."

Women's suffrage likely was a controversial subject in Catawba county as elsewhere in the late nineteenth century and early twentieth century. When the "fairer sex's" emancipation finally came in 1920, it was heralded by Mrs. Bost thus:

"At Last—Women Vote!

"Come, Sarah, Maude, Elizabeth,
"Jane, Mary, Kate and Sue—
"Belle, Gertrude, Helen, Lou—
"Come all! In 1920
"We'll sound a ringing note.
"Though many years in coming,
"This year we go to vote!
"For weeks we've been 'instructed'
"By some well blessed with sense,
"And some who only lately
"Sat uncertain on the fence.
"And some who had fought suffrage
"Stood up (and this is true)
"To tell us ignorant women
"Just what we ought to do.
"But while we see the humor
"And understand the play,
"We'll rise to the occasion,
"And greet the glorious day.
"So come, my fellow citizens,
"A cheer from every throat—
"The second of November
"We go to cast our vote!"

The epilogue of "The Building of Catawba" includes:

"O ye men, of new Catawba,
"You have watched the episodes of time,
"Recalled the heroism of your fathers,
"Watched them build a stately mansion
"On the rock foundation of the ages;
"You now behold your birthright fair and free,
"Your fathers, heroes of the Holy Cross,
"Your fathers, heroes of your country's light;
"Lest you fail to keep the faith they kept,
"Lest you fail to give the light they gave,
"Send forth into the future of Catawba
"The selfsame cross, and the selfsame torch. . . ."

CHAPTER XIX

NOTABLE COMMUNITY INSTITUTIONS

Community agencies of virtually every description have enhanced the attractiveness of Catawbans' lives and have determined that the county should have marked progress, including cultural and social successes. These organizations take many forms, ranging from groups which protect the interests of veterans of America's wars to groups which provide guidance and recreation for youth.

These agencies that seek to promote the welfare, of varying descriptions, of the general citizenry, have flourished lately within the boundaries of the county, and are due credit as forces which promote civic progressiveness. Many tangible results proceed from their operations.

It is, perhaps, a bit strange that the reserved nature of the native Catawban welcomed a commutual movement. Actually, the early settler did not. While he happily aided his neighbor individually, he did not seek inclusion in organizations that purported to philanthropize.

Not until the middle of the nineteenth century did the citizens of Catawba turn to "orders" which formed the nucleus of today's institutions of community service. The period witnessed the disappearance of a frontier and the acceptance of group living; an increase in population and its resulting group problems, a growing feeling of community-ism, state-ism and nationalism; the experience of a locally-fought war; and the edifying realization that individual difficulties often are synonymous and may be overcome by group consultation.

Women are largely responsible for the advent to the Catawba area of agencies that perform community services. In fact, the first "club" endeavors were those devised by women, usually for cultural purposes.

The trend toward united neighborhood living has gained momentum with succeeding years. Citizens now regard the welfare of the community a personal concern of all its members, with the gratifying effect that social, cultural, and even economic, standards are constantly being raised.

Certain institutions, including those which safeguard the community's health and contribute to its financial stability, are due recognition.

THE COUNTY'S LIBRARIES:

The initial Catawba county library was established in Hickory. The Elbert Ivey Memorial library, which contains approximately 35,000 volumes, had its conception in 1893 in the failure of a small bookstore and rental library owned by Charles Graves on Union Square.

A few townspeople, including Colonel C. A. Cilley, Mrs. O. M. Royster and Miss Emily Wheeler, bought the stock of rental books and, with these as a nucleus, opened a small room of a building situated where Deitz Jewelry store now stands. The first library was supported by contributions and by the receipts from a series of ice cream suppers and theatricals, and was operated by volunteer librarians.

In 1907, the Hickory Library Association was formed. Its first meeting was at the home of Mrs. Royster, with Colonel and Mrs. Cilley, Mrs. J. A. Martin, Mrs. C. N. Graves, Misses Amy, Emily, and Julia Wheeler, Miss Josie Person, and Miss Ada Schenck present. The association adopted a constitution and by-laws, and with membership fees and donations from the town and from private citizens, added to the small stock of books. J. D. Elliott gave rent-free a wooden structure on First avenue, SW, near Third Street, SW, as the first Hickory library building. The library occupied successively a building in the Shuford block on Union Square, upstairs quarters over a store on Union Square, and another building furnished rent-free by Elliott, lately occupied by the Clay Printing company.

In the spring of 1917, Mr. and Mrs. Elliott gave a lot on Second street, NW, for a Carnegie library. The $14,000 subsequently received from the Carnegie Commission was the last donation made by the Commission to a public library. Because of the increased cost of building materials, $3,000 had to be raised by public subscription and by the presentation of a pageant arranged by Mrs. W. B. Ramsay.

Before the library, christened the Worth Elliott-Carnegie library, was opened, the people of Hickory had voted a tax of .05c on the $100 property valuation for its support.

CATAWBA COUNTY 465

The library opened August 15, 1922, and was directed ably by Miss Ruby McWhirter, who served until her marriage in 1923; Miss Annie Maude Dawson, who succeeded Miss McWhirter and served until 1926; Miss Emma C. Bonney, who succeeded Miss Dawson and served until her death in 1938; and Miss Grace Patrick, who succeeded Miss Bonney, having served for some time as her assistant, and continues today.

Miss Bonney, whose chief interest is said to have been the welfare and development of "her child," as she referred to the library, fostered the growth of the library until it had increased its attendance, membership, and book stock many times. In 1937, a year prior to her death, the book circulation of the library was 72,668 volumes.

In 1926, the first regular board of trustees of the library was elected by Hickory city officials. The original board consisted of six members: Mrs. J. Worth Elliott, chairman; M. H. Yount, vice-chairman; Mrs. T. A. Mott, secretary and treasurer; Mayor Shuford L. Whitener; Mrs. W. B. Councill; and O. G. Wolff.

The need of additional space prompted the consideration of a new library building. George F. Ivey, industrialist, and his family, gave funds for the purchase of a site for a new structure at 420 Third avenue, NW, and later donated funds for the modern, brick building. The gesture was made in memory of a member of the Ivey family, Elbert A. Ivey, whose name graces the beautiful and utilitarian facility.

Of conservative modern design, the Elbert Ivey library building was first opened to the public on March 29, 1952. The structure was designed by Clemmer and Horton, Hickory architects, and was erected at an approximate cost of $130,000 by Elliott Building company also of Hickory.

Miss Patrick, whose 15 years of service to Hickory and Catawba county through the library have endeared her to all who know her, is presently assisted in the direction of the library by the following who constitute the library's board of trustees: Leon S. Ivey, chairman; Mrs. P. W. Deaton, secretary and treasurer; Alderman Young M. Smith; Mrs. J. A. Moretz; L. C. Gifford; and Miss Mabel Hight.

The story of the building of the Catawba County library and museum at Newton, using the Matthias Barringer house (site of the first court in the county), is one of courage. A tragic ending occurred in 1952 when the historic structure burned to the ground. The same type of courage is today effecting the rebuilding.

It can factually be said that the initial library was born of the determination of a group which, undaunted by lack of funds and materials with which to work, by sheer perseverance, accomplished the end to which it had striven for four years. The group in question is Unit 16 of the American Legion Auxiliary of Newton.

On March 17, 1932, designated as "Community Service Day," during the presidency of Miss Challie Brandon Hall, the Newton Unit voted to sponsor a public library with the belief that such facilities were the most pertinent need of its section, and, for that matter, the entire southern portion of Catawba county. At that time, the sum of $25 was appropriated.

For three years, little significant progress was made. Then, in the fall of 1935, two members of the unit, Miss Hall and Mrs. R. W. James, approached George McCorkle of Washington, D. C., with the plan of the Auxiliary. McCorkle immediately translated his interest into action, and arranged to give to the unit, rent free, two rooms in his building on the southwest corner of the courtsquare to be used as a library. Not only this, but he constructed shelves, repainted and completely remodeled the rooms, making an entrance on A street. Through the courtesy of Edward Haupt, many-times mayor of Newton, who leased the building from McCorkle, the rooms were made available.

As the Auxiliary went into action with the purpose of opening the library to the public, the interest of the public was soon apparent. Enthusiastic response met the Book Drive conducted by the library board during two weeks in January, 1936, and donations of time, labor, materials and help in innumerable ways were given.

The formal opening of the library was arranged for March 17, 1936, exactly four years after the plan was conceived. Due to the inclement weather of that year, however, the opening actually was held on March 20, and books were put in circulation on April 1.

Members of the original library board were Miss Hall, chairman, Mrs. Wade Lefler, Mrs. Cecil Arndt, Mrs. Evans Bost, Mrs. Carl Canipe, Mrs. J. A. Capps, Mrs. Glenn Long, Mrs. Weaver Mann, Mrs. Willie Trott, Mrs. Eli Warlick, Mrs. Wilson Warlick, Mrs. R. W. James, Miss Earl Yoder, Mrs. Delmar Ervin, and Miss Bessie Smith.

In order that the library might become more serviceable to rural Catawba county, the library board desired a bookmobile. So, a school bus was turned over to the Auxiliary for this purpose. Books were supplied from the shelves of the library supplemented by books received at intervals from the North Carolina Library commission and the state-wide WPA library service sponsored by the commission. The Catawba county bookmobile, which was to become an important phase of the library's program, made its first trip on February 18, 1938.

In July, 1939, the Catawba County Commissioners appropriated $2,000 for buying and equipping a Catawba county bookmobile to be operated by the Newton Public library (the official title of the library which later was to become the Catawba County library and museum). The Commission lately purchased a new bookmobile for the Catawba County library in its program of aid to the county's libraries.

Historic interest among members of the Auxiliary, promoted especially by Miss Hall, and on the part of Newton American Legion post, is responsible for the transfer of the old Barringer home, located some two miles east of Newton, to the county seat city for use as a library facility. The decision was to lead to the development of the Catawba County War Memorial Center, located on South Cline avenue, which became one of the county seat city's prime tourist attractions.

Moving the Barringer dwelling in 1945, the rebuilding of the library immediately became an Auxiliary project that attracted county-wide interest. A decision to include a museum was made with the restoration of the old dwelling.

The attention of the North Carolina Library Commission was called to the movement in Newton to furnish library service to, not only the city, but the entire southern Catawba county rural section, and a plan of state-aid was devised. The state's program called for the employment of a librarian who would attend to similar projects in Iredell and Lincoln counties. This now has been changed to a two-county plan, with the librarian dividing his time between Catawba and Lincoln counties.

Miss Hall, who was named librarian soon after the institution was established, was succeeded in 1948 by George Linder, whose extremely creditable services continue today.

The library building and museum had only shortly been devoured by fire when Newtonians and other countians began considering the building of a new structure. Books which were salvaged from the blaze were transferred to a business house on North College avenue, in which the library was immediately again put into operation.

Plans now are underway for the construction of a modern building.

The present Catawba County library board consists of A. L. Shuford, Jr., chairman; Mrs. D. M. Eaton, vice-chairman; Mrs. Evans Bost, secretary-treasurer; Miss Lorene Leonard, Mrs. A. L. Shuford, Sr., Mrs. C. H. Mebane, T. R. Owen, Cowles Gaither, Hugh Moretz, and John F. Carpenter, Sr.

A branch library of the Hickory library serves Negroes, and is the county's third public library. This branch was set up September 17, 1940, under a WPA grant by Miss Patrick, Mrs. Spurgeon Young, Miss Martha Troutman, and Miss Nellie Corpening. Known originally as the Twelfth Street Branch library, the branch was first located in a building owned by Norwood Patterson. Rent was paid by local church groups.

Since the time of its beginning, except for a period from April, 1941, until September, 1942, the branch library has operated continuously. After WPA aid ceased, the facility was stocked with books from the main Hickory library, from Lenoir Rhyne college, and from private sources.

Interest in the branch library continued until books and magazines taxed the capacity of the small quarters. Hence, the Hickory Altrusa club, in 1946, began a project which was to culminate in an attractive structure to house the colored library.

Members of the club organized a drive to raise $10,000 for the construction of the building.

George F. Ivey, who sponsored the Hickory library, purchased a lot at First street and Seventh avenue, SW, and deeded it to the city of Hickory as a site for the proposed library. The Altrusa library project began during the presidency of Mrs. James E. Gaither and was completed a year later during the presidency of Mrs. Karl W. Broome.

Work on the attractive building was supervised by an Altrusan committee under the direction of Mrs. Bobbie C. Landis. The grading of the grounds and planting of shrubbery, donated by the Howard-Hickory Nursery, was done under the supervision of Burgin Finger.

The new Ridgeview Public library was opened in January, 1951.

Miss Menzies Henderson has been in charge of the Ridgeview branch since 1943. She works in cooperation with and under the direction of Miss Patrick and the trustees of the main city library.

THE AMERICAN LEGION

Dedicated to the highest ideals of patriotism and good citizenship, the veterans organization, the American Legion, has superceded its purpose of administering to the needs of men who have borne arms for their country, and their families, and has entered upon a course of general community service. In Catawba county, this service has been particularly noteworthy.

The endeavors of the three posts of the American Legion and their Auxiliary Units of the area have resulted in some of the noblest welfare projects conceivable. Ranging from the sponsorship of financial drives for worthwhile causes to sponsorship of patriotic celebrations, the agency has gained the respect of the citizenry due to the selflessness of its purpose.

Two of the county's three Legion posts appeared quickly following World War One, only within months after the formation of the Legion itself in Paris, France, in March, 1919.

It is a matter of pride to all members of post Sixteen of Newton that it was the second post organized in the whole of Western North Carolina (only Asheville preceded it).

A small group of veterans assembled in the courthouse at Newton on September 17, 1919, and formally organized the post. A charter was granted and the post immediately set forth in activities that have benefitted the county.

G. A. Warlick, Jr., was chosen the first commander. Charter members were, in addition to Warlick, Wilson Warlick, J. Coley Mundy, Julius W. Abernethy, Everette B. Moose, Zeb V. Michael, D. E. Smith, Norman E. Drum, Ross S. Huitt, Charles D. Ramseur, John W. Caldwell, Floyd E. Price, J. Merton Killian, and George R. Powell.

The building of the "hut," which later was to be developed into an attractive building to serve almost all meeting purposes for Newtonians and flanked by Memorial grounds, was done in 1930.

Organization of Hickory Post Forty-Eight followed the organization of the Newton post by less than two months. Veterans of Hickory were called on November 3, 1919, by Major George L. Lyerly to meet in the offices of the chamber of commerce to discuss the establishment of a post.

It was decided to organize a post and application was made to national headquarters for a temporary charter. Those who signed the application for this charter were Major Lyerly, Aldis C. Henderson, Harold G. Deal, Russell M. Yount, E. N. Carr, W. M. Reese, J. Homer Bowles, Weston L. Taylor, Frank L. Cline, William M. Busby, Bascom B. Blackwelder, James C. Shuford, M. Ezra Rink, Joseph E. Cilley, and George C. Warlick. The charter was issued on November 9, and on November 20 the organization meeting was held. Officers were elected, including F. L. Cline, chairman (officers with titles in the vernacular of the Legion were chosen in 1921. Cline actually was the first commander).

At the second meeting, it was decided to make application for a permanent charter and the following signed this application: J. Weston Clinard, Walter C. Taylor, Earl N. Carr, Dr. J. H. Shuford, Herbert C. Childers, Donald S. Menzies, Dr. O. H. Hester, Z. T. Setzer, H. Charles Menzies, Jr., Donald E. Shuford, Lemuel C. Berry, Joseph E. Cilley, Joseph E. Reinhardt, Thomas F. Moose, Richard H. Shuford, J. L. Murphy, Dr. H. C. Menzies, Miss Lillie Hall Crowell, Hugh Miller,

George L. Lyerly, James C. Shuford, S. E. Wright, C. V. Garth, John G. H. Geitner, Cecil T. Bost, James Homer Bowles, Russell M. Yount, Harold G. Deal, C. C. Freeman, George C. Warlick, B. B. Blackwelder, M. Ezra Rink, E. Harold Shuford, W. Marvin Reese, George S. Blackwelder, George L. Huffman, Weston L. Taylor, Laurie A. Deal, A. C. Henderson, N. C. Burns, F. L. Cline, William M. Busby, John Jason Reinhardt, Earl T. Edwards, and H. Lester Flowers.

Legion Post Two Hundred and Forty of Maiden, the newest of the county Legion posts, was formed in 1945. It was the outgrowth of a movement begun by Maiden business leaders to furnish for the municipality a war memorial building. Among the persons who spearheaded the drive were John Whisnant, Leonard Moretz, Dr. H. T. Campbell, A. C. McHargue, E. F. Rose, and D. C. Mosteller.

The post's first commander was E. G. Mauney. The list of the organization's charter members was destroyed in a fire.

Legionnaires opened the doors of their war memorial building in 1950.

Assisting with and oftentimes spearheading the courageous work of the Legion are the women of its Auxiliary. While their efforts largely are dedicated to the disabled of wars, they, like the Legionnaires, have branched out into commendable paths of community service.

Unit Sixteen of the American Legion Auxiliary of Newton, the county's first, was organized May 24, 1920. Mrs. G. A. Warlick, Sr., was the initial president.

Unit Forty-Eight of the American Legion Auxiliary of Hickory was established February 25, 1921. Mrs. J. H. Shuford served as the initial president.

Unit Two Hundred and Forty of the American Legion Auxiliary of Maiden was organized in October, 1947. Mrs. Howard J. Campbell served as the initial president.

The present North Carolina department president of the Auxiliary to the American Legion is Mrs. E. P. Rhyne, a resident of Catawba county. The county also has provided two other state presidents, Mrs. Weaver Mann and Mrs. Karl W. Broome.

Veterans of Foreign Wars of the United States

An agency likewise devoted to the interests of veterans, although more recently formed, is the Veterans of Foreign Wars of the United States. This organization, like the Legion, supplements its regular program by assisting community projects.

Post No. 1957 of Hickory was organized on August 2, 1940, with the following charter members: Christopher C. Annas, William P. Anthony, Robert P. Benfield, George S. Blackwelder, Henry S. Brakefield, Carl L. Brooks, Walter L. Bumgarner, William M. Busby, James C. Byers, Joseph E. Cilley, John G. H. Geitner, A. Gaither Hahn, Charles R. Hawn, Aldis C. Henderson, Preston W. Herman, George L. Huffman, James W. Keever, George L. Lyerly, Glenn McCall, Donald S. Menzies, Joseph L. Murphy, Bailey Patrick, Edward T. Pierce, Walter L. Propst, Hubert K. Setzer, Gus Wade, John G. Wilfong, John S. Wilson, Fred G. Womack, and Calvin C. Wright.

After the Second World War the name of the organization was changed from Catawba to Barb-Hammond-Smith in honor of three Hickory boys who sacrificed their lives in the name of freedom. The men were James Ernest Barb, Frank B. Hammond, and William Henderson Smith. George S. Blackwelder was the first post commander.

Post No. 5305 of Newton was organized on January 8, 1946, with the following charter members: Phil L. Barrier, Richard L. Burgess, Marshall L. Bolick, Albert M. Corpening, George L. Coley, Lawrence L. Coley, Jr., Joseph A. Coley, Jr., Dr. Borden C. Drum, Ben L. Estes, Charles W. Gamble, Floyd N. Griggs, Joe W. Hendrix, J. T. Hewitt, Walter A. Hewitt, Thomas E. Herman, Woodrow Hoke, Wilburn H. Hunsucker, James M. Hewitt, John W. Jordan, James F. Jones, March Kale, John M. Little, Jack H. Lisk, Yates E. Martin, George H. Moose, Archie L. Patterson, Winiford H. Robinson, John T. Saunders, Ralph M. Thomas, George A. Warlick, Rodney L. White, Mose A. White, Charles P. White, Dr. Joseph A. Young, and Paul D. Yount.

The post is named for Donald Lanford Drum, who was killed in the service of his country during World War Two.

John W. Jordan was the first post commander.

CATAWBA COUNTY 473

Women have played an important part in the development of the VFW program. The Hickory post's Auxiliary was formed on October 5, 1946. Miss Jane Abernethy was the first president.

The present North Carolina department president of the Auxiliary to the VFW is Mrs. H. Elvin Reinhardt, a resident of Catawba county. The county also has provided a VFW state commander, Harry Vander Linden.

DAUGHTERS OF THE AMERICAN REVOLUTION

An organization which fosters an appreciation of the founders of America, the soldiers of the Revolution, and their accomplishments, is the Daughters of the American Revolution. The county contains two chapters.

The John Hoyle Chapter of the Daughters of the American Revolution was organized in Hickory on January 31, 1922, with Mrs. E. L. Shuford as Organizing Regent. Charter Number 1697 was issued the chapter on July 20, 1927.

Lieutenant John Hoyle, for whom the chapter was named, was the Revolutionary ancestor of most of the charter members, who are: Esther Shuford Blackwelder, Lucile Shuford Bagby, Florence Porter Boyd, Frances Royer Geitner Crowell, Josie Rowe Courtney, Rose Shuford D'Anna, Mary Shuford Davis, Ada Shuford Geitner, Susie Shuford Geitner, Willie Blackwelder Gibbs, Vera Gibbs, Helen Ramseur Hoyle, Frances Hoyle, Minnie Ballew Herndon, Mamie Virginia Herman, Adelaide Johnston Henry, Ella Shuford Johnston, Mayce Blackwelder Jordan, Lillie Hall Crowell Kenyon, Catherine Menzies, Mildred Shuford Ellis Mott, Ida Baker Mosteller, Elizabeth Hoyle Rucker, Alice Wilson Shuford, Kathryn Campbell Shuford, Elva Crowell Shuford, Magnolia Shuford, Annie Ellis Simpson, Nora Shuford Sell, and Mattie Caroline Wilfong Whitener.

The Hickory Tavern Chapter of the Daughters of the American Revolution was organized on February 13, 1951, at the home of Mrs. J. C. Plonk in Catawba county. Mrs. J. R. Tomlinson was the Organizing Regent. The chapter was moved to Hickory on June 7, 1951.

The chapter was named by Walter W. Hahn for Hickory's first building. Its charter members are Alice Edna Bost Barringer, Marjorie Novella Whitener Bushong, Lura Robinson Cline, Dorothy Rose Robinson Campbell, Linda White Miller Dillard, Carrie Ethel Moose Frye, Peggy Stewart Whitener Goodman, Rachel Ellen White Green, Rosalie Little Murray Hahn, Jennie Little Hefner, Mary Louise Millner Hunt, Mary Viola Lowman Kiser, Alla Pearl Little, Lillian Augusta Little, Mabel Little, Carolyn Rhodes Deal Little, Mary Linda White Miller, Maude Elizabeth Leonard Moretz, Lela Maude Reinhardt Plonk, Auralee Cook Poovey, Pearle Tate Robinson, Maude Yoder Robinson, Margaret Anne Rhyne Setzer, Bessie May Reinhardt Shuford, Helen Virginia Frye Shuford, Kate Reinhardt Staton, Eve Tomlinson Thompson, Pearl Miller Tomlinson, Mildred Ellen Miller Watson, Mabel Rosalie Rowe Weaver, Rose Anne Tomlinson Welton, Gertrude Beatrice Kestler Whitener, Mildred Gertrude Whitener, Ruth Isabel Whitener, and Annie Mae Robinson Woodside.

The United Daughters of the Confederacy perpetuates the memory of the men who fought for Southern independence. This group dedicates itself to historical, memorial, educational, and benevolent work.

First in Catawba county to organize a chapter of the UDC was the city of Newton. The Ransom-Sherrill Chapter was organized on March 18, 1903. It was chartered on June 16, 1903.

The chapter was named in honor of General Matt Ransom, General Robert Ransom, and Lieutenant Frank Sherrill.

Mrs. Fannie Ransom Williams was the chapter's first president. Charter members of the organization are Maude P. Carpenter, Fannie R. Brown, Cora Cowles Gaither, Belle Gill Wilfong, Genevieve Wilfong Gaither, Marie Bost, Isabel Bost Eagles, Mattie Hall Witherspoon, Cora Blanche Abernethy Rowe, M. Ann Robinson Lutz, Sarah A. Rabb, Theresa Westerman Long, Alice P. Ramseur, Fannie Ransom Williams, Mary A. Williams Martin, Minnie Cochrane Mebane, Harriett Harris Seagle, Mary Jane Smyre, Ida Sherrill Trollinger, Sarah M. Finger, Mattie L. Cochrane, and Bessie Yount Feimster.

The second county UDC chapter was formed in Hickory in April, 1901, under the direction of Mrs. O. M. Royster and Mrs. George W. Hall. In choosing its name, the chapter hon-

CATAWBA COUNTY 475

ored Abel A. Shuford. Mrs. O. M. Royster was the chapter's first president.

Charter members of the organization are Mattie Gwaltney Menzies, Susan C. Warlick Johnston, Ruth Ebeltoff Hall, Mary Blout Martin, Esther Gilmer Shuford, Rose Campbell Shuford, Mary Williams Martin, Lucille Shuford, Magnolia McKay Shuford, Pearl Elliott Sherrill, Frances Ferguson Cline, Pattie Mallett Royster, Ada B. Schenck, Margaret Bost, Pheribee Seitz Abernethy, Catherine Shuford Menzies, Mary Stewart Abernethy, Alda Campbell Shuford, Claudia Field Allen, Alice Shuford Abernethy, Anna S. Cilley, Edwina Shearn Chadwick, Bessie Leonard Moretz, Alice Wilson Shuford, and Louise Jones Hall.

Under the leadership of the Abel A. Shuford Chapter, two children's chapters were organized. They are the Dixie Grey, with Mrs. H. C. Menzies as leader, and the James M. Weston, with Mrs. R. A. Grimes as leader. These were organized in 1911. The Belle Wilfong Chapter, Children of the Confederacy, was sponsored by the Ransom-Sherrill Chapter, UDC. It was formed on September 13, 1921, under the leadership of Mrs. W. B. Gaither and Mrs. Glenn Long.

The present Mabel Miller Rowe Chapter, UDC, was organized in 1947-48 as an auxiliary to the Abel A. Shuford Chapter, with Mrs. William Frank Thompson as president, and re-organized and chartered on July 7, 1950, as the Mabel Miller Rowe Chapter, with Mrs. Hume Collins as president.

Charter members of the organization are Katherine Wright Boliek, Naomi Cline Collins, Sarah Drerer Cromer, Dorothy Spratt Crouse, Peggy Stewart Whitener Goodman, Nancy Shuford Haines, Alice Moretz Lee, Evelyn Cline Link, Peggy Setzer Mowry, Elizabeth Mebane Reece, Betty Harris Rhyne, Elizabeth Kincheloe Schriver, Helen Esper Setzer, Helen Biggerstaff Setzer, Helen Frye Shuford, Eve Tomlinson Thompson, Ialeen Geneva Johnson Tillery, Martha Link Frye Vander Linden, Rosalie Franklin Yates Wall, Rose Anne Tomlinson Welton, Mildred Gertrude Whitener, and Virginia Elizabeth Yeager.

The newest UDC chapter, the Cecil Brawley Long Chapter, of Newton, was organized on August 5, 1953. It received its charter on August 27, 1953. Miss Millie Ann Pitts is president.

Charter members of the organization are Nancy Bolick, Augusta Gwendolyn Bost, Janice Wayne Caldwell, Bessie Alice Clapp, Vivian Patterson Clapp, Elizabeth Jude Harrison, Viola Elizabeth Haupt, Christine Sherrill Isenhower, Elizabeth Hill Jarrett, Sara Ruth Jarrett, Sylvia Frazier Kidd, Trudy Deems Lefler, Janice Virginia Little, Joyce Malinda Little, Frances Long, Millie Ann Pitts, Frances Ellen Reynolds, Elizabeth Jordan Saunders, Edna Louise Sigmon, Molly Ray Setzer Sigmon, Barbara Warlick Yount, and Catherine Wolfe Yount.

BOY SCOUTS AND GIRL SCOUTS

On February 9, 1910, the first troop of Boy Scouts of America in North Carolina, and one of the initial troops in the United States, was organized in Hickory.

J. W. Clay of Winston-Salem was the first Scoutmaster, while H. K. (Chip) Setzer is credited as the first Scout. Arthur Moser became the second Scoutmaster, and Rev. Professor Eugene deForrest Heald was the third. Hickory's present Troop One, the first, has operated continuously. It presently is supervised by Claude S. Abernethy, who was one of the area's first Scouts and who has been a booster of the Scouting movement since it was begun.

Scouting in the county has been one of effort, education and growth and it moves forward today as a strong supplement to the home, the church and the school, entrenched in the boy life of the county and supported by the area's elders. The county consistently is a leader among the 11 counties which comprise the Piedmont District of Scouts.

The first Girl Scout troop in Catawba county was organized in Hickory in 1923 by Miss Margaret Wilson, recreation director of the chamber of commerce. Miss Mary Newton and Miss Mildred Whitener were the patrol leaders. The troop's life, however, was short-lived.

The first troop to be officially registered as Troop One was organized in 1930 by Miss Frances Whitney, teacher of education at Lenoir Rhyne college. She continued to act as leader for three years, when the troop lapsed for a year or so. Rev. J. H. Armbrust was instrumental in re-establishing the troop and Miss Rachel Lee and Miss Emma Fritz were secured to act

CATAWBA COUNTY 477

as leaders. The troop has been sponsored by the First Methodist church since that time.

With succeeding years, Girl Scouting has branched throughout the entire county. The county today is a part of the Catawba Valley Area Girl Scout Council.

THE GROWTH OF CATAWBA'S FINANCIAL INSTITUTIONS

The initial Catawba county bank was the Bank of Hickory, organized by D. W. Shuler, formerly of Michigan, in November, 1886. This business operated in a store building on the site of the present post office. The bank failed in July, 1890.

On the following day, A. A. Shuford, O. M. Royster, W. H. Ellis and K. C. Menzies founded the Citizens bank, a private institution. This group applied for a charter as a First National bank and received it in July, 1891. The business was opened in the Shuford Hardware building, now known as the A. M. West building. The bank's authorized capital was $50,000.

The Hickory Banking and Trust company was organized in 1903, with J. F. Abernethy as president and A. Y. Kenyon as cashier. This business continued in operation until May, 1917, when it merged with the Catawba Trust company to become the Consolidated Trust company, which, in February, 1930, was purchased by the First National bank.

The Shuford National bank of Newton was founded in 1906 by A. A. Shuford. A. H. Crowell served as cashier.

The second Newton bank, the Farmers and Merchants bank, was organized in 1907 by Dr. J. H. Yount and Mrs. Virginia Shipp. Dr. Yount was the first president and L. H. Phillips was the first cashier. The bank's authorized capital was $50,000. On May 1, 1946, the Farmers and Merchants bank was consolidated with the Northwestern bank.

The Maiden bank was organized in 1909 by B. M. Spratt. L. A. Carpenter was named president and B. M. Spratt was named cashier. The bank's authorized capital was $20,000. Following the "bank holidays" in March, 1933, this institution did not re-open.

The Citizens bank of Conover was chartered on September 18, 1911, with a capital stock of $10,000. John A. Isenhower was its first president, J. Hunsucker was its first vice-president, and T. M. Minish was its first cashier. The business continued until it merged on July 1, 1946, with the Shuford National bank of Newton and the First National bank of Hickory to form the First National Bank of Catawba County.

The Peoples bank of Catawba was founded in 1912, with a capital stock of $10,000. J. Henry Pitts was its first president, and W. B. Walker its first cashier. The business operated a branch at Claremont for a period of about five years, ending in 1923 or 1924.

The Catawba Trust company was organized in Hickory on January 1, 1917, with G. E. Ransom as president. The business operated until May of the same year when it merged with the Hickory Bank and Trust company under the name of the Consolidated Trust company. The Consolidated Trust company was purchased by the First National bank of Hickory in February, 1930.

In 1919, the First Security Trust company was formed by means of a special dividend from the First National bank of Hickory. On December 30, 1947, the Trust department was purchased from the First Security company by the First National Bank of Catawba County. The charter for trust business therefore was surrendered. The company's name was then changed to the First Security company, purely an insurance agency.

A group of business men of Hickory, feeling the need of a financial institution to serve those in need of borrowing small amounts of money to be repaid in weekly or monthly installments from their income, organized the Hickory Industrial bank in January, 1925. Prior to this time, commercial banks of the county had not installed personal loan departments. The institution continued until February, 1944, when it was converted to a state commercial bank, and the name was changed to the Bank of Hickory, under the same management. On July 1, 1946, the assets of the Bank of Hickory were purchased by the Northwestern Bank of North Wilkesboro, and the Hickory branch of the Northwestern bank was opened. An additional branch followed in Maiden.

Also on July 1, 1946, the First National bank of Hickory, the Shuford National bank of Newton, and the Citizens bank of Conover merged under the name of the First National Bank of Catawba County.

Catawba county is known as a county of home owners. Instrumental in aiding the citizens of the county to own their own homes have been savings and loan associations, which today hold combined assets of approximately $15 million.

The first such organization was formed on April 1, 1874, as its by-laws were adopted on this day. Known as the First Building and Loan of Hickory, the organization's first president was J. G. Hall. It is not known how long the building and loan operated, but it is believed that the company was short-lived.

The oldest existing and largest of the associations in the county is the First Savings and Loan Association of Hickory. It was organized on April 3, 1890, by a group of business men. J. D. Elliott was its first president. In January, 1951, the association's name was changed to the First Savings and Loan Association of Hickory. Present assets are approximately $4½ million.

The second oldest existing association is the Citizens Savings and Loan Association of Newton. Chartered on December 16, 1904, J. C. Smith was its first president. In February, 1950, the name of the association was changed to Citizens Savings and Loan Association of Newton. Today's assets are about $3½ million.

The Fidelity Federal Savings and Loan Association of Hickory was organized on September 12, 1912, under the name of the Mutual Building and Loan Association. J. W. Shuford was the first president. In 1943, the present name of the association was adopted. Today's assets total approximately $4 million.

The First Federal Savings and Loan Association of Catawba county was chartered in 1932, under the name of the Peoples Building and Loan Association. T. W. Saunders has been president since organization. In 1940, the association's name was changed to the First Federal Savings and Loan Association of Conover, and, in 1953, the present name was taken. Today's assets are approximately $3¼ million.

The Establishment of Catawba County Hospitals

Three modern, well-equipped hospitals are tangible evidence of great advances made in Catawba county for the welfare of its people.

The area's first hospital, the Richard Baker hospital of Hickory, was founded in 1911 by Dr. Jacob H. Shuford and named in memory of Dr. Richard Browning Baker, a beloved county physician who served from 1871 until his death in 1906.

The Hickory Memorial hospital was opened in 1936 by Hickory Drs. R. T. Hamrick, H. L. Johnson, J. W. Keever, Dan Stewart, H. C. Menzies, and T. C. Blackburn.

The present Catawba hospital of Newton was established in 1938 by a group of Newton and Conover physicians in response to a need expressed by the people of the community. The organizers, Drs. Glenn Long, Lawrence Caldwell, K. L. Cloninger, Walter Long, and A. F. Klutz, purchased and renovated the building which had been erected and used for a short period as a Catawba county sanatorium.

CHAPTER XX

THE NEW ERA: THE TWENTIETH CENTURY

Evelyn Mebane Odum

Standing at the threshold of his second century, the Catawban today faces the future with confidence, the uncertainties and exigencies of his infant struggles in industrial development since 1900 replaced by a calm assurance.

Whence came this sense of economic security?

For 50 years, since the dawn of the twentieth century, the industrial and agricultural development of Catawba county followed a slow upward curve, halted at intervals by the strains and stresses of periodic general depressions, but each time rising gently to a new higher level. The steady progress burst forth in the period from 1942 to 1952 to reach new heights, as the expansion of the area's productiveness came near to doubling the total wealth as reflected in the tax valuation schedule.

The surge of energy that brought a new prosperity to Catawba county during the first decade of its second century was no mushroom growth, prompted by unnatural developments. Rather one must look into the past, to the preceding 50 years, to discover the deep roots that brought forth abundantly to place Catawba among the ten leading counties of the state's 100 in this year, 1953.

A backward look will reveal that Catawbans literally pulled themselves up both agriculturally and industrially by their own bootstraps. Ninety per cent of the capital invested has come from the pockets of Catawbans, who realized their means from their own ingenuity and business acumen. Leadership has been plentiful, as men of vision and faith in their county again and again have supplied the financial support necessary for development and expansion. While it is evident that each section has produced its outstanding citizens who were instrumental in promoting economic development, it is clear that no community has ever been dominated by an individual or group seeking self-advancement. Thus competitive free enterprise has been encouraged with highly beneficial results.

Because Catawba county is a self-made county, with its capital and labor often representing the same people, it has enjoyed singular freedom from labor strife. With a 90 percent white population, a balance maintained through the years, the benefits of progress as measured by a higher standard of living have extended to the Negro race. Improvements in working conditions and the wage scale have on the whole been made voluntarily, as the basic economy could support the drive toward a better life for all people in a material way.

A survey of the Catawba scene as this county emerges from the first decade of its second century of history will justify the confidence of the Catawban that security is his heritage.

At the mid-twentieth century mark, Catawba had quadrupled its population of 1900. The 1950 Federal Census revealed that 61,794 persons were at home in this fertile area that lies at the foothills of the Blue Ridge mountains. Despite this population growth, Catawba has ample room for future citizens in large numbers, in its 435 square miles.

The population increase from 1940 to 1950 was at the rate of 19.6 percent, better than the increase of 13.7 percent for the State of North Carolina as a whole. The rate of growth has been fairly constant it is shown by the census figures of 51,635 in 1950 and 43,991 in 1940.

Hickory with a 1950 population of 14,755 and boasting populous suburbs, is the county's metropolis. The City of Newton, the county seat, had a population of 6,039, and the six incorporated towns in the county were listed as follows: Longview, 2,291; Maiden, 1,952; Conover, 1,164; Brookford, 768; Claremont, 669; and Catawba, 506.

Ranking eighteenth in the state in population, Catawba county placed eleventh in per capita wealth on the basis of its 1951 tax valuation. In 1952 only four North Carolina counties had a lower tax rate than Catawba's 80c levy.

Admitting the tax valuation figures to be a poor indicator of any county's actual wealth as it does not reflect the investment in farm and business properties, the records on file in Catawba's courthouse nevertheless serve to measure the upward trend and reveal the periods of greatest growth.

Personal and real property valued at $94,481,869 was listed in 1952, divided as follows: real property, $50,135,884; personal property, $41,221,763; and corporate excess, $3,124,222. Extension agricultural workers estimate $19,627,992 of the total represents the county's 3,144 farms, for an average value of $6,243. The county auditor's report shows $42,089,428 is business and manufacturing property.

In 1909, while industrial development was yet in its initial stages, Catawba's tax listings totaled $6,941,020. In less than three decades the total rose to $43,863,049, the tax figure for 1937. The decade from 1942 to 1952 brought an increase from $50,055,755 to $94,481,869, with strong indications the $100,-000,000 mark would soon be passed.

Catawba county is not a county spectacular for concentrations of great wealth. It has its fair share of people of means, but more noteworthy is the fact that a great many people share in the prosperity of its factories and farms.

The annual total buying power of Catawbans in 1953 was estimated at $70,765,000 in an industrial survey made by the Newton-Conover Chamber of Commerce. The total represents $4,187 per family, or $1,107 per capita.

Because the income of Catawbans stems from widely diversified industrial and agricultural operations the county is often described as a well balanced county.

Latest complete reports available show that in 1950, a total of 257 manufacturing plants employed 12,931 people and paid total wages of $20,280,000. The value added by the manufacturing process to materials was $40,966,000. Retail value of the finished products manufactured was estimated at over $100,000,000.

The farm cash income is estimated at well over $3,000,000 annually, but a realistic picture of the actual income that accrues to those engaged in farming must include foods and feed raised and used. Agricultural leaders believe such an addition would place the farm income at over $6,000,000. In 1950 the cash value of cattle and dairy products sold amounted to $1,183,122, with the cash return from all livestock and livestock products sold totaling $1,755,829. All harvested crops sold annually bring in over one and a half million dollars. Crops raised, however, have a value of about three and three-quarter million dollars.

Index to the net returns from retail business may be seen in the amount of goods sold. In the 1951-52 fiscal year retail establishments reported total sales of $47,056,000, or per capita sales of $761.50, giving Catawba sixteenth place in the state. During the same period 13,642 reporting firms paid $842,000 into the state treasury as sales tax.

A survey of the industrial scene at mid-1953 revealed that Catawba had 266 manufacturing plants, according to accurate and up-to-date records in the offices of the North Carolina Employment Security Commission in Hickory and Newton. The two offices serve the entire county.

Of the total, 186 were located in the northwestern or Hickory area, and 80 in the southeastern or Newton area. Ninety-four were engaged in furniture and woodwork, including construction; 98 were hosiery mills, 31 were classified textiles other than hosiery, and 43 engaged in miscellaneous manufacturing activities.

Records in the same two offices showed a total of 25,500 persons employed in 1,270 non-agricultural establishments in the county. Eight hundred sixty of the establishments employing 16,000 people were located in the Hickory area, and 410 employing 9,500 were in the Newton area.

Thus it appears that Catawba industry also supports families residing in neighboring counties, as the 25,500 persons employed represent more than 40 percent of the entire population of Catawba county. However, the Catawba labor supply is not exhausted. Indeed, the outlook is good. The present labor pool for suitable employment includes 2,350 persons, 1,400 in the Hickory area and 950 in the Newton area. It should be noted that this labor pool does not indicate that Catawba county has 2,350 persons needing employment at present. It indicates that industries operating under certain conditions, such as accessibility to homes, would find such a local labor supply available.

Roughly the 266 industries represent more than 40 classifications and include ladies', men's and children's hose; furniture for the home, business, and public buildings, including all-wood

CATAWBA COUNTY

furniture and upholstered lines; textiles of every kind from fabrics used in upholstering to infants' wear, utilizing cotton and synthetic fibers; yarns, tapes, cordage, gloves, and other textile products; foods and feeds including flour, soft drinks, dairy products, meats, bakery products, candies; textile machinery, transportation equipment, concrete products, cleaning preparations, work clothing, precision tools, hand tools, pottery and porcelain. There are printing establishments, wirework plants, ice and fuel companies, construction and steel companies, sawmills, and many others engaged in miscellaneous lines.

The Catawban today, who can factually boast of the diversification of industry in his county, must look into the past to learn how this industrial might was built.

Turning the pages of history back to the beginning of the twentieth century, one sees the tanneries, iron forges, tobacco products plants and some of the other early industries giving way to a new era—an era that was ushered in with the coming of the railroad and the development of industrial machinery.

Showing the farsightedness that has characterized Catawbans since pioneer days, the second generation took a look at the scene and envisioned a future in cotton textiles and woodworking, using products available on the home grounds. This generation was aided in its endeavors by the harnessing of the vast water power of the Catawba river, gift of nature, by the Southern Power company, later the Duke Power company, which has fulfilled the hydroelectric needs of the area since 1913.

Historians have disclosed that the first cotton mill came to Catawba county in 1839, at Long Island, but up until 1867 only one other mill, a Granite Shoal plant, had been founded. By 1884 cotton mills were in operation at Monbo, Long Island, Maiden, and Newton. The Shuford Mills company, founded by Abel A. Shuford, had its beginnings in 1880 in neighboring Caldwell county, at Granite Falls. Soon after the turn of the century the first Catawba mill of the company was established, with three more to follow in ensuing years in Hickory. Before the company was 50 years old it had attained the position of the largest manufacturers of cotton cordage in the world, a position it still holds. The company includes the four Hickory mills, three at Granite Falls, and one plant at Valdese in Burke county. The four Hickory plants of the Shuford Mills company employ approximately 900 people at present.

As early as 1895 the hosiery business was introduced to Catawba county. This branch of the textile industry has outgrown the parent cotton mill industry in Hickory, where employment in hosiery mills outranks that in all other lines. In Newton, birthplace of the county's hosiery business, hosiery mills lead in number, but place third in employment, still preceded by other textiles and pushed from second place by a growing furniture industry.

Records in the courthouse reveal that a group of Newton business men received a charter in 1895 to operate a hosiery mill. Named as incorporators were S. M. Finger, George A. Warlick, J. R. Gaither, J. C. Smith, J. C. Whitesides, D. J. Carpenter, and John M. Mier. The mill was started in a large frame building located on the corner of North Ashe avenue and West Fourth street in Newton, where plug tobacco had formerly been made.

The Newton Hosiery Mill, as it was called, remained in operation for a number of years, but failed to prosper, and George A. Warlick was named receiver. D. J. Carpenter purchased controlling interest in the mill, it is believed around 1900, and greatly expanded the enterprise, making hosiery under the brand name of "Black Crow." It is recalled by Newton residents that the product gained recognition at the Jamestown Exposition in 1907. Some years later, about 1910, the building burned, and the mill passed into the hands of Newton and Statesville banks. A reorganization was effected, a brick building replaced the burned structure, and the mill continued under the name Fidelity Hosiery Mill. The original corporation was dissolved in 1909.

J. A. Cline founded the first hosiery mill in Hickory in 1906.

Just as the hosiery industry has taken the lead in the textile division, furniture manufacturing, one of the big three industries in the county today, early emerged as the most promising specialized line using wood.

George W. Hall of Hickory was the man who pioneered in furniture-making in Catawba county, establishing the Hickory Furniture company in 1901. Not only was he a leader in the county, but also he was among the leaders in the industry in the state. Hall's plant made bedroom suites, continuing this line until 1931 when it was merged with the Hickory Chair company.

This man, known as the father of the furniture industry in the county, also had a hand in the founding of the county's second furniture manufacturing plant, the Martin Furniture company, in Hickory the same year.

How prophetically Hall chose his field in industry is seen today in the semi-annual Furniture Market held in the city of Hickory. This event each spring and fall brings buyers from all over the United States who choose from displays at the city's Community Center and in showrooms of the larger mills.

The work glove industry, another branch of the textile industry, leads in the state in its field. It is centered in the Newton-Conover area. The parent glove mill of the county was founded by Perry Heavner in 1911 near the Banoak school. Later the plant was moved to Connelly Springs, in Burke county, and finally back to this county. The family later entered another line of business. Although the first glove mill was discontinued, four work glove plants today employ around 1,000 men and women of the Newton-Conover section. They are the Newton Glove Manufacturing company, founded in 1916; the Warlong Glove Manufacturing company of Conover, founded in 1916; the Southern Glove company, located on U. S. Highway 321 between Newton and Conover, founded in 1943; and the Carolina Glove company, located east of Newton, organized in 1943.

Limitations of space will not permit examination of beginnings of all industries now of vital importance in the county's economy. Because textiles, hosiery, and furniture manufacturing are the backbone of industrial might in every section of the county, and glove manufacturing leads in its field and gives employment to many, though concentrated in Newton-Conover, these have been selected for special attention. This in no manner minimizes the essentiality of the scores of other manufacturing processes or the others engaged in the three leading lines. It is a tribute to this county's vast industrial power that it is impossible to tell the story briefly. It is a subject for another history.

While Catawba county has been growing industrially, its agricultural development has been steady. For 40 years Catawba county has had a planned program in agriculture. Its effectiveness may be seen in the diversification practiced in planting crops, in the development of the dairy cattle and beef cattle industries, in the mechanization of farms, in the practices used to conserve the fertility of the soil, and in the modernization of farm homes.

Catawbans derived their sustenance from the soil in the pioneer days, and the soil continues to provide one of their greatest reservoirs of strength. Though municipalities in the county list 45.5 percent of the population within the city and the town limits, and claim about 25 percent more in suburbs, the fact remains that Catawbans are still deeply rooted to the soil.

Farming operations in Catawba are carried on by many urbanites, and literally scores are engaged in industrial work while continuing farming. The core of the agricultural industry, however, lies in those people devoted exclusively to the business of farming.

About 225,000 acres of land are classified as farm land, with some 83,000 acres under cultivation in crops, about 20,000 acres in pastures, another 20,000 acres idle, and roughly 100,000 acres in woodlands.

The percentage of farm tenancy in Catawba has declined through the years, until today it is estimated that only 15 percent of those engaged in farming own no part of the land they work. In 1920, when there were fewer farms, 25.2 percent were operated by tenants.

Just as industrial leaders emerged through the years to take the lead in development and expansion, Catawba county has had an excellent rural leadership, with its men of vision foreseeing extra profits in the adoption of modern methods and in making use of the contributions of science to increase crop production and improve livestock.

In their efforts to keep abreast of modern farming methods, Catawbans have had the services of specialists.

As early as 1915 Catawba county employed its first County Farm Agent, and the county farm women have had leadership since 1911 when the first "tomato canning clubs," that developed into the County Home Demonstration clubs, were formed. Rural dwellers have made excellent use of the expert help offered by the farm and home Agricultural Extension Workers. They also took advantage of a county terracing unit, put into operation in 1935, the Soil Conservation program begun in 1935, and the various Federal government programs available to them. Today, they continue to use any of these programs applicable to their individual needs.

That the farm women have profited by the program carried on by a succession of capable Home Demonstration leaders is readily seen in the attractive farm homes, where home grown produce is frozen or processed by the most modern methods and well ordered housekeeping permits time for recreation. Today there are between 700 and 800 members in the 21 County Home Demonstration clubs now active.

Catawba is looking to the future of its farm leadership. Assistant Farm and Home Agents, with the Extension Service, direct 18 4-H clubs for rural boys and girls. Total enrollment at present is 1,530, including 680 boys and 850 girls.

A third Assistant Farm Agent devotes his entire time to farmers engaged in the production and care of livestock.

In addition to these services, rural Catawbans have the use of the expert knowledge of a forester. His duties involve protection of woodlands from fires and reforestation, but he is available to farmers desirous of conserving their forests by correct selection of trees for market. The forestry service was added in 1949 when Catawba joined a Forestry district, thereby gaining state aid.

Soil erosion control gained impetus in Catawba county in 1935, with the establishment of Camp Little, Co. 3415 SCS 15, in Newton. Through an arrangement with the county Soil Conservation head, the 150 to 200 young men enrolled at the camp were kept busy on cooperating farms. They built terraces, cut diversion ditches, filled gullies, set out erosion-checking trees and shrubs, and in many other ways aided in conserving the natural wealth of the soil. After several years the camp was moved to Hickory, where the work continued in that area.

Soil building practices are continued through the Soil Conservation District, formed in 1938 with headquarters in Newton, and also through practices approved by the Agricultural Conservation Program of the United States Department of Agriculture, operated under Production and Marketing Administration officials, located in the county building in Newton. Still another Federal agency active in Catawba county is the Farmers Home Administration, through which farmers facing financing difficulties are aided under approved planned programs.

Rural Catawba county is as deeply imbued with civic consciousness as are the residents of the municipalities. Attractive, well furnished community buildings in every rural area attest to this fact. These centers are the focal point for social and civic activities for young and old. County Home Demonstration clubs initiated most of these movements, finding strong support from men and women, boys and girls in the areas. Grange Chapters are also strong supporters of community improvement programs, often assuming leadership in projects for the general welfare.

It is perhaps due to the planned agricultural program of Catawba county for nearly 40 years that there has been no sudden change in the trend of the agricultural industry. Crop diversification came early to Catawba, and the "Live at Home" movement of the 1920s found a ready and willing response.

The principal cash crops of the county at present are cotton, corn, and wheat, with wheat at the top in acreage. Noteworthy results have been obtained in increasing production per acre, with the most outstanding success gained in producing corn. A recent study of Catawba county revealed that while the area had reduced its acreage 25 percent, an increase of 100 percent was noted in corn produced. The average yield in a normal year is 35 bushels per acre.

Cotton acreage has been reduced in Catawba county markedly. The fiber crop has maintained its position as one of the leaders as a cash crop, however. Reports persist that at one time Catawba had 22,000 acres in cotton, and it is known to have had 16,000 acres devoted to the crop in 1934. The crop control program brought a drop to 12,682 acres in 1937, and in 1949 the acreage was 9,940. The 1953 crop was contained in about 4,500 acres.

CATAWBA COUNTY

The boll weevil struck hard in Catawba county in 1950, cutting the production from the 8,271 bales ginned in 1949 to 1,725 bales. General warfare is still being waged by cotton farmers on the destructive weevil which has cost them thousands of dollars since 1950. Normally the cotton yield of one bale or 500 pounds of lint per acre, together with a favorable price, serve to keep the crop at the top in terms of total financial return.

Other leading crops with the current and 1930 acreage given for comparative purposes are:

Wheat 19,572 acres (1953), 14,078 (1930); corn 15,000 acres (1953), 19,801 acres (1930); oats 12,500 acres (1953), 1,521 acres (1930); hay for all purposes 29,382 acres (1953), 9,359 acres (1930); pastures 18,633 acres (1953), 8,596 acres (1930).

Pastures are much in evidence in this county today, the acreage having been more than doubled in the past 20 years, and increased attention is given to improving pastures.

Catawba, for many years a leader in blooded dairy cattle, is moving into the beef cattle business at a rapid pace. It is estimated that at present there are 12,000 head of cattle, including dairy cattle, beef cattle and calves on Catawba county farms. The movement toward raising beef began about 1939, and in more recent years has found favor with numbers, most of whom are in the operation on a small scale at this time.

The impetus given production of blooded cows for dairy farms in 1935 with the organization of the Catawba Jersey Cattle club has paid well through the years. The trend toward Jersey cows was evident as early as 1882, when the breed was introduced at a sale in Hickory. The County Cow Testing Association was also formed by Jersey breeders in 1935. In recent years the Holstein breed has found favor on some Catawba county farms, but whatever the breed, it can be authoritatively stated that Catawba's dairy farmers have long since bred only blooded dairy cattle.

Catawba county in 1953 had 106 dairies producing Grade A milk, whereas in 1941 only 11 were classified as Grade A milk dairies. An average of from 25 to 30 cows were being milked at the dairies, for a total of approximately 3,180. In 1953 an additional 340 farms were selling milk directly for processing purposes, an outlet for milk producers that opened in neighboring Iredell county in the late 1930s.

The Catawba County Artificial Breeding Association which was formed in 1948 has found widespread approval among Catawba's dairy farmers, who have used the service to breed over 4,000 cows in the last four years.

The poultry business has always flourished in Catawba county, and the census of 1950 counted 90,948 fowls on the farms. In 1953 that number had grown to about 125,000. The annual cash income from poultry is estimated to be $300,000.

As mechanization has come to Catawba's farms, the horse and the mule have been rapidly displaced. Latest census figures indicate 1,259 horses and mules still on the farms, but farm officials believe the number greatly reduced at present. Before mechanization began, in 1915, 6,221 horses and mules were working for and transporting the people of Catawba county.

Any fruit which may be grown in the temperate zone may be grown in Catawba county. While the fruit business is profitable for a number of individuals or groups engaged, the industry does not loom large in the overall picture. Grown for local sale and for some outside markets are peaches, apples and grapes, while berries and small fruits appear principally for home use or for neighborhood markets.

Innumerable other crops are grown in Catawba county, including sweet potatoes, on about 1,000 acres, Irish potatoes, and garden vegetables of all kinds.

It is estimated that 10,000,000 feet of lumber are cut annually from Catawba's 100,000 acres of forest lands. Approximately 300,000,000 board feet were estimated standing in 1953. Principal merchantable species of trees are shortleaf and Virginia pine and oak.

Another industry that derives from the soil in Catawba county is the nursery business, which early moved to the forefront in North Carolina. Because the climate and soil are adapted to shrub and fruit growing, this area as early as 1850 pioneered in the development of choice fruits and trees. A peak was attained in the 1930s, when 50 percent of all the fruit growing trees in the state were raised in Catawba county.

In 1950, 80 percent of the 3,143 farms listed in Catawba county had electricity, placing this area thirty-fourth in the state with 824 miles of rural electric lines. The same year 12 percent of the farms had telephones, for a rank of twenty-second in the state. In 1952, 1,245 rural phones were listed, boosting the percentage of farms with telephones to 39.5.

That these figures will change greatly in the next compilation is obvious from current reports from the three telephone companies that serve the county. Southern Bell Telephone company, which has had a rural expansion program underway for two years, reports that as of July 30, 1953, 1,123 rural phones were in operation through exchanges at Newton, Claremont, and Maiden. The Catawba Telephone company reported 175 rural phones through its exchange in Catawba. The Hickory Telephone company listed 4,417 phones through the Hickory exchange outside the city limits. However, all of these outlets could not be termed rural as a majority were in populous suburban areas. Of the total, 1,403 were on 10-party lines, and many of these would be classified as farm telephones.

North Carolinas' road-building program initiated in the 1920s gave impetus to agriculture and industry alike, in Catawba county. The railroad opened new markets in the 1880s, but the $115,000,000 spent during the 20s for roads in the state opened farm to market roads as well as linked cities and counties of North Carolina. The natural route from Statesville to Asheville directly through Conover and Hickory that brought the battle of the 80s to bring the main line of the North-South railway through Newton again rose to threaten the county seat city's prominence. After a fight that was taken all the way to the State Supreme Court, Newton won its contention that the state's "Main Street," N. C. Highway 10 from Manteo to Murphy, had to pass by the courthouse door.

It was at the mid-century mark that North Carolina entered its second program of road building, which used capital from bonds for the purpose. Approval was given by voters to a $200,000,000 road building plan for secondary roads. The General Assembly of North Carolina soon thereafter gave a boost to municipal road work by passage of the "Powell Act," under which cities and towns in the state share in the state's highway fund under specified conditions.

As of January 1, 1953, Catawba county had 777.3 miles of paved and improved roads, with the figure including state highways in rural areas, in municipalities and municipal roads connecting with the state system. A breakdown of the types of roads shows 99.4 miles of paved state roads in the primary system in the rural sections and 24.3 miles of paved roads in the system in towns and cities. In addition, rural Catawba county had 398.2 miles of treated, but not paved, roads and 233.5 miles of paved roads in the state's secondary highway system. Eighteen and three-tenths miles of paved roads and 3.1 miles of unpaved roads inside municipalities connected with the state highway system. The totals were 376 miles of paved roads and 401.3 miles of unpaved roads.

Along with the farmers' "Live at Home" program came the "Trade at Home" program of the towns. The roads that gave a new life-line for business also offered easy access to big city shopping centers. This situation aroused a new civic consciousness, that gave impetus to the development of civic clubs. These clubs served a dual purpose, as they acted effectively in the capacity of a chamber of commerce. They are yet a vital force. Only Hickory and Newton-Conover have chambers of commerce at present, but each community has its civic group performing similar duties.

Agriculture and industry know no barriers in Catawba county, for often the same people represent both. They have repeatedly jointly supported civic endeavors. It can truly be said that the rural and urban population are similar in interests, standard of living, progressiveness, and emphasis upon cultural and educational advantages.

It has been stated that 90 percent of the capital invested in Catawba county has come from Catawbans. The early development of strong financial institutions meant that farmers and businessmen had access to funds to meet their requirements at home. Sound business practices of banks at Hickory, Newton, Conover and Catawba and of building and loan associations at Hickory, Newton and Conover enabled all to weather the depression storm of the early 30s, thereby giving strong support to the wavering economic structure. That Catawba county came through this period with strength is revealed in the fact that in 1935 it led all counties in the state in retail trade on a per capita basis.

CATAWBA COUNTY 495

Aviation, motor transportation, radio and newspapers, must be added to the factors contributing to the progress of Catawba county.

Air travel came to the county from a movement started in 1937, when the city of Hickory foresaw that an airport would be a necessity if the municipality were to keep pace with a rapidly changing world. As air transportation developed by leaps and bounds, bringing larger commercial aircraft, Hickory again moved to extend the facilities of its airport to meet the requirements set by modern aviation. Today the efforts are rewarded, and people of this and nearby counties have the advantage of both air passenger and air express service.

Motor vehicles registered in Catawba county in 1951 were estimated at 20,635, or about one for every three people. The introduction of motor freight in the 1930s permitted an expansion of industrial areas, as the freight carrier could move to the door of the plant. Presently there are 19 motor freight lines operating regularly in Catawba county, and passenger service through buses amply reaches into every community.

It may be stated authoritatively that Catawba county's people are exceptionally well informed on current events. The ease with which information may be rapidly disseminated the length and breadth of the county was dramatically illustrated in July, 1953. At that time health authorities and local physicians combined forces to check a rapidly spreading epidemic of poliomyelitis, the third such outbreak in the county since 1944. Cooperation of every family in the county was needed in a program to inoculate all children under ten years of age with gamma globulin, a serum found beneficial in combatting the disease. Time to get necessary information to parents was short.

Through the use of the three newspapers in the county and the three radio stations, remarkable results were obtained. It was evident from the response that practically every home in Catawba county has access to either a newspaper or a radio or both. When the results were counted, 14,761 children had been inoculated in two days.

The newspapers and radio stations that serve so effectively are The Daily Catawba News-Enterprise, founded in 1879;

The Hickory Daily Record, founded in 1915; The Newton-Conover Observer, issued tri-weekly, founded in 1933; Radio Station WHKY, Hickory, founded in 1940; Radio Station WNNC, Newton, established in the Spring of 1948; and Radio Station WIRC, Hickory, which began operations December 5, 1948.

Another indication of the alertness of Catawbans is seen in the circulation figures from the three public libraries in the county. In the 1952-53 fiscal year the circulation rose to 286,649 for the three: The Catawba County library in Newton, the Elbert Ivey Memorial library in Hickory, and Ridgeview Public library for Negroes, also in Hickory.

The independent spirit that brought the pioneers to Catawba county, and that led them and succeeding generations to drive toward self-sufficiency is reflected in the county government.

Political observers hesitate to forecast Catawba as a Republican or Democratic county, regardless of the party in power, because the independence of the voters is indicated in every election. History shows that neither major political party can relax in the comfort of victory foreseen.

In 1937 Catawba County Commissioners created the office of county manager. In taking this step they had before them the example of the city of Hickory, which in 1913 had become the first city in North Carolina and among the first in the nation, to employ the services of a manager. The board also in 1937 created a non-partisan tax commission.

Municipalities in the county are not concerned with partisan politics in their selection of officials. The records reveal the administration of public affairs has been uniformly good. Newton now also has the city manager plan, approved by voters in a special election in 1950.

Though emphasis is placed on economy by Catawba county people where their government is concerned it would be a mistake to assume that frugality has been the guide for voters. While they have shown insistence upon value for their tax dollars, they are equally insistent that desirable services be rendered.

Among the services that Catawba county provides with outside aid, state or Federal or both, are public health, education, welfare aid, rural farm and home programs, forestry service, and assistance to public libraries.

The county owns a courthouse, built in 1924 at a cost of approximately $250,000 and still considered one of the most handsome and adequate in the state; a county office and jail building, constructed in 1939 at a cost of $85,000. The county home was discontinued April 1, 1949, and the needy aged are now cared for in nursing homes. Present plans call for a new health center in Hickory, to be located on U. S. Highway 64-70 east of the intersection with South Center street, at a cost of $66,000. Forty-four percent of the cost will be borne by state-Federal aid. In erecting the office building and jail the county was assisted by the Public Works Administration, a Federal agency, which paid 45 percent of the cost.

The State Highway Commission has plans for a headquarters building for the State Highway Patrolmen in this area on U. S. Highway 64-70 between Hickory and Conover.

Offices in the courthouse are those of the Sheriff, County Auditor and Manager, Tax Supervisor, Clerk of Superior Court, County Superintendent of Schools, Register of Deeds, Surveyor, Selective Service Board 18, State Revenue deputies, Western District Federal Judge, and Resident Superior Court Judge. There is also a large courtroom, a commissioners' room, jurors' room, law library, and vaults for records are located in the basement.

The County Welfare Department and District Health Department headquarters occupy the ground floor of the county office building. The second floor houses agricultural Extension workers, with a Home Demonstration kitchen and assembly room. Jail quarters are on the third floor, which has elevator service from the kitchen located in the basement.

Space is rented in Hickory for health and welfare office branches.

Catawba county entered the fiscal year 1953-54 with the largest budget in its history, $1,771,713.33.

More than $1,000,000 of the total was earmarked for schools, with more than half of that amount to be used in a school improvement program which was inaugurated in 1949.

The budget breakdown follows: Schools, $1,093,258.13; General Fund (including county administration, operation of county courthouse, county office building and jail), $257,290.00; Welfare Department, $125,789.20; Health Department, $42,165.00; and Debt Service, $253,211.00.

An examination of recent developments in public education is necessary for a comprehension of the large budget allotment for schools.

Just as in the early 1920s Catawba county, under the superintendency of the Rev. George E. Long, took the lead in North Carolina in the consolidation of its rural schools, so in the year 1949 it was a forerunner in approving a further consolidation under the superintendency of M. C. Campbell.

Friends of education throughout the county voted bonds totaling $3,750,000 for a school improvement program which would result in five rural consolidated high schools, replacing the 11 then in existence. The bonds were also to be used to improve city schools of Newton-Conover and Hickory, with expenditures to be allocated proportionately.

It soon became apparent, however, that a minimum of $5,000,000 would be necessary to complete the program planned, even when stripped to essentials. The county received assistance from a special $50,000,000 bond issue of the state, and allocated surplus funds that had accumulated in the county treasury and drew from the net proceeds from the operation of ABC stores to supplement the bond fund.

Three of the new county high schools were ready for use in 1953, and the other two are to be completed in 1954. Locations are St. Stephens, Maiden, Propst Crossroads, a point near Oxford-Catawba-Claremont, and a point near Balls Creek-Sherrills Ford.

The school improvement program also provided new buildings for the Newton-Conover and Hickory school systems, and a renovation program for existing buildings in all three systems.

The Catawba county rural school system has an enrollment of around 7,000 children. Included in the system with the five consolidated High schools are 13 white elementary schools, three elementary schools for Negroes, and one high school for Negroes, located at Catawba.

The Hickory City school system enrolls some 5,500 children, the physical plants include one Senior High school and one Junior High school for white students, one Negro High school, eight elementary schools for white children and one for Negroes.

The Newton-Conover school system, with approximately 2,200 children enrolled, includes one High school for white children, one for Negroes, three elementary schools for white children and one for Negroes.

Of the more than $1,000,000 allocated for schools in 1953-54, $685,590.91 was earmarked for the school building program. Thus total allocations for operations and regular capital outlay uses amounted to $407,667.22, with $244,753.29 of that amount for current operating expense.

Hickory and Newton-Conover city schools have supplementary funds through special school tax levies, approved by voters in the two districts in 1940.

It is through the County Welfare Department that Catawbans minister to the needs of those requiring assistance.

State and Federal funds provide five-sixths of the allotments approved by the County Welfare Board for Old Age Assistance, Aid to Dependent Children, Aid to the Blind, and Aid to the Permanently Disabled. The county pays all of the funds used in general assistance, for which $30,000 was allocated for the 1953-54 fiscal year, and bears the larger part of the cost of administration. It is estimated that while the county will spend slightly over $100,000 for all phases of welfare work during the current fiscal year, state-Federal contributions will add $290,700.

The county's public health program was inaugurated in 1938, when a county health department was formed, with full-time services of a physician, sanitation officer, public health nurses, and other office personnel. Prior to that time a county health officer served by appointment on a part-time basis. Later the county joined a tri-county health district, which includes Lincoln and Alexander counties. The state gives assistance in the program.

Supplementing the program of the health department in the discovery of tuberculosis is the Alexander-Catawba-Lincoln

District Tuberculosis Association, which holds continuous free X-ray clinics with a mobile X-ray unit in the tri-county area.

This association had its beginnings in 1930, when the Business and Professional Women's Club of Hickory conducted the first mail sale of TB Christmas Seals. Proceeds from this annual sale finance the program.

In the early years, before the formation of the health department, the funds derived were used to employ a public health nurse who worked through the schools. Later a Health Camp for Underprivileged Children was conducted in the summer. It was in 1945 that the Catawba County Tuberculosis Association employed its first full-time executive secretary, and in 1950 the District Association was formed, the first such unit in the state.

Catawba county has four other organizations operating on a county-wide scale financed by voluntary contributions. The Catawba County Chapter of the National Foundation for Infantile Paralysis has been unusually active since 1944 due to the fact that the county has had three poliomyelitis epidemics since that date. The second epidemic struck in 1948, and the third in 1953.

Other organizations concerned with health work in county-wide programs are the Catawba County Unit of the American Cancer Society, and the Catawba County Society for Crippled Children and Adults. The Catawba County Chapter of the American Red Cross is the fifth organization, operating on a county-wide basis.

These five programs received contributions totaling approximately $100,000 in the 1952-53 fiscal year. There are many other organizations supported by voluntary contributions, but without a county organization as a unit.

Looming large on the horizon of Catawba county are its churches. In traversing the area, whether in the municipalities or in the rural section, one is seldom out of sight of one of the more than 100 edifices serving congregations representing many denominations. One is struck with the beauty of the buildings, some constructed of native stone, others of brick, and some of wood. Within recent years most of the churches have added an educational building, housing the church school departments and used as a focal point for social activities, now an integral part of the program of most denominations. Some of the newer churches, built by the larger congregations, have included their educational and recreational facilities under one roof with the sanctuary.

Beauty has become as much a requisite as serviceability for church furnishings. Church grounds are pleasing to the eye, and cemeteries throughout the county are given the care necessary to maintain neatness. These handsome structures that grace Catawba county's countryside are the symbol of the essential spirituality of its people. They have obviously sacrificed to create houses of worship which would fulfill their inner cravings for a physical plant worthy of the high value they place upon spiritual development.

Index to the success of family life of Catawbans may be seen in the marriage and divorce rates for 1950. That year 386 marriages were performed, for a rate of 6.2 per 1,000 population as compared with the United States marriage rate of 11.1 per 1,000. The same year 38 divorces were granted in the county for a rate of .6 per 1,000, a record considerably better than the United States average of 2.6 per 1,000.

Catawba county has been successful in holding its own professional people and drawing others in sufficient numbers to meet the needs of the population.

Approximately 40 lawyers, 20 dentists and 40 physicians and specialists in the medical field were practicing in the county in 1953. In addition to these and scores of educators and ministers, a roster of professional people would include registered nurses, optometrists, physical therapists, pharmacists, chiropractors, chiropodists, veterinarians, and others. Additional specialists available in the county include architects, certified public accountants, photographers, and engravers.

Three hospitals, Richard Baker and Hickory Memorial in Hickory and Catawba Hospital in Newton, have from time to time been enlarged, and offer Catawbans hospital care and professional services rarely found outside large metropolitan areas.

Higher education is available to Catawbans at home, at Lenoir Rhyne college, in Hickory, and vocational and business schools in Hickory. Parochial schools are operated in Conover and at

St. Stephens, and a number of nurseries and kindergartens are in operation in Newton, Conover, and Hickory.

While building a strong financial structure based on manufacturing and agriculture, and straining to fulfill the needs of all the people with educational opportunities and religious training, Catawbans during the twentieth century have not neglected the cultural side of life.

Having found among its people artists, musicians, writers, poets, and other gifted individuals plus a population appreciative of the works resulting from such talent, an effort has been made to encourage the arts.

Hickory with its Museum of Art, its Community Concert Association, and the Community center, headquarters for the city's recreational program, has taken the lead in the county. Newton, prior to the burning of the Catawba County Library in 1952, had used the building for exhibit purposes. The city is in process of establishing a recreation program, supported by a special tax levy. Noteworthy support is given High school bands and Glee Clubs in Newton-Conover and Hickory, and a Hickory Men's Chorus has won fame for itself and has given pleasure to thousands.

In the rural areas, farm organizations, including the county Home Demonstration clubs, Grange Chapters, and 4-H boys' and girls' clubs, foster entertainment featuring use of local talent. The Women's clubs have a Chorus which has attained recognition.

Smaller municipalities in the county have also instituted recreation programs, usually under the sponsorship of a civic club. Through the Boy and Girl Scout organizations leadership is offered the young people in developing natural talents while engaged in citizenship training.

Great interest has developed in flower shows. Hickory annually holds a state Gladiolus Show, and both Conover and Newton hold annual flower shows.

The drama and the romance of the opening of new ventures, and the thrill of introducing colorful, strong, magnetic personalities whose lives determined the course of Catawba's history since 1900 have been sacrificed to permit a broad view of the county's position in industry, agriculture, government, education, and its general characteristics at the middle of the twentieth century.

It will be remembered, however, that the history of an area is only the story of its people. Their determination in overcoming obstacles and disasters as well as their successes in initiating new movements are contained in the panorama of Catawba today.

As he surveys that vast scene, the Catawban is proud of his county. He sees a secure future for himself and his sons and daughters. He is proud of the fact that for generations young Catawbans have taken the helm from their elders to forge steadily forward in an era when the State of North Carolina as a whole was losing too many of its talented young men and women to other states. He visualizes a county that will continue to draw men and women looking for a future, to augment those who have already adopted Catawba as their home. His sense of human values remains keen. He is content that his fellow Catawbans share his convictions that the mind, and the spirit, and the heart as well as the physical body must be nourished. He is quick to lend a helping hand in time of need, but stubborn in resisting any who would misuse his generosity. He welcomes the discoveries of the scientists of the Atomic Age, but he rejects the ideologies of the new era where they threaten his personal dignity and independence.

The Catawban of 1953 in temperament is very like his forefathers of 111 years ago. He has seen the industrial revolution come to his county, he has withstood the shock of wars at home and abroad, and has emerged from periods of depression the stronger for his experience. He has established himself as a solid and dependable citizen among the 100 counties in North Carolina. He stands today with faith in his ability to meet the challenges of the future.

BIBLIOGRAPHY

Personal assistance through interview and/or manuscript, newspaper articles and/or family records was given generously by:

Allison Burch; American Legion Post Number 48; Arndt, Harry M.; Ballard, J. M.; Ballard, Mrs. J. M.; Blackburn, Walter; Bollinger, Raleigh E.; Boyles, H. D.; Bridges, Wake; Brintnall, Earle; Carpenter, John F., Sr.; Carver, Dr. R. W.; Cloninger, C. A.; Davis, Mrs. Mary Shuford; Day, William A.; Deal, Miss Jessie; Deaton, P. W.; Fox, Edgar L.; Gifford, L. C.; Giles, Jesse F.; Gurley, R. N.; Hahn, Walter A.; Hahn, Mrs. Walter A.; Hamilton, W. S.; Hefner, R. L.; Hefner, Mrs. R. L.; Herman, Clyde L.; Hodges, Dr. J. E.; Isenhower, Mrs. J. A.; Kidd, Mrs. L. W.; Killian, J. Yates; Knox, Miss Wylie K.; Latta, Major J. L.; Lefler, Dr. Hugh T.; Linder, George, (and staff of the Catawba County Library); Link, Mrs. Sarah; Long, Mrs. Cecile Brawley; Lowrance, David; McCorkle, M. L.; Marlow, Mrs. W. E.; Mebane, Cyril Long; Miller, Mrs. Cordelia Clay; Moretz, Mrs. J. A.; Mosteller, Miss Nita; Nixon, A.; Nixon, Joseph R.; Olds, Fred A.; Mott, Mrs. T. A.; Patrick, Miss Grace, (and staff of the Elbert Ivey Memorial Library); Plonk, Mrs. J. C.; Pope, George; Poston, Lewis; Robinson, Mrs. Maude Yoder; Ross, Mrs. Helen; Rowe, G. Sam; Rowe, Mrs. Mabel Miller; Shell, Ralph T.; Sherrill, Miles O.; Shuford, Mrs. A. Craig; Shuford, E. L.; Shuford, Mrs. Helen Frye; Sigmon, Mrs. A. Y.; Smith, Rev. C. O.; Steelman, Max R.; Tomlinson, Mrs. Pearl M.; Vander Linden, Frank; Vander Linden, Mrs. Harry; Warlick, Mrs. Virginia; Warlick, J. W.; Warlick, Judge Wilson; Wilfong, Gordon; Willis, Mrs. Mary Elliott Henderson; Yoder, Colonel George M.; and Yoder, Dr. Robert A.

County manuscripts:

Bost, C. C., and Bost, M. M. Diary, published in The Hickory Daily Record from February 18, 1937, to August 31, 1937. (Manuscript is held by Mrs. R. V. Moss.)

Bost, Emma Ingold. *Songs in Many Keys.* Hickory, N. C.

Click, J. F. *The Hickory Baptist Church.* 1927.

Hahn, George W., ed. *The Catawba Soldier of the Civil War.* Hickory, Clay Printing Company, 1911.

Murphy, Joseph L. *A Historical Sketch of Claremont College.*

Setzer, Pearl. *The Building of Catawba.* A historical pageant. 1925, published under the auspices of the Catawba County Fair Association.

Shuford, Julius A. *A Historical Sketch of the Shuford Family.* Hickory, A. L. Crouse and Son, 1902.

Whitener, R. Vance. *Tales of Our Ancestors in Catawba County, North Carolina.*

CATAWBA COUNTY 505

Whitener, Russell W. *The Growth and Development of Education in Catawba County.* (A thesis.)

Yount, H. M. *History of the Work Glove Industry in Catawba County.*

Materials held in the archives of the Catawba County Historical Association:

Answer to inquiry concerning naming of Catawba river (from U. S. Department of Interior).

List of post offices (from U. S. Post Office Department).

Lists of soldiers (from U. S. War Department).

Military records of John Wilfong.

Pension applications of Revolution for 1776 to 1782 (from U. S. National Archives).

Records and documents:

Arndt, Rev. John Godfrey. Journal. (Held by Lenoir Rhyne college.)

Catawba county commission records.

Church records of Grace Lutheran, Olivet Baptist, and St. Peter's Lutheran churches.

County records of Catawba, Lincoln, Rowan, Mecklenburg, Caldwell and Burke counties.

Education records of Catawba county's three school systems: Catawba County Rural, Hickory, and Newton-Conover.

Henkel, Rev. Paul. Diary. (Held by Lenoir Rhyne college.)

North Carolina legislative documents.

North Carolina State Superintendents of Public Instruction, reports of.

Municipal records of Hickory, Newton, Conover, Maiden, Claremont, Brookford, Catawba, and Longview.

Newspapers:

Catawba News-Enterprise.

Hickory Daily Record.

Hickory Democrat.

Hickory Press.

Lincolnton Transcript.

Newton-Conover Observer.

Nut Shell (Hickory).

Press and Carolinian (Hickory).

Times-Mercury (Hickory).

North Carolina reference:

Arnett, Alex Mathews, with the collaboration of Jackson, Walter Clinton. *The Story of North Carolina.* Chapel Hill, The University of North Carolina Press, 1933.

Barringer, Anne. *The Natural Bent, The Memoirs of Dr. Paul B. Barringer.* Chapel Hill, The University of North Carolina Press, 1949.

Branson, Levi, ed. *Branson's North Carolina Business Directory.* For 1867, 1868, 1869, 1872, 1877, 1878, 1884, 1890, and 1896. Raleigh, Branson House (Levi Branson, Office Publisher).

Bynum, Curtis, ed. *Marriage Bonds of Tryon and Lincoln Counties North Carolina.* 1929.

Connor, R. D. W. *Studies in North Carolina History.* Number 1—*Race Elements in the White Population of North Carolina*; Number 2—*Revolutionary Leaders of North Carolina*; Number 3—*Ante-Bellum Builders of North Carolina.* Greensboro, The North Carolina College for Women, 1923.

Coon, Charles L., ed. *The Beginning of Public Education in North Carolina: A Documentary History, 1790-1840*, 2 vols. Publication of the North Carolina Historical Commission. Raleigh, Edwards and Broughton Company, 1908.

Fries, Adelaide L., ed. *Records of the Moravians in North Carolina*, 4 vols. Publications of the North Carolina Historical Commission. Raleigh, Edwards and Broughton Company, 1922-1930.

Graham, William Alexander. *General Joseph Graham and His Papers on North Carolina Revolutionary History.* Raleigh, Edwards and Broughton Company, 1904.

Griffin, Clarence W. *History of Old Tryon and Rutherford Counties, North Carolina.* Asheville, Miller Printing Company, 1937.

Hunter, C. L. *Sketches of Western North Carolina, Historical and Biographical.* Raleigh News steam job print, 1877. Reprinted, Raleigh, Edwards and Broughton Company, 1930.

Johnson, Guion Griffis. *Ante-Bellum North Carolina: A Social History.* Chapel Hill, The University of North Carolina Press, 1937.

Lawson, John. *History of North Carolina.* London, Printed for W. Taylor at the Ship, and F. Baker at the Black Boy, in Pater-Noster Row, 1714. (Second Edition: Frances Latham Harriss, ed. Richmond, Garrett and Massie, 1951.)

Leonard, Jacob Calvin. *History of Catawba College.* Copyright 1927 by the Trustees of Catawba College.

Mebane, C. H. *Biennial Report of the Superintendent of Public Instruction of North Carolina, for the Scholastic Years 1896-'97 and 1897-'98.* Raleigh, Guy V. Barnes, Printer to Council of State, 1898.

Morgan, Jacob L., Brown, Bachman S., Jr., and Hall, John, eds. *History of the Lutheran Church in North Carolina.* Published by the authority of the United Evangelical Lutheran Synod of North Carolina.

North Carolina, A Guide to the Old North State. Compiled and written by the Federal Writers' Project of the Federal Works Agency, Work Projects Administration for the State of North Carolina. Chapel Hill, The University of North Carolina Press, 1939.

North Carolina laws.

North Carolina Resources and Industries. Issued by State Department of Conservation and Development, Raleigh, 1929.

North Carolina, The Land of Opportunity. Compiled and published by the State Board of Agriculture, Raleigh, 1923.

Peattie, Roderick, ed. *The Great Smokies and the Blue Ridge.* New York, The Vanguard Press, 1943.

Rowe, Nellie M. *Discovering North Carolina.* Chapel Hill, The University of North Carolina Press, 1933.

Saunders, William L., ed. *The Colonial Records of North Carolina.* Published under the supervision of the Trustees of the Public Libraries by order of the General Assembly. 10 vols. Raleigh, P. M. Hale Company, 1886-1890.

Schenck, David. *North Carolina 1780-'81.* Raleigh, Edwards and Broughton Company, 1889.

Scott, W. W. *Annals of Caldwell County* and *"Gentleman" John Perkins.* Lenoir, News-Topic Print.

Sherrill, William Lander, *Annals of Lincoln County, North Carolina.* Charlotte, The Observer Printing House, Inc., 1937.

Spencer, Mrs. Cornelia Phillips. *The Last Ninety Days of the War in North Carolina.* New York, Watchman Publishing Company, 1866.

Wager, Paul Woodford. *County Government and Administration in North Carolina.* Chapel Hill, The University of North Carolina Press, 1928.

Wheeler, John H. *Historical Sketches of North Carolina, from 1584 to 1851.* Philadelphia, Lippincott, Grambo and Company, 1851.

——————— ed. *Roster of Soldiers from North Carolina in the American Revolution.* Published by the North Carolina Daughters of the American Revolution. Durham, The Seeman Press, 1932.

United States reference:

Collier's Encyclopedia. Price, Frank W., ed. director, and Barry, Charles P., ed.-in-chief. 20 vols. New York, Collier and Son Corporation, 1952.

Coulter, E. Merton. *The Confederate States of America, 1861-1865.* Baton Rouge, Louisiana State University Press, 1950. *The South During Reconstruction, 1865-1877.* Baton Rouge, Louisiana State University Press, 1947.

Gun Digest. Chicago, 1951.

Hale, William Harlan. *The March of Freedom; A Layman's History of the American People.* New York and London, Harper and Brothers, 1947.

Henry, Robert Selph. *The Story of the Confederacy.* New and revised edition. New York, The New Home Library, 1943.

Hungerford, Edward. *From Covered Wagon to Streamliner.* New York, The Greystone Press, 1941.

Kendrick, Benjamin Burks, and Arnett, Alex Mathews. *The South Looks at Its Past.* Chapel Hill, The University of North Carolina Press, 1935.

Morris, Charles. *A New History of the United States: The Greater Republic.* New Haven, Butler and Alger.

Rights, Douglas LeTell. *The American Indian in North Carolina.* Durham, Duke University Press, 1947.

Source Book. Vols. are perpetual. Source Research Council, Inc., Chicago.

Strassburger, Ralph Beaver, and Hinke, William John, eds. *Pennsylvania German Pioneers: A Publication of the Original Lists of Arrivals in the Port of Philadelphia from 1727 to 1808,* 3 vols. Norristown, Pennsylvania German Society, 1934.

Throm, Edward Louis, ed. *Popular Mechanics' Picture History of American Transportation.* New York, Simon and Schuster, 1952.

United States Census Reports, 1790-1950. Washington, D. C., Government Printing Office.

Watterson, Henry. *History of the Spanish-American War.* New York, Akron, Chicago, The Werner Company, 1898.

Woodward, Comer Vann. *Origins of the New South, 1877-1913.* Baton Rouge, Louisiana State University Press, 1951.

World Book Encyclopedia, The. 18 vols. Chicago, The Quarrie Corporation, 1947.

It is impossible to give due individual credit to all of the people who assisted in compiling the data used in Chapter Twenty of The History of Catawba County. Officials of the county, department heads, municipal leaders, school officials, civic leaders, librarians, state officials, and their office personnel, together with scores of other citizens have all contributed by delving into records and searching their memories. Sometimes the assistance was in the form of directing the writer to the proper source, rather than providing specific information. However, these were valuable contributions, too, and in view of the general splendid cooperation it may be truly said that this chapter is by Catawbans.

INDEX

Abee, Hohn R., 355
Abee, Horace H., 363
Abernathy, David, 191
Abernathy, John D., 185
Abernathy mine, 186
Abernathy, Turner, 185
Abernethy, Rev. Alexander, 106
Abernethy, A. S., 449
Abernethy, Barbara, 430
Abernethy, Berry, 424
Abernethy, Claude S., 476
Abernethy, Dolph, 458
Abernethy, F. M., 114
Abernethy, H. D., 349
Abernethy, Jane, 473
Abernethy, J. F., 351
Abernethy, John Miles, 232, 362
Abernethy, Patrick A., 247
Abernethy, S. M., 189
Abernethy, William, 228
Abolition, 238-40
Academies and early high schools, listed, 148-49
Adams, Phillip, 434
Agriculture, value of (1870), 64; early, 271; in 1890, 67-70; surveys of, 50-70, 488-93
Alexander, Adam, 21
Alexander, James, 435
Alexander, J. L., 347
Alexander, Jule, 449
Alexander, Samuel, 434
Alexander, William, 199
Allen, B. C., 232
Allen, Frank, 368-369
Allen, John, 177
Altrusa library project, 469
Allen iron works, 175
American Legion, 469-73
  Post Sixteen, Newton, history of, 469-70
  Post Forty-Eight, Hickory, history of, 470-71
  Post Two Hundred and Forty, Maiden, history of, 471
American Legion Auxiliary, 471
American Revolution, Catawba Indians in, 27; Catawba County in, 71-87
Amis, Moses N., 200
Armatige, Nathan, 181
Animals, 31
Annals of Catawba County, 429
Anthony, Frony, 93-94, 125
Anthony, Jacob, 435
Anthony, Martin, 434
Anthony, Paul, 93-94, 125, 434
Anthony, Philip, 125
Architecture, 51, 269
Armbrust, Rev. J. H., 476

Arndt, Garland, 460
Arndt, Rev. John Godfrey, 95-98, 101-02
Arndt, H. M., 155
Arney, Christian, 77
Arnt post office, sketch of, postmasters listed, 386
Arwood, W., 361
Asbury, Rev. Daniel, 97, 99-101, 113
Ashe, Samuel, 199
Austin, William P., 363
Avery, Waightstill, 199
Aycock, Charles B., 124, 155, 252

Baily, John L., 233
Baker, Bill, 445
Baker Hospital, 501
Baker, Jacob, 177, 366
Baker, Jones, 188
Baker, Philip, 177
Ballard, A. S., 155
Ballard, Ephraim, 229
Ballew, J. W., 337
Bandys post office, sketch of, postmasters listed, 384
Bandy, T. L., 251
Bandys township, 146, 246
Banoak, 363
Bank of Hickory, sketch of, 477
Banks, Howard, 212
Baptist churches, list of, 116
Baptist ministers, 1842-1900, list of, 119
Barb, James Ernest, 472
Barger, A. L., 341
Barger, Mose, 457
Barrier, Abraham, 435
Barrier, John, 435
Barrier, Julius, 435
Barrier, George Henry, 435
Barn-raising, 59
Barnhill, R. M., 355
Barringer, Catherine, 75, 223
Barringer, C. M., 342
Barringer, John Paul, 414
Barringer, Matthias, 25, 74-75, 81, 124, 222, 414, 424, 426, 427-28
Barringer, Matthias, Jr., 75, 221-23, 228, 243
Barringer muster ground, 221-23, 427
Barringer post office, sketch of, postmasters listed, 378
Barwick, A. J., 362
Baskin, Mattie, 456
Battle, Kemp P., 124
Battle, William H., 233
Beam, M. S., 155
Beard, Nancy Hewitt, 280
Beatties Ford, 370-71

CATAWBA COUNTY 511

Beatties Ford post office, history of, postmasters listed, 379
Beck, J. D., 363
Beekman, Christopher, 74, 191
Beib (Reep), Mary B., 40
Berkeley, J. O., 212
Berrier, David, 130
Berry, H., 363
Berry, J. M., 189
Berryville, N. C., history of, 363
Best, John W., 172-73
Bethel Church, 430
Bethlehem Methodist Church, 108-09
Beulow, Joachim, 96
Bibbs, John, 414
Birds, listed, 31
Black, A. C., 358
Black, Josias, 74
Black, Dr. K. A., 443
Blackwelder, B. B., 354
Blackwelder, George S., 472
Blackwelder, J. W., 251, 354, 456
Blackburn community, 363, 424-25
Blackburn, Daniel, 178
Blackburn, Henry, 424
Blackburn, Robert, 74
Blackburn post office, sketch of, postmasters listed, 387
Blacksmiths, 177
Blair, Hartwell S., 211
Blair, Hugh M., 210
Bogers, Rev., 40
Boggs, R. R., 338
Bolch, Adam, 177, 178
Bolch, David, 179
Bolch, Joseph H., 363 .
Bolick, Caspar, 77
Bolick, Mrs. Charles, 223
Bolick, Henry, 232
Bolick, Marcus A., 337
Bolick, R. K., 342
Bollinger, Henry, 124
Booth, Nancy, 454
Bost, C. C., 68, 351
Bost, Mrs. C. C., 409
Bost, Jonas, 165, 229, 233, 277, 360, 414
Bost, Joseph, 278, 361
Bost, Joshua, 229
Bost, Rosanna, 360
Bost, V. P., 69
Bowles, Benjamin, 77
Bowman, George, 414
Boy Scouts, 476-77
Boyd, Dan, 367
Boyd, John, 180, 233, 355, 357
Boyd, Marcus, 357
Brady, C. R., 342
Brady, G. A., 341-42
Bradburn, John, 161, 342
Brevard, Ephraim, 183, 185
Bridges, J. S., 247
Briggs, Benjamin, 183

Brittain, D. E., 355
Brookford Mills Company, 337
Brookford, N. C., history of, 336-37
Brookford post office, sketch of, postmasters listed, 388
Broome, Mrs. Karl W., 471
Brown, Absalom, 229, 233
Brown, Buckner, 232
Brown, Charity, 85-87
Brown, C. S., and Company, 161-62
Brown, Jacob, 110-11
Brown, James, 251
Brown, J. M., 246
Brown, Matthew, 180
Brown, Osborne, 440
Brown, Sam, 85-87
Bruns, J. H., 345, 354
Bryan, R. K., 211
Buffalo, 19, 28, 30
Bullinger, Henry, 176
Bullinger, Jacob, 176
"Building of Catawba, The," 413
Bunker Hill post office, sketch of, postmasters listed, 379
Burke County, 22, 74, 75, 76, 78, 81, 85, 164, 196, 199, 228, 324, 342, 355, 371, 433, 435
Burkehead, William G., 200, 362
Burns, Otway, 215
Burns, Phillip, 228, 233
Byers, John, 161
Bynum, William P., 199

Cabinet-making, 181
Caldwell County, 76, 200
Caldwell, David, L., 233
Caldwell, Joseph, 124
Caldwell, J. A., 230
Caldwell, John D., 246
Caldwell, Samuel, 77
Caldwell township, 146, 246
Caldwell, William, 358
Campbell, Dr. C. M., 360
Campbell, Mrs. Howard J., 471
Campbell, James R., 361
Campbell, John, 231
Campbell, M. C., 155
Campbell, Nancy, 128
Campbell, Dr. Ogburn, 165, 202, 277, 360, 362
Campbell, Samuel D., 355
Campbell, William, 78
Campgrounds, 113-15
Camp Vance, 169
Cansler, Henry, 225, 414
Capps, J. A., 155
Carolina and North Western Railroad, 173, 438
Carolina Cotton Mills, 358
Carolina Eagle, The, 206, 210, 243
Carolina Glove Company, 487
Carpenter, C. S., 355
Carpenter, D. A., 356

Carpenter, David, 178
Carpenter, D. J., 486
Carpenter, D. M., 356
Carpenter, D. Martin, 358
Carpenter, Henry Franklin, 188, 248, 356
Carpenter, Jacob, 435
Carpenter, John, 222
Carpenter, L. A., 357
Carpenter, Jonathan, 232
Carpenter, J. P., 339
Carpenter, Perry A., 356-57
Carpenter, R. E., 338
Carr, E. N., 354
Carrier, John, 355
Carson post office, sketch of, postmasters listed, 387
Carver, Dr. R. W., 155
Caswell, Richard, 83
Cathey's, Fort, 74-75
Catholic Church, 116
Catawba, meaning of the word, 24
"Catawba Braves," 318
Catawba College, Newton, N. C., history of, 142-43; presidents of, 143; mentioned, 264, 436, 460
Catawba County, first settlers in, 17-19; formation of, 19-24, 219-34; national stocks and early families, 36-49; early agriculture in, 50-58, 68-70; early social activities in, 59-60; travel in early, 61-62; land ownership in, 62-67; mineral deposits in, 67; contributions to American Revolution, 71-87; early religious life in, 88-120; early education in, 121-156; early transportation facilities of, 157-74; early trade and industries, 175-95; early professions in, 196-213; in War of 1812, 214-18; governmental, judicial and political development in, 235-64; in the Confederacy, 265-335; municipalities and villages of, 336-73; post offices of, 374-88; in the Spanish American War, 389-93; in World War I, 394-410; in World War II, 410-12; morals and manners in, 413-62; present day, 481-503
Catawba County Artificial Breeding Association, 492
Catawba County Historical Association, 71, 104, 342
Catawba County Library Board, members listed, 468
Catawba County Library and Museum, 426, 466-68
Catawba County News, The, 207
Catawba County Recorder's Court, 251
Catawba Hospital, 480, 501

Catawba Indians, wars of, 20, 25-27, 178
Catawba Methodist Church, 113
Catawba News-Enterprise, 460
Catawba post office, sketch of, postmasters listed, 382
"Catawba Rifles," 291
Catawba river, various spellings of, 24-25; mentioned, 17-437, passim
Catawba River Lumber Company, 350
Catawba Springs post office, 379
Catawba Station, land ownership in, 62; history of, 337-38; mentioned, 164, 188, 193, 200, 206, 321, 438
Catawba Station post office, sketch of, postmasters listed, 382
Catawba Telephone Company, 493
Catawba Toll Bridge Company, 161
Catawba township, farmers of listed, 64, 247
Catawba Trust Company, sketch of, 478
Catfish post office, sketch of postmasters listed, 358, 430
Cattle and cattle raising, 53, 64, 69, 491
Cawthorn, O. M., 354
Charcoal burning, 184
Chenault, W. W., 321
Cherokee Indians, 25-28, 74-75, 130-31, 222, 418-21, 428, 433
Chester and Lenoir Narrow-Gauge Railroad, 173, 247, 351
Chestnut post office, sketch of, postmasters listed, 379-80, 386
Children of the Confederacy, organizational data, 475
Chronicle post office, sketch of, postmasters listed, 380
Churches, list of early, 91
Cilley, Clinton A., 200, 249
Cilley Hosiery Mill, 281
Cilley, J. H. P., 354
Citizens Bank of Conover, sketch of, 477
Citizens Bank of Hickory, sketch of, 477
Citizens Savings and Loan Association, sketch of, 479
Civil War, Catawbans in, 291-335
Clapp, Dr. J. C., 109, 143, 150, 362
Clapp, Clarence, 362
Clapp, Ernest B., 362
Claremont College, history of, presidents listed, 151
Claremont High School, 151
Claremont, N. C., history of, 339; mentioned 109, 128, 151, 164
Claremont post office, sketch of, postmasters listed, 385
Clark, Jepthae, 110
Clark, Neil W., 363

CATAWBA COUNTY 513

Clay, George P., 179
Clay, Isaac, 128
Clay, J. W., 476
Clay Manufacturing Company, 358
Clay Printing Company, 212-13
Clay, W. L., 211
Clerks of Superior Court, listed, 254-55
Cleveland, Benjamin, 83
Cleveland County, 22-23, 220, 228, 230, 324
Cloninger, Thomas, 232
Clothing, 57-58, 60, 289, 417
Click, J. F., 172, 211
Clinard, F. A., 450, 455
Cline, Alexander, 358
Cline, Boston, 178, 371, 424
Cline, Edward Bost, 200, 249, 354
Cline, F. Lee, 200, 470
Cline, Henry, 229
Cline, J. A., 486
Cline, John, 343
Cline, Jonas, 165, 246-47
Cline, Julius F., 244, 341-42
Cline, Michael, 77
Cline, Miss, 39
Cline, M. L., 277, 354
Cline, M. M., 69
Cline, Paul, 232
Clines township, farmer of listed, 64; mentioned, 146, 246-47
Clinesville post office, sketch of, postmasters listed, 381
Clipper, The, 211
Cobb, Clisby, 184
Cobblers, 177
Cobb, J. S., 184
Cochran, George W., 252
Cochran, M. J., 338
Coffee House tavern, 161
Cole, Charles E., 337
Concordia College, history of, presidents listed, 151-52
Concord Methodist Church, 109-10
Conestoga Wagons, 158
Conley, William G., 126
Connor, Charley, 280
Connor, C. W., 361
Connor, Electious, 181, 229
Connor, Henry W., 238
Connor, R. D. W., 123
Connor, N. C., history of, 339-42; mentioned, 104, 107, 155, 161, 164, 191, 193, 360, 429, 431, 437, 487, 494, 501
Conover post office, sketch of, postmasters listed, 382
Conover township, farmers of listed, 64-65
Conrad, Daniel, 92, 232
Constitutional Convention, members of, listed, 264
Cook, Abram, 98

Cook, Jacob, 69
Cooking, 56
Cook post office, sketch of, postmasters listed, 387
Cooksville, 363
Coon, Charles L., 342
Coons, P. C., 363
Coopers, 177
Copening, A. G., 244-45
Corinth Baptist Church, 112-13
Corn, 52
Cornwallis, Gen. Charles, 79
Coroners, list of, 257-58
Correll, B. A., 358
Cotton, 52, 67, 188, 490-91
Cotton manufacturing, 188
Coulter, Barbara, 92
Coulter, E. P., 132, 145, 288
Coulter, J. H., 338
Coulter, John, 92, 132, 230
Coulter, Martin, 77, 124
Councill, W. B., 249
County administration, 497-98
County Clerks, listed, 252
County Commissioners, listed, 259-61
County Court, 235-37
County Solicitors, listed, 253
County Surveyors, listed, 256-57
County Treasurers, and variations, listed, 258-59
County Trustees, listed, 256
Covington, Wes, 438
Cowles, H. C., 243
Cowpens, Battle of, 79
Cowthon, Mr., 443-45
Coyle, William, 83
Coyner, J. S., 342
Cox, R. C., 155
Crab Orchard School, 155
Craig, Burton, 200, 360
Craige, Kerr, 375
Crawford, J. H., 362
Crawford, John, 41
Creeks and streams, listed, 71
Creek War of 1812, 215, 238
Cricket, The, 211
Crowdertown, 336
Crowder, Ulrich, 370-73
Crossing post office, sketch of, postmasters listed, 385
Crossroads, listed, 373
Crowson, 211
Culbertson, Josiah, 86
Cunningham, John, 178
Curtis, Mrs. E. H., 222

Daily Catawba News-Enterprise, The, 206, 208-09, 495
Daily Record, The, 213
Dale, Fred J., 355
Dancing, 59
Danner, John S., 338

Danville post office, sketch of, postmasters listed, 384-85
Daughters of the American Revolution, 473-74
  John Hoyle Chapter, history of and charter members, 473
  Hickory Tavern Chapter, history of and charter members, 473-74
Davidson, Leon, 178
Davidson, L. W., 361
Davis, George, 251
Davis, Mrs. Mary Shuford, 286
Day, W. A., 61
Deal, Charlie, 432
Deal, Daniel, 246
Deal, E. E., 338
Deal, Eli, 228
Deal, J. A., 339
Deal, Jacob, 259
Deal, James, 429, 432
Deal, John, 124
Deal, Lawson, 430
Deal, Miles, 431
Deal, Mrs. Pearl Setzer, 413
Deal, Perry, 429-31
Deal, Reuben, 432
Deal, Susan, 430
Deal, Thomas, 432
Deal, W. A., 339
Deal, William, 124, 360
Deer skins, trade in, 182
Deitz, Frederick, 126
Deitz, John, 181
Dellinger, David, 360
Dellinger, Henry, 179, 427
Dellinger, James Newton, 360
Dellinger, John, 77, 179, 424
Dellinger, Martha, 360
Denny, Henry C., 200, 353
Dentists, early, listed, 203
Denver community, 100
Dews, Thomas, 227
Dick, Thomas M., 233, 243
Distilling, 54
District schools, early, listed, 149
Dobbins, Rev. Drury, 107
Dobson, John, 77, 435
Dobson, Joseph, 435
Douglas, Isaac, 178
Douglas, James, 178
Douglas, Robert, 243
Downs, Rev., 363
Dowd, W. C., 212
Drum, Donald Lanford, 472
Drum, Frank, 187
Drum, George, 358
Drum, Goss, 358
Drum, John, 177
Drum, Mary, 430
Drum, Mattie, 430
Drum, Peter, 430
Drumville post office, sketch of, postmasters listed, 381

Dunn, John, 199
Dry Ponds post office, 379
Duncan, H. L., 355
Durham, W. K., 339
Dupert, Rev. Richard, 90
Durant, Rev. H. H., 114

Early Grove post office, sketch of, postmasters listed, 378
Eaves, Lawson, 192
Eavesville post office, sketch of, postmasters listed, 378
Ebenezer Methodist Church, 113
Eckard, Elkanah, 341
Edith post office, sketch of, postmasters listed, 285-86
Education, 43, 47, 89, 121-56, 276, 498-99
Edwards, David L., 114
Edwards, Nathaniel, 229
Edwards, William, 109
Elbert Ivey Memorial Library, history of, 464-65
Elias, Kope, 346
Elias, L., 345-46
Elliott, Emma, 367
Elliott, Dr. E. C., 367-68, 370, 440-42
Elliott, Frank, 442
Elliott, H. C., 347
Elliott, J. D., 354, 395
Elliott Springs post office, sketch of, postmasters listed, 380
Ellis, Dr. J. H., 351
Ellis, Dr. J. R., 206, 345-47
Ellis, W. H., 351
Ellis, Mrs. William H., 69
England mine, 186
England, Wilson, 230
Episcopal Churches, listed, 116
Episcopal ministers, 1842-1900, listed, 119
Epps, L. M., 155
Erson, Jane, 95
Ervin, C. W., 338
Ervin, John, 111
Erwin, James, 344
Esaw, 24
Esquire England and Associates, 356
Evangelical and Reformed Churches, listed, 117
Evangelical and Reformed ministers, 1842-1900, listed, 119
Evans, Mollie, 349
Eutaw Springs, battle of, 79

Farabee, S. H., 213
Farmers (1870), 62-67
Farmers and Merchants Bank, sketch of, 477
Farm post office, sketch of, postmasters listed, 384
Farm township, 65
Fay, Jacob, 371

Feimster, W. C., 200, 362
Ferguson, Patrick, 78, 86, 416
Fidelity Federal Savings and Loan Association, sketch of, 479
Fidelity Hosiery Mill, 486
Fink, Dr. Caleb, 192
Finger, Sidney M., 149-50, 362, 486
Firearms, 415-16
First Building and Loan of Hickory, sketch of, 479
First Federal Savings and Loan Association of Catawba County, sketch of, 479
First National Bank of Catawba County, sketch of, 478-79
First National Bank of Hickory, sketch of, 478
First Savings and Loan Association of Hickory, sketch of, 479
First Security Trust Company, sketch of, 478
Fish, listed, 31
Fisher, David, 414
Fisher, Joseph, 228, 233
Fishers post office, sketch of, postmasters listed, 378
Flaum, J., 189
Flax, 52
Flemmings post office, sketch of, postmasters listed, 383
Flemmings township, 65
Flora, listed, 32
Foard, Osborne, 362
Foard-Williams, 366
Foil, Dr. J. A., 150, 436
Foods, 287-88
Fords and bridges, listed, 162-64
Forests and timber products, 29-30, 54
Forney, Daniel M., 227, 344
Fowl and poultry, listed, 31
Fourney, H. A., 362
Fox, A. C., 361
Fox, Alexander, 435
Fox, Dr. A. J., 103, 341
Fox, Arthur T., 363
Foy, J. O., 212
Frazier, John E., 339
French and Indian War, 26-27
Fritchie, Rev. John G., 41, 92, 109
Fritz, Emma, 476
Fruits, listed, 32, 54, 67
Fry, Andrew, 246
Fry, Moses, 232
Fry, Phillip, 74, 77
Frye, C. J., 355
Frye, H. J., 355
Frye, Jacob, 178-79
Frye, Nicholas, 124
Fulbright, Hershel, 355
Fulenwider, John, 182
Fulenwider, William, 183
Fulling Mills, 176-77
Furniture, 55-57, 287

Gabriel, H. C., 362
Gabriel, Robert Harold, 387
Gaither, D. B., 165, 244, 277, 360
Gaither, J. R., 362, 486
Gaither, L. T., 360
Gaither, W. B., 200, 207, 362
Garvin, F. E., 362
Garvin, James A., 361
Gantt, John, 179
Gantt, Willis, 114
Gardens, 52-53
Gaunt, Jesse, 229
Gems, listed, 186-87
German immigrants, 35-44, 121
German Reformed Congregations, 38-40, 90
Geitner, C. H., 354, 450
General Assembly, members of, listed, 262-64
Gifford, L. C., 213
Gilbert, C. B., 338
Gilbert, George, 232
Gilleland, D. Arthur, 358
Girl Scouts, 476-77
Glover, Zula S., 382
Glowers, Dr. George E., 355
Gold mining, 186
Grace, F. A., 348
Grace Lutheran and Reformed Church, 92, 101-04, 126
Grace Union Church, 39-41
Graham, John, 435
Graham, Joseph, 79, 216, 238
Graham, William A., 79, 124, 227
Grains, 490-91
Granite Shoals Cotton Factory, 247
"Great Road" (to Philadelphia), 39
Great Western Stage Line, 162
Greder, Phillipe Henry, 124
Greder, Martin, 126
Greene, A. L., 337
Greene, J. D., 337
Greene, Nathanael, 27, 79
Grindstaff, Michael, 124
Grist mills, 176, 194-95
Gross, Adam, 176, 414
Gross, Henry, 180
Guilford Court House, battle of, 27, 416
Guanzirola, Jerome, 446
Gunsmithing, 179-80
Gurley, R. N., 155

Haas, David, 111
Haas, George, 71
Haas, John, 77, 124, 177
Haas, Simon, 71, 77, 124, 177, 343
Haas, William R., 231
Hahn, Benedict, 77
Hahn, George W., 38, 265, 308, 341
Hahn, Jacob, 98
Hahn, Johannes, 98
Hahn, Joshua, 77

Hahn, Noah, 99
Hahn, S. Augustus, 99
Hahn, Walter A., 161
Haiglar, Chief, 27
Hale, William, 165, 212, 351
Halfway Tavern, 161
Hall, George W., 486
Hall, Mrs. George W., 474
Hall, J. G., 69, 290, 354, 363, 448
Hall, Mrs. P. C., 291
Hall, W., 345-46
Hallman, Benjamin, 361
Hallman, Daniel, 125
Hallman, Henry, 125
Hallman, Philip, 360
Hamilton, Drury, 114, 233, 244-46
Hamilton, H. C., 233
Hamilton, Thomas T., 228
Hamilton township, 146, 246, 248
Hamilton, W. S., 155
Hampton, Thomas, 229
Harbison, Alexander, 434
Harmon, George, 177
Harmon, John, 177
Harmon, Peter, 107
Harmon, William, 229
Harris, Howell, 447
Harris, Stephen, 128
Hart, Charles, 21
Hartley, Joseph, 178
Hartmann, Catharine, 109
Harvey, John, 73
Harwell, James, 83
Hartsell, Isaac A., 351, 354
Harwell, James T., 338
Harwell, T. E., 338
Has, Antoine, 126
Hat manufacturing, 178
Haupt, Edward, 362
Hawn, David, 232
Hawn, John, 22
Hayes, 183
Hayseed post office, sketch of, postmasters listed, 386
Heam, Conrad, 371
Heavner, Perry, 487
Hedrick, Solomon, 232
Heffner, Elias, 108
Heffner, Elizabeth, 108
Heffner, Sarah, 108
Hefner, Charles E., 363
Hefner, John, 181, 233
Hefner, Perry L., 363
Helton, A. J., 188
Helton, Clayton, 460
Helderman, Jacob, 229
Henderson, Lawson, 344
Henderson, Pinkney, 227
Henkel, Rev. David, 105
Henkel, Rev. Paul, 102, 105
Henkel, Rev. Philip, 102, 105
Henkel, Rev. Polycarp C., 105
Henrys Fork river, 157

Herbs, 52, 276, 352-53
Herndon, Col., 83
Herman, Dianah, 340
Herman, Dr. F. L., 244, 247, 341
Herman, Mose, 189, 340
Herman, P. W., 342
Hewitt, J. T., 114
Hewitt, Lucy, 430
Hewitt, M. M., 111
Hickory Banking and Trust Company, sketch of, 477
Hickory Chair Company, 486
Hickory Daily Record, The, 212, 242, 394, 424, 496
Hickory Democrat, The, 212
Hickory Electric Company, 349-50
Hickory Fair, 68-69, 455
Hickory Industrial Bank, sketch of, 478
Hickory Mercury, The, 211
Hickory Memorial Hospital, sketch of, 480, 501
Hickory Municipal Court, 251
Hickory, N. C., (Hickory Tavern), history of, 342-354; mentioned, 90-503, passim
Hickory post office, sketch of, postmasters listed, 381-82
Hickory Tavern, see Hickory, N. C.
Hickory Tavern post office, sketch of, postmasters listed, 381, 456
Hickory Tavern township, 246, 248
Hickory Telephone Company, 493
Hickory township, 65, 146, 248, 251
Hickory Press, The, 211
Hicks, Rev. Berryman, 107
Hicks, Forrest B., 363
Hicks, J. J., 246
Highland Academy, 363
Highland, N. C., history of, 363-64
Hill, Isaac, 192
Hill, J. Henry, 382
Hilton, Evie, 280
Hilton, M. A., 366
Hilton Pottery, 366
Hodges, Dr. J. E., 358
Hofner, Hiram, 189
Hoke, Daniel, 225
Hoke, Frederic, 225, 228-29
Hoke, John, 225
Hoke, Mary Brent, 264
Hoke, Mike, 225, 227
Hoke, Peter, 225
Hoke, Robert F., 264
Hokesville post office, sketch of, postmasters listed, 376
Hoke, W. A., 339
Holbrook, W. E., 212
Holbrook, Henry J., 337
Holcombe, Rev. Hosea, 106
Holshouser, James, 358
Holland, Isaac, 229
Holland, James, 199

CATAWBA COUNTY 517

Hollar, Hattie Miller, 341
Hollar, J. H., 339
Hollar, Mrs. John, 431
Hollar, W. C., 355
Home Demonstration Clubs, 489
Home Guard, 335
Home industry, 55-56
Hoover, Levi, 181
Hop Creek School, 126
Hopewell Methodist Church, 106
Horse racing, 69
Horton, Joseph, 344
Houston, Berry, 363
Houston, Dewey A., 355
Houston, R. B. B., 200
Howard, David L., 337
Howell, J. K., 338
Hoyle, John, 473
Hoyle, Reuben, 232
Hoyle, R. M., 364
Huffman, E. L., 338
Huffman, F., 247
Huffman, George, 232
Huffman, Henry, 180, 414
Huffman, Junius E., 363
Huffman, Martin, 344
Hufham, Thomas M., 200, 354
Hughes, Joseph, 191
Huit, Joseph, 232
Huit, M. M., 244-45
Huit, Moses, 232
Huitt, Madame, 427
Hull, Major, 132, 229, 360
Hunsucker, George E., 358
Hunsucker, Jacob, 178
Hunsucker, J. F., 341-42
Hunsucker, Jonas, 341-42
Hunsucker, R. M., 342
Hunsucker, Lucinda, 436
Hunting and fishing, 53, 59
Husking bee, 60
Hussey, John B., 200, 206, 210, 243
Hutton and Bourbonnais Company, 350

Ikard, Ann, 360
Ikard, Anthony, 360, 362
Ikard, Burt M., 358
Ikerd, Clarence, 438
Ikerd, George A., 111, 231-32, 244, 246
Ikerd, Peter, 74, 124, 177
"In Beautiful Carolina," 413
Industries, modern, 484-87
Ingold, F. B., 449
Ingold, Rev. Jeremiah, 130
Ingold, Lou, 456
Inman, Henry, 435
Iredell County, 61, 89, 206, 216
Iron mining and forging, 182-86, 276
Isahour, Joseph, 107
Isenhower, John A., 342
Isenhower, Mrs. J. A., 339, 429
Isenhower, John L., 340

Isenhower, P. E., 340
Island Ford, 79-80, 86, 128, 221, 247-48, 429

Jackson, Andrew, 215-18
Jacobs Fork post office, sketch of, postmasters listed, 378
Jacobs Fork river, 22, 39, 83, 125-26, 157
Jacobs Fork township, 63, 65, 146, 188-89, 193, 231, 246, 248, 363
Jarrett, Elias, 92
Jarrett, James, 99
Jarrett, Lawrence, 99
Jarrett, Samuel, 126
Jarvis, Thomas J., 124
Jenkins, Leonard, 358
Jenny Lind forge, 183-84, 357
Jonas, John, 435
Jonas, Simon, 435
Jones, Edmund, 395
Jones, Gertrude, 455
Jones, John F., 355, 360
Jones, Lemuel, 83
Jones, Miles, 110
Jones, S. H., 355
Johnson, J. B., 355
Johnson, Jesse, 79
Johnston, Peter, 124
Jordan, John W., 472
Jordan, Samuel H., 200
Jordan, S. H., 342
Joyner, Rev. E. N., 455
Jugtown post office, sketch of, postmasters listed, 383
Jugtown township, 65, 193, 366
Judges, of Catawba County Recorder's Court, listed, 261

Kalberlahn, Hans Martin, 201
Kale, Henry, 109
Keener, Alexander, 358
Keener, Lawson, 184
Keener, G. W., 358
Keever, Dr. A. P., 363
Keever, Henry, 114
Keever, James, 114, 364
Keeversville (Plateau), history of, 364; mentioned, 194
Keeversville post office, sketch of, postmasters listed, 384
Keeversville township, 66
Keisler, Martin, 339
Keller, Martin, 247
Kelley, J. D., 339
Kendall, Rena, 337
Kennon, William, 199
Kile, William, 111
Killian, Andreas, 220
Killian, Andrew, 232
Killian, Catherine, 371
Killian, H. C., 68-69, 363
Killian, Jacob, 220

Killian, Jesse, 220
Killian, John, 220, 225, 229-31, 371, 414
Killian, Joseph, 247
Killian, J. Y., 155
Killian's meeting house, 107
Killian, Rebecca Cresamore, 220
Killian, S. E., 68-69
Killian, W. L., 155
King's Mountain, battle of, 77, 79, 84, 182, 416
Kistler, Paul, 232
Klutz, F. S., 363
Klutz, Dr. Paul J., 357-58
Ku Klux Act, persons indicted under and witnesses, listed, 284-86
Ku Klux Klan, 242-44, 280, 284-86, 347
Kyles, C. P., 358

Lackey, A. L., 114
Lambert, Andrew, 428
Lander, William, 227
Lander, Wilson, 230
Land-ownership (1865), 62
Lanier, George C., 352
Lanier, J. E., 273
Lanier, Leah, 247
Lanier, R. H., 352
Lantz, Rev. John, 362
Latta, J. L., 204, 281, 343, 346, 351-52, 440, 450, 452
Lattimore, Dr. J. L., 357
Lawrence, John M., 353
Lawson, John, 25-26
Layerly (Lyerly), Christopher, 96
Lea, Philip, 24
Lead mining, 187
Leaser, A., 69
Leather and tanning, 55
Lebanon Lutheran Church, 113
Lee, Rachel, 476
Lee, Robert E., 282-83
Lenargin, William, 360
Lenoir Rhyne College, history of, presidents listed, 152-53; mentioned, 95, 151, 363, 468, 476, 501
Lenoir, Walter W., 152
Lentz, Jacob, 109
Lentz, J. A., 354
Leonard, J. T., 337
Leonard, Oscar E., 363
Libraries, 464-69
Lime works, 188
Linebaugh, Frederick, 126
Lineberger, Alexander, 114
Lineberger, Martin, 232
Lincoln, Benjamin, 22
Lincoln County, 22, 28, 74, 76, 81, 85, 95, 97, 100, 104, 113, 125-26, 131-32, 140, 182, 184-85, 196, 214-16, 219-21, 225, 228-30, 248, 324, 342, 344, 371, 379

Lincolnton, N. C., 23, 40, 107, 121, 140, 161, 173, 196, 213, 226-28, 232, 264, 344, 371, 453
Lincolnton Transcript, The, 128
Linden, Frank Vander, 367
Linden, Harry Vander, 473
Lindsay, A. J., 345-46
Link, Aaron, 233
Link, H. W., 345
Link, John, 229
Link, Michael, 98
Link, Sarah, 282
Little, C. E., 339
Little, Daniel, 247
Little, George, 247
Little, Dr. James H., 360
Little, Jane, 360
Little, Joshua, 244-45
Little, Peter, 178
Locke, Francis, 81, 435
Locke, Frank, 355
Log College, 147
Lohr, James, 357
Long, L. F., 362
Long, George, 155
Long, Mrs. Glenn, 291
Long, J. U., 338
Long, Lawson, 186
Long, William, 229, 338
Long Island, 109, 363, 438
Long Island Cotton Mill, 251
Long Island post office, sketch of, postmasters listed, 380
Long Town post office, sketch of, postmasters listed, 381
Longview, N. C., history of, 355
Look Out Dam, 430-31, 437, 440
Lookout section, 429
Lookout Shoals, 85-87
Lore, Valentine, 414
Loretta post office, sketch of, postmasters listed, 387
Loretz, Rev. Andrew H., 40, 97, 102-03
Louise post office, sketch of, postmasters listed, 386
Loughran, Frank, 348
Loughran, Mrs. Frank, 443
Lowe, Alexander, 230
Lowe, Isaac, 229
Lowe, I. W., 233
Lowe, James W., 229
Lowe, Thomas Lafayette, 278-79, 304
Lowenstein, Dr. J., 351
Lowrance, Isaac, 178
Lowrance, Joseph, 228
Lowrance, Lawson, 114, 232
Lowrance, L. H., 338
Lowrance, Mark E., 146, 200, 361
Lowrance Mill post office, sketch of, postmasters listed, 378
Lowrance, William, 338

CATAWBA COUNTY 519

Lutheran Churches, listed, 117; mentioned, 41, 90
Lutheran ministers (1842-1900), listed, 119-20
Lutz, Ambrose, 228
Lutz, Daniel, 77, 178
Lutz, William A., 355
Lyerly, Eubert, 354
Lyerly, George L., 354, 395
Lyerly, Walker, 354
Lynch, A. P., 200
Lytle, Dr. Joseph, 202
Lytton, William, 110

McCaslin, Matthew, 231
McCaslin, William, 233
McComb, R. H., 354
McCorkle, Alexander, 233
McCorkle, Charles Milton, 200, 207, 362
McCorkle, Francis, 74, 77, 81-82
McCorkle, George, 200, 362
McCorkle, Matthew Locke, 129, 142, 165, 200, 221-22, 249, 296, 360-62
McCorkle mine, 186
McDowell, Charles, 74, 78
McDowell County, 74, 76
McDowell, Joseph, 80-81, 425-26
McGee, Jacob, 359
McGimpsie, Thomas, 199
McIntosh, Archer, 353
McIntosh, C. E., 155
McIver, Charles D., 124
McKay, Spruce, 199
McKissick, Daniel, 77, 81, 180, 355
McKrae, D. K., 155
McMullen, William, 178, 342
McNeil, A. H., 338
McRee, Robert M., 383
Mack, Peter, 105
Magistrates (1868), listed, 245-46
Maiden Bank, sketch of, 477
Maiden Creek Forge, 183
Maiden, N. C., history of, 355-58; mentioned, 77, 79, 115, 159, 161, 183, 187, 194, 206-07, 213, 219-20, 268, 336
Maiden post office, sketch of, postmasters listed, 383
Maiden township, 66
Manley, Mathias E., 233
Mann, G. W., 209
Mann, Ione Mebane, 209
Mann, Mrs. Weaver, 471
"Manufactories" of 1884, listed, 189-91
Markel, Frederick, 124
Marlow, L. D., 181
Marshall, A. W., 348, 354
Marshall, Gabriel, 348
Marshall, John, 114
Martin, Alexander, 199
Martin Furniture Company, 487
Martin, J. A., 349

Mauney, E. G., 471
Mauney, Garland E., 358
Mauney, John, 232
Mauney, Samuel D., 379
Mauser, John W., Sr., 363
Mauser, John W., Jr., 363
Maynard, J. M., 363
Mebane, Charles H., 124, 149-50, 155, 208
Mebane, Cyril Long, 209
Mecklenburg County, 21, 199, 216
Medicine, 200-01
Mehaffey post office, sketch of, postmasters listed, 376
Mehaffey, Thomas E., 233
Mehaffey, William L., 229, 232
Memorial Reformed Church, 357
Menzies, D. S., 354
Merchants (1885), listed, 192-94
Mercury, The, 206
Merritt, Dessie Cline, 222
Methodist Churches, listed, 90-91, 100, 117-18
Methodist ministers (1842-1900), listed, 120
Michaels, Sally, 181
Mier, John M., 486
Militia, 75-77, 85, 216, 222, 224-25
Miller, Cordelia Clay, reminiscences of, 139-42
Miller, Rev. Adam, 106
Miller, Frederick, 112
Miller, F. S., 363
Miller, J. F., 212
Miller, Rev. R. J., 108
Miller, S. G., 360
Miller, T. R., 339
Miller, "Uncle Joe," 343
Milling, 54-55
Millstone post office, sketch of, postmasters listed, 387
Minerals, listed, 67, 187-88
Mines (1850-1900), listed, 187-88
Minges, Conrad, 232, 360
Mingus, John, 177
Ministers, prior to 1842, listed, 115-16; denominations unknown, listed, 120; of 1885, listed, 204
Mitchell, Dr. John, 24
Monbo post office, sketch of, postmasters listed, 384
Monbo township, 66
Monday, Wesley W., 229, 233
Montague, Mary, 454
Moore, C. P., 212
Moore, J. F., 68
Moore, John, 344
Morals and manners, 413-62
Moravians, 182, 201, 428
Morden, Robert, 24
Morgan, Daniel, 79-80, 355
Morgan, George H., 355
Morgan, John D., 355

Morgan, Marvin, 355
Morganton, N. C., 26, 79, 161, 169, 196, 336
Morrison, Robert H., 209
Morrow, C. Ray, 339
Morton, E. V., 212
Moser, Arthur, 476
Moser, D. M., 342
Moser, Mrs. F. P., 432
Moser, Henry, 232
Moser, J. H., 339
Moser, Jonathan R., 132
Moser, Lane, 339
Moser, Dr. Marion, 341
Moser, Paul H., 385
Moser, R., 132
Moser, Timothy, 228
Mount Carmel Forge, 185
Mt. Ruhama Baptist Church, 107-08
Mountain Creek post office, sketch of, postmasters of, 376-77
Mountain Creek township, 66, 129, 146, 176, 185, 194, 246
Mountain Grove Church, 106
Mountain Mills post office, sketch of, postmasters listed, 380
Mouser, J. W., 68-69
Mull, Abram, 419
Mull Grove post office, sketch of, postmasters listed, 377
Mull Grove township, 66
Mull, Henry, 432
Mull, Katrina, 418-19, 432
Mull, Peter, 74, 77, 176, 432
Murchison, Alice Penelope, 365
Murphy, Archibald D., 124
Murphy, James, 188
Murphy, Rev. Joseph L., 357, 395
Murray, Dr. Charles, 203
Murray, Harry B., 203
Murray, W. B., 358
Murrill, Hugh A., 211
Murrill, John F., 200, 206, 210-11, 354, 448-49
Murrill, Mrs. J. F., 69
Musgrove, W. M., 338

Names, anglicising of German, 42-43
Newspapers, 206-13
News, The, 206
Newton-Conover Observer, 209-496
Newton Enterprise, The, 207, 361
Newton Fair, 69
Newton, George, 359
Newton Glove Manufacturing Company, 487
Newton Hosiery Mill, 486
Newton, Mary, 476
Newton, N. C., history of, 359-62; mentioned, 71-503, **passim**
Newton Observer, 209
Newton post office, sketch of, postmasters listed, 379

Newton township, 63, 66, 146, 186, 246, 248
Nixon, A., 103
Nixon, Joseph R., 41-42
North Carolina Classis of the Reformed Church, 92
North Carolina Railroad, 165, 172
Norton, W. J., 363
Nurseries, 492
Nussman, Rev. Adulphus, 96
Nuts, list of, 32
Nut Shell, The, 211, 268

Odum, Evelyn Mebane, 209, 481
"Old North State Bitters," 352-53
Old Haas Church, 111
Olds, Fred A., 226
Olivet Baptist Church, 110
Ore banks, listed, 185
Organ Church, 95-97
Orr, William, 22
Oxford post office, sketch of, postmasters listed, 383
Oxford Ford township, 66, 107, 129, 194, 340
Oyama, 365, 438

Paine, John, 181
Pardo, Juan, 25
Park, Benjamin, 434
Park, James, 434
Park, John, 434
Park, Thomas, 434
Parks, William, 434
Partis, Mrs., 360
Payne, Connelly, 211
Payne, Isaac, 185
Pearson, Richmond, 233
Pede, Cyrus, 109
Penland, John, 181
Peoples Bank of Catawba, sketch of, 478
Perjury, early punishment for, 197-98
Perkins, John, 221, 428-29
Peterson, Arthur, 180
Peterson, John, 180
Pharr, John, 342
Phillips, L. H., 362
Physicians (prior to 1900), listed, 202-03
Pickens, Andrew, 79
Pickens, R. S., 212
Piedmont Press, The, 171, 210
Piedmont Wagon Company, 350, 441
Pinkney, Henderson, 363
Pinner, John, 101
Pinner, Winnie, 101
Pioneer families, listed, 46, 48-49
Pitts, David, 188
Pitts, J. H., 338
Pitts, J. L., 338
Pitts, Millie Ann, 475
Plateau, see Keeversville

CATAWBA COUNTY 521

Plateau post office, sketch of, postmasters listed, 384
Pleasant Gardens community, 425-26
Pleasant Hill Academy, 128
Plonk, Levi, 188, 362
Plonk, J. H., 207
Poffh, Mary Mull, 419-20
Pope, George, 124, 280, 290
Pope, Henry, 104
Pope, Mary B., 380
Population trends, 482
Postage rates, early, 375
Postmasters, listed, 376-88
Poston, M. A., 364
Pottery making, 181, 366
Powell, Dr. A. M., 110, 188, 338
Powell, Frank, 338
Powell, George, 362
Powell, Dr. Tate, 111
Presbyterian Churches, listed, 119; mentioned, 46, 88-89, 100
Presbyterian ministers (1842-1900), listed, 120
Press and Carolinian, The, 67-69, 211, 234, 349
Press, The, 211
Pritchet, Buckner, 435
Pritchard, J. C., 354
Processional officers, listed, 252
Property evaluation (1870), 63-64
Propst, E. L., 357
Propst, John, 95
Propst, J. S., 449
Propst post office, sketch of, postmasters listed, 388
Protestant non-denominational church, 119
Providence Cotton Mills, 183
Public Health program, 499-500

Quaker Meadows, massacre at, 74, 78, 80
Quinn, Rev. Edward Hugh, 110

Rabb, Frank, 357
Rabb, George W., 356
Rabb, J. F., 358
Rabb, Logan, 357
Rabb, Pinkney, 357
Rader, Daniel, 232
Ramsaur, Dr. Alex, 357
Ramseur, David, 92
Ramseur, Harriet, 92
Ramseur, Henry F., 92
Ramseur, Ida, 456
Ramseur, W. S., 345, 448
Ramsour, A. L., 188
Ramsour, Alfred, 278
Ramsour, David, 178
Ramsours Mill, battle of, 40, 72, 77, 81-82, 84-85, 182, 416
Rankin, Richard, 225
Ransom, Robert, 395

Ransom-Sherrill Chapter, U. D. C., 290-91
Rauch, M. M., 188
Ray, Dr. Archibald, 128, 225, 227, 229, 414
Reconstruction, county officials of, listed, 240-41; mentioned, 248, 284-90
Rector, Horace, 363
Register of Deeds, listed, 255
Registrars and Election Judges (1868), listed, 245
Rehobeth Methodist Church, 90, 99-101, 221
Reid, C. A., 338
Reid, W. H., 200
Reichert, Henry, 189
Reinhardt, Franklin, 228
Reinhardt, Mrs. H. Elvin, 473
Reinhardt, Joseph A., 228, 233
Reinhardt, Lawson E., 233
Reinhardt, R. P., 69
Reinhardt, William P., 63, 132, 345
Religion, 38, 41, 43, 45-46, 91-92
Renfro, D. C., 355
Reptiles, listed, 32
"Reunion Day," 290-91
Revolutionary soldiers, listed, 81-82
Reynolds, A. O., 460
Reynolds, Reuben, 177
Rhyne, Daniel, 360
Rhyne, D. E., 152
Rhyne, D. W., 360
Rhyne, Mrs. E. P., 471
Rhyne, Kathryn, 360
Rhyne, W. A., 362
Rice, Charles W., 200
Richard Baker Hospital, sketch of, 480
Richmond and Danville Railroad, 172-73, 210
Ridgeview Public Library, 469
Rintleman (Randleman), Christopher, 96
Roads and road-building, early petitioners listed, 159-61, 493-94
Robertson, Richard, 435
Robinson, David, 22
Robinson, Henry, 360, 455
Robinson, Jesse, 344, 421, 424
Robinson, John W., 455
Robinson, J. Parks, 363
Robinson, M. A., 147
Robinson, Manuel, 414
Robinson, William S., 363
Rockett, J. W., 342
Rockett, O. T., 363
Rocket post office, sketch of, postmasters listed, 376
Rock Springs, 100
Rodhiss, 237
Rose, John, 84-85
Roseman, D., 247

Roseman post office, sketch of, postmasters listed, 376
Ross, Benjamin, 435
Ross, Jonathan, 435
Rough and Ready Forge, 185
Routh, G. P., 114
Rowan County, 21, 73, 75, 85, 89, 96, 102, 159, 182, 196, 199, 216, 435
Rowe, C. M., 362
Rowe, D. P., 362
Rowe, J. Dallas, 150, 272, 361
Rowe, Gilbert P., 229
Rowe, Glenn N., 342
Rowe, Lank, 99
Rowe, Mabel Miller, 424
Rowe, M. J., 341, 362
Rowe, S. S., 342
Royster, O. M., 354
Royster, Mrs. O. M., 475
Rudisill, Henry, 252
Rudisill, J. C., 250
Rudisill post office, sketch of, postmasters listed, 386
Rudisill, Robert A., 358
Rufty mine, 186
Rural electrification, 493
Rutherford County, 22-23, 79, 85, 199, 220
Rutherford, Griffith, 74-75, 81, 433

St. James Lutheran Church, 356
St. Johns Lutheran Church, 104-06
St. Matthew's Arbor, 142
St. Paul's Lutheran and Reformed Church, 40, 124-25, 219
St. Peter's Lutheran and Reformed Church, 93-98, 107-08, 111-12
St. Stephen's Lutheran Church, 112, 365
Salem Lutheran and Reformed Church, 231
Salisbury, N. C., 72, 143, 161, 169-70, 172, 191, 196, 280, 308, 335, 337, 417, 430
Sanders, Joseph T., 111
Saunders, A. B., 69
Saunders, Betty, 377
Saul (slave), 18-19
Saw mills, listed, 54-55, 194-95
Scales, Alfred M., 150
Scarborough, Rev. Lewis, 114
Schell, Claude E., 382
School districts, history of, 133-36
Scott, Maria, 435
Scott, Thomas, 435
Scott, W. W., 429
Scronce, Jacob, 360
Seagel, Daniel, 178
Seitz, Abel P., 99
Seitz, Emmett, 124
Seitz, George, 177
Seitz, Jacob, 177
Seitz, John, 177

Seitz, John Q., 340
Seitz, L. P., 69
Self, W. A., 200
Self, W. R., 436
Settle, Thomas, 232, 233, 243
Setzer, Rev. A. W., 206
Setzer, David, 233
Setzer, George, 165, 248, 277, 360
Setzer, John, 77, 223
Setzer, Dr. John F., 361
Setzer, John W., 339
Setzer, J. Milt, 426
Setzer, J. W., 476
Setzer, Mrs. Marshall, 430
Setzer, Mathais, 359
Setzer, Walter, 360
Sevier, John, 78
Shannon, J. H., 206
Shawner post office, sketch of, postmasters listed, 386
Shelby, Isaac, 78
Shell, John, 176
Shell, Michael, 77
Shell, Ralph T., 433
Shell, S. G., 341
Sherford post office, sketch of, postmasters listed, 384
Sheriffs, listed, 253-54
Sherrill, Adam, 17-18, 21, 23, 25, 27-28, 80, 222, 421, 423, 428
Sherrill, Adam, Jr., 17-19
Sherrill, Henderson, 165, 230
Sherrill, J. H., 338
Sherrill, Miles O., 244, 246, 252, 265, 290
Sherrill, Oscar, 338
Sherrill's Ford township, 22, 46, 63, 66-67, 79-80, 99, 106, 110, 125, 159, 161, 194, 222, 365
Sherrill's Ford post office, sketch of, postmasters listed, 377
Sherrill, Uriah, 77
Sherrill, William, 17-18, 77, 84, 99
Sherrill, William, Jr., 17-19
Sherrill, W. L., 338
Shiloh Methodist Church, 113
Shipp, Robert J., 200, 362
Shipp, William M., 199, 229, 361
Shoes and shoe-making, 58
Shook, Henry, 232
Shuford, Abel A., 345, 349, 475, 485
Shuford, A. D., 338, 362
Shuford, Andrew H., 132, 228, 345, 354, 360
Shuford, Ann, 92
Shuford, A. L., 244-45, 345-46
Shuford, Craig, 155
Shuford, David, 73
Shuford, D. W., 69, 349
Shuford, E. L., 281, 337
Shuford, Mrs. E. L., 473
Shuford, Eli, 228-30
Shuford, Elkanah, 191

CATAWBA COUNTY 523

Shuford, E. R., 231
Shuford, George P., 132, 145, 229, 233, 360
Shuford, Jacob, 176, 191
Shuford, Mrs. J. H., 471
Shuford, John, 84-85, 124
Shuford, John G., 109
Shuford, John J., 233
Shuford, John P., 229
Shuford, J. W., 354
Shuford, Martin, 84-85
Shuford Mills Company, 485
Shuford National Bank, sketch of, 477
Shuford, Philip, 92
Shuford, R. L., 69
Shuford, Sarah E., 92
Shufords Ferry post office, sketch of, postmasters listed, 379
Shuford, Solomon, 92
Shuford, W. H., 337
Shuford, W. J., 395
Shull, Anthony, 434
Shull, Frederick, 434
Shull, Thomas Carlton, 434
Sides, Calvin J., 272
Sides, Kate Warlick, 272
Sides School, 125
Sigman, Balser, 435
Sigman, George, 435
Sigman, John, 78
Sigmon, Adolphus, 339
Sigmon, A. Y., 211, 352, 458
Sigmon, Mrs. A. Y., 457
Sigmon, Barnet, 177, 221
Sigmon, Charles E., 342
Sigmon, Edna, 460
Sigmon, George, 177
Sigmon, Hannah, 84, 339
Sigmon, John, 77, 84, 177-78
Sigmon, Martin, 233
Sigmon, N. E., 311
Sigmon, Palsor, 77
"Signs," early, 60
Silversmiths, 180
Simpson, Reuben, 84
Simpson, William, 77, 84
Slagle, John, 125
Slate, F. S., 212
Slaves and slavery, 267, 269-71, 432
Smith, B. B., 114
Smith, Rev. C. O., 105
Smith, Dr. Hildreth H., 264
Smith, Hoke, 225, 264
Smith, J. C., 486
Smith, J. M., 91, 99, 108, 125, 185
Smith, P. F., 341
Smith, Wade F., 358
Smith, William Henderson, 472
Smyre, Clinton Eugene, 339
Smyre, Daniel, 176
Smyre, Francis, 339
Smyre, George, 192, 414
Smyre, John, 95

Smyre, S. J., 362
Smyrna Evangelical and Reformed Church, 109
Snipes, W. S., 155
Soap-making, 58
Social activities, early, 43-44, 59, 289
Soil conservation program, 489-90
Solicitors of Catawba County Recorder's Court, listed, 262
Southern Bell Telephone Company, 493
Southern Glove Company, 487
Southern Power Company, 350
Southern Railway Company, 173
South Fork Church, communicants listed, 97
South Fork river, 40, 157, 371, 427
South Fork community, 39, 72, 77, 83-85, 417, 440
Southerland, Hugh, 456
Sox, J. Loy, 155
Spangenberg, Bishop August Gottleib, 28-30, 428, 433
Spanish American War, Catawbans in, 389-93
Sparkling Catawba Springs, post office, sketch of, postmasters listed, 380-81
Sparkling Catawba Springs township, 66, 194, 366, 440, 443
Speagle, Martin, 98
Spencer, Joseph, 199
Spencer, Pinkney, 339-40
Spencer, Samuel, 199
Stagecoach routes, 160-62
Staley, Charles M., 155
Stamey, Joshua, 229
Stamey, Peter, 229
Standard Keepers, listed, 253
Stanley, William S., 363
Starr, Eli, 232
Startown (Danville), 97, 130, 155, 221, 365
Startown post office, sketch of, postmasters listed, 385
Statesville, N. C., 213, 243, 284, 431
State vs. Amos Sweat, 414
State vs. Covington, 251
State vs. Kale, 251
Steele, Joseph, 177, 191, 360
Steele, Samuel, 434
Stepp, J. Jackson, 337
Stewart, Herbert, 362
Stewart, Joe, 362
Stine, Amzi, 358
Stoneman's raid, 279-80
Streams, listed, 32-35
Stricker, Mary Magdalene, 371
Strohn, John, 158
Sumit, Alex, 360
Summerow, B. J., 207
Summerow, Alice, 362
Sumrow, Daniel, 232

Suttlemyre, Garland, 457
Suttlemyre, Hallman, 457
Suttlemyre, Harvey, 458
Suttlemyre, F. Johnson, 354, 457
Suttlemyre, Philip, 457
Sweat, Amos, 413-14

Tailors, 178
Tanning and tanners, 178
Tar industry, 181
Tarr (Derr), Melchoir, 84-85
Taylor, Hugh, 355
Taylor, W., 361
Teachers, of 1843-1865, listed, 136-39; of 1865-1871, listed, 145-46; Negro, listed, 147; of 1885, listed, 203-04
Temperance Echo, The, 210
Terrell Community, 99-100, 113, 221, 365
Terrell post office, sketch of, postmasters listed, 387
Thessalonica Baptist Church, 108, 231
Thompson, John S., 454
Thorne, D. H., 358
Thornton, John, 24
Thornton, Marcellus Eugene, 200, 211, 350
Threshing machine manufacture, 189
Throneburg, Jacob, 181
Throneburg, Lewis, 177
Tilley, Sam, 354, 443-45
Times-Mercury, The, 211-12, 459
Tippong, Conrad, 77
Tobacco, 67, 171
Todd, M. E., 281
Tomlinson, Mrs. J. R., 473
Tomlinson, J. S., 206, 210
Tomlinson, Mrs. Pearl, 428
Tomlinson, W. T., 210
Tools, early, 51
"Tory Oak," 83
Township and Commissioner plan, 241-42
Travel, early, 60-61, 157-74
Travenstrett, Catherine, 232
Travenstrett, William, 232
Treasurers of Public Buildings, listed, 253
Treholm, George A., 278
Trollinger, J. H., 338
Trollinger, R. H., 338
Turbyfill, John, 77
Tuttle, D. Herndon, 200, 210

Ulrichsburg (Crowdertown), history of, 370-73
Union Baptist Church, 106
United Daughters of the Confederacy, 474-76
    Ransom-Sherrill Chapter, **history of,** charter members listed, 474
    Abel A. Shuford Chapter, history of, charter members listed, 474-75
    Mabel Miller Rowe Chapter, history of, charter members listed, 475
    Cecil Brawley Long Chapter, history of, charter members listed, 475-76
United Merchants and Manufacturers, 337
U. S. Congress, representatives listed, 264

Vale community, 128, 365
Vance, Zebulon B., 69, 124, 170, 281, 346, 353
Van Horn, Isaac, 77-78
Vaughan, Rev. A. S., 142
Vegetables, listed, 53
Veterans of Foreign Wars, 472
    Barb - Hammond - Smith Post No. 1957, history of, charter members listed, 471
    Donald Lanford Drum Post No. 5305, history of, charter members listed, 472
    Auxiliary, 473
Vindicator, The, 206

Wagner, Conrad, 179
Walker, James M., 363
War Between the States, Catawbans in, listed, 291-335; mentioned, 143, 184, 265-334
Ward, Alexander, 229
Ward, Thomas, 225, 227-29
Warlick, Absalom, 229
Warlick, David, 414
Warlick, E. A., 362
Warlick, George A., 207, 487
Warlick, Mrs. G. A., 471
Warlick, John, 69
Warlick, Peter, 229
Warlick, Philip, 165
Warlicks Store post office, sketch of, postmasters of, 378
Warlick, Wilson, 249
Walker, W. B., 338
Warlong Glove Manufacturing Company, 487
Warren, Yodom Y., 337
War of 1812, production of cannon during, 183; roster, 215-17
Waterhouse, Richard, 435
Wealth and income, 483-84
Weaver, Conrad, 98
Weaver, Eugene, 337
Weaver, Jacob, 125, 181, 366
Weaver, Saloma, 98
Weaving, 177
Weddings, 60
Weidner, Henry, 19, 22, 25, 39, 77, 160, 370-71, 414, 417-25, 427
Wesley Chapel Methodist Arbor and Campground, 108

CATAWBA COUNTY 525

Western Carolinian, The, 211
Western Democrat, The, 275
West, Dr. George H., 361
Western North Carolina Railroad, list of persons paid by, 165; early local agents of, listed, 165-66, 170-71; proposed routes for, 166-69; construction reports on, 168-69; schedule and directions of, 171-72; leasing of, 172-73; mentioned, 161, 345, 361, 453, 456
Wheeler, John H., 230, 360
Wheelwrights, 178-79
Whichard, J. R., 211
Whisenant, Banks, 358
Whisnant, A. P., 150
Whisnant, Daniel, 450-51
Whisnant post office, sketch of, postmasters listed, 385
White, James, 225
Whitener, A. A., 200, 354, 395
Whitener, Abram, 77
Whitener, Benjamin, 98, 358
Whitener, Daniel, 77, 125, 233
Whitener, David B., 126
Whitener, Henry, 360
Whitener, Jackson, 228
Whitener, Jesse, 92
Whitener, L. R., 68, 354
Whitener, Mildred, 476
Whitener, Philip, 232, 246
Whitener post office, sketch of, postmasters listed, 387
Whitener, R. Vance, 414
Whitener, S. L., 354
Whitesides, J. C., 486
White Sulphur Springs post office, sketch of, postmasters listed, 380
Whitney, Frances, 476
WHKY, 496
Wike, David, 232
Wilbury, J. C., 69
Wiley, Calvin H., 124
Wiley, F. A., 354
Wilfong, Barbara Evie, 282-83
Wilfong, George, 77, 83-84, 423-24
Wilfong, Henry, 246, 345, 354
Wilfong, Jack, 429, 431
Wilfong, James, 68, 232
Wilfong, John, 30, 77-79, 84, 95, 165, 191, 231-32, 277
Wilfong's Mill, 129, 176, 221
Wilfongs Mill post office, sketch of, postmasters listed, 377
Wilkerson, David, 110
Wilkes County, 76, 85, 200, 353, 435
Wilkie, George, 165, 228, 230, 246
Wilkinson, Rufus P. P., 358
Williams, F. M., 200, 207
Williams, Fannie Ransom, 184, 474
Williams, John, 183, 229, 358
Williams, Richard, 358
Williams, R. R., 155

Williams, William, 183, 188
Willow Grove post office, sketch of, postmasters listed, 377
Wills, Robert, 178
Wilson, Andrew, 77, 85
Wilson, David, 232
Wilson, John, 77, 85
Wilson, Joseph, 228, 232-33, 360
Wilson, Joshua, 219, 228-30
Wilson, Mathew, 22, 233, 299
Wilson, M. M., 361
Wilson, Nathaniel, 219-20, 228-31, 359
Wilson, Newton, 359
Wilson, Rebecca, 219
Windy City (Viewmont), 365
Winebarger, Conrad, 232
Wineberger, Leban, 107
Winkler, Abraham, 457
Winkler, Bard, 457
Winkler, Bill, 457
Winkler, Bob, 457
Winkler, Jeff, 457
Winters, Sam, 339
Winterville post office, sketch of, postmasters listed, 377
WIRC, 496
Wise, Daniel, 84-85
Wise, Isaac, 71-72, 85, 231
Witherspoon, Hoyle, 360
Witherspoon, L. L., 200, 362
WNNC, 496
Woodford, Lyman, 180, 229
Wool, 52, 176-77
World War I, Catawba Indians in, 27; Catawbans serving in, listed, 396-409
World War II, Catawbans who lost lives in, listed, 411-412
Wright, J. W., 200
Wycoff, Isaac B., 233
Wycoff, William A. D., 233

Yadkin river, 27, 86, 175
Yoder, Andrew, 108
Yoder, Charley, 99
Yoder, Conrad, 39-40, 77, 181, 423-24, 434
Yoder, David, 92, 176, 181
Yoder, George M., 39-40, 125
Yoder, John, 39-41, 92, 126
Yoder, John, Jr., 126
Yoder, John A., 92
Yoder, Lavinia, 92
Yoder, Lawrence, 176
Yoder, Levi F., 246
Yoder, Marcus, 345, 354
Yoder post office, sketch of, postmasters listed, 387
Yoder, R. A., 38, 150, 155
Yoder, Reuben, 99, 247
Yoder, Solomon, 181
York, Dr. Brantley, 147
Yount, Dr. D. McD., 341

Yount, Ephraim, 229
Yount, J. A., 340
Yount, John, 219, 225, 229-30, 232
Yount, Mrs. John, 430
Yount, Marshall H., 200, 354
Younts Mill post office, sketch of, postmasters listed, 383
Younts Mill township, 67

Yount, Mrs. Shaw, 430
Yount, Sidney, 252, 431
Yount, S. L., 69
Younts Turnout post office, sketch of, postmasters listed, 381

Zion Lutheran Church, early members listed, 98; mentioned, 90, 125

www.ingramcontent.com/pod-product-compliance
Lightning Source LLC
Chambersburg PA
CBHW020632300426
44112CB00007B/93